Fodor's **2001**

Hawaiʻi

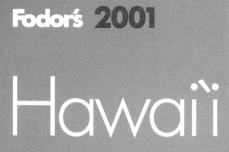

CONTENTS

MAPS

Circled letters in text correspond to letters on the photographs. For more information on the sights pictured, turn to the indicated page number Ⓐ▷ on each photograph.

DESTINATION
HAWAI`I

Just try to describe Hawai`i without saying "paradise." It's nearly impossible. In this place of ineffable beauty, the word is not a cliché but a fact, even an understatement. Eden may greet you on a heroic scale, as at Waimea Canyon on Kaua`i, or may appear in the palm of your hand, as when you hold a native Lokelani rose. The pleasures come in forms that are material and sensual, as well—consider the beguiling shopping and the inspired cuisine created in kitchens energized by world-class chefs. You can also get physical. Go birding, hiking, swimming, or waterskiing, or pursue almost any other outdoor sport known to man—even snow skiing or snowboarding. Or simply head for the nearest perfect crescent of palm-shaded beach and do nothing at all.

O'AHU

O'ahu is the most visited Hawaiian island, yet even here grandeur reveals itself at every turn. The landscape is so rugged and mountainous that many a developer has just shrugged his shoulders and walked away, mumbling in frustration. The monster winter waves along **O'ahu's North Shore** are worth driving from Honolulu to see. Inside the "tube," time stands still: master surfers experience a space like the inside of a glass cathedral, a roar like a jet engine's, and unparalleled exhilaration. Novice-friendly waves roll in at Honolulu's famous ⑧**Waikīkī Beach,** where just about anyone can hang ten on a rented surfboard under the supervision of an experienced instructor. The neighborhood nearby, with its sprawling malls and many diverse boutiques, is a reminder that this Hawaiian Eden has more than one face. ©**King Kamehameha I,** who united the islands in the 1790s, could never have anticipated the busy, modern neighborhood inland from his roost in the capital's ⑩**'Iolani Palace.** Hawaiian royalty called this

⑧ 60

© 50

Victorian structure home between 1882 and 1893, when, on the heels of the uncongenial arrival of 160 U.S. Marines, Queen Lili'uokalani ended the monarchy once and for all. The chill thrown over Hawaiian culture by this event lingered for years.

⑩ 50

O'AHU

Today a cultural renaissance is under way in Hawai'i, and the lively entertainment accompanying the revival of interest in ancient ways will educate, sensitize, and broaden you—particularly as it's on view in Lā'ie at the 40-acre Ⓔ Ⓘ **Polynesian Cultural Center.** Here, amid re-created villages from Tahiti and Samoa, Fiji and the Marquesas, Tonga, and other countries all over the Pacific, you can marvel at the hula and the Samoan Fireknife Dance, both carefully explained. More Hawaiiana is on view at the fine Bishop Museum. Or head for the Waimea Valley in search of the Hawaiian nēnē, the state bird, and to watch an exhibition of cliff-diving. You can also explore waterfalls or just sun yourself on any number of beaches. But it is Pearl Harbor that is, without a doubt, O'ahu's most moving sight. A surprise Japanese air attack on December 7, 1941, crippled the U.S. Navy's Pacific Fleet and prompted America's entry into World War II. Walk the paths lined with memorial stones that front

Ⓔ 59

Ⓕ 58

the ⒻU.S.S. *Bowfin,* namesake of a whole class of submarines from that era; learn the names and read the stories of those who died here on that hellish Sunday morning. Look at their photographs. Not far from the *Bowfin* is a beautiful, massive, white memorial encasing the sunken battleship U.S.S. *Arizona,* which went down with 1,102 crewmen aboard. You will never forget what you see. To end the day, catch the sunset by the pool at Honolulu's ⒼHalekūlani hotel or dine elegantly at ⒽOrchids restaurant.

MAUI

The last two decades have brought golf courses and luxurious hotels, tourists and traffic to the second-largest Hawaiian isle. But the landscape surrounding Ⓐ©**Haleakalā,** the world's largest dormant volcano, remains preternatural in its loveliness. If you wanted to ruin the view, you could fit Manhattan inside its great volcanic bowl. All over the island, but particularly here, lush forests keep company with strikingly red and desertlike terrain, and some of the flora and fauna are rare even in Hawai'i. The stunning silversword plant grows only here and at high elevations on the Big Island. It will bloom just once in its life, near the end of its days. At Ⓑ'**Īao Valley State Park,** wind and water have sculpted impressive rock spires.

Mark Twain may not have thought much of Venice, but he was captivated by this place—and no wonder. All over Maui, rainbows hover over the mists and waterfalls shower the mountainsides. Hop aboard the charming 1890s Ⓓ**Sugarcane Train** and take a ride through the magnificent, lush landscape between Kāʻanapali, on the west coast, and Lahaina, the former whaling town that was once Hawaiʻi's capital and is now the island's main market center. Sugarcane, a mainstay of Maui's economy for years, was a powerful influence on the island's history. Production ceased in 1999, but the train has happily outlived the crop. For local farmers the soil yields other bounties, among them grapes for wine and rich pasture-lands where horses graze. The vineyards and grasslands create another kind of landscape on Maui, one that's intimate, charming, and a perfect counterpoint to nature's grandstanding.

MAUI

Ⓔ▷131

For 19th-century missionaries from New England, Hawai'i represented a golden opportunity to save souls—not just Hawaiian souls but those of fellow New Englanders, whalers drawn to the Pacific by the big profits to be made on whalebone and whale oil. For these roistering mainlanders, Maui and its port of ⒻⒽ**Lahaina** were a red-light district where the bars never closed. The 19th-century buildings where they took their rowdy R&R have been renovated, and much of the town is now a National Historic Landmark. As for the North Pacific's humpback whale population, which once numbered many thousands, only about 1,500

Ⓕ▷118

remain. On winter whale-watching tours from Lahaina you can see them spectacularly breaching and blowing offshore. Under water, along the western and southwestern coasts, the sea yields still other spectacular sights. In the Molokini Crater area, a marine preserve, fish are so tame that they eat right out of a diver's hand. If you're not certified to dive, you can get an idea of the island's submarine wonders at the Ⓙ**Maui Ocean Center** in Mā'alaea. Back on land, West Maui's so-called Golf Coast, north of Lahaina, calls relentlessly to

Ⓖ▷128

⑭ 118

① 160

duffers. The velvety cliff-bound scenery may up your handicap by a stroke or two—the ①**Wailea Golf Club** is just one of the options. Still, just steering a car along a road can be a transcendent experience, as in East Maui on the winding ⑥**Hāna Highway,** one of the most spectacular drives in the world. And it isn't just the hairpin turns that set your heart aflutter, although it might skip a beat or two when a car flies past, seemingly from out of nowhere. It's also the stops along the way—hikes to waterfalls that pour down to virtually deserted swimming holes, or ⑤**Ho`okipa Beach,** where windsurfers ride 15-foot-high waves and take their sport to world-class levels.

① 124

BIG ISLAND

Ⓐ▷ 198

If you like your paradises un-crowded, you'll like the Big Island. (Its formal name, *Hawai'i*, is also the name of the *state*—and something had to give.) Of all the Hawaiian Is-lands, it's the youngest. Inland, ancient Hawaiian ruins and sleepy and not-so-sleepy towns with melodic names punctuate a land-scape of tropical forests, lush pasturelands, and barren lava fields. Rainbows arch over gorges and shimmer near sparkling cascades as at Ⓓ**Rainbow Falls,** outside Hilo, the county seat.

©>198

Ⓓ>194

Here and there you'll see ancient stone heiau and statues, per-haps of the war god Ku. And the volcanic activity that created the entire chain still percolates impressively—over the last 10 years, lava on the coast has added some 70 acres to the Island. Ⓐ**Hawai'i Volcanoes National Park** is the site of Kīlauea, one of the world's most active volcanoes and the only one in the state that's not currently dormant; fireworks displays pale by comparison. The park's bleakly beautiful ©**Devastation Trail** demonstrates what happens when lava gets a bit too frisky: The forest that covered the land in 1959 is completely gone, even some 40 years later. Lava tubes, cinder cones, and barren craters create an otherworldly land-scape along Chain of Craters road. In the park's coastal section, near Ⓑ**Kalapana,** lava flows into the sea—slowly enough for you to get a good close look at it through the steam. Lava flows have even blocked portions of the roads here.

15

BIG ISLAND

On the Big Island you find occasional sparkling white crescents of sand, but many beaches come in colors. Here olive-green, there golden, they are sometimes as black as the lava that formed them, especially on the ⓖ**South Kohala Coast.** Eruptions of Mt. Hualālai 200 years ago created moonscapes that extend to the sea all through the island's northwest corner. Palm trees shading these strands and golf courses at nearby luxury resorts glow especially green against the inky sands and vivid blue waters. The volcanic wonderland extends offshore, where sea turtles and bright fish such as butterfly fish, damselfish, and false moorish idols swim among lava towers, tubes, and caves, as you'll see on trips with organizers like Ⓗ**Red Sail Sports** and at snorkeling destinations such as Punaluʻu Beach Park. Experts can explore a wrecked plane off Keāhole Point. On land, hike along trails blazed by ancient Hawaiians. The hike up

Ⓔ▷ 205

Ⓕ▷ 236

G⟩206

H⟩247

13,680-foot Mauna Loa is one of the state's best-kept secrets. If your timing is right, try to see October's ⒤**Ironman Triathlon,** a 2.4-mile open-ocean swim and a 112-mile bike ride capped with a full 26.2-mile marathon. And on weekday afternoons at the late-19th-century Ⓔ**Huliheʻe Palace** in Kailua-Kona, try to catch a local hula school rehearsing—Hawaiian culture flourishes here as well. Lodging options range from small B&Bs to hotel complexes like the Ⓕ**Kona Village Resort.** Wherever you stay, don't check out without acquiring some rich, smooth macadamia nuts, grown on the Big Island. Or pick up 100% pure Kona coffee, grown just upland of the south Kona shore. The world-famous brews of Kona begin life not as beans but as berries called "cherries." Many of Kona's 600-plus coffee farms permit you to sip their blends gratis, and in a twist that will be novel if you've been to California's wine country, tasting tours in Kona keep you *sober.* These guided visits end, of course, at the plantation's gift shop, and you'll be glad: Some good coffee will help ease the symptoms of "paradise withdrawal" back home.

I⟩248

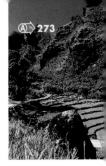

KAUA'I

Ⓑ 282

They call it the Garden Isle, which is saying a lot when you consider the floral splendor of Hawai'i in general. Kaua'i more than lives up to its sobriquet. Then again, as the oldest of the main Hawaiian islands, it's had a few more million years to become splendid. The elemental forces of nature, given a few extra aeons, have given much of Kaua'i a chiseled beauty, including the coastline up north, around the Ⓓ**Hanalei Valley.** Pure glorious scenery is the result—and the reason that many a visitor is drawn to Kaua'i. Yes, you can golf on fine courses here. And yes, there are lovely places to eat, fun places to shop, and varied hostelries, from luxurious resorts to rustic cabins. But Kaua'i is not really about those things. It's about *grandeur*, about Creation outdoing itself. The stunning vistas of the ocean and a mountain named Bali Hai from the Ⓐ**Limahuli Garden,** part of the National Tropical Botanical Garden on the northern coast, will teach you that lesson. So will viewpoints like Canyon Lookout and Kalalau Lookout, with their panorama of jagged moun-

Ⓒ 278

tains and lacy cascades, not
to mention the natural water
show on the south shore at
the ©**Spouting Horn** and
the perfect dunes and spectacular sunsets of the west at
®**Polihale Beach.** If Hawai'i
is paradise, then Kaua'i may
be paradise's prettiest subdivision.

Ⓓ➤**272**

KAUA'I

(E) 272

On Kaua'i, mountain bikers assault the 12-mile-long Power Line Trail, hikers tackle the twisting Kalalau Trail, golfers and tennis players test their skills on any number of resort layouts, outrigger canoeists race offshore, and snorkelers and scuba divers explore the bounty of submarine wonders. Nature lovers have a field day as well. They search for nests of endangered seabirds on the cliffs below the bright white (E)**Kīlauea Lighthouse,** a National Historic Landmark on Kaua'i's north coast, or, in the heart of the island in Kōke'e State Park's (G)**Waimea Canyon,** try to spot the rare jungle fowl, whose ancestors ar-

(F) 274

rived with the Polynesians. (If Mark Twain hadn't called this gorge the "Grand Canyon of the Pacific," someone else would have.) Cascades like ⒻʻŌpaekaʻa Falls, to the east, aren't hard to find either. Obeying gravity over time, these 40 feet of water have carved out many a breathtaking vista on Kauaʻi. Volcanic Mount Waiʻaleʻale, towering over the island's center, is known as the "wettest spot on earth," with almost 500 inches of rain annually. The clever planners of the ⒽPrinceville Hotel made sure that its Horizon Pool appears to flow seamlessly into Hanalei Bay. The Clever Planner of Kauaʻi's west-coast beaches made sure that every day ends with a spectacle.

MOLOKA'I

If, more than anything else, you come to Hawai'i to rest your body and soul, give serious consideration to basing yourself on the "Friendly Isle." This is where Hawaiians themselves vacation, drawn by the island's peace and quiet and its great beauty. It is also where people with Hansen's disease were exiled, beginning in the 1860s, back in the days that its sufferers, then known as lepers, were feared and before drugs could arrest the disease's course. It is a deeply moving experience to visit the settlement, known as Kalaupapa, which is accessible from Pālā'u State Park via

Ⓑ 332

ⓒ⟩ 332

the Ⓐ**Moloka'i Mule Ride.**
Moloka'i is so mellow that
few other sights are musts.
But most visitors do take in at
least part of the 53,000-
acre Moloka'i Ranch for
horseback riding and cul-
tural walks, and Ⓑ**Kaloko'eli
Fishpond** near Kaunakakai,
a distinctive structure built by
the earliest Hawaiians. Many
endangered species survive at

Ⓓ⟩ 336

the Nature Conservancy's lush,
wet Ⓒ**Kamakou Preserve**;
reserve ahead for the rare
guided hikes. The low-key island lifestyle means that your
lodging will in all likelihood
be understated; you even have
the option of sleeping under
canvas at Ⓓ**Paniolo Camp.** The showers there are warmed by
the Hawaiian sun, and the proprietors are accommodating about
packing box lunches for your day trips to splendid beaches such
as Ⓔ**Hālawa Beach Park,** where ancient chieftains once
surfed to unwind.

Ⓔ⟩ 334

LĀNAʻI

A decade ago, the planting, growing, and harvesting of pineapples were the major preoccupation on warm, arid Lānaʻi. Things changed fast after the Great Hawaiian Pineapple Crash of the 1980s. Suddenly, Lānaʻi needed a new economic base. Dole Foods, which owns almost all of the island, is pinning its hopes on the two luxury resorts the company has created to join the venerable, and still charming, Hotel Lānaʻi. Many of the new visitors check out the Ⓐ**Garden of the Gods,** north of Lānaʻi City. The strewn

Ⓓ 353

boulders look merely curious at midday, but as the shadows lengthen, the place becomes eerily beautiful. More poignant than spooky is once prosperous and lovely Ⓑ**Keōmuku,** laid low by an economic crisis in 1901 and finally abandoned in 1954. The Ⓓ**Munro Trail** will take you to Lāna'i's highest point, whose commanding view encompasses most of Hawai'i's other islands. Or sign up with ⒸⒺ**Trilogy Excursions** for a trip to sea— for snorkeling lessons, or just some old-fashioned horsing around.

Ⓔ 357

GREAT ITINERARIES

Ⓐ 58

Highlights of Hawai'i

14 days

NIIHAU

Many Hawai'i visitors simply loll in a chaise longue during their stay. If you would prefer to take a peek at several islands, to get a better feeling for the world's most isolated archipelago, let this itinerary be your guide. You'll travel from O'ahu to Kaua'i, with stops at Moloka'i, Maui, and the Big Island.

O'ahu

3 days

The third largest of the Hawaiian Islands, 608-square-mi O'ahu is a good place to start your tour, with its frequent air service from the mainland and its scores of restaurants and hotels and seemingly endless shopping. It's a lush and beautiful place. Wind and weather have carved dramatic valleys between steep cliffs across the middle of the island, and the temperate, forgiving climate and abundant rainfall keep things a vivid shade of green. On the first morning, rise early to make the steep walk to Diamond Head, the summit of an extinct volcano, for a panorama of the city and the beaches. Once you've soaked up the vista, take in a bit of history at the U.S.S. *Bowfin*, a World War

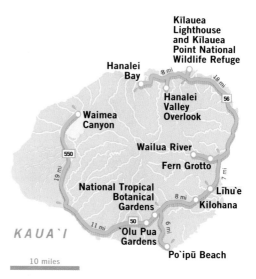

KAUA'I

Kīlauea Lighthouse and Kīlauea Point National Wildlife Refuge

Hanalei Bay — 8 mi — 18 mi

Hanalei Valley Overlook — 56

Waimea Canyon

Wailua River

550

Fern Grotto

19 mi

National Tropical Botanical Gardens — 8 mi — Līhu'e

Kilohana

50

11 mi — 'Olu Pua Gardens

6 mi

Po'ipū Beach

10 miles

II submarine, and the *Arizona* Memorial, commemorating the sinking of this ship on December 7, 1941, with more than a thousand men aboard. Then spend some time exploring the shops, restaurants, and other attractions of Waikīkī—including the Waikīkī Aquarium, which spotlights marine life of Hawai'i and the South Pacific, and the Bishop Museum, which started out as a home for the possessions of King Kamehameha the Great's last direct descendant and is now known for its collection of Polynesiana. On day two, drive around Diamond Head to watch the windsurfers, then follow the coast to Ⓑ Hanauma Bay and the windward town of Kailua. Take side trips to the Nu'uanu Pali Lookout, where the view is spectacular, and the Byodo-In Temple, a replica of the Kyoto original, on your way to the Ⓐ Polynesian Cultural Center, with its Polynesian villages and demonstrations. Pick up a souvenir or two in its open-air shopping village—it has a good selection of Polynesian handicrafts. It's

Ⓑ 63

a long, dark drive back to Waikīkī after the show, so you might want to stay at a local B&B. On your third day continue along the North Shore, stopping at Waimea Valley and Waimea Bay, a popular picnic spot, en route back to Waikīkī. In Honolulu, explore the lei stands and herb shops in the city's Chinatown. Then take a guided tour of America's only royal residence, 'Iolani Palace, and stroll around Mission Houses Museum, the homes of Hawai'i's first missionaries (who arrived in 1820), and Kawaiaha'o Church, built out of local coral blocks and used for royal ceremonies.

Kaua'i
2 days

On the Garden Isle, begin by making the 90-minute drive from Līhu'e around the south shore of the island and up to spectacular ⒹWaimea Canyon, nicknamed the "Grand Canyon of the Pacific." Lookouts en route give you wonderful views of the entire panorama. Kōke'e State Park is at the northern end of the canyon, a true wilderness full of colorful flowers. Return the way you came, stopping en route as time permits to visit one of the tropical botanical gardens along the road (12-acre 'Olu Pua Gardens and the 186-acre National Tropical Botanical Gardens) and the eclectic shops at Kilohana. Plan your trip to allow time to arrive at Po'ipū Beach and catch the sunset over the Pacific—a sight you won't soon forget. On your final day, cruise up the Wailua River to the Fern Grotto, take a flightseeing tour, and stop at Kīlauea Light-house, built in 1913 and towering over the Kīlauea Point National Wildlife Refuge, and the Hanalei Valley Overlook, where fields of taro stretch before you almost as far as you can see. Spend your last evening watching the sun set at Hanalei Bay, a spectacular way to bring your island sojourn to a close.

Moloka'i
2 days

This long, small island doesn't take long to explore. The best strategy is to see just a little each day to allow time to

Ohia Lodge. Its restaurant, although the most formal on the island, is casual and comfortable, and if you eat before the sun goes down you can marvel at the spectacular ocean vista through the big picture windows. The next day—and it will be a full one—reserve ahead to tour

Ⓒ▷337

kick back and relax. West Moloka'i is mostly given over to 53,000-acre Moloka'i Ranch, the largest local landholder. In tiny Maunaloa, which anchors the area, start by stopping at the old market and kite shop, on the brief main street. Later head for wide ⒸPāpōhaku Beach, the island's nicest and most private strand and one of the state's most sensational, with its stunning white sand. At dinnertime head for nearby

Kalaupapa, to which people afflicted with Hansen's disease were once relegated; make the tortuous 2-mi trip via the Moloka'i Mule Ride. Father Damien, a Catholic priest, cared for the community's residents until he succumbed to the disease in 1889. Before you catch an evening flight to Maui, take in the stupendous view of the peninsula from Pālā'au State Park.

27

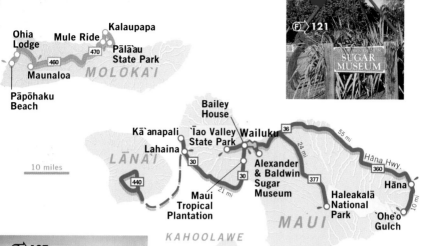

(F) > 121

Ohia Lodge
Kalaupapa
Mule Ride
470
Pālā'au State Park
460
Maunaloa
MOLOKA'I
Pāpōhaku Beach

Bailey House
Kā'anapali 'Iao Valley **Wailuku** 36
Lahaina State Park
LĀNA'I 30
55 mi
24 mi
Hāna Hwy.
440 **Alexander & Baldwin Sugar Museum** 360
10 miles 30 377 **Hāna**
21 mi **Haleakalā National Park**
Maui Tropical Plantation MAUI **'Ohe'o Gulch**
KAHOOLAWE

(E) > 127

Maui
4 days

Maui, which inspires people to call it the Valley Isle, is the second-largest landfall in the state. Start your Maui sojourn in 'Iao Valley State Park, where a 2,000-ft-high spire known as the 'Iao Needle rises astonishingly from the valley floor and easy hikes lead through jungly forests. The peripatetic Mark Twain, stopping in the area during his peregrinations through the islands, dubbed it the Yosemite of the Pacific. Nothing less did justice to its charismatic grandeur. Afterward take 'Iao Valley Road into Wailuku, where it becomes Main Street. Many of the old buildings in this dozy little town are on the National Register of Historic Places. Bailey House, former home of prominent 19th-century missionaries Edward and Caroline Bailey, displays period furniture and artifacts. Then follow Highway 30 south a couple of miles to the 120-acre Maui Tropical Plantation, a sort of agricultural theme park, to tour former sugarcane fields, get an overview of the growing processes, and catch lively demonstrations of activities like lei-making and coconut-husking. Then head over to the (F)Alexander & Baldwin Sugar Museum in Kahului. The next day, if it's sunny, make the fabulous 4-hr drive to Hāna. It's a spectacular 55 mi of bridges and turns and vistas showcasing classic Hawaiian scenery. Keep an eye out en route for waterfalls, pools, swimming holes, hiking trails, lookout points, and other stopping places. Overnight in Hāna, a onetime company town devoted to the sugar industry that's now almost entirely focused on tourism. In the morning visit aviator Charles Lindbergh's grave and 'Ohe'o Gulch, where there are many waterfalls more than 100 ft high with idyllic pools at the bottom. The place is perfect for picnicking and sunbathing and can get very crowded. Backtracking along the Hāna Highway, end the day exploring historic Lahaina, the famous restored former whaling town where crusty sailors just back from many months at sea clashed with New England missionaries whose single-minded goal was to save the men's souls. After you've explored its antique buildings, go on to Kā'anapali to spend the night. The next morning, get up early for a sailing-and-snorkeling cruise out of Lahaina to Lāna'i. Then get to bed early, because the following day you'll rise before dawn to see the sun rise over the immense crater of (E)Haleakalā, the volcano whose lava flow created all of East Maui. The crater is now the centerpiece of Haleakalā National Park, which is full of hiking trails. At lovely Hosmer Grove, a forested area, you can pick up a trail map. The Sliding Sands trail off the top of the crater shows off some amazingly colorful scenery that's almost lunar.

Big Island
3 days

After arriving in Hilo, the county seat of the island and the fourth-largest city in the state, drive up Waiānuenue Avenue about a mile (stay to the right) as far as exquisite (H)Rainbow Falls. It's beautiful when the sun is shining, and rainbows form above the mist if the sun is right in the morning. Then travel north of Hilo for 7 mi along Highway 19, and turn right onto the 4-mi scenic bypass that skirts Hawai'i Tropical Botanical Garden, 17 acres crowded with exotic species like ginger and heliconia, before rejoining the highway. Next turn left inland toward the small and unprepossessing town of Honomū and drive 4 mi to 'Akaka Falls State Park, where a 20-min walk yields the rewarding sight of the park's two cascades—the 100-ft Kahuna Falls and the 420-ft 'Akaka Falls. At this point one option would keep you in Honomū to have lunch and stroll amid its galleries

and flea market. But it's better to spend the afternoon in ⒼHawai'i Volcanoes National Park, exploring its lava tubes and mineral formations, steam vents and tropical plants—and, if you're lucky, to catch the sight of lava flowing from Kīlauea Volcano. It would take years to see everything in this 359-square-mi preserve, but you can get a feel for the volcanic terrain in just a short time with a visit to Halema'uma'u Crater, a steam-clouded pit inside the Kīlauea Caldera, or with a hike along the blackened Devastation Trail. Begin the next day with a drive up the Hāmākua Coast to Waimea, to see the Hawaiiana in the Kamuela Museum and tour the Parker Ranch Visitor Center. The ranch was founded in 1847 and grew up around 2 acres of land given to John Palmer Parker by King Kamehameha I; one of Parker's descendants collected some very fine art, and a Utrillo and Renoir are on display. En route to the Kohala Coast resorts—don't miss the nearby petroglyph carvings—look for the snow-capped summit of Mauna Ke'a. (The next morning head south through Hōlualoa, Kealakekua, and Captain Cook, stopping for a bit at

Pu'uhonua o Hōnaunau National Historic Park, about 20 mi south of Kailua-Kona. Games and crafts demonstrations, among other activities there, teach you a lot about Hawaiian history. When you've seen it all, head back to Kailua-Kona and the Astronaut Ellison S. Onizuka Space Center, a tribute to Hawai'i's first astronaut. You can spend the rest of the day sightseeing, shopping, and relaxing in Kailua-Kona.

Kamuela Museum

Parker Ranch Visitor Center

Kohala Coast

Waimea

41 mi

19

19

Hāmākua Coast

10 mi

Petroglyph Carvings

19

Honomū

'Akaka Falls State Park

4 mi

Scenic Drive

19

Mauna Ke'a

7 mi

Hawai'i Tropical Botanical Garden

32 mi

Airport

Astronaut Ellison S. Onizuka Space Center

Rainbow Falls

Hilo

1 mi

HAWAI'I

Kailua-Kona

11

27 mi

11

Hōlualoa

Kealakekua

20 mi

Hawai'i Volcanoes National Park/ Kīlauea Volcano

Captain Cook

Halema'uma'u Crater

Devastation Trail

Pu'uhonua o Hōnaunau National Historic Park

10 miles

Ⓗ 199

FODOR'S
CHOICE

Honolulu
City and Harbor

Bellows Field

Even with so many special places in Hawai'i, Fodor's writers and editors have their favorites. Here are a few that stand out.

QUINTESSENTIAL HAWAI'I

Ⓗ **Arizona Memorial, O'ahu.** For practically every visitor this is a must-see, with its gleaming white memorial and powerful presentation. ☞ p. 57

Big Island sunsets. On the Kohala Coast, the sun consistently sets as a blazing red orb, casting fiery orange and magenta hues across an ocean view broken only by an occasional billowing sail. ☞ p. 180

Garden of the Gods, Lāna'i. For photography it's hard to top this surreal landscape scattered with red and black lava formations and rocks, with the blue Pacific in the background. ☞ p. 352

Hiking on the Big Island. In Hawai'i Volcanoes National Park, trek into fern forests to watch fresh lava hit the Pacific amid billowing steam—and new land being created. ☞ p. 244

Ⓐ **Maui and Kaua'i flight-seeing.** Gaze down on the moonscape craters of Maui's Haleakalā volcano or zoom over rain forests, waterfalls, beaches, and emerald-green carpeted canyons. ☞ p. 175

Surfing O'ahu's North Shore. Winter brings giant waves to Sunset Beach and Waimea Bay, and the world's top pros and hundreds of spectators gather for surfing's major competitions. ☞ p. 61

Whale-watching off Maui. Humpback whales breach and blow right offshore between November and May. ☞ p. 179

BEACHES

Ⓘ **Hāpuna Beach, Big Island.** In summer this clean, wide white-sand beach is perfect for snorkeling and scuba-diving. Kids can romp alongside the tidal pools in a cove at the north end. ☞ p. 212

Ⓕ **Hulopo'e Beach, Lāna'i.** The island's only swimming beach is great for snorkeling. ☞ p. 353

Kahaloa and Ulukou Beaches, O'ahu. The swimming stands out at these strands fronting Waikīkī's Royal Hawaiian and Sheraton Moana Surfrider hotels. ☞ p. 60

Nāpili Beach, Maui. This sparkling white beach forms a secluded cove that's tailor-made for romantics. ☞ p. 134

Ⓑ **Pāpōhaku Beach, Moloka'i.** You can always find a private section of glorious white sand on Hawai'i's longest beach. ☞ p. 334

Polihale Beach Park, Kaua'i. Come for the breathtaking views of rugged cliffs; surf and currents make swimming dangerous. ☞ p. 282

FLAVORS

Formal Dining Room, Lodge at Kō'ele, Lāna'i. Fresh local ingredients create an inventive island cuisine in this elegant Upcountry restaurant. $$$$ ☞ p. 354

Ⓙ **Pahu i'a at Four Seasons Resort Huālalai, Big Island.** Meals are imaginative and beautifully presented; at night, spotlights illuminate the surf just feet from your table. $$$–$$$$ ☞ p. 221

A Pacific Cafe, Maui. Hawaiian Regional cuisine is at its best here. Rather than simply adding a tropical flourish to traditional fare, these chefs create new flavors with innovative combinations that reflect Hawai'i's cultural diversity. $$–$$$ ☞ p. 142

Trattoria Ha'ikū, Maui. This dinner house, once a mess hall for pineapple cannery workers, brings white linens to the jungle and serves country-style Italian fare made from local ingredients. $$–$$$ ☞ p. 143

A Pacific Cafe O'ahu, at Ward Centre, O'ahu. Chef Jean-Marie Josselin's splendidly creative cuisine is served up in a setting that's modern and whimsical. $$ ☞ p. 71

Hamura Saimin, Līhu'e, Kaua'i. Do as approximately 999 other diners do each day: Order a steaming bowl of *saimin* (broth and noodle soup

with pork, fish cake, wonton, or other ingredients)—and enjoy. $ ☞ p. 277

Kanemitsu Bakery and Restaurant, Kaunakakai, Moloka'i. Don't miss the round Moloka'i bread baked on the premises. $ ☞ p. 330

COMFORTS

Four Seasons Resort Huālalai, Big Island. This is a resort that movie moguls only dream of, with accommodations in two-story bungalows arranged around swimming pools by the ocean's edge and connected by torch-lit paths. $$$$ ☞ p. 235

Halekūlani, O'ahu. The gorgeous setting, top-rated service, spectacular dining, and beautiful guest rooms (every one with a lānai) make this retreat one of the world's most sumptuous resorts. $$$$ ☞ p. 75

Ⓒ **Kāhala Mandarin Oriental, O'ahu.** For luxurious privacy, great food, and lovely rooms near Waikīkī shopping and attractions, this hotel fills the bill—beautifully. $$$$ ☞ p. 82

Ⓔ **Lodge at Kō'ele, Lāna'i City, Lāna'i.** Fireplaces warm this sprawling mountain retreat in the cool highlands; local artwork and rare Pacific artifacts embellish the interiors. $$$$ ☞ p. 355

Ⓓ **Princeville Hotel, Kaua'i.** In Kaua'i's most romantic retreat, a spectacular cliffside property, mountain peaks frame breathtaking views across Hanalei Bay and the Pacific. Service and facilities are unrivaled, the golf course world-class. $$$$ ☞ p. 294

Ritz-Carlton, Kapalua, Maui. A magnificent setting, terraced swimming pools, refined cuisine, exemplary service, and beautifully appointed rooms (most with ocean views over landscaped golf courses) make for an island idyll. $$$$ ☞ p. 145

Ⓖ **The Camps at Moloka'i Ranch, Moloka'i.** Moloka'i Ranch's three upscale camps offer meals, many activities, and evening entertainment by the local paniolo. City slickers never had it this good. $$$–$$$$ ☞ p. 336

1 O'AHU

O'ahu is where the spirit of Aloha was born, and it's still Hawai'i's most exciting, cosmopolitan gathering place with an eclectic blend of people, customs, and cuisines. Here's all the tropical splendor for which the Islands are famous, plus the urbanity of Honolulu. But sparkling Waikīkī Beach is just the beginning of this island's allure. O'ahu may be the seat of government and the commercial center for the Hawaiian Islands, but those who live here know that in a matter of minutes you can leave urban life behind and wander through some of Hawai'i's most beautiful forest reserves, mountain areas, and beach parks.

Updated by
Maggie
Wunsch

F OR THOSE WHO LOVE the sophistication of the city but yearn for the pleasures of nature's most abundant beauty, O'ahu has become the island to return to again and again. Part of its dramatic appearance lies in its majestic highlands: the western Wai'anae Mountains rise 4,000 ft above sea level, and the verdant Ko'olau Mountains cross the island's midsection at elevations of more than 3,000 ft. Eons of erosion by wind and weather have carved these ranges' sculptured, jagged peaks, deep valleys, sheer green cliffs, and dynamic vistas. At the base of these mountains more than 50 beach parks lie draped like a beautiful lei, each known for a different activity, be it snorkeling, surfing, swimming, or sunbathing.

Third-largest of the Hawaiian Islands and covering 608 square mi, O'ahu was formed by two volcanoes that erupted 4 to 6 million years ago. Honolulu, the nation's eleventh-largest city, is here, and 75% of Hawai'i's 1.1 million residents call the island home. Somehow, amid all this urban development, you are never more than a glimpse away from an ocean or mountain view that can take your breath away.

Hawai'i's last kings and queens ruled from Honolulu's 'Iolani Palace, near the present downtown. It was at 'Iolani that the American flag first flew over the Islands. Even in those days of royalty, the virtues of Waikīkī as a vacation destination were recognized. Long processions of *ali'i* (nobility) made their way across streams and swamps, past the duck ponds, to the coconut groves and the beach.

By the 1880s guest houses were scattered along the south shore like so many seashells. The first hotel, the Moana (now the Sheraton Moana Surfrider), was built at the turn of the 20th century. Christened "The First Lady of Waikīkī," the Moana's inaugural room rates of $1.50 per night were the talk of the town. At that time Waikīkī was connected to the rest of Honolulu by tram, which brought townspeople to the shore. In 1927 the "Pink Palace of the Pacific," the Royal Hawaiian Hotel, was built by the Matson Navigation Company to accommodate travelers arriving on luxury liners. It was opened with a grand ball, and Waikīkī was launched as a first-class tourist destination: duck ponds, taro patches, and all.

December 7, 1941, brought that era to a close, with the bombing of Pearl Harbor and America's entry into the war in the Pacific. The Royal Hawaiian was turned over to American military forces and became a respite for war-weary soldiers and sailors. But with victory came the postwar boom, and by 1952 Waikīkī had 2,000 hotel rooms. Today, hundreds of thousands of visitors sleep in the more than 31,000 rooms of Waikīkī's nearly 120 hotels and condominiums. As this new millennium began, Waikīkī spent the year 2000 making improvements, some needed—like infrastructure improvements—and others to ensure that it remains a top destination for fun and tropical enchantment. At press time, wider beach expanses, a beach center, a historic Waikīkī walking trail, and more was on the horizon. With Waikīkī leading the way, O'ahu maintains its status as an exciting destination, with more things to see, more places to eat, and more things to do than on all the other Hawaiian Islands combined.

Pleasures and Pastimes

Dining

O'ahu's cuisines are as diverse as its population, with Asian, European, and Pacific flavors most prevalent. Here, the Asian influence can even be found at the corner fast-food restaurant, where the McDonald's menu is posted in both English and kanji, the universal script of the Orient. In addition to its regular fare, McDonald's serves *saimin,* a Japanese noodle soup that ranks as the local favorite snack. German, Italian, French, and Portuguese cultures have also all left their mark on the island, and you'll find their influences as well throughout its restaurants. While you're exploring O'ahu's banquet of choices, be sure to sample Hawai'i regional cuisine, also known variously as Euro-Asian or Pacific Rim. Created by a new generation of Hawai'i chefs, it marries European culinary influences with "local kine" foods—flavors and products that are the tradition of the Islands.

Driving

A walk on the sand at sunset may epitomize the romance of O'ahu, but a drive around the island brings you face-to-face with its sheer natural beauty. Roll past the wave-dashed coastline of the eastern shore, with its photogenic beaches, islands, and cliffs. Drive through the central plains past acres of red soil, once rich in pineapple and now supporting diversified crops, such as coffee. Head to the North Shore, a reflection of old O'ahu with its rickety storefronts and trees hanging heavy with bananas and papaya. Forget the air-conditioning, roll down the windows, and smell the salt air along the windward coast, where the view is dominated by mountains chiseled by centuries of winds, rains, and waterfalls.

Lodging

O'ahu's lodgings range from sprawling resorts that seem to be cities unto themselves to intimate, low-rise hideaways. First-time visitors who wish to be in the heart of the island's activity can find it all in Waikīkī. Guests do well by this South Shore tourist mecca, since shops, restaurants, nightlife, and the beach are all just a stroll away. Business travelers like to stay on the eastern edge of Waikīkī, near the Hawai'i Convention Center, or in downtown Honolulu's sole hotel. Windward and North Shore digs are casual and shorter on amenities but have charms all their own.

Shopping

Honolulu is experiencing a retail boom, from the expansion of existing shopping centers to the construction of new ones. The Ala Moana Shopping Center just outside Waikīkī recently completed a renovation that added a third level of stores and restaurants. Duty Free Shoppers has plans for an additional $65 million retail complex in Waikīkī on the corner of Royal Hawaiian and Kalakaua avenues, designed to be reminiscent of the "Old Hawai'i style." It is scheduled to open in March 2001. What makes shopping on O'ahu additionally interesting is the rich cultural diversity of its products and the many items unique to Hawai'i, such as bowls made of koa wood and jewelry fashioned from rare shells from the island of Ni'ihau. Waikīkī, Honolulu proper, and Hale'iwa on the North Shore are particularly good places to find handmade Hawaiian souvenirs.

Water Sports

Whether you soar above them, sail on them, or dive into them, the waters surrounding O'ahu are an ocean lover's dream. The seas off Waikīkī call to those looking for a surfing lesson and outrigger canoe ride, while the North Shore is the headquarters for accomplished wave riders. Snorkeling and scuba diving at Hanauma Bay, on the island's eastern tip, bring you face to face with a rainbow of sea creatures. Honolulu's Kewalo Basin is the starting point for most fishing charters and the Honolulu harborfront piers serve as home port for many of the new luxury cruise excursions. Windsurfers and ocean kayakers head to the beaches of the windward side, Lanikai in particular, for equip-

ment rentals and lessons in near-perfect conditions. Year-round and island-wide, the water temperature is conducive to a dip, but don't so
much as wade if the waves and currents are threatening.

EXPLORING OʻAHU

Oʻahu is a mixed bag, with enough attractions and adventures to fill
an entire vacation. Waikīkī is the center of the island's visitor industry and home to its largest concentration of accommodations, stores,
restaurants, and nightclubs. Dominated by Diamond Head crater,
Waikīkī's less populated eastern end includes a zoo, an aquarium, and
a beautiful park designed for sports from jogging to kite-flying. West
of Waikīkī is Honolulu, Hawaiʻi's capital city, a bustling blend of history and modern-day commerce. The photogenic East Oʻahu coast is
fringed with white-sand beaches and turquoise seas, and you can drive
right over the top of the Koʻolau Mountains. Finally, a circle-island tour
takes you to central, northern, and windward Oʻahu, where shoes and
cell phones give way to sandy toes and Hawaiian time.

To stay oriented on the island, you need to remember just a few simple things. Directions on Oʻahu are often given as *mauka* (toward the
mountains) or *makai* (toward the ocean). In Honolulu and Waikīkī,
you may also hear people referring to "Diamond Head" (toward that
landmark) and *ʻewa*—away from Diamond Head.

*Numbers in the text correspond to numbers in the margin and on the
Waikīkī, Downtown Honolulu, and Oʻahu maps.*

Great Itineraries

IF YOU HAVE 1 DAY

If you have a short layover on your way to another island or if you
can tear yourself away from a convention (or a honeymoon resort) for
just one day of sightseeing, the first thing you should do is treat yourself to a dawn hike up **Diamond Head** ⑳, then have breakfast at one
of Waikīkī's beachfront restaurants. Next, take the bus or drive to nearby
Ala Moana Shopping Center (☞ Shopping Centers *in* Shopping, *below*),
which has stores to satisfy all souvenir needs. Buy a carryout lunch from
its eclectic, international food court, cross Ala Moana Boulevard, and
picnic, sun, and swim at **Ala Moana Beach Park** (☞ Beaches Around
Oʻahu *in* Beaches, *below*). Go on a late-afternoon outrigger canoe ride
with one of Waikīkī's beachboys, followed by *mai tais* (potent rum drinks
with orange and lime juice) and Hawaiian music at sunset at the
Halekūlani ⑦ or **Royal Hawaiian Hotel** ⑧.

IF YOU HAVE 3 DAYS

On your first day, dig in by following the Waikīkī and/or Kapiʻolani
Park tours described below. Start the second day at the **Hawaiʻi Maritime Center** ㉑ in downtown Honolulu, followed by shopping and
lunch at the adjacent **Aloha Tower Marketplace** ㉒. For a view from
atop the building that was once the tallest structure in Honolulu, go
next door for a short elevator ride to the **Aloha Tower's** observation
deck. Explore historic downtown Honolulu before heading back to
Waikīkī for sunset and dinner. On day three, get an early start so you
arrive at **Hanauma Bay** ㊵ by 7:30. Get a break from the sun with a
stop a little farther north along the coast at **Sea Life Park** ㊲, which features some splashy marine shows. From here, follow the East Oʻahu
Ring tour in reverse, back to Waikīkī.

IF YOU HAVE 5 DAYS

Devote the first day to Waikīkī, the second to downtown Honolulu,
and the third to East Oʻahu. On day four, get an early start in order to

see the **Arizona Memorial** and **Battleship _Missouri_ Memorial** ㊹, since the waiting lines lengthen throughout the morning. Or take the early morning boat tour to Pearl Harbor courtesy of Dream Cruises (☞ Contacts and Resources _in_ O'ahu A to Z, _below_). From there, drive to the **Bishop Museum** ㊷ and spend some time immersed in Hawaiiana. Keep the rest of the day low-key until evening, when you can take in a cocktail or dinner show followed by dancing. Devote day five to the North Shore. Drive to **Hale'iwa** ㊼ for breakfast and shopping, then tour **Waimea Valley and Adventures Park** ㊽, and finish with a late-afternoon or early evening visit to the **Polynesian Cultural Center** ㊿.

When to Tour O'ahu

The ideal seasons to visit O'ahu are spring and fall, when fewer tourists are around and the weather is warm, but not too warm. Fall is additionally fun thanks to the Aloha Festivals, a monthlong program of free Hawaiian-style celebrations and special events. Festival highlights on O'ahu include a floral parade and evening block parties downtown and in Waikīkī. Since many families travel in the summer, most every O'ahu hotel offers children's programs from June through August. Come December, downtown Honolulu is a veritable wonderland during its holiday festival of lights.

Waikīkī

If Hawai'i is America's most exotic, most unusual state, then Waikīkī is its generator, keeping everything humming. On the dry, sunny side of O'ahu, it incorporates all the natural splendors of the Islands and synthesizes them with elegance and daring into an international playground in the middle of the vast blue Pacific.

A tropical retreat since the days of Hawai'i's kings and queens, Waikīkī sparkles along 2½ mi of spangled sea from the famous Diamond Head crater on the east to the Ala Wai Yacht Harbor on the west. Separated on its northern boundary from the sprawling city of Honolulu by the broad Ala Wai Canal, Waikīkī is 3½ mi from downtown Honolulu and worlds apart from any other city in the world. Nowhere else is there such a salad of cultures so artfully tossed, each one retaining its distinct flavor. You'll find yourself saying things like _aloha_ and _mahalo_ (thank you), and in no time you will be planning your next trip back as you laze on its sunny, hypnotic shores.

A Good Walk

A good place to start a Waikīkī walking tour is the **Ala Wai Yacht Harbor** ①, home to an armada of pleasure boats and two members-only yacht clubs. It's just makai of the 'Ilikai Hotel Nikko Waikīkī at 1777 Ala Moana Boulevard. From here head toward the main intersection of Ala Moana Boulevard and Kālia Road, turn right at the big sign to **Hilton Hawaiian Village** ②, and wander through this lush, 20-acre resort complex past gardens and waterfalls.

Continue makai on Kālia Road to Ft. DeRussy, home of the **U.S. Army Museum** ③. Across the street, on Saratoga Road, nestled snugly amid the commerce of Waikīkī, is an oasis of tranquillity: the tea house at the **Urasenke Foundation** ④, where the art of Hawaiian hospitality bows to the art of the centuries-old Japanese tea ceremony.

With a little taste of the Orient and some Zen for the road, head mauka until you reach Kalākaua Avenue. Then turn right toward Diamond Head. At the intersection with Lewers Street, stop and peer into the lobby of the **First Hawaiian Bank** ⑤ for a quick view of the island's history in six massive wall murals. Diagonally across Kalākaua Avenue is one of Waikīkī's architectural landmarks, the **Gump Building** ⑥.

38

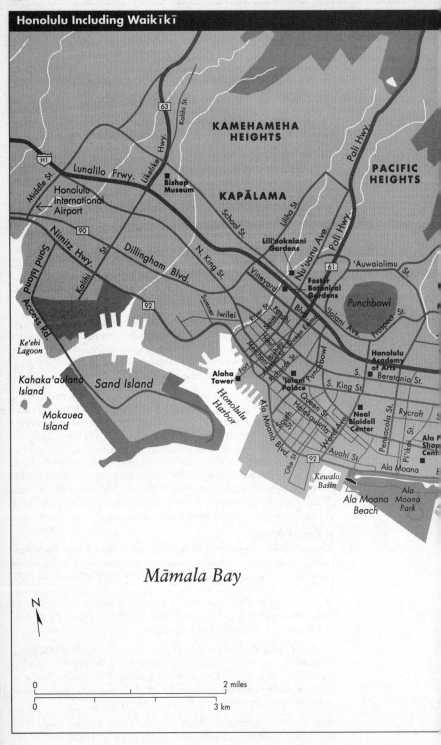

KAMEHAMEHA HEIGHTS

PACIFIC HEIGHTS

Lunalilo Frwy.

Honolulu International Airport

Bishop Museum

KAPĀLAMA

Middle St.

Kalihi St.

Likelike Hwy.

63

H1

90

Nimitz Hwy.

Kalihi St.

Dillingham Blvd.

School St.

N. King St.

Vineyard

Lili'uokalani Gardens

Nu'uanu Ave.

Liliha St.

Pali Hwy.

'Auwaiolimu St.

Foster Botanical Gardens

61

Punchbowl

Prospect St.

'Iolani Ave.

Summer

Iwilei

92

Ke'ehi Lagoon

Sand Island Access Rd.

River St.

Pauahi St.

Smith St.

Hotel St.

Merchant

Beretania

Queen Emma

Nu'uanu

Bishop St.

King St.

Punchbowl

Honolulu Academy of Arts

Beretania St.

Kahaka'aulana Island

Sand Island

Aloha Tower

Fort

Richards St.

'Iolani Palace

S. King St.

Rycroft

Mokauea Island

Honolulu Harbor

Ala Moana Blvd.

South St.

Queen St.

Helekauwila

Ward Ave.

Neal Blaidell Center

Penacola St.

Piikoi St.

Ala Shop Cent.

Ohe St.

Auahi St.

92

Ala Moana

Kewalo Basin

Ala Moana Beach

Ala Moana Park

Māmala Bay

N

0   2 miles

0   3 km

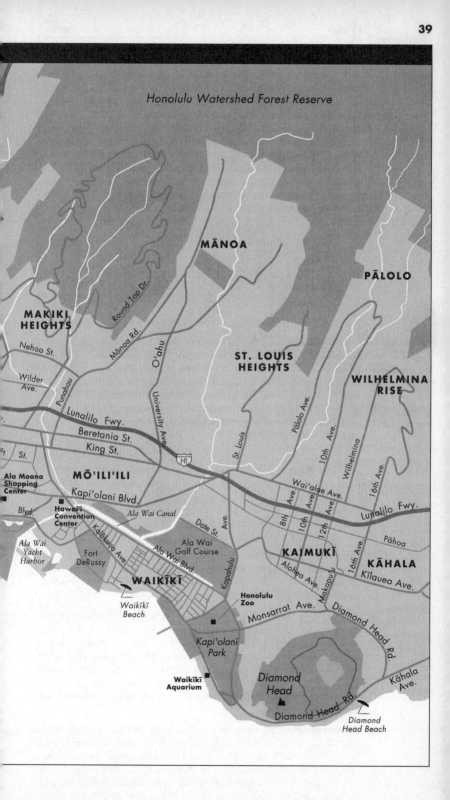

Honolulu Watershed Forest Reserve

MĀNOA

PĀLOLO

MAKIKI
HEIGHTS

ST. LOUIS
HEIGHTS

WILHELMINA
RISE

Nehoa St.

Round Top Dr.

Mānoa Rd.

Wilder
Ave.

Punahou

Oʻahu

University Ave.

St. Louis

Pālolo Ave.

10th Ave.

Wilhelmina

16th Ave.

Lunalilo Fwy.

Beretania St.

King St.

H1

Ala Moana
Shopping
Center

MŌʻILIʻILI

Kapiʻolani Blvd.

Hawaiʻi
Convention
Center

Ala Wai Canal

Blvd.

Waiʻalae Ave.

8th Ave.

10th Ave.

12th Ave.

Lunalilo Fwy.

Pāhoa

Kalākaua Ave.

Fort
DeRussy

Ala Wai
Yacht
Harbor

Ala Wai Blvd.

Date St.

Ave.

Ala Wai
Golf Course

Kapahulu

KAIMUKĪ

Alohea Ave.

Makapuu

16th Ave.

KĀHALA

Kīlauea Ave.

WAIKĪKĪ

Waikīkī
Beach

Honolulu
Zoo

Monsarrat Ave.

Diamond Head Rd.

Kāhala
Ave.

Kapiʻolani
Park

Waikīkī
Aquarium

Diamond
Head

Diamond Head Rd.

Diamond
Head Beach

Walk down Lewers Street toward the ocean. It dead-ends at the impressive **Halekūlani** ⑦, one of Waikīkī's most prestigious hotels, famed for its elegant hospitality. From the Halekūlani stroll toward Diamond Head along the paved oceanside walkway. It leads past the Sheraton Waikīkī to the gracious, historic, and very pink **Royal Hawaiian Hotel** ⑧. Back on the mauka side of Kalākaua Avenue, walk two blocks 'ewa and one block mauka to the **IMAX Waikīkī Theater** ⑨, home of continuous huge-screen films. Return to Kalākaua Avenue and walk toward Diamond Head. Your next stop on the mauka side of the street is the **International Market Place** ⑩, home to shops, stalls, and artisans who display their wares in an open-air bazaar setting. Catch some shade beneath the banyan tree that features its very own Swiss Family Robinson–style tree house.

Across Kalākaua Avenue is the oldest hotel in Waikīkī, the venerable **Sheraton Moana Surfrider** ⑪. Wander through the breezy lobby to the wide back porch, called the Banyan Veranda, or take a quick tour through tourism history in the Moana's second-floor historical room. From here, walk down the beach and head toward Diamond Head. Next to Kalakaua Avenue you'll find the four **Kahuna (Wizard) Stones of Waikīkī** ⑫. Said to hold magical powers, they are often overlooked and, more often than not, irreverently draped with wet towels.

Continue your walk four blocks farther down Kalākaua Avenue toward Diamond Head, then turn mauka onto 'Ōhua Avenue and you'll find the only church in Waikīkī with its own building, the Roman Catholic St. Augustine's. In the back of the church is the **Damien Museum** ⑬, a small but fascinating exhibition on the life of Father Damien, a Belgian priest who died while ministering to the victims of Hansen's disease (leprosy) on the island of Moloka'i.

TIMING

Allow yourself at least one full day for this walk, and time it so that you'll wind up on Waikīkī Beach at sunset. Many shops and attractions are open every day of the year from sunup to way past sundown, to cater to the body clocks and pocketbooks of tourists from around the world. Still, Waikīkī is most inviting in the cool of the early morning. The weather is sunny and pleasant almost every day of the year, so you'll rarely need a jacket or umbrella.

Sights to See

☜ *following the text of a review is your signal that the property has a Web site where you will find details and, usually, images; for a link, visit www.fodors.com/urls.*

❶ **Ala Wai Yacht Harbor.** Every other summer the Trans-Pacific yacht race from Los Angeles makes its colorful finish here, complete with flags and onboard parties. The first Trans-Pac of this new century is estimated to arrive in July of 2001. No matter when you visit Hawai'i, if you want a taste of what life on the water could be like, stroll around the docks and check out the variety of craft, from houseboats to luxury cruisers. ⊠ *1777 Ala Moana Blvd., oceanside across from 'Ilikai Hotel Nikko Waikīkī.*

❶ **Damien Museum.** This tiny two-room museum behind St. Augustine's Church contains low-key exhibits about Father Damien, the Belgian priest who worked with those afflicted with Hansen's disease (leprosy) and exiled to the Hawaiian island of Moloka'i during the late 1800s. Ask to see the museum's 20-minute videotape. It's low-budget but well done and emotionally gripping. ⊠ *130 'Ōhua Ave.,* ☎ *808/923–2690.* ☜ *Free.* ☉ *Weekdays 9–3.*

⑤ First Hawaiian Bank. Get a glimpse of Hawaiian history kept safe in this Waikīkī bank. Half a dozen murals depict the evolution of Hawaiian culture, from Hawaiian arts before contact with the Western world to the introduction of the first printing press to the Islands in 1872. The impressive panels were painted between 1951 and '52 by Jean Charlot (1898–1979), whose work is represented in Florence at the Uffizi Gallery and in New York at both the Metropolitan Museum and the Museum of Modern Art. The murals are beautifully lit at night, with some panels visible from the street. ✉ *2181 Kalākaua Ave.,* ☎ *808/ 943–4670.* ✍ *Free.* ☯ *Mon.–Thurs. 8:30–4, Fri. 8:30–6.*

⑥ Gump Building. Built in 1929 in Hawaiian-colonial style, with Asian architectural motifs and a blue-tile roof, this structure once housed Hawai'i's premier store, Gump's (known for high-quality Asian and Hawaiian objects). It's now home to a Louis Vuitton boutique. ✉ *2200 Kalākaua Ave.*

❼ Halekūlani. Keeping an air of mystery within its tranquil setting, the modern Halekūlani is centered around a portion of its original (1917) beachfront estate, immortalized as the setting for the first of the Charlie Chan detective novels, *The House Without a Key.* For a view of an orchid blossom that is like no other, take a peek at the swimming pool with its huge orchid mosaic on the bottom. ✉ *2199 Kālia Rd.,* ☎ *808/ 923–2311.*

NEED A BREAK? If it's lunchtime or close to sunset, linger at the **Halekulani** and get a table at **House Without a Key** (☞ Waikīkī *in* Dining, *below*). Offering a view of Diamond Head from most every table, it has a light lunch menu and serves wonderful tropical drinks and *pūpū* (appetizers) before dinner. Enjoy the view, the sounds of the Hawaiian steel guitar, and see graceful hula performed nightly beneath the centuries-old *kiawe* tree (kiawe is a mesquite-type wood).

❷ Hilton Hawaiian Village. This 20-acre Waikīkī resort is the quintessential tropical getaway, complete with a little island in Kahanamoku Lagoon and palm trees all around. Look for the penguin pond in the back of the main lobby. The village is a hodgepodge of Asian architecture, with a Chinese moon gate, a pagoda, and a Japanese farmhouse with a waterwheel, all dominated by a tall mosaic mural of the hotel's Rainbow Tower. The **Rainbow Bazaar** here is a good place to browse for souvenirs in all price ranges. ✉ *2005 Kālia Rd.,* ☎ *808/949–4321.*

❾ IMAX Waikīkī Theater. Immerse yourself in what is on a screen five stories high and 70 ft wide while surrounding yourself with digital stereo sound. The IMAX is managed by Consolidated Theatres, so call or consult local newspapers for shows and times. ✉ *325 Seaside Ave.,* ☎ *808/ 923–4629.* ✍ *$8.50, 2 films on same day $13, 3 films $16.* ☯ *Daily 11:30–9:30.* ✎

❿ International Market Place. The tropical open-air setting is fun to wander through, with wood-carvers, basket-weavers, and other artisans from various Pacific islands hawking their handicrafts. Intrepid shoppers find fun souvenirs here, and at the adjacent Duke's Lane. ✉ *2330 Kalākaua Ave.,* ☎ *808/923–9871.*

⓬ Kahuna (Wizard) Stones of Waikīkī. According to legend, these boulders preserve the magnetic legacy of four sorcerers—Kapaemahu, Kinohi, Kapuni, and Kahaloa—who came here from Tahiti sometime before the 16th century. Before leaving the Islands they transferred their mystic knowledge and healing powers to these rock-solid totems. Just to the west of these revered rocks is the **Duke Kahanamoku Statue,** erected

Waikīkī

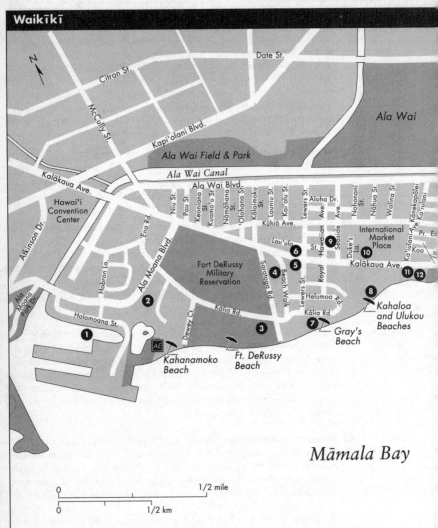

Māmala Bay

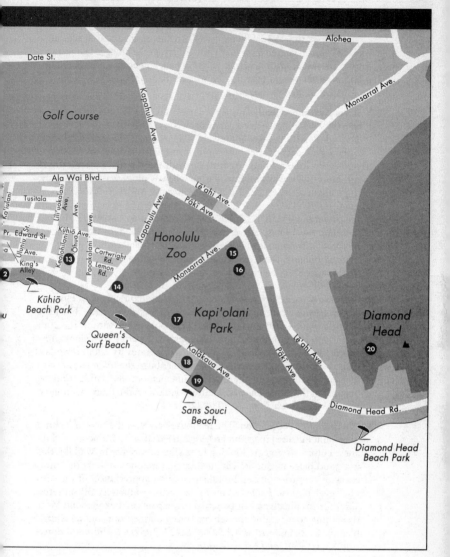

Alohea

Date St.

Monsarrat Ave.

Golf Course

Kapahulu Ave.

Ala Wai Blvd.

Tusitala

Liliʻuokalani Ave.

Kaʻiulani Ave.

Leʻahi Ave.

Pāki Ave.

Pr. Edward St.

Kūhiō Ave.

Kapahulu Ave.

Honolulu Zoo

ʻŌhua Ave.

Ulunu St.

Ave.

Kealohilani

Paoakalani Ave.

Cartwright Rd.

Lemon Rd.

13

King's Alley

Monsarrat Ave.

15

16

2

14

Kūhiō Beach Park

17

Kapiʻolani Park

Diamond Head

20

Queen's Surf Beach

Kalākaua Ave.

Pāki Ave.

Leʻahi Ave.

18

19

Sans Souci Beach

Diamond Head Rd.

Diamond Head Beach Park

in honor of Hawai'i's celebrated surfer and swimmer. Known as the "father of modern surfing," Duke won a gold medal for the 100-m freestyle at the 1912 Olympics. When the bronze statue was first placed here, it caused a wave of controversy, as the Duke is facing away from the water with his back to the ocean, something no safety-conscious surfer would ever do. ⊠ *Waikīkī Beach, Diamond Head side of Sheraton Moana Surfrider.*

❽ Royal Hawaiian Hotel. This legendary hotel sticks out amid the high-rises on Waikīkī Beach like a candy confection. Affectionately nicknamed the Pink Palace, the Royal Hawaiian opened in 1927, and the lobby, with its pink decor, is reminiscent of an era when visitors to the Islands arrived on luxury liners. A stroll through the Royal's coconut grove garden is like a walk back to a time when Waikīkī was still a sleepy, tropical paradise. ⊠ *2259 Kalākaua Ave.,* ☎ *808/923–7311.*

NEED A BREAK?   The **Island Snow** kiosk (⊠ Royal Hawaiian Shopping Center, 2201 Kalākaua Ave.) serves shave ice—a local favorite and the Hawaiian version of a snow cone. It comes in such exotic fruit flavors as guava, coconut, banana, litchi, and mango. To really go native, try it with ice cream and adzuki beans.

★ **⓫ Sheraton Moana Surfrider.** Listed on the National Register of Historic Places, this intricate beaux arts–style hotel was christened "The First Lady of Waikīkī" when she opened her doors at the turn of the 20th century. In 2001, this renovated landmark with period furnishings, historical exhibits, and plenty of nostalgia celebrates its 100th birthday. Visit the **Historical Room** in the rotunda above the main entrance to see the collection of old photographs and memorabilia dating from the opening of the hotel. Then enjoy afternoon tea on the **Banyan Veranda.** ⊠ *2365 Kalākaua Ave.,* ☎ *808/922–3111.*

❹ The Urasenke Foundation. The teahouse here was the first of its kind to be built outside Japan and provides an excellent introduction to Japanese culture. If you are looking for a slice of serenity in Waikīkī, this is a good place to find it. The meditative ceremony reflects the influences of centuries of Zen Buddhism and an appreciation of the simplicity of nature. Each ceremony lasts approximately 30 minutes. Visitors can either watch or be actual participants in the ceremony. Wear something comfortable enough for sitting on the floor (but no shorts, please). ⊠ *245 Saratoga Rd.,* ☎ *808/923–3059.* 🖃 *Minimum donation $2.* ☉ *Wed. and Fri. 10–noon.*

☾ **❸ U.S. Army Museum.** This museum at Ft. DeRussy houses an intimidating collection of war paraphernalia. The major focus is on World War II memorabilia, but exhibits range from ancient Hawaiian weaponry to displays relating to the Vietnam War. It's within Battery Randolf (Building 32), a bunker built in 1911 as a key to the defense of Pearl Harbor and Honolulu. Some of its walls are 22 ft thick. Guided group tours can be arranged. ⊠ *Ft. DeRussy, Bldg. 32, Kālia Rd.,* ☎ *808/438–2822.* 🖃 *Free.* ☉ *Tues.–Sun. 10–4:30.*

Kapi'olani Park and Diamond Head

Established during the late 1800s by King Kalākaua and named after his queen, Kapi'olani Park is a 500-acre expanse where you can play all sorts of sports, enjoy a picnic, see wild animals, or hear live music. It lies in the shadow of Diamond Head, Hawai'i's most famous natural landmark. Diamond Head got its name from sailors who thought they had found precious gems on its slopes. The diamonds proved to be volcanic refuse.

A Good Walk

The ʻewa end of Kapiʻolani Park is occupied by the **Honolulu Zoo** ⑭, on the corner of Kalākaua and Kapahulu avenues. Its 40 acres are home to 2,000 furry and finned creatures. On weekends look for the Zoo Fence Art Mart, on Monsarrat Avenue outside the zoo, on the Diamond Head side. You might find some affordable works by contemporary artists and craftspeople that make better Hawaiʻi keepsakes than the ashtrays and monkeypod bowls carved in the Philippines.

Across Monsarrat Avenue, between Kalākaua Avenue and Pākī Avenue in Kapiʻolani Park, is the **Waikīkī Shell** ⑮, Honolulu's outdoor concert arena. Next to the Shell is the site of the **Kodak Hula Show** ⑯. Cut across the park toward the ocean to the **Kapiʻolani Bandstand** ⑰, where you'll hear more free island tunes on days when community events are taking place.

Cross Kalākaua Avenue toward the ocean to the **Waikīkī Aquarium** ⑱ and its neighbor, the **Waikīkī War Memorial Natatorium** ⑲, an open-air swimming stadium built in 1927 to commemorate lives lost in World War I.

As it leaves Kapiʻolani Park, Kalākaua Avenue forks into Diamond Head Road, a scenic 2-mi stretch popular with walkers and joggers, and winds around the base of Diamond Head alongside the ocean, passing handsome Diamond Head Lighthouse (not open to the public). Lookout areas offer views of the surfers and windsurfers below. For those willing to undertake more strenuous walking, the hike to the summit of **Diamond Head** ⑳, Hawaiʻi's most famous landmark, offers a marvelous view. To save time and energy, drive, don't walk, along Diamond Head Road, turn left at Monsarrat Avenue, head a mile up the hill, and look for a sign on the left to the entrance to the crater. Drive through the tunnel to the inside of the crater. The trail begins at the parking lot.

TIMING

Budget a full day to see Kapiʻolani Park and Diamond Head. If you want to hike up to the crater's summit, do it before breakfast. That way you beat not only the heat but the crowds. Hiking Diamond Head takes an hour round-trip, but factor in some extra time to enjoy the views from the top. Keep an eye on your watch if you're there at day's end, because the gates close promptly at 6. If you want to see the Honolulu Zoo, it's best to get there right when it opens, since the animals are livelier in the cool of the morning. Give the aquarium an hour, including 10 minutes in its Sea Vision Theater. For the best seats at the 10 AM Kodak Hula Show, get there by 8 or so.

Sights to See

★ ⑳ **Diamond Head.** Once a military fortification, this 760-ft extinct volcanic peak provides the ideal 360-degree Oʻahu perspective for first-time visitors. Panoramas sweep from across Waikīkī and Honolulu in one direction and out to Koko Head in the other, with surfers and windsurfers scattered like confetti on the cresting waves below. Most guidebooks say there are 99 steps on the trail to the top. That's true of one flight, but there are four flights altogether. Bring a flashlight to see your way through a narrow tunnel and up a very dark flight of winding stairs. ⊠ *Monsarrat Ave. at 18th Ave.* 🎫 *$1.* 🕙 *Daily 6–6.*

☼ ⑭ **Honolulu Zoo.** There are bigger and better zoos, but this one is pretty, and on Wednesday evening in summer, the zoo puts on "The Wildest Show in Town," a free program of song, dance, and island entertainment. If you're visiting during a full moon, check out the zoo's Night Walks. Call or check the local newspaper for information about special events. The best part of the zoo is its 7½-acre African savanna, where animals roam freely on the other side of hidden rails and moats. ⊠ *151 Kapahulu Ave.,* ☎ *808/971–7171.* ☞ *$6.* ۞ *Daily 9–4:30.*

⑰ Kapi'olani Bandstand. At press time, the old Kapi'olani Bandstand had been torn down to make way for a new one reminiscent of the park's original Victorian-style bandstand. Scheduled for completion by mid-2000, it will host entertainment like the free Sunday-afternoon Royal Hawaiian Bands concerts offered in the past. Check the local newspaper for entertainment information. ⊠ *'Ewa end of Kapi'olani Park, mauka side of Kalākaua Ave.*

★ ⑯ Kodak Hula Show. This one-hour show, in the bleachers adjacent to the Waikīkī Shell, is colorful, lively, and fun. It has been wowing crowds since 1937. For the best viewpoints, come early for good seating. It's a great opportunity to take photographs. ⊠ *2805 Monsarrat Ave.,* ☎ *808/627–3379.* ☞ *Free.* ۞ *Tues.–Thurs. at 10.*

★ ☾ ⑱ Waikīkī Aquarium. This amazing little attraction harbors more than 300 species of Hawaiian and South Pacific marine life, including the giant clam, the chambered nautilus, and sharks. A recent $3 million renovation has added a Hawaiian Reef Habitat. Check out the Sea Visions Theater and ask about the new educational audio tour. ⊠ *2777 Kalākaua Ave.,* ☎ *808/923–9741.* ☞ *$7.* ۞ *Daily 9–5.*

⑮ Waikīkī Shell. Local people bring a picnic and get "grass seats" (lawn seating). Here's a chance to enjoy a magical night underneath the stars with some of Hawai'i's best musicians as well as visiting guest artists. Most concerts are held May 1 to Labor Day. Check the newspapers to see what's playing. ⊠ *2805 Monsarrat Ave.,* ☎ *808/924–8934.*

⑲ Waikīkī War Memorial Natatorium. This 1927 World War I monument stands proudly, its outer wall lighted at night, showing off what's left of the pair of eagle statues that sit atop the entrance. The natatorium facade was undergoing restoration at press time. The 100-m saltwater swimming pool remains closed to the public, and no determination has yet been made as to whether the pool will escape the wrecker's ball. ⊠ *2777 Kalākaua Ave.*

NEED A BREAK?   Next to the Waikīkī War Memorial Natatorium, you can enjoy breakfast, lunch, or dinner outdoors beneath the shade of a hau tree at the New Otani Kaimana Beach Hotel. Dubbed the **Hau Tree Lānai** (⊠ 2863 Kalākaua Ave., ☎ 808/921–7066), it's a little jewel if you want oceanfront refreshment.

Downtown Honolulu

Honolulu's past and present play a delightful counterpoint throughout the downtown sector. Modern skyscrapers stand directly across from the Aloha Tower, which was built in 1926 and was, until the early 1960s, the tallest structure in Honolulu. Old structures have found new meaning here. For instance, today's governor's mansion, built in 1846, was the home of Queen Lili'uokalani until her death in 1917.

To reach downtown Honolulu from Waikīkī by car, take Ala Moana Boulevard to Alakea Street. There are public parking lots (50¢ per half hour for the first two hours) in buildings along Alakea Street and Bethel Street, two blocks 'ewa. Keep in mind that parking in most downtown lots is expensive ($3 per half hour).

A Good Walk

Begin at the **Hawai'i Maritime Center** ㉑ at the harbor front, across Ala Moana Boulevard from Alakea Street in downtown Honolulu. This

Downtown Honolulu

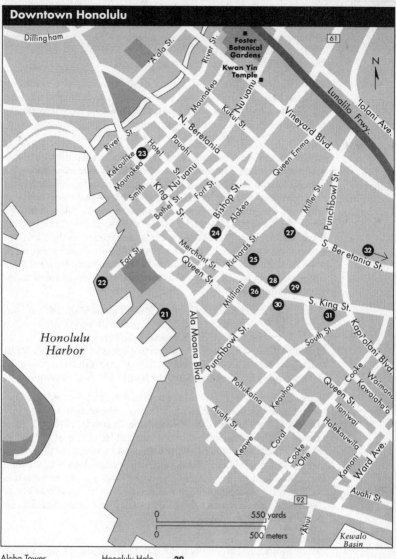

Honolulu Harbor

Foster Botanical Gardens

Kwan Yin Temple

0   550 yards

0   500 meters

Kewalo Basin

museum traces the history of Hawai'i's love affair with the sea. Just 'ewa of the Hawai'i Maritime Center is **Aloha Tower Marketplace** ㉒, a complex of harborside shops and restaurants where you can also view the luxury cruise liners in port and the traditional Hawaiian Boat Days celebrations that greet each arrival.

Cross Ala Moana Boulevard, walk a block 'ewa, and turn mauka on Ft. Street Mall, a pedestrian walkway, until you reach King Street. Turn left, and in a few blocks you'll reach **Chinatown** ㉓, the old section of downtown Honolulu. This area is crammed with mom-and-pop shops, art galleries, ethnic restaurants, and a big open market.

Walk back toward Diamond Head along King Street until it intersects with Bishop Street. On the mauka side is lovely **Tamarind Park** ㉔, a popular lunchtime picnic spot for Honolulu's workforce, which gathers under its shady plumeria, kukui, and monkeypod trees—and one tamarind. Continue down King Street until you reach **'Iolani Palace** ㉕, on the mauka side. This graceful Victorian structure was built by King David Kalākaua in 1882. Also on the palace grounds is the Kalākaua Coronation Bandstand, where the Royal Hawaiian Band performs at noon most Fridays. Past the palace is the massive stone **Hawai'i State Library** ㉘, built in 1913 and renovated in 1992, a showcase of architectural restoration.

Across King Street from 'Iolani Palace is Ali'iōlani Hale, the old judiciary building that served as the parliament hall during the kingship era. In front of it is the gilded **Kamehameha I Statue** ㉖, which honors Hawai'i's greatest monarch. Walk one block mauka up Richards Street to tour the **Hawai'i State Capitol** ㉗. Almost across the street from the state capitol is Washington Place, the home of Hawai'i's governor.

Return to King Street, stay on the mauka side, and proceed in a Diamond Head direction. At Punchbowl Street is **Honolulu Hale** ㉙, or City Hall. Across the street is the **Kawaiaha'o Church** ㉚, Hawai'i's most famous religious structure. On the Diamond Head side of the Kawaiaha'o Church is the **Mission Houses Museum** ㉛, where the first American missionaries in Hawai'i lived. From here it's three long blocks toward Diamond Head to Ward Avenue and one block mauka to Beretania Street, but the **Honolulu Academy of Arts** ㉜ is worth the extra mileage (you might choose to drive there instead). It houses a world-class collection of Western and Asian art.

TIMING

Downtown Honolulu merits a full day of your time. Be sure to stop by the palace Tuesday through Saturday, the only days tours are offered. Remember that the Mission Houses Museum is closed Sunday and Monday and the Honolulu Academy of Arts is closed Monday. Saturday morning is the best time to walk through Chinatown. That's when the open-air markets do their biggest business with local families. A walk through Chinatown can take an hour, as can tours of the Mission Houses and 'Iolani Palace. Wrap up your day at sunset with refreshments or dinner back at the Aloha Tower Marketplace, which stays open late into the evening, with live entertainment on the docks.

Sights to See

🖑 ㉒ **Aloha Tower Marketplace.** Two stories of shops, kiosks, indoor and outdoor restaurants, and live entertainment are here at the Honolulu Harbor with Aloha Tower as its anchor. For a bird's-eye view of this working harbor, take the free ride up to the tower's observation deck. The Marketplace's location makes it an ideal spot for watching the arrival of cruise ships. On Hawaiian Boat Days, the waterfront comes alive with entertainment and hula dancers who greet the arriving ships.

⊠ *101 Ala Moana Blvd., at Piers 8, 9, and 10,* ☎ *808/528–5700.* ⊙ *Daily 9–9, restaurants 9 AM–2 AM.*

㉓ **Chinatown.** Slightly on the tawdry side, this historic neighborhood has everything from art galleries in renovated structures to lei stands, herb shops, acupuncture studios, noodle factories, and Chinese and Thai restaurants. A major highlight is the colorful O'ahu Market, an open-air emporium with hanging pigs' heads, display cases of fresh fish, row after row of exotic fruits and vegetables, and vendors of all ethnic backgrounds. Check out the Chinese Cultural Plaza's Moongate stage for cultural events, especially around Chinese New Year's. ⊠ *King St. between Smith and River Sts.*

NEED A BREAK? There are Chinese, Thai, Japanese, Korean, and Italian food stalls at **Maunakea Marketplace** (⊠ 1120 Maunakea St., ☎ 808/524–3409), one block mauka of King Street. The food offerings are usually flavorful and reasonably priced. A courtyard has some seating.

☞ ㉑ **Hawai'i Maritime Center.** The main exhibits (some of which are interactive) are in the **Kalākaua Boat House,** where you learn about Hawai'i's whaling days, the history of Honolulu Harbor, the Clipper seaplane, and surfing and windsurfing in Hawai'i. Moored next to the Boat House are the *Falls of Clyde,* a century-old, four-masted, square-rigged ship now used as a museum; and the *Hōkūle'a,* a reproduction of an ancient Polynesian double-hull voyaging canoe. The *Hōkūle'a* has completed several journeys throughout the Pacific, during which the crew used only the stars and the sea as a navigational guide. ⊠ *Ala Moana Blvd., at Pier 7,* ☎ *808/536–6373.* ▣ *$7.50.* ⊙ *Daily 8:30–5.*

㉗ **Hawai'i State Capitol.** The capitol's architecture is richly symbolic: The columns look like palm trees, the legislative chambers are shaped like volcanic cinder cones, and the central court is open to the sky, representing Hawai'i's open society. The building is surrounded by reflecting pools, just as the Islands are embraced by water. ⊠ *215 S. Beretania St.,* ☎ *808/586–0178.* ▣ *Free.* ⊙ *Guided tour weekdays at 1:30.*

㉘ **Hawai'i State Library.** This beautifully renovated main library is wonderful to explore. Its "Asia and the Pacific" room has a fascinating collection of books old and new about Hawai'i. The center courtyard offers a respite from busy downtown. ⊠ *478 King St.,* ☎ *808/586–3500.* ▣ *Free.* ⊙ *Mon. and Fri.–Sat. 9–5, Tues. and Thurs. 9–8, Wed. 10–5.*

㉜ **Honolulu Academy of Arts.** Dating to 1927, the Academy has an impressive permanent collection including the James Michener collection of Hiroshige's Ukiyoe Japanese prints, Italian Renaissance paintings, and American and European art. Six open-air courtyards provide a casual counterpart to the more formal interior galleries. The Luce Pavilion complex, under construction at press time and scheduled to open in January 2001, will include 8,000 additional square ft of exhibition area, a larger café, and a gift shop. Call about special exhibits, concerts, and films. ⊠ *900 S. Beretania St.,* ☎ *808/532–8700.* ▣ *$7.* ⊙ *Tues.–Sat. 10–4:30, Sun. 1–5.* ▣

㉙ **Honolulu Hale.** The center of city government, this Mediterranean-Renaissance–style building was constructed in 1929. Stroll through the cool, open-ceiling lobby with exhibits of local artists, and time your visit to coincide with one of the free concerts sometimes offered in the evening, when the building stays open later. During the winter holiday season, the Hale becomes the focal point for the annual Honolulu City Lights Festival program. ⊠ *530 S. King St.,* ☎ *808/527–5666 for concert information.* ▣ *Free.* ⊙ *Weekdays 8–4:30.*

㉕ **'Iolani Palace.** Built in 1882 on the site of an earlier palace and beautifully restored today, this is America's only royal residence. It contains the thrones of King Kalākaua and his successor (and sister) Queen Lili'uokalani. The palace is open for guided tours only. Reservations are essential. Take a look at the gift shop, formerly the 'Iolani Barracks, built to house the Royal Guard. ⊠ *King and Richards Sts.,* ☎ *808/522–0832.* ☜ *$15.* ⊙ *Tues.–Sat. 9–2:15.*

NEED A BREAK?	For a quick pick-me-up, stop by **Lion Coffee** (⊠ 222 Merchant St., between Alakea and Richards Sts.) for an espresso, cappuccino, latte, or plain ol' cuppa joe along with a fresh-baked muffin, scone, or cookie. Lion Coffee shares space with Native Books & Beautiful Things, a lovely shop selling Hawaiian crafts and publications.

㉖ **Kamehameha I Statue.** This downtown landmark pays tribute to the Big Island chieftain who united all the warring Hawaiian Islands into one kingdom. He stands with one arm outstretched in welcome. The original version is in Kapa'au, on the Big Island, near the king's birthplace. Each year on June 11, his birthday, the statue is draped in leis. ⊠ *417 S. King St., outside Ali'iōlani Hale.*

㉚ **Kawaiaha'o Church.** Fancifully called Hawai'i's Westminster Abbey, this 14,000 coral-block house of worship witnessed the coronations, weddings, and funerals of generations of Hawaiian royalty. The graves of missionaries and of King Lunalilo are in the yard. The upper gallery has an exhibit of paintings of the royal families. Services in English and Hawaiian are held each Sunday. Although there are no guided tours, you can look around the church at no cost. ⊠ *957 Punchbowl St., at King St.,* ☎ *808/522–1333.* ☜ *Free.* ⊙ *Service Sun. at 8 AM, in Hawaiian at 10:30 AM, Wed. at 6 PM.*

㉛ **Mission Houses Museum.** The stalwart Hawai'i missionaries arrived in 1820, gaining royal favor and influencing every aspect of island life. Their descendants have become leaders in government and business. You can walk through their original dwellings, including a white-frame house that was prefabricated in New England, shipped around the Horn, and is today Hawai'i's oldest wooden structure. The museum hosts a variety of events throughout the year, including living history programs and holiday craft fairs. Certain areas of the museum may be seen only on a 1-hr guided tour. ⊠ *553 S. King St.,* ☎ *808/531–0481.* ☜ *$8.* ⊙ *Tues.–Sat. 9–4; guided tours at 9:45, 11:15, 1, and 2:30.*

㉔ **Tamarind Park.** From jazz and Hawaiian tunes to the strains of the U.S. Marine Band, music fills this pretty park at noon on Friday. Do as the locals do: Pick up lunch at one of the many carryout restaurants and find a bench or patch of grass. ⊠ *S. King St. between Bishop and Alakea Sts.,* ☎ *808/527–5666 for concert information.* ☜ *Free.*

The East O'ahu Ring

At once historic and contemporary, serene and active, the east end of O'ahu holds remarkable variety within its relatively small area, and its scenery includes windswept cliffs and wave-dashed shores. When touring this side of the island, don't forget the camera!

A Good Drive

From Waikīkī there are two routes to Lunalilo Freeway (H-1). On the Diamond Head end, go mauka on Kapahulu Avenue and follow the signs to the freeway. On the 'ewa end, take Ala Wai Boulevard and turn mauka at Kalākaua Avenue, staying on it until it ends at Beretania Street, which is one-way going left. Turn right off Beretania Street at Pi'ikoi Street, and the signs will direct you onto the freeway heading west.

Take the freeway exit marked Pali Highway (Hwy. 61), one of three roads that cut through the Ko'olau Mountains. On the right is the **Queen Emma Summer Palace** ㉝. The colonial-style white mansion, which once served as the summer retreat of King Kamehameha IV and his wife, Queen Emma, is now a museum.

As you drive toward the summit of the highway, the road is lined with sweet ginger in summer and red poinsettias in winter. If it has been raining, waterfalls will be tumbling down the chiseled cliffs of the Ko'olau. If it is very windy, those waterfalls can look as if they are traveling up the cliffs, not down, making them a sight to behold.

Watch for the turn to the **Nu'uanu Pali Lookout** ㉞. There is a small parking lot and a lookout wall from which you can see all the way up and down the windward coast—a view that Mark Twain called the most beautiful in the world.

As you follow the highway down the other side of the mountain, continue straight along what becomes Kailua Road. If you are interested in Hawaiian history, look for the YMCA at the Castle Hospital junction of Kalaniana'ole Highway and Kailua Road. Behind it is **Ulupō Heiau** ㉟, an ancient outdoor shrine. Ready for a detour? Head straight on Kailua Road to Kailua Beach Park (☞ Beaches Around O'ahu *in* Beaches, *below*), which many people consider the best on the island. The road twists and turns, so watch the signs.

Retracing your route back to Castle Junction, turn left at the intersection onto Kalaniana'ole Highway. Soon you will come to the simple town of **Waimānalo** ㊱. Waimānalo's two beaches are Bellows Beach, great for swimming and bodysurfing, and Waimānalo Beach Park, also safe for swimming (☞ Beaches Around O'ahu *in* Beaches, *below*).

Another mile along the highway, on the right, is **Sea Life Park** ㊲, home to the world's only "wholphin," the offspring of a whale and a dolphin. Across the highway from Sea Life Park is Makapu'u Beach (☞ Beaches Around O'ahu *in* Beaches, *below*), a beautiful cove that is great for seasoned bodysurfers but treacherous for weak swimmers. The road winds up a hill, at the top of which is a turnoff on the makai side to **Makapu'u Point** ㊳, a fabulous photo opportunity.

Next you'll see a long stretch of inviting sand called Sandy Beach (☞ Beaches Around O'ahu *in* Beaches, *below*). Tempting as this beach looks, it is not advisable to swim here because the waves are powerful and the rip currents more than tricky. From here the road twists and turns next to steep cliffs along the Koko Head shoreline. Offshore, the islands of Moloka'i and Lāna'i call like distant sirens, and every once in a while Maui is visible in blue silhouette. For the best photos, pull into the parking lot at **Hālona Blowhole** ㊴. At the top of the hill on the makai side of the road is the entrance to **Hanauma Bay** ㊵.

From here back to Waikīkī the highway passes several residential communities called Hawai'i Kai, Niu Valley, and 'Āina Haina, each of which has a small shopping center if you need a soda or a snack. Right before you turn off from Kalaniana'ole Highway you'll notice a long stretch of green on the makai side. This is the private Wai'alae Country Club, scene of the televised annual Sony Hawaiian Open Golf Tournament (☞ Spectator Sports *in* Outdoor Activities and Sports, *below*).

Take the Kīlauea Avenue exit. Turn left at the stoplight onto Kīlauea Avenue. Here you'll see Kāhala Mall (☞ Shopping Centers *in* Shopping,

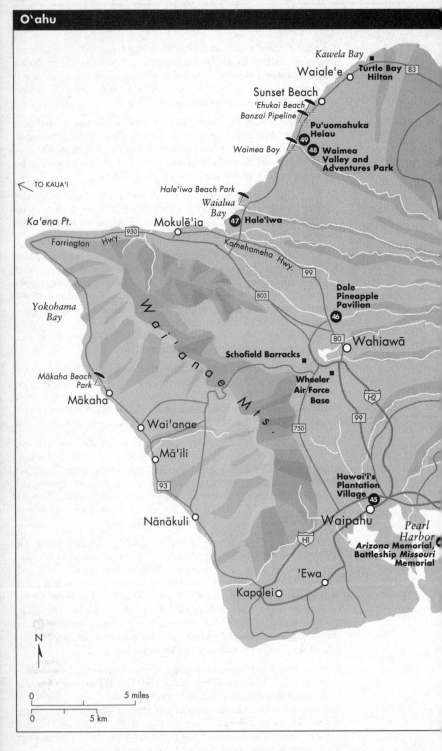

Kawela Bay

Waiale'e

Turtle Bay Hilton 83

Sunset Beach

'Ehukai Beach
Banzai Pipeline

Pu'uomahuka Heiau

49

Waimea Bay

48 **Waimea Valley and Adventures Park**

← TO KAUA'I

Hale'iwa Beach Park

Waialua Bay

Ka'ena Pt.

Mokulē'ia

47 **Hale'iwa**

Farrington Hwy.

930

Kamehameha Hwy.

99

803

Dole Pineapple Pavilion

46

Yokohama Bay

Waiʻanae Mts.

80 Wahiawā

Schofield Barracks

Mākaha Beach Park

Mākaha

Wheeler Air Force Base

H2

99

750

Wai'anae

Mā'ili

93

Hawai'i's Plantation Village

45

Nānākuli

Waipahu

Pearl Harbor

H1

Arizona **Memorial, Battleship** *Missouri* **Memorial**

'Ewa

Kapolei

N

| 0 | | 5 miles |
| 0 | | 5 km |

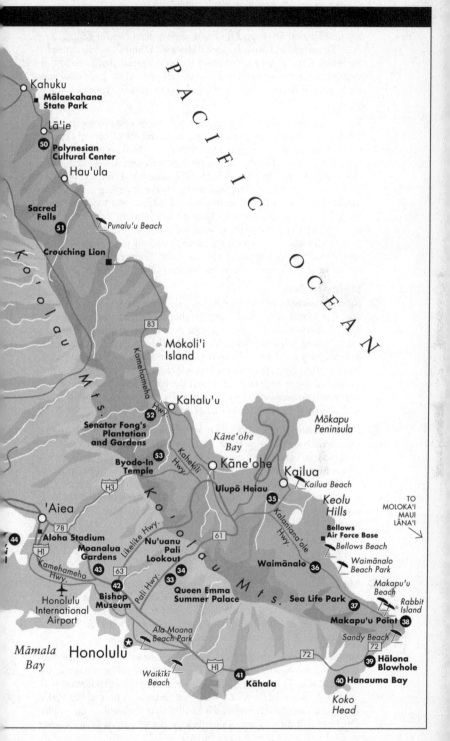

PACIFIC OCEAN

Kahuku
Mālaekahana State Park
Lā'ie
50 **Polynesian Cultural Center**
Hau'ula
Sacred Falls
51
Punalu'u Beach
Crouching Lion

K·o·'o·l·a·u M·t·s·

83
Kamehameha Hwy.

Mokoli'i Island

Kahalu'u
52
Senator Fong's Plantation and Gardens
Byodo-In Temple **53**
H3

Kahekili Hwy.

Kāne'ohe Bay

Mōkapu Peninsula

Kāne'ohe
Kailua
Ulupō Heiau
Kailua Beach

'Aiea
78
Aloha Stadium
Moanalua Gardens
Nu'uanu Pali Lookout
H1
44
43 63
42
Bishop Museum
34 33
Queen Emma Summer Palace

Likelike Hwy.
Kamehameha Hwy.
Poli Hwy.
61

Keolu Hills
35
Bellows Air Force Base
Bellows Beach
Waimānalo
Waimānalo Beach Park
36

Kalaniana'ole Hwy.

TO MOLOKA'I MAUI LĀNA'I

Makapu'u Beach
Rabbit Island
Sea Life Park
37
Makapu'u Point **38**
Sandy Beach
72
39 **Hālona Blowhole**

Honolulu International Airport

Mālama Bay

Honolulu ★
Ala Moana Beach Park

Waikīkī Beach
H1
41
Kāhala
72
40 **Hanauma Bay**

Koko Head

below), an upscale shopping complex with yuppie eateries, high-fashion stores, and eight movie theaters. A few blocks past the mall, take a left on Hunakai Street and follow it until it dead-ends at Kāhala Avenue. Turn right and drive through **Kāhala** ④, O'ahu's wealthiest neighborhood. Kāhala Avenue becomes Diamond Head Road. Follow it straight to Kapi'olani Park. Stay on the right side of the park until you hit Kapahulu Avenue. Take a left, and you're back in Waikīkī.

TIMING

Take your time, take all day, and enjoy a few beaches along the way. The weather is sunny and warm year-round, and the scenery of O'ahu's east side is too miraculous to rush through. If Hanauma Bay is your main focus, avoid Tuesday, when the park is closed. Also note that the bay is best in the early hours before the waters are churned up. You could reverse the above directions and get there first thing in the morning, before the crowds. Allow two hours for Hanauma Bay, two hours for Sea Life Park, and one for Queen Emma Summer Palace. Another tip: Look up to the top of the mountains and, if it's clear, head directly to the Pali Lookout. It's a shame to get there only to find the view obscured by clouds or fog. Bring a jacket along. Temperatures at the summit are several degrees cooler than in warm Waikīkī.

Sights to See

㊴ Hālona Blowhole. Below a scenic turnout along the Koko Head shoreline, this oft-photographed lava tube that sucks the ocean in and spits it out in lofty plumes may or may not perform, depending on the currents. Nearby is the tiny beach used to film the wave-washed love scene in *From Here to Eternity*. As you face the blowhole and the ocean, look down to your far right to see the beach. This beach is not recommended for swimming or even wading. Also, take your valuables with you and lock your car, because this scenic location is a hot spot for petty thieves. ⊠ *Kalaniana'ole Hwy., 1 mi east of Hanauma Bay.*

㊵ Hanauma Bay. One of O'ahu's most famous snorkeling destinations, this partially collapsed volcanic crater is home to more than 50 species of Hawaiian fish. Even from the overlook, the horseshoe-shape bay is a beauty, and you can easily see the reefs through the clear aqua waters. The wide beach is a great place for sunbathing and picnics. This is a marine conservation district, and new regulations prohibit the feeding of the fish. Come early to get parking as the number of visitors allowed per day is limited. Call for current conditions. The beach is closed to visitors on Tuesday. ⊠ *7455 Kalaniana'ole Hwy.,* ☎ *808/396–4229.* 🎫 *Donation $3; parking $1; mask, fins, and snorkel rental $6.* ⊙ *Wed.–Mon. 6–6.*

㊶ Kāhala. O'ahu's wealthiest neighborhood has streets lined with multimillion-dollar homes, and the classy **Kāhala Mandarin Oriental Hawai'i** hotel attracts a prestigious clientele. At intervals along tree-lined Kāhala Avenue are narrow lanes that provide public access to Kāhala Beach. ⊠ *East of Diamond Head.*

㊳ Makapu'u Point. This spot has breathtaking views of the ocean, mountains, and the windward islands. The peninsula jutting out in the distance is **Mōkapu**, site of a U.S. Marine base. The spired mountain peak is **Mt. Olomana**. In front of you on the long pier is part of the **Makai Undersea Test Range**, a research facility that is closed to the public. Offshore is **Rabbit Island**, a picturesque cay so named because some think it looks like a swimming bunny.

Nestled in the cliff face is the **Makapu'u Lighthouse,** which is closed to the public. Near the Makapu'u Point turnout, you'll find the start of a mile-long paved road (closed to traffic). Hike up it to the top of the 647-ft bluff for a closer view of the lighthouse and, during the winter months, a great whale-watching vantage point. ⊠ *Kalaniana'ole Hwy., turnout above Makapu'u Beach.*

③④ Nu'uanu Pali Lookout. This panoramic perch looks out to windward O'ahu. It was in this region that King Kamehameha I drove defending forces over the edges of the 1,000-ft-high cliffs, thus winning the decisive battle for control of O'ahu. It's a windy spot, so hang on to your hat. Lock your car if you get out, because break-ins have occurred here. ⊠ *Top of Pali Hwy.*

③③ Queen Emma Summer Palace. Built in 1848, this stately white home was used by Queen Emma and her family as a retreat from the rigors of court life in hot and dusty Honolulu during the mid-1800s. It has an eclectic mix of European, Victorian, and Hawaiian furnishings and has excellent examples of Hawaiian quilts and koa-wood furniture as well as the queen's wedding dress and other memorabilia. ⊠ *2913 Pali Hwy.,* ☎ *808/595–3167.* ⊡ *$5.* ☉ *Guided tours daily 9–4.*

☾ ③⑦ Sea Life Park. Dolphins leap and spin, penguins frolic, and a killer whale performs impressive tricks at the shows in this marine-life attraction. There's also a 300,000-gallon Hawaiian reef tank where you can come nose-to-nose with hundreds of marine creatures. The Pacific Whaling Museum, Hawaiian Monk Seal Care Center, Sea Turtle Lagoon, and a variety of interactive programs entertain and educate visitors about marine animals unique to Hawai'i. Even if you've seen trained cetaceans at other marine parks, the distinctively Hawaiian flavor makes this place special. The setting alone, right across from the ocean, is worth the price of admission. ⊠ *Kalaniana'ole Hwy., Waimānalo,* ☎ *808/259–7933.* ⊡ *$25.* ☉ *Daily 9:30–5.*

③⑤ Ulupō Heiau. Though they may look like piles of rocks to the uninitiated, *heiau* are sacred stone platforms for the worship of the gods and date from ancient times. *Ulupō* means "night inspiration," referring to the legendary *menehune,* a mythical race of diminutive people who supposedly built the heiau under the cloak of darkness. ⊠ *Behind YMCA at Kalaniana'ole Hwy. and Kailua Rd.*

....

NEED A
BREAK?
Generations of children have purchased their beach snacks and sodas at **Kalapawai Market** (⊠ 306 S. Kalāheo Ave.), near Kailua Beach. A windward landmark since 1932, the green-and-white market has distinctive charm. It's a good source for your carryout lunch, since there's no concession stand at the beach.

....

③⑥ Waimānalo. This modest little seaside town flanked by chiseled cliffs is worth a visit. Its biggest draw is its beautiful beach, offering glorious views to the windward side. Down the side roads, heading mauka, are little farms that grow a variety of fruits and flowers. Toward the back of the valley are small ranches with grazing horses. If you see any trucks selling corn and you're staying at a place where you can cook it, be sure to get some in Waimānalo. It may be the sweetest you'll ever eat, and the price is the lowest on O'ahu. ⊠ *Kalaniana'ole Hwy.*

Around the Island

After visiting three historic attractions in populated West Honolulu, you'll find that the O'ahu landscape turns increasingly rural as you head north. The center of the island is carpeted in pineapple and sugarcane plantations, which are slowly being phased out in favor of diversified agriculture. On the North Shore there are ranches, banana farms, and fields of exotic flowers grown for export. The plantation towns are small.

Some have become cute with boutiques and little art galleries. Others are just themselves—old, wooden, and picturesque—the small homes surrounded by a riot of flowers and tropical-fruit trees.

A Good Drive

Follow H-1 Freeway heading west. Take the exit for Likelike Highway. Stay in the right lane and look for signs to the **Bishop Museum** ㊷. The building alone, with its huge Victorian turrets and immense stone walls, is worth seeing. Once you're back on the freeway heading west, the road merges into the Moanalua Freeway (Rte. 78). Stay on this past the Pu'uloa Road–Tripler Hospital exit for **Moanalua Gardens** ㊸, a lovely park with huge, spreading monkeypod trees.

Continuing on the freeway, up over what is known as "Red Hill," you'll pass Aloha Stadium, a 50,000-seat arena that hosts the annual NFL Pro Bowl, local football and baseball games, and big-name rock concerts. The Aloha Flea Market (☞ Shopping Centers *in* Shopping, *below*) is also held here. As you approach the stadium on the freeway, bear right at the sign to 'Aiea, and then merge left onto Kamehameha Highway (Rte. 99), going south to Pearl Harbor. Turn right at the Hālawa Gate for a tour of the **Arizona Memorial, Battleship Missouri Memorial** ㊹, and the U.S.S. *Bowfin*.

Follow H-1 west to Waipahu (Exit 8B) and onto Farrington Highway. Turn right at Waipahu Depot Road and left onto Waipahu Street to reach **Hawai'i's Plantation Village** ㊺, a collection of restored original and replicated homes from a 19th-century plantation town.

Take H-1 to H-2 to Highway 80 (Kamehameha Hwy.), heading to Wahiawā, home of the U.S. Army base at Schofield Barracks. Head north until Highway 80 meets Highway 99, where you'll see a scrubby patch called the Del Monte Pineapple Variety Garden. Unpromising as it looks, it's actually quite interesting, with varieties of the ubiquitous fruit ranging from thumb-size pink ones to big golden ones.

Merge left on Kamehameha Highway and you'll see the **Dole Pineapple Pavilion** ㊻. From here, Kamehameha Highway cuts through pineapple and sugarcane fields. Close to the bottom of the hill, a traffic-light intersection invites you to take the Hale'iwa bypass road to save time. Don't. Turn left instead and drive to the traffic circle. Go around the circle and continue 7 mi to Mokulē'ia on Route 930. Soon you'll come to Dillingham Airfield, where you can fly in a glider (☞ Contacts and Resources *in* O'ahu A to Z, *below*).

Back at the traffic circle, follow the signs to **Hale'iwa** ㊼, a sleepy plantation town that has come of age with fashion boutiques, surf shops, restaurants, and the best grilled *mahimahi* sandwich (mild-flavored dolphinfish) on the North Shore at Kua 'Aina Sandwich (☞ Around the Island *in* Dining, *below*). Leaving Hale'iwa and continuing along Kamehameha Highway (Rte. 83), you'll pass the famous North Shore beaches, where the winter surf comes in size extra extra large. The first of these is the famous big surf spot Waimea Bay (☞ Beaches Around O'ahu *in* Beaches, *below*). Across the street, on the mauka side of the road, is **Waimea Valley and Adventures Park** ㊽. If you're interested in seeing a fine example of an ancient Hawaiian heiau, turn mauka at the Foodland store and take Pūpūkea Road up the steep climb, not quite a mile, to the dirt road on the right, leading to the **Pu'uomahuka Heiau** ㊾.

Continue along the coastal road past more famous surfing beaches, including 'Ehukai and Sunset (☞ Beaches Around O'ahu *in* Beaches, *below*). If it's wintertime, keep clear of those waves, which sometimes rise as high as 30 ft. Leave the sea to the daring (some say crazy) surfers who ride the towering waves with astounding grace. The only hotel of any consequence in these parts is your next landmark: the Turtle Bay Hilton (☞ Around the Island *in* Lodging, *below*). If it's Sunday between 10 and 2, you might want to stop for its incredibly extensive champagne brunch, served in a pretty oceanside dining room. Along this stretch of Kamehameha Highway, there is often a small lean-to set up with Kahuku watermelons for sale. By all means, buy one. They're the juiciest, sweetest melons you'll find in the Islands.

As you approach the town of Lāʻie, there is a long stretch of pine trees on the makai side. Look for the entrance to Mālaekahana State Park (☞ Beaches Around Oʻahu *in* Beaches, *below*). Coming up on the mauka side is the sprawling **Polynesian Cultural Center** ㊿.

As you continue driving along the shoreline, notice the picturesque little island of Mokoliʻi ("little lizard"), a 208-ft-high sea stack. According to Hawaiian legend, the goddess Hiʻiaka, sister of Pele, slew the dragon Mokoliʻi and flung its tail into the sea, forming the distinct islet. Other dragon body parts—in the form of rocks, of course—were scattered along the base of nearby Kualoa Ridge.

Continue straight on Kahekili Highway (Rte. 83) and look on your right for **Senator Fong's Plantation and Gardens** ㉒. Two miles farther on the right is the Valley of the Temples and its lovely **Byodo-In Temple** ㉓, a replica of a 900-year-old temple in Kyoto, Japan.

Follow Kahekili Highway to Likelike Highway (Hwy. 63), where you turn mauka and head back toward Honolulu through the Wilson Tunnel. The highway leads to Lunalilo Freeway going east. Exit at Pali Highway and go south through downtown Honolulu on Bishop Street. Then turn left on Ala Moana Boulevard, which leads to Kalākaua Avenue in Waikīkī.

TIMING

Unless you don't plan on stopping at any of the sights, allot nothing less than a day to circle the island. Try to factor in two or three different excursions and time-outs along this scenic North Shore. Don't rush through the Polynesian Cultural Center, because you'll miss much of what makes it so well done. Instead, devote an afternoon and evening to the center, perhaps stopping first for a morning at Waimea Valley. Note that the center is closed Sunday.

On another day, allow a full afternoon for the Bishop Museum. Inquire also about the "Behind-the-Scenes" museum tour. Afternoons, you may have to wait as long as two hours to see the *Arizona* Memorial. The best bet is to head out there early in the day. Haleʻiwa deserves two hours: Factor in some extra North Shore time for hiking, relaxing on a beach, going kayaking, taking a glider ride, and having a snack. Wear flip-flops but bring a pair of walking shoes as well.

The weather is mercurial on the North Shore. It can be sunny and clear in Waikīkī and cloudy in the country. Carry along a light jacket, a hat, and sunscreen. Then you're ready for anything.

Sights to See

★ ㊹   *Arizona* Memorial. A simple, gleaming white structure shields the hulk of the U.S.S. *Arizona,* which sank with 1,102 men aboard when the Japanese attacked Pearl Harbor on December 7, 1941. The tour includes a 20-minute documentary with actual news footage from the day of the attack and a shuttle-boat ride to the memorial. Appropriate dress is required (no bathing suits, slippers, or bare feet). ⊠ *National Park Service, Pearl Harbor,* ☎ *808/422–0561.* ☞ *Free. Tour tickets distributed on a first-come, first-served basis, with 1- to 3-hr waits common.* ⊙ *Daily 8–3.* ☜

④④ **Battleship *Missouri* Memorial.** The U.S.S. *Missouri*, which saw action from World War II to the Persian Gulf War, and on whose decks the agreement for Japanese surrender to end World War II was signed, was towed from Bremerton, Washington, to Pearl Harbor in 1998. The famed battleship, now moored about a 1,000 ft from the *Arizona*, opened as a museum and interactive educational center in 1999. Tours start at the visitor center located between the *Arizona* and U.S.S. *Bowfin* Memorial. A trolley transports you to the Navy's Ford Island, where you can board the "Mighty Mo," tour the educational exhibits, and see how 2,400 sailors lived and worked together in the shadow of its 16-inch guns. ⊠ *Pearl Harbor,* ☏ *808/545–2263 or 888/877–6477.* 🎫 *$12, guided tours $20, self-guided tours $14.* ☉ *Daily 9–5.* 🐾

OFF THE
BEATEN PATH

U.S.S. *BOWFIN* – Dubbed "the Pearl Harbor Avenger" and moored near the *Arizona* Memorial visitor center (☞ *above*), the *Bowfin* is one of only 15 World War II subs in existence. Children under four are not admitted. ⊠ *11 Arizona Memorial Dr., at Pearl Harbor,* ☏ *808/423–1342.* 🎫 *$8.* ☉ *Daily 9–5.* 🐾

---

④② **Bishop Museum.** Founded in 1889 by Charles R. Bishop as a memorial to his wife, Princess Bernice Pauahi, the museum began as a repository for the royal possessions of this last direct descendant of King Kamehameha the Great. Today it is the Hawaiʻi State Museum of Natural and Cultural History, with world-famous displays of Polynesian artifacts: lustrous feather capes; the skeleton of a giant sperm whale; an authentic, well-preserved grass house; and photography and crafts displays. Also visit the planetarium, hula and Hawaiian craft demonstrations, and special exhibits. ⊠ *1525 Bernice St.,* ☏ *808/847–3511.* 🎫 *$14.95.* ☉ *Daily 9–5.* 🐾

⑤③ **Byodo-In Temple.** Tucked away in the back of the Valley of the Temples cemetery is a replica of the Temple at Uji in Japan. A 2-ton statue of the Buddha presides inside the main temple building and alongside a meditation house and gardens set dramatically against the sheer, green cliffs of the Koʻolau Mountains. Visitors have the opportunity to ring the 5-ft, 3-ton brass bell for good luck and may also feed some 10,000 carp that inhabit the garden's ponds. ⊠ *47-200 Kahekili Hwy., Kāneʻohe,* ☏ *808/239–8811.* 🎫 *$2.* ☉ *Daily 8–4:30.*

④⑥ **Dole Pineapple Pavilion.** Celebrate Hawaiʻi's famous golden fruit at this promotional, tourist-oriented center with exhibits, a 10,000-square-ft gift shop, snack concession, agricultural display, and the world's largest maze. Although much more sophisticated than its original 1950 fruit stand, the Pavilion is filled with souvenir options galore and kids love the 1.7-mi "Pineapple Maze" made up of 11,400 colorful Hawaiian plants. ⊠ *64-1550 Kamehameha Hwy.,* ☏ *808/621–8408.* 🎫 *Pavilion free, maze $4.50.* ☉ *Daily 9–6.*

④⑦ **Haleʻiwa.** During the 1920s this seaside hamlet was a trendy retreat at the end of a railroad line. During the '60s hippies gathered here, followed by surfers. Today Haleʻiwa is a fun mix, with old general stores and contemporary boutiques, galleries, and eateries. Be sure to stop in at **Liliʻuokalani Protestant Church,** founded by missionaries in the 1830s. It's fronted by a large, stone archway built in 1910 and covered with night-blooming cereus. ⊠ *Follow H-1 west from Honolulu to H-2 north, exit at Wahiawā, follow Kamehameha Hwy. 6 mi, turn left at signaled intersection, then right into Haleʻiwa.*

NEED A
BREAK?

For a real slice of Haleʻiwa life, stop at **Matsumoto's** (⊠ 66-087 Kamehameha Hwy.), a family-run business. In a building dating to 1910, it sells shave ice, a tropical snow cone that costs about $1. They shave the ice right before your eyes and offer every flavor imaginable, including banana, mango, papaya, coconut, and strawberry.

....

45 Hawai'i's Plantation Village. Displays and authentically furnished buildings, both original and replicated, re-create Hawai'i's sugar plantation era. Tour a Chinese social hall, Japanese shrine, sumo ring, saimin stand, dental office, and historic homes at this "living museum" 30 minutes from downtown Honolulu. ⊠ *Waipahu Cultural Gardens Park, 94-695 Waipahu St., Waipahu,* ☎ *808/677–0110.* ⛟ *$5.* ⊙ *Mon.–Fri. 9–4, Sat. 10–4 with guided tours hourly.*

43 Moanalua Gardens. This lovely park is the site of a major hula festival on the third weekend in July. Throughout the year, the Moanalua Gardens Foundation sponsors hikes that leave from here to Moanalua Valley. Call for specific times. ⊠ *1401 Mahiole St., Honolulu,* ☎ *808/ 839–5334.* ⛟ *Free.* ⊙ *Weekdays 8–4.*

☝ 50 Polynesian Cultural Center. Re-created villages here represent Hawai'i, Tahiti, Samoa, Fiji, the Marquesas, New Zealand, and Tonga. This 42-acre center, founded in 1963 by the Church of Jesus Christ of Latter-Day Saints, showcases the lifestyles of the Pacific Rim cultures. Shows, restaurants, lū'aus, and cultural demonstrations enliven the area, and there's a spectacular IMAX film about the sea. Its expansive open-air shopping village features Polynesian handicrafts. If you're staying in Honolulu, it's better to see the center as part of a van tour so you won't have to drive home after the two-hour evening show. Various packages are available, from basic admission with no transportation to an all-inclusive deal. ⊠ *55-370 Kamehameha Hwy., Lā'ie,* ☎ *808/293– 3333 or 808/923–1861.* ⛟ *$27–$95.* ⊙ *Mon.–Sat. 12:30–9:30.*

49 Pu'uomahuka Heiau. Worth a stop for its spectacular views from a bluff high above the ocean overlooking Waimea Bay, this sacred spot was once the site of human sacrifices. It's now on the National Register of Historic Places. ⊠ *½ mi north of Waimea Bay on Rte. 83, turn right on Pūpūkea Rd. and drive 1 mi uphill.*

51 Sacred Falls. At press time, this popular hiking spot remains closed to the public after a landslide in 1999 caused fatalities and injuries. The Hawai'i State Department of Land and Natural Resources is still assessing the impact and had not yet determined if the area would reopen to hikers. Prior to this incident, a strenuous 2-mi hike led visitors to a gorgeous 80-ft-high waterfall. A swim in the pool beneath the falls was your reward at trail's end. To check on the status of this area, contact the Department of Land and Natural Resources, Parks Division Information, at the number listed below. If the park has reopened, be sure to go with someone else, and don't attempt the hike if there has been rain. The valley is subject to flash flooding, and the trail can be slippery. ⊠ *Kamehameha Hwy., Hau'ula,* ☎ *808/587–0300.* ⛟ *Free.*

52 Senator Fong's Plantation and Gardens. Hiram Fong, the first Asian-American to be elected to Congress, hasn't been a senator for many years, but this enterprising elder statesman still watches over his estate. At his 700-acre plantation there's a 45-minute guided tram tour of the landscaped grounds, including human-made ponds fed by natural springs. The visitor center has a snack bar and gift shop. ⊠ *47- 285 Pūlama Rd., off Kahekili Hwy., 2 mi north of Byodo-In Temple, Kahalu'u,* ☎ *808/239–6775.* ⛟ *$10.* ⊙ *Tram tours daily 9–4.*

☝ 48 Waimea Valley and Adventures Park. At this 1,800-acre attraction, remnants of an early Hawaiian civilization are surrounded by more than 2,500 species of flora from around the world. The garden trails are well marked, and the plants are labeled. You might spot a Hawaiian nēnē, the state bird. There's a spectacular show of cliff-diving from 45-ft-high falls, and you can take part in Hawaiian games and dances. Tour the backcountry on horseback or by kayak, mountain bike, or all-terrain vehicle. Free "moonwalks" are held two nights at the time of each full moon. ⊠ *59-864 Kamehameha Hwy., Hale'iwa,* ☎ *808/ 638–8511.* ⌨ *$24.* ☉ *Daily 10–5:30.*

BEACHES

For South Seas sun, fun, and surf, O'ahu is a dream destination, but first some words of caution: When approaching any Hawaiian beach, take notice of the signs! If they warn of dangerous surf conditions or currents, pay attention. Most beaches have lifeguards, although two exceptions are Kahana and Mālaekahano. Waikīkī is only 21 degrees north of the equator, so be aware that the sun here is very strong. No alcoholic beverages are allowed, and no matter which beach you choose, lock your car and never, ever leave your valuables unattended.

Waikīkī Beaches

The 2½-mi strand called **Waikīkī Beach** actually extends from Hilton Hawaiian Village on one end to Kapi'olani Park and Diamond Head on the other. Areas along this sandy strip have separate names but subtle differences. Beach areas are listed here from west to east.

Kahanamoku Beach. Named for Hawai'i's famous Olympic swimming champion, Duke Kahanamoku, this beach has decent snorkeling and swimming and a gentle surf. Its sandy bottom slopes gradually. The area has a snack concession, showers, a beach-gear and surfboard rental shop, catamaran cruises, and a sand volleyball court. ⊠ *In front of Hilton Hawaiian Village.*

★ **Ft. DeRussy Beach.** Sunbathers, swimmers, and windsurfers enjoy this beach fronting the military hotel, the Hale Koa, and the U.S. Army Museum. It is one of the widest in Waikīkī. It trails off to a coral ocean bottom with fairly good snorkeling sights. The beach is frequented by military personnel but is open to everyone. There are volleyball courts, food stands, picnic tables, dressing rooms, and showers. ⊠ *In front of Ft. DeRussy and Hale Koa Hotel.*

Gray's Beach. Named for a little lodging house called Gray's-by-the-Sea, which stood here in the 1920s, this beach is known for two good surfing spots called Paradise and Number Threes just beyond its reef. High tides often cover the narrow beach. Hawaiians used to consider this a place for spiritual healing and baptism and called it *Kawehewehe* ("the removal"). You'll find food stands, surfboard and beach-gear rental, and canoe and catamaran rides. ⊠ *In front of Halekūlani.*

★ **Kahaloa and Ulukou Beaches.** A lot of activities and possibly the best swimming are available along this little stretch of Waikīkī Beach. Take a catamaran or outrigger canoe ride out into the bay, unless you're ready to try your skill at surfing at this most popular beach. ⊠ *In front of Royal Hawaiian Hotel and Sheraton Moana Surfrider.*

★ **Kūhiō Beach Park.** This beach is named for Prince Jonah Kūhiō Kalaniana'ole, a distinguished native statesman who once had his home here on Waikīkī's shore. At press time, the area surrounding this beach was undergoing a major renovation to provide new facilities as well as a wider, sandier beach. Offshore you can see boogie boarders and bodysurfers enthusiastically riding the waves. It is also a great place to pick up dinner from the fast-food places across the street and head back to watch the sun set into the Pacific. ⊠ *Past the Sheraton Moana Surfrider Hotel to Kapahulu Ave. pier.*

Queen's Surf. A great place for a sunset picnic, this beach is beyond the seawall, toward Diamond Head, at what's known as the "other end of Waikīkī." It was once the site of Queen Liliʻuokalani's beach house, hence the name. A mix of families and gays gather here, and it seems as if someone is always playing a bongo drum. There are good shade trees, picnic tables, and a changing house with showers. ⊠ *Across from entrance to Honolulu Zoo.*

Sans Souci. Nicknamed Dig-Me Beach because of its outlandish display of skimpy bathing suits, this small rectangle of sand is nonetheless a good sunning spot for all ages. Children enjoy its shallow, safe waters, and the shore draws many ocean kayakers and outrigger canoeists. Serious swimmers and triathletes also swim in the channel here, beyond the reef. There's no food concession, but near one end is the Hau Tree Lānai restaurant. ⊠ *Makai side of Kapiʻolani Park, between New Otani Kaimana Beach Hotel and Waikīkī War Memorial Natatorium.*

Beaches Around Oʻahu

Here are Oʻahu's finer beaches, listed in alphabetical order.

Ala Moana Beach Park. Ala Moana has a protective reef, which keeps the waters calm and perfect for swimming. After Waikīkī, this is the most popular beach among visitors. To the Waikīkī side is a peninsula called Magic Island, with picnic tables, shady trees, and paved sidewalks ideal for jogging. Ala Moana also has playing fields, changing houses, indoor and outdoor showers, lifeguards, concession stands, and tennis courts. This beach is for everyone, but only in the daytime. It's a high-crime area after dark. ⊠ *Honolulu, makai side of Ala Moana Shopping Center and Ala Moana Blvd.; from Waikīkī take Bus 8 to shopping center and cross Ala Moana Blvd.*

Bellows Beach. The waves here are great for bodysurfing. Locals come here for the fine swimming on weekends (and holidays), when the Air Force opens the beach to civilians. There are showers, abundant parking, and plenty of spots for picnicking underneath shady ironwood trees. There is no food concession, but McDonald's and other take-out fare is available right outside the entrance gate. ⊠ *Entrance on Kalanianaʻole Hwy. near Waimānalo town center, signs on makai side of road.*

ʻEhukai Beach Park. ʻEhukai is part of a series of beaches running for many mi along the North Shore. What sets it apart is the view of the famous Banzai Pipeline, where the waves curl into magnificent tubes making it an experienced wave riders dream. In spring and summer, the waves are more accommodating to the average swimmer, but the winter waves are fierce and should not be challenged. The long, wide, and generally uncrowded beach has a changing house with toilets and an outdoor shower and water fountain. Bring along drinks because there is very little shade here, and the nearest store is a mile away. ⊠ *North Shore, 1 mi north of Foodland store at Pūpūkea, turn makai off Kamehameha Hwy. directly into the small parking lot bordering highway.*

Haleʻiwa Beach Park. The winter waves are impressive here, but in summer the ocean is like a lake, ideal for family swimming. The beach itself is big and often full of locals. Its broad lawns off the highway invite volleyball and Frisbee games and groups of barbecuers. There is a changing house with showers but no food concessions. Haleʻiwa has everything you need for provisions. ⊠ *North Shore, makai side of Kamehameha Hwy., north of Haleʻiwa town center and past harbor.*

★ **Hanauma Bay.** The main attraction here is snorkeling. The coral reefs are clearly visible through the turquoise waters of this sunken volcanic crater half open to the ocean. It is a designated marine preserve and closed one day a week to the public. Although the fish are the tamest you'll view while snorkeling, feeding them is no longer allowed. The bay is best early in the morning (around 7), before the crowds arrive. It can be difficult to park later in the day. There is a busy food and snorkel-equipment concession on the beach, plus changing rooms and showers. No smoking is allowed on the beach. Hanauma Bay Snorkeling Excursions (☎ 808/373–5060) run to and from Waikīkī. ⊠ *7455 Kalaniana'ole Hwy.,* ☎ *808/396–4229.* 🎫 *Donation $3; parking $1; mask, snorkel, and fins rental $6.* ⊘ *Wed.–Mon. 6 AM–7 PM.*

Kahana Bay Beach Park. Local parents often bring their children to wade in safety at this pretty beach cove with very shallow, protected waters. A grove of tall ironwood and pandanus trees keeps the area cool, shady, and ideal for a picnic. An ancient Hawaiian fishpond, which was in use until the '20s, is visible nearby. There are changing houses, showers, and picnic tables. Across the highway is Kahana Valley, burgeoning with banana, breadfruit, and mango trees. ⊠ *Windward side of island, makai of Kamehameha Hwy., north of Kualoa Park.*

★ **Kailua Beach Park.** Steady breezes attract windsurfers by the dozens to this long, palm-fringed beach with gently sloping sands. You can rent equipment in Kailua and try it yourself. This is a local favorite, so if you want the beach to yourself, head there on a weekday. There are showers, changing rooms, picnic areas, and a concession stand. Buy your picnic provisions at the Kalapawai Market nearby. ⊠ *Windward side, makai of Kailua town, turn right on Kailua Rd. at market, cross bridge, then turn left into beach parking lot.*

Kualoa Regional Park. This is one of the island's most beautiful picnic, camping, and beach areas. Grassy expanses border a long, narrow stretch of beach with spectacular views of Kāne'ohe Bay and the Ko'olau Mountains. Dominating the view is an islet called Mokoli'i, which rises 206 ft above the water. The one drawback is that it's usually windy. Bring a cooler because no refreshments are sold here. There are places to shower, change, and picnic in the shade of palm trees. ⊠ *Windward side, makai of Kamehameha Hwy., north of Waiāhole.*

Mākaha Beach Park. Because it's off the tourist track, this beach provides a slice of local life most visitors don't see. Families string up tarps for the day, fire up hibachis, set up lawn chairs, get out the fishing gear, and strum 'ukulele while they "talk story" (chat). The swimming is generally decent in the summer, but avoid the big winter waves. The ¼-mi beach has a changing house and showers and is the site of a yearly big-board surf meet. ⊠ *Wai'anae Coast, 1½ hrs west of Honolulu on H-1 Fwy. and Farrington Hwy., makai side of highway.*

Makapu'u Beach. Swimming at Makapu'u should be attempted only by strong strokers and bodysurfers, because the swells can be overwhelmingly big and powerful. Instead, consider this tiny crescent cove—popular with the locals—as a prime sunbathing spot. Finding parking in the small lot can be tricky. In a pinch, try parking on the narrow shoulder and walking down to the beach. There is a changing house with indoor and outdoor showers. ⊠ *Makai of Kalaniana'ole Hwy., across from Sea Life Park, 2 mi south of Waimānalo.*

Mālaekahana Beach Park. The big attraction here is tiny Goat Island, a bird sanctuary just offshore. At low tide the water is shallow enough—never more than waist high—so that you can wade out to it. Wear sneakers so you don't cut yourself on the coral. Families love to camp in the groves of ironwood trees at Mālaekahana State Park. The shade provides a welcome respite from the heat of the day. The beach itself is fairly narrow but long enough for a 20-minute stroll, one way. The waves are never too big, and sometimes they're just right for the beginning bodysurfer. There are changing houses, showers, and picnic tables. Note that the entrance gates are easy to miss because you can't see the beach from the road. ⊠ *Windward side, entrance gates are makai of Kamehameha Hwy., ½ mi north of Lā'ie.*

Sandy Beach. Strong, steady winds make "Sandy's" a kite-flyer's paradise. But the shore break is vicious here, and this beach has a reputation as one of the leading sites for injury to those who lack knowledge of how to handle rough surf. Do not swim here. Sandy's is a popular spot for the high school and college crowd. There's a changing house with indoor and outdoor showers but no food concessions. ⊠ *Makai of Kalaniana'ole Hwy., 2 mi east of Hanauma Bay.*

Sunset Beach. This is another link in the chain of North Shore beaches that extends for miles. It is popular for its gentle summer waves and crashing winter surf. The beach is broad, and the sand is soft. Lining the adjacent highway there are usually carryout truck stands selling shave ice, plate lunches, and sodas. ⊠ *North shore, 1 mi north of 'Ehukai Beach Park on makai side of Kamehameha Hwy.*

★ **Waimānalo Beach Park.** Boogie boarders and bodysurfers enjoy the predictably gentle waves of this beach. The lawn at Waimānalo attracts hundreds of local people who set up minicamps for the weekend, complete with hibachis, radios, lawn chairs, coolers, and shade tarps. Sometimes these folks are not very friendly to tourists, but the beach itself is welcoming, and from here you can walk a mile along the shore for fantastic windward and mountain views. The grassy, shady grounds have picnic tables and shower houses. ⊠ *Windward side, look for signs makai of Kalaniana'ole Hwy., south of Waimānalo town.*

★ **Waimea Bay.** Made popular in that old Beach Boys song "Surfin' U.S.A.," Waimea Bay is a slice of hang-ten heaven and home to the king-size 25- to 30-ft winter waves. Summer is the time to swim and snorkel in the calm waters. The beach is a broad crescent of soft sand backed by a shady area with tables, a changing house, and showers. Parking is almost impossible in the lot on weekends, so folks just park along the road and walk down. ⊠ *North shore across from Waimea Valley, 3 mi north of Hale'iwa on makai side of Kamehameha Hwy.*

Yokohama Bay. You'll be one of the few outsiders at this Wai'anae Coast beach at the very end of the road. It feels and looks remote and untouched, which may explain its lack of crowds. Locals come here to fish and swim in waters that are calm enough for children in summer. The beach is narrow and rocky in places. Bring provisions, because the nearest town is a 15-minute drive away. There's a changing house and showers, plus a small parking lot, but most folks just pull over and park on the side of the bumpy road. ⊠ *Wai'anae Coast, northern end of Farrington Hwy. about 7 mi north of Mākaha.*

DINING

If you are looking for a meal with a view, explore the restaurants at the upscale hotels and resorts that line O'ahu's shores. Settings can be as casual as a "barefoot bar" or as elegant as a romantic dinner for two under the stars. Beyond Waikīkī are culinary jewels tucked away in shopping centers and residential neighborhoods that specialize in ethnic cuisines. You'll almost never go wrong if you sample the offerings at any establishment whose name ends in the words "Drive Inn." Here you will find the local grinds, which are the staples of the Hawaiian diet: seafood plate lunches and noodle saimin soups. For snacks and fast food around the island, look for the lunch wagons, usually parked roadside near the beaches.

For an explanation of price categories, *see* Dining *in* Smart Travel Tips A to Z at the back of the book.

Waikīkī

Chinese

$$–$$$ ✕ **Golden Dragon.** Nearly 50 à la carte dishes and a six-course Sig-
★ nature Selection dinner make up the menu of fine Cantonese, Szechuan,
and nouvelle-Chinese dishes prepared by chef Steve Chiang. The restaurant, overlooking the lagoon on the mezzanine of the Hilton Hawaiian Village's Rainbow Tower, has a stunning red-and-black color
scheme, and there are lazy Susans on each table for easy sampling of
your companion's choices. Signature dishes include stir-fried lobster
with curry sauce and Szechuan beef. Two of the house specialties—the
Imperial Peking duck and Imperial beggar's chicken (whole chicken
wrapped in lotus leaves and baked in a clay pot)—must be ordered 24
hours in advance. ⊠ *Hilton Hawaiian Village, 2005 Kālia Rd., ☎ 808/
946–5336. Reservations essential. AE, D, DC, MC, V. No lunch.*

Contemporary

$$$ ✕ **Bali by the Sea.** In the Hilton Hawaiian Village, this restaurant is
★ breeze-swept and pretty, with an oceanside setting offering glorious views
of Waikīkī Beach. Overseeing the dining room is Chef Jean-Luc Voegele
from the Michelin three-star restaurant Le Crocodile in Strasborg,
France. The menu is a blend of French and Asian influences, with such
entrées as casserole of Hawaiian lobster and 'ōpakapaka (blue snap-
per) with Kaffir lime sauce. Another favorite is the rack of lamb crusted
with macadamia nuts and herbs. ⊠ *Hilton Hawaiian Village, 2005 Kālia
Rd., ☎ 808/941–2254. Reservations essential. AE, D, DC, MC, V. No
dinner Sun.*

$$–$$$ ✕ **Cascada.** This Waikīkī hideaway restaurant, in the Royal Garden
at Waikīkī hotel, was designed in the style of dining terraces found in
the villas of Southern Italy and France. The dining room has a hand-
painted trompe l'oeil ceiling and tables spilling out onto a marble ter-
race with tropical gardens and a cascading waterfall. Island flair goes
into the Mediterranean dishes created by Chef Matt Stephenson.
Grilled prawns, Royal crab cake served with Asian pesto aioli and rouille,
veal Milanese with arugula and mozzarella, and chicken Napoleon
saltimbocca style are a few of the popular choices. ⊠ *Royal Garden
at Waikīkī, 440 'Olohana St., ☎ 808/943–0202. AE, D, DC, MC, V.*

$$–$$$ ✕ **Duke's Canoe Club.** Beachfront in the Outrigger Waikīkī, and named
after Hawai'i's famous surfer Duke Kahanamoku, this eatery is casual
and usually crowded (reserve ahead or you'll probably wait for a table).
The entertainment is Hawaiian, and on weekend evenings the restau-
rant hosts sunset "concerts on the beach" on its outdoor terrace. Duke's
offers moderate prices with seafood and steak at the heart of its menu.
Fish can be served up Duke's style, which is baked in a garlic, lemon,
and sweet basil glaze to keep it tender and moist. The chef will also grill,
sauté, roast, or hibachi your fish selection. Other Duke's specialties in-
clude Caesar salad and macadamia-and-crab wontons. There is also a
barefoot bar. Duke's is very popular, so even though reservations are
not essential, be sure to call ahead. ⊠ *Outrigger Waikīkī on the Beach,
2335 Kalākaua Ave., ☎ 808/922–2268. AE, D, DC, MC, V.*

$$–$$$ ✕ **Hau Tree Lānai.** Dining out of doors next to the ocean is what a va-
cation in Hawai'i is all about, and this is a great place to do it. At break-
fast, lunch, or dinner you can dine under graceful hau trees right beside
the sand at Kaimana Beach and hear the whisper of the waves. Break-
fast offerings include a huge helping of eggs Benedict, fluffy Belgian
waffles with your choice of toppings (strawberries, bananas, or
macadamia nuts), and a tasty fresh salmon omelet. Two standout din-
ner entrées are the jumbo shrimp with mushrooms, tomatoes, Maui
onions, and white wine over fettuccine and a sesame-crusted hoisin rack

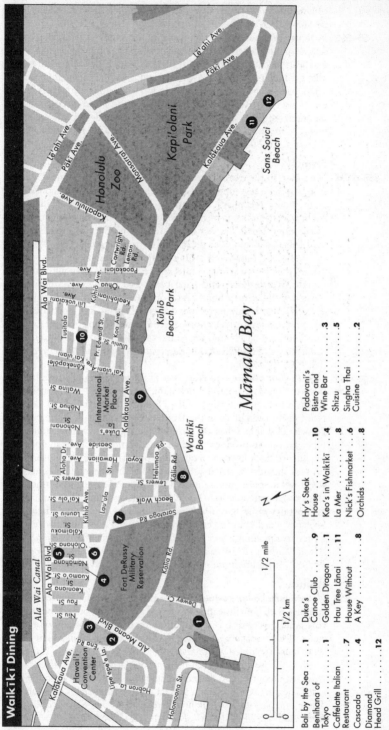

Waikīkī Dining

Bali by the Sea 1
Benihana of Tokyo 1
Caffelatte Italian Restaurant 7
Cascada 4
Diamond Head Grill 12
Duke's Canoe Club 9
Golden Dragon 1
Hau Tree Lānai 11
House Without A Key 8
Hy's Steak House 10
Keo's in Waikīkī 4
La Mer 8
Nick's Fishmarket 6
Orchids 8
Padovani's Bistro and Wine Bar 3
Shizu 5
Singha Thai Cuisine 2

Ala Wai Canal

Ala Wai Blvd.

Ala Wai Blvd.

Hawai'i Convention Center

Kalākaua Ave.

Lili'uokalani Ave.

Tusitala

Kūhiō Ave.

'Ōhua Ave.

Paokalani Ave.

Cartwright Rd.
Lemon Rd.

Kapahulu Ave.

Honolulu Zoo

Kapi'olani Park

Iē'ahi Ave.

Pākī Ave.

Monsarrat Ave.

Kalākaua Ave.

Sans Souci Beach

Kūhiō Beach Park

Waikīkī Beach

International Market Place

Duke's Ln.

Kalākaua Ave.

Nohonani St.
Nāhua St.
Walina St.
Kāneakapolei St.
Ka'iulani Ave.
Pr. Edward St.
Uluniu Ave.
Liliu St.
Koa Ave.

Seaside Ave.
Hawaiian Ave.
Aloha Dr.
Royal Hawaiian Ave.
Lewers St.
Lau'ula St.
Kai'olu St.
Beach Walk
Saratoga Rd.
Helumoa Rd.
Kālia Rd.

Fort DeRussy Military Reservation

Kālia Rd.

Ala Moana Blvd.

Niu St.
Pau St.
Ke'eaumoku St.
Kuamo'o St.
Nāhua St.
Olohana St.
Kalamoku St.
Kūhiō Ave.

Holomoana St.
Hobron La.
Lipe'epe'e La.
Kalākaua Ave.
'Ena Rd.

Dewey Ct.

Māmala Bay

N

0   1/2 mile
0   1/2 km

of lamb. ⊠ *New Otani Kaimana Beach Hotel, 2863 Kalākaua Ave.,* ☎ *808/921–7066. Reservations essential. AE, D, DC, MC, V.*

$$–$$$ ✕ **House Without a Key.** This is one of the jewels of Waikīkī, a casual seaside spot in the serene Halekulani hotel and serving salads, sandwiches, and hearty meals. Special meat, fish, pasta, and chicken entrées are available for lunch or dinner. Favorites include Joy's Sandwich (crabmeat salad, bacon, and avocado on whole-wheat bread) and the beef burger on a kaiser roll. With the ocean and Diamond Head in view, this is a mesmerizing place at sunset, when there's wonderful live entertainment. A breakfast buffet is served daily 7–10:30. ⊠ *Halekūlani, 2199 Kālia Rd.,* ☎ *808/923–2311. Reservations not accepted. AE, MC, V.*

French

$$$–$$$$ ✕ **La Mer.** In the exotic, oceanfront atmosphere of a Mandalay man-
★ sion, you'll be served neoclassic French cuisine that many consider to be the finest in Hawai'i. Here, on the grounds of the Halekulani, is a room as luscious as its menu. Open to the ocean with sweeping views of Diamond Head, La Mer celebrates the marriage of French and Island cuisines. Begin your meal with tartares of *hamachi* (yellowtail), *'ahi* (yellowfin tuna), and salmon with three caviars. Entrées include *onaga* (pink or red snapper) fillet cooked skin-side crisp with confit of tomato, truffle juice, and fried basil, and breast of Barbary duck roasted with lavender honey. A favorite sweet is the symphony of four desserts. Also highly recommended is the cheese and port course. In addition to à la carte selections, there are two complete dinner menus: four courses for $85 and six courses for $105. ⊠ *Halekūlani, 2199 Kālia Rd.,* ☎ *808/923–2311. Reservations essential. Jacket required. AE, MC, V. No lunch.*

$$–$$$ ✕ **Padovani's Bistro and Wine Bar.** Philippe Padovani gained fame at
★ three top Hawai'i hotels (Halekūlani, Ritz-Carlton, and Mānele Bay) and as a founding member of the Hawai'i Regional Cuisine Council. Now, at his own place in the Doubletree Alana Waikīkī, he presents French food that relies on local seafood, greens, herbs, fruits, and other Hawaiian products. The chef's specialties include an appetizer of panfried duck liver and a tart of onion marmalade and mushrooms. Entrées include panfried venison loin with ginger plum sauce and sweet-potato purée, and sautéed tiger shrimp with mushroom-herb polenta and tomato and basil sauce. The room is small and romantic, and an upstairs wine bar offers 50 varietals by the glass, single-malt Scotches, snacks, and an enclosed cigar room. Padovani's also features a prix-fixe menu for $45 and a tasting menu for $85. ⊠ *Doubletree Alana Waikīkī, 1956 Ala Moana Blvd.,* ☎ *808/946–3456 or 808/ 947–1236. Reservations essential. AE, D, DC, MC, V.*

Italian

$$$ ✕ **Caffelatte Italian Restaurant.** A family from Milan operates this tiny trattoria with limited seating inside and a few tables outside on the narrow lānai. Every dish is worth ordering, from the gnocchi in a thick, rich sauce of Gorgonzola cheese to the veal scallopini in a light white-wine sauce sprinkled with parsley. For dessert, the tiramisù is the best in town. Be aware that each person must order three courses (appetizer, main course, and dessert), a rule that keeps the tab on the high side. The chef will prepare a special mystery dinner for two for $60. There's no parking, so walk here if you can. ⊠ *339 Saratoga Rd., 2nd level,* ☎ *808/924–1414. AE, DC, MC, V. Closed Tues.*

Japanese

$$–$$$ ✕ **Shizu.** Come here for traditional Japanese cooking in a contemporary setting overlooking an extensive Japanese rock garden. The two *teppanyaki* rooms, which seat 8 and 10 people respectively, have spec-

tacular stained-glass windows with vibrant irises. Teppanyaki diners sit around a massive iron grill on which a dexterous chef slices and cooks sizzling meats and vegetables. An elaborate 10-course teppanyaki dinner is one of the offerings. There's also a sushi bar and other traditional dishes such as tempura. Try green-tea cheesecake for dessert. ⊠ *Royal Garden at Waikīkī, 440 'Olohana St., 4th floor,* ☎ *808/943–0202. AE, D, DC, MC, V.*

$–$$ ✕ **Benihana of Tokyo.** These restaurants are as famous for their cutting-board theatrics at the *teppan* (iron grill) tables as they are for their food. If you don't mind being seated with people you have not yet met, and love to watch your meal being sliced, diced, tossed, and sautéed before your eyes, this might be a nice alternative to formal restaurant dining. There's not much variety to the menu, but it's still a lot of fun. Finish off the meal with some green-tea ice cream, a Benihana tradition. ⊠ *Hilton Hawaiian Village, 2005 Kālia Rd.,* ☎ *808/955–5955. Reservations essential. AE, D, DC, MC, V.*

Seafood

$$$–$$$$ ✕ **Orchids.** It seems only fitting that you can hear the waves from this
★   oceanfront dining room that lays out the best seafood bar in town, including sashimi, *poke* (marinated raw fish), and shellfish. Recommended menu offerings include pistachio-crusted *hapuupūu* sea bass and a hearty paella that combines fresh-caught fish, mussels, jumbo shrimp, squid, and saffron rice. Meat and poultry dishes include a mustard-herb roasted Colorado lamb rack and tandoori-roasted island chicken. Outdoor and indoor seating is available, with the best views from the lānai. ⊠ *Halekūlani, 2199 Kālia Rd.,* ☎ *808/923–2311. Reservations essential. AE, MC, V.*

$$–$$$$ ✕ **Nick's Fishmarket.** It's a little old-fashioned, perhaps—black booths,
★   candlelight, and formal table settings—but it's hard to beat Nick's seafood. The bouillabaisse is an outstanding combination of lobster, crab, prawns, mussels, clams, and fish. Nick's is one of the few places with abalone on the menu. Here it's sautéed and served with lobster risotto. Nick's is also the place for *imu*-style seafood: Ti leaves and hot lava rocks line the cooking pot to steam such delicacies as Tristan lobster tail, scallops, and salmon. Leave room for Vanbana Pie, a decadent combination of bananas, vanilla Swiss-almond ice cream, and hot caramel sauce. ⊠ *Waikīkī Gateway Hotel, 2070 Kalākaua Ave.,* ☎ *808/955–6333. Reservations essential. AE, D, DC, MC, V.*

Steak

$$–$$$$ ✕ **Hy's Steak House.** Things always seem to go well at Hy's, from the filet mignon tartare and oysters Rockefeller right through to the flaming desserts. The atmosphere is snug and librarylike, and you can watch the chef perform behind glass. Tuxedoed waiters make helpful suggestions about the menu. Hy's is famous for its kiawe-broiled New York strip steak, cold-water lobster tail, and rack of lamb. The Caesar salad is excellent, as are the panfried O'Brien potatoes. ⊠ *Waikīkī Park Heights Hotel, 2440 Kūhiō Ave.,* ☎ *808/922–5555. Reservations essential. AE, DC, MC, V. No lunch.*

Thai

$$–$$$ ✕ **Singha Thai Cuisine.** Dishes here are prepared in traditional Thai
★   fashion, with just a sprinkling of Hawaiian regional flavorings. Seafood, vegetarian curry dishes, and the Thai chili are wonderful. Singha's beautiful Royal Thai dancers dressed in traditional costume add to the occasion, performing nightly center stage in the restaurant. ⊠ *1910 Ala Moana Blvd.,* ☎ *808/941–2898. Reservations essential. AE, D, DC, MC, V. No lunch.*

$$ ✕ **Keo's in Waikīkī.** Hollywood celebrities have discovered this twin-
★   kling nook with tables set amid lighted trees, big paper umbrellas, and
sprays of orchids everywhere. In fact, photos of Keo with different star
patrons are displayed on one wall. What many may not know is that
many of the herbs, vegetables, fruits, and flowers found at Keo's are
grown on his O'ahu North Shore farm. Favorite dishes include Evil Jun-
gle Prince (shrimp, vegetables, or chicken in a sauce flavored with basil,
coconut milk, and red chili) and *chiang mai* salad (chicken salad sea-
soned with lemongrass, red chili, mint, and fish sauce). Consider or-
dering your food mild or medium. It'll still be hot, but not as hot as it
could be. For dessert, the apple bananas (small, tart bananas grown
in Hawai'i) in coconut milk are wonderful. ✉ *2028 Kūhiō Ave.,* ☎
808/951–9355. Reservations essential. AE, D, DC, MC, V. No lunch.

Honolulu

American/Casual

$-$$ ✕ **California Pizza Kitchen.** This trio of dining and watering holes for
young fast-trackers is worth the likely wait for a table. At the Kāhala
site, a glass atrium with tiled and mirrored walls and one side open to
the shopping mall creates a sidewalk-café effect. Its newest location,
on the top level of the Ala Moana Center, offers a great respite for the
weary shopper. The pizzas have unusual toppings, such as Thai chicken,
Peking duck, and Caribbean shrimp. The pastas are made fresh daily.
✉ *Kāhala Mall, 4211 Wai'alae Ave.,* ☎ *808/737–9446;* ✉ *Ala Moana
Shopping Center, 1940 Ala Moana Blvd.,* ☎ *808/941–7715;* ✉ *554
Pearlridge Center Downtown, 'Aiea,* ☎ *808/487–7741. Reservations
not accepted. AE, D, DC, MC, V.*

$-$$ ✕ **Hard Rock Cafe.** The Honolulu branch of this international chain
has rock-and-roll memorabilia along with surfboards and aloha shirts
for local color. The Hard Rock has always sold more T-shirts than T-
bones, so don't expect culinary surprises on its formula menu. The por-
tion-controlled quarter-pound burgers hold sway, but don't overlook
the 'ahi steak sandwiches or the watermelon baby-back ribs. French
fries are, of course, a must. The decibel level of the oldies playing over
the sound system is set at "too loud," and you'll probably have to wait
for a table. ✉ *1837 Kapi'olani Blvd.,* ☎ *808/955–7383. Reservations
not accepted. AE, MC, V.*

$ ✕ **L & L Drive Inn.** In the Kāhala Mall, and at more than 40 neighborhood
locations throughout the island, the "drive inn" serves up an impressive mix of Asian-American and Hawaiian-style barbecue plate lunches.
Chicken *katsu* (cutlet), beef curry, and seafood mix plates include two
scoops of rice and macaroni salad. There are also "mini" versions of
the large-portion plates that include just one scoop of starch. This is
great casual island dining, with prices that are very affordable. Great
for takeout: Pick up lunch and head to the nearest beach park. ✉ *Kāhala
Mall Shopping Center, 4211 Waialae Ave.,* ☎ *808/732–4042. Reservations not accepted. No credit cards.*

Barbecue

$-$$ ✕ **Dixie Grill.** This southern-inspired eatery emphasizes just how much
fun food can be. Why, there's even an outdoor sandbox for the kids!
Dixie Grill specializes in baby back ribs, smoked barbecue chicken, whole
Dungeness crab, campfire steak, and fried catfish. Recipes for the bar-
becue sauces come from Memphis, the Carolinas, Georgia, and Texas.
Sandwiches, salads, and comfort foods like meat loaf round out the
dinner menu. Save room for the Georgia peach cobbler. ✉ *404 Ward
Ave.,* ☎ *808/596–8359. AE, D, DC, MC, V.*

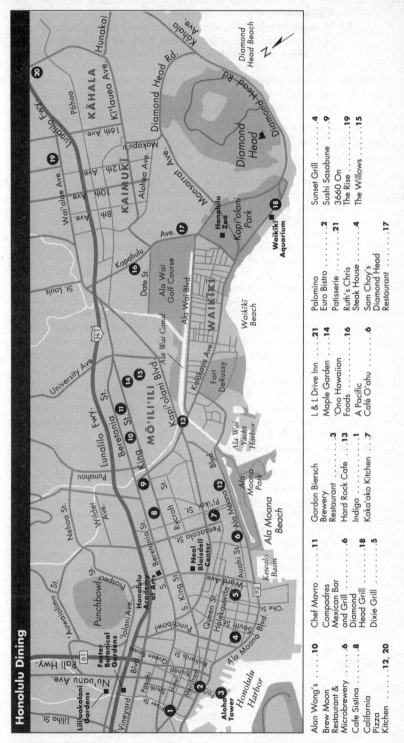

Honolulu Dining

Alan Wong's **10**
Brew Moon
Restaurant &
Microbrewery **6**
Cafe Sistina **8**
California
Pizza
Kitchen **12, 20**

Chef Mavro **11**
Compadres
Mexican Bar
and Grill **6**
Diamond
Head Grill **18**
Dixie Grill **5**

Gordon Biersch
Brewery
Restaurant **3**
Hard Rock Cafe . . **13**
Indigo **1**
Kaka'ako Kitchen . . **7**

L & L Drive Inn . . . **21**
Maple Garden . . . **14**
'Ono Hawaiian
Foods **16**
A Pacific
Café O'ahu **7**

Palomino
Euro Bistro **2**
Patisserie **21**
Ruth's Chris
Steak House **4**
Sam Choy's
Diamond Head
Restaurant **17**

Sunset Grill **4**
Sushi Sasabune . . . **9**
3660 On
The Rise **19**
The Willows **15**

Chinese

$–$$ ✕ **Maple Garden.** The reputation of Maple Garden is founded on spicy Mandarin cuisine, not on decor. There are some booths, an Oriental screen or two, and lights that are a little too bright. It's comfortable, however, and that's all that matters, because the food is delicious. Consistent favorites are the eggplant in a tantalizing hot garlic sauce, lobster in black-bean sauce, and a Peking duck that must be ordered 24 hours in advance. ✉ *909 Isenberg St.,* ☎ *808/941–6641. MC, V.*

Contemporary

$$$–$$$$
★   ✕ **Chef Mavro.** Named for chef-owner George Mavrothalassitis, formerly of the Four Seasons Maui and Halekūlani, this high-end bistro marries island ingredients with contemporary French techniques. The chef bakes onaga in a crust of Hawaiian salt, herbs, and *ogo* (seaweed), and his terrine of marinated Waimānalo vegetables comes with diced Japanese pickles. Three prix-fixe menus are accompanied by suggested wines by the glass. The menu changes monthly, a testament to Chef Mavro's creativity and commitment to local, seasonal ingredients. ✉ *1969 S. King St.,* ☎ *808/944–4714. Reservations essential. AE, DC, MC, V. No lunch.*

$$–$$$$
★   ✕ **Alan Wong's.** Wong focuses heavily on Hawaiian-grown products to keep the flavors super fresh, and he's utterly creative, turning local grinds into beautifully presented gourmet treats. For starters, get "Da Bag," a puffed-up foil bag that's punctured at the table, revealing steamed clams, *kālua* (roasted) pork, spinach, and shiitake mushrooms. Garlic-mashed potatoes come with a black-bean salsa, grilled pork chops with a coconut-ginger sweet potato purée. Don't miss the coconut sorbet served in a chocolate-and-macadamia-nut shell and surrounded by exotic fruits. The dining room is low-key, and there's a display kitchen. Finding the restaurant can be difficult: Look for a white apartment building and a small sign after a parking garage where your car can be valet parked. ✉ *McCully Court, 1857 S. King St., 3rd floor,* ☎ *808/949–2526. AE, MC, V. No lunch.*

$$–$$$ ✕ **Diamond Head Grill.** When the Colony Surf Hotel became a Starwood W hotel, this restaurant, formerly David Paul's Diamond Head Grill, became home to one of Hawai'i's newest generation of hot chefs: David Reardon, the former executive chef of the Orchid at Mauna Lani. The grill is open daily for breakfast and dinner and for lunch on weekdays. The breakfast menu features macadamia-and-ginger waffles with *pohā*-berry butter (poha is Hawaiian for cape gooseberry), crab and egg crepes, and a local-style fried rice with Portuguese sausage and two fried eggs. Lunch and dinner appetizers include a kālua pork *lumpia* (spring roll) with mango guacamole and spicy mustard sauce and a coconut curry seafood chowder. Entrées like grilled yellowfin tuna with hot-and-sour lobster soy broth, sweet Kahuku corn-and-carrot risotto, and guava-and-mustard-crusted rack of lamb round out the menu. There's a serpentine martini bar and a baby grand piano for live evening entertainment. ✉ *W Honolulu–Diamond Head Hotel, 2885 Kalākaua Ave.,* ☎ *808/922–3734. Reservations essential. AE, D, MC, V.*

$$–$$$
★   ✕ **Sam Choy's Diamond Head Restaurant.** His motto is "Never trust a skinny chef," and indeed, Choy's broad girth and even broader smile let you know you'll be well taken care of here. The theme is upscale local, as the Hawai'i-born chef contemporizes the foods he grew up with. The result? Deep-fried, Brie-stuffed wontons with pineapple marmalade; fresh fish and vegetables wrapped in ti leaves; seared 'ahi seasoned with ginger; and roasted duck with a Big Island orange sauce. Portions are huge. Two people can easily split an entrée. ✉ *449 Kapahulu Ave., 2nd fl.,* ☎ *808/732–8645. AE, MC, V. No lunch.*

$$-$$$ ✕ **Sunset Grill.** The sweet smell of wood smoke greets you as you enter the Sunset Grill, which specializes in kiawe-broiled foods. The place is supposed to feel unfinished, with the marble bar top and white tablecloths contrasting nicely with the concrete floors. The salade niçoise, big enough for a whole dinner, includes marinated grilled 'ahi. The trout and scallops, cooked in a wood oven, are both very good. The grilled ribs and the daily specials, especially the pastas, accompanied with a glass of wine from its extensive 400-bottle wine list, are definitely worth a try. ✉ *Restaurant Row, 500 Ala Moana Blvd.,* ☎ *808/521–4409. AE, DC, MC, V.*

$$-$$$ ✕ **3660 on the Rise.** This stellar eatery is a 10-minute drive from
★ Waikīkī in the up-and-coming culinary mecca of Kaimukī. Light hardwoods, frosted glass, green marble, and black granite mix in a leisurely fashion here, and there's almost always a full house in the 90-seat dining room (with room for 20 on a street-side lānai outside). Homegrown ingredients are combined with European flavors: Dungeness crab cakes are prepared in a nest of angel hair and served with a ginger-cilantro aioli, and *pūlehu* (broiled) lamb chops are intensified by garlic, pepper, rosemary, and thyme. The restaurant is also known for its spectacular desserts, so save room for the warm chocolate soufflé cake with espresso sauce and vanilla ice cream. ✉ *3660 Wai'alae Ave.,* ☎ *808/ 737–1177. AE, DC, MC, V.*

$-$$$ ✕ **Palomino Euro-Bistro.** A relative newcomer to the downtown Hon-
★ olulu dining scene, Palomino is developing a loyal clientele with its menu fusing French, Spanish, and Italian cuisines. Entrées from the woodburning oven include mahimahi with creamy polenta, fig-caper-olive relish, and mussels, and Basque-style chicken. For seafood, consider the seafood ravioli or the crab cakes with pesto beurre blanc. If pasta is your preference, go for the fusilli with hot Portuguese sausage. The restaurant's art-deco decor includes handblown glass chandeliers, a grand staircase, American and African woods, and a 50-ft marble-and-mahogany bar. ✉ *Harbor Court, 66 Queen St., 3rd floor,* ☎ *808/528– 2400. AE, D, DC, MC, V.*

$$ ✕ **Brew Moon Restaurant & Microbrewery.** The menu states "A vision for food, a passion for beer," and Brew Moon lives up to both promises. Entrées are varied and creative, from sesame-seared 'ahi to fire-roasted ribs and grilled pizzas. The molasses and cumin-charred pork tenderloin comes with garlic mashed potatoes, and there's a spicy curry chicken. Large picture windows show off the brewery and fermentation room where six beers are crafted, including a low-calorie light-alcohol brew and a rich copper-color ale. The dessert specialty is a float made with fresh-brewed root beer. This is a favorite spot for business lunches and after-work drinks, so expect a high-energy atmosphere. Vie for a table on the 150-seat lānai if you want a more relaxed setting for cocktails and snacks. On Sundays, Brew Moon is the site of a Jazz brunch featuring live entertainment. ✉ *Ward Centre, 1200 Ala Moana Blvd.,* ☎ *808/593–0088. AE, D, DC, MC, V.*

$$ ✕ **Indigo.** Local boy Glenn Chu turned Honolulu on its ear by daring
★ to open a trendy restaurant in a seedy downtown neighborhood—and succeeding. The decor emphasizes wicker and track lighting, and there's a charming back lānai that shields you from the downtown hubbub. Chu's variations on foods from his Chinese heritage include crispy wontons stuffed with hot goat cheese, Szechuan peppered beef loin in black-bean sauce, and prawns with hot chili-garlic sauce. The restaurant is within walking distance of the Hawai'i Theatre. ✉ *1121 Nu'uanu Ave.,* ☎ *808/521–2900. AE, D, DC, MC, V.*

$$ ✕ **A Pacific Café O'ahu.** Take Asian, Mediterranean, and Indian cuisines
★ and combine them with a love of Hawai'i's homegrown products. The result: chef Jean-Marie Josselin's award-winning menu, a true O'ahu

standout. Lunch highlights include a shiitake mushroom sandwich with mozzarella, and a mixed green salad with grilled Japanese eggplant, goat cheese, and chili vinaigrette. At dinner the wok-charred mahimahi with a garlic-sesame crust and lime-ginger beurre blanc is superb. It's easy to see why chef Josselin's restaurants are favorites on three Hawaiian islands. ⊠ *Ward Centre, 1200 Ala Moana Blvd.,* ☎ *808/593–0035. AE, DC, MC, V.*

$–$$ ✕ **Gordon Biersch Brewery Restaurant.** Snuggling up to Honolulu
★ Harbor, this indoor-outdoor eatery, part of a West Coast–based chain of microbreweries, is Aloha Tower Marketplace's busiest. The menu is American with an island twist, from chicken skewers in a hot peanut-coconut sauce to fresh-seared 'ahi in a *sansho* (Japanese pepper) crust. There is also a variety of pastas and pizzas. You can smell the garlic fries the moment you walk in. All that spicy food goes well with the beer. Ask for tastes of the dark, medium, and light brews before choosing your favorite. ⊠ *Aloha Tower Marketplace, 1 Aloha Tower Dr.,* ☎ *808/599–4877. AE, D, DC, MC, V.*

$ ✕ **Kaka'ako Kitchen.** The floors of this converted warehouse are concrete, the furniture is plastic, and the plates are Styrofoam. But this is where the owners of the eatery 3660 on the Rise (☞ *above*) turned their talents to perfecting the art of "plate lunch." Fresh fish entrées mix with vegetarian offerings such as tofu burgers, pan-seared chicken salad, teriyaki chicken sandwich, and sautéed mahimahi. You can even order brown rice and a side of mesclun greens. Best yet, you can order takeout and head to the nearest beach park for a gourmet meal with a view. ⊠ *1216 Waimanu St.,* ☎ *808/596–7488. Reservations not accepted. No credit cards. Closed Sun. No dinner.*

German

$ ✕ **Patisserie.** By day, this bakery in the Kāhala Mall is a deli dominated by fluorescent lights and a shining display case, but five nights a week it turns into a 24-seat restaurant with great German food, a rarity in Hawai'i. The menu is small—only 10 entrées—but any choice is a good one. The Wiener schnitzel is juicy within its crispy crust, and veal ribs are garnished with a sprig of rosemary. Try the potato pancakes, crisp outside and soft inside, joined by a healthy spoonful of applesauce. Tossed salad and European-style breads are included in the price. No liquor is served, but you can bring your own. ⊠ *Kāhala Mall, 4211 Wai'alae Ave.,* ☎ *808/735–4402. Reservations not accepted. MC, V. Closed Sun.–Mon.*

Hawaiian

$$ ✕ **The Willows.** Originally opened in 1944, this restaurant was tucked away amid low-rise apartment buildings and gave little clue as to the wonderful ambiance that waited within its walls. Willows underwent extensive renovation and reopened in 1993 with a renewed reputation for historic Hawaiian hospitality. Man-made ponds meander between the thatched dining pavilions, and there's also a tiny wedding chapel and a gallery gift shop. The food is served buffet style, with the trademark Willows' curry back on the menu, along with roasted Portobello mushrooms, *laulau* (a steamed bundle of ti leaves containing pork, butterfish, and taro tops), and pineapple-mango barbecued ribs. ⊠ *901 Hausten St.,* ☎ *808/952–9200. Reservations essential. AE, D, MC, V.*

$ ✕ **'Ono Hawaiian Foods.** The adventurous in search of a real "local food" experience should head to this no-frills hangout. You know it has to be good if residents are waiting in line to get in. Here you can sample poi, *lomilomi* salmon (salmon massaged until tender and served with minced onions and tomatoes), laulau, kālua pork, and *haupia* (a light, gelatinlike dessert made from coconut). Appropriately enough, the Hawaiian word *'ono* means delicious. You may not like every island delicacy you try since some, like poi, are acquired tastes, but you're sure to find at least one authentically Hawaiian food that you can declare "onolicious." ⊠ *726 Kapahulu Ave.,* ☎ *808/737–2275. Reservations not accepted. No credit cards. Closed Sun.*

Italian

$–$$ ✕ **Cafe Sistina.** Step off a busy Honolulu street and right into this tiny, artistic café. Sergio Mitrotti has gained quite a following with his inventive Italian-Mediterranean cuisine. He's concocted an appetizer of goat cheese, chili peppers, garlic, prosciutto, and Greek olives, and he fills ravioli with such delights as Gorgonzola, porcini mushrooms, red peppers, and pancetta cream. Linguine *alla puttanesca* comes alive with tomatoes, onions, capers, and kalamata olives. Fresh chewy bread comes with a pesto butter to die for. A graphic artist by training, Mitrotti has painted the café's walls with Italianesque scenes. ⊠ *1314 S. King St.,* ☎ *808/596–0061. AE, MC, V.*

Japanese

$$–$$$ ✕ **Sushi Sasabune.** This tiny sushi bar is the home of the island's most famous "trust me" sushi. Sit at the bar, and you eat what the chef chooses for you. And don't expect a California roll. It might be something as exotic as teriyaki octopus. Sasabune's sushi specials also include crab, salmon, and tuna, and come with miso soup, seaweed salad, and adzuki-bean ice cream. The sushi is authentically Japanese, with fish and seafood flown in from around the globe. ⊠ *1419 S. King St.,* ☎ *808/947–3800. Reservations essential. AE, D, DC, MC, V.*

Mexican

$–$$ ✕ **Compadres Mexican Bar and Grill.** The after-work crowd gathers here for potent margaritas and yummy pūpū. An outdoor terrace with is best for cocktails and chips. Inside, the wooden floors, colorful photographs, and lively paintings create a festive setting for imaginative Mexican specialties. Fajitas, baby-back ribs, *huevos rancheros* (eggs with salsa, beans, and guacamole and served on a tortilla), and grilled shrimp are just a few of the many offerings. ⊠ *Ward Centre, 1200 Ala Moana Blvd.,* ☎ *808/591–8307. D, MC, V.*

Steak

$$–$$$ ✕ **Ruth's Chris Steak House.** Here's a steak joint that doesn't look like one. This pastel-hued dining room on Restaurant Row caters to meat lovers by serving top-of-the-line steak cuts. The portions are large, so bring an appetite. Side orders include generous salads and an ultracreamy spinach au gratin. Charbroiled fish, veal, and lamb chops provide tasty alternatives to the steaks. For dessert, try the house special, a bread pudding happily soaked in whiskey sauce. ⊠ *Restaurant Row, 500 Ala Moana Ave.,* ☎ *808/599–3860. AE, DC, MC, V.*

Around the Island

Hale'iwa

AMERICAN/CASUAL

$ ✕ **Kua 'Aina Sandwich.** A must-stop spot during a drive around the island, this tiny North Shore eatery has a few tables inside and a few more on the lānai next to the road. Burgers are heaped with bacon, cheese, salsa, or pineapple, and the grilled mahimahi sandwich comes with a homemade tartar sauce. Do try the French fries. You can also check out Kua 'Aina's newest location across from the Ward Centre (⊠ 1116 Auahi St., 808/591–9133). Expect a crowd, and once you've tasted these burgers you'll know why. ⊠ *66-214 Kamehameha Hwy.,* ☎ *808/637–6067. Reservations not accepted. No credit cards.*

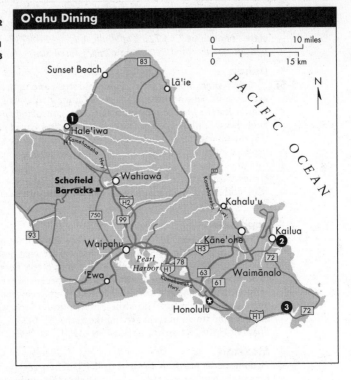

O'ahu Dining

Hawai'i Kai
CONTEMPORARY

$$ ✕ **Roy's.** Two walls of windows offer views of Maunalua Bay and Diamond Head in the distance, and a glassed-in kitchen affords views of what is cooking at Roy Yamaguchi's Hawai'i Kai venture. This is a noisy two-story restaurant with a devoted following. Roy also has branches on the Big Island, Maui, and Kaua'i. The menu matches Hawai'i flavors with Euro-Asian accents. It's hard to find a better blackened 'ahi in a hot, soy-mustard butter sauce. Of the individual pizzas, the best is topped with vine-ripened tomatoes, goat cheese, and roasted garlic. ⊠ *Hawai'i Kai Corporate Plaza, 6600 Kalaniana'ole Hwy.,* ☎ *808/396–7697. AE, D, DC, MC, V.*

Kailua
MEXICAN

$ ✕ **Bueno Nalo.** Long a Waimānalo landmark, this family-run eatery moved to the windward side of the island in 1998. It's still run by the same owners, who are dedicated to healthy Mexican cuisine. Velvet paintings and piñatas add a fun, funky flavor to the setting. The food is reliably good. *Topopo* salad is a heap of greens, tomatoes, onions, tuna, olives, cheese, and beans on top of a tortilla. Combination plates with tacos, enchiladas, and tamales are bargains, and the chili rellenos are expertly seasoned. Families will appreciate the *keiki* (child's) menu for diners 10 and under. Reservations for parties of fewer than six are not accepted. ⊠ *20 Kainehe St.,* ☎ *808/263–1999. AE, MC, V.*

LODGING

O'ahu has a wide range of accommodations, so it pays to plan ahead to find your perfect vacation home-away-from-home. First consider whether your dream vacation includes getting away from the usual hustle and bustle. If so, look at the listings in the "Around the Island" category. If you prefer proximity to the action, go for a hotel or condominium in or near Waikīkī, where most of the island's lodgings are. Except for the peak months of January, February, and August, you'll have little trouble getting a room if you call in advance. Don't be intimidated by published rates. Most hotels offer a variety of package options and special deals, such as sports, honeymoon, room and car, and kids stay/eat free promotions. These extras can make vacations even more affordable, so ask about them when you book.

Below is a selective list of lodging choices in each price category. For an explanation of price categories, *see* Lodging *in* Smart Travel Tips A to Z at the back of the book. For a complete list of every hotel and condominium on the island, write or call the Hawai'i Visitors & Convention Bureau for a free *Accommodation Guide* (☞ Contacts and Resources *in* O'ahu A to Z, *below*). It details amenities and gives each hotel's proximity to the beach.

Waikīkī

$$$$ 🏨 **Aston Waikīkī Beach Tower.** On Kalakaua Avenue, but set back from the street on the mauka side, this 39-story luxury condominium resort has the atmosphere of an intimate vest-pocket hotel. Here guests can find the amenities, oversize rooms, and views of Waikīkī that you would expect from a larger beachfront resort, but in a serene, quiet hideaway. It has stylish one- and two-bedroom suites with microwaves, dishwashers, wet bars, washer-dryers, and private lānai. There is twice-daily maid service. ⊠ *2470 Kalākaua Ave., Honolulu 96815,* ☎ *808/926–6400 or 800/922–7866,* ℻ *808/926–7380. 140 suites. Kitchenettes, minibars, room service, pool, sauna, concierge. AE, D, DC, MC, V.* 🐾

$$$$ 🏨 **Halekūlani.** Today's sleek, modern, and luxurious oceanside Halekūlani
★   still lives up to the translation of its name—the "House Befitting Heaven." A masterful blend of the past and present was created in an architectural design that incorporates the original estate's main building and terrace. The mood is serene and tranquil amid the frenetic activity of Waikīkī. Guest rooms are spacious, artfully appointed in marble and wood. Ninety percent have ocean views, and each has its own lānai, sitting area, terrific toiletries, and dozens of little touches that are sure to please. The hotel has three of the finest restaurants in Honolulu and an oceanside pool with a giant orchid mosaic. ⊠ *2199 Kālia Rd., Honolulu 96815,* ☎ *808/923–2311 or 800/367–2343,* ℻ *808/926–8004. 412 rooms, 44 suites. 3 restaurants, 3 bars, minibars, room service, pool, exercise room, beach, concierge, business services, meeting rooms. AE, DC, MC, V.* 🐾

$$$$ 🏨 **Hawai'i Prince Hotel Waikīkī.** The Prince is a sleek high-rise with the sort of sophisticated interior design generally reserved for a city hotel. You know you're in Waikīkī, however, when you look out your window at the Ala Wai Yacht Harbor. Guest rooms offer high-tech phone systems and data ports along with floor-to-ceiling windows offering ocean views. Hotel restaurants include the elegant Prince Court restaurant and Hakone, which serves some of the best authentic Japanese food on the island, including a 10-course *kaiseki* dinner (a traditional meal of small, artful, bite-size portions). Within walking distance to the Ala Moana Shopping Center and the Hawai'i Convention Center, this hotel also has its own 27-hole Arnold Palmer–designed golf course in Ewa Beach, about a 45-minute hotel shuttle ride from Waikīki. There's also a free shuttle to the beach and downtown. ⊠ *100 Holomoana St., Honolulu 96815,* ☎ *808/956–1111 or 800/321–6248,* ℻ *808/946–0811. 467 rooms, 54 suites. 3 restaurants, lobby lounge, minibars, room service, pool, beauty salon, 27-hole golf course, concierge, business services, meeting rooms. AE, DC, MC, V.* 🐾

76

Waikīkī Lodging

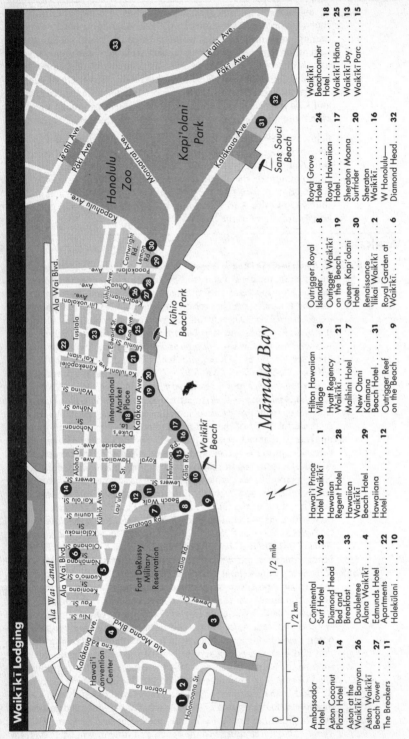

Māmala Bay

Ambassador Hotel **5**
Aston Coconut Plaza Hotel **14**
Aston at the Waikīkī Banyan . . . **26**
Aston Waikīkī Beach Tower **27**
The Breakers **11**

Continental Surf Hotel **23**
Diamond Head Bed and Breakfast **33**
Doubletree Alana Waikīkī **4**
Edmunds Hotel Apartments **22**
Halekūlani **10**

Hawai'i Prince Hotel Waikīkī **1**
Hawaiian Regent Hotel . . . **28**
Hawaiian Waikīkī Beach Hotel **29**
Hawaiiana Hotel **12**

Hilton Hawaiian Village **3**
Hyatt Regency Waikīkī **21**
Malihini Hotel **7**
New Otani Kaimana Beach Hotel . . . **31**
Outrigger Reef on the Beach . . . **9**

Outrigger Royal Islander **8**
Outrigger Waikīkī on the Beach . . . **19**
Queen Kapi'olani Hotel **30**
Renaissance 'Ilikai Waikīkī . . . **2**
Royal Garden at Waikīkī **6**

Royal Grove Hotel **24**
Royal Hawaiian Hotel **17**
Sheraton Moana Surfrider **20**
Sheraton Waikīkī **16**
W Honolulu—Diamond Head . . **32**

Waikīkī Beachcomber Hotel **18**
Waikīkī Hāna **25**
Waikīkī Joy **13**
Waikīkī Parc **15**

$$$$ ▣ **Hilton Hawaiian Village.** Each year Hilton spends a bundle to maintain this lavishly landscaped, 20-acre oceanfront resort, the largest in
★   Waikīkī. Surrounding its towers are cascading waterfalls, a 10,000-square-ft super pool, colorful fish and birds, and even a botanical garden with labeled flora. The hotel also features the Rainbow Bazaar, an international shopping arcade. Guest rooms are decorated in attractive raspberry or aqua shades, with rattan and bamboo furnishings. Scheduled to open in 2001 is the 24-story Kalia Tower, adding an additional 453 guest rooms and suites, each equipped with its own work space to accommodate technology needs. It will also house a three-level health and wellness spa and a Hawaiian Interactive Cultural Center. ✉ *2005 Kālia Rd., Honolulu 96815,* ☎ *808/949–4321 or 800/445–8667,* FAX *808/947–7898. 2,180 rooms, 365 suites. 6 restaurants, 5 lounges, minibars, room service, 3 pools, exercise room, beach, shops, children's programs (ages 5–12), concierge, business services, meeting rooms. AE, D, DC, MC, V.* ❧

$$$$ ▣ **Hyatt Regency Waikīkī.** A 10-story atrium with a two-story waterfall and mammoth metal sculpture, shops, live music, and Harry's Bar make this one of the liveliest lobbies anywhere, though you may get lost in it. The Ciao Mein restaurant serves both Italian and Chinese food, and the Texas Rock 'N Roll Sushi Bar is where East meets western. Each guest room has a private lānai. The hotel is across from the beach and a short walk from Kapi'olani Park. ✉ *2424 Kalākaua Ave., Honolulu 96815,* ☎ *808/923–1234 or 800/233–1234,* FAX *808/923–7839. 1,212 rooms, 18 suites. 4 restaurants, 2 lobby lounges, minibars, room service, pool, spa, shops, children's programs (ages 5–12), concierge, business services. AE, D, DC, MC, V.* ❧

$$$$ ▣ **Renaissance 'Ilikai Waikīkī.** It's not on the beach, but it's one of the closest hotels to Ala Moana Shopping Center, Ala Moana Beach Park, and the Hawai'i Convention Center. It's also the acknowledged tennis hotel of Waikīkī (courts are on the rooftops). Guest rooms are spacious and each offers Internet access using in-room television screens and cordless keyboards. There are three towers and a huge esplanade, which is always busy, and crowds gather at sunset for the torch lighting, hula dancing, and live Hawaiian music. For sky-high dining, there's Sarento's Top of the 'I' Italian restaurant. As the sun goes down there are all-you-can-eat pūpū at the Paddles Bar. ✉ *1777 Ala Moana Blvd., Honolulu 96815,* ☎ *808/949–3811 or 800/645–5687,* FAX *808/947–0892. 728 rooms, 51 suites. 4 restaurants, 2 lobby lounges, minibars, room service, 2 pools, 7 tennis courts, business services, meeting rooms. AE, D, DC, MC, V.* ❧

$$$$ ▣ **Royal Hawaiian Hotel.** One of the hotels that made Waikīkī famous,
★   it has been host since 1927 to movie stars, royalty, and some of the world's wealthiest travelers. Called the "Pink Palace of the Pacific" due to its architecture and pink exterior, the Royal was built in an age of leisurely travel when people sailed here on luxury liners and spent months. The hotel retains the feel of that historic time with its high ceilings and period furniture. Pink telephones in each room and corridors of pink carpeting add a dreamy quality. The modern wing is more expensive, but for charm—and the tinkle of massive crystal chandeliers—the rooms in the Historic Wing are a treasure. You can dine by the water's edge at the Surf Room, sip a mai tai at the bar that made that drink famous, or lounge on the sand in the hotel's private beach section. ✉ *2259 Kalākaua Ave., Honolulu 96815.* ☎ *808/923–7311 or 800/782–9488,* FAX *808/924–7098. 472 rooms, 53 suites. 3 restaurants, bar, minibars, room service, pool, concierge, business services, meeting rooms. AE, DC, MC, V.* ❧

$$$$ ▣ **Sheraton Moana Surfrider.** The first hotel built on Waikīkī Beach, the Moana opened its doors in 1901. Today it has merged with the

newer Surfrider next door and celebrates its 100th birthday in 2001 with special events all year long. To get the historical experience, request a room in the Moana Banyan Wing. Although these rooms are small by today's standards, they are well-appointed and charming. For more spacious accommodations with a modern feel, the Diamond and Tower Wings are a better choice. The Banyan Court is the focal point for beachfront activity, and you can relax on the gracious veranda for high tea. ⊠ *2365 Kalākaua Ave., Honolulu 96815,* ☎ *808/922–3111 or 800/782–9488,* FAX *808/923–0308. 750 rooms, 41 suites. 3 restaurants, bar, 3 lobby lounges, snack bar, minibars, room service, pool, beach, concierge, meeting rooms. AE, DC, MC, V.*

\$\$\$\$ ⛰ **Sheraton Waikīkī.** Towering over its neighbors, the Sheraton takes center stage on Waikīkī Beach. If you like constant activity, the Sheraton Waikīkī has it: entertainment venues, poolside hula, year-round children's programs, and the host of many meetings and conventions. Guest rooms are spacious, and many have grand views of Diamond Head. The hotel is just steps away from the multilevel Royal Hawaiian Shopping Center and next to the Royal Hawaiian Hotel. Be sure to take the glass-walled elevator up to the Hanohano Room, an elegant dining room with breathtaking panoramas of the ocean and Waikīkī. The hotel features amenities such as a children's center, fitness center, hospitality center for early arriving and late departing guests, and historical tours, one of which spotlights the Honu sea turtles that can be viewed in the Pacific waters at the hotel's edge. ⊠ *2255 Kalākaua Ave., Honolulu 96815,* ☎ *808/922–4422 or 800/325–3535,* FAX *808/923–8785. 1,709 rooms, 130 suites. 5 restaurants, 3 lobby lounges, minibars, room service, 2 pools, health club, beach, children's programs (ages 5–12), concierge, business services, meeting rooms. AE, DC, MC, V.* ✆

\$\$\$\$ ⛰ **W Honolulu—Diamond Head.** Located beachfront on the quiet edge of Waikīkī across from Kapiʻolani Park, this Starwood Resort property has opened in the former Colony Surf. Created with the business traveler in mind, W Honolulu offers 24-hour concierge and room service, and each guest room features a private balcony and amenities such as in-room data ports, CD players, and VCRs with video library. The luxurious trademark W beds wrap you in 250-thread-count sheets, and rooms are elegantly appointed with teak furnishings, a Balinese island motif, and spectacular oceanfront views. The hotel's signature restaurant is the Diamond Head Grill (☞ Honolulu *in Dining, above*). ⊠ *2885 Kalākaua Ave., Honolulu 96815,* ☎ *808/922–1700 or 888/528–9465,* FAX *808/791–5110. 44 rooms, 4 suites. Restaurant, room service, in-room data ports, in-room VCRs, beach, dry cleaning, laundry service, concierge, business services. AE, D, DC, MC, V.*

\$\$\$–\$\$\$\$ ⛰ **Aston at the Waikīkī Banyan.** Families enjoy this high-rise condominium resort near Diamond Head, one block from Waikīkī Beach and two blocks from the Honolulu Zoo. One-bedroom suites have daily maid service and private lānai. Look for the fishpond in the lobby area. The Banyan also features a guest activities deck, tennis, outdoor barbecues, and a children's playground. ⊠ *201 ʻŌhua Ave., Honolulu 96815,* ☎ *808/922–0555 or 800/922–7866,* FAX *808/922–0906. 307 suites. Snack bar, kitchenettes, pool, sauna, tennis court. AE, D, DC, MC, V.* ✆

\$\$\$–\$\$\$\$ ⛰ **Doubletree Alana Waikīkī.** Leisure and business travelers like this hotel's location on the west edge of Waikīkī, two blocks from Ala Moana Shopping Center, Ala Moana Beach Park, the Hawaiʻi Convention Center, and 4 mi from downtown Honolulu. Public areas of the 19-story high-rise are modern and attractive, with rotating exhibits of local artists' work in the lobby. Guest rooms have private lānai with panoramic views of the mountains or ocean. The staff of this boutique property has a reputation for hospitality, and service is attentive, plus you get the trademark Doubletree chocolate-chip cookies upon arrival. Those doing business globally will like the 24-hour business-center services. Also open round-the-clock is the fitness center. ✉ *1956 Ala Moana Blvd., Honolulu 96815,* ☎ *808/941–7275 or 800/367–6070,* FAX *808/949–0996. 268 rooms, 45 suites. Restaurant, lobby lounge, minibars, room service, pool, exercise room, concierge, business services. AE, D, MC, V.*

$$$–$$$$ 🏨 **Hawaiian Regent Hotel.** On the eastern edge of Waikīkī, the Hawaiian Regent is close to Kapi'olani Park, the zoo, and the aquarium. Its two towers and two lobbies and courtyards are open to ocean breezes, sunlight, and tropical feeling. A \$21 million renovation of the hotel's Kalākaua Tower was undertaken in 2000, and that Tower's oversize guest rooms not only capture the feeling of the tropical Hawai'i in the 1950s era, but the private lānai offer unparalleled views of either the Waikīkī strip or Diamond Head. Families should inquire about rooms that sleep six and include two bathrooms. Several dining choices include two Japanese restaurants and a cutting-edge Mediterranean dining room called Acqua. The shopping arcade has 20 shops and boutiques. ✉ *2552 Kalākaua Ave., Honolulu 96815,* ☎ *808/922–6611 or 800/367–5370,* FAX *808/921–5222. 1,337 rooms, 9 suites. 5 restaurants, 2 lobby lounges, minibars, room service, 2 pools, tennis court, exercise room, dance club, concierge, business services, meeting rooms. AE, D, MC, V.*

$$$–$$$$ 🏨 **Hawaiian Waikīkī Beach Hotel.** Across the street from the beach, on the Diamond Head end of Waikīkī, this hotel is within walking distance of the zoo and Kapi'olani Park. The seawall in front of the hotel offers the best sunset views. The mauka tower offers mainly ocean views. The rooms have rattan furniture, right down to the headboards, and each has a private lānai. The Captain's Table serves meals in casual surroundings modeled after an old-time luxury liners. ✉ *2570 Kalākaua Ave., Honolulu 96815,* ☎ *808/922–2511 or 800/877–7666,* FAX *808/ 923–3656. 673 rooms, 40 suites. 2 restaurants, 3 lobby lounges, minibars, room service, pool. AE, D, DC, MC, V.*

$$$–$$$$ 🏨 **New Otani Kaimana Beach Hotel.** Polished to a shine, this hotel is
★   open to the trade winds and furnished with big, comfortable chairs. The ambience is cheerful and charming, and the lobby has a happy, unpretentious feel. Best of all, it's right on the beach at the quiet end of Waikīkī, practically at the foot of Diamond Head. Rooms are smallish but very nicely appointed, with soothing pastel decor and off-white furnishings. Get a room with an ocean view and dine at least once at the Hau Tree Lānai. ✉ *2863 Kalākaua Ave., Honolulu 96815,* ☎ *808/ 923–1555 or 800/356–8264,* FAX *808/922–9404. 119 rooms, 6 suites. 2 restaurants, lobby lounge, minibars, room service, meeting rooms. AE, D, DC, MC, V.*

$$$–$$$$ 🏨 **Outrigger Reef on the Beach.** Right on the beach near Ft. DeRussy Park, the Reef is the official hotel for the Honolulu Marathon each December. Guest rooms and suites feature refrigerators, coffeemakers, and personal amenities such as hair dryers. The rooms are done in soft mauves and pinks and many have lānai. Ask for an ocean view; the other rooms have decidedly less delightful overlooks. ✉ *2169 Kālia Rd., Honolulu 96815,* ☎ *808/923–3111 or 800/688–7444,* FAX *808/924–4957. 846 rooms, 39 suites. 2 restaurants, 4 bars, no-smoking rooms, refrigerators, room service, pool, exercise room, beach, nightclub, children's programs (ages 5–12), meeting rooms. AE, D, DC, MC, V.*

$$$–$$$$ 🏨 **Outrigger Waikīkī on the Beach.** Outrigger Hotels & Resorts' star property, on Kalākaua Avenue in the heart of the best shopping and dining action, stands next to some of the nicest sands in Waikīkī. Rooms have a Polynesian motif, and each has a lānai. The top four floors are for members of the Voyager Club and include a guest lounge that offers Continental breakfast and sunset appetizers daily. For more than 25 years, the main ballroom has been home to the sizzling Soci-

ety of Seven entertainers. The beachfront Duke's Canoe Club is a dining hot spot. ⊠ *2335 Kalākaua Ave., Honolulu 96815,* ☎ *808/923–0711 or 800/688–7444,* 𝖥𝖠𝖷 *800/622–4852. 500 rooms, 30 suites. 6 restaurants, 5 bars, lobby lounge, kitchenettes, minibars, room service, pool. AE, D, DC, MC, V.* ✥

$$$–$$$$ 🏨 **Royal Garden at Waikīkī.** From the outside, this 25-story boutique hotel looks like your average Waikīkī high-rise. But step inside and it whispers elegance, from the marble and etched glass in the lobby to the genuine graciousness of the staff. Guest rooms have sitting areas, private lānai, and marble and brass baths. There's a free shuttle service to and from Kapi'olani Park, Ala Moana Shopping Center, Royal Hawaiian Shopping Center, and duty-free shops. ⊠ *440 'Olohana St., Honolulu 96815,* ☎ *808/943–0202 or 800/367–5666,* 𝖥𝖠𝖷 *808/946–8777. 202 rooms, 18 suites. 2 restaurants, lobby lounge, in-room safes, refrigerators, room service, 2 pools, business services, meeting rooms. AE, D, DC, MC, V.* ✥

$$$–$$$$ 🏨 **Waikīkī Beachcomber Hotel.** With an excellent location right across
★ the street from Waikīkī Beach, it's also a short walk from the Royal Hawaiian Shopping Center and the International Market Place. Rooms have simple island-style rattan furnishings, prints by local artists, and private lānai. Two evening shows are presented here: the venerable "Don Ho" and "The Magic of Polynesia." ⊠ *2300 Kalākaua Ave., Honolulu 96815,* ☎ *808/922–4646 or 800/622–4646,* 𝖥𝖠𝖷 *808/923–4889. 487 rooms, 11 suites. Restaurant, lobby lounge, snack bar, no-smoking rooms, minibars, refrigerators, room service, pool. AE, DC, MC, V.* ✥

$$$–$$$$ 🏨 **Waikīkī Joy.** This boutique hotel is a lesser-known gem. One tower has all suites, and another has standard hotel rooms. Units have either ocean or partial ocean views. Each has a lānai, a whirlpool bath, a deluxe stereo system with Bose speakers, and a control panel by the bed. The location is great, tucked away on a quiet side street yet still close to Waikīkī's restaurants, shops, and entertainment. ⊠ *320 Lewers St., Honolulu 96815,* ☎ *808/923–2300 or 800/922–7866,* 𝖥𝖠𝖷 *808/924–4010. 50 rooms, 44 suites. Lobby lounge, kitchenettes, minibars, pool, sauna. AE, D, DC, MC, V.* ✥

$$$–$$$$ 🏨 **Waikīkī Parc.** Billed as an executive boutique hotel and owned and
★ managed by the same group who manages the Halekūlani (☞ *above*) across the street, where guests have signing privileges, the Parc offers guests the same attention to detail in service and architectural design but lacks its beachfront location. The lobby is light and airy, and guest rooms are done in cool blues and whites and lots of rattan. The hotel has a fine Japanese restaurant called Kacho, and the lovely Parc Café is known for its reasonably priced all-you-can-eat theme buffets. Business travelers can depend on the 24-hour services of the business center, which includes a boardroom. ⊠ *2233 Helumoa Rd., Honolulu 96815,* ☎ *808/921–7272 or 800/422–0450,* 𝖥𝖠𝖷 *808/931–6638. 298 rooms. 2 restaurants, in-room safes, minibars, room service, pool, concierge, business services. AE, D, DC, MC, V.* ✥

$$–$$$ 🏨 **Ambassador Hotel.** The Ambassador's west-Waikīkī location puts guests in a good position. It's within walking distance of the beach and all that Waikīkī has to offer and close to the new convention center, the Ala Wai Canal, and the Ala Moana Shopping Center. There's nothing glamorous about the exterior of this high-rise hotel, but the carpeting, fixtures, and furnishings look fresh. All rooms have private lānai, and superior units come with a stove and oven. ⊠ *2040 Kūhiō Ave., Honolulu 96815,* ☎ *808/941–7777 or 800/923–2620,* 𝖥𝖠𝖷 *808/ 941–4717. 187 rooms, 34 suites. Restaurant, in-room safes, kitchenettes, refrigerators, pool. AE, D, DC, MC, V.*

$$–$$$ 🏨 **Hawaiiana Hotel.** This intimate, low-rise hideaway a few blocks from
★ the beach takes you back in time to Old Hawai'i. The hotel is surrounded

by a garden of lush tropicals, and a giant tiki god carving greets you at the entry. Hawaiian musical entertainment is featured each week. The hotel's centerpiece is the pool, and every morning guests are served Kona coffee here. Each room features both a double and single bed as well as a kitchenette and view of the gardens below. Upon departure, women receive a farewell floral lei. ⊠ *260 Beach Walk, Honolulu 96815,* ☎ *808/923–3811,* FAX *808/926–5728. 95 rooms. Pool, coin laundry. AE, D, DC, MC, V.*

$$–$$$ 🏨 **Queen Kapi'olani Hotel.** Built in 1969, this 19-story hotel a half-block from the beach appeals to those in search of clean, basic accommodations within walking distance of the beach and Waikīkī's main attractions. Some rooms have kitchenettes, and there's a large pool and sundeck on the third floor. ⊠ *150 Kapahulu Ave., Honolulu 96815,* ☎ *808/922–1941 or 800/367–5004,* FAX *808/922-2694. 308 rooms, 7 suites. 2 restaurants, bar, refrigerators, room service, pool, meeting rooms. AE, D, DC, MC, V.* 🏊

$$ 🏨 **Diamond Head Bed and Breakfast.** On the southeastern edge of Kapi'olani Park, this home features two guest rooms. Both are large, have private bath, are tropical in style, and open to a lānai and large backyard that makes the hustle and bustle of Waikīkī seem light years away. Hostess Joanne Trotter has filled the large living spaces with modern artwork and furnishings created for tropic comfort. ⊠ *3240 Noela Dr., Honolulu 96815,* ☎ *808/885–4550,* FAX *808/885–0559. Reservations: Hawai'i's Best Bed and Breakfasts, Box 563, Kamuela, 96743,* ☎ *808/885–4550 or 800/262–9912,* FAX *808/885–0559. 2 rooms. No credit cards.* 🏊

$$ 🏨 **Outrigger Royal Islander.** This is one of the new Ohana Hotels in the Outrigger chain. Ohana hotels promise clean, comfortable accommodations, with conveniences such as refrigerators and laundry services, at a value price. The Royal Islander is just a two-minute walk from a very nice section of Waikīkī Beach. The rooms have tapa-print bedspreads, and there are island-inspired pictures on the walls. Each room also has a private lānai. Choose between studios, one-bedroom apartments, and suites. The staff is helpful in arranging activities such as golf, scuba, and sightseeing tours. Guests have access to pools at other Outrigger hotels. ⊠ *2164 Kālia Rd., Honolulu 96815,* ☎ *808/ 922–1961 or 800/688–7444,* FAX *808/923–4632. 94 rooms, 7 suites. In-room safes, coin laundry. AE, D, DC, MC, V.* 🏊

$–$$ 🏨 **Aston Coconut Plaza Hotel.** With its intimate size and service, Coconut Plaza is a true boutique hotel. On the Ala Wai Canal, three blocks from the beach, its tropical plantation decor features rattan furnishings and floral bedspreads. Guest rooms have private lānai, and all except standard-view rooms come with kitchenettes. Free Continental breakfast is served daily on the lobby veranda. ⊠ *450 Lewers St., Honolulu 96815,* ☎ *808/923–8828 or 800/882–9696,* FAX *808/923–3473. 70 rooms, 11 suites. Kitchenettes, pool, coin laundry, meeting rooms. AE, D, DC, MC, V.* 🏊

$–$$ 🏨 **The Breakers.** This hotel's two-story buildings surround the pool and look out over gardens filled with exotic tropical flowers. A throwback to the early 1960s, guest rooms feature Japanese-style shoji doors and carefully chosen interior decor. Rooms come with kitchenettes, bath with shower only, and lānai. Guests return here year after year to soak up the laid-back Old Hawai'i atmosphere. It's a couple blocks from the beach and from Waikīkī restaurants. ⊠ *250 Beach Walk, Honolulu 96815,* ☎ *808/923–3181,* FAX *808/923–7174. 64 units. Kitchenettes, pool. AE, DC, MC, V.* 🏊

$–$$ 🏨 **Continental Surf Hotel.** One of the better budget hotels of Waikīkī, this appealing high-rise is along the Kūhiō Avenue strip, two blocks from the ocean and convenient to many shops and restaurants. The lobby is large and breezy, and the comfortable rooms are decorated in Polynesian hues of browns and golds. The units have limited views and no lānai. Guests may use the facilities of its sister hotel, the Miramar, 1½ blocks away. ⊠ 2426 Kūhiō Ave., Honolulu 96815, ☎ 808/922–2232, FAX 808/923–9487. 141 rooms. Kitchenettes. AE, MC, V.

$–$$ 🏨 **Waikīkī Hāna.** Smack dab in the middle of Waikīkī and a block away from the beach, this eight-story hotel is convenient for exploring just about every shop, restaurant, and activity in O'ahu's tourist hub. Accommodations are clean and plain. Many have their own lānai. Pay a little extra per day and you can rent a refrigerator. ⊠ 2424 Koa Ave., Honolulu 96815, ☎ 808/926–8841 or 800/367–5004, FAX 808/596–0158. 70 rooms, 2 suites. Restaurant, lobby lounge, in-room safes, kitchenettes, coin laundry. AE, DC, MC, V.

$ 🏨 **Edmunds Hotel Apartments.** On the Ala Wai Canal, four blocks from the ocean, this has been a budget alternative for decades. Long lānai wrap around the building, so each room has its own view of the pretty canal and glorious Manoa Valley beyond—views that look especially lovely at night, when lights are twinkling up the mountain ridges. If you can put up with the constant sounds of traffic on the boulevard this is a real bargain. ⊠ 2411 Ala Wai Blvd., Honolulu 96815, ☎ 808/923–8381 or 808/732–5169. 8 rooms. Kitchenettes. No credit cards.

$ 🏨 **Malihini Hotel.** There's no pool, it's not on the beach, none of the units have a TV or air-conditioning, and the rooms are spartan. Still, the atmosphere of this low-rise complex is cool and pleasant, and the gardens are well maintained. All rooms are either studios or one-bedrooms, and all have kitchenettes and daily maid service. The low prices and good location make this a popular place, so be sure to book well in advance. ⊠ 217 Saratoga Rd., Honolulu 96815, ☎ 808/923–9644. 21 rooms, 9 suites. Kitchenettes. No credit cards.

$ 🏨 **Royal Grove Hotel.** This flamingo-pink family-oriented hotel is reminiscent of Miami. With just six floors, it is one of Waikīkī's smaller hotels. The lobby is comfortable. The rooms, though agreeably furnished, have neither themes nor views. Go for the higher priced rooms if possible because the economy rooms offer no air-conditioning and more street noise. The hotel is about 2 blocks from the beach, and the pool area is bright with tropical flowers. ⊠ 15 Uluniu Ave., Honolulu 96815, ☎ 808/923–7691, FAX 808/922–7508. 78 rooms, 7 suites. Kitchenettes, pool. AE, D, DC, MC, V.

Honolulu

$$$$ 🏨 **Kāhala Mandarin Oriental Hawai'i.** Minutes away from Waikīkī, ★ on the quiet side of Diamond Head, this elegant oceanfront hotel is hidden in the wealthy neighborhood of Kāhala. Formerly the Kāhala Hilton, it reopened in 1996 after a $75-million renovation. The room decor combines touches of Asia and Old Hawai'i, with mahogany furniture, teak parquet floors, hand-loomed area rugs, local art, and grass-cloth wall coverings. Stop by to see the daily dolphin feedings in the hotel's impressive 26,000-square-ft lagoon. ⊠ 5000 Kāhala Ave., 96816, ☎ 808/739–8888 or 800/367–2525, FAX 808/739–8800. 341 rooms, 29 suites. 3 restaurants, 2 lobby lounges, minibars, room service, pool, outdoor hot tub, sauna, steam room, exercise room, beach, dive shop, snorkeling, concierge, business services, meeting rooms. AE, D, DC, MC, V. ❧

$$$–$$$$ 🏨 **Ala Moana Hotel.** This long-standing landmark has an excellent location, right next to the popular Ala Moana Shopping Center (they're connected by a pedestrian ramp) and Hawai'i Convention Center and one block from Ala Moana Beach Park. Each room in this 36-story high-rise has a lānai with a view of either the ocean, the Ko'olau

Mountains, or Diamond Head. Amenities are modern. For instance, you can order room service at the touch of a remote control button. Rooms on the 29th to 35th floors provide concierge service, in-room whirlpool baths, and free use of the conference room. The hotel's nightclub, Rumours, is a preferred spot for the after-work crowd. ⊠ *410 Atkinson Dr., 96814,* ☎ *808/955–4811 or 800/367–6025,* FAX *808/ 944–6839. 1,102 rooms, 67 suites. 4 restaurants, bar, 2 lobby lounges, in-room safes, minibars, room service, pool, dance club, nightclub, meeting rooms. AE, DC, MC, V.* ✎

$$$–$$$$ 🏨 **Aston at the Executive Centre Hotel.** Here's a great option for the corporate traveler who wants to avoid Waikīkī. Downtown Honolulu's only hotel is an all-suite high-rise in the center of the business district, within walking distance of the Aloha Tower Marketplace and 10 minutes from Honolulu International Airport. Suites are on the top 10 floors of a 40-story glass-walled tower, providing views of downtown and Honolulu Harbor. Each unit has a separate living area and kitchenette stocked with cold beverages. Some units have washer-dryers. Continental breakfast is included. ⊠ *1088 Bishop St., 96813,* ☎ *808/539–3000 or 800/922–7866,* FAX *808/523–1088. 116 suites. Restaurant, in-room safes, kitchenettes, pool, exercise room, business services, meeting rooms. AE, DC, MC, V.* ✎

$$–$$$ 🏨 **Mānoa Valley Inn.** Here's an intimate surprise tucked away in Mānoa Valley, just 2 mi from Waikīkī. Built in 1919, this stately home is on the National Register of Historic Places. Linger over the complimentary Continental breakfast buffet on a shady lānai in the morning and enjoy fresh tropical fruit and cheese in the afternoon. Rooms are furnished in country-inn style, with antique four-poster beds, marble-top dressers, patterned wallpaper, and fresh flowers. There's a reading room with a TV and VCR. ⊠ *2001 Vancouver Dr., Honolulu 96822,* ☎ *808/947–6019 or 800/535–0085,* FAX *808/922–2421. 8 rooms, 4 with bath; 1 cottage. AE, DC, MC, V.*

$$–$$$ 🏨 **Pagoda Hotel.** Minutes away from Ala Moana Shopping Center and Ala Moana Beach Park, the Pagoda is well placed. A free shuttle bus makes the trip between the hotel and its sister property, the Pacific Beach in Waikīkī. The location and moderate rates make this a good choice if you're simply looking for a place to sleep and catch a couple of meals. Studios include a full-size refrigerator, a stove, and cooking utensils. There are no memorable views since the hotel is surrounded by high-rises. The Pagoda's floating restaurant is notable for its Japanese gardens and carp-filled waterways. ⊠ *1525 Rycroft St., Honolulu 96814,* ☎ *808/941–6611 or 800/472–4632,* FAX *808/955–5067. 364 rooms. 2 restaurants, refrigerators, pool. AE, D, DC, MC, V.*

Around the Island

$$$$ 🏨 **'Ihilani Resort & Spa.** At press time, 'Ihilani was in the process of
★ conversion to a JW Marriott Resort, making it only the 10th Marriott hotel to carry this designation. On O'ahu's western shore, 'Ihilani is a 25-minute drive from Honolulu International Airport. The resort has a sleek 15-story hotel illuminated by a glass-dome atrium. Guest rooms have marble bathrooms with deep soaking tubs, private lānai, teak furnishings, in-room CD players with a selection of CDs, and a high-tech control system (lights, temperature controls, and more) built into the telephones. Most rooms have ocean views. The 35,000-square-ft 'Ihilani Spa offers everything from seaweed baths to stair-climbers, and there's a Ted Robinson–designed 18-hole championship golf facility. ⊠ *92-1001 'Ōlani St., Kapolei 96707,* ☎ *808/679–0079 or 800/626– 4446,* FAX *808/679–0295. 333 rooms, 54 suites. 4 restaurants, minibars, room service, 2 pools, spa, 18-hole golf course, 6 tennis courts,*

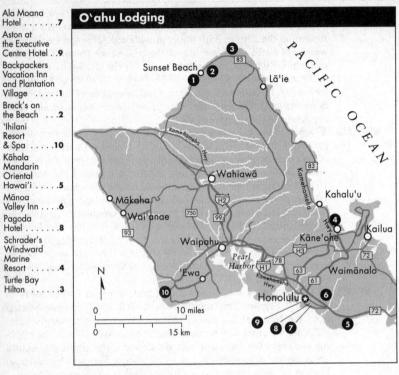

O'ahu Lodging

baby-sitting, children's programs (ages 5–12), concierge, meeting rooms. AE, DC, MC, V.

$$$–$$$$ 🏨 **Turtle Bay Hilton.** Although it is in need of more than a face-lift to restore it to a standard that matches the natural beauty of its setting, this oceanside retreat continues to offer an abundance of activities and a relaxing stay away from town. Guests can enjoy an ocean full of water sports, horseback ride along the spectacular shoreline, play golf and tennis, or relax by either of the hotel's two pools. The rooms, in three wings, have private lānai and are furnished in wicker. Check out the hotel's mammoth Sunday champagne brunch, and dine next to huge windows with views of the crashing surf. Adjacent to the hotel are studio cabanas that are also in need of renovation. Although they offer more privacy, the main building rooms afford better views. ⊠ 57-091 Kamehameha Hwy. (Box 187), Kahuku 96731, ☎ 808/293–8811 or 800/445–8667, FAX 808/293–9147. 450 rooms, 30 suites, 86 cabanas. 2 restaurants, lobby lounge, refrigerators, room service, pool, 2 18-hole golf courses, 10 tennis courts, exercise room, horseback riding, beach, children's programs (ages 5–12), meeting rooms. AE, D, DC, MC, V. 🐾

$–$$$ 🏨 **Schrader's Windward Marine Resort.** In a setting that is more roadside motel than resort, Schrader's provides a moderately priced lodging alternative for guests who want to spend less on accommodations and more on activities. You'll find fewer amenities than you would in Waikīkī, but perhaps a little more personalized attention. Schrader's proximity to the U.S. Marine base makes it popular with military families. Some rooms open onto Kāne'ohe Bay, which is so close that people have been known to fish right off their lānai. Other rooms face the Ko'olau Mountains. One- to three-bedroom accommodations are available. This is a popular spot for water activities. ⊠ 47-039 Lihikai Dr., Kāne'ohe 96744, ☎ 808/239–5711 or 800/735–5711, FAX 808/239–6658. 57 rooms. Kitchenettes, pool. AE, D, DC, MC, V.

$–$$ 🏨 **Backpackers Vacation Inn and Plantation Village.** Spartan in furnishings and definitely very casual in spirit, Backpackers is a surfer's kind of place to catch some sleep between wave sets. It's near Waimea Bay on the North Shore and offers double rooms (some with a double bed, others with two single beds), hostel accommodations, and cottages. Some accommodations have kitchenettes. It's a three-minute walk to the supermarket. ✉ *59-788 Kamehameha Hwy., Haleʻiwa 96712,* ☎ *808/638–7838,* FAX *808/638–7515. 25 rooms. MC, V.*

$ 🏨 **Breck's on the Beach Hostel.** Just north of Sunset Beach Park, Breck's offers a great location, with rooms ranging from basic dormitory to ocean-view balcony apartments that sleep eight people. Guests, usually a blend of surfer types from many continents, have access to free bodyboards and snorkeling equipment. Bicycles and surfboards are also available. Studio apartments have refrigerator and private bath, and the larger balcony apartments include kitchens. Airport pickup is available. Three-night minimum stay required. ✉ *59-043 Huelo St., Sunset Beach 96712,* ☎ *808/638–7873. 21 units. No credit cards.*

NIGHTLIFE AND THE ARTS

Nightlife on Oʻahu can be as simple as a barefoot stroll in the sand or as elaborate as a dinner show with all the glitter of a Las Vegas production. You can view the vibrant hues of a Honolulu sunset during a cocktail cruise or hear the melodies of ancient chants at a lūʻau on a remote west-shore beach.

Waikīkī is where nearly all Oʻahu's night action takes place, and what action there is! Kalākaua and Kūhiō avenues come to life when the sun goes down and the lights go on. Outside Honolulu, offerings are slimmer but equally diverse. You can dance the two-step at a waterfront café one night, boogie to live bands in a tiny second-story windward bar the next, or kick back to the sounds of North Shore–style slack-key guitar and the lilting falsetto voice stylings of local artists. Wafting through the night air of Oʻahu is the sound of music of every kind—from classical to contemporary. Music has been the language of Hawaiʻi from the beginning, and Oʻahu has the best selection. Everywhere there is hula, whether dancers wear sequin skirts in Waikīkī or authentic ti-leaf skirts at Paradise Cove.

The arts thrive right alongside the tourist industry in Oʻahu's balmy climate. The island has an established symphony, a thriving opera company, chamber music groups, and community theaters. Major Broadway shows, dance companies, and rock stars also make their way to Honolulu. Check the local newspapers—the morning *Honolulu Advertiser,* the afternoon *Honolulu Star-Bulletin,* or the *Honolulu Weekly*—for the latest happenings.

Bars, Cabarets, and Clubs

Drinking age is 21 on Oʻahu and throughout Hawaiʻi. Many bars will admit younger people but will not serve them alcohol. By law, all establishments that serve alcoholic beverages must close at 2 AM. The only exceptions are those with a cabaret license, which have a 4 AM curfew. Though billed as discotheques, they are required to have live music. Most places have a cover charge of $2–$5.

Waikīkī

Aaron's at the Top of the Ala Moana. A splendid view, good contemporary dance music, and a well-dressed crowd come together at this Honolulu nightclub. ✉ *Ala Moana Hotel, 410 Atkinson Dr.,* ☎ *808/ 955–4466.* ☉ *Dancing Sun.–Thurs. 9:30–2, Fri.–Sat. 10–2.*

Banyan Veranda. Such Hawaiian entertainers as Jerry Santos and Pumehana Davis perform on the open-air lānai here. It is from this location that the radio program "Hawaii Calls" first broadcast the sounds of Hawaiian music and the rolling surf across to the U.S. mainland. ⊠ *Sheraton Moana Surfrider, 2365 Kalākaua Ave.,* ☎ *808/922–3111.* ◷ *Nightly 5:30–11.*

Esprit. Honolulu, an all-male octet, performs music from the big-band era of the 1930s up through current pop hits, with Broadway numbers, too. This club, with its central location in the heart of Waikīkī, is a popular dance spot, and features the high-energy singers "The Krush." ⊠ *Sheraton Waikīkī, 2255 Kalākaua Ave.,* ☎ *808/922–4422.* ◷ *Sat.–Mon. 8:30–2.*

Hanohano Room. World-class views 30 stories above Waikīkī, combined with late-night jazz and weekly jam sessions by some of Hawai'i's best musicians, make this a romantic spot for music lovers and those who like to dance close and slow. ⊠ *Sheraton Waikīkī, 2255 Kalākaua Ave., 30th floor,* ☎ *808/922–4422.* ◷ *Sat. 11–1.*

Lewers Lounge. Bruce Hamada and friends perform contemporary jazz and standards here at Halekūlani hotel from Tuesday through Saturday evenings. A vocalist-pianist sits in Sunday and Monday. A dessert menu is offered. ⊠ *Halekūlani, 2199 Kālia Rd.,* ☎ *808/923–2311.* ◷ *Entertainment nightly 10:30–midnight.*

Lobby Bar. In the partially open-air main lobby of the Hawaiian Regent, this is the home of legendary Hawaiian musical treasures like Aunty Genoa Keawe. Slack key guitar can also be heard here. The hotel's Ocean Terrace is the site of a summer concert jam series featuring the island's up-and-coming contemporary artists. ⊠ *Hawaiian Regent, 2552 Kalakaua Ave.,* ☎ *808/922–6611.* ◷ *Nightly from 5:30.*

Mai Tai Bar. Keith and Carmen Haugen sing island duets at this open-air Waikīkī Beach bar. Carmen's hula is a thing of beauty. Catch them in the early evenings Tuesday through Sunday. Entertainers vary on other nights. ⊠ *Royal Hawaiian Hotel, 2259 Kalākaua Ave.,* ☎ *808/923–7311.* ◷ *Entertainment nightly 5:30–7:30.*

Moose McGillycuddy's Pub and Cafe. Loud bands play for the beach-and-beer gang in a blue-jeans-and-T-shirt setting. ⊠ *310 Lewers St.,* ☎ *808/923–0751.* ◷ *Nightly 9–1:30.*

Nashville Waikīkī. Country music in the tropics? You bet! Put on your *paniolo* (Hawaiian cowboy) duds and mosey on out to the giant dance floor. There are pool tables, dart boards, line dancing, and free dance lessons to boot. ⊠ *Outrigger West Hotel, 2330 Kūhiō Ave.,* ☎ *808/926–7911.* ◷ *Daily 4–4; dance lessons nightly at 7.*

Nick's Fishmarket. This is probably the most comfortable of Waikīkī's upscale dance lounges, with an elegant crowd, smooth music, and an intimate atmosphere. There is some singles action here. ⊠ *Waikīkī Gateway Motel, 2070 Kalākaua Ave.,* ☎ *808/955–6333.* ◷ *Nightly 10–2.*

Paradise Lounge. A variety of acts, including the longtime band Olomana, perform in this pretty outdoor club. ⊠ *Hilton Hawaiian Village, 2005 Kālia Rd.,* ☎ *808/949–4321.* ◷ *Fri.–Sat. 8–midnight.*

Pool Stage. Various local performers present outstanding Hawaiian song and dance by the Sheraton Waikīkī's oceanfront pool. One of the most popular is 'ukulele wizard Moe Keale, familiar to TV viewers from his roles on *Hawai'i Five-O.* ⊠ *Sheraton Waikīkī, 2255 Kalākaua Ave.,* ☎ *808/922–4422.* ◷ *Nightly 6–8:30.*

Royal Garden at Waikīkī. Some of O'ahu's top jazz stylists like singing in the elegant, intimate lobby lounge of this sophisticated hotel. ⊠ *Royal Garden at Waikīkī, 444 'Olohana St.,* ☎ *808/943–0202.* ◷ *Tues.–Sun. 8–11.*

Rumours. The after-work crowd loves this spot, which has dance videos, disco, and throbbing lights. On Saturday "Little Chill" nights the club plays oldies from the '70s and '80s and serves free pūpū. There is ballroom dancing Sunday evening from 5 to 9. ⊠ *Ala Moana Hotel, 410 Atkinson St.,* ☎ *808/955–4811.* ☉ *Wed.–Fri. 5–2, Sat. 8–4.*

Shore Bird Beach Broiler. This Waikīkī beachfront disco spills right out onto the sand. It features a large dance floor and 10-ft video screen. Karaoke sing-alongs are held nightly. ⊠ *Outrigger Reef Hotel on the Beach, 2169 Kālia Rd.,* ☎ *808/922–2887.* ☉ *Nightly 9–2.*

Virtual Experience. Calling itself a place to escape, this posh, high-tech club has 12 oversized screens for exploring computerized worlds, an atmosphere conducive to quiet conversation, with drinks and pūpū to heighten the experience. ⊠ *311 Lewers St.,* ☎ *808/847–8825.* ☉ *Nightly 6–4. Live entertainment Tues. and Thurs.*

Wave Waikīkī. Dance to live rock and roll until 1:30, recorded music after that. It can be a rough scene, but the bands are tops. ⊠ *1877 Kalākaua Ave.,* ☎ *808/941–0424.* ☉ *Nightly 9–4.*

Honolulu

Anna Bannana's. Generations of Hawai'i college students have spent more than an evening or two at this legendary two-story, smoky dive. Here, the live music is fresh, loud, and sometimes experimental. Different local favorites deliver ultracreative dancing music, and the likes of blues singer Taj Mahal have been known to slip in for a set or two. ⊠ *2440 S. Beretania St.,* ☎ *808/946–5190.* ☉ *Nightly 11:30–2, live music Thurs.–Sat. 9–2.*

Gordon Biersch Brewery Restaurant. Live duos and trios serenade patrons of the outside bar that flanks Honolulu Harbor. While there's no dancing, this is the place in Honolulu to see and be seen. ⊠ *Aloha Tower Marketplace, 101 Ala Moana Blvd.,* ☎ *808/599–4877.* ☉ *Wed.–Sat. 7–1.*

Honu Bar and Terrace. Sophisticated and swank, this lobby lounge presents light jazz and island ensembles during the cocktail and sunset hours. ⊠ *Kāhala Mandarin Oriental Hawai'i, 5000 Kāhala Ave.,* ☎ *808/739–8888.* ☉ *Mon.–Thurs. 4:30–6:30, Fri.–Sun. 5–7.*

Pier Bar. Here's one of the few places in Honolulu to hear live music outdoors and dance underneath the stars. It attracts a grab bag of groups; call ahead to find out who's playing. ⊠ *Aloha Tower Marketplace, 101 Ala Moana Blvd.,* ☎ *808/536–2166.* ☉ *Nightly 6:30–4.*

Row Bar. Restaurant Row's outdoor gathering place mixes it up each weekend with live reggae, rock, and rhythm-and-blues. Single professionals meet here *pau hana* (after work). ⊠ *500 Ala Moana Blvd.,* ☎ *808/528–2345.* ☉ *Fri.–Sat. 8–11:45, Sun. jazz 5:30–8:30.*

Venus Nightclub. This high-energy social bar features pūpū and dancing nightly, with live entertainment five nights a week. Attention, ladies: "The Spectacular Male Revue" is a Honolulu experience. ⊠ *1349 Kapi'olani Blvd.,* ☎ *808/955–2640.* ☉ *Nightly 8–4.*

World Cafe. Honolulu's only upscale billiards nightclub also has a sports bar and dancing to Top 40 tunes. ⊠ *500 Ala Moana Blvd.,* ☎ *808/ 599–4450.* ☉ *Mon.–Thurs. 11:30–2, Fri.–Sat. 11:30–4, Sun. 3–2.*

'Aiea

Pecos River Cafe. Billing itself as Hawai'i's premier country-and-western nightclub, this easygoing establishment has live music nightly. ⊠ *99-016 Kamehameha Hwy.,* ☎ *808/487–7980.* ☉ *Nightly 9–2.*

Kahuku

Bayview Lounge. A beautiful place to watch the sun set over the North Shore water, this lounge inside the Turtle Bay Hilton hosts a variety of local bands that play contemporary Hawaiian tunes. ⊠ *Turtle Bay Hilton, 57-091 Kamehameha Hwy.,* ☎ *808/293–8811.* ☉ *Nightly 6–9.*

Cocktail and Dinner Cruises

Dinner cruises depart either from the piers adjacent to the Aloha Tower Marketplace in downtown Honolulu or from Kewalo Basin, just 'ewa of Ala Moana Beach Park, and head along the coast toward Diamond Head. There's usually dinner, dancing, drinks, and a sensational sunset. Except as noted, dinner cruises cost approximately $50–$60, cocktail cruises $20–$30. Most major credit cards are accepted.

Ali'i Kai Catamaran. Patterned after an ancient Polynesian vessel, this huge catamaran casts off from historic Aloha Tower with 1,000 passengers. The deluxe dinner cruise has two open bars, a huge dinner, and an authentic Polynesian show with colorful hula music. The food is good, the after-dinner show loud and fun, and everyone dances on the way back to shore. ⊠ *Pier 5, street level, Honolulu,* ☎ *808/539–9400.* ۞ *Nightly at 5:30.*

Dream Cruises. The 100-ft motor yacht *American Dream* handles up to 225 guests for evening cruises off the shores of Waikīkī. Decks have plenty of outdoor space for views of the twinkling city lights. The dinner cruise includes one mai tai, buffet, and soft drinks. You pay for extra booze. After a hula demonstration with audience participation, a disc jockey spins dancing tunes from the '50s through the '70s. ⊠ *1020 Auahi St., Honolulu,* ☎ *808/592–5200.* ۞

Paradise Cruises. Prices vary depending on which deck you choose on the 1,600-passenger, four-deck *Star of Honolulu.* For instance, a seven-course French dinner on the top costs $199. A steak and crab feast on level two costs $72. Evening excursions also take place on the 340-passenger *Starlet I* and 230-passenger *Starlet II.* ⊠ *1540 S. King St., Honolulu,* ☎ *808/983–7827.*

Royal Hawaiian Cruises. The sleek *Navatek* is a revolutionary craft designed to sail smoothly in rough waters. That allows it to power farther along Waikīkī's coastline than its competitors. During the cocktail cruise, there's sizzling entertainment by such local singers as Nohelani Cypriano, and the dinner cruise includes gourmet food by acclaimed Honolulu chef George Mavrothalassitis. ⊠ *Honolulu Harbor,* ☎ *808/848–6360.* ۞ *Dinner cruise nightly 5:30–8.*

Cocktail and Dinner Shows

Some O'ahu entertainers have been around for years, and others have just arrived on the scene. Either way, the dinner-show food is usually buffet-style with a definite local accent. If you want to dine on your own and then take in a show, sign up for a cocktail show. Dinner shows are all in the $45–$60 range. Cocktail shows run $30–$35. The prices usually include one cocktail, tax, and gratuity. In all cases, reservations are essential, and most major credit cards are accepted. Be sure to call in advance. You never know when an artist may have switched venues.

Creation: A Polynesian Odyssey. From the battles of New Zealand and Fiji warriors to 1940s luxury liners and contemporary Hawaiian lifestyle, this show takes audiences on a musical tour of Polynesia. The highlight is a daring Samoan fire knife dancer. ⊠ *'Āinahau Showroom, Sheraton Princess Ka'iulani Hotel, 120 Ka'iulani Ave.,* ☎ *808/922–5811.* ۞ *Dinner seatings nightly at 5:15 and 8, cocktail seatings nightly at 5:45 and 8:15, shows nightly at 6 and 8:30.*

Don Ho. The singer who made tiny bubbles famous, he is the entertainer visitors ask about first when it comes to Waikīkī entertainment. His show, a Polynesian revue (with a cast of young and attractive Hawaiian performers), has found the perfect home in this intimate club setting inside the Waikīkī Beachcomber Hotel. ⊠ *Waikīkī Beachcomber*

HAWAIIAN MUSIC

ASK MOST VISITORS ABOUT Hawaiian music and they'll likely break into a lighthearted rendition of "Little Grass Shack." When they're done, lead them directly to a stereo.

First, play them a recording of singer Kekuhi Kanahele, whose compositions combine ancient Hawaiian chants with modern melodies. Then ask them to listen to a CD by guitarist Keola Beamer, who loosens his strings and plays slack-key tunings dating back to the 1830s.

Share a recording by falsetto virtuoso Amy Hanaiali'i Gilliom, one of the very few singers perpetuating the upper-register vocal style. Then take them to a concert by Henry Kapono, who writes and sings of the pride—and pain—of being pure Hawaiian.

These artists, like many others, are proving just how multifaceted Hawaiian music has become. They're unearthing their island roots in the form of revered songs and chants, and they're reinterpreting them for today's audiences. It's "chicken-skin" (goose-bumps) stuff, to be sure, and it's made only in Hawai'i.

Granted, "Little Grass Shack" does have its place in the history books. After Hawai'i became a U.S. territory in 1900, the world discovered its music thanks to touring ensembles who turned heads with swaying hips, steel guitars, and pseudo-Hawaiian lyrics. Once radio and movies got into the act, dreams of Hawai'i came with a saccharine Hollywood sound track.

But Hawaiian music is far more complex. It harks back to the sounds of the ancient Islanders who beat rough-hewn drums, blew haunting calls on conch shells, and intoned repetitive chants for their gods. It recalls the voices of 19th-century Christian missionaries who taught Islanders how to sing in four-part harmony, a style that's still popular today.

The music takes on international overtones thanks to gifts from foreign immigrants: the 'ukulele from Portuguese laborers, for instance, and the guitar from Mexican traders. And it's enlivened by a million renderings of "Tiny Bubbles," as mainstream entertainers like Don Ho croon Hawaiian-pop hits for Waikīkī tourists.

Island music came full circle in the late 1960s and '70s, a time termed the Hawaiian Renaissance. While the rest of the world was rocking 'n' rolling, a few dedicated artists began giving voice to a resurgence of interest in Hawaiian culture, history, and traditions.

Today's artistic trailblazers are digging deep to explore their heritage, and their music reflects that thoughtful search. They go one step further by incorporating such time-honored instruments as nose flutes and gourds, helping them keep pace with the past.

Why is Hawaiian music such a well-kept secret? Simply put, it's rarely played outside of the Islands. A handful of local performers are making their mark on the mainland and in Japan. But if you want to experience the true essence of Hawaiian music, you must come to Hawai'i. Check ads and listings in local papers for information on concerts, which take place in indoor and outdoor theaters, hotel ballrooms, and cozy nightclubs. When you hear the sound, you'll know it's Hawaiian because it'll make you feel right at home.

Hotel, 2300 Kalākaua Ave., ☎ *808/923–3981.* ⊗ *Shows Sun.–Thurs. at 7, with cocktail and dinner seatings.*

The Love Notes "Fabulous Fifties" Show. If you like to doo-wop and rock-and-roll and wax nostalgic for the music of the '50s and '60s, head to the Backstage Showroom at the 'Ilikai for this energetic show that re-creates the era when music was king. ⊠ *'Ilikai Hotel Nikko Waikīkī, 1777 Ala Moana Blvd.,* ☎ *808/949–3811.* ⊗ *Nightly at 8:30.*

Magic of Polynesia. Magician John Hirokawa displays mystifying sleight of hand in this highly entertaining show, which also includes the requisite hula and island music. ⊠ *Waikīkī Beachcomber Hotel, 2300 Kalākaua Ave.,* ☎ *808/539–9460.* ⊗ *Nightly at 6:30 and 8:45.*

Polynesian Cultural Center. Easily one of the best on the Islands, this show has soaring moments and an "erupting volcano." The actors are students from Brigham Young University's Hawai'i campus. ⊠ *55-370 Kamehameha Hwy., Lā'ie,* ☎ *808/293–3333.* ⊗ *Dinner seating Mon.–Sat. at 4:30; show Apr.–May and Sept.–Christmas, Mon.–Sat. at 7:30, and Christmas–Mar. and June–Aug., Mon.–Sat. at 6 and 7:45.* ✎

Society of Seven. This lively, popular septet has great staying power and, after more than 25 years, continues to put on one of the best shows in Waikīkī. They sing, dance, do impersonations, play instruments, and, above all, entertain with their contemporary sound. ⊠ *Outrigger Waikīkī Hotel, 2335 Kalākaua Ave.,* ☎ *808/923–7469.* ⊗ *Mon. at 8:30; Tues.–Sat. at 6:30 and 8:30.*

Yes! Acrobats, magicians, clowns, mimes, and dancers gather onstage in this international nightclub revue. Highlights include tumblers clad in gold from head to toe, a life-size Raggedy Ann, exotic birds, and a giant slinky flipping and sliding across the stage. It's a one-of-a-kind act in Waikīkī. ⊠ *Polynesian Palace, Outrigger Reef Towers Hotel, 227 Lewers St.,* ☎ *808/923–7469.* ⊗ *Tues.–Sun. at 6:30 and 8:30.*

Dance

Every year at least one of mainland America's finer ballet troupes makes the trip to Honolulu for a series of dance performances at the **Neal Blaisdell Center Concert Hall** (⊠ Ward Ave. at King St., Honolulu, ☎ 808/591–2211). A local company, **Ballet Hawai'i** (☎ 808/988–7578), is active during the holiday season with its annual production of *The Nutcracker,* which is usually held at the Mamiya Theater (⊠ 3142 Wai'alae Ave., Chaminade University, Honolulu).

Film

Art, international, classic, and silent films are screened at the little theater at the **Honolulu Academy of Arts** (⊠ 900 S. Beretania St., Honolulu, ☎ 808/532–8768). The **Hawai'i International Film Festival** (⊠ 1001 Bishop St., Suite 745, Honolulu, ☎ 808/528–3456) may not be Cannes, but it is unique and exciting. During the weeklong festival, held from the end of November to early December, top films from the United States, Asia, and the Pacific are screened day and night at several theaters on O'ahu. **Varsity Theater** (⊠ 1106 University Ave., Honolulu, ☎ 808/973–5834) is a two-theater art house that brings internationally acclaimed motion pictures to Honolulu. Waikīkī generally gets the first-run films at its trio of theaters dubbed, appropriately, the **Waikīkī 1, Waikīkī 2,** and **Waikīkī 3** (☎ 808/971–5033). Check newspapers for what's playing. **Kāhala Mall** (⊠ 4211 Wai'alae Ave., Honolulu, ☎ 808/733–6233) has eight movie theaters showing a diverse range of films. It's a 10-minute drive from Waikīkī.

Lū'au

Here are some good lū'au that emphasize fun over strict adherence to tradition. They generally cost $40–$75. Reservations are essential, and most major credit cards are accepted.

Germaine's Lū'au. This lū'au is billed as being "100 years away from Waikīkī." Expect a lively crowd as you are bused to a private beach near an industrial area 35 minutes from Waikīkī. The bus ride is actually a lot of fun, and the beach and the sunset are pleasant. The service is brisk in order to feed everyone on time, and the food is the usual multicourse, all-you-can-eat buffet, but the show is warm and friendly. The bus collects passengers from 13 Waikīkī hotels. Lū'au start at 6. ☎ 808/941–3338. ⊘ *Tues.–Sun. at 6.*

Paradise Cove Lū'au. This is another mass-produced event for 1,000 or so. A bus takes you from one of six Waikīkī hotel pickup points to a remote beachfront estate beside a picturesque cove on the western side of the island, 27 mi from Waikīkī. There are palms and a glorious sunset, and the pageantry is fun, even informative. The food—well, you didn't come for the food, did you? ☎ 808/973–5828. ⊘ *Daily at 5:30, doors open at 5.*

Polynesian Cultural Center Lū'au. An hour's drive from Honolulu, this North Shore O'ahu attraction takes place amid seven re-created villages of Polynesia. Dinner is all-you-can-eat, followed by a world-class revue. ☎ 808/923–1861. ⊘ *Mon.–Sat. at 5:30.*

Royal Hawaiian Lū'au. This is a notch above the rest of the commercial lū'au on O'ahu, with a feast that is more upscale and exotic. It takes place oceanside on Waikīkī Beach at the venerable Pink Palace. With the setting sun, Diamond Head, the Pacific Ocean, and the enjoyable entertainment, who cares if the lū'au isn't totally authentic? ☎ 808/923–7311. ⊘ *Mon. at 6.*

Music

Chamber Music Hawai'i (☎ 808/947–1975) gives 25 concerts a year at the Honolulu Lutheran Church (⊠ 1730 Punahou St., Honolulu), Honolulu Academy of Arts (⊠ 900 S. Beretania St., Honolulu), and other locations around the island.

Hawai'i Opera Theater's season spans January through March and includes such works as *The Barber of Seville, Tristan,* and *Madame Butterfly.* All are performed in their original language with projected English translation. ⊠ *Neal Blaisdell Concert Hall, Ward Ave. and King St., Honolulu,* ☎ 808/596–7858. ⊡ *$23–$77 at box office.*

Honolulu Symphony Orchestra, led by a young and dynamic conductor named Samuel Wong, this is a top-notch ensemble whether it's playing by itself or backing up a guest artist. International performers are headlined from time to time, and pops programs are also offered, some underneath the stars during the summer nights at the Waikīkī Shell. Write or call for a complete schedule. Shows take place at the Blaisdell Center and Hawai'i Theatre Center. ⊠ *677 Ala Moana Blvd., Honolulu,* ☎ 808/524–0815. ⊡ *$10–$50.* ✎

Rock concerts are usually performed at the cavernous **Neal Blaisdell Center Arena** (☎ 808/591–2211). Internationally famous performers pack them in at **Aloha Stadium** (☎ 808/486–9300). Check newspapers for upcoming events.

Theater

Because the Islands are so expensive to get to and stay on, major touring companies seldom come to Hawai'i. As a result, O'ahu has developed several excellent local theater troupes, which present first-rate entertainment on an amateur and semiprofessional level all year long.

Army Community Theatre. This is a favorite for its revivals of musical theater classics, presented in an 800-seat house. The casts are talented, and the fare is great for families. ⊠ *Richardson Theater, Fort Shafter, Honolulu,* ☎ *808/438–4480.* ▨ *$12–$15.*

Diamond Head Theater. This company is in residence five minutes from Waikīkī, right next to Diamond Head. Its repertoire includes a little of everything: musicals, dramas, experimental, and classics. ⊠ *520 Makapu'u Ave., Honolulu,* ☎ *808/734–0274.* ▨ *$10–$40.*

Hawai'i Theatre Center. Beautifully restored, this downtown Honolulu theater built in the 1920s hosts a wide range of events, including theatrical productions. ⊠ *1130 Bethel St., Honolulu,* ☎ *808/528–0506.* ▨ *Prices vary.*

☞ **Honolulu Theater for Youth.** This group stages delightful productions for children around the Islands from July to May. Write or call for a schedule. ⊠ *2846 Ualena St., Honolulu,* ☎ *808/839–9885.* ▨ *$10.*

John F. Kennedy Theater. This space at the University of Hawai'i's Manoa campus is the setting for eclectic dramatic offerings—everything from musical theater to Kabuki, Noh, and Chinese opera. ⊠ *1770 East–West Rd., Honolulu,* ☎ *808/956–7655.* ▨ *$9–$12.*

Kumu Kahua. This is the only troupe presenting shows and plays written on and about the Islands. It stages five or six productions a year. ⊠ *46 Merchant St., Honolulu,* ☎ *808/536–4441.* ▨ *$12–$15.*

Manoa Valley Theater. Wonderful nonprofessional performances are put on in this intimate theater in Manoa Valley from September to July. ⊠ *2833 E. Manoa Rd., Honolulu,* ☎ *808/988–6131.* ▨ *$17–$20.*

OUTDOOR ACTIVITIES AND SPORTS

Participant Sports

Biking

The good news is that the coastal roads are flat and well paved. On the downside, they're also awash in vehicular traffic. Frankly, biking is no fun in either Waikīkī or Honolulu, but things are a bit better outside the city. Be sure to take along a nylon jacket for the frequent showers on the windward side and remember that Hawai'i is Paradise after the Fall: Lock up your bike.

Mountain bikes are available for rent at **Blue Sky Rentals & Sports Center** (⊠ 1920 Ala Moana Blvd., across from the Hilton Hawaiian Village, ☎ 808/947–0101). Rates are $15 a day (8–6), $20 for 24 hours, and $75 per week, plus a $25 deposit. This price includes a bike, a helmet, a lock, and a water bottle.

You can buy a bike or, if you brought your own, you can get it repaired at **Eki Cyclery Shop** (⊠ 1603 Dillingham Blvd., Honolulu, ☎ 808/847–2005). For biking information and maps, contact the Honolulu City and County Bike Coordinator (☎ 808/527–5044). If you want to know more about what it is like to "bike" the islands, check out the Web site listed below.

If you want to find some biking buddies, write ahead to the **Hawai'i Bicycling League** (⊠ Box 4403, Honolulu 96813, ☎ 808/735–5756, ✍), which can tell you about upcoming races and club rides (frequent on all the Islands).

Camping and Hiking

Oʻahu has 33 major trails that offer choices for all skill levels and a number of camping options in different settings. The **Hawaiʻi State Department of Land and Natural Resources** (✉ 1151 Punchbowl St., Room 130, Honolulu 96813, ☎ 808/587–0300) offers a free Oʻahu recreation map.

For a complimentary hiking safety guide, contact the City and County of Honolulu's **Trails and Access Manager** (☎ 808/973–9782). Ask for a copy of "Hiking on Oʻahu: The Official Guide."

For families, the **Hawaiʻi Nature Center** (✉ 2131 Makiki Heights Dr., Honolulu, 96822, ☎ 808/955–0100) in upper Makiki Valley conducts a number of programs for both adults and children. The center offers guided hikes into tropical settings that reveal hidden waterfalls and protected forest reserves. **Oahu Nature Tours** (☎ 800/861–6018 or 808/924–2473) offers glorious sunrise, rain forest, and volcanic walking tours with an escort who will explain the wealth of native flora and fauna that is your companion along the way.

Camping on Oahu is available at four state parks, 12 county beach parks, and within the grounds of one county botanic garden. Stays are restricted to five nights per month in all beach and state recreation areas, and parks are closed to campers on Wednesday and Thursday evenings. To obtain a free camping permit for state parks, write to **Department of Land and Natural Resources, State Parks Division,** ✉ Box 621, Honolulu, 96809, ☎ 808/587–0300. For county and beach parks, contact the **Honolulu Department of Parks and Recreation,** ✉ 650 S. King St., Honolulu 96813, ☎ 808/523–4525. A word of caution: Although some Oaʻhu recreation areas have caretakers and gates that close in the evening for your safety, many others can be quite isolated at night.

Mālaekahana State Park on the North Shore is a local favorite camping spot and offers a beachfront setting with two areas that include rest rooms, showers, picnic tables, and drinking water. It's on Kamehameha Highway between Laie and Kahuku. On the windward coast, **Hoomaluhia Botanic Gardens,** (✉ 45-680 Luluku Rd., Kaneohe, ☎ 808/523–4525) offers a safe, scenic camping setting at the base of the majestic Koolau Mountains. Five grassy camping areas with rest rooms, showers, and drinking water are available on Friday, Saturday, and Sunday evenings only. Permits are free and are issued at the garden daily between 9 and 4.

For camping supplies, visit **The Bike Shop** (✉ 1149 S. King St., Honolulu, ☎ 808/595–0588) or **Omar the Tent Man** (✉ 95-l58 Leoole St., Waipahu, ☎ 808/677–8785).

Fitness Centers

Clark Hatch Physical Fitness Center. This club has weight-training facilities, an indoor pool, a racquetball court, aerobics classes, and treadmills. ✉ *745 Fort St., Honolulu,* ☎ *808/536–7205.* ☞ *About $10 per day.* ☉ *Weekdays 6 AM–8 PM, Sat. 7:30–5:30.*

ʻIhilani Resort & Spa. About 25 minutes from the airport, this is Oʻahu's largest health and fitness center. There's 35,000 square ft of space for classes, weight rooms, relaxation programs, hydrotherapies—you name it. Call for prices and to arrange nonguest privileges. ✉ *Ko Olina Resort, Kapolei,* ☎ *808/679–0079.*

24-Hour Fitness. Waikīkī's most accessible fitness center. Weight-training machines, cardiovascular equipment, free weights, and a pro shop are offered. ✉ *Pacific Beach Hotel, 2nd floor, 2490 Kalākaua Ave.,* ☎ *808/971–4653.* ☞ *$10 per day for guests of many Waikīkī hotels (call for list), $20 for nonguests.* ☉ *Daily.*

Golf

Ala Wai Golf Course. One of the most popular of the island's facilities is on Waikīkī's mauka end, across the Ala Wai Canal. It's par-70 on 6,424 yards and has a pro shop and a restaurant. The waiting list is long, so if you plan to play, call the minute you land. ⊠ *404 Kapahulu Ave.,* ☎ *808/733–7387.* ⊡ *Greens fee $40, cart $14.*

Hawai'i Kai Championship Course. Advance reservations are recommended at this 18-hole, 6,222-yard course and the neighboring 18-hole, 2,386-yard Hawai'i Kai Executive Course. ⊠ *8902 Kalaniana'ole Hwy., Honolulu,* ☎ *808/395–2358.* ⊡ *Greens fee weekdays $100 and $37, respectively; weekends and holidays $120 and $42; cart included.*

Hawai'i Prince Golf Club. This 27-hole course welcomes visiting players. ⊠ *91-1200 Ft. Weaver Rd., 'Ewa Beach,* ☎ *808/944–4567.* ⊡ *Greens fee $90 guests, $135 nonguests; cart included.*

Kahuku Golf Course. The 9-hole walking-only course is played more by locals than by visitors. ⊠ *Kahuku,* ☎ *808/293–5842.* ⊡ *Greens fee $20 for nonresidents.*

Ko Olina Golf Club. Affiliated with the 'Ihilani Resort is this club on O'ahu's west side. Its 18 holes are beautifully landscaped with waterfalls and ponds where black and white swans serve as your gallery. ⊠ *Ko Olina Resort, 92-1220 Ali'inui Dr., Kapolei,* ☎ *808/676–5300.* ⊡ *Greens fee $145; cart included.*

Links at Kuilima. The 18 holes here were designed by Arnold Palmer. ⊠ *Turtle Bay Hilton, 57-091 Kamehameha Hwy., Kahuku,* ☎ *808/ 293–8574.* ⊡ *Greens fee $75 guests, $125 nonguests; separate 9-hole course $25; cart included.*

Sheraton Mākaha Country Club. Two exceptional 18-hole courses here offer a beautiful valley setting. ⊠ *84-626 Mākaha Valley Rd., Wai'anae,* ☎ *808/695–9544.* ⊡ *Greens fee $160 until noon, $90 noon–2:30, $50 2:30–closing; cart included.*

Horseback Riding

Kualoa Ranch. This ranch across from Kualoa Beach Park leads trail rides in Ka'a'awa, one of the most beautiful valleys in all Hawai'i. Kualoa has other activities as well, like windsurfing and jet skiing. Try one of its all-inclusive packages, starting at $79, with transportation from Waikīkī and a choice of activities. ⊠ *49-560 Kamehameha Hwy., Ka'a'awa,* ☎ *808/237–8515, 808/538–7636 in Honolulu.*

Turtle Bay Hilton has 75 acres of hotel property—including a private beach—for exploring on horseback at a cost of $35 for 45 minutes. ⊠ *57-091 Kamehameha Hwy., Kahuku,* ☎ *808/293–8811.*

Jogging

In Honolulu, the most popular places are the two parks, **Kapi'olani** and **Ala Moana,** at either end of Waikīkī. In both cases, the loop around the park is just under 2 mi. You can run a 4½-mi ring around **Diamond Head crater,** past scenic views, luxurious homes, and herds of other joggers. If you jog along the 1½-mi **Ala Wai Canal,** you'll probably glimpse outrigger-canoe teams practicing on the canal. If you're looking for jogging companions, show up for the free **Honolulu Marathon Clinic,** which starts at the Kapi'olani Park Bandstand from March to November, Sunday at 7:30 AM.

Once you leave Honolulu, it gets trickier to find places to jog that are scenic as well as safe. Best to stick to the well-traveled routes, or ask the experienced folks at the **Running Room** (⊠ 819 Kapahulu Ave., Honolulu, ☎ 808/737–2422) for advice.

Rock Climbing

The Mokulē'ia Wall on the North Shore is one of the world's best venues for rock climbing. This 900-ft vertical trail is as challenging as any in the world. Those skilled enough to make it to the top get glorious views of the coastline. From Farrington Highway (Hwy. 930), west of Haleiwa, there is a trail leading to the base of the Mokulēʻia Wall, but the trailhead is poorly marked and easy to miss. For help in finding it, call or visit the experts at **Climbers Paradise** (⊠ 214 Sand Island Rd., Honolulu, ☎ 808/842–7625), an indoor climbing center that also rents gear and offers lessons.

Tennis

In the Waikīkī area, there are four free public courts at **Kapiʻolani Tennis Courts** (⊠ 2748 Kalākaua Ave., ☎ 808/971–2525); 9 at the **Diamond Head Tennis Center** (⊠ 3908 Pākī Ave., ☎ 808/971–7150); and 10 at **Ala Moana Park** (⊠ makai side of Ala Moana Blvd., ☎ 808/522–7031).

Several Waikīkī hotels have tennis facilities open to nonguests, but guests have first priority. The **ʻIlikai Hotel Nikko Waikīkī** (⊠ 1777 Ala Moana Blvd., ☎ 808/949–3811) has seven courts, one lighted for night play, plus a pro shop, tennis clinics, and a ball machine. The hotel also offers special tennis packages. There's one championship tennis court at the **Hawaiian Regent Hotel** (⊠ 2552 Kalākaua Ave., ☎ 808/ 922–6611). There are two courts at the **Pacific Beach Hotel** (⊠ 2490 Kalākaua Ave., ☎ 808/922–1233); instruction is available. The **Hawaiʻi Prince Golf Club** (⊠ 91-1200 Ft. Weaver Rd., ʻEwa Beach, ☎ 808/944–4567) has two tennis courts.

Water Park

Hawaiian Adventures Water Park. Get wet and wild at this 25-acre water-theme park that features a football field–size wave pool, a continuous river for tube cruising, four- and seven-story waterslides, four double tube slides, and a children's interactive pool full of waterfalls, minislides, and animal floaties. There is a food court, gift shop, and locker rentals. It's in Kapolei, mauka of the H-1 Freeway on Farrington Highway, 15 minutes from the Honolulu International Airport. ⊠ *400 Farrington Hwy., Kapolei,* ☎ *808/674–9283.* ☜ *$30.* ◷ *10:30–5:30, longer hours in summer.* ☺

Water Sports

The seemingly endless ocean options can be arranged through any hotel travel desk or beach concession. Try the **Waikīkī Beach Center,** next to the Sheraton Moana Surfrider, or the **C & K Beach Service,** by the Hilton Hawaiian Village (no telephones).

DEEP-SEA FISHING

For fun on the high seas try **Island Charters** (☎ 808/593–9455), **Tradewind Charters** (☎ 808/973–0311 or 800/829–4899), or **Maggie Joe** (☎ 808/591–8888). All are berthed in Honolulu's Kewalo Basin. On the North Shore call **Kuʻuloa Kai Charters** (☎ 808/637–5783).

Plan to spend from $100 to $115 per person to share a boat for a full day (6:30–3). Half-day (five-hour) rates are $95. Boat charters start at about $550 for a full day and $450 for a half day. All fishing gear is included, but lunch is not. The captain usually expects to keep the fish. Tipping is customary.

OCEAN KAYAKING

This dynamic sport is catching on fast in the Islands. You sit on top of a board and paddle on both sides; it's great fun for catching waves or just exploring the coastline. Bob Twogood, a name that is synonymous with Oʻahu kayaking, runs a shop called **Twogood Kayaks Hawaiʻi** (⊠ 345 Hahani St., Kailua, ☎ 808/262–5656), which makes, rents, and sells the fiberglass craft. Twogood rents solo kayaks for $25 a half day, and $32 for a full day. Tandems are $32 a half day and $42 for a full day, including kayak delivery and pickup across from Kailua Beach. On the North Shore, kayak lessons are available from **Kayak Oahu Adventures** (⊠ Waimea Valley Adventures Park, 59-894 Kamehameha Hwy., ☎ 808/638–8189).

SCUBA DIVING AND SNORKELING

For scuba diving, **South Seas Aquatics** (⊠ 2155 Kalākaua Ave., Suite 112, Honolulu, ☎ 808/922–0852) offers two-tank boat dives for $75. Several certification courses are available; call for rates. **Captain Bruce's Scuba Charters** (☎ 808/395–3590) focuses on intimate trips for experienced divers. Led by a naturalist guide, charters run out of O'ahu's west coast, known for its great scuba sites. A two-tank dive costs $96 including transportation from Waikīkī, equipment, and refreshments.

The most famous snorkeling spot in Hawai'i is Hanauma Bay. **Hanauma Bay Snorkeling Excursions** (☎ 808/373–5060) runs to and from Waikīkī and costs $20 round-trip, including park admission, snorkeling gear, and lessons. You can also get masks, fins, and snorkels at the **rental stand** right at the park (☎ 808/395–4725).

DIVE SITES

Hanauma Bay. East of Koko Head, this bay is an underwater state park and a popular dive site. The shallow inner reef gradually drops from 10 ft to 70 ft at the outer reef. Among the tame, colorful tropical fish you'll see here are butterfly fish, goatfish, parrot fish, and surgeon fish. There are also sea turtles.

Mahi Wai'anae. This 165-ft minesweeper was sunk in 1982 to create an artificial reef. It's intact and penetrable. Goatfish, tame lemon butterfly fish, blue-striped snapper, and a 6-ft moray eel can be seen hanging about. Depths are from 50 ft to 90 ft.

Maunalua Bay. East of Diamond Head, Maunalua Bay has several sites, including Turtle Canyon, with lava flow ridges and sandy canyons teeming with green sea turtles of all sizes; *Kāhala Barge,* a penetrable, 200-ft sunken vessel; Big Eel Reef, with many varieties of moray eels; and Fantasy Reef, a series of lava ledges and archways populated with barracuda and eels.

Shark's Cove. This North Shore site is diveable in the summer months only and should be explored only by experienced divers. There are large, roomy caverns where sunlight from above creates a stained-glass effect. Easily accessible from shore, the cove's depths range from 15 ft to 45 ft. This is the most popular cavern dive on the island.

Three Tables. Named for the trio of flat rocks that break the surface near the beach, this North Shore site has easy access from the shore. Beneath the waves are large rock formations, caverns, and ledges. It's diveable only in the summer months.

SURFING

To rent a board in Waikīkī, contact **C&K Beach Service,** on the beach fronting the Hilton Hawaiian Village (☎ no phone). Rentals cost $8–$10 per hour, depending on the size of the board, and $12 for two hours. Lessons are $30 per hour with board, and they promise to have you riding the waves by lesson's end.

On the North Shore, rent a short board for $5 an hour or a long board for $7 from a shop called **Surf 'N' Sea** (☎ 808/637–9887). Its surfing lessons cost $65 for three hours and start daily at 1 PM.

WATERSKIING

Hawai'i Water Sports and Water Ski Center (⊠ Koko Marina Shopping Center, 7192 Kalaniana'ole Hwy., Hawai'i Kai, ☎ 808/395–3773) has a package with round-trip transportation from Waikīkī and a half day of waterskiing in Hawai'i Kai Marina for $110 per hour per person (two-person minimum), with lessons. There are also rides in inflatable banana boats and bumper tubes for kids of all ages.

WINDSURFING

This sport was born in Hawai'i, and O'ahu's Kailua Beach is its cradle. World champion Robby Naish and his family build and sell boards, rent equipment, provide accommodation referrals, and offer both windsurfing and kite-flying instruction out of **Naish Hawai'i** (✉ 155A Hāmākua Dr., Kailua, ☎ 808/261–6067). A four-hour package, including 90 minutes of instruction, costs $55.

Kailua Sailboard and Kayaks Company (✉ 130 Kailua Rd., Kailua, ☎ 808/262–2555) rents equipment and transports it to the waterfront five minutes away. On the North Shore, **Surf 'N' Sea** (✉ Hale'iwa, ☎ 808/637–9887) rents windsurfing gear for $12 per hour; a two-hour windsurfing lesson costs $58. Or try **Windsurfing School North Shore** (✉ Hale'iwa, ☎ 808/638–8198).

Spectator Sports

Football

The nationally televised **Jeep Aloha Bowl Football Classic,** held on Christmas Day at Aloha Stadium in Honolulu (☎ 808/486–9300), is a sports tradition bringing together powerhouse college teams from the PAC-10 and BIG-12 conferences. For local action the **University of Hawai'i Rainbows** take to the field at Aloha Stadium in season, with a big local following. There are often express buses from Kapi'olani Park (☎ 808/956–6508 for details).

Golf

The giants of the greens return to Hawai'i every January or February (depending on the TV scheduling) to compete in the **Sony Hawaiian Open Golf Tournament** (☎ 808/831–5400), a PGA tour regular with a $1 million purse. It is held at the exclusive Wai'alae Country Club near Waikīkī, and it's always a crowd-pleaser.

Mountain Biking

Professional mountain bikers come to O'ahu each year for the **Outrigger Hotels Hawaiian Mountain Tour,** a four-day, five-stage race across the most rugged terrain of the windward coast.

Running

The **Honolulu Marathon** is a thrilling event to watch as well as to participate in. Join the throngs who cheer at the finish line at Kapi'olani Park as internationally famous and local runners tackle the 26.2-mi challenge. It's held on the second Sunday in early December and is sponsored by the Honolulu Marathon Association (☎ 808/734–7200).

Surfing

For two weekends each March, **Buffalo's Annual Big-Board Surfing Classic** fills Mākaha Beach with Hawaiian entertainment, food booths, and the best in big-board surfing (☎ 808/696–3878). In winter be sure to head out to the North Shore to watch the best surfers in the world hang ten during the **Triple Crown Hawaiian Pro Surfing Championships.** This two-day event, scheduled according to wave conditions, is generally held at the Banzai Pipeline and Sunset Beach during November and December. Watch newspapers for details.

Triathlon

Swim-bike-run events are gaining in popularity and number in Hawai'i. Most fun to watch (or compete in) is the **Tinman Triathlon** (☎ 808/732–7311), held in mid-July in Waikīkī.

Volleyball

This is extremely popular in the Islands, and no wonder. Both the men's and women's teams of the **University of Hawai'i** have blasted to a number-one ranking in years past. Crowded, noisy, and very exciting home games are played September to December (women's) and January to April (men's) in the university's 10,000-seat special-events arena. ⊠ *Lower Campus Rd., Honolulu,* ☎ *808/956–4481.* ☒ *$8.*

Windsurfing

Watch the pros jump and spin on the waves during July's **Pan Am Hawaiian Windsurfing World Cup** off Kailua Beach. There are also windsurfing competitions off Diamond Head point, including August's **Wahine Classic,** featuring the world's best female boardsailors. Consult the sports section of the daily newspaper for details on these events.

SHOPPING

As the capital of the 50th state, Honolulu is the number-one shopping spot in the Islands and an international crossroads of the shopping scene. It has sprawling shopping malls, unique boutiques, hotel arcades, neighborhood businesses, and a variety of other enterprises. Major shopping malls are generally open daily from 10 to 9, smaller neighborhood boutiques are usually 9-to-5 operations.

Shopping Centers

In Waikīkī

DFS Galleria Waikīkī (⊠ 330 Royal Hawaiian Ave., ☎ 808/931–2655), across from the entrance to the Sheraton Waikīkī, is open to the general public and features three themed floors. Destination World is for take-home Hawai'i gift products and food. Fashion World features the upscale designer retailers like Ralph Lauren, Calvin Klein, Anna Sui, and Chanel. The third level is for duty-free shopping for overseas travelers. The Galleria offers free double-decker trolley service to Waikīkī hotels every 30 minutes.

The fashionable **King Kalākaua Plaza** (⊠ 2080 Kalākaua Ave.), one of Waikīkī's newest shopping destinations, features flagship stores Banana Republic and Nike Town and the Official All Star Cafe.

Royal Hawaiian Shopping Center (⊠ 2201 Kalākaua Ave., ☎ 808/922–0588 for information on free hula lessons, crafts demonstrations, and other special events), fronting the Royal Hawaiian and Sheraton Waikīkī hotels, is three blocks long and contains 120 stores on three levels. There are such upscale establishments as Chanel and Cartier, as well as local arts and crafts from the Little Hawaiian Craft Shop, which features Bishop Museum reproductions, Ni'ihau shell leis (those beautiful, super-expensive leis from the island of Ni'ihau), feather hatbands, and South Pacific art. Bijoux Jewelers has a fun collection of baubles, bangles, and beads for your perusal. Royal Hawaiian Gems fashions gold bracelets, necklaces, and rings with Hawaiian names engraved in them. Bike buffs can check out the Harley-Davidson MotorClothes and Collectibles Boutique.

Waikīkī Shopping Plaza (⊠ 2270 Kalākaua Ave.) is across the street from the Royal Hawaiian Shopping Center. Its landmark is a 75-ft-high water-sculpture gizmo, which looks great when it's working. Sawada Pro Golf Shop is one of 50 shops and restaurants on six floors.

Waikīkī Trade Center (⊠ Corner of Kūhiō and Seaside Aves.) is slightly out of the action and has shops only on the first floor. Need some water sportswear? Stop by the Town & Country Surf Shop.

Waikīkī has three theme park–style shopping centers. Right in the heart of the area is the **International Market Place** (⊠ 2330 Kalākaua Ave.), a tangle of 200 souvenir shops and stalls under a giant banyan tree. **Waikīkī Town Center** (⊠ 2301 Kūhiō Ave.) an open-air complex with a variety of shops ranging from fashions to jewelry. There are also free hula shows Monday, Wednesday, Friday, and Saturday at 7 PM. **King's Village** (⊠ 131 Ka'iulani Ave., ☎ 808/944–6855 for special-events information) is an eclectic mix of resort wear and jewelry shops, souvenir stores, fast-food places, and Japanese restaurants. It looks like a Hollywood stage set of monarchy-era Honolulu, complete with a changing-of-the-guard ceremony every evening at 6:15.

Around Honolulu

Ala Moana Shopping Center (⊠ 1450 Ala Moana Blvd., ☎ 808/946–2811 for special-events information) is a gigantic open-air mall just five minutes from Waikīkī by bus. The 50-acre, 200-shop center is on the corner of Atkinson and Ala Moana boulevards. All of Hawai'i's major department stores are here, including Neiman Marcus, Sears, and JCPenney. Liberty House is highly recommended for its selection of stylish Hawaiian wear. Upscale fashions are available at Gucci, Ann Taylor, Louis Vuitton, Gianni Versace, and Emporio Armani. For stunning Hawaiian prints, try the Art Board, and buy your local footwear at the Slipper House.

Ala Moana also has a huge assortment of local-style souvenir shops, such as Hawaiian Island Creations, Irene's Hawaiian Gifts, and Products of Hawai'i. Makai Market is a large international food bazaar. Stores at Ala Moana open their doors daily at 9:30. The shopping center closes Monday through Saturday at 9 and Sunday at 5, with longer hours during the Christmas holidays.

Heading west from Waikīkī, toward downtown Honolulu, you'll run into **Ward Warehouse** (⊠ 1050 Ala Moana Blvd.), a two-story mall with 65 shops and restaurants, among them Hoelzel Fashion, Mamo Howell, and Native Books and Beautiful Things. **Ward Centre** (⊠ 1200 Ala Moana Blvd.) has 30 upscale boutiques and eateries, including Kamehameha Garment Co. and A Pacific Island Cafe-O'ahu.

Restaurant Row (⊠ 500 Ala Moana Blvd., between South and Punchbowl Sts., ☎ 808/538–1441 for special-events information) is a trendy conglomeration of fun retailers and eateries. Stop by Gifts of Aloha Snack Store or Honolulu Chocolate Company for the best sweets this side of paradise.

Aloha Tower Marketplace (⊠ 101 Ala Moana Blvd., at Piers 8, 9, and 10, ☎ 808/528–5700 for special-events information) cozies up to Honolulu Harbor and bills itself as a festival marketplace. Along with restaurants and entertainment venues, it has shops and kiosks selling mostly visitor-oriented merchandise, from expensive sunglasses to souvenir refrigerator magnets. It is also the new home of **Don Ho's Island Grill,** featuring Hawaiian entertainment and food harborside.

Aloha Flea Market is a thrice-weekly outdoor bazaar that attracts hundreds of merchants and thousands of bargain hunters. Operations range from slick tents with rows of neatly stacked, new wares to blankets spread on the pavement, covered with rusty tools and cracked china. You'll find gold trinkets, antique furniture, digital watches, Japanese fishing floats, T-shirts, mu'umu'u, and palm-frond hats. Price haggling—in moderation—is the order of the day. ⊠ *99-500 Salt Lake Blvd.,* ☎ *808/732–9611.* ☑ *$6, including round-trip shuttle from Waikīkī.* ☉ *Wed. and weekends 6–3.*

Kāhala Mall (⊠ 4211 Wai'alae Ave.) is 10 minutes by car from Waikīkī in the chic residential neighborhood of Kāhala, near the slopes of Diamond Head. This mall features such clothing stores as Liberty House and Gap. Reyn's is the acknowledged place to go for men's resort wear. Its aloha shirts have muted colors and button-down collars, suitable for most social occasions. Banana Republic has outdoor wear. Along with an assortment of gift shops, Kāhala Mall also has eight movie theaters (☎ 808/733–6233) for post-shopping entertainment.

The **Waikele Premium Outlets** (⊠ H-1 Fwy., Waikele, 30 minutes west of downtown Honolulu) reflects Hawai'i's latest craze: warehouse shopping at discount prices. Among its occupants are the Anne Klein Factory, Donna Karan Company Store, Villeroy & Boch, and Saks Fifth Avenue.

Specialty Stores

Clothing

HIGH FASHION

Neiman Marcus (⊠ Ala Moana Shopping Center, ☎ 808/951–8887) is the trendy end of the high-fashion scene. For the latest in footwear, **Nordstrom Shoes** (⊠ Ala Moana Shopping Center, ☎ 808/973–4620) displays an elegant array of pricey styles. Top-of-the-line international fashions for men and women are available at **Mandalay Imports** (⊠ Halekūlani, 2199 Kālia Rd., ☎ 808/922–7766), home of Star of Siam silks and cottons, Anne Namba couture, and designs by Choisy, who works out of Bangkok. **Pzazz** (⊠ 1419 Kalākaua Ave., ☎ 808/955–5800), which sells high fashion at low prices, is nicknamed the Ann Taylor of consignment shops.

RESORT WEAR

For stylish Hawaiian wear, the kind worn by local men and women, look in one of the **Liberty House** branches at Ala Moana Shopping Center, Kāhala Mall (☞ Around Honolulu *in* Shopping Centers, *above*), or in downtown Honolulu (⊠ 2314 Kalākaua Ave., Waikīkī, ☎ 808/941–2345 for all stores). **Carol & Mary** (⊠ Halekūlani, ☎ 808/971–4269; ⊠ Hilton Hawaiian Village, ☎ 808/973–5395; ⊠ Royal Hawaiian Hotel, ☎ 808/971–4262) sells high-end resort wear for women. For menswear, try **Reyn's** (⊠ Ala Moana Shopping Center, ☎ 808/949–5929; ⊠ Kāhala Mall, ☎ 808/737–8313; ⊠ Sheraton Waikīkī Hotel, ☎ 808/923–0331). **Native Books and Beautiful Things** (⊠ Ward Warehouse, ☎ 808/537–2926) and **Ohelo Road** (⊠ Kāhala Mall, ☎ 808/735–5525) both carry one-of-a-kind island print dresses.

If you are looking for aloha wear that ranges from the bright-and-bold to the cool-and-classy, try **Hilo Hattie** (⊠ 700 N. Nimitz Hwy., ☎ 808/537–2926), the world's largest manufacturer of Hawaiian and tropical fashions. For convenience, it offers free shuttle service from Waikīkī. For vintage aloha shirts, try **Bailey's Antique Clothing and Thrift Shop** (⊠ 517 Kapahulu Ave., ☎ 808/734–7628), on the edge of Waikīkī.

McInerny has several locations (⊠ Ala Moana Shopping Center, ☎ 808/973–5380; ⊠ Hilton Hawaiian Village, ☎ 808/973–5392; ⊠ Royal Hawaiian Hotel, ☎ 808/971–4263; ⊠ Royal Hawaiian Shopping Center, ☎ 808/971–4275) where you can find a wide selection of colorful resort wear for men and women, with styles for day and evening.

Food

Bring home some fresh pineapple, papaya, or coconut to savor or share with your friends and family. Jam comes in flavors like pohā, passion fruit, and guava. Kona coffee beans have an international following. There are such dried-food products as saimin, haupia, and teriyaki barbecue sauce. All kinds of cookies are available, as well as exotic teas, drink mixes, and pancake syrups. And don't forget the macadamia nuts, from plain to chocolate-covered and brittled. By law, all fresh-fruit products must be inspected by the Department of Agriculture before export. For cheap prices on local delicacies, try one of the many **Long's Drugs** stores (⊠ Ala Moana Shopping Center, 1450 Ala Moana Blvd., 2nd level, ☎ 808/941–4433; ⊠ Kāhala Mall, ☎ 808/732–0784; ⊠ 1088 Bishop Street Mall, downtown, ☎ 808/536–4551). **Tropical Fruits Distributors of Hawai'i** (⊠ 651 Ilalo St., Honolulu, ☎ 808/874–3234) specializes in packing inspected pineapple and papaya; it will deliver to your hotel and to the airport baggage check-in counter or ship to the mainland United States and Canada.

Gifts

Robyn Buntin Galleries (⊠ 820 S. Beretania St., Honolulu, ☎ 808/545–5572) presents Chinese nephrite jade carvings, Japanese lacquer and screens, Buddhist sculptures, and other international pieces. **Takenoya Arts** (⊠ Halekūlani, 2199 Kālia Rd., ☎ 808/926–1939) specializes in intricately carved *netsuke* (toggles used to fasten containers to kimonos), both antique and contemporary, and one-of-a-kind necklaces. **Following Sea** (⊠ Kāhala Mall, ☎ 808/734–4425) sells beautiful handmade jewelry and pottery.

Hawaiian Art and Crafts

One of the nicest gifts is something handcrafted of native Hawaiian wood. Koa and milo each have a beautiful color and grain. The great koa forests are disappearing because of environmental factors, so the wood is becoming valuable.

The best selection of Hawaiian arts and crafts in Waikīkī is at the **Little Hawaiian Craft Shop** (⊠ Royal Hawaiian Shopping Center, ☎ 808/926–2662). Some items are Bishop Museum reproductions, with a portion of the profits going to the museum. The shop also has a good selection of Ni'ihau shell leis, feather hatbands, and South Pacific arts.

For hula costumes and instruments, try **Hula Supply Center** (⊠ 2346 S. King St., ☎ 808/941–5379). For traditional island comforters, try **Quilts Hawai'i** (⊠ 2338 S. King St., ☎ 808/942–3195). For high-end collector's items, head to **Martin & MacArthur** (⊠ Aloha Tower Marketplace, ☎ 808/524–6066), specialists in koa furniture.

Jewelry

You can buy gold chains by the inch on the street corner, and jade and coral trinkets by the dozen. **Bernard Hurtig's** (⊠ Hilton Hawaiian Village Ali'i Tower, ☎ 808/947–9399) has fine jewelry with an emphasis on 18-karat gold and antique jade. Hawaiian heirloom jewelry is popular with island residents. Bracelets, earrings, and necklaces are imprinted with distinctive black letters that spell out your name in Hawaiian. In Waikīkī, try **Hawaiian Heirloom Jewelry Factory** (⊠ Royal Hawaiian Shopping Center, ☎ 808/924–7972. **Haimoff & Haimoff Creations in Gold** (⊠ Halekūlani, 2199 Kālia Rd., ☎ 808/923–8777) sells the work of award-winning jewelry designer Harry Haimoff.

O'AHU A TO Z

Arriving and Departing

By Plane

FROM THE MAINLAND UNITED STATES

Honolulu International Airport (☎ 808/836–6413) is one of the busiest in the nation. It is only a 20-minute drive from Waikīkī. Most flights originate in Los Angeles or San Francisco, which, of course, means they are nonstop. Flying time from the West Coast is 4½–5 hours.

American carriers coming into Honolulu include **American** (☎ 808/833–7600 or 800/433–7300), **Continental** (☎ 800/525–0280), **Delta** (☎ 800/221–1212), **Hawaiian** (☎ 808/838–1555 or 800/367–5320), **Northwest** (☎ 808/955–2255 or 800/225–2525), **TWA** (☎ 800/221–2000), and **United** (☎ 800/241–6522).

FROM THE UNITED KINGDOM

Air New Zealand (☎ 800/262–1234), **American** (☎ 808/833–7600 or 800/433–7300), **Continental** (☎ 800/525–0280), **Delta** (☎ 800/221–1212), and **United** (☎ 800/241–6522) are among the airlines that fly to Honolulu from the United Kingdom. Rates for an APEX ticket vary. Check around for the best offer.

DISCOUNT FLIGHTS

Charter flights are the least expensive and the least reliable—with chronically late departures and occasional cancellations. They also tend to depart less frequently (usually once a week) than do regularly scheduled flights. If the savings are worth the potential annoyance, charter flights serving Honolulu International Airport include **American Trans Air** (☎ 800/435–9282) and **Hawaiian Airlines** (☎ 808/838–1555 or 800/367–5320). Consult your local travel agent for information.

BETWEEN THE AIRPORT AND WAIKĪKĪ

There are taxis right at the airport baggage claim exit. At $1.50 start-up plus $1.50 for each mile, the fare to Waikīkī will run approximately $20, plus tip. Drivers are also allowed to charge 30¢ per suitcase. **Trans Hawaiian Services** (☎ 808/566–7333) runs an airport shuttle service to Waikīkī. Fare is $7 one-way, $13 round-trip. The municipal bus is only $1, but you are allowed only one bag, which must fit on your lap. Some hotels have their own pickup service. Check when you book.

If you do find yourself waiting at the airport with extra time on your hands, be sure to visit the **Pacific Aerospace Museum** in the central waiting lobby of the main terminal. It includes a 1,700-square-ft, three-dimensional, multimedia theater presenting the history of flight in Hawai'i, and a full-scale space shuttle flight deck. Hands-on exhibits include a mission-control computer program tracing flights in the Pacific. ☎ 808/839–0777. ⊒ $3. ☉ Daily 8:30–6.

By Ship

Boat Day used to be the biggest day of the week. Jet travel has almost obscured that custom, and it's too bad, because arriving in Hawai'i by ship is a great experience. If you have the time, it is one sure way to unwind. Many cruises are planned a year or more in advance and fill up fast. Most cruise-ship companies offer a fare that includes round-trip air travel to the point of embarkation.

Cunard/N.A.C. Line, Royal Cruises, P & O/Princess Cruises, and **Royal Viking** have cruise ships passing through Honolulu once or twice a year. The **S.S.** *Independence* stops in Honolulu each Saturday morning and departs each Saturday night on its weeklong interisland cruises. You can also book three- and four-day packages on the Hawai'i-based luxury liner. At press time, there was talk of American Hawai'i Cruises adding another vessel in Hawaiian waters sometime within the next year. ⊠ *American Hawai'i Cruises, 1380 Port of New Orleans Pl., Robin St. Wharf, New Orleans, LA 70130,* ☎ *504/586–0631 or 800/543–7637.* ✆

Getting Around

Waikīkī is only 2½ mi long and ½ mi wide, which means you can usually walk to where you are going.

By Bus

You can go all around the island or just down Kalākaua Avenue for $1 on Honolulu's municipal transportation system, affectionately known as **TheBus** (☎ 808/848–5555). You are also entitled to one free transfer per fare if you ask for it when boarding. Board at the front of the bus. Exact change is required, and dollar bills are accepted. A four-day pass for visitors costs $10 and is sold at the more than 30 ABC stores (Hawaiian chain stores that sell sundries and are geared to tourists) in Waikīkī. Monthly passes cost $25.

There are no official bus-route maps, but you can find privately published booklets at most drugstores and other convenience outlets. The important route numbers for Waikīkī are 2, 4, 8, 19, 20, and 58. If you venture afield, you can always get back on one of these.

There are also a number of brightly painted private buses, many free, that will take you to such commercial attractions as dinner cruises, garment factories, and the like.

By Car

O'ahu's drivers are generally courteous, and you rarely hear a horn. People will slow down and let you into traffic with a wave of the hand. A friendly wave back is customary. If a driver sticks a hand out the window in a fist with the thumb and pinky sticking straight out, this is a good thing: The Hawaiian symbol for "hang loose," it's called the *shaka* and is often used to say "thanks," as well. Hawai'i has a seat-belt law for front-seat passengers, and children under 40 pounds must be in a car seat, available from your car-rental agency.

It's hard to get lost on O'ahu. Roads and streets, although they may be unpronounceable to the visitor (Kalaniana'ole Highway, for example), are at least well marked. Major attractions and scenic spots are marked by the distinctive HVCB sign with its red-caped warrior. Although it's hard to get lost, driving in Honolulu can be frustrating, as many streets are one-way.

Driving in rush-hour traffic (6:30–8:30 and 3:30–5:30) can be exasperating, because left turns are prohibited at many intersections. Parking along many streets is curtailed during these hours, and towing is strictly enforced. Read the curbside parking signs before leaving your vehicle, even at a meter. Remember not to leave valuables in your car. Tourists and rental cars can be targets for thieves.

By Limousine

Cloud Nine Limousine Service (☎ 808/524–7999 or 800/524–7999) will provide red-carpet treatment in its chauffeur-driven superstretch limousines. Riding in such style costs $60 an hour, plus tax and tip, with a two-hour minimum service required. Another reliable company is **Lowy Limousine Service** (☎ 808/455–2444), which specializes in Lincoln stretch limos starting at $50 per hour, with a two-hour minimum.

By Moped, Motorcycle, and Bicycle

Island Motorcycle (☎ 808/957–0517) rents a variety of motorcycles for $129 to $149 a day. **Blue Sky Rentals & Sports Center** (✉ 1920 Ala Moana Blvd., across from Hilton Hawaiian Village, ☎ 808/947–0101) rents mopeds for $20 a day (8–6) and $25 for 24 hours. Mountain bikes cost $15 a day, $20 for 24 hours, and $75 for the week, plus a $25 deposit, including helmet, lock, and water bottle.

By Taxi

You can usually get one right outside your hotel. Most restaurants will call a taxi for you. Rates are $1.50 at the drop of the flag, plus $1.50 per mile. Drivers are generally courteous, and the cars are in good condition, many of them air-conditioned. The two biggest taxicab companies are **Charley's** (☎ 808/531–1333), a fleet of company-owned cabs, and **SIDA of Hawai'i, Inc.** (☎ 808/836–0011), an association of individually owned cabs.

By Trolley

The **Waikīkī Trolley** (☎ 808/596–2199) cruises Waikīkī, Ala Moana, and downtown, making 20 stops along a two-hour route. The trolley ride provides a good orientation. The conductor narrates, pointing out sights as well as shopping and dining along the way. The trolley departs from the Royal Hawaiian Shopping Center every 15 minutes daily 8–4:30. Buy an all-day pass from the conductor for $18.

Contacts and Resources

Car Rentals

If you plan to tour O'ahu itself, and not just restrict your visit to Waikīkī, renting a car is essential. During peak seasons—summer, Christmas vacations, and February—reservations are necessary.

Rental agencies abound in and around the Honolulu International Airport and in Waikīkī. Often it is cheaper to rent in Waikīkī than at the airport. **Avis** (☎ 808/834–5524 or 800/333–1212), **Budget** (☎ 800/527–0700 or 808/838–1111), **Dollar** (☎ 800/367–7006), **Hertz** (☎ 808/523–5176 or 800/654–8200), **National** (☎ 808/831–0270 or 800/227–7368), and **Thrifty** (☎ 808/733–5188 or 800/367–2277) have airport and downtown offices. Local budget and used rental-car companies include **JN Car and Truck Rentals** (☎ 808/831–2724), with a line of luxury cars, convertibles, passenger vans, and trucks; and **VIP** (☎ 808/922–4605), at the airport and in Waikīkī.

Doctors

At **Doctors on Call** a doctor, laboratory-radiology technician, and nurses are always on duty. Appointments are recommended but not necessary. Services include diagnosis and treatment of illness and injury, laboratory testing, X ray on-site, and referral, when necessary. Dozens of kinds of medical insurance are accepted, including Medicare, Medicaid, and most kinds of travel insurance. ✉ *Nicos Bldg., 2222 Kalākaua Ave., 2nd floor,* ☎ *808/971–6000.*

HOSPITALS

Castle Medical Center (✉ 640 Ulukahiki, Kailua, ☎ 808/263–5500). **Kapiolani Medical Center for Women and Children** (✉ 1319 Punahou St., Honolulu, ☎ 808/973–8511). **Queen's Medical Center** (✉ 1301 Punchbowl St., Honolulu, ☎ 808/538–9011). **Saint Francis Medical Center–West** (✉ 91-2141 Ft. Weaver Rd., 'Ewa Beach, ☎ 808/678–7000). **Straub Clinic** (✉ 888 S. King St., Honolulu, ☎ 808/522–4000).

Emergencies

Police, fire department, and **ambulance** (☎ 911). **Coast Guard Rescue Center** (☎ 800/552–6458).

Guided Tours

AERIAL TOURS

Biplane Rides. After suiting up with goggles and leather helmets, you can climb into an open cockpit of a restored Stearman biplane for loops, rolls, hammer heads, and other aerobatic maneuvers above O'ahu's North Shore. Only one person can go up at a time. ✉ *Dillingham Airfield, Mokulē'ia,* ☎ *808/637–4461.* 🕐 *20 mins $125, 40 mins $175.* ☼ *Daily 10:30–5:30.*

Glider Rides. Through the bubble top of a sleek sail plane you get aerial views of O'ahu's North Shore with its coral pools, sugarcane fields, windsurfers, and, in winter, humpback whales. On-board live video-taping is available. Reservations are not accepted. ⊠ *Dillingham Airfield, Mokulē'ia,* ☎ *808/677–3404.* ☒ *1 passenger $90, 2 passengers $120.* ☉ *Daily 10–5, 20- and 30-min flights every 20 mins.*

EXCURSIONS AND TOUR COMPANIES

There are many ground-tour companies in Oa'hu who handle day-long sightseeing excursions. Depending on the size of the tour, travel may be by air-conditioned bus or smaller vans. Vans are recommended because less time is spent picking up passengers, and you get to know your fellow passengers and your tour guide. Whether you go by bus or van, you'll probably be touring in top-of-the-line equipment, as the competition among these companies is fierce and everyone has to keep up. If you're booking through your hotel travel desk, ask whether you'll be on a bus or a van and exactly what the tour includes in the way of actual "get-off-the-bus" stops and "window sights." Most of the tour guides have been in the business for years. Many have taken special Hawaiiana classes to learn their history and lore. Tipping ($2 per person at least) is customary. The following companies are recommended: **American Express Tours and Activities Center** (☎ 808/521–7283) books through several tour companies and can help you choose which tour best suits your needs. **E Noa Tours** (☎ 808/591–2561) uses minibuses and trolleys and likes to get you into the great outdoors. **Polynesian Adventure Tours** (☎ 808/833–3000) has motorcoaches, vans, and minicoaches. **Polynesian Hospitality** (☎ 808/526–3565) provides narrated tours. **Roberts Hawai'i** (☎ 808/539–9400) has equipment ranging from vans to presidential limousines. **Trans Hawaiian Services** (☎ 808/566–7420) offers multilingual tours.

Most tour companies offer some version of the following standard Oa'hu tours listed below:

Circle Island Tour. There are several variations on this theme. Read Exploring O'ahu (☞ *above*) to decide what is important to you, and then choose a tour package that comes the closest to matching your desires. Some of these all-day tours include lunch. Transport is either bus or minibus, the latter being slightly more expensive. ☒ *$45–$65.*

Little Circle Tour. These tours cover the territory discussed in the East O'ahu Ring (☞ Exploring O'ahu, *above*). Most are the same, no matter what the company. This is a half-day tour. ☒ *$25–$40.*

Pearl Harbor and City. This comprehensive tour includes the boat tour to Pearl Harbor run by the National Park Service (☞ Around the Island *in* Exploring O'ahu, *above*). ☒ *$25–$40.*

Polynesian Cultural Center. One of the advantages of the tour is that you don't have to drive yourself back to Waikīkī after dark if you take in the evening show (☞ Around the Island *in* Exploring O'ahu, *above*). ☒ *$70–$80.*

SEA TOURS

Dream Cruises. Dream Cruises offers tours of Pearl Harbor aboard the 100-ft motor yacht *American Dream.* The trip takes place in the early morning to coincide with the time that Pearl Harbor was attacked on December 7, 1941. It includes a stop near the U.S.S. *Arizona* Memorial, where the captain conducts a brief memorial service and lei placement ceremony. Narration and videos help describe the sights. In winter, this cruise is paired with a whale-watch. ⊠ *1020 Auahi St.,* ☎ *808/592–5200.* ☒ *$21.95.* ☉ *Daily 7:30–10:30 AM.*

Tradewind Charters. This is a good bet for half-day private charter tours for sailing, snorkeling, and whale-watching. These luxury yachts not only eliminate crowds, but guests also have the opportunity to "take the helm" if they wish. The cruise also features snorkeling at an exclusive anchorage as well as hands-on snorkeling and sailing instruction. Charter prices are approximately $495 and accommodate up to six passengers. ⊠ *796 Kalanipuu St., Honolulu 96825,* ☎ *800/829–4899.* ✍

UNDERWATER TOURS

Atlantis Submarines. This company operates two vessels off Waikīkī: a 65-ft, 80-ton sub carrying up to 48 passengers and a newer 102-ft, 64-passenger craft. Rides are popular with children; a trip includes a catamaran ride to the dive site, providing great views of the Waikīkī and Diamond Head shoreline. The subs dive up to 100 ft to see a sunken navy-yard oiler and an artificial reef populated by brilliant fish. While the man-made concrete reef looks more like a fish tenement, it is drawing reef fish back to the area. You get a two-hour cruise with informative narration. The dive itself lasts about one hour. Children must be at least 3-ft tall to board. Note: Flash photography will not work; use film speed ASA 200 or above without flash. ⊠ *1600 Kapi'olani Blvd., Suite 1630, Honolulu 96814,* ☎ *808/973–9811.* 🖃 *$89 –$99, depending on which sub (48- or 64-passenger) you go on.*

Voyager Submarines. A roomy, air-conditioned yellow submarine takes you to the depths of the underwater world. The tour features a high-tech laser video show and narration of the volcanic reefs by marine-life specialists. For the more adventurous, the company also operates Hawaii Ocean Thrills, offering extreme marine sports including jet skis and jet-propelled Formula One racing boats. ⊠ *1085 Ala Moana Blvd., Honolulu 96814,* ☎ *808/592–7850.* 🖃 *$89.*

WALKING TOURS

Chinatown Walking Tour. Meet at the Chinese Chamber of Commerce (⊠ 42 N. King St.) for a fascinating peek into herbal shops, an acupuncturist's office, open-air markets, and specialty stores. The 2½-hour tour is sponsored by the Chinese Chamber of Commerce. Reservations are required. ☎ *808/533–3181.* 🖃 *$5.* ☉ *Tues. at 9:30.*

Historic Downtown Walking Tour. Volunteers from the Mission Houses Museum (⊠ 553 S. King St.) take you on a two-hour walk through Honolulu, where historic sites stand side by side with modern business towers. During the first hour, you get a tour of the Mission Houses themselves. Reservations are required. ☎ *808/531–0481.* 🖃 *$8.* ☉ *Thurs. and Fri. 9:30 AM–12:30 PM.*

Honolulu Time Walks. History springs to life for young and old alike during these fun jaunts, which come with appropriately costumed narrators. Tours include "Haunted Honolulu," "Honolulu's Crime Beat," "Mysteries of Mō'ili'ili," "Mark Twain's Honolulu," and the "Old Hawai'i Saloon Walk." The company also presents theater shows and films about the Islands. ☎ *808/943–0371.* 🖃 *$7–$45.*

Late-Night Pharmacies

Kuhio Pharmacy (⊠ Outrigger West Hotel, 2330 Kuhio Ave., ☎ 808/923–4466) is Waikīkī's only pharmacy and handles prescription requests only till 4:30 PM. **Long's Drugs** (⊠ Ala Moana Shopping Center, 1450 Ala Moana Blvd., 2nd level, ☎ 808/949–4010; ⊠ 2220 S. King St., ☎ 808/947–2651) is open evenings at its Ala Moana location and 24 hours at its S. King Street location (15 minutes from Waikīkī by car).

Visitor Information

Hawai'i Visitors & Convention Bureau (⊠ Waikīkī Business Plaza, 2270 Kalākaua Ave., Suite 801, Honolulu 96815, ☎ 808/923–1811 or 800/464–2924, ✍). **O'ahu Visitor Bureau** (☎ 888/464–6665, ✍). **Hawai'i Attractions Association** (☎ 808/596–7733, ✍). **Surf Report** (☎ 808/596–7873). **Weather** (☎ 808/973–4381) for O'ahu weather.

2 MAUI

The three planned resort communities along Maui's lee shore—Kapalua, Kā'anapali, and Wailea—offer self-contained environments of such luxury and beauty that the effect is almost surreal. With its golf courses, beaches, glorious sunsets, and (in winter) leaping humpback whales, leeward Maui is justifiably one of the top beach-vacation spots in the world. But there's more to the story—the curious history of Lahaina, the national park at Haleakalā, the towns and ranches Upcountry, and the dramatic rain-forest drive to Hāna.

Updated by
Pablo Madera

MAUI NŌ KA ʻOI IS WHAT THE LOCALS SAY—it's the best, the most, the top of the heap. Visitors agree. Readers of *Condé Nast Traveler* have voted Maui "Best Island in the World" for six years in a row and "Top Travel Destination" for three. To those who know Maui well, there's good reason for the superlatives. The second-largest island in the Hawaiian chain, Maui has made an international name for itself with its tropical allure, its arts and cultural activities, and miles of perfect-tan beaches. Maui weaves a spell over the more than 2 million people who visit its shores each year, and many visitors decide to return for good.

Maui residents have quite a bit to do with their island's successful tourism story. In the mid-1970s, savvy marketers on Maui saw a way to increase their sleepy island's economy by positioning it as an island apart. Community leaders started promoting their Valley Isle separately from the rest of the state. They nicknamed West Maui "the Golf Coast," luring in heavyweight tournaments that, in turn, would bring more visitors. They attracted some of the finest resorts and hotels in the world, and they became the state's condominium experts, emphasizing the luxurious privacy these accommodations can provide. Maui's visitor count swelled, putting it far ahead of that of the other Neighbor Islands.

Quick growth has led to its share of problems. During the busy seasons— from Christmas to Easter and then again during the summer—West Maui can be overly crowded. Although Maui has widened the road that connects Lahaina and Kāʻanapali, the occasional traffic congestion here might not be what you bargained for. And East Maui's Kīhei still has trouble keeping traffic in motion along its one seaside main drive.

But then consider Maui's natural resources. The island is made up of two volcanoes, one now extinct and the other dormant, that both erupted long ago and joined into one island. The resulting depression between the two is what gives Maui its nickname, the Valley Isle. West Maui's 5,788-ft Puʻu Kukui was the first volcano to form, a distinction that gives that area's mountainous topography a more weathered look. Rainbows seem to grow wild over this terrain as gentle mists fill the deeply eroded canyons.

The Valley Isle's second volcano is the 10,023-ft Haleakalā, a mammoth mountain. If you hike its slopes or peer into its enormous crater, you'll witness an impressive variety of nature, with desertlike terrain butted up against tropical forests.

The island's volcanic history gives Maui much of its beauty. The roads around the island are lined with rich red soil, the fertile foothold for sugarcane. Sugar has disappeared from West Maui, as it has nearly everywhere in the state. But Central Maui is still carpeted with grassy green, thanks to HC&S with its working mills at Puʻunēnē and Pāʻia. As the deep blue of ocean and sky mingles with the red and green of Maui's topography, it looks as if an artist has been busy painting the landscape. Indeed, visual artists love Maui.

Farmers also appreciate the Valley Isle. On the slopes of Haleakalā, the volcanic richness of the soil has yielded lush results. Sweetly scented flowers bloom large and healthy. Grapes cultivated on Haleakalā's slopes are squeezed for wine and champagne. Horses graze languidly on rolling meadows of the best Upcountry grasses, while jacaranda trees dot the hillsides with spurts of luscious lavender. As the big brute of a volcano slides east and becomes the town of Hāna, the rains that lavishly fall there turn the soil into a jungle and waterfalls cascade down the crags.

Pleasures and Pastimes

Beaches

Maui's beaches win awards for being the best in the world. (Yes, there are awards for beaches.) Those of Wailea and Kapalua lead the pack. Maui residents particularly revere Mākena Beach, beyond Wailea—so much so that they launched a successful grassroots campaign to have it preserved as a state park. Don't expect to find the island ringed with sand. In fact, most of the coastline is dramatically craggy. Beaches tend to be pockets. Each one has a personality of its own and can be completely explored in half a day. The thin, clean strand of Kā'anapali, though, goes on for three miles, past resort after resort. Offshore here, yachts, catamarans, and parasail riders drift across brilliant porcelain-blue water. Many of Maui's beaches are a little difficult to spot from the road, especially where homes and hotels have taken up shoreline property. Just remember that you can go to any beach you want. Access to the sea is a sacred trust in Hawai'i, preserved from ancient times. Sometimes you have to poke around to find the beach. Then again, maybe those are the ones you want.

Culture

Maui people like the arts so much that they built the $32-million Maui Arts & Cultural Center, with its well-designed 1,200-seat Castle Theater and its Schaefer International Art Gallery. The island also has one of the oldest community-theater groups in the country and one of the highest per capita populations of painters anywhere. Friday night is Art Night in Lahaina, where commercial galleries line Front Street. But many artists have retreated to the Upcountry region, making Makawao their hub. Up here, Hui No'eau Visual Arts Center has been providing classes, studios, and exhibits since the 1930s. The resorts, too, are lined with splendid art collections. The hotels also perpetuate Hawaiian culture. The best at this are the Ritz-Carlton, Kapalua and the Kā'anapali Beach Hotel. The best way to explore Maui's curious history and mixed cultures is to tour the small museums—Baldwin Home in Lahaina, Bailey House in Wailuku, the Alexander & Baldwin (A&B) Sugar Museum in Pu'nēnē, the Hāna Cultural Center Museum, and the 'Ulupalakua Ranch History Room at the Tedeschi Vineyards and Winery, to name a handful. Or go to the local events, the festivals and benefit concerts, a Japanese o-bon dance or a Portuguese church bazaar. There's always something going on. Check *The Maui News* on Thursday ("The Scene") and Sunday ("Currents").

Dining

On Maui you can eat a great meal every night for two months without ever dining twice in the same place. The resorts set very high standards, and restaurants elsewhere have risen to the challenge. Maui continues to attract fine chefs, several of whom are known for their trendsetting Hawai'i regional cuisine. This growing movement uses fruits and vegetables unique to Hawai'i in classic European or Asian ways—spawning such dishes as 'ahi (yellowfin tuna) carpaccio, breadfruit soufflé, and papaya cheesecake. Of course, you can find plain old local-style cooking on the Valley Isle—particularly if you wander into the less-touristy areas of Wailuku or Kahului, for example. A good "plate lunch" will fulfill your daily requirement of carbohydrates: macaroni salad, two scoops of rice, and an entrée of, say, curry stew, teriyaki beef, or *kālua* (roasted) pig and cabbage.

Driving

Maui is blessed with bad roads in beautiful places. Lots of visitors take a break from the beach and just go driving, usually taking day trips from their lodgings around Lahaina or Kīhei. Maui's landscape is extraordinarily diverse for such a small island. Your sense of place (and the weather) will seem to change every few miles. If you drive to the top of

Haleakalā you rise from palm-lined beaches to the rare world inhabited by airplanes in only an hour and a half. The road to Hāna takes you into the tropical rain forest, testing your reflexes behind the wheel on the rain-gouged windward side. Upcountry—around Makawao and Ha'ikū—you can drive into and out of the rain, with rainbows that seem to land on the hood of your car. Older, smaller West Maui has its own moods. 'Īao Valley in Wailuku captures the spirit of these mountains best.

Lodging

The resorts here re-create whatever is beautiful about Maui on the premises, doing their best to improve on nature. And their best is pretty amazing—opulent gardens, fantasy swimming pools with slide-down waterfalls and hidden grottoes (sometimes with swim-up bars in them), spas, cultural events, championship golf courses, priceless art collections, tennis clubs. . . . They make it hard to work up the willpower to leave the resort and go see the real thing. Kā'anapali, the grande dame, sits next to Lahaina's action. Kapalua, farther north, is more private and serene—and catches a bit more wind and rain. Sprawling Wailea on the South Shore has excellent beaches and designer golf courses, each with a distinct personality. Resort prices are not for everyone. Many visitors compromise on the luxury and find condominium apartments in Nāpili and Kahana (for West Maui) or in Kīhei (East Maui). With a few exceptions, you'll find that accommodations are all clustered along these leeward shores. If you want to stay elsewhere on the island—say, Upcountry or in Hāna (without using the Hotel Hāna-Maui)—seek out a bed-and-breakfast.

Water Sports

The West Maui vacation coast (from Lahaina to Kapalua) centers on Lahaina Harbor, where you can find boats for snorkeling, scuba diving, deep-sea fishing, whale-watching, parasailing, and sunset cocktail–partying. At the harbor, you can learn to surf or you can ride a submarine; catch a ferry ride to Lāna'i or grab a seat on a fast inflatable and explore all the way around it. The East Maui vacation coast has Mā'alaea Harbor and the great snorkeling beaches of Kīhei and Wailea. If you want to walk through the ocean without getting wet, visit the top-notch aquarium in Mā'alaea. If you'd rather watch, drive to Ho'okipa, near Pā'ia, for surfers and windsurfers.

Whale-Watching

One of the best signs of the high intelligence of humpback whales is that they return to Maui every year. Having fattened themselves in sub-arctic waters all summer, they migrate south in the winter to breed, and thousands of them cruise the Lahaina Roadstead (that is, the leeward Maui sea channel) in particular. From December 15 to May 1 the Pacific Whale Foundation has naturalists stationed in two places (on the rooftop of their headquarters and at the scenic viewpoint on the *pali*, or cliffside stretch, of the highway into Lahaina). The foundation also runs whale-watch boats that depart every hour of the day. In fact, every boat on the island will go out of its way to watch humpbacks when the opportunity arises—which it does often, as the whales themselves seem to have a penchant for people-watching.

EXPLORING MAUI

There is plenty to see and do on the Valley Isle besides spending time on the beach. The island can be split up into five exploring areas—West Maui, Central Maui, the South Shore, Upcountry (including Haleakalā), and the Road to Hāna (East Maui). You can spend half a day to a full day or more in each area, depending on how long you have to visit. The best way to see the whole island is by car, but there are opportunities for good walking tours.

To get yourself oriented, first look at a map of the island. You will notice two distinct circular landmasses. These are volcanic in origin. The smaller landmass, on the western part of the island, consists of 5,788-ft Pu'u Kukui and the West Maui Mountains. The interior of these mountains is one of the earth's wettest spots. Annual rainfall of 400 inches has sliced the land into impassable gorges and razor-sharp ridges. Oddly enough, the area's leeward shore—what most people mean when they say "West Maui"—is sunny and warm year-round.

The large landmass on the eastern portion of Maui was created by Haleakalā, the cloud-wreathed volcanic peak at its center. One of the best-known mountains in the world, Haleakalā is popular with hikers and sightseers. This larger region of the island is called East Maui. Its dry, leeward South Shore is flanked with resorts, condominiums, beaches, and the busy town of Kīhei. Its windward shore, largely one great rain forest, is traversed by the Road to Hāna.

Between the two mountain areas is Central Maui, the location of the county seat of Wailuku, from which the islands of Maui, Lāna'i, Moloka'i, and Kaho'olawe are governed. It's also the base for much of the island's commerce and industry.

In the Islands, the directions *mauka* (toward the mountains) and *makai* (toward the ocean) are often used.

Great Itineraries

Many visitors never get over the spell of the sea, and never go inland to explore the island and its people. Those who do, though, launch out early from their beachside hotel or condo, loop through a district, then wind up back "home" for sunsets and *mai tais* (potent rum drinks with orange and lime juice). When you live on an island, you get used to going in circles. Don't be too goal-oriented as you travel around. If you rush to "get there," you might find you've missed the point of going, which is to encounter one of the most beautiful islands in the world, still largely unpopulated.

Numbers in the text correspond to numbers in the margin and on the Maui, Lahaina, and Kahului-Wailuku maps.

IF YOU HAVE 1 DAY

This is a tough choice. But how can you miss the opportunity to see **Haleakalā National Park** ㊳ and the volcano's enormous, otherworldly crater? Sunrise at the summit has become the thing to do. It's quite dramatic (and chilly), but there are drawbacks. Namely, you miss seeing the landscape and views on the way up in the dark. You also have to get up early. How early? You'll need an hour and a half from the bottom of **Haleakalā Highway** (Highway 37) ㊲ to the summit. Add to that the time of travel to the highway—at least 45 minutes from Lahaina or Kīhei. *The Maui News* posts the hour of sunrise every day. The best experience of the crater takes all day and good legs. Start at the summit, hike down Sliding Sands trail, cross the crater floor, and come back up the Halemau'u switchbacks. (This works out best if you leave your car at the Halemau'u trailhead parking lot and get a lift for the last 20-minute drive to the mountaintop.) All you need is a packed lunch, water, and decent walking shoes. If you don't hike, leave the mountain early enough to go explore **'Īao Valley State Park** ㉙ above Wailuku. This will show you the island's jungle landscape and will compensate for the fact that you're missing the drive to Hāna.

IF YOU HAVE 3 DAYS

Give yourself the Haleakalā volcano experience one day, and then rest up a little with a beach-snorkel-exploring jaunt on either East or West Maui. The East Maui trip will have to include the **Maui Ocean**

Center ㉜ at Māʻalaea. Then drive the South Shore, sampling the little beaches in **Wailea** ㉞ and getting a good dose of big, golden **Mākena Beach State Park** ㉟. Be sure to drive on past Mākena into the rough lava fields, the site of Maui's last lava flows, which formed rugged **La Pérouse Bay** ㊱. The ʻĀhihi-Kīnaʻu Marine Preserve has no beach, but it's a rich spot for snorkeling.

Or take the West Maui trip over the pali through Olowalu, **Lahaina** ④–⑰, and **Kāʻanapali** ③, and dodge off the highway to find small beaches in Nāpili, Kahana, **Kapalua** ①, and beyond. The road gets narrow and sensational around **Kahakuloa** ②. If you're enjoying it, keep circling West Maui and return through the Central Valley.

On your third day, explore **Hāna** ㊹. Stop in **Pāʻia** ㊹ for a meal, pause at **Hoʻokipa Beach** ㊺ for the surf action, and savor the sight of the taro fields of **Keʻanae Arboretum** ㊿ and **Wailua Overlook** ㊾. Nearly everyone keeps going past Hāna town to **ʻOheʻo Gulch** ㊿, the "seven pools."

IF YOU HAVE 5 DAYS
Explore Upcountry. Get to **Makawao** ㊷ and use that as your pivot point. Head north at the town's crossroads and drive around **Haʻikū** ㊻ by turning left at the first street (Kokomo Road), right at Haʻikū Road, then coming back uphill on any of those leafy, twisting gulch-country roads. After you've explored Makawao town, drive out to Kula on the Kula Highway. This is farmland, with fields of flowers and vegetables and small ranches with well-nourished cattle. Stop in little Kēōkea for coffee, and keep driving on Highway 37 to the ʻUlupalakua Ranch History Room at the **Tedeschi Vineyards and Winery** ㊵. Add some time in Central Maui to really get to the heart of things, especially **Wailuku** ㉓–㉖, with its old buildings and curious shops. From here you can loop out to **Pāʻia** ㊹ and spend some time enjoying beaches in the Spreckelsville area and poking around the shops of this old plantation town.

When to Tour Maui

Although Maui has the usual temperate-zone shift of seasons—a bit rainier in the winter, hotter and drier in the summer—these seasonal changes are negligible on the leeward coasts, where most visitors stay. The only season worth mentioning is tourist season, when the roads around Lahaina and Kīhei get crowded. Peak visitor activity occurs from Christmas to March and picks up again in summer. If traffic is bothering you, get out of town and explore the countryside. During high season, the Road to Hāna tends to clog—well, not clog exactly, but develop little choo-choo trains of cars, with everyone in a line of six or a dozen driving as slowly as the first car. The solution: Leave early (dawn) and return late (dusk). And if you find yourself playing the role of locomotive, pull over and let the other drivers pass.

West Maui

West Maui, anchored by the amusing old whaling town of Lahaina, was the focus of development when Maui set out to become a premier tourist destination. The condo-filled beach towns of Nāpili, Kahana, and Honokōwai are arrayed between the stunning resorts of Kapalua and Kāʻanapali, north of Lahaina.

A Good Drive

Begin this tour in **Kapalua** ①. Even if you're not staying there, you'll want to have a look around the renowned Kapalua Bay Hotel and enjoy a meal or snack before you begin exploring. From Kapalua drive north on the Honoapiʻilani Highway (Hwy. 30). This road is paved, but storms now and then make it partly impassable, especially on the winding

8-mi stretch that is only one lane wide, with no shoulder and a sheer drop off into the ocean. However, you'll discover some gorgeous photo opportunities along the road, and if you go far enough, you'll come to **Kahakuloa** ②, a sleepy fishing village tucked into a cleft in the mountain. The road pushes on to Wailuku, but you may be tired of the narrow and precipitously winding course you have to take.

From Kahakuloa turn around and go back in the direction from which you came—south toward Kāʻanapali and Lahaina, past the beach towns of Nāpili, Kahana, and Honokōwai. If you wish to explore these towns, get off the Upper Honoapiʻilani Highway and drive closer to the water. If you're not staying there, you may want to visit the planned resort community of **Kāʻanapali** ③, especially the Hyatt Regency Maui and the Westin Maui. To reach them, turn right at Kāʻanapali Parkway. Next, head for Lahaina. Before you start your Lahaina trek, take a short detour by turning left from Honoapiʻilani Highway onto Lahainaluna Road, and stop at the **Hale Paʻi** ④, the printing shop built by Protestant missionaries in 1837. Return down Lahainaluna Road until you reach Front Street and turn left.

Since Lahaina is best explored on foot, use the drive along Front Street to get oriented and then park at or near **505 Front Street** ⑤, at the south end of the town's historic and colorful commercial area. Heading back into town, turn onto Prison Street and you'll come to the **Hale Paʻahao** ⑥, which was built from coral blocks. Then return to Front Street, where it's a short stroll to the **Banyan Tree** ⑦, one of the town's best-known landmarks, and behind it, the old **Court House** ⑧. Next door, also in Banyan Park, stand the reconstructed remains of the waterfront **Fort** ⑨. About a half block northwest, you'll find the site of Kamehameha's **Brick Palace** ⑩. **Brig Carthaginian II** ⑪ is anchored at the dock nearby and is open to visitors. If you walk from the brig to the corner of Front and Dickenson streets, you'll find the **Baldwin Home** ⑫, restored to reflect the decor of the early 19th century and now home to the Lahaina Restoration Foundation. Next door is the **Master's Reading Room** ⑬, Maui's oldest building.

Wander north or south on Front Street to explore Lahaina's commercial side. At the Wharf Cinema Center, you can see the **Spring House** ⑭, built over a freshwater spring. If you continue north on Front Street, you'll come to the **Wo Hing Museum** ⑮. Walk another two blocks north, and you'll find the **Seamen's Hospital** ⑯. If it's before dusk and you still have a hankering for just one more stop, try the **Waiola Church and Cemetery** ⑰. Walk south down Front Street, make a left onto Dickenson Street, and then make a right onto Waineʻe Street and walk another few blocks.

TIMING

You can walk the length of Lahaina's Front Street in less than 30 minutes if you don't stop along the way. Just *try* not to be intrigued by the town's colorful shops and historic sites. Realistically, you'll need at least half a day—and can easily spend a full day—to check out the area's coastal beaches, towns, and resorts. The Banyan Tree in Lahaina is a terrific spot to be when the sun sets—mynah birds settle in here for a screeching symphony, which can be an event in itself. If you arrange to spend a Friday afternoon exploring Front Street, you can dine in town and hang around for Art Night, when the galleries stay open into the evening and entertainment fills the streets.

Sights to See

✎ following the text of a review is your signal that the property has a Web site where you will find details and, usually, images; for a link, visit www.fodors.com/urls.

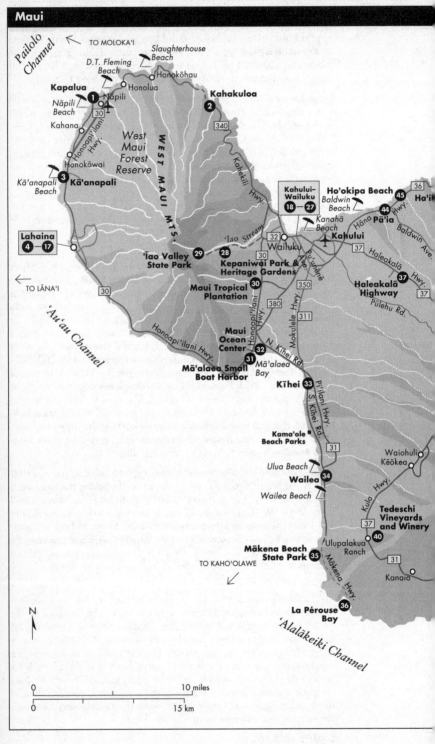

Pailolo Channel

TO MOLOKA'I

Slaughterhouse Beach

D.T. Fleming Beach

Kapalua ①

Nāpili Beach

Nāpili

Honolua

Honokōhau

Kahakuloa ②

30

Kahana

Hono'api'ilani Hwy.

West Maui Forest Reserve

340

Honokōwai

Kā'anapali ③

Kā'anapali Beach

Kahekili Hwy.

Kahului–Wailuku 18 — 27

Ho'okipa Beach 45 **Ha'i**

Baldwin Beach

36

Pā'ia 44

Kanahā Beach

WEST MAUI MTS.

Lahaina 4 — 17

'Īao Stream

32

Wailuku

Kahului

37

Hāna Hwy.

Baldwin Ave.

Haleakalā Hwy.

TO LĀNA'I

'Īao Valley State Park 29

28

Kepaniwai Park & Heritage Gardens

30

Pū'unēnē

Pū'unēnē Ave.

350

Haleakalā Highway 37

37

30

Maui Tropical Plantation

30

380

Hono'api'ilani Hwy.

311

Mokulele Hwy.

Pūlehu Rd.

Maui Ocean Center 32

31

N. Kīhei Rd.

Mā'alaea Small Boat Harbor

Mā'alaea Bay

Kīhei 33

Pi'ilani Hwy.

S. Kīhei Rd.

'Au'au Channel

Kama'ole Beach Parks

31

Waiohuli

Kēōkea

Ulua Beach

Wailea 34

Wailea Beach

Kula Hwy.

Tedeschi Vineyards and Winery 40

37

Mākena Beach State Park 35

Ulupalakua Ranch

TO KAHO'OLAWE

Mākena Hwy.

31

Kanaio

La Pérouse Bay 36

'Alalākeiki Channel

N

0 _____ 10 miles
0 _____ 15 km

PACIFIC OCEAN

46 kū

Ulumalu Rd.

Huelo

47

Kailua

360

365

Puahokamoa Stream

Kaumahina State Wayside Park

48

49

Hui No'eau Visual Arts Center

Honomanū Bay

50

Ke'anae Arboretum

51

Wailua

43

Kokomo

42

Makawao

Pukalani

52

Ke'anae Overlook

53

Wailua Overlook

Nāhiku

54

Enchanting Floral Gardens

Waikāne Falls

55

41

377

Kōolau Forest Reserve

360

Hāna Hwy.

Haleakalā Crater Rd.

Hāna Airport

37

Haleakalā National Park Headquarters Visitor Center

Pi'ilanihale Heiau

56

Wai'ānapanapa State Park

57

378

Leleiwi Overlook

38

Hāna Forest Reserve

Hotel Hāna-Maui

59

39

Kula Botanical Gardens

Kalahaku Overlook

Hāna

58

Haleakalā

Haleakalā National Park

Pu'u 'Ula'ula Overlook

Haleakalā Visitor Center

Koki Beach

Hāmoa Beach

Mū'olea

Kahikinui Forest Reserve

'Ohe'o Gulch

60

Kīpahulu

61

Grave of Charles Lindbergh

Kaupō

Pi'ilani Hwy.

31

Kaupō

'Alenuihāhā Channel

TO THE BIG ISLAND OF HAWAI'I

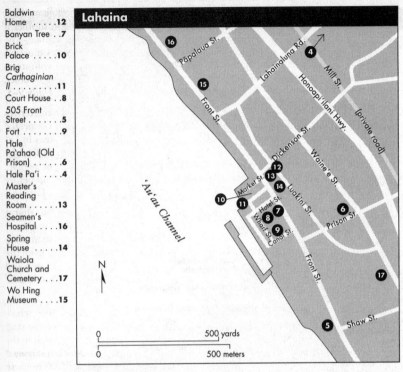

★ **⑫ Baldwin Home.** In 1835 an early missionary to Lahaina, Ephraim Spauld-ing, built this attractive thick-walled house of coral and stone. In 1836 Dr. Dwight Baldwin—also a missionary—moved in with his family. The home has been restored and furnished to reflect the period. You can view the living room with the family's grand piano, the dining room, and Dr. Baldwin's dispensary. The Lahaina Restoration Foundation occupies the building, and its knowledgeable staff is here to answer almost any question about historic sites in town. Ask for its walking-tour brochure. ✉ *696 Front St., Lahaina,* ☎ *808/661–3262.* 💲 *$3.* ⊙ *Daily 10–4.*

⑦ Banyan Tree. This massive tree, a popular and hard-to-miss meeting place if your party splits up for independent exploring, was planted in 1873. It is the largest of its kind in the state and provides a welcome retreat for the weary who come to sit under its awesome branches. ✉ *Front St., between Hotel and Canal Sts., Lahaina.*

⑩ Brick Palace. All that's left of the palace built by King Kamehameha I around 1802 to welcome the captains of visiting ships are the ex-cavated cornerstones and foundation in front of the Pioneer Inn. Hawai'i's first king lived only one year in the palace because his fa-vorite wife, Ka'ahumanu, refused to stay there. It was then used as a warehouse, storeroom, and meeting house for 70 years, until it col-lapsed. ✉ *Makai end of Market St., Lahaina.*

★ **⑪ Brig *Carthaginian II*.** This vessel's sailing days are over, but it makes an interesting museum. It was built in Germany in the 1920s and is a replica of the type of ship that brought the New England missionar-ies around Cape Horn to Hawai'i in the early 1800s. A small museum belowdecks features the "World of the Whale," a colorful multimedia exhibit about whaling and local sea life. ✉ *At dock opposite north end of Wharf St., Lahaina,* ☎ *808/661–3262.* 💲 *$3.* ⊙ *Daily 10–4.*

❽ Court House. This old civic building was erected in 1859, rebuilt in 1925, and restored to its 1925 condition in 1999. At one time or another it served as a customs house, post office, vault and collector's office, governor's office, police court, and courtroom. Now it houses museum displays, the Lahaina Arts Society, a visitor center—where volunteers will answer your questions—and, perhaps best of all, a water cooler. ✉ *649 Wharf St., Lahaina,* ☎ *808/661–0111.* ⚃ *Free.* ☾ *Daily 9–5.*

❺ 505 Front Street. Quaint New England–style architecture characterizes this mall, which houses small shops and casual restaurants connected by a wooden sidewalk. It isn't as crowded as some other areas in Lahaina, probably because between here and the nearby Banyan Tree the town turns into a sleepy residential neighborhood and some people, walking from the more bustling center of Front Street, give up before they reach the mall. ✉ *South end of Front St. near Shaw St., Lahaina.*

❾ Fort. Used mostly as a prison, this fortress was positioned so that it could police the whaling ships that crowded the harbor. It was built after sailors, angered by a law forbidding local women from swimming out to ships, lobbed cannonballs at the town. Cannons raised from the wreck of a warship in Honolulu Harbor were brought to Lahaina and placed in front of the fort, where they still sit today. The building itself is an eloquent ruin. ✉ *Canal and Wharf Sts., Lahaina.*

❻ Hale Pa'ahao (Old Prison). This jailhouse dates back to rowdy whaling days. Its name means "stuck-in-irons house," referring to the wall shackles and ball-and-chain restraints. The compound was built in the 1850s by convict laborers out of blocks of coral that had been salvaged from the demolished waterfront ☞ **Fort.** Most prisoners were there for desertion, drunkenness, or reckless horse riding. Today, a wax figure representing an imprisoned old sailor tells visitors his recorded tale of woe. ✉ *Waine'e and Prison Sts., Lahaina.* ⚃ *Free.* ☾ *Daily 8–5.*

❹ Hale Pa'i. Six years after the Protestant missionaries established Lahainaluna Seminary as a center of learning and enlightenment in 1831, they built this printing shop. Here at the press they and their young native scholars created a written Hawaiian language and used it to produce a Bible, history texts, and a newspaper. An exhibit features a replica of the original Rampage press and facsimiles of early printing. The oldest U.S. educational institution west of the Rockies, the seminary now serves as Lahaina's public high school. ✉ *980 Lahainaluna Rd., Lahaina.* ⚃ *Donation.* ☾ *Weekdays 10–3.*

❸ Ka'anapali. The theatrical look of Hawai'i tourism—planned resort communities where luxury homes mix with high-rise hotels, fantasy swimming pools, and a theme-park landscape—all began right here in the 1960s. Three miles of uninterrupted white beach and placid water form the front yard for this artificial utopia, with its 40 tennis courts and two championship golf courses. The six major hotels here are all worth visiting just for a look around, especially the Hyatt Regency Maui, which has a multimillion-dollar art collection. At the Whalers Village shopping complex, a small **Whaling Museum** tells the story of the 19th-century *Moby-Dick* era. ✉ *2435 Kā'anapali Pkwy., Suite H16,* ☎ *808/661–5992.* ⚃ *Donation.* ☾ *Daily 9:30 AM–10 PM.*

❷ Kahakuloa. This tiny fishing village seems lost in time. Untouched by progress, it's a relic of pre–jet travel Maui. Many remote villages similar to Kahakuloa used to be tucked away in the valleys of this area. This is the wild side of West Maui. True adventurers will find terrific snorkeling and swimming along this coast, as well as some good hiking trails. ✉ *North end of Honoapi'ilani Hwy.*

❶ Kapalua. This resort, set in a beautifully secluded spot surrounded by pineapple fields, got its first big boost in 1978, when the Maui Land & Pineapple Company built the luxurious Kapalua Bay Hotel. It was joined in 1992 by a dazzling Ritz-Carlton. The hotels host dedicated golfers, celebrities who want to be left alone, and some of the world's richest folks. Kapalua's shops and restaurants are among Maui's finest, but expect to pay big bucks. By contrast, the old **Honolua Store** serves informal plate lunches, popular with locals. ⊠ *Bay Dr., Kapalua.*

Lahaina. This little whaling town has a notorious past. There are stories of lusty whalers who met head-on with missionaries bent on saving souls. Both groups journeyed to Lahaina from New England in the early 1800s. At first, Lahaina might look touristy, but there's a lot that's genuine here as well. The town has renovated most of its old buildings, which date from the time when it was Hawai'i's capital. Much of the town has been designated a National Historic Landmark, and any new buildings must conform in style to those built before 1920. ⊠ *Honoapi'ilani Hwy., 3 mi south of Kā'anapali.*

❻ Lahaina–Kā'anapali & Pacific Railroad. Affectionately called the Sugarcane Train, this is Maui's only passenger train. It's an 1890s-vintage railway that once shuttled sugar but now moves sightseers between Kā'anapali and Lahaina. This quaint little attraction with its singing conductor is a big deal for Hawai'i but probably not much of a thrill for those more accustomed to trains. The kids will like it. ⊠ *1½ blocks north of the Lahainaluna Rd. stoplight on Honoapi'ilani Hwy., Lahaina,* ☎ *808/661–0089.* ☞ *$14.50.* ☉ *Daily 9–5:30.*

⓭ Master's Reading Room. This could be Maui's oldest residential building, constructed in 1834. In those days the ground floor was a mission's storeroom, and the reading room upstairs was for sailors. ⊠ *Front and Dickenson Sts., Lahaina,* ☎ *808/661–3262.*

⓰ Seamen's Hospital. Built in the 1830s to house King Kamehameha III's royal court, this property was later turned over to the U.S. government, which used it as a hospital for whalers. Next door is a typical **sugar plantation camp residence**, circa 1900. ⊠ *1024 Front St., Lahaina,* ☎ *808/661–3262.*

⓮ Spring House. Built by missionaries to shelter a freshwater spring, this historic structure is now home to a huge Fresnel lens, once used in a local lighthouse that guided ships to Lahaina. ⊠ *Wharf Cinema Center, 658 Front St., Lahaina.*

NEED A BREAK? The sandwiches have real Gruyère and Emmentaler cheese at **Maui Swiss Cafe** (⊠ 640 Front St., Lahaina, ☎ 808/661–6776)—expensive ingredients with affordable results. The friendly owner scoops the best and cheapest locally made ice cream in Lahaina. Daily lunch specials are less than $6. Courtyard tables are set back from Front Street. Open from 9 to 7 daily, this is an informal local favorite.

⓱ Waiola Church and Cemetery. The Waiola Cemetery is actually older than the neighboring church, dating from the time when Kamehameha's sacred wife, Queen Keōpūolani, died and was buried there in 1823. The first church here was erected in 1832 by Hawaiian chiefs and was originally named Ebenezer by the queen's second husband and widower, Governor Hoapili. Aptly immortalized in James Michener's *Hawai'i* as the church that wouldn't stand, it was burned down twice and demolished in two windstorms. The present structure was put up in 1953 and named Waiola (water of life). ⊠ *535 Waine'e St., Lahaina,* ☎ *808/661–4349.*

⑮ **Wo Hing Museum.** Built by the Wo Hing Society in 1912 as a fraternal society for Chinese residents, this eye-catching building now contains Chinese artifacts and a historic theater that features Thomas Edison's films of Hawai'i, circa 1898. Upstairs is the only public Taoist altar on Maui. ⊠ *858 Front St., Lahaina,* ☎ *808/661–5553.* ✉ *Donation.* ⏰ *Daily 10–4.*

Central Maui

Kahului, an industrial and commercial town in the center of the island, is home to many of Maui's permanent residents, who find their jobs close by. The area was developed in the early '50s to meet the housing needs of workers for the large sugarcane interests here, specifically those of Alexander & Baldwin. The large company was tired of playing landlord to its many plantation workers and sold land to a developer who promised to create affordable housing. The scheme worked, and Kahului became the first planned city in Hawai'i. Ka'ahumanu Avenue (Hwy. 32), Kahului's main street, runs from the harbor to the hills. It's the logical place to begin your exploration of Central Maui.

A Good Tour

Begin at the **Alexander & Baldwin Sugar Museum** ⑱ in Pu'unēnē, directly across from the HC&S sugar mill. The mill has been processing cane and belching steam and smoke since it opened in 1902. For a while it was the biggest sugar mill in the world. By 1930 Pu'unēnē had a population of 10,000 workers and families living in "camps" around the mill, and it had a school, churches, and a bowling alley. All of that is gone today, but the museum tells the story of these people and of the industry they helped create.

From here, explore **Kahului,** which looks nothing like the lush tropical paradise most people envision as Hawai'i. Head back on Pu'unēnē Avenue all the way to its end at Ka'ahumanu Avenue and turn left. Three blocks ahead you'll see the sputniklike canvas domes of Ka'ahumanu Center, Maui's largest shopping center. If you turn right at the signal just before that, you'll follow the curve of Kahului Beach Road and see many ships in port at **Kahului Harbor** ⑲. On your left are the cream-and-brown buildings of **Maui Arts & Cultural Center** ⑳. Continue past the harbor, turn right at Waiehu Beach Road, and about a mile later as you cross the 'Iao Stream you'll see **Haleki'i-Pihana Heiau State Monument** ㉑ on the hilltop to your left. Return along the harbor road and make a right turn at Kanaloa Avenue. Return to Ka'ahumanu Avenue on this road, passing the new **Keōpūolani Park** ㉒ and the War Memorial Stadium, site of the annual Hula Bowl game. Turn right to reach Wailuku (Ka'ahumanu eventually becomes Wailuku's Main Street). To get a closer look at **Wailuku's Historic District** ㉓, turn right from Main Street onto Market Street, where you can park for free within view of the landmark '**Iao Theater** ㉔. The theater is a good place to begin your walking tour. Many amusing shops line **Market Street** ㉕ between Vineyard and Main streets. From here, it's a short walk along Main Street to **Ka'ahumanu Church** ㉖ on High Street, just around the corner from Main and across the way from the County Court House. Retrieve your car and return to Main Street, where you'll turn right. After a few blocks, on your left, you'll see **Bailey House** ㉗.

Continue driving uphill, into the mountains. Main Street turns into 'Iao Valley Road, the air cools, and the hilly terrain gets more lush. Soon you'll come to **Kepaniwai Park & Heritage Gardens** ㉘. 'Iao Valley Road ends at '**Iao Valley State Park** ㉙, home of the erosion-formed gray and moss-green rock called 'Iao Needle. This is a great place to picnic, wade in the stream, and explore the paths. Then return to Wailuku and, at the traffic light, turn right onto Highway 30. Drive south a couple of miles to the **Maui Tropical Plantation & Country Store** ㉚.

120

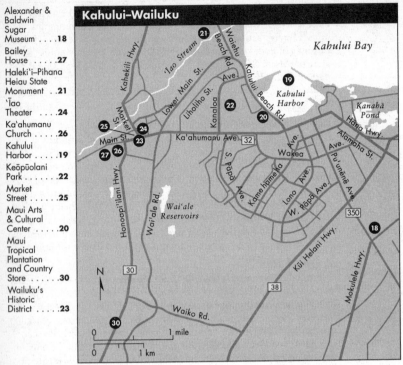

TIMING

The complete itinerary will take a full day. But you can explore Central Maui comfortably in little more than half a day if you whiz through the Maui Tropical Plantation, or save it for another day. If you want to combine sightseeing with shopping, this is a good itinerary for it, but you'll need more time. Hikers may want to expand their outing to a full day to explore 'Iao Valley State Park.

Sights to See

★ ⑱ **Alexander & Baldwin Sugar Museum.** "A&B," Maui's largest landowner, was one of five companies known collectively as the Big Five that spearheaded the planting, harvesting, and processing of the valuable agricultural product sugarcane. Although Hawaiian cane sugar is now being supplanted by cheaper foreign versions—as well as by sugar derived from inexpensive sugar beets—the crop was for many years the mainstay of the Hawaiian economy. You'll find the museum in a small, restored plantation manager's house next to the post office and the still-operating sugar refinery (black smoke billows up when cane is burning). Historic photos, artifacts, and documents explain the introduction of sugarcane to Hawai'i and how plantation managers brought in laborers from other countries, thereby changing the Islands' ethnic mix. Exhibits also describe the sugar-making process. ⊠ *3957 Hansen Rd., Pu'unēnē,* ☎ *808/871–8058.* ☜ *$4.* ⊙ *Mon.–Sat. 9:30–4:30.*

★ ㉗ **Bailey House.** This was the home of Edward and Caroline Bailey, two prominent missionaries who came to Wailuku to run the first Hawaiian girls' school on the island, the Wailuku Female Seminary. The school's main function was to train the girls in the "feminine arts." It once stood next door to the Baileys' home, which they called Halehō'ike'ike (House of Display), but locals always called it the Bailey House, and the sign painters eventually gave in. Construction of the house, between 1833 and 1850, was supervised by Edward Bailey himself. The Maui Historical Society runs a museum in the plastered stone house, with a small collection of artifacts from before and after the missionaries' arrival and with Mr. Bailey's paintings of Wailuku. Some rooms have missionary-period furniture. The Hawaiian Room has exhibits on the making of tapa cloth, as well as samples of pre–Captain Cook weaponry. ⊠ *2375A Main St., Wailuku,* ☎ *808/244–3326.* ⌦ *$4.* ☉ *Mon.–Sat. 10–4.* ✋

㉑ **Halekiʻi-Pihana Heiau State Monument.** Stand here at either of the two *heiau* (ancient temple platforms) and imagine the king of Maui surveying his domain. That's what Kahekili, Maui's last fierce king, did, and so did Kamehameha the Great after he defeated Kahekili's soldiers. Today the view is most instructive. Below, the once-powerful ʻIao Stream has been sucked dry and boxed in by concrete. Before you is the urban heart of the island. The suburban community behind you is all Hawaiian Homelands. ⊠ *End of Hea Place, off Kuhio Place from Waiehu Beach Road (Hwy. 340), Kahului,* ⌦ *Free.* ☉ *Daily 7–7.*

㉔ **ʻIao Theater.** One of Wailuku's most-photographed landmarks, this charming movie house went up in 1927 and served as a community gathering spot. When restoration work was completed in 1996, the Maui Community Theatre resumed its longtime residence here in its historic Wailuku headquarters. The Art Deco building is now the showpiece of Wailuku's Main Street. ⊠ *68 N. Market St., Wailuku,* ☎ *808/242–6969.*

NEED A BREAK?
Maui Bake Shop & Deli Ltd. (⊠ 2092 Vineyard St., Wailuku, ☎ 808/242–0064) serves salads, sandwiches, and a variety of light entrées, but what you're really going to crave are the pastries—a feast for the eyes as well as the palate. The pastel-frosted frogs, chicks, rabbits, and mice, made of orange butter-cream cookie dough, are irresistible.

★ ㉙ **ʻIao Valley State Park.** When Mark Twain saw this park, he dubbed it the Yosemite of the Pacific. Yosemite it's not, but it is a lovely deep valley with the curious ʻIao Needle, a spire that rises more than 2,000 ft from the valley floor. You can take one of several easy hikes from the parking lot across ʻIao Stream and explore the junglelike area. This park offers a beautiful network of well-maintained walks, where you can stop and meditate by the edge of a stream or marvel at the native plants and flowers. Mist occasionally rises if there has been a rain, which makes being here even more magical. ⊠ *Western end of Hwy. 32.* ⌦ *Free.* ☉ *Daily 7–7.*

㉖ **Kaʻahumanu Church.** It's said that Queen Kaʻahumanu attended services on this site in 1832 and requested that a permanent structure be erected. Builders first tried adobe, which dissolved in the rain, then stone. The present wooden structure, built in 1876, is classic New England style, with white exterior walls and striking green trim. You won't be able to see the interior, however, unless you attend Sunday services. There's a service entirely in the Hawaiian language each Sunday morning at 9:30. ⊠ *Main and High Sts., Wailuku,* ☎ *808/244–5189.*

Kahului. The town of Kahului is the industrial and commercial center for Maui's year-round residents, as close to a bustling urban center as Maui gets. Most visitors arrive at the airport here and see all they will see of the town as they drive on to their hotels. But this is the home of Maui's largest mall, Kaʻahumanu Center, which is virtually the social center of island life. It's also the site of the newly revived Maui Mall (with a 12-theater "megaplex") and the island's big mainland-style box stores, which are all visible on the main road from the airport.

⑲ **Kahului Harbor.** This is Maui's chief port, since it's the island's only deep-draft harbor. American-Hawaii's 800-passenger S.S. *Indepen-*

dence and S.S. *Constitution* each stop here once a week, as do cargo ships and smaller vessels, including the occasional yacht. Surfers sometimes use this spot to catch some good waves, but it's not a good swimming beach. ⊠ *Kahului Beach Rd., Kahului.*

㉒ Keōpūolani Park. Maui's new "Central Park" covers 101 acres, and—reflecting Maui residents' traditional love of sports—it has seven playing fields. Named for the great Maui queen who was born near here and is buried in Lahaina's Waiola Church cemetery, the park is planted with native species that will take a few years to reach their potential. The park also includes a native-plant botanical garden and a 3-mi walking path. ⊠ *Kanaloa Ave. next to the YMCA.*

㉘ Kepaniwai Park & Heritage Gardens. This county park is a memorial to Maui's cultural roots, with picnic facilities and ethnic displays dotting the landscape. There's an early Hawaiian shack, a New England–style saltbox, a Portuguese-style villa with gardens, and dwellings from such other cultures as China and the Philippines. Next door the **Hawai'i Nature Center** has an interactive exhibit and hikes good for children.

The peacefulness here belies the history of the area. During his quest for domination, King Kamehameha I brought his troops from the Big Island of Hawai'i to the Valley Isle in 1790 and engaged in a particularly bloody battle against the son of Maui's chief, Kahekili, near Kepaniwai Park. An earlier battle at the site had pitted Kahekili himself against an older Big Island chief, Kalani'ōpu'u. Kahekili prevailed, but the carnage was so great that the nearby stream became known as Wailuku (water of destruction) and the place where fallen warriors choked the stream's flow was called Kepaniwai (the water dam). ⊠ *Valley Rd., Wailuku.* ⌨ *Free.* ☉ *Daily 7–7.*

NEED A BREAK? If you're in Central Maui at lunchtime, try local favorite **Cafe O'Lei** (⊠ 2051 Main St., Wailuku, ☎ 808/244–6816), right in downtown Wailuku. The food is healthy, fresh, and tasty. The prices are great, and the people are friendly.

㉕ Market Street. An idiosyncratic assortment of shops—with proprietors to match—makes Wailuku's Market Street a delightful place for a stroll. Shops like the Good Fortune Trading Company and Brown-Kobayashi have affordable antiques and home furnishings. Merchants are happy to recommend a restaurant and offer advice or directions.

★ ⑳ Maui Arts & Cultural Center. This $32-million facility opened in 1994 after an epic fund drive led by the citizens of Maui. The top-of-the-line Castle Theater seats 1,200 people on orchestra, mezzanine, and balcony levels. Rock stars play the A&B Amphitheater. The Center (as it's called) also includes a small black box theater, an art gallery with interesting exhibits, and classrooms. The building itself is worth the visit. It incorporates work by Maui artists, and its signature lava-rock wall pays tribute to the skills of the Hawaiians. ⊠ *Above the harbor on Kahului Beach Rd., Kahului,* ☎ *808/242–2787; 808/242–7469 box office.* ☉ *Weekdays 9–5.*

㉚ Maui Tropical Plantation & Country Store. When Maui's once-paramount crop declined in importance, a group of visionaries decided to open an agricultural theme park on the site of this former sugarcane field. The 60-acre preserve, on Highway 30 just outside Wailuku, offers a 30-minute tram ride through its fields with an informative narration covering growing processes and plant types. Children will probably enjoy the historical-characters exhibit, as well as fruit-testing, coconut-husking, and lei-making demonstrations, not to mention some entertaining spider monkeys. There's a restaurant on the property and a "country store" specializing in "Made In Maui" products. ⊠ *Honoapi'ilani Hwy.*

(Hwy. 30), Waikapu, ☎ *808/244–7643.* ⌑ *Free; tram ride with narrated tour $9.50.* ☉ *Daily 9–5.*

㉓ **Wailuku's Historic District.** The National Register of Historic Places lists many of this area's old buildings. You can pick up a free brochure that describes a self-guided walking tour when you stop into Wailuku Main Street Association (2062 Main St., ☎ 808/244–3888). Over all the little town is sleepy, and one wouldn't guess that it's Maui's county seat. The mayor sits on the top floor of the tallest building in town, on the corner of Main and High streets. ⊠ *High, Vineyard, and Market Sts., Wailuku.*

The South Shore

Twenty years ago almost no one lived in Kīhei. Now about one-third of the Maui population lives here in what was, for a while, one of the fastest-growing towns in America. Traffic lights and mini-malls may not fit your notion of tropical paradise, but Kīhei does offer sun, heat, and excellent beaches. Besides that, the town's relatively inexpensive condos and small hotels make this a home base for many Maui visitors. At one end of this populous strip, you have Māʻalaea Small Boat Harbor and the Maui Ocean Center, a world-class seawater aquarium. At the other end, lovely Wailea—a resort community to rival those on West Maui—gives way to truly unspoiled coastline.

A Good Drive

Start with a look at **Māʻalaea Small Boat Harbor** ㉛, the setting-out place for many whale-watch trips, snorkel excursions (often out to the tiny crescent island Molokini), and sunset dinner cruises. Then tour the **Maui Ocean Center** ㉜, an aquarium dedicated to the sea life of the North Pacific. When you leave the aquarium, turn right onto Highway 30 and then turn right again at the first traffic signal—Highway 31 or North Kīhei Road. You're headed toward the town of **Kīhei** ㉝ on a straight road following the long sandy coastline of Māʻalaea Bay. On your left is marshy Keālia Pond, a state-managed wildlife sanctuary. On your right, ecologically fragile dunes run between the road and the sea. A turnout provides some parking stalls, information about the dunes, and a boardwalk so you can cross the dunes and use the beach. When you get to the long, thin town of Kīhei, you have a choice. You can turn right at the fork in the road and experience the colorful stop-and-go beach route of South Kīhei Road. Or you can turn left and bypass the town on the Piʻilani Highway, hastening to the resort community of **Wailea** ㉞. If you're looking for the best beach, you might as well flip a coin. There are great beaches all along this coast. At Wailea, you'll drive past grand resorts interspersed with stretches of golf courses and access roads leading down to small but excellent beaches. Then the manicured look of Wailea gives way to wildness and, after a couple of miles, to **Mākena Beach State Park** ㉟. Mākena is such a big beach that it has two paved parking areas. Beyond this point the landscape gets wilder and the road gradually fades away in black fields of cracked lava. This is **La Pérouse Bay** ㊱.

TIMING

Because it includes so many fine beach choices, this is definitely an all-day excursion—especially if you include a visit to the aquarium. A good way to do this trip is to get active in the morning with exploring and snorkeling, then shower in a beach park, dress up a little, and enjoy the cool luxury of the Wailea resorts. At sunset, settle in for dinner at one of the area's many fine restaurants.

Sights to See

㉝ **Kīhei.** This is a community that's still discovering itself. Much of it is less than 10 years old, inhabited by recent Maui immigrants. An abundance of condos, moderately priced hotels, and sprawl-malls makes the town convenient for visitors. The beaches and the reliably sunny weather make it a draw. The county beach parks such as Kamaʻole One, Two, and Three provide lawns, showers, and picnic tables. Remember: Beach park or no beach park, the public has a right to the entire coastal strand, and this one in Kīhei has many off-road delights.

㊱ La Pérouse Bay. Beyond Mākena Beach, the road fades away into a vast territory of black lava flows, the result of Haleakalā's last eruption some 200 years ago. This is where Maui received its first official visit by a European explorer—the French admiral Jean-François de Galaup, Comte de La Pérouse, in 1786. Before it ends, the road passes through ʻĀhihi-Kīnaʻu Marine Preserve, an excellent place for morning snorkel adventures.

㉛ Māʻalaea Small Boat Harbor. With only 89 slips and so many good reasons to take people out on the water, this active little harbor needs to be expanded. The Army Corps of Engineers has a plan to do so, but harbor-users are fighting it—particularly the surfers, who say the plan would destroy their surf breaks. In fact, the surf here is world renowned, especially the break to the left of the harbor called "freight train," said to be the fastest anywhere.

★ ㉟ Mākena Beach State Park. "Big Beach" they call it—a huge stretch of coarse golden sand without a house or hotel for miles. A decade ago, Maui citizens campaigned successfully to preserve this beloved beach from development. At the right-hand end of the beach rises the beautiful hill called Puʻu Ōlaʻi, a perfect cinder cone. A climb over the rocks at this end leads to "Little Beach," where the (technically illegal) clothing-optional attitude prevails.

★ ㉜ Maui Ocean Center. This aquarium, which focuses on Hawaii and the Pacific, will make you feel as though you're walking from the seashore down to the bottom of the reef, and then through an acrylic tunnel in the middle of the sea. Special tanks get you close up with turtles, rays, and the bizarre creatures of the tide pools. ⊠ *Enter from Honoapiʻilani Hwy. (Hwy. 30) as it curves past Māʻalaea Harbor, Māʻalaea,* ☎ *808/270–7000.* ☑ *$17.50.* ☉ *Daily 9–5.*

★ ㉞ Wailea. Wailea is to Kīhei as Kāʻanapali—Maui's original fantasy resort development—is to the town of Lahaina. In both cases, the town is real and the resort community is ideal. The luxury of the Grand Wailea, the Moorish near-silliness of the Kea Lani, the simple grandeur of the Four Seasons, the public displays of fine art and architecture make Wailea a unique Maui attraction. A handful of perfect little beaches all have public access, and a paved beachwalk allows you to stroll between all the properties, restaurants, and sandy coves.

Haleakalā and Upcountry

The west-facing upper slopes of Haleakalā are locally called "Upcountry." This region is responsible for much of Hawaiʻi's produce—lettuce, tomatoes, and sweet Maui onions—but the area is also a big flower producer. As you drive along you'll notice cactus thickets mingled with purple jacaranda, wild hibiscus, and towering eucalyptus trees. Upcountry is also fertile ranch land, with such spreads as the historic 20,000-acre ʻUlupalakua Ranch and 32,000-acre Haleakalā Ranch. In Makawao each July 4, the Maui Roping Club throws its annual rodeo and parade.

A Good Drive
Take the **Haleakalā Highway** ㊲ (Hwy. 37) to **Haleakalā National Park** ㊳ and the mountain's breathtaking summit. Make sure you have a full gas tank. There are no service stations above Kula.

Watch the signs: Haleakalā Highway divides. If you go straight it becomes Kula Highway, which is still Highway 37. If you veer to the left it becomes Highway 377, the road you want. After about 6 mi, make a left onto Highway 378. The switchbacks begin here. Near the top of the mountain is the Park Headquarters/Visitor Center, a good spot to stretch your legs and learn a little bit about the park.

Continuing up the mountain, you'll come to several overlooks, including Leleiwi Overlook and Kalahaku Overlook, both with views into the crater. Not far from Kalahaku Overlook you'll find the Haleakalā Visitor Center. Eventually you'll reach the highest point on Maui, the Puʻu ʻUlaʻula Overlook.

On the return trip, turn left when you reach Highway 377. Go about 2 mi, and you'll come to **Kula Botanical Gardens** ㊴ on your left. It's worth a stop here to admire the abundant tropical flora. Continue on Highway 377, away from Kahului, and you'll soon join Highway 37 again. Turn left and, about 8 mi farther on, you'll reach ʻUlupalakua Ranch headquarters and **Tedeschi Vineyards and Winery** ㊵, where you can sample Hawaiʻi's only homemade wines.

Return toward Kahului on Highway 37, the Kula Highway. **Enchanting Floral Gardens** ㊶ is clearly visible on the right side of the road near Mile Marker 10, about 2 mi before the Highway 37/377 junction. If you're pressed for time you can take Highway 37 from here back to Kahului. Otherwise, head north on Highway 365 toward **Makawao** ㊷, a classic old Hawaiian town. The **Hui Noʻeau Visual Arts Center** ㊸ is about a mile from the Makawao crossroads as you head down Baldwin Avenue. From here it's a 7-mi drive down toward the ocean to the Hāna Highway at the town of Pāʻia. Make a left on the Hāna Highway to return to Kahului.

TIMING

This can be an all-day outing even without the detours to Tedeschi Vineyards and Makawao. If you start early enough to catch the sunrise from Haleakalā's summit, you'll have plenty of time to explore the mountain, have lunch in Kula or at ʻUlupalakua Ranch, and end your day with dinner in Makawao or Haʻikū.

Sights to See

㊶ **Enchanting Floral Gardens.** This 8-acre flower garden shines with blooms from every part of the globe. There are excellent collections of bromeliads and proteas, but this garden doesn't specialize. You'll find some of everything, and the signage is very good. A paved path winds through the display, under blooming arbors, and past three colorful gazebos that are often used for weddings. ⊠ *Hwy. 37 near Omaopio Rd., Kula,* ☎ *808/878–2531,* ℻ *808/878–1805.* ▨ *$5.* ⊙ *Daily 9–5.*

㊲ **Haleakalā Highway.** On this road, you'll travel from sea level to an elevation of 10,023 ft in only 38 mi—a feat you won't be able to repeat on any other car route in the world. It's not a quick drive, however. It'll take you about two hours—longer if you can't resist the temptation to stop and enjoy the spectacular views. ⊠ *Hwy. 37.*

★ ㊳ **Haleakalā National Park.** Haleakalā Crater is the centerpiece of this 27,284-acre national park, first established in 1916. The crater is actually an "erosional valley," flushed out by water pouring from the summit through two enormous "gaps." The small hills within the crater are volcanic cinder cones (called *puʻu* in Hawaiian), each with a small crater at its top, and each the site of a former eruption. The mountain has terrific camping and hiking opportunities, including a trail that loops through the crater.

Before you head up Haleakalā, call for the latest park weather conditions (☎ 808/871–5054). Extreme gusty winds, heavy rain, and even snow in winter are not uncommon—even if it's paradise as usual down at beach level. Because of the high altitude, the mountaintop temperature is often as much as 30 degrees cooler than that at sea level. Be sure to pack an extra jacket.

You can learn something of the volcano's origins and eruption history at the Park Headquarters/Visitor Center, at 7,000-ft elevation on Haleakalā Highway. Maps, posters, and other memorabilia are available at the gift shop here.

Leleiwi Overlook, at about an 8,800-ft elevation on Haleakalā, is one of several lookout areas in the park. If you're here in the late afternoon, it's possible you'll experience a phenomenon called the Brocken Specter. Named after a similar occurrence in East Germany's Harz Mountains, the "specter" allows you to see yourself reflected on the clouds and encircled by a rainbow. Don't wait all day for this, because it's not a daily occurrence.

The famous silversword plant grows amid the desertlike surroundings at **Kalahaku Overlook,** at the 9,000-ft level on Haleakalā. This endangered flowering plant grows only here in the crater at the summit of this mountain. The silversword looks like a member of the yucca family and produces a 3- to 8-ft-tall stalk with several hundred purple sunflowers. At this lookout the silversword is kept in an enclosure to protect it from souvenir hunters and nibbling wildlife.

The **Haleakalā Visitor Center,** at 9,740-ft elevation on Haleakalā, has exhibits inside, and a trail from here leads to White Hill—a short, easy walk that will give you an even better view of the valley. Hosmer Grove, just off the highway before you get to the visitor center, has campsites and interpretive trails. Park rangers maintain a changing schedule of talks and hikes both here and at the top of the mountain. Call the park for current schedules.

Just before the summit, the **Crater Observatory** offers warmth and shelter, informative displays, and an eye-popping view of the cinder-cone-studded, 7-mi by 3-mi crater. The highest point on Maui is the **Puʻu ʻUlaʻula Overlook,** at the 10,023-ft summit. Here you'll find a glass-enclosed lookout with a 360-degree view. The building is open 24 hours a day, and this is where visitors gather for the best sunrise view. Dawn begins between 5:45 and 7, depending on the time of year. On a clear day you can see the islands of Molokaʻi, Lānaʻi, Kahoʻolawe, and Hawaiʻi. On a *really* clear day you can even spot Oʻahu glimmering in the distance.

On a small hill nearby, you'll see **Science City,** a research and communications center straight out of an espionage thriller. The University of Hawaiʻi and the Department of Defense don't allow visitors to enter the facility. The university maintains an observatory here, and the Department of Defense tracks satellites. ✉ *Haleakalā Crater Rd. (Hwy. 378), Makawao,* ☎ *808/572–4400.* ☎ *$10 per car.* ☉ *Park Headquarters/Visitor Center daily 7:30–4; Haleakalā visitor center daily sunrise–3.*

NEED A
BREAK?   **Kula Lodge** (✉ Haleakalā Hwy., Kula, ☎ 808/878–2517) serves hearty breakfasts from 6:30 to 11:15, a favorite with visitors coming down from a sunrise visit to Haleakalā's summit, as well as those on their way up for a later-morning tramp in the crater. Spectacular ocean views fill the windows of this mountainside lodge (☞ East Maui *in* Lodging, *below*).

 Hui Noʻeau Visual Arts Center. This nonprofit cultural center is on the old Baldwin estate, just outside the town of Makawao. The main house,

Close-Up

HAWAI'I'S FLORA AND FAUNA

HAWAI'I HAS THE DUBIOUS distinction of claiming more extinct and endangered animal species than all of the North American continent. The Hawaiian crow, or 'alalā, for example, has been reduced to a population of only 15 birds, and most of these have been raised in captivity on the Big Island. The 'alalā is now facing a serious threat from another endangered bird—the 'io, or Hawaiian hawk. Still "protected" although making a comeback from its former endangered status, the nēnē goose, Hawai'i's state bird, roams freely in parts of Maui, Kaua'i, and the Big Island, where mating pairs are often spotted ambling across roads in Hawai'i Volcanoes National Park.

The mongoose is not endangered, although some residents wish it were. Alert drivers can catch a glimpse of the ferretlike mongoose darting across country roads. The mongoose was brought to Hawai'i in 1883 in an attempt to control the rat population, but the plan had only limited success, since the hunter and hunted rarely met: Mongooses are active during the day, rats at night. Another creature, the rock wallaby, arrived in Honolulu in 1916 after being purchased from the Sydney Zoological Garden. Two escaped, and today about 50 of the small, reclusive marsupials live in remote areas of Kalihi Valley.

At the Kīlauea Point National Wildlife Refuge on Kaua'i, hundreds of Laysan albatross, wedge-tail shearwaters, red-footed boobies, and other marine birds glide and soar within photo-op distance of visitors to Kīlauea Lighthouse. Boobie chicks hatch in the fall and emerge from nests burrowed into cliffside dirt banks and even under stairs—any launching pad from which

the fledgling flyer can catch the nearest air current.

Hawai'i has only two native mammals. Threatened with extinction, the rare Hawaiian bat hangs out primarily at Kealakekua Bay on the Big Island. Also on the endangered species list, doe-eyed Hawaiian monk seals breed in northwestern Islands. With only 1,500 left in the wild, you won't catch many lounging on the beaches of Hawai'i's populated islands, but you can see rescued pups and adults along with "threatened" Hawaiian green sea turtles at Sea Life Park and the Waikīkī Aquarium on O'ahu.

Tropical flowers such as plumeria, orchids, hibiscus, red ginger, heliconia, and anthuriums grow wild on all islands. Pīkake blossoms make the most fragrant leis, and fragile orange 'ilima (once reserved only for royalty) the most elegant leis. The lovely wood rose is actually the dried seed pod of a species of morning glory. Mountain apple, Hawaiian raspberry, thimbleberry, and strawberry guava provide refreshing snacks for hikers; and giant banyan trees, hundreds of years old, spread their canopies over families picnicking in parks, inviting youngsters to swing from their hanging vines.

Sprouting ruby pom-pomlike lehua blossoms— thought to be the favorite flower of Pele, the volcano goddess—'ōhi'a trees bury their roots in fields of once-molten lava. Also growing on the Big Island as well as the outer slopes of Maui's Haleakalā, exotic protea flourish only at an elevation of 4,000 ft; within Haleakalā's moonscape crater, the rare and otherworldly silversword— a 7-ft stalk with a single white spike and pale yellow flower found nowhere else on earth—blooms once and then dies.

an elegant two-story Mediterranean-style villa designed in the 1920s by the defining Hawai'i architect C. W. Dickey, shines from the efforts of renovations. "The Hui," more than 60 years old, is the grande dame of Maui's well-known arts scene. The acreage seems like a botanical garden, and the nonstop exhibits are always satisfying. The Hui also offers classes and maintains working artists' studios. ⊠ *2841 Baldwin Ave., Makawao,* ☎ *808/572–6560.* ☒ *Free.* ⊙ *Tues.–Sun. 10–4.*

㉟ Kula Botanical Gardens. This well-kept 35-year-old garden has assimilated itself naturally into its craggy 6-acre habitat. There are beautiful trees here, including native koa (prized by woodworkers) and kukui (the state tree, a symbol of enlightenment). There's also a good selection of proteas, the flowering shrubs that have become a signature flower crop of Upcountry Maui. A natural stream feeds into a koi pond, which is also home to a pair of African cranes. ⊠ *R.R. 2, Upper Kula Rd., Kula,* ☎ *808/878–1715.* ☒ *$4.* ⊙ *Daily 9–4.*

㊷ Makawao. This once-tiny town has managed to hang on to its country charm (and eccentricity) as it has grown in popularity. The district was settled originally by Portuguese and Japanese immigrants, who came to Maui to work the sugar plantations and then moved "Upcountry" to establish small farms, ranches, and stores. Descendants now work the neighboring Haleakalā and 'Ulupalakua ranches. Every July 4 the *paniolo* (Hawaiian cowboy) set comes out in force for the Makawao Rodeo. The crossroads of town, lined with places to shop, see art, and get food, reflects a growing population of people who came here just because they liked it. ⊠ *Hwy. 365, East Maui.*

NEED A BREAK?
One of Makawao's most famous landmarks is **Komoda Store & Bakery** (⊠ 3674 Baldwin Ave., ☎ 808/572–7261)—a classic mom-and-pop store that has changed little in more than 70 years—where you can get a delicious cream puff if you arrive early enough in the day. They make hundreds, but sell out each day.

★ ㊵ Tedeschi Vineyards and Winery. You can take a tour of the winery and its historic grounds, the former Rose Ranch, and sample the island's only wines: a pleasant Maui Blush, the Maui Brut-Blanc de Noirs Hawaiian Champagne, and Tedeschi's annual Maui Nouveau. The top-selling products, however, are pineapple wines. The tasting room is a cottage built in the late 1800s for the frequent visits of King Kalākaua. The cottage also contains the 'Ulupalakua Ranch History Room, which tells colorful stories of the ranch's owners, the paniolo tradition that developed here, and Maui's polo teams. The old General Store may look like a museum, but in fact it's an excellent pit stop. The ranch and winery are not too out of the way when you're returning from a visit to Haleakalā, and they're definitely worth a stop. ⊠ *Kula Hwy., 'Ulupalakua Ranch,* ☎ *808/878–6058.* ☒ *Free.* ⊙ *Daily 9–5, tours daily 9–2:30.*

The Road to Hāna

Don't let anyone tell you the Hāna Highway is impassable, frightening, or otherwise unadvisable. Because of all the hype, you're bound to be a little nervous approaching it for the first time. But once you try it, you'll wonder if maybe there's somebody out there making it sound tough just to keep out the hordes. The 55-mi road begins in Kahului, where it is a well-paved highway. The eastern half of the road is challenging, because it is riddled with turns and bridges, and you'll want to stop often so the driver can enjoy the view, too. But it's not a grueling all-day drive. The challenging part of the road takes only an hour and a half.

A Good Drive

The Hāna Highway is the main street in the little town of **Pā'ia** ㊹. You'll want to begin with a full tank of gas. There are no gas stations along the Hāna Highway, and the stations in Hāna close by 6 PM. You can also pick up a picnic lunch here. Lunch and snack choices along the way are limited to local fare from rustic fruit stands. Once the road gets twisty, remember that many residents make this trip frequently. You'll recognize them because they're the ones who'll be zipping around every curve. They've seen this so many times before that they don't care to linger. Pull over to let them pass.

Two miles east of Pā'ia you'll see **Ho'okipa Beach** ㊺, arguably the wind-surfing capital of the world. Two miles later the bottom of Ha'ikū Road offers a right-turn side trip to **Ha'ikū** ㊻, Maui's verdant gulch country. About 6 mi later, at the bottom of Kaupakalua Road, the roadside mileposts begin measuring the 36 mi to Hāna town. The road's trademark noodling starts about 3 mi after that. All along this stretch of road, waterfalls are abundant. Open the windows to enjoy the sounds and smells. There are plenty of places to pull off and park. You'll want to plan on doing this a few times, since the road's curves make driving without a break difficult. When it's raining (which is often), the drive is particularly beautiful.

As you drive on you'll pass the sleepy country villages of **Huelo** and **Kailua** ㊼. At about Mile Marker 11 you can stop at the bridge over **Puahokamoa Stream** ㊽, where there are more pools and waterfalls. If you'd rather stretch your legs and use a flush toilet, continue another mile to the **Kaumahina State Wayside Park** ㊾. Near Mile Marker 13 you'll find yourself driving along a cliffside down into deep, lush **Honomanū Bay** ㊿. Another 4 mi brings you to the **Ke'anae Arboretum** ⑤, where you can add to your botanical education or enjoy a challenging hike into a forest. Nearby you'll find the **Ke'anae Overlook** ㊾. Coming up is the halfway mark to Hāna. If you've had enough scenery, this is as good a time as any to turn around and head back to civilization.

Don't expect a booming city when you get to Hāna. It's the road that's the draw. Continue from Mile Marker 20 for about ¾ mi to **Wailua Overlook** ㊾. After another ½ mi you'll hit the best falls on the entire drive to Hāna, **Waikāne Falls** ㊾. At about Mile Marker 25 you'll see a road that heads down toward the ocean and the village of **Nāhiku** ㊾, once a populous native settlement. Just after Mile Marker 31, the left turn at 'Ula'ino Road doubles back for a mile, loses its pavement, and even crosses a streambed just before Kahanu Garden and **Pi'ilanihale Heiau** ㊾, the largest in the state. Back on the road and less than ½ mi farther is the turnoff for Hāna Airport. Just beyond Mile Marker 32 you'll pass **Wai'ānapanapa State Park** ㊾. Stop at the black-sand beach for a swim. **Hāna** ㊾ is just minutes away from here. **Hotel Hāna-Maui** ㊾, with its surrounding ranch, is the mainstay of Hāna's economy.

Once you've seen Hāna, you might want to drive 10 mi past the town to the pools at **'Ohe'o Gulch** ㊿. Many people travel the mile past 'Ohe'o Gulch to see the **Grave of Charles Lindbergh** ㊿. You'll see a ruined sugar mill with a big chimney on the right side of the road and then, on the left, a rutted track leading to Palapala Ho'omau Congregational Church. The simple one-room church sits on a bluff over the sea, with the small graveyard on the ocean side. From here, you'll want to return the way you came. The road ahead is quite rough and not recommended for rental cars.

TIMING

With stops, the drive from Pā'ia to Hāna should take you between two and three hours. Lunching in Hāna, hiking, and swimming can easily turn the round-trip into a full-day outing. Since there's so much lush scenery to take in, try to plan your Road to Hāna drive for a day that promises fair, sunny weather. And be prepared for car trains that form spontaneously during the busier tourist seasons. (If you find one forming behind you, pull over and let the other drivers pass.)

Sights to See

⑥ Grave of Charles Lindbergh. The world-renowned aviator chose to be buried here because he and his wife, writer Anne Morrow Lindbergh, spent a lot of time living in the area in a home they'd built. He was buried here in 1974, next to Palapala Ho'omau Congregational Church. Since this is a churchyard, be considerate and leave everything exactly as you found it. Next to the churchyard on the ocean side is a small county park, a good place for a peaceful picnic. ⊠ *Palapala Ho'omau Congregational Church, Kīpahulu.*

OFF THE BEATEN PATH **KAUPŌ ROAD –** The road to Hāna continues all the way around Haleakalā's "back side" through 'Ulupalakua Ranch and into Kula. It's a bad road, sometimes impassable in winter. The car-rental agencies are smart to call it off-limits to their passenger cars. Most of the residents along the road in these wild reaches also prefer that you stick to the windward side of the mountain. The danger and dust from increasing numbers of speeding jeep drivers are making life tough for the natives, especially in Kaupō, with its 4 mi of unpaved road. The small communities around East Maui cling tenuously to the old ways. Please keep them in mind if you do pass this way.

㊻ Ha'ikū. At one time this town vibrated around a couple of enormous pineapple canneries. Now the place is reawakening and becoming a self-reliant community. At the town center, the old cannery has been turned into a rustic mall. Nearby warehouses are following suit. Continue 2 mi up Kokomo Road to see a large pu'u capped with a grove of columnar pines, and the 4th Marine Division Memorial Park. During World War II American GIs trained here for battles on Iwo Jima and Saipan. Locals have nicknamed the cinder cone "Giggle Hill," because it was a popular place for Maui girls to entertain their favorite servicemen. You might want to return to Hāna Highway by following Ha'ikū Road east. This is one of Maui's prettiest drives, and it passes West Kuiaha Road, where a left turn will bring you to a second renovated cannery. ⊠ *Intersection of Ha'ikū and Kokomo Rds.*

★ ㊾ **Hāna.** For many years, the ☞ Hotel Hāna-Maui was the only attraction for diners and shoppers determined to spend some time and money in Hāna after their long drive. The **Hāna Cultural Center Museum** (☎ 808/248–8622), on Ukea Street, helps to meet that need. Besides operating a well-stocked gift shop, it displays artifacts, quilts, a replica of an authentic *kauhale* (an ancient Hawaiian living complex, with thatched huts and food gardens), and other Hawaiiana. The knowledgeable staff can explain it all to you.

Keep in mind that this is a company town. Although sugar was once the mainstay of Hāna's economy, the last plantation shut down in the '40s. In 1946 rancher Paul Fagan built the Hotel Hāna-Maui and stocked the surrounding pastureland with cattle. Suddenly, it was the ranch and its hotel that were putting food on most tables. The cross you'll see on the hill above the hotel was put there in memory of Fagan.

The town centers on its lovely circular bay, dominated on the right-hand shore by a pu'u called Ka'uiki. A short trail here leads to a cave, the birthplace of Queen Kā'ahumanu. Two miles beyond town another pu'u presides over a loop road that passes Hāna's two best beaches—

Koki and Hāmoa. The hill is called Ka Iwi O Pele (Pele's Bone). This area is rich in Hawaiian history and legend. Offshore here, at tiny 'Ālau Island, the demigod Maui supposedly fished up the Hawaiian islands. ⊠ *Hāna Hwy., Mile Marker 35.*

Hāna Airport. Think of Amelia Earhart. Think of Waldo Pepper. If these picket-fence runways don't turn your thoughts to the derring-do of barnstorming pilots, you haven't seen enough old movies. Only the smallest planes can land and depart here, and when none of them happen to be around, the lonely wind sock is the only evidence that this is a working airfield. ⊠ *Hāna Hwy. past Mile Marker 30,* ☎ *808/248–8208.*

⑩ Honomanū Bay. At Mile Marker 14 the Hāna Highway drops into and out of this enormous valley, with its rocky black-sand beach. The Honomanū Valley was carved by erosion during Haleakalā's first dormant period. At the canyon's head there are 3,000-ft cliffs and a 1,000-ft waterfall, but don't try to reach them. There's not much of a trail, and what does exist is practically impassable. ⊠ *Hāna Hwy. before Ke'anae.*

★ **㊺ Ho'okipa Beach.** There is no better place on this or any other island to watch the world's best windsurfers in action. The surfers know five different surf breaks here by name. Unless it's a rare day without wind or waves, you're sure to get a show. It's not safe to park on the shoulder. Use the ample parking lot at the county park entrance. ⊠ *2 mi past Pā'ia on Hwy. 36.*

㊾ Hotel Hāna-Maui. It's pleasant to stroll around the lobby of this low-key but beautiful property, perhaps on the way to dinner at the restaurant, drinks at the bar, or shopping in the gift stores. The newer Sea Ranch cottages across the road are also part of the Hāna-Maui. The cottages were built to look like authentic plantation housing, but only from the outside. ⊠ *Hāna Hwy., Hāna,* ☎ *808/248–8211.*

㊼ Huelo. This sleepy little farm town has two quaint and lovely churches but little else of interest. Yet it's a good place to meet local residents and learn about a rural lifestyle you might not have expected to find in the Islands. The same could be said, minus the churches, for nearby **Kailua** (Mile Marker 6), home to Alexander & Baldwin's irrigation employees. ⊠ *Hāna Hwy. near Mile Marker 5.*

㊾ Kaumahina State Wayside Park. The park has a picnic area, rest rooms, and a lovely overlook to the Ke'anae Peninsula. Hardier souls can camp here, with a permit. ⊠ *Hāna Hwy., Mile Marker 12, Kailua,* ☎ *808/984–8109.* 🎫 *Free.* ☉ *Weekdays 8–4.*

㊿ Ke'anae Arboretum. Here's a place to learn the names of the many plants and trees now considered native to Hawai'i. The meandering Pi'ina'au Stream adds a graceful touch to the arboretum and provides a swimming pond besides. You can take a fairly rigorous hike from the arboretum, if you can find the trail at one side of the large taro patch. Be careful not to lose the trail once you're on it. A lovely forest waits at the end of the hike. ⊠ *Hāna Hwy., Mile Marker 17, Ke'anae.* 🎫 *Free.*

㉒ Ke'anae Overlook. From this observation point, you'll notice the patchwork-quilt effect the taro farms create below. The people of Ke'anae are working hard to revive this Hawaiian agricultural art and the traditional cultural values that the crop represents. The ocean provides a dramatic backdrop for the farms. In the other direction there are awesome views of Haleakalā through the foliage. This is a great spot for photos. ⊠ *Hāna Hwy. near Mile Marker 17, Ke'anae.*

㊻ Nāhiku. This was a busy settlement in ancient times, with hundreds of residents. Now only about 80 people live in Nāhiku, mostly native

Hawaiians and some back-to-the-land types. A rubber grower planted trees here in the early 1900s. The experiment didn't work out, so Nāhiku was essentially abandoned. The road ends at the sea in a pretty landing. This is the rainiest, densest part of the East Maui rain forest. ⊠ *Makai side of Hāna Hwy., Mile Marker 25.*

★ ⑥⓪ **'Ohe'o Gulch.** One branch of Haleakalā National Park runs down the mountain from the crater and reaches the sea here, where a basalt-lined stream cascades from one pool to the next. Tour guides used to call this area by the silly name "Seven Sacred Pools." You can park here and walk to the lowest pools for a cool swim. The place gets crowded, though, since most people who drive the Hāna Road make this their last stop. If you can hike at all, go up the stream on the 2-mi hike to **Waimoku Falls**. The trail crosses a spectacular gorge, then turns into a boardwalk that takes you through an amazing bamboo forest. You can pitch a tent in the grassy campground down by the sea. *Pi'ilani Hwy., 10 mi south of Hāna.*

★ ④④ **Pā'ia.** This little town on Maui's north shore was once a sugarcane enclave, with a mill and plantation camps. Shrewd immigrants quickly opened shops to serve the workers, who probably found it easier to buy supplies near home. The town boomed during World War II when the marines set up camp in nearby Ha'ikū. The HC&S sugar mill, on Baldwin Avenue about a mile above the traffic light at Hāna Highway, is still in full production. After the war, however, workers moved to other parts of Maui, and the town's population began to dwindle. In the '70s Pā'ia became a hippie town as dropouts headed for Maui to open boutiques, galleries, and unusual eateries. In the '80s windsurfers discovered nearby Ho'okipa Beach and brought an international flavor to Pā'ia. You can see this in the youth of the town and in the budget inns that have cropped up to offer accommodations to those who windsurf for a living. Pā'ia is certainly a fun place.

If you want to do some shopping, you can find clothing and handcrafted keepsakes or snacks and sweets in abundance in the friendly town of Pā'ia. Pā'ia is also home to Lama Tenzin, a Tibetan monk who lives and teaches at a small open temple called **Karma Rimay O Sal Ling**, on Baldwin Avenue half a mile from the traffic light. ⊠ *Hwys. 390 and 36, north shore.*

NEED A
BREAK?
Pā'ia has become a great place to find food. It used to be that **Picnics** (☎ 808/579–8021) was the one place to eat on Baldwin Avenue, and **Charley's Saloon** (☎ 808/579–8085), an easygoing local hangout with pool tables, was the place on Hāna Road. Now, right near the intersection of Baldwin Avenue and Hāna Road, you have a number of choices. **Pā'ia Fishmarket** (☎ 808/579–8030) specializes in fresh island fish both by the pound and served as tasty lunches and dinners. **Anthony's Coffee Company** (☎ 808/579–8340) serves ice cream, smoothies, and picnic lunches. The little town also has an excellent wine store, **The Wine Corner** (☎ 808/579–8940), and an admirable natural-foods store called **Mana Foods** (☎ 808/579–8078).

★ ⑤⑥ **Pi'ilanihale Heiau.** The largest prehistoric monument in Hawai'i, this temple platform was built for a great 16th-century Maui king named Pi'ilani and his heirs. This king also supervised the construction of a 10-ft-wide road that completely encircled the island. (That's why his name is part of most of Maui's difficult-to-pronounce highway titles.) Hawaiian families continue to maintain and protect this sacred site as they have for centuries, and they have not been eager to turn it into a tourist attraction. However, they now offer a brochure so you can tour the property yourself. Parties of four or more can reserve a guided tour by calling 48 hours in advance. Tours include 122-acre **Kahanu Garden**, a federally funded research center focusing on the ethnobotany of the Pacific. ⊠ *Left on 'Ula'ino Rd. at Mile Marker 31; the road turns to gravel; continue 1½ mi,* ☎ *808/ 248–8912.* ⊡ *$5 self-guided tours, $10 guided.* ⊙ *Weekdays 9–3.*

48 Puahokamoa Stream. The bridge over Puahokamoa Stream is one of many you'll cross en route from Pā'ia to Hāna. It spans pools and waterfalls. Picnic tables are available, so many people favor this as a stopping point, but there are no rest rooms. ⊠ *Hāna Hwy. near Mile Marker 11.*

★ **57 Wai'ānapanapa State Park.** The park is right on the ocean, and it's a lovely spot to picnic, hike, or swim. An ancient burial site is nearby, as well as a heiau. Wai'ānapanapa also has one of Maui's only black-sand beaches and some freshwater caves for adventurous swimmers to explore. With a permit you can stay in state-run (and rather shabby) cabins here for less than $30 a night—the price varies depending on the number of people—but reserve early. They often book up a year in advance. ⊠ *Hāna Hwy. near Mile Marker 32, Hāna,* ☎ *808/984–8109.* ⊡ *Free.*

54 Waikāne Falls. Though not necessarily bigger or taller than the other falls, these are the most dramatic—some say the best—falls you'll find on the road to Hāna. That's partly because the water is not diverted for sugar irrigation. The taro farmers in Wailua need all the runoff. This is a particularly good spot for photos. ⊠ *Hāna Hwy. past Mile Marker 21, Wailua.*

53 Wailua Overlook. From the parking lot you can see Wailua Canyon, but you'll have to walk up steps to get a view of Wailua Village. The landmark in Wailua Village is a church made of coral, built in 1860. Once called St. Gabriel's Catholic Church, the current Our Lady of Fatima Shrine has an interesting legend surrounding it. As the story goes, a storm washed just enough coral up onto the shore to build the church but then took any extra coral back to sea. ⊠ *Hāna Hwy. near Mile Marker 21, Wailua.*

BEACHES

All of Hawai'i's beaches are free and open to the public—even those that grace the front yards of fancy hotels—so you can make yourself at home on any one of them. Blue beach-access signs indicate rights-of-way through condominium and resort properties.

Although they don't appear often, be sure to pay attention to any signs or warning flags on the beaches. Warnings of high surf or rough currents should be taken seriously. Before you seek shade under a coconut palm, be aware that the trade winds are strong enough to knock fruit off the trees and onto your head. Drinking alcoholic beverages on beaches in Hawai'i isn't allowed.

West Maui

"Slaughterhouse" Beach. The island's northernmost beach is part of the Honolua-Mokuleia Marine Life Conservation District. "Slaughterhouse" is the surfers' nickname for what is officially Mokuleia. When the weather permits, this is a great place for bodysurfing and sunbathing. Concrete steps and a green-painted railing help you get down the sheer cliff to the sand. The next bay over, Honolua, has no beach but offers one of the best surf breaks in Hawai'i. Often you'll see competitions happening there, with cars pulled off the road and parked in the pineapple field. There are no facilities at this wild area. ⊠ *Mile Marker 32 on the road past Kapalua.*

D. T. Fleming Beach. This charming, mile-long sandy cove is better for sunbathing than for swimming because the current can be quite strong. Still it's one of the island's most popular, and there are rest rooms, showers, picnic tables, grills, and paved parking. Part of the

beach runs along the front of the Ritz-Carlton, Kapalua. ⊠ *Hwy. 30,
1 mi north of Kapalua Resort.*

Kapalua Beach. On the northern side of Nāpili Bay is small, pristine
Kapalua Beach. You may have to share sand space with a number of
other beachgoers, however, because the area is quite popular for laz-
ing, swimming, and snorkeling. There are showers, rest rooms, and a
paved parking lot. ⊠ *Past Bay Club restaurant off Lower Honoapi'ilani
Hwy., before Kapalua Bay Hotel.*

★ **Nāpili Beach.** This sparkling white crescent makes a perfect cove for
strolling and sunbathing. It's right outside the Nāpili Kai Beach Club,
a popular little resort for honeymooners, but despite this and other condominiums and development around the bay, the facilities here are min-
imal. There are showers at the far right end of the beach and a tap by
the beach-access entrance, where you can wash the sand off your feet,
and you're only a few miles south of Kapalua. ⊠ *5900 Lower
Honoapi'ilani Hwy.; from upper highway follow cutoff road closest
to Kapalua Resort and look for Nāpili Pl. or Hui Dr.*

★ **Kā'anapali Beach.** This is not the beach if you're looking for peace and
quiet, but if you want lots of action, lay out your towel here. It fronts
the big hotels at Kā'anapali and is one of Maui's best people-watching spots: Cruises, windsurfers, and parasailers head out from here while
the beautiful people take in the scenery. Although no facilities are
available, the nearby hotels have rest rooms and some, like the Marriott, have outdoor showers. You're also close to plenty of shops and
concessions. ⊠ *Follow any of 3 Kā'anapali exits from Honoapi'ilani
Hwy. and park at any of the hotels.*

The South Shore

Kīhei has excellent beaches right in town, including three beach parks
called **Kama'ole I, II,** and **III,** which have showers, rest rooms, picnic tables, and barbecues. Good snorkeling can be done along the rocky borders of the parks. If Kīhei is excellent, though, Wailea is better. Look for
a little road and parking lot between the first two big resorts—the Renaissance and the Outrigger. This gets you to **Mokapu** and **Ulua beaches.**

★ A similar road just after the Grand Wailea gets you to **Wailea Beach.** Then,
after the Kea Lani, you find **Polo Beach.** Each beach is a pocket-size beauty
with wonderful snorkeling, also showers and rest rooms.

★ **Mākena.** Just south of Wailea is the state park at Mākena, with two good
beaches. Big Beach is 3,000 ft long and 100 ft wide. The water off Big
Beach is fine for swimming and snorkeling, and you'll find showers, rest
rooms, and paved parking here. If you walk over the cinder cone at Big
Beach, you'll reach Little Beach, which is clothing-optional by popular
practice. Officially, nude sunbathing is illegal in Hawai'i, but several bathers
who've pushed their arrests through the courts have found their cases
dismissed. Understand, though, that you take your chances if you decide to indulge in this favorite local practice at Little Mākena.

The North Shore

Kanahā Beach. Local folk and windsurfers like this long golden strip
of sand bordered by a wide grassy area. This is a popular Kahului spot
for joggers and picnicking Maui families. Kanahā Beach has toilets,
showers, picnic tables, and grills. ⊠ *Drive through airport and back
out to car-rental road (Koeheke), turn right, and keep going.*

Baldwin Beach. Another local favorite, just west of Pā'ia town, this beach
is a big body of comfortable sand. There's not much wave action for bodysurfing, but this is good place to stretch out and swim or jog. The county
park at the right side of the beach has picnic areas, rest rooms, showers,
and sometimes even a lifeguard. ⊠ *Hāna Rd., 1 mi west of Baldwin Ave.*

★ **Ho'okipa Beach.** If you want to see some of the world's finest windsurfers,
stop at this beach along on the Hāna Highway. The sport has become

an art—and a career, to some—and its popularity was largely developed right at Hoʻokipa. It's also one of Maui's hottest surfing spots, with waves as high as 15 ft. This is not a good swimming beach, nor the place to learn windsurfing yourself, but plenty of picnic tables and barbecue grills are available for hanging out. ⊠ *Hwy. 36, 1 mi past Pāʻia.*

Hāna

Kōkī Beach. This beach in Hāna offers unusually good bodysurfing because the sandy bottom stays shallow for a long way out. On the down side, there are no facilities here. But this is a wild place rich in Hawaiian lore. Watch conditions because the riptides here can be mean. Just down the road is the beach James Michener called the best in the Pacific—crescent-shape Hāmoa Beach. Park on the roadside and walk down either one of the steep paths. Hotel Hāna-Maui keeps facilities here for its guests but has politely included a shower and rest room for the public. ⊠ *Haneoʻo Loop Rd., 2 mi east of Hāna town.*

DINING

In the resorts you'll find some of Maui's finest Continental restaurants and some good cafés and bistros as well. In addition, because many of the upscale hotels sit right on the beach, you'll often have the benefit of an oceanfront ambience. Outside the resorts, you'll find great places to dine formally or grab a bite informally (to use the pidgin term, "grind").

Except as noted, reservations are not required, but it's never a bad idea to phone ahead to book a table. Restaurants are open daily unless otherwise noted. Few restaurants on Maui require jackets. An aloha shirt and pants for men and a simple dress or pants for women are acceptable in all but the fanciest establishments. For price category explanations, *see* Smart Travel Tips A to Z at the back of the book.

West Maui

American

$$–$$$ ✕ **Longhi's.** This Lahaina establishment has been around since 1976, serv-
★ ing great Italian pasta as well as sandwiches, seafood, beef, and chicken dishes. All the pasta is homemade, and the in-house bakery turns out breakfast pastries, desserts, and fresh bread. Even on a warm day, you won't need air-conditioning here with two spacious, breezy, open-air levels to choose from. The black-and-white tile floors are a nice touch. ⊠ *888 Front St., Lahaina,* ☎ *808/667–2288. AE, D, DC, MC, V.*

$–$$ ✕ **Lahaina Coolers.** This breezy little café with a surfboard hanging
★ from its ceiling serves such tantalizing fare as Evil Jungle Pasta (grilled chicken in spicy Thai peanut sauce) and linguine with prawns, basil, garlic, and cream. It also has pizzas, steaks, burgers, and such desserts as a chocolate taco filled with tropical fruit and berry salsa. Pastas are made fresh in-house. Don't be surprised to see a local fisherman walk through the dining area with a freshly caught snapper, or a harbor captain reeling in a hearty breakfast. ⊠ *180 Dickenson St., Lahaina,* ☎ *808/661–7082. AE, MC, V.*

Chinese

$–$$ ✕ **Red Lantern.** This true Maui novelty is a good place to eat that stays open until 2 AM. This oceanfront restaurant wins a lot of local awards, and for good reason. The owners are native Chinese and they are serious about food. The menu lists 138 items, including specials like shark fin or sea cucumber in oyster sauce, but less-adventurous dishes are numerous as well. Dim sum is one of the specialties. Takeout is available, too. ⊠ *1312 Front St., Lahaina,* ☎ *808/667–1884. AE, D, DC, MC, V.*

136

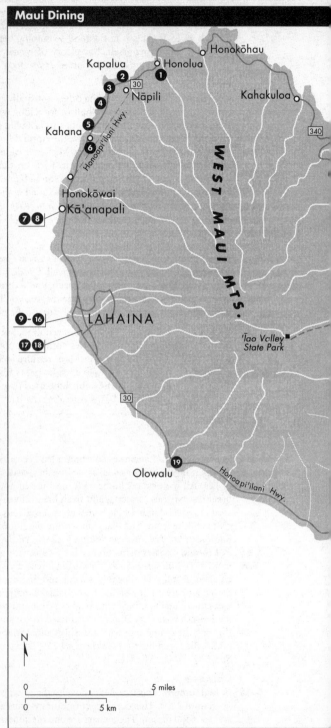

Maui Dining

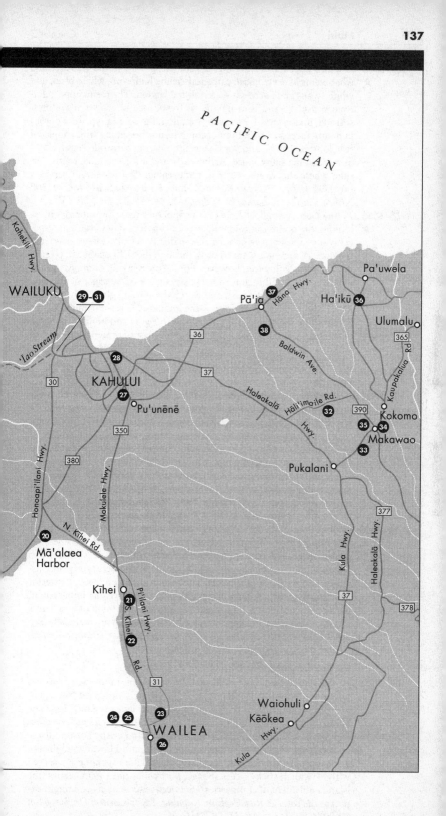

PACIFIC OCEAN

WAILUKU

29 31

'Īao Stream

28

30

KAHULUI

27

Pu'unēnē

Kahekili Hwy.

350

380

Honoapi'ilani Hwy.

Mokulele Hwy.

N. Kīhei Rd.

20

Mā'alaea
Harbor

Kīhei

21

22

S. Kīhei Rd.

Pi'ilani Hwy.

31

24 25

26

WAILEA

23

Pā'ia

37

Hāna Hwy.

38

36

37

Baldwin Ave.

Haleakalā Hwy.

Hāli'imaile Rd.

32

Pa'uwela

Ha'ikū

36

Ulumalu

365

Kaupakalua Rd.

390

Kokomo

35 34

Makawao

33

Pukalani

377

Kula Hwy.

Haleakalā Hwy.

37

378

Waiohuli

Kēōkea

Kula Hwy.

Kula

Continental

$$$-$$$$ ✕ **Swan Court.** You enter this elegant eatery via a grand staircase and
★   what seems like a tropical, cathedral-ceiling ballroom, where black and
white swans glide across a waterfall-fed lagoon. The menu applies Eu-
ropean and Pacific Rim flavors to fresh, locally grown vegetables,
seafood, and meats. Try the crispy scallop dim sum (a type of wonton)
in plum sauce; creamy lobster-coconut bisque brimming with chunks of
fish, lobster, shrimp, and button mushrooms; or charbroiled lamb chops
in macadamia satay sauce. Arrive early and ask for a table on the left
side, where the swans linger in the evening. The restaurant serves a
breakfast buffet. ⊠ *Hyatt Regency Maui, Kā'anapali Beach Resort, 200
Nohea Kai Dr., Lahaina,* ☎ *808/661–1234. AE, D, DC, MC, V.*

$$-$$$$ ✕ **Bay Club.** A candlelit dinner at this spot on a rocky promontory over-
★   looking the ocean is a romantic way to cap off a day in the sun, espe-
cially if you've been swimming at Kapalua Beach just a few yards from
the door. You won't want to walk through the richly paneled, elegant
interior with sandy feet, however. For a truly relaxing evening, shower
and dress first and then lean back, sip a glass of cabernet or Riesling
from the excellent wine list, and watch the sun slip gloriously past the
Maui horizon. Island seafood is the emphasis here, starting with appetizers like the seared 'ahi tartare and foie gras and building to main
courses such as the Hawaiian seafood pan roast of prawns, lobster, and
scallops cooked in sweet basil broth. ⊠ *Kapalua Bay Hotel, 1 Bay Dr.,
Kapalua,* ☎ *808/669–5656. AE, D, DC, MC, V.*

French

$$$-$$$$ ✕ **Gerard's.** Owner and celebrated chef Gerard Reversade started cook-
★   ing at the age of 10, and at 12 he was baking croissants. Since 1982 he
has been honoring the French tradition at this charming restaurant with
such exquisitely prepared dishes as rack of lamb in mint crust with thyme
jus; venison cutlets in a port sauce with confit of chestnuts, walnuts, fen-
nel, and pearl onions; and impeccably fresh fish. The menu changes once
a year, but many favorites—such as the sinfully good crème brûlée—re-
main. A first-class wine list, a lovely room, and celebrity-spotting round
out the experience. ⊠ *Plantation Inn, 174 Lahainaluna Rd., Lahaina,*
☎ *808/661–8939. AE, D, DC, MC, V. No lunch.*

$$-$$$$ ✕ **Chez Paul.** Since 1975 this tiny roadside restaurant between Lahaina
★   and Mā'alaea in Olowalu has served excellent French cuisine to a
packed house of repeat customers. Such dishes as fresh local fish
poached in white wine with shallots, cream, and capers typify the classical menu with island touches. The restaurant's nondescript exterior
belies the fine art, 14 linen-draped tables, 22-seat private dining room,
wine cellar, and charming atmosphere inside. Don't blink or you'll miss
this small group of buildings huddled in the middle of nowhere. ⊠ *Hwy.
30, 4 mi south of Lahaina,* ☎ *808/661–3843. Reservations essential.
AE, D, MC, V. No lunch.*

Hawaiian/Pacific Rim

$$$-$$$$ ✕ **'Ānuenue Room.** In Hawaiian, *'ānuenue* means rainbow. The name,
however, doesn't really characterize the Ritz-Carlton's elegant signa-
ture restaurant, with its dark wood walls and massive chandeliers. The
cuisine is pure Hawaiian, inventively elevated. Appetizers include *opihi*
(sea snail) with island goat cheese in pastry, and crispy corn-and-sea-
urchin fritters served with shrimp, seaweed, and Hawaiian chili-lob-
ster sauce. For the main course, how about kālua suckling pig served
with Hawaiian sticky rice, cabbage, port wine, and *'ohelo* berries (the
island equivalent of cranberries)? Service is excellent, as you might ex-
pect at the Ritz. ⊠ *Ritz-Carlton, Kapalua, 1 Ritz-Carlton Dr., Kapalua,*
☎ *808/669–1665. AE, D, DC, MC, V.*

$$–$$$$ ✕ **David Paul's Lahaina Grill.** This beautifully designed restaurant sits arm-
★ in-arm with the elegant Lahaina Inn in a historic, creaky building on La-
hainaluna Road. It's won numerous awards since it opened in 1990,
including *Honolulu* magazine's selection as "Best Restaurant on Maui"
seven years in a row. It offers an extensive wine cellar, an in-house bak-
ery, and a baby grand in the lounge. The chef's celebrated menu is revised
seasonally, but you can count on finding the signature tequila shrimp and
firecracker rice along with such scrumptious desserts as triple-berry pie.
⊠ *127 Lahainaluna Rd., Lahaina,* ☎ *808/667–5117. AE, DC, MC, V.*

$$–$$$ ✕ **Hula Grill.** This bustling, family-oriented restaurant is the informal coun-
terpart to genial chef-restaurateur Peter Merriman's first popular eatery,
Merriman's, on the Big Island, and the food is every bit as good. South
Pacific snapper is baked with tomato, chili, and cumin aioli and served
with black bean, Maui onion, and avocado relish. Spare ribs are steamed
in banana leaves, then grilled with mango barbecue sauce over mesquite-
like *kiawe.* The restaurant is set in a re-created 1930s Hawaiian beach
house, and every table has an ocean-beach view. Or you can actually dine
on the beach, toes in the sand, at the Barefoot Bar, where Hawaiian en-
tertainment is presented every evening. ⊠ *Whalers Village, 2435 Kāʻana-
pali Pkwy., Kāʻanapali,* ☎ *808/667–6636. AE, DC, MC, V.*

$$–$$$ ✕ **Iʻo.** Opened in 1999, this restaurant immediately established itself as
the hippest place in Lahaina—both for its theatrical, sculpted interior de-
signed by the artist Dado and for its eclectic menu of contemporary Pa-
cific cuisine. The most popular appetizer is the "silken purse"—steamed
wontons stuffed with roasted peppers, mushrooms, macadamia nuts, and
tofu and served with jalapeño-scented tomato sauce and yogurt purée.
Favorite dinners include the crispy ʻahi, sashimi-grade tuna wrapped in
nori and served with a salad of green papaya and sweet peppers; and lemon-
grass-coconut fish served with fresh hearts-of-palm salad and chilled spicy
soba noodles. ⊠ *505 Front St., Lahaina,* ☎ *808/661–8422,* 🖷 *808/661–
8399. AE, D, DC, MC, V. No lunch.*

$$–$$$ ✕ **Plantation House Restaurant.** It's hard to decide which is best here,
the food or the view. Rolling hills, grassy volcanic ridges lined with
pine trees, and fairways that appear to drop off into the ocean pro-
vide an idyllic setting. The specialty is fresh island fish prepared ac-
cording to different "tastes"—Upcountry Maui, Asian-Pacific, Provence,
and others. The "Taste of the Rich Forest" includes roasted wild mush-
rooms served on tender tot soi greens and garlic mashed potatoes with
a Maui onion meunière. The breeze through the large shuttered win-
dows can be cool, so you may want to bring a sweater or sit by the
fireplace. ⊠ *Plantation Course Clubhouse, 2000 Plantation Club Dr.,
past Kapalua,* ☎ *808/669–6299. AE, MC, V.*

$$–$$$ ✕ **Roy's Kahana Bar & Grill.** Anyone who's ever eaten at one of Roy
Yamaguchi's restaurants knows how good the food is, and this Roy's is
no exception. Such Asian-Pacific specialties as shrimp with sweet-and-
spicy chili sauce keep regulars returning for more. Locals find this is a
great place to get together with friends for fun and good food. Next door
is the somewhat quieter Roy Yamaguchi's Nicolina, which caters to a
spice-loving crowd with grilled Southwestern-style chicken with chili hash
and smoked tomato sauce, and smoked-and-peppered duck with gingered
sweet potatoes and Szechuan-Mandarin sauce. ⊠ *Kahana Gateway
Shopping Center, 4405 Honoapiʻilani Hwy., Kahana,* ☎ *808/669–6999
(Roy's); 808/669–5000 (Nicolina). AE, D, DC, MC, V.*

Italian

$–$$ ✕ **BJ's Chicago Pizza.** If you're in the mood for pizza, this is the place
to go on Maui. Residents have consistently voted it the island's best,
and *Bon Appétit* magazine even went so far as to call it one of the country's best. The restaurant sits right on the seawall in Lahaina. The sound

of live music by contemporary island stars tempts you inside because it all looks like so much fun. It is. ⊠ *730 Front St., Lahaina,* ☎ *808/661–0700. AE, DC, MC, V.*

Seafood

$$–$$$ ✕ **Erik's Seafood Grotto.** This seafood diner is so proud of its large selection of fresh fish that it displays the whole offering nightly as a photo opportunity. Additional house specialties include bouillabaisse brimming with clams, scallops, lobster, shrimp, and fish and served with toasted garlic bread; and *cioppino,* a seafood stew served over homemade fettuccine. A stop at the oyster bar is a worthwhile detour. Try half shells topped with horseradish mayonnaise and baked with Gruyère cheese. Come to this nautical spot between 5 and 6 and catch the $12.95–$13.95 early bird specials. ⊠ *Kahana Villas, 4242 Lower Honoapi'ilani Hwy., Kahana,* ☎ *808/669–4806. AE, D, DC, MC, V.*

$$–$$$ ✕ **Pacific'O.** You can sit outdoors at umbrella-shaded tables near the water's edge, or find a spot in the breezy, marble-floored interior. The menu is exciting, with the likes of a fresh 'ahi-and-*ono* tempura (ono is a makerel-like fish), in which the two kinds of fish are wrapped around *tobiko* (flying-fish roe), then in nori, and wok-fried. There's a great lamb dish, too—a whole rack of sweet New Zealand lamb, sesame-crusted and served with roasted macadamia sauce and Hawaiian chutney. Live jazz is offered Thursday through Saturday nights from 9 to midnight. George Benson likes to sit in. ⊠ *505 Front St., Lahaina,* ☎ *808/667–4341. AE, D, DC, MC, V.*

$–$$ ✕ **Kimo's.** Outstanding seafood is just one of the options here. Also good are Hawaiian-style chicken and pork dishes, burgers, sandwiches, vegetarian pasta, and sashimi. The smoked marlin appetizer is especially tasty. On a warm Lahaina summer day, it's a treat to relax at an umbrella-shaded table on the open-air lānai, sip a pineapple-passion-fruit-guava drink, and watch sailboats and parasailers glide in and out of the harbor. Try the signature dessert, hula pie: vanilla–macadamia-nut ice cream topped with chocolate fudge and whipped cream in an Oreo-cookie crust. ⊠ *845 Front St., Lahaina,* ☎ *808/661–4811. AE, DC, MC, V.*

Steak

$$–$$$$ ✕ **Ruth's Chris Steak House.** This chain claims to be the "home of serious steaks"—corn-fed midwestern beef, and only the top 2% of the cuts. When you hear your own immense, broiled-to-order portion sizzling as it approaches from across the room, you may believe the claim. The meat cuts like butter, and butter is a main feature of the '40s-style, classic steak house menu (creamed spinach, scalloped potatoes). The ambience is appropriately old-fashioned and elegant: candlelight, lots of wood, and etched glass. The windows look right out over the Lahaina seawall. ⊠ *Lahaina Shopping Center, 900 Front St., Lahaina,* ☎ *808/661–8815. AE, DC, MC, V.*

Thai

$–$$ ✕ **Orient Express.** Have your Thai food hot, medium, or mild at this decidedly Asian locale with red lacquer and yellow flowers evident everywhere. Eating Thai is always an adventure with such menu choices as beef satay marinated in coconut milk and spices, skewered on bamboo sticks and grilled; or shrimp cooked with bamboo shoots, water chestnuts, and dried chilies. ⊠ *Nāpili Shores Resort, 5316 Lower Honoapi'ilani Hwy., Nāpili,* ☎ *808/669–8077. AE, MC, V. No lunch.*

Central Maui

Italian

$$ ✕ **Marco's Grill & Deli.** This convenient eatery outside the Kahului airport (look for the green awning) is home to some of the best-priced and best-tasting Italian fare on Maui. Fettuccine Alfredo, linguine with sausage, and vodka rigatoni are all on the extensive menu, along with an unforgettably good Reuben sandwich and the best Greek salad you'll ever find. The local business crowd fills the place for breakfast, lunch, and dinner. ⊠ *444 Hāna Hwy., Kahului,* ☎ *808/877–4446. AE, D, DC, MC, V.*

Japanese

$ ✕ **Restaurant Matsu.** The Maui Mall just got a face-lift and a movie megaplex, but it's fortunately held on to a few real gems from the old days—including this tiny, nondescript kitchen and lunch room. Sit at a common table and eat authentic Japanese fare along with the locals—*katsus* (cutlets) and curries served with white rice, or bowls of saimin or udon noodles with tempura. ⊠ *Maui Mall, Ka'ahumanu Ave., Kahului,* ☎ *808/871–0822. No credit cards.*

Thai

$–$$ ✕ **Saeng's Thai Cuisine.** Making a choice from the six-page menu here requires determination, but the food is worth the effort, and most dishes can be tailored to your taste buds: hot, medium, or mild. Begin with spring rolls and a dipping sauce, move on to such entrées as Evil Prince Chicken (cooked in coconut sauce with Thai herbs) or red curry shrimp, and finish up with tea and tapioca pudding. The dining room is decorated with Asian artifacts, flowers, and a waterfall, and tables on a veranda will satisfy outdoor lovers. ⊠ *2119 Vineyard, Wailuku,* ☎ *808/244–1567. AE, MC, V.*

$–$$ ✕ **Siam Thai.** Behind a slightly weathered storefront you'll find some of the best Thai food on Maui. This local favorite serves traditional chicken-coconut soup, beef and chicken sautéed with ginger and bamboo shoots, curries, and vegetarian dishes—about 60 selections in all. The food tends to be spicy, the portions small, and huge crowds arrive at lunchtime. Some patrons opt for takeout because there's not much in the way of decor. ⊠ *123 Market St., Wailuku,* ☎ *808/244–3817. AE, D, DC, MC, V.*

Vietnamese

$–$$ ✕ **A Saigon Café.** The only storefront sign announcing this small, delightful hideaway is one reading OPEN. Once you find it, treat yourself to *banh hoi chao tom,* more commonly called "shrimp pops burritos" (ground marinated shrimp, steamed and grilled on a stick of sugarcane). It's fun and messy. Vegetarian fare is also well represented here. The white interior serves as a backdrop for Vietnamese carvings and other interesting artwork. ⊠ *1792 Main St., Wailuku,* ☎ *808/243–9560. D, MC, V.*

The South Shore

American

$$–$$$ ✕ **Joe's Bar & Grill.** With friendly service; a great view of Lāna'i; and such dishes as New York strip steak with caramelized onions, wild mushrooms, and Gorgonzola cheese crumble, there are lots of reasons to stop in at this spacious, breezy spot. Owners Joe and Bev Gannon, who run the immensely popular Hāli'imaile General Store (☞ East Maui, *below*), have brought their flair for food home to roost in this comfortable treetop-level restaurant at the Wailea Tennis Club, where you can dine while watching court action from a balcony seat. ⊠ *131 Wailea Ike Pl., Wailea,* ☎ *808/875–7767. AE, MC, V.*

$–$$ ✕ **Hapa's Brewhaus & Restaurant.** This friendly place has an assortment of great eats that includes pizza, calzones, pastas, chicken-teriyaki burgers, vegetarian stir-fry, sashimi, and lobster bisque. There are seven kinds of beer on tap, including Kona Longboard Lager. The adjoining room, Hapa's Rockin' Sushi, is open till one in the morning. ⊠ *Lipoa Center, 41 E. Lipoa St., Kīhei,* ☎ *808/879–9001. D, DC, MC, V.*

Eclectic

$$$$ ✕ **Seasons.** Acclaimed executive chef George Mavrothalassitis prepares standout dishes that marry fresh island ingredients with flavors from his native Provence as well as from China, Japan, Thailand, and the Pacific islands. Consider, for example, *onaga* (pink or red snapper) and summer truffles with braised leeks, or shaved hamachi sashimi served with a tomato and peppercorn gelée and citrus *shoyu* (sweet soy sauce). As befits the Four Seasons Resort, this is a restaurant of understated elegance, with talbes set with white linen and French china and a decor that emphasizes natural materials. A trio of island musicians and sensational ocean vistas add to the delicious ambience. ⊠ *Four Seasons Resort Maui, 3900 Wailea Alanui, Wailea,* ☎ *808/874–8000. AE, D, DC, MC, V. No lunch.*

Hawaiian/Pacific Rim

$$–$$$ ✕ **Hula Moons.** This delightful oceanside spot is full of memorabilia chronicling the island life of Don Blanding, a writer, artist, and poet who became Hawai'i's unofficial ambassador of aloha in the 1930s. The outstanding menu blends locally grown produce with Pacific Rim and European preparations. Try the scallops with Chinese black-bean sauce, charbroiled T-bone steak with pineapple compote and Moloka'i sweet potatoes, or the just-off-the-boat catch of the day. You can dine inside, poolside, or outside on the terrace while you choose your vintage from an extensive wine list. ⊠ *Aston Wailea Resort, 3700 Wailea Alanui, Wailea,* ☎ *808/879–1922. AE, D, DC, MC, V.*

$$–$$$ ✕ **A Pacific Cafe.** Hawai'i regional cuisine began with a few innovative
★ island chefs, including Jean-Marie Josselin. With the assistance of corporate chef George Gomes, Jr., who was born and raised in the Islands, Josselin now serves this innovative cuisine in five island locations, two on Maui. Flavorful combinations include pan-seared *mahimahi* (mild-flavored dolphinfish) with a garlic sesame crust and ginger-lime sauce; Chinese roasted duck with baked sour-cherry *manapua* (dough wrapped around diced pork), charred baby eggplant, and *liliko'i*–star anise sauce ("liliko'i" is Hawaiian for passion fruit); and "the original" tiger-eye 'ahi sushi tempura with pear tomato salad and Chinese mustard sauce. The restaurant's tropical, whimsical decor has been described as "the Flintstones meet the Jetsons." ⊠ *Azeka Place II Shopping Center, 1279 S. Kīhei Rd., Kīhei,* ☎ *808/879–0069;* ⊠ *3350 Lower Honoapi'ilani Rd., Lahaina,* ☎ *808/669–2724. AE, D, DC, MC, V. No lunch.*

Italian

$$ ✕ **Bella Luna Ristorante.** Best sunset view on the island—who could dare to claim such a title? Bella Luna does, and deservedly so. This is a small place (40 seats), where you dine looking out over a golf course and the open sea at the very quiet, off-the-beaten-path Diamond Resort. It's an informal and friendly place, with seafood, Italian dishes, and a wine list with decent, affordable selections. It's a great place for a date. The owners also serve three meals a day out of the Wailea Blue Clubhouse just down the street. ⊠ *Diamond Resort, 555 Kaukahi St., Wailea,* ☎ *808/879–8255. AE, DC, MC, V. No lunch.*

Seafood

$$–$$$$ ✕ **Mā'alaea Waterfront Restaurant.** At this harborside establishment
★ fresh fish is prepared in a host of sumptuous ways: baked in buttered parchment paper; imprisoned in ribbons of angel-hair potato; or topped with tomato salsa, smoked chili pepper, and avocado. The varied menu also offers outstanding rack of lamb and veal scallopini. Tourists come early to dine at sunset on the outdoor patio. Enter Mā'alaea at the Maui Ocean Center and then follow the blue WATERFRONT RESTAURANT signs to the third condominium. ⊠ *50 Hau'oli St., Mā'alaea,* ☎ *808/244–9028. AE, D, DC, MC, V.*

East Maui

Hawaiian/Pacific Rim

$$–$$$ ✕ **Hāli'imaile General Store.** What do you do with a lofty wooden build-
★ ing that used to be a camp store in the 1920s and is surrounded by a tiny
town in the middle of sugarcane and pineapple fields? If you're Bev and
Joe Gannon, you turn it into a legendary restaurant. The Szechuan bar-
becued salmon and rack of lamb Hunan style are classics. For a filling
and innovative appetizer, try the sashimi napoleon: a tower of crispy wonton layered with smoked salmon. The outstanding house salad is topped
with Maui onions, mandarin oranges, walnuts, and crumbled blue cheese
on request. ✉ *900 Hāli'imaile Rd., left at exit off Hwy. 37, 5 mi from
Hāna Hwy., Hāli'imaile,* ☎ *808/572–2666. MC, V.*

Italian

$$–$$$ ✕ **Casanova Italian Restaurant & Deli.** This is a good Italian dinner house
in an out-of-the-way location—Makawao. The pizzas are skimpy, but
they're baked in a brick, wood-burning oven imported from Italy.
Casanova is also known for its daytime deli and, at night, for its extra-
large dance floor and entertainment by well-known island and mainland
musicians (☞ Bars and Clubs *in* Nightlife and the Arts, *below*). ✉ *1188
Makawao Ave., Makawao,* ☎ *808/572–0220. D, DC, MC, V.*

$$–$$$ ✕ **Trattoria Ha'ikū.** Here the rural hills of Tuscany and the leafy gulches
★ of Ha'ikū not only look alike but also taste alike. The house itself is a
renovated 1920s mess hall, built for workers at the adjacent pineapple cannery. With a little understated drama—white linens and splashing fountains—it does a wonderful job of interpreting the classic Italian
trattoria. Fresh local ingredients are used whenever possible (they
make the marinara from vine-ripened Maui tomatoes), as specialty products are imported from Italy. ✉ *Olde Ha'ikū Cannery, Ha'ikū and
Kokomo Rds., Ha'ikū,* ☎ *808/575–2820. MC, V.*

Mexican

$–$$ ✕ **Polli's.** This Mexican restaurant in the paniolo town of Makawao
★ not only has a wide selection of such delicious taste treats as seafood
enchiladas, chimichangas, quesadillas, and fajitas, but also offers to
prepare any item on the menu with seasoned tofu or vegetarian taco
mix instead of meat—and the meatless dishes are just as good. A special treat are the *bunuelos*—light pastries topped with cinnamon,
maple syrup, and a scoop of ice cream. The intimate interior is plastered with colorful sombreros and other cantina knickknacks. ✉ *1202
Makawao Ave., Makawao,* ☎ *808/572–7808. AE, D, DC, MC, V.*

Seafood

$$–$$$ ✕ **Mama's Fish House.** As you enjoy the landscaped grounds and
★ ocean views at this cliff-top restaurant, check out the stone path engraved with whimsical Hawaiian geckos. But the real treat here is the
fish, prepared in seven mouthwatering ways—baked in a creamy herb
sauce, sautéed with macadamia nuts, or grilled with spicy wasabi butter, for example. That's why this thatched-hut restaurant with a Hawaiian nautical theme is packed every evening. The chicken, steak, and
kālua pig dishes are worth trying as well. About 1½ mi east of Pa'ia
on the Hāna Highway, look for Mama's classic '40s-era Ford trucks
parked on grassy knolls at both entrances. ✉ *799 Poho Pl., Kū'au,* ☎
808/579–8488. Reservations essential. AE, D, DC, MC, V.

Steak

$$ ✕ **Makawao Steak House.** A restored 1927 house on the slopes of
Haleakalā houses this paniolo restaurant that serves consistently good
prime rib, rack of lamb, and fresh fish. Three fireplaces, friendly ser-
vice, and an intimate lounge create a cozy, welcoming atmosphere.

✉ *3612 Baldwin Ave., Makawao,* ☎ *808/572–8711,* Ⅸ *808/572-7103. D, DC, MC, V. No lunch.*

LODGING

Maui has the highest percentage of upscale hotel rooms and the highest average accommodation cost of any Hawaiian island. The quality level—and the opulence quotient—are way up there, making this one of the best places in the world to indulge in a first-class resort vacation. But Maui also has the state's highest concentration of condominium units; many are oceanfront and offer the ambience of a hotel suite without the cost.

The county officially sanctions relatively few B&Bs, not wanting to siphon business from the hotels. However, many alternative accommodations offer seclusion and a countryside experience, especially Upcountry and in Hāna. The majority of these are better described as guest cottages—or guest houses—that skip the breakfast part of B&B and offer instead provisions and privacy. Most are a departure from the typical resort-style accommodations associated with the island. Rates for most B&Bs range from $40 to as much as $150 per night.

For price category explanations, *see* Smart Travel Tips A to Z at the back of the book. For further information about Maui B&Bs and condos, *see* Contacts and Resources *in* Maui A to Z, *below*.

West Maui

$$$$ 🏨 **Hyatt Regency Maui.** When this trendsetting property was developed in 1980, it set a new standard for luxury resorts: a museum-quality art collection; a seemingly endless swimming pool, with swim-through grottoes and a 130-ft water slide; fantasy landscaping (the builders used 10,000 tons of rock to fabricate the environment) with splashing waterfalls; and a collection of exotic creatures, even penguins. The Hyatt remains Kā'anapali's premier property. Improved access for people with disabilities and the addition of some new facilities—an outdoor Jacuzzi, a wedding gazebo, and a beachfront bar—have kept this oasis competitive with any resort on the island. ✉ *Kā'anapali Beach Resort, 200 Nohea Kai Dr., Lahaina 96761,* ☎ *808/661–1234 or 800/233–1234,* Ⅸ *808/667–4499. 815 rooms. 4 restaurants, 6 bars, in-room safes, 12 no-smoking floors, pool, 2 18-hole golf courses, 6 tennis courts, health club, beach, library, children's programs (ages 3–12), chapel. AE, D, DC, MC, V.* 🐾

$$$$ 🏨 **Kā'anapali Ali'i.** Yes, this is a condominium, but you'd never know it; the four 11-story buildings are put together so well you still have the feeling of seclusion. Instead of tiny rooms you can choose between one- and two-bedroom apartments. Each features lovely amenities: a chaise in an alcove, a bidet, a sunken living room, a whirlpool, oak kitchen cabinets, and a separate dining room. The Kā'anapali Ali'i is maintained like a hotel, with daily maid service, an activities desk, and a 24-hour front desk. ✉ *50 Nohea Kai Dr., Lahaina 96761,* ☎ *808/667–1400 or 800/ 642–6284,* Ⅸ *808/661–1025. 264 units. 2 pools, sauna, 18-hole golf course, 6 tennis courts, beach. AE, D, DC, MC, V.* 🐾

$$$$ 🏨 **Kapalua Bay Hotel.** Built in 1978 fronting what was once voted America's best beach, at lovely Kapalua Bay, this hotel has a real Maui feel to it. The exterior is understated white and natural wood, and the open lobby, filled with flowering vanda and dendrobium orchids, has a view of the ocean. The plantation-style rooms are decorated in earth tones, and all have views of Lāna'i and Moloka'i. A shopping plaza outside the main hotel entrance has some fine restaurants and boutiques. Guests receive preferred rates and tee times at three golf courses in Kapalua. ✉ *1 Bay Dr., Kapalua 96761,* ☎ *808/669–5656 or 800/367–8000,*

FAX *808/669–4694. 209 rooms. 3 restaurants, 2 pools, 6 tennis courts, beach. AE, DC, MC, V.*

$$$$ ☷ **Kapalua Bay Villas.** This harmoniously designed complex of two- and three-story buildings seems to cascade down the cliffs to the sea. Privately owned and individually decorated one- and two-bedroom units may be rented through the Kapalua Bay Hotel (☞ *above*). Condos are assigned to one of five luxury categories and regularly inspected to ensure that standards are maintained. The ocean views are great, with the island of Moloka'i in the distance and humpback whales (in season) passing close to shore. Renters enjoy a free shuttle to the hotel and guest rates for golf, tennis, and other hotel amenities. ⊠ *1 Bay Dr., Kapalua 96761,* ☎ *808/669–5656 or 800/367–8000,* FAX *808/669–4694. 125 units. Golf privileges. AE, D, DC, MC, V.*

$$$$ ☷ **Maui Marriott.** Rooms here are large and tastefully done in pastel tones and bamboo furnishings, and nearly 90% have ocean views. Besides having access to a beachside massage tent and privileges at two 18-hole golf courses in Kā'anapali, guests can join classes featuring aerobics; hula; Hawaiian arts, crafts, and language; food preparation; and a number of sports. The best thing here, however, is the service: The staff is genuinely friendly and helpful. ⊠ *100 Nohea Kai Dr., Lahaina 96761,* ☎ *808/667–1200 or 800/228–9290,* FAX *808/667–8300. 720 rooms. 4 restaurants, 2 lobby lounges, 2 pools, 2 hot tubs, massage, golf privileges, 5 tennis courts, health club, beach, bicycles, children's programs (ages 5–12). AE, D, DC, MC, V.* ✎

$$$$ ☷ **Nāpili Kai Beach Club.** These lodgings on 10 beautiful beachfront acres appeal to a loyal following. Hawaiian-style rooms are done in sea-foam green, mauve, and rattan; shoji doors open onto your lānai, with the beach and ocean right outside. The property also includes two 18-hole putting greens, four swimming pools, and an extra-large whirlpool. This is a family-friendly place, with kids' programs as well as free classes in hula and lei-making. Packages that include a car, breakfast, and other extras are available if you stay five nights or longer. ⊠ *5900 Lower Honoapi'ilani Rd., Nāpili Bay 96761,* ☎ *808/669–6271 or 800/367–5030,* FAX *808/669–5740. 162 rooms. Kitchenettes, 4 pools, hot tub, 2 putting greens, beach. AE, MC, V.* ✎

$$$$ ☷ **Ritz-Carlton, Kapalua.** This beachfront hotel features spacious, com-
★ fortable rooms with oversize marble bathrooms, lānai overlooking the three-level pool, and all the grace, elegance, and service that this hotel chain is known for. Most rooms have ocean views. Guests on the Club floors have a private lounge with complimentary snack and beverage service all day long. All guests have golf privileges at three 18-hole courses in Kapalua. ⊠ *1 Ritz-Carlton Dr., Kapalua 96761,* ☎ *808/669–6200 or 800/262–8440,* FAX *808/665–0026. 548 rooms. 4 restaurants, 5 lobby lounges, pool, beauty salon, golf privileges, 10 tennis courts, health club, beach, children's programs (ages 5–12). AE, D, DC, MC, V.* ✎

$$$$ ☷ **Royal Lahaina Resort.** The lānai at this Hawaiian Hotels & Resorts property afford stunning ocean or golf-course views. What distinguishes the Royal Lahaina are the two-story cottages, each divided into four units; the bedrooms open to the trade winds on two sides. The upstairs units each have a private lānai, and downstairs units share. The walkway to the courtyard wedding gazebo is lined with stepping stones engraved with the names of past brides and grooms and their wedding dates. ⊠ *2780 Keka'a Dr., Lahaina 96761,* ☎ *808/661–3611 or 800/447–6925,* FAX *808/661–3538. 592 rooms. 3 restaurants, 3 pools, 18-hole golf course, 11 tennis courts, beach. AE, D, DC, MC, V.* ✎

$$$$ ☷ **Sheraton Maui.** This beautiful resort consists of six buildings, each six stories or fewer, set in lush gardens on Kā'anapali's best stretch of beach. The resort sits next to 80-ft-high "Black Rock," from which divers leap in a nightly torch-lighting ritual. One of the two swimming

Maui Lodging

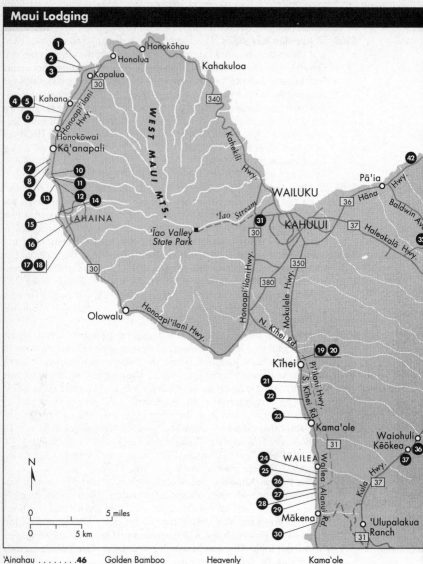

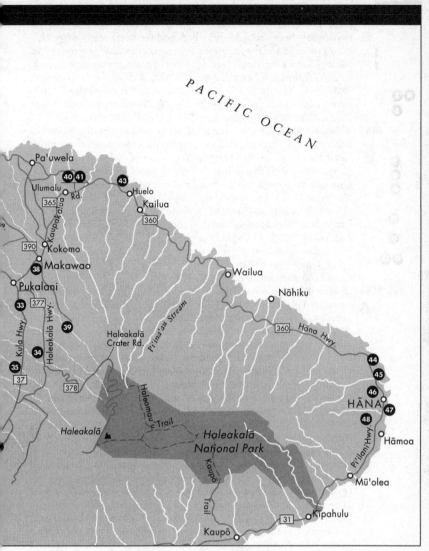

pools looks like a natural lagoon, with rock waterways and wooden bridges. The Sheraton has family appeal—a number of rooms provide two double beds and a Murphy bed, and the hotel offers a free children's programs in the summer. Conveniences include generous room amenities and a "no-hassle" check-in that bypasses the registration desk. ✉ 2605 Kā'anapali Pkwy., Lahaina 97671, ☎ 808/661–0031 or 800/ 782–9488, FAX 808/661–0458. 510 rooms. 3 restaurants, 3 lobby lounges, in-room safes, refrigerators, pool, 3 tennis courts, health club, beach, children's programs (ages 5–12). AE, D, DC, MC, V. ✺

$$$$ 🖭 **Westin Maui.** This is a hotel for active people who like to be out and about and won't spend all their time in their rooms, which are rather small for the price. But compensations are provided—an "aquatic playground" with five heated swimming pools, privileges at two 18-hole golf courses in Kā'anapali, and the central-most position on Kā'anapali Beach. The landscaping is lush. There are abundant waterfalls (15 at last count) and lagoons. A valuable Asian and Pacific art collection is displayed throughout the property. ✉ 2365 Kā'anapali Pkwy., Lahaina 96761, ☎ 808/667–2525 or 800/228–3000, FAX 808/661–5831. 761 rooms. 3 restaurants, 4 lobby lounges, 5 pools, beauty salon, hot tub, golf privileges, health club, beach, baby-sitting, children's programs (ages 12 and under). AE, D, DC, MC, V. ✺

$$$–$$$$ 🖭 **Plantation Inn.** Charm and luxury set apart this inn reminiscent of
★   a southern plantation home. Filled with Victorian and Far Eastern furnishings, it's set on a quiet street in the heart of Lahaina. Secluded lānai draped with hanging plants face a central courtyard, pool, and garden pavilion perfect for morning coffee. Each guest room or suite is decorated differently, with hardwood floors, French doors, antiques, four-poster beds, and ceiling fans. Some have kitchenettes and whirlpool baths. A generous breakfast is included in the room rate. One of Hawai'i's best French restaurants, Gerard's (☞ West Maui in Dining, above), adds to the allure. ✉ 174 Lahainaluna Rd., Lahaina 96761, ☎ 808/667–9225 or 800/433–6815, FAX 808/667–9293. 18 rooms. Restaurant, refrigerators, pool, hot tub. AE, MC, V. ✺

$$$ 🖭 **Kā'anapali Beach Hotel.** This attractive, old-fashioned hotel is full of
★   aloha and the good-natured spirit of Maui, and the employees' chorus entertains joyously most afternoons. In addition, this happy place is recognized as one of the best values on the West Side. The vintage-style "Mixed Plate" restaurant, known locally for its Hawaiian food, is decorated with displays honoring the many cultural traditions represented on the staff. The employees themselves contributed the artifacts. There are complimentary classes in hula, lei-making, and 'ukulele-playing—and guests have privileges at the two 18-hole Kā'anapali golf courses. ✉ 2525 Kā'anapali Pkwy., Lahaina 96761, ☎ 808/661–0011 or 800/262–8450, FAX 808/ 667–5978. 430 rooms. 2 restaurants, lobby lounge, pool, golf privileges, beach. AE, D, DC, MC, V. ✺

$$$ 🖭 **Mauian Hotel.** This quiet place way out in Nāpili is for quiet people. The simple two-story buildings date from 1959, but the current owners have renovated the place for comfort and convenience, including fully equipped kitchens. The rooms, however, have neither televisions nor telephones. Such noisy devices are relegated to the 'Ohana Room, where a Continental breakfast is served daily. Best of all, the two-acre property opens out onto lovely Napīli Bay. ✉ 5441 Lower Honoapi'ilani Rd., Napīli 96761, ☎ 808/669–6205 or 800/367–5034, FAX 808/669– 0129. 44 rooms. Pool, shuffleboard, coin laundry. AE, D, MC, V. ✺

$$$ 🖭 **Papakea Beach Resort.** This resort is an active place to stay if you consider all the classes held here, such as swimming, snorkeling, and pineapple cutting. In Honokōwai, Papakea has built-in privacy because its units are spread out among 11 low-rise buildings on some 13 acres of land. You aren't really aware that you're sharing the property with

364 other units. Bamboo-lined walkways between buildings and fish-stocked ponds create a serene mood. There's a two-day minimum stay. Despite its name, there is no beach on the premises, although there are several nearby. ⊠ *3543 Honoapiʻilani Hwy., Lahaina 96761,* ☎ *808/ 669–4848 or 800/367–5637,* FAX *808/669–0751. 36 studios; 224 1-bed-room and 104 2-bedroom units. 2 pools, hot tub, saunas, putting green, 4 tennis courts. AE, MC, V.* ✑

$$–$$$ 🏨 **Lahaina Inn.** This antique jewel is classic Lahaina—a two-story
★ wooden building that will transport you back to the turn of the last century. The nine small rooms and three suites shine with authentic period restoration and furnishings, including quilted bedcovers, antique lamps, and Oriental carpets—no televisions. You can sit in a wicker chair on your balcony right in the heart of town. An excellent Continental breakfast is left in the parlor for your convenience. ⊠ *127 Lahainaluna Rd., Lahaina 96761,* ☎ *808/661–0577 or 800/669–3444,* FAX *808/667–9480. 12 rooms. AE, D, MC, V.*

$$–$$$ 🏨 **Pioneer Inn.** Known officially as the Best Western Pioneer Inn-Maui, this historic building has occupied its ringside seat on Lahaina's action since 1901. Its dockside ambience capitalizes on Lahaina's 19th-century whaling days. All rooms are air-conditioned, and New England–style mahogany furnishings recapture Lahaina's missionary era. It's often possible to stay in one of the small rooms for under $100 a night. You might not want to spend your entire vacation here, as the area can be a bit noisy in the evening, but for a night or two of bargain-price historic atmosphere, the place can't be beat. ⊠ *658 Wharf St., Lahaina 96761,* ☎ *808/661–3636 or 800/457–5457,* FAX *808/667–5708. 34 rooms. 3 restaurants. AE, D, DC, MC, V.* ✑

The South Shore

$$$$ 🏨 **Four Seasons Resort.** This is a Maui favorite, partially because of
★ its location, on one of the Valley Isle's finest beaches with all the amenities of the well-groomed Wailea Resort. Access to three 18-hole golf courses and "Wimbledon West," with 11 championship tennis courts, is included. The property itself has great appeal, with terraces, courtyards, gardens, waterfalls, and fountains. Nearly all the rooms have an ocean view and combine traditional style with tropical touches. You'll find terry robes and whole-bean coffee grinders in each room. ⊠ *3900 Wailea Alanui, Wailea 96753,* ☎ *808/874–8000 or 800/334–6284,* FAX *808/874–6449. 380 rooms. 3 restaurants, 2 bars, pool, 2 tennis courts, golf privileges, health club, beach. AE, D, DC, MC, V.* ✑

$$$$ 🏨 **Grand Wailea.** Sunny opulence is everywhere at this 40-acre resort.
★ Elaborate water features include a 2,000-ft multilevel "canyon river-pool" with slides and grottoes. The Spa Grande cossets guests with rejuvenating offerings, from aerobics classes to exotic water-and-massage therapies. Luxury pervades the spacious ocean-view rooms, beautifully outfitted with such amenities as an overstuffed chaise longue, a comfortable writing desk, and an oversize tub and separate shower. Guests have access to three 18-hole golf courses, and tennis privileges are available. ⊠ *3850 Wailea Alanui Dr., Wailea 96753,* ☎ *808/875–1234 or 800/888–6100,* FAX *808/874–2442. 779 rooms. 5 restaurants, 6 bars, 3 pools, golf privileges, health club, beach, children's programs (ages 5–12), chapel. AE, D, DC, MC, V.* ✑

$$$$ 🏨 **Kamaʻole Sands.** This is a huge property for Kīhei—11 four-story buildings wrap around a grassy slope on which are clustered swimming and wading pools, a small waterfall, whirlpool baths, and barbecues. All units have kitchens, laundries, and private lānai. Managed by Castle Resorts & Hotels, this condominium property has a 24-hour front desk and an activities desk, and it is across the road from Kīhei

Beach. ⊠ *2695 S. Kīhei Rd., Kīhei 96753,* ☎ *808/874–8700 or 800/ 367–5004,* FAX *808/879–3273. 11 studios; 211 1-bedroom, 83 2-bedroom, and 4 3-bedroom units. Restaurant, pool, wading pool, 4 tennis courts. AE, D, DC, MC, V.* 🕭

$$$$ 🏨 **Kea Lani Hotel Suites & Villas.** This Moorish-domed, all-suite resort offers seclusion and privacy in oceanside two- and three-bedroom villas, each with its own small pool and within easy reach of attractions in Wailea and West Maui. Accommodations in the main hotel are spacious one-bedroom suites with dining lānai and marble bathrooms. Guests have access to three 18-hole golf courses, and tennis privileges are available. ⊠ *4100 Wailea Alanui, Wailea 96753,* ☎ *808/875– 4100 or 800/882–4100,* FAX *808/875–1200. 413 suites, 37 villas. 3 restaurants, deli, 2 lobby lounges, in-room VCRs, refrigerators, 3 pools, beauty salon, 2 hot tubs, golf privileges, health club, beach, shops, children's programs (ages 5–12). AE, D, DC, MC, V.* 🕭

$$$$ 🏨 **Maui Prince.** The attention to service, style, and presentation is apparent from the minute you walk into the delightful open-air lobby of this hotel. Rooms on three levels surround the courtyard, which is home to a Japanese garden with a bubbling stream. Each evening a small ensemble performs chamber music in the courtyard. Room decoration is understated, in tones of mauve and beige. Unfortunately, there's an earth berm between the hotel and the beach—part of the agreement the hotel had to make with the zoning commission and local residents— so an ocean view isn't possible from the first floor. ⊠ *5400 Mākena Alanui Rd., Mākena 96753,* ☎ *808/874–1111 or 800/321–6284,* FAX *808/879–8763. 290 rooms. 4 restaurants, pool, 2 18-hole golf courses, 6 tennis courts, beach. AE, DC, MC, V.*

$$$$ 🏨 **Outrigger Wailea Resort.** The tropical lobby and interior spaces showcase a remarkable collection of Hawaiian and Pacific Rim artifacts. All of the spacious rooms have private lānai and are styled with a tropical theme. The grounds are beautiful, with walks along paths accented with palm, banana, and torch ginger. There are golf privileges at three nearby courses, as well as tennis privileges at the Wailea Tennis Club. The resort also offers a game bar, two Jacuzzis, children's programs, and a Hawaiian cultural program. ⊠ *3700 Wailea Alanui Dr., Wailea 96753,* ☎ *808/879–1922 or 800/922–7866,* FAX *808/874–8331. 516 rooms. 2 restaurants, 3 pools, 2 hot tubs, beach, children's programs (ages 5–12). AE, D, DC, MC, V.* 🕭

$$$–$$$$ 🏨 **Maui Coast Hotel.** This is a classy seven-story hotel that you would never notice because it's set back off the street. The standard rooms are fine—very clean and modern—but the best deal is to pay a little more for one of the suites. In these you'll get an enjoyable amount of space and jet nozzles in the bathtub. And the suites adapt well to families. You can lounge by the large pool and order food and drinks from neighboring Jameson's Grill & Bar. Or walk across the street to Kama'ole Beach. There's an activities desk, too, to help you plan your time. ⊠ *2259 S. Kīhei Rd., Kīhei, 96753,* ☎ *808/874–6284, 800/895–6284, or 800/426–0670,* FAX *808/875–4731. 265 rooms, 114 suites. Restaurant, in-room safes, refrigerators, pool, dry cleaning, laundry service. AE, D, DC, MC, V.*

$$$–$$$$ 🏨 **Renaissance Wailea Beach Resort.** Most of this hotel's rooms, positioned on fantastic Mōkapu Beach, are contained in a seven-story, T-shape building. Tapestries and gorgeous carpets enhance the public areas. Outside, you'll find exotic gardens, waterfalls, and reflecting ponds. The VIP Mōkapu Beach Club building houses 26 luxury accommodations and has its own concierge, pool, and beach cabanas. Guest rooms are decorated in shades of cream and each has a lānai. Guests have access to the nearby golf and tennis facilities. ⊠ *3550 Wailea Alanui Dr., Wailea 96753,* ☎ *808/879–4900 or 800/992–4532,* FAX *808/874–6128. 345 rooms. 4 restaurants, lobby lounge, refrigerators, 2 pools, hot tub,*

basketball, health club, Ping-Pong, shuffleboard, beach, children's programs. AE, D, DC, MC, V. 🍴

$$$–$$$$ 🏨 **Wailea Villas.** The Wailea Resort has three fine condominiums, calling them, appropriately, Wailea 'Ekahi, Wailea 'Elua, and Wailea 'Ekolu (Wailea One, Two, and Three). Since then, Wailea has added the Grand Champions Villas, and the adjoining Mākena Resort has built Mākena Surf and Polo Beach Club. All have beautifully landscaped grounds, large units with exceptional views, and access to five of the island's best beaches. The Wailea 'Elua Village, Polo Beach Club, and Mākena Surf are the more luxurious properties, with rates to match. The three original villas are an expansive property, with all the amenities of the fine Wailea Resort, including daily maid service and a concierge. ✉ 3750 Wailea Alanui Dr., Wailea 96753, ☎ 808/879–1595 or 800/367–5246, ℻ 808/874–3554. 9 studios; 94 1-bedroom, 157 2-bedroom, and 10 3-bedroom apartments. 6 pools. AE, MC, V. 🍴

$$–$$$ 🏨 **Luana Kai.** Here's a prime example of the condominium-by-the-sea, perfect for setting up household for at least four days (the required minimum). There are three different room plans, suited for couples, families, or friends traveling together. Each one comes with everything you need to move in and make yourself at home—a fully stocked kitchen, dishwasher, laundry, television, and video and stereo equipment. The pool's a social place, with five gas grills, a full outdoor kitchen, and saunas for men and women. There's no beach on site—for that, you have to go down the road a ways—but the place adjoins a grassy county park with tennis courts. ✉ 940 S. Kīhei Rd., Kīhei, 96753, ☎ 808/ 879–1268 or 800/669–1127, ℻ 808/879–1455. 113 units. Pool, sauna, putting green, 4 tennis courts, shuffleboard. AE, DC, MC, V. 🍴

$$ 🏨 **Maui Lu Resort.** The first hotel in Kīhei and now operated by Aston Resorts, this place is reminiscent of a rustic lodge. The main lobby was the summer home of the original owner, a Canadian logger. Over the years the Maui Lu has added numerous wooden buildings and cottages to its 28 acres. Of the 120 rooms, 50 are right on the beach, and some have their own private coves. The rest are across Kīhei Road on the main property. ✉ 575 S. Kīhei Rd., Kīhei 96753, ☎ 808/879–5881 or 800/ 922–7866, ℻ 808/879–4627. 120 rooms. Restaurant, lounge, in-room safes, refrigerators, 2 tennis courts, beach. AE, D, DC, MC, V. 🍴

East Maui

$$$$ 🏨 **Hotel Hāna-Maui.** One of the best places to stay in Hawai'i—and a
★ departure from the usual resort-style accommodations—is this small, secluded hotel in Hāna surrounded by a 7,000-acre ranch. The original hotel buildings have white plaster walls and trellised verandas. Inside, the spacious rooms have bleach-wood floors, furniture upholstered in natural fabrics, and such welcome touches as fine art and orchids. The newer Sea Ranch Cottages across the road surround a state-of-the-art fitness center. A shuttle carries guests to a secluded beach nearby. ✉ Box 9, Hāna 96713, ☎ 808/248–8211 or 800/321–4262, ℻ 808/248–7264. 96 units. Restaurant, bar, 2 pools, massage, 2 tennis courts, exercise room, horseback riding, jogging, beach, library. AE, D, DC, MC, V.

$$–$$$ 🏨 **Kula Lodge.** This venue isn't typically Hawaiian: The lodge resembles a chalet in the Swiss Alps, and two of its five units have a gas fireplace. Charming and cozy in spite of the nontropical ambience, this is a perfect spot for a romantic stay. Units are in two wooden cabins; four have lofts in addition to the ample bed space downstairs, but none have phones or TVs. On three wooded acres, the lodge has views of the valley and ocean enhanced by the surrounding forest and tropical gardens. The property has a restaurant and lounge, as well as a gift shop and a protea store that will pack flowers for you to take home. ✉ R.R. 1,

Box 475, Kula 96790, ☎ *808/878–2517 or 800/233–1535,* FAX *808/ 878–2518. 5 units. Restaurant. AE, MC, V.* ✎

$$ ⌨ **Heavenly Hāna Inn.** An impressive Japanese gate marks the entrance to this small upscale inn. The three suites, one a two-bedroom unit, all have TVs. Decor is spare, with Japanese overtones. The furniture was built by Hāna residents. ✉ *Box 790, Hāna 96713,* ☎ *808/248– 8442. 3 suites. AE, D, MC, V.*

Guest Houses and Bed-and-Breakfasts

Despite the traditional name bed-and-breakfast, many of these small-scale accommodations (both rooms and cottages) choose not to interrupt your privacy with breakfast. Instead they'll provide you with lush Up-country or tropical surroundings that will enchant you and a kitchen that will let you do your own thing.

$$$–$$$$ ⌨ **Ekena.** This idyllic setting (Ekena means Garden of Eden in Hawaiian) is full of tropical fruit trees and exotic flowers, and it sits on a hillside near the town of Hāna with a commanding view of sea and land. There are two houses, each with a fully equipped kitchen and all necessities. Jasmine, the smaller of the two, is suited to parties of two or four. The main house, Sea Breeze, is huge (2,600 square ft), with two large master suites, but the owners restrict its occupancy to a maximum of four people. In order to ensure privacy, they also rent to only one party at a time. There's a minimum stay of three days, and children are not allowed. ✉ *Box 728, Hāna 96713,* ☎ FAX *808/248–7047. 2 houses. No credit cards.* ✎

$$$ ⌨ **'Ainahau.** Hidden away next to Hāna Bay, this cottage looks so-so
★ till you get inside and start looking around. The place is ingeniously and lovingly crafted and furnished with works of art. The kitchen is set up with all the details of home, including a loaded spice rack and a coffee grinder, and the cottage is equipped with cable TV and a CD player. Nature at its most benign lies around you, and the bed is both theatrical and sensuous. Hāna Settings manages this and several other getaways, provides gourmet catered meals at your order, and organizes custom Hāna weddings. ✉ *Box 970, Hāna 96713,* ☎ *808/248–7849,* FAX *808/248–8267. 1 room. Kitchenette, in-room VCR. AE, MC, V.*

$$$ ⌨ **Hāmoa Bay House & Bungalow.** This Balinese-inspired property is
★ sensuous and secluded, a private sanctuary in a fragrant jungle. There are two buildings. The main house is 1,300 sq ft and contains two bedrooms, one of them a suite set apart by a breezeway; there's a screened veranda with ocean view and also an outdoor lava-rock shower. The 600-square-ft bungalow is a treetop perch with a giant bamboo bed and a hot tub on the veranda. Both accommodations come with complete kitchen and laundry and VCRs. Hāmoa Beach is a short walk away. ✉ *Box 773, Hāna 96713,* ☎ *808/248–7884,* FAX *808/248–7047. 2 rooms, 1 bungalow. No credit cards.*

$$–$$$ ⌨ **Bloom Cottage.** The name comes from the abundance of roses and other flowers that surround this well-run, classic bed-and-breakfast. This is life in the slow lane, with privacy and quiet and a fireplace when the evenings are nippy. The furnishings are very Ralph Lauren with a cowhide flourish suited to this ranch-country locale six mi from Tedeschi Winery. The house, a 1906 antique, has three rooms and is good for four to six people willing to share a single bathroom. The cottage is ideal for a couple. ✉ *229 Kula Hwy., Kula 96790,* ☎ *808/ 878–1425,* FAX *661/393–5015. 3 rooms; 1 cottage. AE, D, MC, V.*

$$–$$$ ⌨ **Old Wailuku Inn.** This historic home, built in 1924, has been lov-
★ ingly renovated and may be the ultimate Hawaiian bed-and-breakfast. Each room is decorated on the theme of a Hawaiian flower, and the flower motif is worked into the heirloom Hawaiian quilt on each bed.

Other features include 10-ft ceilings, floors of native hardwoods, VCRs, and (depending on the room) some delightful bathtubs. The first-floor rooms have private gardens. A hearty breakfast is included. ⊠ *2199 Kaho'okele St., Wailuku 96793, ☎ 808/244–5897 or 800/305–4899. 7 rooms. AE, D, DC, MC, V. In-room VCRs.* ❧

$$–$$$ 🏠 **Olinda Country Cottage & Inn.** The restored Tudor home and adjacent cottage are so far up Olinda Road above Makawao you'll keep thinking you must have passed it, but keep driving to reach the inn, which sits amid an 8½-acre protea farm surrounded by forest and some wonderful hiking trails. There are three delightful accommodations in the inn: two upstairs bedrooms with private baths; the downstairs Pineapple Sweet with its French doors; and best of all the ultraromantic cottage, which looks like a dollhouse from the outside. It would be easy to settle in for a long winter here, but bring slippers and warm clothes—the mountain air can be chilly. ⊠ *536 Olinda Rd., Makawao 96768, ☎ FAX 808/572–1453 or ☎ 800/932–3435. 2 rooms with bath, 1 room shares bath, 2 cottages. No credit cards.*

$$–$$$ 🏠 **Silver Cloud Guest Ranch.** Silver Cloud is in cowboy country, on the
★ high mountainside beyond Kula and just five mi before 'Ulupalakua Ranch. The noble "Plantation House," with six rooms, surveys pasture lands and a spellbinding panorama of islands and sea. Silence is a chief attraction in this offbeat but magnificent part of Maui. Besides the main house, the ranch has a separate "Lānai Cottage" and five studios with kitchenettes (good for families) arranged like a bunkhouse in a horseshoe shape. A complete breakfast with fresh fruit and juice is served out of the Plantation House kitchen every morning. ⊠ *R.R. 2, Box 201, Kula 96790, ☎ 800/532–1111 or 808/878–6101, FAX 808/ 878–2132. 12 rooms. Horseback riding. AE, D, DC, MC, V.*

$$ 🏠 **Bambula Inn.** This casual sprawling house in a quiet Lahaina residential area has two studio apartments, one attached to the house and one freestanding. No breakfast is served; this is a move-in-and-hang-out beach house. Just across the street is a small beach, and moored just offshore is a sailboat, the *Bambula*—hand-built by the Frenchman who owns the inn. He likes to take his guests out for whale-watching and sunset sails, no charge. He also provides bicycles and snorkel equipment. This is a friendly, easygoing way to visit Lahaina. ⊠ *518 Ilikahi St., Lahaina 96761, ☎ 808/667–6753 or 800/544–5524, FAX 808/667–0979. 2 studios. Kitchenettes. D, MC, V.* ❧

$$ 🏠 **By the Sea B&B.** If you want to stay in a bed-and-breakfast in Kīhei, this is a pretty one. You'll be amazed at the lushness and romance that the owner has managed to create in a small lot hemmed in by apartments and commercial buildings. The private yard is a cool little Eden with a large pond and waterfall—a good place to hang out in the hammock by day or the hot tub by night. There are three self-contained apartments in the house. The honeymoon-style "Palm Room" on the second floor has a king bed and its own lānai. All accommodations have separate entrances and designated parking slots, and the owners provide beach equipment, fishing gear, and Continental breakfast. ⊠ *20 Wailana Pl., Kīhei 96753, ☎ 808/879–2700 or 888/879–2700, FAX 808/879–5540. 3 rooms. Coin laundry. AE, DC, MC, V.* ❧

$$ 🏠 **Golden Bamboo Ranch.** This secluded 7-acre estate lies in the edge-of-the-rain-forest lushness of rural Ha'ikū. The owners scrupulously maintain four units—one cottage, a studio, and two suites. Each has a kitchen or kitchenette and unobstructed views across a brilliant green landscape to the sea. ⊠ *422 Kaupakalua Rd., Ha'ikū 96708, ☎ 800/344–1238 or 808/572–7824, FAX 808/572–7824. 4 units. Kitchenettes. AE, D, DC, MC, V.* ❧

$$ 🏠 **Hale Ho'okipa Inn.** This handsome 80-year-old Craftsman-style house is right in the heart of Makawao town, a good home base for excursions to the crater or to Hāna. The owner has lovingly renovated the old place and furnished it with antique furniture and fine art. (She's also a certified tour guide who likes to take guests on hikes.) She has divided the house into three single rooms, each prettier than the next, and the "South Wing," which sleeps four and includes the kitchen. All rooms have private bath, and Continental breakfast is served. This inn matches everybody's mythical notion of grandma and grandpa's house. ⊠ *32 Pakani Pl., Makawao 96768,* ☎ *808/572–6698,* FAX *808/ 572–2580. 3 rooms, 1 2-bedroom suite. No credit cards.* ✍

$$ 🏠 **Kū'au Cove Plantation.** Here's a rare and handy location for a Maui visit—on a secluded cove midway between the town of Pā'ia and Ho'okipa Beach Park. The home is quite handsome, dating from the late 1930s and lovingly renovated by the current owners. Furnishings emphasize wicker and rattan and have quilted floral bedcovers. In classic bed-and-breakfast style, the owners rent two large bedrooms in the main house, both set apart from the family living area and each with private baths and queen-size beds. They also have two private studio apartments with kitchens. Continental breakfast is served. ⊠ *2 Wa'a Pl., Kū'au, 96779,* ☎ *808/579– 8988,* FAX *808/579–8710. 2 rooms, 2 apartments. MC, V.* ✍

$$ 🏠 **Kula View.** This affordable home-away-from-home sits in comfortable, peaceful rural Kula. The 2,000-ft elevation makes for a pleasantly temperate climate and a panorama that takes in the West Maui mountains and the ocean on either side. Guests stay in the entire upper floor of a simple but tastefully decorated house—Laura Ashley fabrics, a breakfast nook full of wicker furnishings, a private entrance, and a deck. The hostess puts an emphasis on hospitality, providing a welcoming "amenity basket," a very popular Continental breakfast, advice on touring, and even beach towels or warm clothes for your crater trip. This is a quiet, refreshing place to return to after a day on the road. ⊠ *140 Holopuni Rd., Kula 96790,* ☎ *808/878–6736. 1 room. No credit cards.* ✍

$–$$ 🏠 **Island View.** For that warm-sky, Upcountry-ranch feeling, head for this property not far from Pukalani. The owner is a master builder, and this sprawling house has obviously been a labor of love. There are bonuses for animal lovers: You'll have the company of a Dr. Dolittle–inspired assortment of animals, including Ollie, a surfing dog. The property includes two bed-and-breakfast rooms and one beautifully designed vacation "house" (one bedroom and two stories) for stays of four nights or longer. ⊠ *692 Naele Rd., Kula 96790,* ☎ *808/878–6739,* FAX *808/ 572–2265. 2 rooms, 1 cottage. No credit cards.* ✍

$–$$ 🏠 **Peace of Maui.** The small Upcountry community of Hali'imaile, 2 mi closer to the coast than Makawao and near both Baldwin Avenue and the Haleakalā Highway, is well situated for accessing the rest of the island. This small inn is a good choice for budget-minded travelers who want to be out and active all day. Six rooms in a "lodge" setting have pantries and mini-refrigerators. The kitchen and bathroom are shared. There's also a separate cottage with its own kitchen and facilities. You'll have sweeping views of the north shore and the mountains here. ⊠ *1290 Hali'imaile Rd., Hali'imaile 96768,* ☎ *888/475– 5045 or 808/572–5045. 7 rooms. No credit cards.* ✍

$ 🏠 **Aloha Lani Inn.** This accommodation operates rather like the classic European homestay. You share a bathroom with another guest, or perhaps with the home owners, and you're welcome to the kitchen, the lānai, the laundry facilities, the phone, the snorkel gear, the kayak, and so on. It's a casual, friendly, and inexpensive way to visit the West Side. The inn is in a quiet neighborhood within walking distance of Lahaina town. There's a two-night minimum stay. ⊠ *13 Kauaula Rd., Lahaina 96761,* ☎ *808/662–0812 or 800/57–ALOHA,* FAX *808/661– 8045. 3 rooms. AE, D, MC, V.* ✍

$ ⌂ **Halfway to Hāna House.** A private studio set in the country on Maui's lush rural north coast, this serene retreat comes with surrounding gardens and great ocean views. It's a short walk from here to natural pools and waterfalls, hiking areas, and horseback riding. The room comes with optional Continental breakfast and a well-supplied kitchenette—all the equipment you need to do your own thing. ⊠ *Box 675, Ha'ikū 96708,* ☎ *808/572–1176,* FAX *808/572–3609. 1 room. No credit cards.* ✎

$ ⌂ **Makani 'Olu'olu Cottage.** Actually, these folks offer both a cottage and an *'ohana* (an apartment attached to the house). The location is unusual—the heart of lush rural Ha'ikū, where the *makani* (winds) are *'olu'olu* (pleasant). Both rentals are suited to one or two people, with queen beds, complete kitchens, and delightful frescoes on the walls depicting tropical scenes—original works by the multitalented landlady. The tiled 'ohana is downstairs, with its own entrance and a lānai that looks over green pastures. The cottage has decoupage shelves and an antique upright piano. ⊠ *925 Kaupakalua Rd., Ha'ikū 96708,* ☎ *808/ 572–8383. 2 rooms. No credit cards.* ✎

NIGHTLIFE AND THE ARTS

Nightlife on Maui might be better labeled "evening life." Quiet Maui has little of Waikīkī's after-hours decadence. But before 10 PM there's a lot on offer, from lū'au shows and dinner cruises to concerts at "The Center." Lahaina still tries to uphold its reputation as a party town, and succeeds wildly every Halloween when thousands converge on Front Street.

Since it opened in 1994, the **Maui Arts & Cultural Center** (⊠ Maui Central Park, Kahului, ☎ 808/242–2787) has become the venue for more and more of the island's best live entertainment. The complex includes the 1,200-seat Castle Theater, which hosts classical, country, and world-beat concerts by touring musicians; a 4,000-seat amphitheater for large outdoor concerts; and the 350-seat McCoy Theater for plays and recitals. For information on current programs, check the Events Box Office (☎ 808/242–7469) or the daily newspaper, the *Maui News.* Most major credit cards are accepted at the venues listed below.

For nightlife of a different sort, children and astronomy buffs will enjoy stargazing at **Tour of the Stars,** a one-hour program held nightly on the roof of the Hyatt Regency Maui in Kā'anapali. You can look through giant binoculars and a deep-space telescope. The program is run by an astronomer. Check in at the hotel lobby 15 minutes prior to starting time. ⊠ *Lahaina Tower, Hyatt Regency Maui, 200 Nohea Kai Dr., Kā'anapali,* ☎ *808/661–1234, ext. 4727.* ☞ *$20.* ☽ *Nightly at 8, 9, and 10.*

Bars and Clubs

Contemporary Music

Kahale's Beach Club. A friendly, informal hangout, Kahale's offers live music (usually Hawaiian), bar drinks, burgers, fries, and artichokes every day from 10 AM till 2 in the morning. ⊠ *36 Keala Pl., Kīhei,* ☎ *808/875–7711.*

Makai Bar. Live Hawaiian and contemporary music nightly, awesome sunset views, and the best *pūpū* (appetizers) on Maui are at this comfortable spot on the Kā'anapali coast. ⊠ *Lahaina Tower, Hyatt Regency Maui, Kā'anapali Beach Resort,* ☎ *808/667–1200.*

Molokini Lounge. This is a pleasant bar with an ocean view, and you can even see Molokini Island before the sun goes down. Live music is presented, often Hawaiian in theme. There's a dance floor for late-night revelry. ⊠ *Lahaina Tower, Hyatt Regency Maui, Kā'anapali Beach Resort,* ☎ *808/667–1200.*

Jazz

Pacific'O. This highly recommended restaurant (☞ West Maui *in* Dining, *above*) is also the most reliable place to hear live jazz on the beach. It's a mellow, pacific sort of jazz—naturally—and it plays from 9 until midnight Thursday through Saturday. Guests musicians— George Benson, for example—often sit in. ⊠ *505 Front St., Lahaina,* ☎ *808/667–4341.*

Rock

Casanova Italian Restaurant & Deli. Casanova, voted "Best Late Night on Maui" in a *Maui News* readers' survey, claims to be the best place on the island for singles to meet. When a DJ is not spinning hits, contemporary musicians rock on with blues, country-western, rock-and-roll, and reggae. Past favorites have included Kool and the Gang, Los Lobos, and Taj Mahal. Expect a cover charge on nights featuring live entertainment. ⊠ *1188 Makawao Ave., Makawao,* ☎ *808/572–0220.*

Cheeseburger in Paradise. This Front Street hangout is known for—what else?—big beefy cheeseburgers (not to mention a great spinach-nut burger). Locals also know it as a great place to tune in to live bands playing rock-and-roll, Top 40, and oldies sounds from 4:30 PM to closing. There's no dance floor, but the second-floor balcony is a good place to watch Lahaina's Front Street action. ⊠ *811 Front St., Lahaina,* ☎ *808/661–4855.*

Hapa's Brewhaus & Restaurant. Good food and some fine brews are on the menu here, along with sports TV, rock and funk bands, disco, hula shows, and comedy. These folks have gone all out to create a first-rate club with a large stage, roomy dance floor, state-of-the-art lighting and sound systems, and tier seating so that everyone gets a good view. Even nonsmokers will find the club comfortable: The air-conditioning system removes secondhand smoke. ⊠ *Lipoa Center, 41 E. Lipoa St., Kihei,* ☎ *808/879–9001.*

Hard Rock Cafe. Maui's version of the Hard Rock is popular with young locals as well as visitors who like their music *loud.* ⊠ *Lahaina Center, 900 Front St., Lahaina,* ☎ *808/667–740.*

Maui Brews. Live bands serve up Top 40, reggae, salsa, or some kind of rock every night—a DJ on the weekends. This "island bistro and nightclub" is a big hangout place. They do a complete bar menu of appetizers, pastas, burgers, and entrées, and there are 16 kinds of draft beer, 10 specialty martinis, and a menu for kids. ⊠ *Lahaina Center, 900 Front St.,* ☎ *808/667–7794.*

Moose McGillycuddy's. The Moose offers no-cover live music on Tuesday and Thursday. Otherwise, it's recorded music, but it's played so loud you'd swear it's live. This entertaining place tends to draw a young crowd that comes to enjoy the burgers and beer, to dance, and to meet one another. Specials include a pound-and-a-half king crab dinner and, on other nights, a 22-ounce porterhouse. ⊠ *844 Front St., Lahaina,* ☎ *808/667–7758.*

Tsunami. You can dance to recorded Top 40 hits in this sophisticated, high-tech disco, where laser beams zigzag high above a futuristic dance floor. The music plays from 9 to 2 on Thursday, Friday, and Saturday nights. On other nights, the room is used for private parties. Tsunami has pool tables and a dress code: no beach wear, jeans, or T-shirts. Expect a $5 cover charge. ⊠ *Grand Wailea, 3850 Wailea Alanui Dr., Wailea,* ☎ *808/875–1234.*

Dinner and Sunset Cruises

America II Sunset Sail. The star of this two-hour cruise is the craft itself—a 1987 America's Cup 12-m class contender that is exceptionally smooth and steady, thanks to its renowned winged-keel design. ⊠ *Lahaina Harbor, Lahaina,* ☎ *808/667–2195.* 🖃 *$25.*

***Kaulana* Cocktail Cruise.** This two-hour sunset cruise (with a bit of whale-watching thrown in, in season) features a pūpū menu, open bar, and live music. ⊠ *Lahaina Harbor, Lahaina,* ☎ *808/871–1144.* ⛴ *$39.*

Pride Charters. A 65-ft catamaran built specifically for Maui's waters, the *Pride of Maui* features a large cabin, a large upper sundeck for un-obstructed viewing, and a stable, comfortable ride. Breakfast, lunch, and beverages are provided. For later departures, there is an optional barbecue. ⊠ *Māʻalaea Harbor, Māʻalaea,* ☎ *808/242–0955.* ⛴ *$40.*

Scotch Mist Charters. A two-hour champagne sunset sail is offered on the 25-passenger Santa Cruz 50 sloop *Scotch Mist II.* ⊠ *Lahaina Harbor, Lahaina,* ☎ *808/661–0386.* ⛴ *$38.*

Windjammer Cruises. This cruise includes a prime rib and Alaskan salmon dinner and live entertainment on the 70-ft, 93-passenger *Spirit of Windjammer,* a three-masted schooner. ⊠ *283 Wili Ko Pl., Suite 1, Lahaina,* ☎ *808/661–8600.* ⛴ *$69.*

Film

Maui Film Festival. This ongoing celebration offers weekly screenings of quality films that may not show up at the local megaplex. Most screenings are in Maui's most luxurious movie house—Castle Theater at Maui Arts & Cultural Center. On Wednesday night the usual movies are followed by live music and poetry readings in the "Candlelight Cafe." But the schedule varies, and the program is expanding. In summer the festival comes to Wailea for cinema under the stars in a program that includes music, hula, and Hawaiian storytelling. For recorded program information call ☎ 808/572–FILM or check the Web site: www.mauifilmfestival.com.

Lūʻau and Revues

Maui Myth & Magic Theatre. Maui's newest live theater opened in 1999 with the debut of ʻUlalena, a 75-minute musical extravaganza that is well received by audiences and Hawaiian-culture experts alike. The ensemble cast (20 singer/dancers and a 5-musician orchestra) mixes native rhythms and stories with acrobatic performance and high-tech stage wizardry to give an inspiring introduction to island culture. It's movie-style seating with beer and wine for sale at the popcorn line. They also offer dinner-theater packages in conjunction with top Lahaina restaurants. ⊠ *878 Front St., Lahaina,* ☎ *808/661–9913 or 877/688–4800,* ℻ *808/661–5363. Reservations essential.* ⛴ *$35.* ☉ *Tues.–Sat. 6:30 and 9.*

Nāpili Kai Beach Club Keiki Hula Show. Expect to be charmed as well as entertained when 30 children ages 6 to 17 take you on a dance tour of Hawaiʻi, New Zealand, Tahiti, Samoa, and other Polynesian islands. The talented youngsters make their own ti-leaf skirts and fresh-flower leis. They give the leis to the audience at the end of the show. This is a nonprofessional but delightfully engaging review, and the 80-seat oceanfront room is usually sold out. ⊠ *Nāpili Kai Beach Club, 5900 Honoapiʻilani Hwy., Nāpili,* ☎ *808/669–6271.* ⛴ *$35.* ☉ *Dinner Fri. at 6, show at 7:30.*

Old Lahaina Lūʻau. This is the best lūʻau you'll find on Maui. It's small, personal, and authentic. Its new home is an outdoor theater designed specifically for traditional Hawaiian entertainment. It feels like an old seaside village. In addition to fresh fish and grilled steak and chicken, you'll get all-you-can-eat traditional lūʻau fare: kālua pig, chicken long rice, *lomilomi* salmon (massaged until tender and served with minced onions and tomatoes), *haupia* (coconut pudding), and other treats. You'll also get all you can drink. Guests sit either on tatami mats or at tables. Then there's the entertainment, featuring a musical journey from old Hawaiʻi to the present with hula dancing, chanting, and singing. ⊠ *1251 Front St., Lahaina (makai of the Lahaina Cannery Mall),* ☎ *808/667–1998.* ⛴ *$65.* ☉ *Nightly 5:30–8:30.*

The Feast at Lele. "Lele" is an older, more traditional name for Lahaina. This "feast" is redefining the lūʻau by crossing it with fine dining island-style in an intimate beach setting. Both the show and the three-course gourmet meal express the spirit of a specific island culture—Hawaiian, Samoan, Tongan, or Tahitian. The wine list and liquor selections are excellent. This may be the trend of the future for would-be Polynesian royalty. ⊠ *505 Front St., Lahaina,* ☎ *808/667–5353,* FAX *808/661–8399. Reservations essential.* ✍ *$89.* ☉ *Tues., Thurs., and Sat. (more often in high season), 5:30 in winter and 6:30 in summer.*

Warren & Annabelle's. Magician Warren Gibson entices his guests into a swank nightclub setting with red carpets and a gleaming mahogany bar, then plies them with appetizers (coconut shrimp, crab cakes), desserts (rum cake, crème brûlée), and "smoking cocktails." Then he performs table-side magic while his ghostly assistant, Annabelle, tickles the ivories. The show is fun, and all the better for being not too slick. Note that this is a nightclub, so no one under 21 is allowed. ⊠ *Lahaina Center, 900 Front St.,* ☎ *808/667–6244. Reservations essential.* ✍ *$36.* ☉ *Mon.–Sat., 7 and 8:30.*

Music

Maui Philharmonic Society. The Society has presented such prestigious performers as Ballet Hispanico, the Shostakovich String Quartet, and the New Age pianist-composer Philip Glass. Performances take place in various spots around the island. ⊠ *J. Walter Cameron Center, 95 Mahalani St., Wailuku 96793,* ☎ *808/244–3771.*

Maui Symphony Orchestra (☎ *808/244–5439*). The symphony orchestra usually performs at the Maui Arts & Cultural Center (⊠ Maui Central Park, Kahului, ☎ 808/242–2787; box office 808/242–7469), offering five seasonal concerts and a few special musical sensations as well. The regular season includes a Christmas concert, an opera gala, a classical concert, and two pops concerts outdoors.

Theater

Baldwin Theatre Guild. Dramas, comedies, and musicals are presented by this group about eight times a year. The guild has staged such favorites as *The Glass Menagerie, Brigadoon,* and *The Miser.* Musicals are held in the Community Auditorium, which seats 1,200. All other plays are presented in the Baldwin High School Mini Theatre. ⊠ *1650 Kaʻahumanu Ave., Kahului,* ☎ *808/984–5673.* ✍ *$8.*

Maui Academy of Performing Arts. For a quarter-century this group has offered fine performances as well as dance and drama classes for children and adults. It has presented such plays as *Peter Pan, Jesus Christ Superstar,* and *The Nutcracker.* MAPA has secured a new home in Wailuku at the old National Dollar Store building. They hope to occupy the new theater and two dance studios in mid 2001. *Main and Market Sts., Wailuku,* ☎ *808/244–8760.* ✍ *$10–$12.*

Maui Community Theatre. Now staging about six plays a year, this is the oldest dramatic group on the island, started in the early 1900s. Each July the group also holds a fund-raising variety show, which can be a hoot. ⊠ *ʻIao Theatre, 68 N. Market St., Wailuku,* ☎ *808/242–6969.* ✍ *Musicals $10–$15, nonmusicals $8–$13.*

Seabury Hall Performance Studio. This college-preparatory school above Makawao town offers a season of often supercharged shows in its satisfying small theater and two dance studios. The school's formula is to mix talented kids with seasoned adults and innovative, even offbeat, concepts. Dance concerts are always a hit. ⊠ *480 Olinda Rd., 1 mi north of Makawao crossroads,* ☎ *808/573–1257.* ✍ *$7–$12.*

OUTDOOR ACTIVITIES AND SPORTS

Participant Sports

Biking

Maui County has designated hundreds of miles of bikeways on Maui's roads, making biking safer and more convenient than in the past. Painted bike lanes make it possible for a rider to travel all the way from Mākena to Kapalua, and you'll see dozens of hardy souls pedaling under the hot Maui sun. Some visitors rent a bike just to ride around the resort where they're staying. Whatever your preference, you have several rental choices, including **Island Biker** (⊠ 415 Dairy Rd., Kahului, ☎ 808/877–7744), **Maui Sports and Cycle** (⊠ Long's Center, Kīhei, ☎ 808/875–8448, **South Maui Bicycles** (⊠ Island Surf building, Kīhei, ☎ 808/874–0068), and **West Maui Cycles** (⊠ 840 Waine'e St., Lahaina, ☎ 808/661–9005). Bikes rent for $10 to $20 a day. Several companies offer downhill bike tours from the top of Haleakalā all the way to the coast (☞ Contacts and Resources *in* Maui A to Z, *below*).

Camping and Hiking

Let's start with the best—hiking **Haleakalā Crater.** The recommended way to explore the crater is to leave your car at the head of Halemau'u Trail and hitchhike the last few miles up to the summit, or else go in two cars and ferry yourselves back and forth. This way, you can hike from the summit down Sliding Sands Trail, cross the crater floor, investigate the Bottomless Pit and Pele's Paint Pot, then climb out on the switchback trail (Halemau'u). When you emerge, the shelter of your waiting car will be very welcome. Give yourself eight hours for the hike; wear jogging-type shoes and take a backpack with lunch, water, and a reliable jacket for the beginning and end of the hike. This is a demanding trip, but you will never regret or forget it.

If you want to stay longer than a day, plan to shelter in one of the national park's three cabins or two campgrounds. The cabins are equipped with bunk beds, wood-burning stoves, fake logs, and kitchen gear. To reserve a cabin you have to think at least three months in advance and hope the lottery system is kind to you. Contact the National Park Service (⊠ Box 369, Makawao 96768, ☎ 808/572–9306). The tent campsites are easy to reserve on a first-come, first-served basis. Just make sure to stop at park headquarters to register on your way in.

Just as you enter the national park, **Hosmer Grove** offers an hour-long loop trail into the "cloud forest" that will give you insight into Hawai'i's fragile ecology. You can pick up a map at the trailhead. Park rangers offer guided hikes on a changing schedule. There are six campsites (no permit needed), pit toilets, drinking water, and cooking shelters.

Another good hiking spot—and something totally unexpected on a tropical island—is **Polipoli Forest.** During the Great Depression, the government began a program to reforest the mountain, and soon cedar, pine, cypress, and even redwood took hold. It's cold here and foggy, often wet or at least misty. To reach the forest, take Highway 37 all the way out to the far end of Kula. Then turn left at Highway 377. In about half a mile, turn right at Waipoli Road. Then up you go. First it's switchbacks. Then it's just plain bad—but passable. There are wonderful trails, also a small campground and a cabin that you can rent from the Division of State Parks. Write far in advance for the cabin (⊠ Box 1049, Wailuku 96793, ☎ 808/244–4354); for the campground, you can wait until you arrive in Wailuku and visit the State Parks office (⊠ 54 High St.).

Past Hāna you contact the national park again at **ʻOheʻo Gulch.** This is the starting point of one of the best hikes on Maui—the 2-mi trek upstream to 400-ft **Waimoku Falls.** Along the way you can take side trips and swim in the stream's basalt-lined pools. Then the trail bridges a sensational gorge and passes onto a boardwalk through a clonking, mystifying forest of giant bamboo. Down at the grassy sea cliffs, you can camp, no permit required, although you can stay only three nights. Toilets, grills, and tables are available here, but no water and no open fires.

In ʻĪao Valley, the **Hawaiʻi Nature Center** (⊠ 875 ʻĪao Valley Rd., Wailuku, 96793, ☎ 808/244–6500) leads interpretive hikes for children and their families.

Fitness Centers

Most fitness centers on Maui are in hotels. If your hotel does not have a facility, ask if privileges are available at other hotels. Outside the resorts, the most convenient and best equipped are **24 Hour Fitness** (⊠ 150 Hāna Hwy., Kahului, ☎ 808/877–7474) and **World Gym** (⊠ Kīhei Commercial Center, 300 Ohukai Rd., G-112, Kīhei, ☎ 808/879–1326), which both have complete fitness facilities. Or contact the **Maui Family YMCA** (⊠ 250 Kanaloa Ave., Kahului, ☎ 808/242–9007).

Golf

How do you keep your mind on the game in a place like Maui? It's very hard, because you can't ignore the view, but Maui has become one of the world's premier golf-vacation destinations. The island's major resorts all have golf courses, each of them stunning. They're all open to the public, and most lower their greens fees after 2:30 on weekday afternoons.

Elleair Golf Course. Formerly Silversword Golf Course, this privately owned course independent of the resorts was designed by Bill Newis to take advantage of its lofty location above Kīhei town. You'll get panoramic views not only out to sea but also across Haleakalā. ⊠ 1345 Piʻilani Hwy., Kīhei, ☎ 808/874–0777. ☜ Greens fee $75, including cart.

Kāʻanapali Golf Courses. Two of Maui's most famous courses are here. The layout consists of the North Course, designed by Robert Trent Jones, Sr., and the South Course, laid out by Arthur Jack Snyder. ⊠ Kāʻanapali Beach Resort, Kāʻanapali, ☎ 808/661–3691. ☜ Greens fee $100 guests, $120 nonguests, including cart.

Kapalua Golf Club. The club has three 18-holers—the Village Course and the Bay Course, both designed by Arnold Palmer, and the Plantation Course, designed by Ben Crenshaw. Kapalua is well-known to television-sports watchers. ⊠ 300 Kapalua Dr., Kapalua, ☎ 808/669–8044. ☜ Greens fee $95–$100 guests, $140–$150 nonguests, including cart; club rental $30–$40.

Mākena Golf Course. There are two lovely 18-hole courses here, North and South, designed by Robert Trent Jones, Jr. Of all the resort courses, this one is the most remote. At one point, golfers must cross a main road, but there are so few cars that this poses no problem. ⊠ 5415 Mākena Alanui Rd., Kīhei, ☎ 808/879–3344. ☜ Greens fee $80 guests, $140 nonguests, including cart.

Sandalwood Golf Course. Sandalwood offers a unique location on the slopes of the West Maui mountains just south of Wailuku, with elevated views of Haleakalā. ⊠ 2500 Honoapiʻilani Hwy., Wailuku, ☎ 808/242–4653. ☜ Greens fee $75, including cart.

Wailea Golf Club. The club has three courses: the Gold and the Blue, which were designed by Arthur Jack Snyder, and the newer Emerald, designed by Robert Trent Jones, Jr. In his design, Snyder incorporated ancient lava-rock walls to create an unusual golfing experience.

✉ *100 Wailea Golf Club Dr., Wailea,* ☎ *808/875–5111.* ⛳ *Greens fee $110 guests, $140 nonguests, including cart.*

Maui also has municipal courses, where the fees are lower. Be forewarned, however, that the weather can be cool and wet, and the locations may not be convenient. The **Waiehu Municipal Golf Course** is on the northeast coast of Maui a few miles past Wailuku. ✉ *Off Hwy. 340, West Maui,* ☎ *808/244–5934.* ⛳ *Greens fee $25 weekdays, $30 weekends; cart $15.*

Hang Gliding
USHGA instructor Armin Engert of **Hang Gliding Maui** (☎ 808/572–6557, ✎) will teach you the basics of weight-shift control while he takes you on a tandem hang-gliding experience from the top of Haleakalā to the green pastures of Kula. He has a 100% safety record. The soundless, practically effortless flight lasts anywhere from 30 to 90 minutes, depending on the thermal activity. There's a weight limit of 200 pounds for this trip, which costs $300 and includes 24 snapshots of your adventure taken by a wing-mounted camera.

Parasailing
If you have a yen to be floating in the sky like a bird but lack the derring-do of a barnstormer, parasailing is the perfect alternative to skydiving (you gently rise several hundred feet from the ground instead of leaping out of an aircraft at 10,000 ft) or hang gliding (the safety rope holds you in your flight pattern). This is an easy and fun way to earn your wings: Just strap on a harness attached to a parachute and a power boat pulls you up and over the ocean from a launching dock or from a boat's platform. To reduce interference with whales, no "thrill craft"—including parasails—are allowed in Maui waters from December 15 to April 15.

Several companies on Maui will take you for a ride that usually lasts about 10 minutes and costs $30 to $50. For safety reasons, **West Maui Para-Sail** (☎ 808/661–4060) requires that passengers weigh more than 100 pounds, or two must be strapped together in tandem. **Lahaina Para-Sail** (☎ 808/661–4887) lays claim to the only parasail vessel on Maui that is Coast Guard certified for 25 passengers and has bathroom facilities on board. The group will be glad to let you experience a "toe dip" or "freefall" if you request it, and the minimum weight to fly alone is 75 pounds.

Sporting Clays
Skillfully designed to fit inside the crater of a large cinder cone, **Papaka Sporting Clays** (✉ 1325 S. Kīhei Rd., ☎ 808/879–5649) is an outdoor arcade dedicated to the art of shotgun shooting. The 40 stations include "Springing Teal," "High Pheasant," and "Busting Bunnies" (no real bunnies involved; the targets are clay disks). Certified instructors outfit you with a vest, earplugs, eye protection, a shotgun, and instruction. They pick you up in the Kīhei–Wailea area or at ʻUlupalakua Ranch by appointment any morning or afternoon. The cost is $95 for 75 targets. Spectators can come along for free.

Tennis
There are other facilities around the island besides those listed below, usually one or two courts in smaller hotels or condos. Most of them, however, are open only to their guests. The best free courts are the five at the **Lahaina Civic Center** (✉ 1840 Honoapiʻilani Hwy., Lahaina, ☎ 808/661–4685), near Wahikuli State Park. They're available on a first-come, first-served basis.

Hyatt Regency Maui. The Hyatt has six courts, with rentals and instruction. All-day passes cost $15 for guests, $20 for nonguests. ✉ *200 Nohea Kai Dr., Kāʻanapali,* ☎ *808/661–1234 ext. 3174.*

Kapalua Tennis Garden. This complex serves the Kapalua Resort with 10 courts and a pro shop. You'll pay $10 an hour if you're a guest, $12 if you're not, and you're welcome to stay longer for free if there is no one waiting. ⊠ *100 Kapalua Dr., Kapalua,* ☎ *808/669–5677.*

Mākena Tennis Club. This club at the Mākena Resort, just south of Wailea, has six courts. Rates are $16 per court hour for guests, $18 for nonguests. After an hour, if there's space available, there's no charge. ⊠ *5400 Mākena Alanui Rd., Kīhei,* ☎ *808/879–8777.*

Maui Beach & Tennis Club. The Maui Marriott's club has five Plexipave courts, with three lighted for night play, and a pro shop. Daily rates are $10 for guests and $12 for nonguests. ⊠ *100 Nohea Kai Dr., Kā'anapali,* ☎ *808/667–1200, ext. 8689.*

Royal Lahaina Tennis Ranch. In the Kā'anapali Beach Resort on West Maui, the Royal Lahaina offers 11 recently resurfaced courts and a pro shop. Rates are a flat $10 per person per day whether you are a guest or not. ⊠ *2780 Keka'a Dr.,* ☎ *808/661–3611 ext. 2296.*

Wailea Tennis Club. These are the state's finest tennis facilities, often called "Wimbledon West" because of the two grass courts. There are also 11 Plexipave courts and a pro shop. You'll pay $25 an hour per person for the hard courts. The grass courts are by well-in-advance reservation only. On weekday mornings clinics are given to help you improve your ground strokes, serve, volley, or doubles strategy. ⊠ *131 Wailea Ike Pl., Kīhei,* ☎ *808/879–1958 or 800/332–1614.*

Water Sports

Note that to reduce interference with whales, no "thrill craft"—specifically parasails and Jet Skis—are allowed in Maui waters from December 15 to April 15.

DEEP-SEA FISHING

If fishing is your sport, Maui is the place for it. You'll be able to throw in hook and bait for fish like 'ahi, *aku* (skipjack tuna), barracuda, bonefish, *kawakawa* (bonito), mahimahi, Pacific blue marlin, *ono* (wahoo), and *ulua* (jack crevalle). On Maui you can fish throughout the year, and you don't need a license.

Plenty of fishing boats run out of Lahaina and Mā'alaea harbors. If you charter a boat by yourself, expect to spend in the neighborhood of $600 a day. But you can share the boat with others who are interested in fishing the same day for about $100 each. Although there are at least 10 companies running boats on a regular basis, these are the most reliable: **Finest Kind Inc.** (⊠ Lahaina Harbor, Slip 7, Box 10481, Lahaina 96767, ☎ 808/661–0338), **Hinatea Sportfishing** (⊠ Lahaina Harbor, Slip 27, Lahaina 96761, ☎ 808/667–7548), and **Lucky Strike Charters** (⊠ Box 1502, Lahaina 96767, ☎ 808/661–4606). **Ocean Activities Center** (⊠ 1847 S. Kīhei Rd., Suite 203A, Kīhei 96753, ☎ 808/879–4485 or 800/798–0652) can arrange fishing charters as well. You're responsible for finding your own transportation to the harbor.

KAYAKING

The sport has been gaining popularity on the island. Kayaking off the coast of Maui can be a leisurely paddle or it can be a challenge. This depends on your location, your inclination, and the weather of the day. The company to contact is **Maui Sea Kayaking** (☎ 808/572–6299, FAX 808/572–6151, ✍). They take small parties to secret spots. They like the idea of customizing their outings. For example, the guides accommodate kayakers with disabilities as well as senior kayakers, and they also offer kid-size gear. They're also into kayak surfing. And they offer a honeymoon/vow-renewal experience that could make Tarzan rekindle his appreciation for Jane.

RAFTING

These high-speed inflatable craft are nothing like the raft that Huck Finn used to drift down the Mississippi. While passengers grip straps, these rafts fly, skimming and bouncing, across the top of the sea. Because they're so maneuverable, they go where the big boats can't—secret coves, sea caves, and unvisited beaches. **Blue Water Rafting** (⌂ Box 1865, Kīhei 96753, ☎ 808/661–4743 or 800/874–2666) leaves from the Kīhei boat ramp and explores the rugged coast beyond La Pérouse Bay. **Ocean Riders** (⌂ 96767, Lahaina 96767, ☎ 808/661–3586), in Lahaina, takes people all the way around the island of Lāna'i. For snorkeling or gawking, the "back side" of Lāna'i is one of Hawai'i's unsung marvels.

SAILING

Because of its proximity to the smaller islands of Moloka'i, Lāna'i, Kaho'olawe, and Molokini, Maui can provide some of Hawai'i's best sailing experiences. Most sailing operations like to combine their tours with a meal, some throw in snorkeling or whale-watching, and others offer a sunset cruise.

The best and longest-running operation is the Coon family's **Trilogy Excursions** (⌂ 180 Lahainaluna Rd., Lahaina 96761, ☎ 808/661–4743 or 800/874–2666). They have six beautiful multihulled sailing craft, and the crews treat passengers with genuine warmth and affection. A full-day catamaran cruise to Lāna'i includes a guided van tour of the island, a barbecue lunch, beach volleyball, and a "Snorkeling 101" class, in which you can test your skills in the waters of Hulopo'e Marine Preserve. (Trilogy has exclusive commercial access.) Snorkeling gear is supplied. It also offers a Molokini snorkel cruise.

Comparable to Trilogy in its service, good food, and comfortable catamaran cruise is the **Mahana Na'ia** (⌂ Mā'alaea Harbor, ☎ 808/871–8636). This boat specializes in snorkel trips to Molokini. In a slip nearby at Mā'alaea Harbor, you'll find a beautiful monohull luxury yacht called **Cinderella** (☎ 808/244–0009), which is available for charters and for customized tours. Another sleek yacht that offers the exhilaration of fast sailing is the 65-ft cutter-rigged **World Class** (☎ 808/667–7733), which picks up passengers on the sand at Kā'anapali.

Other companies offering cruises include **Maui–Moloka'i Sea Cruises** (⌂ 831 Eha St., Suite 101, Wailuku 96793, ☎ 808/242–8777), **Sail Hawai'i** (☎ 808/879–2201), **Scotch Mist Charters** (☎ 808/661–0386), and the Hyatt Regency Maui's **Kiele V** (⌂ 200 Nohea Kai Dr., Lahaina, ☎ 808/661–1234).

SCUBA DIVING

Maui is just as scenic underwater as it is above. In fact, some of the finest diving spots in Hawai'i lie along the Valley Isle's western and southwestern shores. If you're a certified diver, you can rent gear at any Maui dive shop simply by showing your PADI or NAUI card. Unless you're familiar with the area, however, it's probably best to hook up with a dive shop for an underwater tour.

Maui has no lodging facilities tailored to divers, but there are many dive shops that sell and rent equipment and give lessons and certification. Before signing on with any of these outfitters, however, it's a good idea to ask a few pointed questions.

Some popular outfitters include **Ed Robinson's Diving Adventures** (⌂ Kīhei, ☎ 808/879–3584 or 800/635–1273), **Happy Divers** (⌂ 840 Waine'e St., Suite 106, Lahaina, ☎ 808/669–0123), **Lahaina Divers** (⌂ 143 Dickenson St., Lahaina, ☎ 808/667–7496), **Maui Dive Shop** (⌂ Honokōwai Marketplace, ☎ 808/661–0268; ⌂ 1455 S. Kīhei Rd Kīhei, ☎ 808/879–0843), and **Pacific Dive Shop** (⌂ 150 Dickenson St.,

Lahaina, ☎ 808/667–5331). All provide equipment with proof of certification, as well as introductory dives for those who aren't certified. Introductory boat dives generally run about $80.

Area dive sites include the following:

Honolua Bay. In West Maui, this marine preserve is alive with many varieties of coral and tame tropical fish, including large ulua, *kāhala*, barracuda, and manta rays. With depths of 20 ft to 50 ft, this is a popular spot for introductory dives. Dives are generally made only during the summer months.

Molokini Crater. At 'Alalākeiki Channel, this is a crescent-shape islet formed by the top of a volcano. This marine preserve's depth range (10 ft to 80 ft), combined with the attraction of the numerous tame fish dwelling here that can be fed by hand, makes it a popular introductory dive site.

SNORKELING

If you want a personal introduction to Maui's undersea universe, the undisputable authority is **Ann Fielding's Snorkel Maui.** A marine biologist, Fielding—formerly with University of Hawai'i, Waikīkī Aquarium, and the Bishop Museum and the author of several guides to island sealife—is the Carl Sagan of Hawai'i's reef cosmos. She'll not only show you fish, but she'll also introduce you to *individual* fish. This is a good first experience for dry-behind-the-ears types. Snorkel trips include lunch. ⊠ *Box 1107, Makawao 96768,* ☎ *808/572–8437.* 🖃 *$75 adults, $65 children.*

Of course the same dive companies that take scuba aficionados on tours will take snorkelers as well. One of Maui's most popular snorkeling spots can be reached only by boat: Molokini Crater, that little bowl of land off the coast of Wailea. For about $55, you can spend half a day at Molokini, with meals provided.

Ocean Activities Center (⊠ 1847 S. Kīhei Rd., Suite 203A, Kīhei, ☎ 808/879–4485) does a great job, although other companies also offer a Molokini snorkel tour.

You can find some good snorkeling spots on your own. If you need gear, **Snorkel Bob's** (⊠ Nāpili Village Hotel, 5425 Lower Honoapi'ilani Rd., Nāpili, ☎ 808/669–9603; ⊠ 34 Keala Pl., Kīhei, ☎ 808/879–7449; ⊠ 161 Lahainaluna Rd., Lahaina, ☎ 808/661–4421) will rent you a mask, fins, and snorkel and throw in a carrying bag, map, and snorkel tips for as little as $5 per day.

Secluded **Windmill Beach** (⊠ Take Hwy. 30 3½ mi north of Kapalua; then turn onto the dirt road to the left) has a superb reef for snorkeling. A little more than 2 mi south, another dirt road leads to **Honolua Bay.** The coral formations on the right side of the bay are particularly dramatic. You'll find **Nāpili Bay,** one beach south of the Kapalua Resort, also quite good for snorkeling.

Almost the entire coastline from Kā'anapali south to Olowalu offers fine snorkeling. Favorite sites include the area just out from the cemetery north of Wahikuli State Park, near the lava cone called **Black Rock,** on which Kā'anapali's Sheraton Maui Hotel is built, and the shallow coral reef south of Olowalu General Store.

The coastline from Wailea to Mākena is also generally good for snorkeling. The best is found near the rocky fringes of Wailea's **Mōkapu, Ulua, Wailea,** and **Polo** beaches.

Between Polo Beach and Mākena Beach (turn right on Mākena Road just past Mākena Surf Condo) lies **Five Caves,** where you'll find a maze of underwater grottoes below offshore rocks. This spot is recommended for experienced snorkelers only, since the tides can get rough. At Mākena, the waters around the **Pu'u Ōla'i** cinder cone provide great snorkeling.

SURFING

Although on land it may not look as if there are seasons on Maui, the tides tell another story. In winter the surf is up on the northern shores of the Hawaiian Islands, and summer brings big swells to the southern side. Near-perfect winter waves on Maui can be found at **Honolua Bay,** on the northern tip of West Maui. To get there, continue 2 mi north of D. T. Fleming Park on Highway 30 and take a left onto the dirt road next to a pineapple field; a path takes you down the cliff to the beach.

Next best for surfing is **Ho'okipa Beach Park** (⊠ Off Hwy. 36, a short distance east of Pā'ia), where the modern-day sport began on Maui. This is the easiest place to watch surfing, because there are paved parking areas and picnic pavilions in the park. A word of warning: The surfers who come here are pros, and if you're not, they may not take kindly to your getting in their way.

Pushing the envelope of big-wave surfing has reached a new level here in the channel waters off Maui, where surfers get pulled out to sea and then whipped into the big waves. At Ho'okipa Beach Park, viewers with a good pair of binoculars might be able to see out past the windsurfers to view an example of tow-in surfing: Jet Ski pilots pull state-of-the-art big-wave surfers out to the 1-mi marker, where the waves can average 30 ft to 40 ft during winter swells. Amazing grace!

You can rent surfboards and boogie boards at many surf shops, such as **Second Wind** (⊠ 111 Hāna Hwy., Kahului, ☎ 808/877–7467), **Lightning Bolt Maui** (⊠ 55 Ka'ahumanu Ave., Kahului, ☎ 808/877–3484), and **Ole Surfboards** (⊠ 277 Wili Ko Pl., Lahaina, ☎ 808/661–3459).

WINDSURFING

It's been about 20 years since Ho'okipa Bay was discovered by board-sailors, who gave this windy beach 10 mi east of Kahului an international reputation. The spot is blessed with optimal wave-sailing wind and sea conditions and, for experienced windsurfers, can offer the ultimate experience. Other locations around Maui are good for windsurfing as well—Honolua Bay, for example—but Ho'okipa is absolutely unrivaled.

Even if you're a windsurfing aficionado, chances are good you didn't bring your equipment. You can rent it—or get lessons—from these shops: **Maui Ocean Activities** (⊠ Whalers Village, Kā'anapali, ☎ 808/667–1964), **Maui Windsurf Company** (⊠ 22 Hāna Hwy., Kahului, ☎ 808/877–4816), **Ocean Activities Center** (⊠ 1847 S. Kīhei Rd., Suite 203A, Kīhei, ☎ 808/879–4485), and **Maui Windsurfari** (⊠ 425 Koloa St., Kahului, ☎ 808/871–7766 or 800/736–6284). Lessons range from $30 to $60 and can last anywhere from one to three hours. Equipment rental also varies—from no charge with lessons to $20 an hour. For the latest prices and special deals, it's best to call around once you've arrived.

Spectator Sports

Golf

Maui has a number of golf tournaments, most of which are of professional caliber and worth watching. Many are also televised nationally. One of those attention-getters is the **Mercedes Championships** (☎ 808/669–2440), formerly called the Lincoln-Mercury Kapalua International, held now in January. This is the first official PGA tour event, held on Kapalua's Plantation Course. The Aloha Section of the Professional Golfers Association of America hosts the **GTE Hawaiian Tel Hall of Fame** (☎ 808/669–8877) championship at the Plantation

Course in May and a clambake feast on the beach tops off the **Kapalua Clambake Pro-Am** (☎ 808/669–8812) in July.

At Kā'anapali the **EMC Maui Kā'anapali Classic SENIOR PGA Golf Tournament** pits veteran professionals in a battle for a $1 million purse each October.

Over in Wailea, in June, on the longest day of the year, self-proclaimed "lunatic" golfers start out at first light to play 100 holes of golf in the annual **Ka Lima O Maui,** a fund-raiser for local charities. In January, 2001, the Wailea resort is adding the **Senior Skins** game, a nationally televised competition that pits four of the most respected Senior PGA players against one another.

Outrigger-Canoe Races

Polynesians first traveled to Hawai'i by outrigger canoe, and racing the traditional craft has always been a favorite pastime in the Islands. Canoes were revered in old Hawai'i, and no voyage could begin without a blessing, ceremonial chanting, and a hula performance to ensure a safe journey. At Whalers Village in May, the two-day launch festivities for the **Ho'omana'o Challenge Outrigger Sailing Canoe World Championship** (☎ 808/661–3271) also include a torch-lighting ceremony, arts-and-crafts demonstrations, and a chance to observe how the vessels are rigged—as well as the start of the race.

Polo

Polo is popular with Mauians. From April to June Haleakalā Ranch hosts "indoor" contests on a field flanked by side boards. The field is on Highway 377, 1 mi from Highway 37. During the "outdoor" polo season, mid-August to the end of October, matches are held at Olinda Field, 1 mi above Makawao on Olinda Road. There is a $3 admission charge for most games, which start at 1 PM on Sunday. The sport has two special events. One is the **Oskie Rice Memorial Tournament** on Memorial Day. The other—the **High Goal Benefit,** held on the last Sunday in October—draws challengers from Argentina, England, South Africa, New Zealand, and Australia. For information, contact Emiliano (☎ 808/572–4915).

Rodeos

With dozens of working cattle ranches throughout the Islands, many youngsters learn to ride a horse before they can drive a car. Mauians love their rodeos and put on several for students at local high schools throughout the year. Paniolos get in on the act, too, at three major annual events: the **Oskie Rice Memorial Rodeo,** usually staged the weekend after Labor Day; the **Cancer Benefit Rodeo** in April, held at an arena 3 mi east of Pā'ia; and Maui's biggest event, drawing competitors from all islands as well as the U.S. mainland, the **4th of July Rodeo,** which comes with a full-on parade and other festivities that last for days. Spectator admission fees to the competitions vary from free to $7. Cowboys are a tough bunch to tie down to a phone, but you can try calling the **Maui Roping Club** (☎ 808/572–2076) for information.

Surfing and Windsurfing

Not many places can lay claim to as many windsurfing tournaments as Maui. The Valley Isle is generally thought to be the world's preeminent windsurfing location and draws boardsailing experts from around the globe who want to compete on its waves. In March the **Hawaiian Pro Am Windsurfing** competition gets under way. In April the **Da Kine Hawaiian Pro Am** lures top windsurfers, and the **Aloha Classic World Wave Sailing Championships** takes place in October. All are held at Ho'okipa Bay, right outside the town of Pā'ia, near Kahului. For competitions featuring amateurs as well as professionals, check out the **Maui Race Series** (☎ 808/877–2111), six events held at Kanahā Beach in Kahului in summer when winds are the strongest and lack of big waves makes conditions excellent for the slalom (speed-racing) course. Competitors maneuver their boards close to shore, and the huge beach provides plenty of seating and viewing space. Hoʻokipa Bay's large waves are also prime territory for surfers. The **Local Motion Surfing** competition heats up the action in May, and in January the **Maui Rusty Pro,** held jointly at Honolua Bay, invites professionals to compete for a $40,000 purse.

Tennis
At the **Kapalua Jr. Vet/Sr. Tennis Championships** in May, where the minimum age is 30, players have been competing in singles and doubles events since 1979. On Labor Day, the **Wilson Kapalua Open Tennis Tournament,** Maui's grand prix of tennis, calls Hawaiʻi's hottest hitters to volley for a $12,000 purse at Kapalua's Tennis Garden and Village Tennis Center. Also at the Tennis Center, Women's International Tennis Association professionals rally with avid amateurs in a week of pro-am and pro-doubles competition during the **Kapalua Betsy Nagelsen Tennis Invitational** in December. All events are put on by the **Kapalua Tennis Club** (☎ 808/669–5677).

In East Maui, 2000 marks the 16th year for the Wailea Open Tennis Championship, held in July on the Plexipave courts at the **Wailea Tennis Club** (☎ 808/879–1958).

SHOPPING

Whether you head for one of the malls or opt for the boutiques hidden around the Valley Isle, one thing you should have no problem finding is clothing made in Hawaiʻi. The Hawaiian garment industry is now the state's third-largest economic sector, after tourism and agriculture.

Maui has an abundance of locally made art and crafts in a range of prices. A group that calls itself Made on Maui exists solely to promote the products of its members—items that range from pottery and paintings to Hawaiian teas and macadamia caramel corn. You can identify the group by its distinctive Haleakalā logo.

Business hours for individual shops on the island are usually 9–5, seven days a week. Shopping centers tend to stay open later (until 9 or 10 at least one night of the week).

Shopping Centers
Azeka Place Shopping Center (⊠ 1280 S. Kīhei Rd.). Kīhei offers this large and bustling place. Azeka I is the older half, on the makai side of the street. Azeka II, on the mauka side, has a **Long's Drugs** and several good lunch stops. Residents, however, favor the locally owned shops at the small Kamaʻole Shopping Center (⊠ 2463 S. Kīhei Rd.). Another place to rub elbows with Kīhei locals is Rainbow Mall (⊠ 2439 S. Kīhei Rd.).
Kaʻahumanu Center (⊠ 275 Kaʻahumanu Ave., Kahului, ☎ 808/877–3369). An expansion turned this into Maui's largest mall and a showplace with more than 75 stores and a gorgeous glass-enclosed atrium entrance topped by an umbrella-shaded food court. Stop at Camellia Seed Shop for what the locals call "crack seed," a delicacy made from dried fruits, nuts, and sugar. Other interesting stops here include Shirokiya, a popular Japanese retailer; Maui Hands, purveyor of prints, paintings, woodwork, and jewelry by some of the island's finest artists; and such mall standards as Foot Locker, Mrs. Field's Cookies, and Kinney Shoes.
Lahaina Cannery Mall (⊠ 1221 Honoapiʻilani Hwy., Lahaina, ☎ 808/661–5304). The 50 shops here are set in a building reminiscent of an old pineapple cannery. Unlike many other shopping centers in Hawaiʻi, the Lahaina Cannery isn't open-air, but it is air-conditioned. Recommended

stops include Hawaiian Island Gems, featuring striking Hawaiian heirloom jewelry and pearls; Superwhale, with a good selection of children's tropical wear; and Kite Fantasy, one of the best kite shops on Maui.

Lahaina Center (⊠ 900 Front St., Lahaina, ☎ 808/667–9216). Island department store Hilo Hattie anchors the center and puts on a free hula show at 2 PM every Wednesday and Friday. An additional 10,000 square ft of parking lot space here have been transformed into an ancient Hawaiian village complete with three full-size thatch huts built with 10,000 linear ft of 'ōhi'a wood from the Big Island, 20 tons of *pili* grass, and more than 4 mi of handwoven coconut *senit* (twine). Indoor entertainment is found at a four-screen cinema. The roster of shops and restaurants include World Cafe and the Hard Rock Cafe for eats and Banana Republic and Waterwear for clothing.

Maui Mall (⊠ 70 Ka'ahumanu Ave., Kahului, ☎ 808/877–7559). Perhaps spurred by new competition from Ka'ahumanu Center, this place has given itself a face-lift and added a whimsically designed 12-screen megaplex, and these improvements have started attracting new tenants. The anchor stores are still Long's Drugs and Star Market, and they've kept a good Japanese diner named Restaurant Matsu (☞ Central Maui *in* Dining, *above*). The Tasaka Guri Guri Shop is an oddity. It's been around a hundred years, selling an ice cream–like confection called "guri guri" that you will find nowhere else in the world.

Maui Marketplace (⊠ 270 Dairy Rd., Kahului, ☎ 808/873–0400). At this 20-acre complex several outlet stores and big retailers, such as Eagle Hardware, Sports Authority, and Borders Books & Music, have made their first expansion to a Neighbor Island. The center couldn't have a more convenient location. It's at the busy intersection of Hāna Highway and Dairy Road, close to Kahului Airport.

The Shops at Wailea (⊠ Between the Aston Wailea Resort and the Grand Wailea). The Wailea resort has taken a couple of years to completely re-create its shopping. The place has an old-world piazza design that covers 150,000 sq ft and includes a central stage for shows. Tenants include Louis Vuitton, Tiffany & Co., several art galleries, and a new Longhi's restaurant.

Whalers Village (⊠ 2435 Kā'anapali Pkwy., Kā'anapali, ☎ 808/661–4567). Chic and trendy, Whalers Village has grown into a major West Maui shopping center, with a whaling museum and more than 50 restaurants and shops. Upscale haunts include Louis Vuitton, Prada, Ferragamo, Hunting World, and Chanel Boutique. The complex also offers some interesting diversions: Hawaiian artisans display their crafts daily, hula dancers perform on an outdoor stage weeknights from 7 to 8, and a free slide show spotlighting whales and other marine life takes place at the Whale Center of the Pacific on Tuesday and Thursday at 7.

Grocery Stores

If you need groceries to take back to your condo, the following are conveniently located and offer good selections and extended hours.

Foodland (⊠ 1881 S. Kīhei Rd., Kīhei, ☎ 808/879–9350). In Kīhei town center, this is the most convenient supermarket for visitors staying in Wailea. It's open around the clock.

Lahaina Square Shopping Center Foodland (⊠ 840 Waine'e St., Lahaina, ☎ 808/661–0975). This Foodland serves West Maui and is open daily from 6 AM to midnight.

Safeway (⊠ Lahaina Cannery Mall, Honoapi'ilani Hwy., Lahaina, ☎ 808/667–4392; ⊠ 170 E. Kamehameha Ave., Kahului, ☎ 808/877–3377). Safeway has two stores on the island open 24 hours daily. The one in Lahaina serves West Maui, and the one in Kahului provides a convenient stop for visitors shopping at Ka'ahumanu Center or touring the historic sites of Central Maui before returning to Wailea lodgings.

Specialty Stores

Art

Maui has more art per square mile than any other Hawaiian island— maybe more than any other U.S. county. There are artists' guilds and co-ops and galleries galore all over the island. Art shows are held throughout the year at the Maui Arts & Cultural Center. Marine sculptors and painters showcase their work during **Celebration of Whales** at the Four Seasons Resort Wailea in January. The Lahaina Arts Society presents **Art in the Park** under the town's historic banyan tree every Friday and Saturday from 9 to 5. Moreover, the town of Lahaina hosts **Art Night** every Friday from 7 to 10. Galleries open their doors (some serve refreshments) and musicians stroll the streets.

Hot Island Glassblowing Studio & Gallery (⊠ 3620 Baldwin Ave., Makawao, ☎ 808/572–4527). This is an exciting place to visit, with the glass-melting furnaces glowing bright orange and the shop loaded with mesmerizing sculptures and functional pieces. Set back from Makawao's main street in " The Courtyard," the working studio is owned by a family of award-winning glassblowers.

Hui No'eau Visual Arts Center (⊠ 2841 Baldwin Ave., Makawao, ☎ 808/572–6560). The center presents juried and nonjuried exhibits by local artists.

Lahaina Galleries (⊠ 728 Front St., Lahaina, ☎ 808/667–2152; ⊠ Kapalua Resort, ☎ 808/669–0202). The gallery has two locations in West Maui offering a mixed collection of the works of both national and international artists.

Martin Lawrence Galleries (⊠ Lahaina Market Place, Front St. and Lahainaluna Rd., Lahaina, ☎ 808/661–1788). Martin Lawrence represents noted mainland artists, including Andy Warhol and Keith Haring, in a bright and friendly gallery open since 1991.

Maui Crafts Guild (⊠ 43 Hāna Hwy., Pā'ia, ☎ 808/579–9697). This is one of the most interesting galleries on Maui. Set in a two-story wooden building alongside the highway, the Guild is crammed with work by local artists. The best pieces are the pottery and sculpture. Upstairs antique kimonos, hand-painted silks, and batik fabric are on display.

Maui Hands (⊠ 3620 Baldwin Ave., Makawao, ☎ 808/572–5194; ⊠ Ka'ahumanu Center, Kahului, ☎ 808/877–0368). This gallery shows work by dozens of local artists, including paniolo-theme lithographs by Sharon Shigekawa, who knows whereof she paints: She rides each year in the Kaupō Roundup. The shop is in the town's old theater.

Viewpoints (⊠ 3620 Baldwin Ave., Makawao, ☎ 808/572–5979). Viewpoints calls itself Maui's only fine-arts collective; it is a cooperative venture of about two dozen Maui painters and sculptors, representing a wide variety of styles.

Village Gallery (⊠ 120 Dickenson St., Lahaina, ☎ 808/661–4402; ⊠ Ritz-Carlton, 1 Ritz-Carlton Dr., Kapalua, ☎ 808/669–1800). This gallery, with two locations on the island, features such popular local artists as Betty Hay Freeland, Wailehua Gray, Margaret Bedell, George Allen, Joyce Clark, Pamela Andelin, Stephen Burr, and Macario Pascual.

Clothing

ISLAND WEAR

Hilo Hattie (⊠ Lahaina Center, Lahaina, ☎ 808/661–8457). Hawai'i's largest manufacturer of aloha shirts and mu'umu'u. They also carry brightly colored blouses, skirts, and children's clothing.

Liberty House. Liberty House has the kind of island wear—colorful shirts and mu'umu'u as well as other graceful styles—worn by people who live year-round on Maui. The store has several branches on the island, including shops at the Hyatt Regency and at the Four Seasons Wailea, but the largest is the one at Ka'ahumanu Center in Kahului (☎ 808/877–3361).

Reyn's (⊠ Kapalua Bay Hotel, Kapalua, ☎ 808/669–5260; ⊠ Hyatt Regency Maui, Kā'anapali, ☎ 808/661–0215; ⊠ Whalers Village, Kā'anapali, ☎ 808/661–9032). This is the place to go for high-quality aloha shirts in the subtler shades that local men favor for business attire.

RESORT WEAR

Not all of Maui's casual clothing is floral. You can find island-worthy sportswear in shops all over the Valley Isle, including most of the stores that sell island wear, as well as these:

Honolua Surf Company (⊠ 845 Front St., Lahaina, ☎ 808/661–8848; ⊠ Whalers Village, Kā'anapali, ☎ 808/661–5455; ⊠ Lahaina Cannery Mall, Lahaina, ☎ 808/661–5777; ⊠ 2411 S. Kīhei Rd., Kīhei, ☎ 808/874–0999). This chain is popular with young women for casual clothing and sportswear.

SGT Leisure (⊠ 855B Front St., Lahaina, ☎ 808/667–0661; ⊠ Whalers Village, Kā'anapali, ☎ 808/667–9433). These shops carry resort wear by Tori Richards and other designers. Primarily, though, they sell their own line of informal apparel—sweatshirts, T-shirts, and accessories such as beach bags and hats—bearing their big fish logo.

Tropical Tantrum Outlet Store (⊠ Azeka Place Shopping Center, Kīhei, ☎ 808/874–3835; ⊠ Ka'ahumanu Center, Kahului, ☎ 808/871–8088; ⊠ Kama'ole Shopping Center, Kīhei, ☎ 808/875–4433). This well-known outfitter has three retail stores on Maui, but here at the outlets you'll find a wide selection of stylish resort wear, aloha shirts, and mu'umu'u for 50% less than at the company's retail stores.

Flea Market

Maui Swap Meet. This Saturday flea market is the biggest bargain on Maui, with crafts, gifts, souvenirs, fruit, flowers, jewelry, antiques, art, shells, and lots more. ⊠ *Hwy. 350, off S. Pu'unēnē Ave., Kahului.* ☎ *50¢.* ⊗ *Sat. 5:30–noon.*

Food

Many visitors to Hawai'i opt to take home some of the local produce: pineapples, papayas, coconut, or Maui onions. You can find jams and jellies—some of them "Made on Maui" products—in a wide variety of tropical flavors. Cook Kwee's Maui Cookies have gained quite a following, as have Maui Potato Chips. Both are available in most Valley Isle grocery stores. Coffee sellers now have Maui-grown and -roasted beans alongside the better-known Kona varieties.

Remember that fresh fruit must be inspected by the U.S. Department of Agriculture before it can leave the state, so it's safer to buy a box that has already passed muster.

Airport Flower & Fruit Co. (☎ 808/243–9367 or 800/922–9352). Ready-to-ship pineapples, Maui onions, papayas, and fresh coconuts are available by phone.

Take Home Maui (⊠ 121 Dickenson St., Lahaina, ☎ 808/661–8067 or 800/545–6284). These folks will supply, pack, and deliver produce free to the airport or your hotel.

Gifts

Lahaina Printsellers Ltd. (⊠ Lahaina Cannery Mall, 1221 Honoapi'ilani Hwy., Lahaina, ☎ 808/667–7843). Hawai'i's largest selection of original antique maps and prints pertaining to Hawai'i and the Pacific are available here. They also sell museum-quality reproductions and original oil paintings from the Pacific Artists Guild. Two smaller shops are also at Whalers Village in Kā'anapali and at the Grand Wailea Resort in Wailea.

Maui's Best (✉ Ka'ahumanu Center, Kahului, ☎ 808/877–7959; ✉ Azeka Place Shopping Center, Kīhei, ☎ 808/874–9216). This a good stop for a wide selection of gifts from Maui and around the world.
Ola's Makawao (✉ 1156 Makawao Ave., Makawao, ☎ 808/573–1334). Ola's has a delightful assortment of whimsical gifts and affordable, functional contemporary art made by artists from Hawai'i and the U.S. mainland. It is also the exclusive western-U.S. distributor for chocolates by JoMart Candies.

Hawaiian Crafts

The arts and crafts native to Hawai'i are first on the list for many visiting shoppers. Such woods as koa and milo grow only in certain parts of the world, and because of their increasing scarcity, prices are rising. Artisans turn the woods into bowls, trays, and jewelry boxes that will last for years. Look for them in galleries and museum shops.

Hāna Cultural Center (✉ Ukea St., Hāna, ☎ 808/248–8622). The culture center sells distinctive island quilts and other Hawaiian crafts.
Kīhei Kalama Village Marketplace (✉ 1941 S. Kīhei Rd., Kīhei, ☎ 808/879–6610). This is a fun place to investigate. A shaded collection of outdoor stalls sells everything from printed and hand-painted T-shirts and sundresses to jewelry, pottery, wood carvings, fruit, and gaudily painted coconut husks—all made by local craftspeople.
Quilters Corner (✉ 1000 Limahana Pl., Lahaina, ☎ 808/661–0944). Here you'll find a huge selection of Hawaiian quilts and needlepoint, as well as plenty of tropical-print fabrics, silver jewelry, and other local crafts and gift items.

Jewelry

Haimoff & Haimoff Creations in Gold (✉ Kapalua Resort, ☎ 808/669–5213). This shop features the original work of several jewelry designers, including the award-winning Harry Haimoff.
Jessica's Gems (✉ Whalers Village, Kā'anapali, ☎ 808/661–4223; ✉ 858 Front St., Lahaina, ☎ 808/661–9200). Jessica's has a good selection of Hawaiian heirloom jewelry, and its Lahaina store specializes in black pearls.
Lahaina Scrimshaw (✉ 845A Front St., Lahaina, ☎ 808/661–8820; ✉ Whalers Village, Kā'anapali, ☎ 808/661–4034). Here you can buy brooches, rings, pendants, cuff links, tie tacks, and collector's items adorned with this intricately carved sailors' art.
Master Touch Gallery (✉ 3655 Baldwin Ave., Makawao, ☎ 808/572–6000). The exterior of this shop is as rustic as all the old buildings of Makawao, so there's no way to prepare yourself for the elegance and sensuousness of the handcrafted jewelry displayed within. Owner David Sacco truly has the "master touch."
Maui Divers (✉ 640 Front St., Lahaina, ☎ 808/661–0988). This company has been crafting gold and coral into jewelry for more than 20 years.

MAUI A TO Z

Arriving and Departing

By Plane

Kahului Airport (☎ 808/872–3800 or 808/872–3830) is efficient and remarkably easy to navigate. Its main disadvantage is its distance from the major resort destinations in West Maui. It will take you about an hour, with traffic in your favor, to get to a hotel in Kapalua or Kā'anapali but only 20 to 30 minutes to go to Kīhei or Wailea. However, Kahului is the only airport on Maui that has direct service from the mainland.

If you're staying in West Maui, you might be better off flying into the **Kapalua–West Maui Airport** (☎ 808/669–0623). The only way to get to the Kapalua–West Maui Airport is on an interisland flight from Honolulu since the short runway accommodates only small planes. The little airport is set in the midst of a pineapple field with a terrific view of the ocean far below and provides one of the most pleasant ways to arrive on the Valley Isle. Three rental-car companies have courtesy phones inside the terminal. Shuttles also run between the airport and the Kā'anapali and Kapalua resorts.

Hāna Airport (☎ 808/248–8208) isn't much more than a landing strip. Only commuter Aloha Island Air flies here, landing twice a day from Honolulu (via Moloka'i and Kahului) and departing 10 minutes later. The morning flight originates in Princeville, Kaua'i. When there is no flight, the tiny terminal usually stands eerily empty, with no gate agents, ticket takers, or other people in sight. If you are staying at the Hotel Hāna-Maui, your flight will be met. If you have reserved a rental car, the agent will usually know your arrival time and meet you. Otherwise you can call Dollar Rent A Car (☎ 808/248–8237) to pick you up.

FLIGHTS FROM THE MAINLAND UNITED STATES

United (☎ 800/241–6522) flies nonstop to Kahului from Los Angeles and San Francisco. **American** (☎ 800/433–7300) also flies into Kahului, with one stop in Honolulu, from Dallas and Chicago and nonstop from Los Angeles. **Delta** (☎ 800/221–1212) has through service to Maui daily from Salt Lake City, Atlanta, and Los Angeles and one nonstop daily from Los Angeles. **Hawaiian Airlines** (☎ 800/882–8811) has direct flights to Kahului from the U.S. West Coast.

Flight time from the West Coast to Maui is about 5 hours; from the Midwest, expect about an 8-hour flight; and coming from the East Coast will take about 10 hours, not including layovers.

FLIGHTS FROM HONOLULU

Continental (☎ 800/525–0280), **Hawaiian** (☎ 800/882–8811), **Northwest** (☎ 800/225–2525), and **TWA** (☎ 800/221–2000) fly from the mainland to Honolulu, where Maui-bound passengers can connect with a 40-minute interisland flight. Maui is the most visited of the Neighbor Islands and therefore the easiest to connect to on an interisland flight. Honolulu–Kahului is one of the most heavily traveled air routes in the nation. Flights generally run about $50 one-way between Honolulu and Maui and are available from **Hawaiian Airlines** (☎ 808/871–6132 or 800/367–5320), **Aloha Airlines** (☎ 808/244–9071; 800/367–5250 from the U.S. mainland), and **Island Air** (☎ 800/652–6541).

BETWEEN THE AIRPORT AND HOTELS

By Car. The best way to get from the airport to your destination—and to see the island itself—is in your own rental car. Most major car-rental companies have desks or courtesy phones at each airport (☞ Car Rentals *in* Contacts and Resources, *below*). They also can provide a map and directions to your hotel from the airport.

By Shuttle. If you're staying at the Kā'anapali Beach Resort and fly into the Kapalua–West Maui Airport, you can take advantage of the resort's free shuttle and go back to the airport later to pick up your car. During daylight hours, the shuttle passes through the airport at regular intervals.

The **Trans Hawaiian Airporter Shuttle** (☎ 808/877–7308) runs between Kahului Airport and the West Maui hotels daily 8–4. One-way fare for adults is $13. You should call 24 hours prior to departure.

By Taxi. Maui has more than two dozen taxi companies, and they make frequent passes through the airport. If you don't see a cab, you can call **Yellow Cab of Maui** (☎ 808/877–7000) or **La Bella Taxi** (☎ 808/242–8011) for islandwide service from the airport. Call **Kīhei Taxi** (☎ 808/879–3000) if you're staying in the Kīhei, Wailea, or Mākena areas. Charges from Kahului Airport to Kāʻanapali run about $49; to Wailea, about $31; and to Lahaina, about $42.

By Ship

Approaching the Valley Isle on the deck of a ship is an unforgettable experience. Watching the land loom ever larger conjures up the same kinds of feelings the early Polynesians probably had on their first voyage—except they didn't get the kind of lavish treatment those on board a luxury cruise ship routinely receive. You can book passage through **American Hawaiʻi Cruises** (✉ 2 North Riverside Plaza, Chicago, IL 60606, ☎ 312/466–6000 or 800/765–7000), which offers seven-day interisland cruises departing from Honolulu on the S.S. *Constitution* and the S.S. *Independence*. Or ask about the company's seven-day cruise-resort combination packages.

Getting Around

By Bus

Although Maui has no public transit system, a private company, **Trans-Hawaiian Services** (☎ 808/877–7308), transports visitors around the West Maui and South Maui areas. One-way, round-trip, and all-day passes are available.

By Car

Maui has some 120 mi of coastline, not all of which is accessible. Less than one-quarter of its land mass is inhabited. To see the island, your best bet is a car (☞ Car Rentals *in* Contacts and Resources, *below*). Most of the roads on the island have two lanes. If you're going to attempt the partially paved, patched, and bumpy road between Hāna and ʻUlupalakua, you'll be better off with a four-wheel-drive vehicle, but be forewarned: Rental-car companies prohibit travel on roads they've determined might damage the car, so if you break down, you're on your own for repairs. There are two other difficult roads on Maui: One is Highway 36, or the Hāna Highway, which runs 56 mi between Kahului and Hāna and includes more twists and turns than a person can count. The other is an 8-mi scenic stretch of one-lane highway between Kapalua and Wailuku on the north side of the West Maui mountains.

ROAD SERVICE

For emergency road service, **AAA** members may call ☎ 800/222–4357. A Honolulu-based dispatcher will send a tow truck, but you will need to tell the driver where to take your car. Don't forget to carry your membership card with you.

By Limousine

Arthur's Limousine Service (✉ 283H Lalo St., Kahului 96732, ☎ 808/871–5555 or 800/345–4667) offers a chauffeured superstretch Lincoln complete with bar and two TVs for $88 per hour. Arthur's fleet also includes less grandiose Lincoln Town Cars for $65 per hour with a two-hour minimum. If you want to stretch out with a company on the South Shore, call **Wailea Limousine Service** (☎ 808/875–4114). Despite the name, this company also provides limousines to the Lahaina area (☎ 808/661–4114).

By Moped

You can rent mopeds on the West Side at **Wheels R Us** (✉ 741 Waineʻe St., Lahaina, ☎ 808/667–7751) for $36 a day. On the South Shore, try **Wheels USA** at Rainbow Mall (✉ 2439 S. Kīhei Rd., Kīhei, ☎ 808/875–1221). Rates are $25 for four hours or $31 until 4:30. Be especially careful navigating roads where there are no designated bicycle lanes. Note that helmets are optional on Maui, but eye protection is not.

By Shuttle

If you're staying in the right hotel or condo, there are a few shuttles that can get you around the area. The double-decker **West Maui Shopping Express** ferries passengers to and from Kāʻanapali, Kapalua, Honokōwai, and Lahaina from 8 AM to 10 PM. The fare is $1 per person each way, and schedules are available at most hotels.

The **Kāʻanapali Trolley Shuttle** runs within the resort between 9 AM and 11 PM and stops automatically at all hotels and at condos when requested. It's free. All Kāʻanapali hotels have copies of schedules, or you can call the Kāʻanapali Operation Association (☎ 808/661–7370).

The **Wailea Shuttle** and the **Kapalua Shuttle** run within their respective resorts and are free. Schedules are available throughout each resort.

By Taxi

For short hops between hotels and restaurants, this can be a convenient way to go, but you'll have to call ahead. Even busy West Maui doesn't have curbside taxi service. **West Maui Taxi** (✉ 761 Kumukahi St., Lahaina, ☎ 808/667–2605) and **Yellow Cab of Maui** (✉ Kahului Airport, ☎ 808/877–7000) service the entire island, but you'd be smart to consider using them just for the areas where they're located. **Aliʻi Cab** (✉ 75 Kūʻai Pl., Lahaina, ☎ 808/661–3688) specializes in West Maui, and **Kīhei Taxi** (✉ Kīhei, ☎ 808/879–3000) serves Central Maui.

Contacts and Resources

Bed-and-Breakfast Reservation Services

The Maui Visitors Bureau refers callers to **Bed & Breakfast Hawaiʻi** (☎ 808/733–1632). **Bed and Breakfast Honolulu** (☎ 808/595–7533 or 800/288–4666) has statewide listings, with about 50 B&Bs on Maui. **Bed & Breakfast Maui-Style** (☎ 808/879–7865, FAX 808/874–0831) has listings for about 50 B&Bs on Maui. **Island Bed & Breakfast** (☎ 808/822–7771 or 800/733–1632), headquartered on Kauaʻi, has listings throughout the state and handles about 35 B&Bs on Maui. A directory is available for $12.95.

Car Rentals

During peak seasons—summer and Christmas through Easter—be sure to reserve your car well ahead of time if you haven't booked a room-car package with your hotel. Expect to pay about $35 a day—before taxes, insurance, and extras—for a compact car from one of the major companies. You can get a less-expensive deal from one of the locally owned budget companies. You'll probably have to call for a shuttle from the airport, since few of these companies have rental desks there. There is a $2 daily road tax on all rental cars in Hawaiʻi.

Budget (☎ 800/527–0700; 800/268–8900 in Canada), **Dollar** (☎ 800/800–4000), and **National** (☎ 800/227–7368) have courtesy phones at the Kapalua–West Maui Airport; **Hertz** (☎ 800/654–3131; 800/263–0600 in Canada) and **Alamo** (☎ 800/327–9633) are nearby. All of the above, plus **Avis** (☎ 800/331–1212; 800/879–2847 in Canada), have desks at or near Maui's major airport in Kahului. **Roberts Tours** (☎ 808/523–9323) offers car rentals through package tours. Quite a few locally owned companies rent cars on Maui, including **Rent-A-Jeep** (☎ 808/877–6626), which will pick you up at Kahului Airport.

Doctors

Doctors on Call (✉ Hyatt Regency Maui, Nāpili Tower, Suite 100, Kāʻanapali, ☎ 808/667–7676) serves West Maui.

A walk-in clinic at Whalers Village, **West Maui Health Care Center** was created by two doctors in 1980 to treat visitors to West Maui. ⊠ *2435 Kāʻanapali Pkwy., Suite H-7, Kāʻanapali,* ☎ *808/667–9721.* ☉ *Daily 8 AM–10 PM.*

Kīhei Clinic Medical Services (⊠ 2349 S. Kīhei Rd., Suite D, Kīhei, ☎ 808/879–1440) is in the central part of the Valley Isle and geared toward working with visitors in Kīhei and Wailea.

HOSPITALS

Hāna Medical Center (⊠ Hāna Hwy., Hāna, ☎ 808/248–8294). **Kula Hospital** (⊠ 204 Kula Hwy., Kula, ☎ 808/878–1221). **Maui Memorial Hospital** (⊠ 221 Mahalani, Wailuku, ☎ 808/244–9056).

Emergencies

Police, fire, or ambulance, ☎ 911. **Coast Guard Rescue Center,** ☎ 800/552–6458.

Guided Tours

AERIAL TOURS

Helicopter flight-seeing excursions can take you over the West Maui mountains, Hāna, and Haleakalā. This is a beautiful, exciting way to see the island, and the *only* way to see some of its most dramatic areas. Tour prices usually include a videotape of your trip so you can relive the experience at home. Prices run from about $100 for a half-hour rain-forest tour to $250 for a two-hour mega-experience that includes a champagne toast on landing.

It takes about 90 minutes to travel inside the volcano, then down to the village of Hāna. Some companies stop in secluded areas for refreshments. Helicopter-tour operators throughout the state come under sharp scrutiny for passenger safety and equipment maintenance. Noise levels are a concern as well; residents have become pretty vocal about regulating this kind of pollution. Don't be afraid to ask about a company's safety record, flight paths, age of equipment, and level of operator experience.

Blue Hawaiian Helicopters (⊠ Kahului Heliport, Hangar 105, Kahului 96732, ☎ 808/871–8844). This company has provided aerial adventures in Hawaiʻi since 1985, and it has the best service and safety record. Its ASTAR helicopters are air-conditioned and have noise-canceling headsets for all passengers. Highly recommended.
Hawaiʻi Helicopters (⊠ Kahului Heliport, Hangar 106, Kahului 96732, ☎ 808/877–3900, 800/994–9099, or 800/367–7095). Hawaiʻi Helicopters flies fast, twin-engine jet helicopters.
Sunshine Helicopters (⊠ Kahului Heliport, Hangar 107, Kahului 96732, ☎ 808/871–0722 or 800/544–2520). Sunshine offers a Molokaʻi flight in its "Black Beauty" aircraft.

GROUND TOURS

This is a big island to see in one day, so tour companies combine various sections—either Haleakalā, ʻIao Needle, and Central Maui, or West Maui and its environs—in various tour packages. Contact companies for a brochure of their current offerings. Very often your hotel has a tour desk to facilitate arrangements.

A tour of **Haleakalā** and **Upcountry** is usually a half-day excursion, and is offered in several versions by different companies for about $50 and up. The trip often includes stops at a protea farm and at Tedeschi Vineyards and Winery, the only place in Hawaiʻi where wine is made. A Haleakalā sunrise tour starts before dawn so that visitors get to the top of the dormant volcano before the sun peeks over the horizon. Some companies throw in champagne to greet the sunrise.

A tour of **Hāna** is almost always done in a van, since the winding road to Hāna just doesn't provide a comfortable ride in bigger buses. Of late, Hāna has so many of these one-day tours that it seems as if there are more vans than cars on the road. Still, to many it's a more relaxing way to do the drive than behind the wheel of a car. Guides decide where you stop for photos. Tour costs run $70–$120.

Ground tour companies are usually statewide and have a whole fleet of vehicles. Some use air-conditioned buses, whileothers prefer smaller vans. Then you've got your minivans, your microbuses, and your mini-coaches. The key is how many passengers each will hold. Be sure to ask how many stops you'll get on your tour, or you may be disappointed to find that all your sightseeing is done through a window.

Most of the tour guides have been in the business for years. Some were born in the Islands and have taken special classes to learn more about their culture and lore. They expect a tip ($1 per person at least), but they're just as cordial without one.

Polynesian Adventure Tours (⊠ 400 Hāna Hwy., Kahului 96732, ☎ 808/877–4242 or 800/622–3011). This company uses large buses with floor-to-ceiling windows. The drivers are fun characters who really know the island.

Roberts Hawai'i Tours (⊠ Box 247, Kahului 96732, ☎ 808/871–6226 or 800/767–7551). This is one of the state's largest tour companies, and its staff can arrange tours with bilingual guides if asked ahead of time.

Trans Hawaiian Services (⊠ 720 Iwilei Rd., Suite 101, Honolulu 96817, ☎ 800/533–8765). Despite its size, this tour operator manages to keep its tours personal.

HIKING TOURS

Hike Maui (⊠ Box 330969, Kahului 96733, ☎ 808/879–5270, ℻ 808/893–2515, ✎). This is the oldest hiking company in the Islands, and its rain-forest, mountain-ridge, crater, coastline, and archaeological-snorkel hikes are led by such knowledgeable folk as ethnobotanists and marine biologists. Prices range from $75 to $125 for hikes of five to 10 hours, including lunch. Hike Maui supplies waterproof day packs, rain ponchos, first-aid gear, and water bottles.

HORSEBACK TOURS

Several companies on Maui offer horseback riding that's far more appealing than the typical hour-long trudge over a boring trail with 50 other horses.

Adventures on Horseback. Frank Levinson started this company in the '80s with five-hour outings into secluded parts of Maui. The tours traverse ocean cliffs on Maui's north shore, follow the slopes of Haleakalā, and pass along streams, through rain forests, and near waterfalls, where riders can stop for a dip in a freshwater pool. ⊠ *Box 1771, Makawao 96768,* ☎ *808/242–7445.* ✎ *$175 including breakfast, lunch, and refreshments.*

Charley's Trail Rides & Pack Trips. These trips require a stout physical nature—but not a stout physique: Riders must weigh under 200 pounds. Charley's overnighters go from Kaupō—a *tiny* village nearly 20 mi past Hāna—up the slopes of Haleakalā to the crater. ⊠ *c/o Kaupō Ranch, Kaupō 96713,* ☎ *808/248–8209.* ✎ *$40–$160.*

Pony Express Tours. Pony Express will take you on horseback into Haleakalā Crater. The half-day ride goes down to the crater floor for a picnic lunch. The full-day excursion covers 12 mi of terrain and visits some of the crater's weird formations. You don't need to be an experienced rider, but the longer ride can be tough if you're unathletic. The company also offers one- and two-hour rides on Haleakalā Ranch. ✉ *Box 535, Kulā 96790,* ☎ *808/667–2200 or 808/878–6698.* 🎫 *$40–$160.*

Rent-a-Local. This is *the* best way to see Maui—through the eyes of the locals. Started by Laurie Robello, who is part Hawaiian, the company now has excellent guides who will drive your car on a tour tailored to your interests. ✉ *333 Dairy Rd., #102, Kahului 96732,* ☎ *808/877–4042 or 800/228–6284.* 🎫 *$199 for 2 people, $25 for each additional person.*

Temptation Tours. Company president Dave Campbell has targeted members of the affluent older crowd (though almost anyone would enjoy these tours) who don't want to be herded onto a crowded bus. He provides exclusive tours in his plush six-passenger limovan and specializes in full-day tours to Haleakalā and Hāna. Dave's "Ultimate" Hāna tour includes lunch at Hotel Hāna-Maui. ✉ *211 'Āhinahina Pl., Kula 96790,* ☎ *808/877–8888.* 🎫 *$110–$249.*

Once you have your bearings, you may want a tour that's a bit more specialized. For example, you might want to bike down a volcano, ride a mule, or immerse yourself in art. Here are some options:

Art Tours. A free guided tour of the **Hyatt Regency Maui's art collection and gardens** (✉ 200 Nokea Kai Dr., Kā'anapali, ☎ 808/661–1234) starts at 11 on Monday, Wednesday, and Friday. It takes you through the Hyatt's public spaces, adorned with a constantly changing multimillion-dollar collection of Asian and Pacific art. Among the treasures to be found are Chinese cloisonné; Japanese dragon pots; Thai elephant bells; Hawaiian quilts; battle shields and masks from Papua, New Guinea; and such contemporary work as *The Acrobats,* a bronze sculpture by Australian artist John Robinson. If you're not fond of group tours, just pick up a copy of the hotel's "Art Guide" for a fascinating do-it-yourself experience. Exploring the spectacular $30 million art collection housed on the grounds of the **Grand Wailea** (✉ 3850 Wailea Alanui Dr., Wailea, ☎ 808/875–1234) is like entering an international art museum. Sculptures, artifacts, stained-glass windows, a 200,000-piece ceramic tile mosaic, paintings, and assorted works by Fernand Léger, Andy Warhol, Picasso, Fernando Botero, and noted Hawaiian artists make this excursion a must for art lovers. The tour leaves from the resort's Napua Art Gallery at 10 every Tuesday and Friday and is free for guests of the resort. Nonguests pay $6.

Crater Bound Tours. Groups assemble at a Haleakalā ranger station at 7:30, then walk 4–10 mi to where Craig Moore (☎ 808/878–1743) and his crew have unpacked the horses, set up the campsite, and organized a social hour. A second day is spent exploring the crater. The third day is a hike back out of the crater. Gourmet breakfasts and dinners are served. A basic three-day, two-night package is $500 per person, or talk to Moore about special arrangements and interests, including shorter treks, hikes, van tours, and his Haleakalā crater mule rides.

Maui Downhill. After instruction in safety fundamentals, you don a helmet, get on a bicycle atop Haleakalā volcano, and coast down. Lunch or breakfast is included, depending on what time you start. ✉ *199 Dairy Rd., Kahului 96732,* ☎ *808/871–2155 or 800/535–2453.* 🎫 *$95–$115.*

Maui Mountain Cruisers. This is another company that will put you on a bicycle at the top of Haleakalā and let you coast down. Safety precautions are a top priority, so riders wear helmets. Meals are provided. ☎ *808/871–6014.* 🎫 *$86–$99, van riders $55.*

Maui Pineapple Plantation Tour. This plantation tour takes you right into the fields in a company van. The 2½-hour trip gives you firsthand experience of the operation and its history, some incredible views of the island, and the chance to pick a fresh pineapple for yourself. Tours go out morning and afternoon, weekdays, from the Kapalua Logo Shop. ⊠ *Kapalua Resort Activity Desk,* ☎ *808/669–8088.* ⊡ *$26.*

WALKING TOURS

The **Lahaina Restoration Foundation** (⊠ Baldwin Home, 696 Front St., Lahaina, ☎ 808/661–3262) has published a walking-tour map for interested visitors. The map will guide you to the most historic sites of Lahaina, some renovated and some not. Highlights of the walk include the Jodo Mission, the Brig *Carthaginian II,* the Baldwin Home, and the Old Court House. These are all sights you could find yourself, but the map is free and full of historical tidbits, and it makes the walk easier.

Rental Agents

Besides the condos listed in Lodging (☞ *above*), which operate like hotels and offer hotel-like amenities, Maui has condos you can rent through central booking agents. Most agents represent more than one condo complex (some handle single-family homes as well), so be specific about what kind of price, space, facilities, and amenities you want. The following are multiproperty agents.

Ameri Resort Management, Inc. (⊠ 5500 Honoapi'ilani Rd., Kapalua 96761, ☎ 808/669–5635 or 800/786–7387). **Aston Hotels & Resorts** (⊠ 2255 Kūhiō Ave., 18th fl., Honolulu 96815, ☎ 800/342–1551). **Destination Resorts** (⊠ 3750 Wailea Alanui Dr., Wailea 96753, ☎ 800/367–5246). **Hawaiian Apartment Leasing Enterprises** (⊠ 479 Ocean Ave., Laguna Beach, CA 92651, ☎ 714/497–4253 or 800/854–8843). **Hawaiian Resorts, Inc.** (⊠ 1270 Ala Moana Blvd., Honolulu 96814, ☎ 800/367–7040; 800/877–7331 in Canada). **Hawai'i Condo Exchange** (⊠ 1817 El Cerrito Pl., Los Angeles 90068, ☎ 800/442–0404). **Kīhei Maui Vacations** (⊠ Box 1055, Kīhei 96753, ☎ 800/542–6284). **Marc Resorts Hawai'i** (⊠ 2155 Kalakaua Ave., Suite 706, Honolulu 96815, ☎ 800/535–0085). **Maui Windsurfari** (⊠ 425 Koloa St., Kahului 96732, ☎ 808/871–7766 or 800/736–6284). **Vacation Locations Hawai'i** (⊠ Box 1689, Kīhei, Maui 96753, ☎ 808/874–0077 or 800/522–2757).

Visitor Information

Maui Visitors Bureau (⊠ 1727 Wili Pā Loop, Wailuku 96793, ☎ 808/244–3530, ℻ 808/244–1337, ✎). **Aunty Aloha's Breakfast Lū'au** (⊠ Kā'anapali Beach Hotel, Kā'anapali, ☎ 808/242–8437 or 800/993–8338) is a fun and tasty way to learn about exciting and often unpublicized things to do on Maui. The orientation includes live Hawaiian music, a hula show, a comical slide show, and an all-you-can-eat island-style breakfast and runs weekdays at 8:15 AM. The cost is $13.95, and you can get two tickets for the price of one if you attend on their first morning in Maui. **Visitor Channel Seven** televises visitor information 24 hours a day, including video tours, restaurant previews, and activities information.

Weather

Haleakalā Weather Forecast (☎ 808/871–5054) gives up-to-date reports on sea conditions, also a weather forecast for the road to Hāna and for 'Īao Valley State Park. **National Weather Service/Maui Forecast** (☎ 808/877–5111) covers the islands of Maui, Moloka'i, and Lāna'i.

WHALE-WATCHING

APPEALING TO BOTH CHILDREN and adults, whale-watching is one of the most exciting activities in the United States. During the right time of year on Maui—between November and April—you can see whales breaching and blowing just offshore. The humpback whales' attraction to Maui is legendary. More than half the North Pacific's humpback population winters in Hawai'i, as they've been doing for years. At one time there were thousands of the huge mammals, but the world population has dwindled to about 1,500. In 1966 they were put on the endangered species list, which restricts boats and airplanes from getting too close.

Experts believe the humpbacks keep returning to Hawaiian waters because of the warmth. Winter is calving time for the behemoths, and the young whales, born with little blubber, probably couldn't survive in the frigid Alaskan waters. No one has ever seen a whale give birth, but the experts studying whales off Maui know that calving is their main winter activity, since the 1- and 2-ton youngsters suddenly appear while the whales are in residence.

Quite a few operations run whale-watching excursions off the coast of Maui, with many boats departing from the wharves at Lahaina and Mā'alaea each day. **Pacific Whale Foundation** (✉ Kealia Beach Plaza, 101 N. Kīhei Rd., Kīhei 96753, ☎ 808/879–8811) pioneered whale-watching back in 1979 and now runs four boats, plus sea kayaks and special trips to encounter turtles and dolphins. During humpback season (Dec. 15–May 1) PWF has a marine naturalist stationed at McGregor Point Lookout (on the cliffs heading into Lahaina) and also weekdays at 12:15 on the observation deck of its Kīhei office.

Also offering whale-watching in season are **Ocean Activities Center** (✉ 1847 S. Kīhei Rd., Suite 203A, Kīhei 96753, ☎ 808/879–4485); **Island Marine** (✉ 113 Prison St., Lahaina 96761, ☎ 808/661–8397); and **Pride Charters** (✉ 208 Kenolio Rd., Kīhei, ☎ 808/874–8835), whose two-hour whale-watch cruise is narrated by a naturalist from Whales Alive and Keiko (Free Willie) Foundation. Ticket prices average $22–$35.

3 THE BIG ISLAND OF HAWAI'I

THE VOLCANO ISLE

The Big Island is the youngest and largest
island of the Hawaiian chain, and still
growing: Fresh lava has added black-sand
beaches and more than 70 acres of land on
its southeast side in the last decade alone.
An enviable 266 mi of coastline offers
splendid multicolored beaches, but this
is also an island of cool, mountainous
countryside; rain forest; and coffee, orchid,
and macadamia-nut plantations. In addition
to fabulous resorts and world-class golf
courses, adventures await in volcanic craters
and blue waters, along mountainous trails,
on cowboy ranches, and on the towering
summit of Mauna Ke'a.

By Betty
Fullard-Leo

Updated by
Sophia
Schweitzer

NEARLY TWICE AS LARGE AS ALL THE OTHER Hawaiian Islands combined, the Big Island is used to setting records. Perhaps most dramatically, it has the world's most active volcano: The east rift zone below Halema'uma'u on Kīlauea has been spewing lava intermittently since January 3, 1983. The island's southern tip is the southernmost point in the United States, although to the southeast, far beneath the ocean's surface, Lōihi, a sea mount bubbling lava, is slowly building another Hawaiian island, due to emerge in about 10,000 years. If you measure Mauna Ke'a from its origins 32,000 ft beneath the ocean's surface to its 13,796-ft peak, it is the tallest mountain in the world. The Keck Observatory on its summit, one of the world's most powerful telescopes, searches the universe from the clearest place on earth for peering into the heavens.

With its diverse climate and terrain, the Big Island offers skiing (but only for experts) in winter and year-round sunshine on its southern and western shores, where the temperature averages 69°F–84°F in July and 53°F–75°F in January. Yet there is so much rain near Hilo, its major city, that its only zoo is right in the middle of a rain forest, whereas land along the Kona-Kohala Coast is generally dry, with uninhabited stretches of lava.

In earlier times, Hawai'i's kings and queens lived and played along the Kona-Kohala Coast. King Kamehameha I was born close to its northern shores, near Mo'okini Heiau, built around the end of the 5th century. All along the water's edge are reminders of earlier inhabitants. At Kawaihae, two *heiaus* (stone platforms that were the site of worship)—Pu'ukoholā and Mailekini—mark the site of Kamehameha's final victory in 1810 in his battle to unite the Hawaiian Islands.

Most developers are aware of the reverence the Hawaiian people feel for their *'āina* (land), and they attempt to preserve and restore the bits and pieces of Hawaiian history that come to light when a bulldozer rakes the land. You'll find historic markers scattered along trails and roadways, at hotel grounds and in parks. Resorts, such as the Outrigger Waikoloa Beach, the Orchid at Mauna Lani, and Kona Village, conduct tours of petroglyph fields. The Outrigger Waikoloa Beach at 'Anaeho'omalu Bay, the Four Seasons Resort Hualālai, and the Mauna Lani Resort have restored the fishponds that once supplied the tables of Hawaiian royalty. The Orchid offers a botanical tour of traditional Hawaiian plants growing in its lush gardens.

In the calm tranquillity of the Kohala Mountains to the north, where the *paniolo* (Hawaiian cowboys) ride, or at the windswept isolation of South Point—thought to have been populated as early as AD 750—you can reflect on the lives of the early Hawaiians who crossed this land on foot. Did they bring their gods and goddesses from their ancient homeland in Tahiti and the Marquesas? Or was the goddess Pele conceived as an explanation for some violent volcanic eruption?

Five volcanoes formed the Big Island perhaps a half-million years ago: Kohala, Hualālai, Mauna Ke'a (white mountain), Mauna Loa (long mountain), and Kīlauea, which is currently active. Early Hawaiians believed that Pele lived in whichever crater was erupting. Even today, eerie stories are repeated as fact. They tell of a woman hitchhiker who dresses in red and wanders the volcano area accompanied by a small white dog. "My neighbor gave her a ride, but when he looked in the mirror she was gone!" is how one oft-repeated tale goes. Just a mere 42 years ago, Kīlauea exploded in a cascading fountain of fire 1,900 ft in height. Even if the past two decades have been relatively

The Big Island of Hawai'i *(Boxes Refer to Detail Maps)*

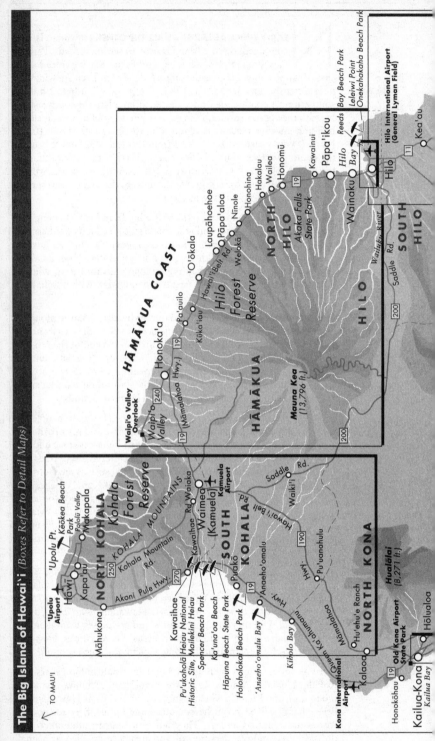

← TO MAUI

NORTH KOHALA

'Upolu Pt.
'Upolu Airport
Hāwī
Kapa'au
Keōkea Beach Park
Pololū Valley
Makapala
Māhukona

Kohala Forest Reserve

KOHALA MOUNTAINS

Kohala Mountain Rd.

Akoni Pule Hwy.

250

270

Kawaihae
Pu'ukoholā Heiau National Historic Site, Mailekini Heiau
Spencer Beach Park
Ka'una'oa Beach
Hāpuna Beach State Park
Holoholokai Beach Park
'Anaeho'omalu Bay

Kona International Airport

Honokōhau

19

Kailua-Kona
Kailua Bay

Old Kona Airport State Park

Kalaoa

Kīholo Bay

Queen Ka'ahumanu Hwy.

'Anaeho'omalu

Hōlualoa

Puakō

Kawaihae Rd
Waikoloa
Waimea (Kamuela)
Kamuela Airport

SOUTH KOHALA

Saddle Rd.
Waiki'i

Hawai'i Belt Rd.

190

Pu'uanahulu

Hu'ehu'e Ranch

Māmalahoa Hwy.

NORTH KONA

Hualālai
(8,271 ft.)

HĀMĀKUA COAST

Waipi'o Valley Overlook
Waipi'o Valley

240

19
(Māmalahoa Hwy.)

Honoka'a

Kūka'iau

Pa'auilo

'O'ōkala

Laupāhoehoe
Pāpa'aloa
Ninole
Welokā
Hawai'i Belt Rd.

Hilo Forest Reserve

HĀMĀKUA

Mauna Kea
(13,796 ft.)

200

Honohina
Hakalau
Wailea
Honomū
Kalalau

Akaka Falls State Park

NORTH HILO

19

Kawainui

Pāpa'ikou
Reeds

Hilo Bay

Wainaku

Hilo

Bay Beach Park
Leleiwi Point
Onekahakaha Beach Park

Hilo International Airport
(General Lyman Field)

Kea'au
11

SOUTH HILO

HILO

Wailuku River

Saddle Rd.

200

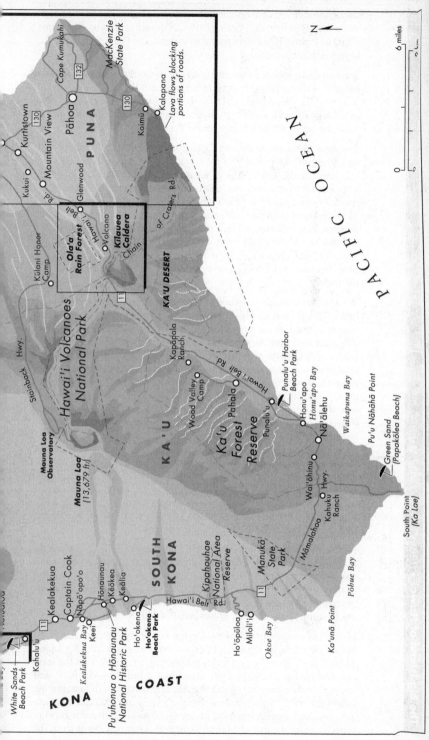

PACIFIC OCEAN

N

6 miles

MacKenzie State Park

Cape Kumukahi

132

Pāhoa

PUNA

130

Kalapana
Lava flows blocking
portions of roads.

Kurtistown

130

Kaimū

Mountain View

Kukui

Glenwood

Kūlani Honor Camp

Hawaii Belt Rd.

Olaʻa Rain Forest

Volcano

Kīlauea Caldera

Chain of Crater's Rd.

Hawaiʻi Volcanoes National Park

KAʻU DESERT

11

Stainback Hwy.

Kapāpala Ranch

Mauna Loa Observatory

Mauna Loa (13,679 ft.)

Wood Valley Camp

Kaʻu Forest Reserve

Pāhala

Punaluʻu

Punaluʻu Harbor Beach Park

Honuʻapo

Honuʻapo Bay

Nāʻālehu

Waikapuna Bay

KAʻU

Hawaiʻi Belt Rd.

Puʻu Nāhāhā Point

Green Sand (Papakōlea Beach)

Waiʻōhinu

Kahuku Ranch

Māmalahoa Hwy.

South Point (Ka Lae)

Pōhue Bay

SOUTH KONA

Kealakekua

Captain Cook

Nāpoʻopoʻo

Hōnaunau

Keōkea

Keālia

Keei

Kealakekua Bay

Puʻuhonua o Hōnaunau National Historic Park

Hoʻokena

Hoʻokena Beach Park

Kipahoehoe National Area Reserve

Hawaiʻi Belt Rd.

Manukā State Park

11

Hoʻōpūloa

Miloliʻi

Okoe Bay

Kaʻunā Point

White Sands Beach Park

Kahaluʻu

11

KONA COAST

unglamorous in comparison, with lava flowing from rift zones through 'ōhi'a forests or into the ocean, nearly 200 housing units as well as the Chain of Craters Road were forced to surrender to Pele's rage. No lives, however, have been lost.

You can drive almost to the end of Chain of Craters Road, leave your car, and walk to where molten lava flows into the ocean. It's not always visible. Helicopters carry sightseers over the 2½-mi lava lake called Kupaianaha, an 800-ft cinder cone, to view steam clouds rising from the ocean as the hot lava meets the sea.

The drive along the Hāmākua Coast to Hilo, the island's county seat and the fourth-largest city in the state, calls attention to modern development on the island. Fields of sugarcane no longer wave in the breeze. They have been replaced by orchards of macadamia nut trees and other specialty crops raised for chefs who prepare Hawai'i regional cuisine. Macadamia nuts are big business on the Big Island, supplying 90% of the state's yield. Kona coffee, anthuriums and orchids, *pakalōlō* (marijuana—at one time said to be the state's biggest income-producing, though illegal, crop), and, since 1999, kava—used in the pharmaceutical industry—are adding a new chapter to the agricultural history of the state.

While Kīlauea Volcano remains the greatest attraction to visitors, one other thing is certain: Business owners in all sections of the economy have combined efforts to make the island exciting, welcoming, and fun. The increased number of flights with direct service to the mainland, Japan, and Canada reflect their success. Upcountry Waimea accommodates more restaurants and shops than ever before, has added an old-fashioned wagon tour to Parker Ranch activities, and has opened its own visitor center. Hilo's Kamehameha Avenue has undergone renovations and, despite the rain, its farmers' market remains the most inspiring in the state, displaying colorful produce reflecting the island's full range of climates and ethnic traditions. The new Pacific Tsunami Museum, in one of its historic buildings, explores the devastating world of tsunamis and honors the many men, women, and children whose lives have been lost to them. North Kohala saw the grand reopening of the Old Nanbu Hotel, built in 1898 and doomed to be torn down only a couple of years ago. Visitors can marvel over the work of contemporary artists or savor an espresso there where old-timers tied their horses, drank beer, and played pool.

New attractions on the island are by and large culturally aware. In Hāmākua, the train museum examines the sugar plantation days and has restored part of the authentic track, and on the resort side of the island you can sail a voyaging canoe at the Orchid, learn about Hawaiian culture at ancient Pu'ukoholā Heiau, or visit the Four Seasons' Hawaiian Cultural Center, which grows coral as one of its projects.

Hawai'i is sometimes called the Orchid Isle or the Volcano Isle (both apt descriptions, by the way), but residents always say "the Big Island of Hawai'i," since the entire chain of islands that makes up the state is called Hawai'i as well. True, nightlife is a little low-key here, and there is a silly rumor that good beaches are scarce, but in fact, the Big Island excites the senses and inspires the adventurer. You can hike into a crater, catch marlin weighing hundreds of pounds, discover another universe from the top of Mauna Ke'a, and outstare a shark from the safety of a submarine porthole.

Pleasures and Pastimes

Dining

Hotels along the Kohala Coast invariably employ cutting-edge chefs who cook with the freshest local produce, fish, and herbs, creating intriguing blends of flavors that reflect the island's varied ethnic background. Events such as the Winter Wine Escapes at Mauna Ke'a Beach Resort and Cuisines of the Sun at Mauna Lani Bay Hotel draw hundreds of guests to starlit open-air dinners celebrating the bounty of the Isle's land and waters.

Fishing

A big lure for visiting fishing enthusiasts is deep-sea trolling for marlin, especially off the shores of the Big Island. Each morning an entire fleet of sportfishing boats leaves Kona in search of the elusive game fish. If the marlin aren't biting, reels are often whining with catches of local 'ahi (yellowfin tuna) and ono (wahoo).

Golf

Not to be outdone when it comes to scenic golf, many of the Big Island's courses are emerald oases in the midst of black, barren lava fields. They were designed by world-renowned architects, and on several of the 19 courses the challenges are as extraordinary as the views. They range from mountainside meccas to green seaside havens. Towering over them is snow-capped, 13,796-ft Mauna Ke'a, home of Poli'ahu, the Hawaiian snow goddess. Mauna Lani has been host to the prestigious Senior Skins tournaments for more than a decade, and the course at Hualālai is home to the Senior MasterCard Tournament.

Hiking

The ancient Hawaiians blazed a wide variety of trails across their archipelago, and many of these paths can still be hiked today. Part of the King's Trail at 'Anaeho'omalu, on the Big Island, winds through a field of lava rocks covered with prehistoric carvings meant to communicate stories of births, deaths, marriages, and other family events. In Hawai'i Volcanoes National Park, trails crisscross the volcanic landscape. You can choose to enter a lava tube or circle a kīpuka (verdant island surrounded by lava), home to rare Hawaiian honeycreepers. Puffs of steam warm the lava beneath your feet on the caldera hike. The serenity of remote beaches, such as the black-sand beach at Pololū in North Kohala, is only accessible to hikers. But a word of caution: Hiking in Hawai'i is not without danger and you should not risk trails, cliffs, or areas that appear no longer in use.

Horseback Riding

With its paniolo heritage, the Big Island is a mecca for equestrians. Riders can gallop through green Upcountry pastures, ride to Kealakekua Bay to see the Captain Cook monument, saunter into Waipi'o Valley for a taste of old Hawai'i, or venture the steep descent into Pololū Valley on mules.

Lodging

Accommodations on the Big Island vary tremendously: from sunny "total-destination" resorts to condominiums on cool mountaintops and family-style bed-and-breakfasts in green little towns geared more toward fishing and farming than vacationing. This is the beauty of a trip to this island: You can sample that elusive thing called "the real Hawai'i" and also have time to experience the ultimate luxury vacation. But be aware that you'll need a car or a taxi if you choose to stay overnight in one of the many bed-and-breakfast units or small inns that are outside the resort areas. These places provide a more intimate vacation experience than the big hotels, but the quality and prices vary enormously. For more information about B&Bs, *see* Contacts and Resources *in* Big Island A to Z, *below.*

Scuba Diving

Diving on the Big Island is as good as it gets. Aquarium, in Kealakekua Bay, is a state underwater park with depths from 15 ft to 110 ft and a popular place for introductory boat dives. Pine Trees, in North Kona, is an area that includes such sites as Carpenter's House, Golden Arches, and Pyramid Pinnacles—two underwater lava towers with tubes, arches, false Moorish idols, and large schools of butterfly fish. Depths run from 10 ft to 50 ft. Plane Wreck Point, off Keāhole Point, is for expert divers only. Damselfish, fantail, and filefish hover around in the shadows. Red Hill, south of the Kona Surf Hotel, encompasses six different sites of large caverns and lava tubes. Sea life in the area includes encrusting sponges, octopus, shells, sleeping reef sharks, and abundant tropical fishes. Depths range from 25 ft to 70 ft.

Shopping

An inordinate number of talented artists seek out the solitude and beauty of the Big Island. Galleries abound in Kailua-Kona, North Kohala, Waimea, Holualoa, Volcano, Hilo, and even in such out-of-the-way burgs as Kukuihaele and Honomū, where you can purchase wonderful original artwork, fine woodwork, and other handmade crafts. Coffee drinkers will also want to bring back some Kona coffee, grown on the western slopes of the Big Island. Kona coffee has a long-standing reputation as a gourmet grind and retails for perhaps twice as much as regular brands. Be aware that blends need only contain 10% Kona coffee to bear the prestigious label. Another local product that makes a great gift are macadamia nuts. You'll find them everywhere and treated in every way—from chocolate-covered to garlic-dusted.

Skiing

Believe it or not, you can ski in Hawai'i—atop the Big Island's Mauna Ke'a volcano. It's for hardy souls only. There are no lifts, and after schussing down, you must herringbone your way back up the slope. The months of December through February are your best bets for skiing Hawaiian style, and currently only one guide company is operating.

EXPLORING THE BIG ISLAND

The first secret to enjoying the Big Island to the max is: Rent a car! The second: Stay more than three days, or return again and again until you have seen all the facets of this fascinating place. With 266 mi of coastline made up of white-coral, black-lava, and a dusting of green-olivine beaches, and with its cliffs of lava and emerald gorges slashing into jutting mountains, the Big Island is so large and so varied that it is easiest to split your stay and your sightseeing into excursions from Hilo and excursions from Kona when planning a visit.

If your schedule allows a week or 10 days on the island, you might want to spend a night or two in the county seat of Hilo, a night at a bed-and-breakfast after exploring Hawai'i Volcanoes National Park, and another in Waimea before finishing up your vacation at a resort on the sunny side of the island. It's best to follow this in east coast–to–west coast order for accommodations so you won't go home with memories of Hilo's often gray skies. If you are short of time, give Hilo the once-over lightly and then see Hawai'i Volcanoes National Park on your first day, traveling the Hāmākua Coast route and making your new base in Kailua-Kona that night.

The sections below divide the island into an exploration of Hilo; a car trip from Hilo to the volcano area; a tour of the Hāmākua Coast; a walking tour of Kailua-Kona; and a trip around the northwest, including Waimea and the Kohala Mountains. Later in this chapter, we've included a section on the beaches you won't want to drive past.

Directions on the island are often referred to as *mauka* (toward the mountains) and *makai* (toward the ocean).

Numbers in the text correspond to numbers in the margin and on the Hilo Vicinity, Hawai'i Volcanoes National Park and Puna, Hāmākua Coast, Kailua-Kona, and Kohala District maps.

IF YOU HAVE 1 DAY

If you just have one day for the Big Island, fly directly to Hilo and rent a car or take a prearranged tour and concentrate on seeing **Hawai'i Volcanoes National Park** ⑲. At the Kīlauea Visitor Center, watch the film on Kīlauea's eruptions, and find out about the possibility of seeing the lava flow by driving down Chain of Craters Road. Ask about area hikes, and then enjoy your day exploring Halema'uma'u Crater, Thurston Lava Tube, fern forests, Devastation Trail, and other natural phenomena.

IF YOU HAVE 3 DAYS

Three days will give you barely enough time to sample a few of the Big Island's myriad pleasures. It might be best to fly into Kailua-Kona and settle in a hotel, a condominium, or one of the elegant resorts on this, the sunniest side of the island.

Start in **Kailua-Kona** ㉘–㉇, learning about Big Island history by taking in Hulihe'e Palace, Moku'aikaua Church, and Ahu'ena Heiau. Then spend the afternoon at a lovely beach, such as 'Anaeho'omalu, Hāpuna, or Kauna'oa on the Kohala Coast. Indulge yourself that first evening with *mai tais* (potent rum drinks with orange and lime juice) by the sea and a leisurely dinner, but get enough rest so you can take off at high speed in the morning.

On day two, head for Hawai'i Volcanoes National Park early so you'll have time to sightsee along the way. Take Queen Ka'ahumanu Highway, turning inland to **Waimea** ㊾–㊼. Stop at the Gallery of Great Things or Cook's Discoveries to purchase exquisite Hawaiian-made crafts. Then continue on with a side trip to the **Waipi'o Valley Overlook** ㊲. Finally, zip through **Hilo** ①–⑯—unless it's a Wednesday or Saturday morning, when the farmers' market adds local color to the town. From Hilo, it's about half an hour's drive to **Hawai'i Volcanoes National Park** ⑲ (☞ If You Have 1 Day, *above*). Return via the same route, as the drive around South Point takes forever.

On your third day, consider a morning snorkel cruise to Kealakekua Bay, south of Kailua-Kona. This is a real joy and gives you the opportunity to see where Captain Cook was killed in 1779. If you would prefer to sightsee, consider a drive to the end of the road (Highway 270) toward North Kohala, which offers a variety of interesting stops along the way. At the Mauna Lani Bay Hotel and Bungalows you'll find the Puakō Petroglyph Park (☞ Holoholokai Beach Park *in* Beaches, *below*). Take along a bottle of water to make the 20-minute hike to the petroglyph fields bearable. Drive on to Kawaihae and stop just before the intersection at **Pu'ukoholā Visitor Center** ㊽ to take in the Pu'ukoholā Heiau and learn more about King Kamehameha's feats. At Kawaihae, several restaurants and ice-cream shops with local flavors guarantee a satisfactory lunch break. You'll enjoy the open vistas of ocean and barren land on the way to the two sugar plantation towns,

Hāwī and Kapa'au (54), where several little shops, galleries, and the Bamboo Restaurant are worth investigating. Pause in Kapa'au to snap a photo of the **King Kamehameha Statue** (55) and then continue directly to the **Pololū Valley** (56) overlook. Here, a steep but newly improved trail leads to a black-sand beach with a restless surf. Save some film for this fabulous view, and then head for home.

IF YOU HAVE 8 DAYS

With this much time, you might consider splitting your stay into three hotels. Stay the first night in **Hilo** ①–⑯ and spend your first day exploring this old plantation town. Visit the farmers' market, shop on Kamehameha Avenue, wander through **Lyman Mission House and Museum** ⑦, and drive up to **Rainbow Falls** ⑮ and **Pe'epe'e Falls** ⑯, also known as Boiling Pots. Plant lovers will want to visit either the **Hawai'i Tropical Botanical Garden** ㉙ for its misty, rain-forest appeal or the Nani Mau Gardens, with its more manicured patches of tropical flowers.

Rise early on the morning of the second day to check out the **Suisan Fish Market** ④. Have breakfast and pack for your move to new accommodations around the volcano, but on the way spend much of your day on a leisurely side trip to **Pāhoa** ㉖ and Puna. Splurge on dinner at Kīlauea Lodge. Reserve your third day for a thorough exploration of **Hawai'i Volcanoes National Park** ⑲, including the drive down Chain of Craters Road at dusk to see the lava flow.

On day four, move on to a hotel on the Big Island's southwestern shore. Drive back through Hilo to enjoy sightseeing—**'Akaka Falls State Park** ㉛, **Honoka'a** ㊱, **Waipi'o Valley Overlook** ㊲—along the Hāmākua Coast. Stop for lunch in the town of Parker Ranch in Upcountry **Waimea** ㊾–(52). Make day five primarily a beach day, adding only a snorkel cruise or a little run into **Kailua-Kona** ㊳–㊼ for lunch, a visit to **Hulihe'e Palace** ㊶, and some souvenir shopping. Save the morning of day six to discover North Kohala. If you're a hiker, biker, or horseback rider, you might want to book an activity that takes place in this area. For more sedate types, a tour into Waipi'o Valley (☞ Contacts and Resources *in* Big Island A to Z, *below*) is a memorable experience. After your morning adventure, the galleries and lunch spots in the little towns of **Hāwī and Kapa'au** (54) are alluring, and on the return drive to your hotel, history comes alive at **Mo'okini Heiau** (57), **Lapakahi State Historical Park** (58), and the **Pu'ukoholā Visitor Center** ㊽ for the Pu'ukoholā Heiau.

On day seven, take the high road through coffee country and head south from Kailua-Kona via the artists' colony of Hōlualoa to Captain Cook, Kealakekua, and Hōnaunau. Spend an hour or so at Pu'uhonua o Hōnaunau, and while you're in the area, check out the Painted Church as well. The drive to South Point is long, through awesome stretches of lava fields. Once you reach the scenic point of Ka Lae, you'll feel the eerie isolation the first Hawaiian explorers must have experienced on landing at this remote outpost. Day eight, departure day, should be one of rest and relaxation—a leisurely breakfast, a brief trip to the beach, golf, or last-minute shopping.

When to Tour the Big Island

Touring the Big Island is appealing at any time of year. There are seldom traffic jams, and the weather remains basically stable year-round. It's a rare day when Kailua-Kona and the Kohala Coast are not sunny and warm; however, deluges can occur in January and February. It's difficult to predict weather in Hilo. If you are traveling in winter, you are apt to get wet in Hilo. The volcano area is always cooler because of the higher elevation, so you'll want a sweater or light jacket.

Hilo

Hilo is a town of both modern and rustic buildings stretching from the banks of the Wailuku River to Hilo Bay, where a few hotels rim stately Banyan Drive. Nearby, the 31-acre Lili'uokalani Gardens, a Japanese-style park with arched bridges and waterways, was established as a safety zone after a devastating tidal wave swept away businesses and homes on May 22, 1960, killing 60 people. Residents don't worry much about a tidal wave recurring, but they haven't built anything except hotels, the park, and a golf course in that area, either.

Though the center of government and commerce for the island, Hilo is primarily a residential town. Mansions with perfectly kept yards of lush tropical foliage surround older wooden houses with rusty corrugated roofs. It's a friendly community, populated primarily by descendants of the contract laborers—Japanese, Chinese, Filipino, Puerto Rican, and Portuguese—brought in to work the sugarcane fields during the 1800s. Bring your umbrella—the rainfall averages 139 inches per year!

When the sun shines and the snow glistens on Mauna Ke'a, 25 mi in the distance, Hilo sparkles. In the rain the town takes on the look of an impressionist painting—greenery muted alongside weather-worn brown, red, and blue buildings. Several of these buildings have been spruced up to revitalize the downtown area and attract more businesses and visitors. The whole town has fewer than 1,000 hotel rooms, most of them strung along Banyan Drive. By contrast, the eight Kohala Coast resorts alone boast over 3,704 rooms combined. Nonetheless, Hilo (with a population of 46,000 in the entire district) is the fourth-largest city in the state and home to a branch of the University of Hawai'i. Often the rain blows away by noon and a colorful arch appears in the sky. One of Hilo's nicknames is the City of Rainbows.

A Good Drive

Begin this excursion driving southwest from the cluster of hotels along **Banyan Drive** ①, which loops around a peninsula jutting into Hilo Bay. On the right, **Lili'uokalani Gardens** ② has Oriental gardens and an arched footbridge to **Coconut Island** ③. At the western end of Banyan Drive, early risers who want to see a major local-style fish auction should head for **Suisan Fish Market** ④ at about 7:30. The market is a great place to "talk story" (chat) and listen to the almost unintelligible bidding that takes place in pidgin English. Continue to **Wailoa Center** ⑤ to enjoy a current art show or view the poignant history of the 1960 tsunami.

Drive across town to the Hilo Public Library on Waiānuenue Avenue, leave your car, and explore downtown Hilo on foot. In front of the library are the ponderous **Naha and Pinao stones** ⑥, which legend says King Kamehameha I was able to lift as a teenager, thus foretelling that someday he would be a powerful king. Stroll southeast along Kapi'olani Street and then turn right on Haili Street to visit the historic **Lyman Mission House and Museum** ⑦. The restored house was built in 1839 by missionaries who came from Boston to run a school for boys. Returning on Haili Street, you'll come across **Haili Church** ⑧, where Protestant sermons and hymns are rendered in both Hawaiian and English. Farther down Haili Street, stop at the **Big Island Visitors Bureau** ⑨ for maps and brochures.

If you're in the mood for a quick pick-me-up, return northwest along **Keawe Street** ⑩, inspecting the plantation-style architecture along the way. By the time you reach Kalākaua Street the benches in **Kalākaua Park** ⑪ will seem a perfect respite. A statue in the park honors the popular 19th-century king—known as the Merrie Monarch—who so much reinspired Hawaiian cultural values.

Continue makai on Kalākaua Street to visit the new **Pacific Tsunami Museum** ⑫ in the former First Hawaiian Bank Building. After three blocks you'll come across the **New S. Hata Building** ⑬, which houses interesting shops and restaurants; just next door, on either side of Mamo Street, the **Hilo Farmers' Market** ⑭ adds local color to the otherwise businesslike streets every Wednesday and Saturday.

You'll need your car for two popular sights a couple of miles west of town. Drive up Waiānuenue Avenue about a mile, angling to the right when the road forks, to reach **Rainbow Falls** ⑮. After a Hilo downpour, it thunders into Wailuku River Gorge. Two miles or so farther up the road, also on the right, is a green sign for **Pe'epe'e Falls** ⑯, also known as Boiling Pots because of the turbulent action of the water in potholes at the base of the falls.

TIMING

It rains in Hilo. You'll face less of a chance of getting wet, however, if you avoid the months of January, February, or March. Allow a full day to explore Hilo if you try to take in all the sights, less if you skip the Lyman Mission House and Museum and have little interest in shopping. Remember that morning hours are generally cooler for walking the streets than late afternoon, when the humidity can soar. You may want to return more than once to peel away the many layers of this leisurely little town. It's definitely worth timing a visit for a Wednesday or Saturday, when the farmers' market is in full swing.

Sights to See

✎ *following the text of a review is your signal that the property has a Web site where you will find details and, usually, images; for a link, visit www.fodors.com/urls.*

❶ Banyan Drive. The 46 big, leafy banyan trees with aerial roots dangling from the limbs were planted along here in the '30s by visiting celebrities; you will find such names as Amelia Earhart and Franklin Delano Roosevelt on plaques on the trees. ✉ *Begin at Hawai'i Naniloa Resort, 93 Banyan Dr.,* ☎ *808/969–3333.*

❾ Big Island Visitors Bureau. Marked by a red-and-white Hawaiian-warrior sign, the bureau is worth a visit, especially if you are just beginning your stay on the Big Island. Brochures, maps, and advice are dispensed with friendly aloha spirit. ✉ *250 Keawe St.,* ☎ *808/961–5797.* ✎

NEED A
BREAK?

For a quick cup of coffee or an early breakfast before starting your day, try Queen's Court at the **Hilo Hawaiian Hotel** (✉ 71 Banyan Dr., ☎ 808/935–9361). Both the window seats and the raised booths set back from the windows have good views of Hilo Bay. Hilo hosts most of the island's intrastate business travelers, so prices here are not exorbitant.

❸ Coconut Island. In ancient times a place of healing, just offshore from Lili'uokalani Gardens and across a footbridge, this small (approximately 1 acre) island draws children to play in the tidal pools while fishermen try their luck. ✉ *Lili'uokalani Gardens, Banyan Dr.*

❽ Haili Church. Originally constructed in 1859 by New England missionaries, this church was rebuilt in 1979 following a fire. Haili Church is known for its choir, which sings hymns in Hawaiian. ✉ *211 Haili St.,* ☎ *808/935–4847.*

⑭ Hilo Farmers' Market. This abundant and colorful market draws farmers and shoppers from all over the island. Two days a week, bright orchids, anthuriums, and birds of paradise, as well as exotic vegetables,

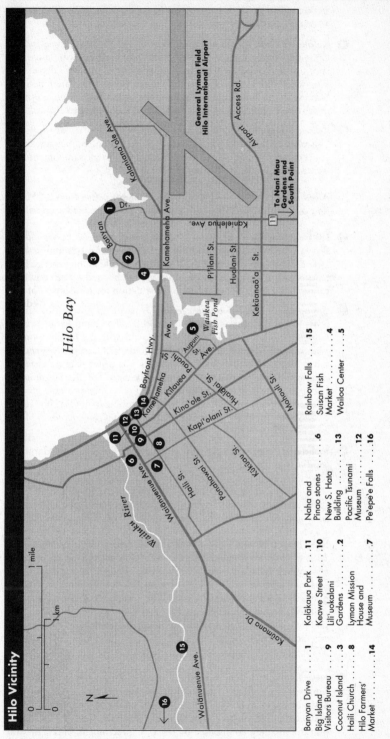

Hilo Vicinity

Hilo Bay

General Lyman Field
Hilo International Airport

To Nani Mau
Gardens and
South Point

Kaumana Dr.

Waiānuenue Ave.

Wailuku River

N

1 mile
1 km

tropical fruits, and an array of baked goods, offer a feast for the eye. ⊠ *Mamo and Kamehameha Sts.* ⊙ *Wed. and Sat. 6:30–2:30.*

⑪ **Kalākaua Park.** King Kalākaua, who revived the hula dance and became the inspiration for Hilo's Merrie Monarch Festival, chose this spot to create a park. A bronze statue, sculpted in 1988, depicts the king with a taro leaf in his left hand to signify the Hawaiian peoples' bond with the land. In his right hand the king holds an *ipu*, a symbol of Hawaiian culture, chants, and hula. ⊠ *Kalākaua and Kino'ole Sts.*

⑩ **Keawe Street.** Buildings here have been restored in original 1920s and '30s plantation styles. While most shopping is along Kamehameha Avenue, the ambience on Keawe Street offers a nostalgic sampling of Hilo as it might have been 80 years ago.

NEED A   A few sips of fresh-brewed Kona coffee at **Bear's Coffee Shop** (⊠ 106
BREAK?   Keawe St., ☎ 808/935–0708) are sure to revive the tired shopper.

❷ **Lili'uokalani Gardens.** This 30-acre public park on either side of Banyan Drive was home to Hilo businesses until a tsunami in 1960 swept them away and took the lives of 60 people in the process. Fish-stocked streams and half-moon bridges, pagodas, and a ceremonial tea-house make this a favorite Sunday destination for residents.

★ ❼ **Lyman Mission House and Museum.** Of particular interest to history buffs, Lyman House was built in 1839 by David and Sarah Lyman, Congregationalist missionaries. It's the oldest frame building on the island. The adjacent museum, dedicated in 1973, recently opened the Earth Heritage Gallery, which includes a realistic magma chamber and displays the Earth's formation and the arrival of life. The museum houses unique artifacts of Hawaiian and other major ethnic groups. The gift shop sells an educational walking-tour map of Old Hilo Town. ⊠ *276 Haili St.,* ☎ *808/935–5021.* 🎫 *$7 includes guided tour.* ⊙ *Mon.–Sat. 9–4:30.*

❻ **Naha and Pinao stones.** In front of the public library are two large oblong stones, the legendary Naha and Pinao stones. The Pinao stone is reportedly an entrance pillar of an ancient temple built near the Wailuku River. Kamehameha I is said to have moved the 5,000-pound Naha stone when he was still in his teens. Legend decreed that he who did so would become king of all the islands. ⊠ *300 Waiānuenue Ave.*

OFF THE   **NANI MAU GARDENS –** About 4 mi from the center of Hilo on Highway
BEATEN PATH   11 is this tropical wonderland. Nani Mau Gardens has numerous vari-
               eties of fruit trees and hundreds of varieties of ginger, orchids, anthuri-
               ums, and other tropicals. The 20 acres include a Hawaiian cultural
               garden, a botanical museum, waterways, and waterfalls, as well as
               palm and orchid gardens. A guided tour by tram is available. The light
               and airy restaurant is open daily for lunch. The garden can be used for
               catered affairs. ⊠ 421 Makalika St., Hilo, ☎ 808/959–3541. 🎫
               $7.50, guided tour via tram $5. ⊙ Daily 8–5.

⑬ **New S. Hata Building.** This historic structure houses shops, restaurants, a bakery, and offices. The building was erected as a general store in 1912 by the Hata family. The "S" stands for the first name of the original builder, Sadanosuke. During World War II the Hatas were interned and the building confiscated by the U.S. government. When the war was over, a daughter repurchased it for $100,000. With its arched windows and decorative moldings, it is a beautiful example of renaissance-revival architecture and won an award from the state for the authenticity of its restoration. ⊠ *308 Kamehameha Ave., at Mamo St.*

HULA, THE DANCE OF HAWAI'I

LEGENDS IMMORTALIZE LAKA AS the goddess of hula, portraying her as a gentle deity who journeyed from island to island, sharing the dance with all who were willing to learn. Laka's graceful movements, spiritual and layered with meaning, brought to life the history, the traditions, and the genealogy of the islanders. Ultimately taught by parents to children and by *kumu* (teachers) to students, the hula preserved without a written language the culture of these ancient peoples.

Some legends trace the origins of hula to Moloka'i, where a family named La'ila'i was said to have established the dance at Ka'ana. Eventually the youngest sister of the fifth generation of La'ila'i was given the name Laka, and she carried the dance to all the Islands in the Hawaiian chain.

Another legend credits Hi'iaka, the volcano goddess Pele's youngest sister, as having danced the first hula in the hala groves of Puna on the Big Island. Hi'iaka and possibly even Pele were thought to have learned the dance from Hōpoe, a mortal and a poet also credited as the originator of the dance.

In any case, hula thrived until the arrival of puritanical New England missionaries, who with the support of Queen Ka'ahumanu, an early Christian convert, attempted to ban the dance as an immoral activity throughout the 19th century.

Though hula may not have been publicly performed, it remained a spiritual and poetic art form, as well as a lively celebration of life presented during special celebrations in many Hawaiian homes. David Kalākaua, the popular "Merrie Monarch" who was king from 1874 to 1891, revived the hula. Dancers were called to perform at official functions. In 1906, Nathaniel Emerson wrote about hula, "Its view of life was idyllic, and it gave itself to the celebration of those mythical times when gods and goddesses moved on earth as men and women, and when men and women were as gods."

Gradually, ancient hula, called *kahiko*, was replaced with a lively, updated form of dance called '*auana* (modern). Modern costumes of fresh ti-leaf or raffia skirts replaced the voluminous *pa'u* skirts made of *kapa* (cloth made of beaten bark), and the music became more melodic, as opposed to earlier chanted routines accompanied by *pahu* (drums), '*ili 'ili* (rocks used as castanets), and other percussion instruments. Such tunes as "Lovely Hula Hands," "Little Grass Shack," and the "Hawaiian Wedding Song" are considered hula '*auana*. Dancers might wear graceful *holomu'u* with short trains, or ti-leaf skirts with coconut bra tops.

In 1963 the Merrie Monarch Festival was established in Hilo on the Big Island and has since become the most prestigious hula competition in the state. It's staged annually the weekend after Easter, and contestants of various *halau* (hula schools) from Hawai'i and the mainland compete in the categories of Miss Aloha Hula, hula kahiko (ancient), and hula '*auana* (modern). For more information, contact the **Merrie Monarch Hula Festival** (✉ Hawai'i Naniloa Resort, 93 Banyan Dr., Hilo 96720, ☎ 808/935–9168).

Moloka'i stages its own Ka Hula Piko festival to celebrate the birth of hula every May. Singers, musicians, and dancers perform in a shaded glen at Papohaku Beach State Park, and nearby, islanders sell food and Hawaiian crafts. During the week preceding the festival, John Kaimikaua, the founder, and his halau present hula demonstrations, lectures, and storytelling at various Moloka'i sites.

For more information, contact the **Moloka'i Visitors Association** (✉ Box 960, Kaunakakai 96748, ☎ 808/553–3876 or 800/800–6367).

NEED A BREAK?   Wander inside the New S. Hata Building and pause to enjoy a grilled Italian-style sandwich or a healthy salad. Not hungry? Treat yourself to a superb espresso drink instead. Tables face the large windows of old O'-Keefe bakery at **Canoes Café** (⌧ 308 Kamehameha Ave., ☎ 808/935–4070), open Monday to Saturday 8 to 2:45, Sunday 10 to 2. Herbed carrot bread is only one of many breads provided daily by O'-Keefe.

⑫ Pacific Tsunami Museum. This small museum offers a poignant history of the tragedies that have visited this side of the island and a memorial to all who lost their lives. In a 1931 C. W. Dickey–designed building, the museum also has an interactive computer center, a science room, a video room, a replica of Old Hilo Town, and a knowledgeable, friendly staff. In the background, a striking quilt made by students in Laupāhoehoe tells a silent story. ⌧ *130 Kamehameha Ave.,* ☎ *808/935–0926.* ⌸ *$5.* ☉ *Mon.–Sat. 10–4.* ✍

⑯ Pe'epe'e Falls. The falls drop in four streams of water into a series of circular pools, and the resultant turbulent action (best seen after a good rain when the water is high) has earned them the name Boiling Pots. ⌧ *3 mi west of Hilo on Waiānuenue Ave.; keep to the right when road splits and look for a green sign.*

⑮ Rainbow Falls. After a Hilo rain, these falls thunder into Wailuku River gorge. If the sun peeks out in the morning hours, rainbows form above the mist. This quiet area surrounded by tropical vegetation is great for photos. ⌧ *Take Waiānuenue Ave. west of town 1 mi; when road forks, stay on right of Waiānuenue Ave.; look for Hawaiian-warrior sign.*

OFF THE BEATEN PATH   **SOUTH POINT –** The southernmost point of land in the United States, Ka Lae is easily accessible for a self-guided excursion by car, but it's a long, long drive with few amenities along the way. Count on 3½ hours for the 126-mi Highway 11 route from Hilo to Kona. The turn to South Point is just beyond Nā'ālehu, the southernmost U.S. town. Take a break here at Punalu'u Bakeshop and Visitor Center (☎ 808/929–7343) for some fragrant sweet bread before going the 12 mi down a narrow road to treeless, windswept Ka Lae. Here you'll find the small Kalalea Heiau and abandoned structures once used to lower cattle and to produce ships anchored below the cliffs. Old canoe-mooring holes were carved through the rocks, possibly by settlers from Tahiti as early as AD 750. If you're driving a four-wheel-drive vehicle, follow the road 3 mi along the shoreline to Mahana, or Green Sand Beach. At the base of a low sea cliff, the beach has a green tint from the glassy olivine formed by the minerals that combine when hot 'a'a (chunky, cinder-type lava) hits the sea. Please remember, the rip current is dangerous!

❹ Suisan Fish Market. The liveliest action in town takes place at this fish auction mornings from about 7 or 8, Monday through Saturday. This is the place for local sights and sounds. ⌧ *85 Lihiwai St. (Banyan Dr. turns left onto Lihiwai St.),* ☎ *808/935–8051.*

❺ Wailoa Center. Adjacent to the Wailoa State Park, the Wailoa Center features changing exhibits by local artists. There's also a photographic exhibit of the 1946 and 1960 tidal waves. ⌧ *Pi'opi'o St.,* ☎ *808/933–0416.* ☉ *Mon.–Tues. and Thurs.–Fri. 8:30–4:30, Wed. noon–4:30.*

Hawai'i Volcanoes National Park and Puna

The most popular attraction on the Big Island, Hawai'i Volcanoes National Park is home to active Kīlauea Volcano. Even when there is no fiery display or lava flowing, you'll have plenty to see in the park, which includes the summit caldera and gently sloping northeast flank of 13,677-ft Mauna Loa volcano. The lush greenery of tree ferns and other tropical plants, lava tubes, cinder cones, odd mineral formations, steam vents, and the vast barren craters along Chain of Craters Road make this the ultimate ecotour. Don't forget to take a sweater (or a jacket in winter), as temperatures can get nippy at the park's 3,700-ft elevation. Also take a flashlight if you plan to visit the shoreline lava flow after sunset.

A Good Drive

In Hilo take Highway 11, Kanoelehua Avenue, which takes you directly to the park, 30 mi to the southeast. Along the way, distinctive red-and-white Hawaiian-warrior markers (installed by the Hawai'i Visitors and Convention Bureau) designate visitor attractions. On the right of the road you'll see a sign for **Pana'ewa Rain Forest Zoo** ⑰. Just five minutes up Stainback Highway, it's a great stop for kids—home to lively monkeys and solemn nēnē (the state bird).

About 5 mi south of Hilo on the left of Highway 11 is the marker for **Mauna Loa Macadamia Factory** ⑱. The entry road wanders miles through macadamia trees to a macadamia-nut processing plant with large viewing windows, a large visitor center, and a gift shop.

Follow Highway 11 through the towns of Mountain View and Glenwood to the entrance sign of **Hawai'i Volcanoes National Park** ⑲. The 359-square-mi park, established in 1916, remains a vast showcase of nature's powerful beauty. Stop first at the Kīlauea Visitor Center to find the latest information on volcanic activity. From here, walk over to **Volcano Art Center** ⑳ to see the work of Big Island artists. Across the street from the art center is **Volcano House** ㉑, a charming lodge dating from 1941 with a huge stone fireplace. Its dining room windows edge Kīlauea and, in the center of the caldera, you'll see the steaming fire pit, called Halema'uma'u Crater. Currently the volcano is not erupting from here but from a rift zone on the flanks of Kīlauea. Hiking trails starting at the lodge lead you around and into the crater.

You can also drive the crater's circumference via the 11 mi of Crater Rim Drive. Scenic stops include the yellow, acrid-smelling sulfur banks; steam vents; and the park's Thomas A. Jaggar Museum, on the edge of Kīlauea Caldera. You'll find several easy walks along the way: Halema'uma'u Overlook (a 10-minute walk); Devastation Trail (30 minutes), and Thurston Lava Tube (20 minutes).

If you have time, drive from the center of the park down **Chain of Craters Road** ㉒—aptly named after the huge depressions. The road through awesome historic lava flows offers breathtaking ocean views. A sign midway down on the left marks a trail across the lava to **Pu'u Loa Petroglyphs** ㉓, a field of lava etchings left by early Hawaiians. It's about a 25-minute walk.

Approximately 28 mi from Kīlauea Visitor Center, on the makai side, the Waha'ula Visitor Center and the 13th-century sacrificial Waha'ula Heiau were demolished by lava in 1989 and 1997 respectively. Just beyond the area, lava has overflowed the road repeatedly since 1984. It's now closed. At road's end you can walk (1–5 mi, depending on where you park) to where lava spills intermittently into the ocean. Bring drinking water and wear hiking boots. It's a long, hot trek, often over very difficult terrain, and there are no facilities.

Return via Chain of Craters Road to exit the park; turning left onto Highway 11, take the first cross road to the right toward the Volcano

Hawai'i Volcanoes National Park and Puna

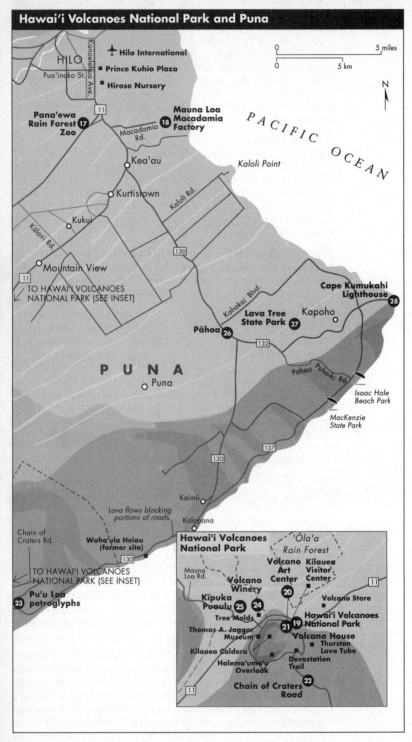

HILO

Pua'inako St.

Kanoelehua Ave.

✈ Hilo International
■ Prince Kuhio Plaza
■ Hirose Nursery

5 miles
5 km

N

PACIFIC OCEAN

Pana'ewa Rain Forest Zoo 17

11

Mauna Loa Macadamia Factory 18

Macadamia Rd.

Kea'au

Kaloli Point

Kurtistown

Kaloli Rd.

Kukui

Kūlani Rd.

130

Mountain View

11

TO HAWAI'I VOLCANOES NATIONAL PARK (SEE INSET)

Cape Kumukahi Lighthouse

Kohokai Blvd.

Lava Tree State Park 27

Kapoho

28

Pāhoa 26

132

PUNA

Puna

Pahoa Pohoiki Rd.

Isaac Hale Beach Park

MacKenzie State Park

137

130

Kaimū

Lava flows blocking portions of roads

Kalapana

Chain of Craters Rd.

Waha'ula Heiau (former site)

130

TO HAWAI'I VOLCANOES NATIONAL PARK (SEE INSET)

Pu'u Loa petroglyphs 23

Hawai'i Volcanoes National Park

'Ōla'a Rain Forest

Mauna Loa Rd.

Volcano Art Center

Kilauea Visitor Center

11

Volcano Winery 20

Volcano Store

Kīpuka Puaulu 25 24

Hawai'i Volcanoes National Park 21 19

Tree Molds

Thomas A. Jaggar Museum

Volcano House

Thurston Lava Tube

Kilauea Caldera

Halema'uma'u Overlook

Devastation Trail

11

Chain of Craters Road 22

Golf & Country Club. Less than a mile beyond you'll find **Volcano Winery** ㉔, with a gift shop and tasting room.

Back on Highway 11 drive in a southwesterly direction to the next right and turn onto Mauna Loa Road. A sign marks Tree Molds. Each chimneylike formation was created when molten lava hardened around a tree, burning it away in the process. Farther on is a little park with picnic tables, and at the end of the road you can take a self-guided mile-long walk around **Kīpuka Puaulu** ㉕, also known as Bird Park and famous for its many native species.

Head back toward Hilo via the Old Volcano Highway, which runs parallel to Highway 11. Pause at Volcano Store for excellent bargains in cut flowers. On the road again, notice the yellow and white ginger (the aromatic flower prized for lei) and tiny, purple wild orchids that grow in profusion. Along Highway 11, several nurseries proudly sell and display bright red, pink, white, and varicolored anthuriums. The round wooden water tanks beside weathered houses indicate this area's catchment system; the city supplies water only closer to Kurtistown.

If you have spent a night at Volcano, you might have enough extra time to take a side trip to Puna, where farmers grow everything from flowers to bananas, papayas, and pakalōlō. Turn right onto Highway 130 at Keaʻau and drive 11 mi to **Pāhoa** ㉖. With its wooden boardwalks and rickety old buildings, this tired town is reminiscent of the Wild West. It has hole-in-the-wall restaurants, trinket shops, the island's oldest (Akebono) theater, and an assortment of '60s-era characters.

From Pāhoa, angle left onto Highway 132 and continue to **Lava Tree State Park** ㉗, where some of the cylindrical black tree molds rise 12 ft in the cool air—the only reminder of an ʻōhiʻa forest taken by Mauna Loa's eruption in 1790. Eventually you'll reach the coast beyond Kapoho, a now nonexistent town where two roads cross: In 1960 it was covered with lava. Luckily, everyone was safely evacuated. After 2 mi on an unpaved road you'll come across lonely-looking **Cape Kumukahi Lighthouse** ㉘. Returning to the Kapoho crossroads, turn left to follow Highway 137 along the coast, taking a break at either Isaac Hale Beach Park or MacKenzie State Recreation Area (☞ Beaches, *below*). Get back onto Highway 130 for the hour drive back to Hilo.

TIMING

To explore Hawaiʻi Volcanoes National Park in depth could take a lifetime. Winter temperatures can dip below the cotton-shirt comfort level and misty weather prevails over clear skies and balmy afternoons, but the park is worth visiting at any time and day of the year. Open daily, this is a national park, ideal for families and therefore busier during the summer months, holidays, and weekends. Count on spending at least three-quarters of a day at the park, but if you wish to see the lava flow after dark or visit the Puna District plan an overnight stay at one of the charming B&Bs tucked into the fern forest.

It'll take you about 45 minutes to drive the distance from Hilo to the park. Allow two hours for the trip up and back down the 24 mi of the Chain of Craters Road to the Kalapana coastal district of the park, where the flowing lava hits the ocean in giant billowing clouds of steam. Add an hour or so to hike to the edge of the flow and back.

Sights to See

㉘ **Cape Kumukahi Lighthouse.** This lonely lighthouse stands encircled by lava that stopped 6 ft from its base and tumbled into the sea on either side, as if the quixotic goddess Pele had suddenly changed her mind about its destruction. ⊠ *Hwy. 132, near coast beyond crossroads marked Kapoho on many maps.*

㉒ Chain of Craters Road. No food, water, or gasoline is available along this road, which descends 3,700 ft in 24 mi to the Kalapana Coast. Be sure to stock up before you head out. At road's end, you can walk to where the lava flows into the ocean. ⊠ *Begins in Hawai'i Volcanoes National Park.*

★ **⑲ Hawai'i Volcanoes National Park.** The 359-square-mi park, established in 1916, provides an unmatched volcanic experience. The park and Chain of Craters Road are open 24 hours a day, but visitors must obtain a backcountry hiker's permit to remain in the park area overnight. The Kīlauea Visitor Center (☎ 808/985–6011 or 985–6000, ✆), open daily 6:45–5, lies just beyond the park's entry booth. You can learn here about park wildlife and vegetation. If you can't see a real eruption, don't miss the hourly movie shown from 9 to 4. The center posts the latest news on volcanic activity, and hikers can obtain trail information as well as information about ranger-escorted scenic walks and camping permits.

Within the park, Halema'uma'u Crater is the steaming pit within gaping Kīlauea Caldera. You can hike around or into the crater. Then return to your car for the 11-mi drive around the crater's circumference to **Halema'uma'u Overlook** for another view. Children will enjoy the hands-on fun at the free **Thomas A. Jaggar Museum** (⊠ Crater Rim Dr., ☎ 808/985–6049; ♥ daily 8:30–5) at the edge of Kīlauea Caldera. Seismographs that measure the earth's movement will also record a child's footfall. Or you can watch fascinating filmstrips of current and previous eruptions.

Nearby **Devastation Trail** was created after a 1959 eruption, when fiery lava from the smaller, adjacent Kīlauea Iki Crater burned the surrounding 'ōhi'a forest. The 30-minute walk off **Crater Rim Drive** is self-guided. If you are in the park for a full day or more, you could venture on an exhilarating hike into Kīlauea Iki (*iki* means little). It takes less than half a day, but get information and maps first at the Kīlauea Visitor Center. A jaunt through a fern forest connects with a boardwalk that leads through to an eerie, barren landscape that may make you feel you're on another planet. A 20-minute walk will take you 450 ft into **Thurston Lava Tube**, a natural tunnel about 10 ft high that formed when the cooling top and sides of a lava flow hardened and the lava inside drained away.

Yellow, acrid-smelling sulfur banks and gaping vents emitting warm steam are found throughout the cool environs of the park. Pregnant women and anyone with heart or respiratory problems should avoid both the sulfur banks and the fumes. ⊠ *Hawai'i Volcanoes National Park, Highway Belt Rd. (Hwy. 11), 96718,* ☎ *808/985–6000 for volcano activity updates and general information.* ✆ *$10 per car for 7 days.* ✆

㉕ Kīpuka Puaulu. A *kīpuka* is a forested island surrounded by a sea of lava. This sight is also known as Bird Park. Let your kids identify a koa tree and search for native birds, such as the 'apapane and the 'elepaio. A written guide with numbers that correspond to sites along the kīpuka's trail is available at the Kīlauea Visitor Center (☞ Hawai'i Volcanoes National Park, *above*). ⊠ *Hawai'i Volcanoes National Park, Mauna Loa Rd.*

㉗ Lava Tree State Park. Tree molds that rise like blackened smokestacks formed here in 1790 when a lava flow swept through the 'ōhi'a forest. ⊠ *Hwy. 132, Puna District,* ☎ *808/974–6200.* ✆ *Free.* ♥ *Daily 30 min before sunrise–30 min after sunset.*

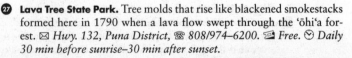

⑱ **Mauna Loa Macadamia Factory.** Acres of macadamia trees lead to a processing plant with viewing windows. A videotape describes the harvesting and preparation of the nuts, and there are free samples in the roomy visitor center. Children can run off their energy on the nature trail. Feel free to bring your own picnic lunch. ✉ *Macadamia Rd. on Hwy. 11, 5 mi south of Hilo,* ☎ *808/966–8618.* ⌕ *Self-guided tour free.* ☉ *Daily 8:30–5.* ✎

㉖ **Pāhoa.** This little town has wooden boardwalks and rickety buildings reminiscent of the Wild West. The few restaurants, antiques shops, secondhand stores, tie-dye clothing boutiques, and art galleries in quaint old buildings are fun to wander through. ✉ *Turn southeast onto Hwy. 130 at Kea'au, drive 11 mi to right turn marked Pāhoa.*

🖐 ⑰ **Pana'ewa Rain Forest Zoo.** Children enjoy the monkeys and tigers in this quiet, often wet, low-key zoo, which also hosts native Hawaiian species. Trails have been paved, but take an umbrella for protection from the frequent showers. ✉ *Stainback Hwy. off Hwy. 11,* ☎ *808/959–7224.* ⌕ *Free.* ☉ *Daily 9–4.*

㉓ **Pu'u Loa Petroglyphs.** Midway down Chain of Craters Road, a sign on the left marks Pu'u Loa Petroglyphs. It's a 25-minute walk across the lava to where etchings of people, boats, and animals made by early Hawaiians are spread over a vast area of black lava. The round depressions are thought to be piko holes, where umbilical cords of newborns were buried. ✉ *Hawai'i Volcanoes National Park, Chain of Craters Rd.*

⑳ **Volcano Art Center.** The building was constructed to be the Volcano House in 1877, replacing a thatched-roof hut built in 1846. Now a celebrated art center, it features the work of Big Island photographers, artists, and craftspeople. Be sure to take a look at the block prints depicting Hawaiian legends by Dietrich Varez. ✉ *Hawai'i Volcanoes National Park, Crater Rim Dr.,* ☎ *808/967–7565.* ☉ *Daily 9–5.*

㉑ **Volcano House.** This charming old lodge, with its huge stone fireplace, 42 rooms for rent, the Ka 'Ōhelo Dining Room, and a snack bar dates from 1941. The dining room is busy with tour groups at lunchtime, but dinner can be a quieter experience. ✉ *Hawai'i Volcanoes National Park, Crater Rim Dr.,* ☎ *808/967–7321.*

NEED A BREAK? The **Steam Vent Café** (✉ Behind Volcano Store in Volcano Village, ☎ 808/985–8744) serves lattes and distributes leaflets on accommodations and activities. Drop by for coffee, pastries, sandwiches, a last-minute gift, or some simple good cheer. If you're looking for something a bit more substantial and need Internet access, behind Kīlauea General Store is the **Lava Rock Café** (✉ Old Volcano Hwy., ☎ 808/967–8526), which serves full breakfasts and lunch daily and dinner Tuesday through Saturday in a breezy, pinewood-lattice setting. You'll find a variety of choices, from chicken salad to New York steak, cappuccino to brandy.

㉔ **Volcano Winery.** There's a gift shop and tasting room at this unusual winery that creates pleasant white table wines made from Symphony grapes grown nearby. Also on offer are honey wines, a red Pele Delight, Guava or Passion Chablis, and Volcano Blush. ✉ *35 Pi'imauna Dr., Volcano,* ☎ *808/967–7479.* ☉ *Daily 10–5:30.* ✎

NEED A BREAK? Coffee and a steaming bowl of saimin at **Volcano Golf & Country Club Restaurant** (✉ Volcano Golf & Country Club, 35 Pi'imauna Dr., Volcano, ☎ 808/967–8228) can be a soul-saving snack on a cool, wet day. The restaurant, which serves breakfast and lunch, has big plate-glass windows that afford a view of mist-shrouded golf greens, rare golden-blossom lehua trees, and an occasional nēnē goose.

Hāmākua Coast

The Hilo–Hāmākua Heritage Coast leads past green cliffs and gorges, jungle vegetation, open emerald fields, and stunning ocean scenery along Highway 19, which runs north-northwest from Hilo. The 47-mi drive winds through little plantation towns, Pāpa'ikou, Honomū, Laupāhoehoe, and Honoka'a, to the end of the road at the Waipi'o Valley Overlook. The lush valley floor has maintained the ways of old Hawai'i, with taro patches, wild horses, and isolated little houses that can be reached only by hiking or by taking four-wheel-drive vehicles. (For companies that offer escorted tours, wagon rides, and horseback rides, *see* Participant Sports *in* Outdoor Activities and Sports, *below,* and Contacts and Resources *in* Big Island A to Z, *below.*) If you continue to Kailua-Kona, it is a total of 95 mi via this shorter of the two coastal routes from Hilo.

A Good Drive

Seven miles north of Hilo, turn right off Highway 19 onto a 4-mi scenic drive to reach **Hawai'i Tropical Botanical Garden** ㉙, a 17-acre rain forest preserve showcasing more than 2,000 species of plants and a profusion of flowers beside Onomea Bay. After the scenic drive rejoins Highway 19, turn left toward **Honomū** ㉚ to travel 4 mi inland to **'Akaka Falls State Park** ㉛. An interesting wayside stop along the way, Honomū has wooden buildings that reflect a plantation past replaced by tourism-geared shops and restaurants. At the park, two falls, 'Akaka and Kahuna, are even more breathtaking after you've walked the hilly 20-minute trail to see them.

Enjoy the ride through sleepy little villages with music in their names: Honohina, Ni'nole, Pāpa'aloa. If you say every letter and pronounce *i* as "ee" and *e* as in "hey," you'll come close to the correct pronunciation. In 1946 a 56-ft tidal wave, which caused 159 deaths, crashed into this scenic coastline and washed out one of the most expensive railways ever built. The **Laupāhoehoe Train Museum** ㉝ takes you back to the time when sugar reigned along the Hāmākua Coast.

Here you'll also come across three parks: **Kolekole Beach Park** ㉜, with changing rooms and picnic facilities; **Laupāhoehoe Point Park** ㉞, for fishing; and the inland **Kalōpā State Park** ㉟, for hiking.

In 1995 the Honoka'a Sugar Company was the last to discontinue operations on this coast, and today you'll see more macadamia orchards than waving fields of cane as you near **Honoka'a** ㊱, hailed as the macadamia capital of the world. Secondhand and antiques stores, with dusty dishes, fabrics, and crafts, line Honoka'a's main street.

Just before the road (Rte. 240) ends, 8 mi beyond Honoka'a, a sign directs you to the right to Kukuihaele, on a loop with no street name, where you'll find Waipi'o Valley Artworks, a gallery. Here you can make arrangements for tours departing from **Waipi'o Valley Overlook** ㊲ (☞ Contacts and Resources *in* Big Island A to Z, *below*) to the floor of the 6-mi-deep valley. At the end of the road, the once heavily populated valley is a tropical Eden bounded by 2,000-ft cliffs.

TIMING

If you've stopped to explore the quiet little villages with wooden boardwalks and dogs dozing in backyards, or if you've spent several hours in Waipi'o Valley, night will undoubtedly be falling by the time you complete this journey. Don't worry: The return to Hilo via Highway 19 takes only about an hour, or you can continue on the same road to Waimea (20 minutes) and then to the Kohala Coast resorts (another 25 minutes). Highways may be more heavily traveled during the weekends, but basically this is open country, easy to navigate any time of the week or year. Hopping in and out of the

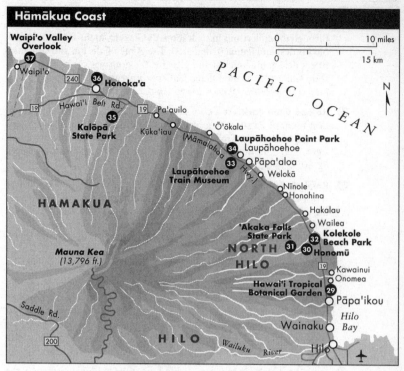

Hāmākua Coast

car during the cooler winter months may be more comfortable than in the heat of summer.

Sights to See

★ ③ **'Akaka Falls State Park.** You have to walk about 20 minutes to see the two falls, **'Akaka** and **Kahuna**. The easier downhill trail to your right takes you to the 400-ft Kahuna Falls first. 'Akaka Falls drops more than 420 ft, tumbling far below into a pool drained by Kolekole Stream amid a profusion of fragrant white, yellow, and red torch ginger. ⊠ *4 mi inland off Hwy. 19, near Honomū,* ☎ *808/974–6200.* 🎫 *Free.* ☉ *Daily 30 min before sunrise–30 min after sunset.*

② **Hawai'i Tropical Botanical Garden.** Seven miles outside of Hilo, stunning coastline views appear around each curve of the 4-mi scenic drive, lined with lush vegetation, which accesses the privately owned, non-profit, 17-acre nature preserve beside Onomea Bay. Pathways lead past waterfalls, ponds, and more than 2,000 species of plants and flowers, including palms, bromeliads, ginger, heleconia, orchids, and ornamentals. ⊠ *27-717 Old Mamalahoa Hwy., Pāpa'ikou,* ☎ *808/964–5233.* 🎫 *$15, family membership $35.* ☉ *Daily 9–5.* 🐾

③ **Honoka'a.** This is the place where, in 1881, Australian William Purvis planted the first macadamia-nut trees in Hawai'i. Called the macadamia capital of the world, Honoka'a is now better known for its secondhand and antiques stores. ⊠ *Hwy. 240/Mamane St.*

NEED A BREAK? A quick stop at **Tex Drive Inn** (⊠ Pakalana St. and Hwy. 19, ☎ 808/775–0598) will give you a chance to taste the snack it is famous for: *malasada,* a puffy, doughy Portuguese doughnut (sans hole), deep-fried and rolled in sugar and best eaten hot. For mouthwatering pastries and a strong espresso in Honoka'a, stop in at **Mamane Street Bakery** (⊠ Mamane St., ☎ 808/775–9478), where residents from as far as Waimea and Hilo gladly shop.

③⓪ Honomū. A plantation past is reflected in the wooden boardwalks and tin-roof buildings of this small, struggling town. It's fun to poke through the collections in such shops as Glass from the Past (filled with old bottles) and Panua (tribal arts). The 'Akaka Falls Inn and Gift Shop offers delectable lunches and gifts for the gourmet cook. The Woodshop Gallery/Café and Ohana Gallery showcase fine local art. ⊠ *2 mi inland from Hwy. 19 en route to 'Akaka Falls State Park.*

③⑤ Kalōpā State Park. At a cool 2,000-ft elevation, past the old plantation town of Pa'auilo, is a lush, forested area with picnic tables, rest rooms, and cabins. Trails are bordered with plants identified by small signs. ⊠ *12 mi north of Laupāhoehoe and 2 mi inland off Hwy. 19,* ☎ *808/974–6200.* ☞ *Free.* ⊙ *Daily 7–7 or by permit.*

③② Kolekole Beach Park. This beach at the mouth of the Kolekole River is not safe for inexperienced swimmers or surfers. Leave the locals surfing offshore and hike 4 mi up the river to a waterfall and pond for a chilly, refreshing dip. Facilities at the park include changing rooms, barbecue pits, and covered picnic areas. ⊠ *Off Hwy. 19,* ☎ *808/961–8311.* ☞ *Free.* ⊙ *Daily until 11 PM.*

③④ Laupāhoehoe Point Park. This is not a safe place for swimming. Surf pounds the jagged black rocks at the base of the stunning point. Still vivid in the minds of longtime Hilo residents is the 1946 tragedy during which 20 schoolchildren and four teachers were swept to sea by a tidal wave. **Laupāhoehoe Harbor** has bathrooms, showers, picnic tables, and stone barbecue pits. ⊠ *On northeast coastline, Hwy. 19, makai side, north of Laupāhoehoe.* ☞ *Free.* ⊙ *Daily 7 AM–sunset.*

③③ Laupāhoehoe Train Museum. Behind the stone loading platform of the once-famous Hilo Railroad, constructed around the turn of the 20th century, the former manager's house is home to a poignant display of the era when sugar was king. The railroad, believed to be one of the most expensive ever built, was washed away by the tidal wave of 1946, destroying an important part of Hāmākua's history. ⊠ *Hwy. 19, Laupāhoehoe, mauka side,* ☎ *808/962–6300.* ☞ *Suggested donation $2.* ⊙ *Daily 9–4:30.*

③⑦ Waipi'o Valley Overlook. Bounded by 2,000-ft cliffs, the Valley of the Kings—Waipi'o—was once a favorite retreat of Hawaiian royalty. Waterfalls drop 1,200 ft from the Kohala Mountains to the valley floor. Sheer cliffs make access difficult. A few residents still cultivate taro in the pastoral valley, a handful of families enjoy the isolation, and horses roam among the flowers, lotus ponds, and rivers. A crescent of black sand makes it a popular spot for surfers. ⊠ *Follow Hwy. 240 8 mi northwest of Honoka'a.*

OFF THE BEATEN PATH

WAIPI'O VALLEY – In 1823, the first white visitors found 1,500 people living in this Edenlike environment amid wild fruit trees, banana patches, taro fields, and fishponds. Here, in 1780, Kamehameha I was singled out as a future ruler by reigning chiefs. In 1791 he fought Kahekili in his first naval battle at the mouth of the valley. Now, as then, waterfalls frame the landscape.

The no-name hotel (no electricity or running water, either)—sometimes it's called the Waipi'o Hotel—is the only hotellike accommodation for overnighters. Consider it a roof over your head. Arrangements must be made in advance. You need to pack your own food and bring mosquito repellent and mosquito coils (locally called "punks"). You can walk into the valley or arrange to be dropped off by one of the four-wheel-drive tours that run daily. ⊠ *For hotel write to Tom Araki, 25 Malana Pl., Hilo 96720,* ☎ *808/775–0368. 5 rooms. No credit cards.*

Kailua-Kona

The touristy seaside village of Kailua-Kona has many historic sites tucked between the open-air shops and restaurants that line Ali'i Drive, its main oceanfront street. At the base of the 8,271-ft Mt. Hualālai, Kailua-Kona is where King Kamehameha I died in 1819 and where his successor, Liholiho, broke the *kapu* (taboo) system, a rigid set of laws that had provided the framework for Hawaiian government. The following year, on April 4, 1820, the first Christian missionaries from New England came ashore at Kailua-Kona.

The easiest place to park your car (a fee is charged) is at King Kamehameha's Kona Beach Hotel, but free parking is available if you enter Kailua via Palani Road, or Highway 190. Turn left onto Kuakini Highway; in half a block turn right and then immediately left into the parking lot. Walk makai on Likana Lane half a block to Ali'i Drive.

A Good Walk

Begin the ½-mi walk at **King Kamehameha's Kona Beach Hotel** ㊳ at the northern end of town, where artifacts and pictures of early kings are displayed in the lobby. The hotel offers free tours of **Ahu'ena Heiau** ㊴, or you can wander around the two stone platforms at the ocean's edge to view a reconstructed grass hut on your own. Next, investigate **Kailua Pier** ㊵ and the seawall where fishermen cast their lines in the afternoon and weavers make bowls and hats of coconut fronds. A submarine ride departs from the pier (☞ Contacts and Resources *in* Big Island A to Z, *below*). Then take in **Hulihe'e Palace** ㊶, one of only three royal palaces in the United States, and **Moku'aikaua Church** ㊷, the first Christian church in the state of Hawai'i. Tackle a plethora of shops filled with tropical clothing, souvenir T-shirts, jewelry, and local crafts in the block-long, oceanfront **Kona Inn Shopping Village** ㊸. Much of the shopping area is converted from the old Kona Inn, a once-prestigious hotel and now a symbol of a more gracious era; Kona Inn Restaurant is still a popular gathering place for cocktails at sunset. At the southern end of Ali'i Drive, **Hale Hālāwai Beach Park** ㊹ and the **Waterfront Row** ㊺ restaurant complex provide welcome respites. End your walk either a few steps to the south at **St. Michael's Church** ㊻, next to the site of the first Catholic church built in Kona in the 1840s, or a few blocks down at **Coconut Plaza** ㊼, a little shopping square with affordable ethnic restaurants, contemporary boutiques, and a gallery filled with some of the finest Big Island art.

Ali'i Drive continues for 6 mi along the oceanfront, past Disappearing Sands Beach Park, the tiny blue-and-white St. Peter's Catholic Church, the ruins of a heiau, and Kahalu'u Beach Park. Elegant condos with beautifully landscaped grounds, the golf course of the Kona Country Club, and the Keauhou Shopping Center are all part of the scenery before the road ends.

TIMING

You can walk the whole ½-mi length of "downtown" Kailua-Kona and back again in 45 minutes, or else spend an entire day here, taking time to browse in the shops, do the historical tours, have lunch, and breathe in the atmosphere. If you want to know more about Kailua's fascinating past, arrange for a guided tour by the Kona Historical Society (☞ Contacts and Resources *in* Big Island A to Z, *below*).

Kailua-Kona enjoys year-round sunshine—except for the rare deluge. Mornings offer cooler weather, smaller crowds, and more birds singing in the banyan trees, but afternoon outings are great for cool drinks while gazing out over the ocean.

204

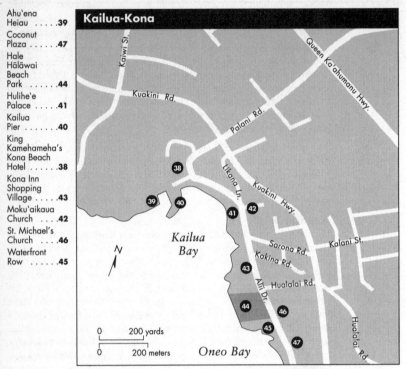

Sights to See

OFF THE BEATEN PATH

Before you start your day, have breakfast at the **Kona Ranch House** (☒ 75-5653 Olioli St., ☎ 808/329–7061). Up on the hill from King Kamehameha's Kona Beach Hotel, this pleasant plantation-style restaurant with wicker furniture and a café-style decor has been the traditional location for Kailua-Kona residents to enjoy everything from plain oatmeal to full-on omelets, fragrant breads, and waffles topped with fruit.

39 **Ahu'ena Heiau.** This spiritual site has been one of the few heiaus on the Islands to be restored. Beside the lagoon on Kamakahonu Beach, just outside King Kamehameha's Kona Beach Hotel, this is the area where King Kamehameha I spent his last years—from 1813 till his death in 1819. Built by early Hawaiians, the stone platforms of heiaus often had grass huts on top. Free tours start from King Kamehameha's Kona Beach Hotel. ☒ *75-5660 Palani Rd.,* ☎ *808/329–2911.* ☒ *Free.* ☼ *Tours weekdays at 1:30.*

OFF THE BEATEN PATH

ASTRONAUT ELLISON S. ONIZUKA SPACE CENTER — This informative museum 7 mi north of Kailua-Kona, at the airport, was opened in 1991 as a tribute to Hawai'i's first astronaut, who was killed in the 1986 *Challenger* disaster. The space center has computer-interactive exhibits. You can launch a miniature rocket and rendezvous with an object in space, feel the effects of gyroscopic stabilization, participate in hands-on science activities, and view educational films. ☒ *Kona International Airport, Kailua-Kona,* ☎ *808/329–3441.* ☒ *$3.* ☼ *Daily 8:30–4:30.* ☣

47 **Coconut Plaza.** Kona's latest development hides coffee shops, boutiques, ethnic restaurants, and an exquisite gallery in its meandering labyrinth of airy buildings. There's also a Hard Rock Cafe, impossible to miss. ☒ *75-5795–75-5825 Ali'i Dr.*

NEED A
BREAK?
Island Lava Java (⊠ 75-5799 Ali'i Dr., ☎ 808/327–2161) is a dandy place for a cappuccino, a mocha java accompanied by a fresh-baked muffin or bagel, or a scoop of Tropical Dreams ice cream.

㊹ Hale Hālāwai Beach Park. Benches under the trees at the ocean's edge are a perfect place to soak up the view and enjoy a calm respite from shopping in town. ⊠ *Southern end of Ali'i Dr.*

★ ㊶ Hulihe'e Palace. Fronted by a wrought-iron gate decorated with the royal crest, Hulihe'e Palace is one of only three royal palaces in America. The two-story residence was built of lava, coral, koa wood, and 'ōhi'a timbers in 1838 by the island's governor, John Adams Kuakini, a year after he completed Moku'aikaua Church. During the 1880s it served as King David Kalākaua's summer palace. The oversize doors and koa-wood furniture are witness to the size of some of the Hawaiian people. During weekday afternoons hula *hālau* (schools) rehearse on the grounds. ⊠ 75-5718 *Ali'i Dr.*, ☎ 808/329–1877. ☒ *$5.* ☉ *Weekdays 9–4, weekends 10–4.*

㊵ Kailua Pier. Built in 1918, Kailua Pier is a hub of ocean activity. Outrigger canoe teams practice and tour boats depart. Though most fishermen use Honokōhau Harbor, north of Kailua-Kona, pier activity increases during marlin tournament season in August and September. Each October close to 1,500 international athletes swim 2.4 mi from the pier to begin the grueling Ironman Triathlon competition.

Along the **seawall** fishermen and children daily cast their lines. For youngsters, a bamboo pole and hook are easy to come by in the village, and plenty of locals are willing to give pointers. ⊠ *Next to King Kamehameha's Kona Beach Hotel; the seawall is between Kailua Pier and Hulihe'e Palace on Ali'i Dr.*

㊳ King Kamehameha's Kona Beach Hotel. Stroll through the high-ceiling lobby, reminiscent of a covered shopping mall, to view museum-quality displays of Hawaiian artifacts and mounted marlin and trophies from past Hawaiian International Billfish tournaments. The 1986 winner of the tournament, a marlin that weighed in at 1,062 pounds, hangs on one wall. The 1,166-pound 1993 record-setter is a floor display. ⊠ 75-5660 *Palani Rd., Kailua-Kona,* ☎ 808/329–2911.

OFF THE
BEATEN PATH
KONA BREWING COMPANY & BREWPUB — A few blocks mauka of King Kamehameha's Kona Beach Hotel, Kona Brewing Company offers thirst-quenching tours and tastings. Its wheat ale, flavored with *liliko'i* (passion fruit), is a staple of the company's pub. A breezy and eclectic space with a koa-wood bar and a historic tin roof, the pub uses local and organic produce for its gourmet pizzas. For nonbeer drinkers, an exquisite sparkling ginger ale will hit the spot. ⊠ *North Kona Shopping Center, 75-5629 Kuakini Hwy., Kailua-Kona,* ☎ 808/334–1133 or 808/334–2739. ☒ *Free.* ☉ *Weekdays 11–10, Sat. 10 AM–11 PM, Sun. 4–10.*

㊸ Kona Inn Shopping Village. Much of this shopping arcade was once Kona Inn, a hotel built in 1929 that was a longtime landmark. The boardwalk is bordered with shops and restaurants. Prior to the construction of the inn, the personal heiau of King Liholiho was on this shore. Broad lawns with coconut trees on the ocean side are lovely for afternoon picnics. Some visitors bring lawn chairs and stretch out with a good book. ⊠ 75-5744 *Ali'i Dr.*

NEED A
BREAK?
The **Kona Coffee Café** (⊠ 75-5744 Ali'i Dr., ☎ 808/329–7131) serves 100% Kona coffee as well as locally made cookies. For cocktails at sunset, go next door to the **Kona Inn Restaurant** (⊠ 75-5744 Ali'i Dr., ☎ 808/329–4455), a traditional favorite.

★ **42 Moku'aikaua Church.** Also known as the Church of the Chimes—they sound on the hour—the present church was built in 1836, though the original was founded in 1820 by Hawai'i's first missionaries and was the earliest Christian church in the Islands. Moku'aikaua Church is built of black stone from an abandoned heiau. The stone was mortared with white coral and topped by an impressive steeple. Inside, at the back, behind a panel of gleaming koa wood, is a model of the brig *Thaddeus.* ⊠ 75-5713 Ali'i Dr., ☎ 808/329–0655.

OFF THE ✓ **PU'UHONUA O HŌNAUNAU** – About 20 mi south of Kailua-Kona, this
BEATEN PATH 180-acre national historic park was, in early times, a place of refuge and healing. It was a safe haven for women in times of war, and if a kapu breaker, criminal, or prisoner of war escaped and reached this site, he was allowed to live and to avoid punishment, purified by the priests who lived within the walls. Hale-o-Keawe Heiau, built in 1650, has been restored, and wood images of Hawaiian gods have been replaced. Demonstrations of Hawaiian skills, games, poi pounding, canoe making, and more are frequently scheduled. There are tidal pools and a picnic area in this park heavy with history. In the evenings clear skies add depth to scheduled events. ⊠ *Follow Hwy. 11 south of Kailua-Kona to Hōnaunau, turn right, and follow Hwy. 160 3½ mi,* ☎ *808/328–2326.* ⚐ *$2.* ☉ *Weekdays 7:30 AM–11 PM, weekends 7:30 AM–8 PM.* ✑

NEED A It doesn't look like much, this small restaurant in what used to be a
BREAK? seafood market. Make no mistake! The **Ke'ei Café** (⊠ Hwy. 11, Hōnaunau, ☎ 808/328–8451) serves delicious dinners with Brazilian flavors in its clean, teal-toned space. Small local farmers provide a fresh selection of ingredients. This is the only place south of Kailua-Kona for a fine meal. Reservations are essential, credit cards are not accepted, and the restaurant is closed Sunday and Monday.

46 St. Michael's Church. The site of the first Catholic church built in Kona in 1840 is marked by a small thatched structure to the left of the present pink church at the entrance to a neglected graveyard. In front of the church a grotto shrine holds a statue of the Virgin Mary. ⊠ 75-5769 Ali'i Dr., ☎ 808/326–7771.

45 Waterfront Row. Built in the early 1990s, this wooden complex houses several restaurants, including the popular Chart House, reliable for steak and seafood. A view tower and benches are in the two-level complex for those who want to enjoy the ocean vista. ⊠ 75-5770 Ali'i Dr.

The Kohala District

Along the roadside of Highway 19, brightly colored bougainvillea stands out in relief against the chunky black-lava landscape that stretches as far as the eye can see. Most of the lava flows, spreading from the mountain to the sea, are from the last eruptions of Mt. Hualālai, in 1800–01. They are interrupted only by the green oases of irrigated golf courses surrounding the glamorous luxury resorts rising along the Kona-Kohala Coast. The landscape along this long stretch of coastline changes considerably, from the cool 2,500-ft altitude of the cowboy town of Waimea to the incredibly green rolling fields that compose much of North Kohala. During the winter months, glistening humpback whales cleave the waters just offshore. On the coast you'll see ancient stone heiau and the remains of a fishing village, moving legacies of the Hawaiian people who still inhabit the area.

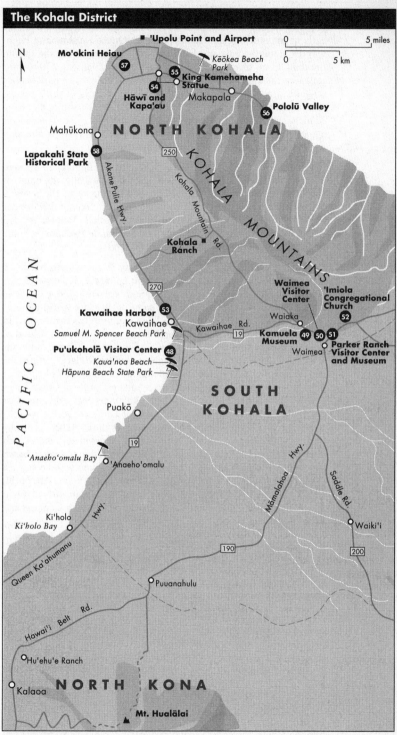

The Kohala District

'Upolu Point and Airport

Mo'okini Heiau

Kēōkea Beach Park

57

55 King Kamehameha Statue

54

Hāwī and Kapa'au

Makapala

56 Pololū Valley

Mahūkona

NORTH KOHALA

Lapakahi State Historical Park

58

250

KOHALA MOUNTAIN

Akone Pulie Hwy.

Kohala Mountain Rd.

Kohala Ranch

270

MOUNTAINS

Waimea Visitor Center

'Imiola Congregational Church

52

Kawaihae Harbor

53

Kawaihae

Samuel M. Spencer Beach Park

Kawaihae Rd.

19

Waiaka

Kamuela Museum

49 50 51

Pu'ukoholā Visitor Center

48

Waimea

Parker Ranch Visitor Center and Museum

Kaua'noa Beach

Hāpuna Beach State Park

SOUTH KOHALA

PACIFIC OCEAN

Puakō

Māmalahoa Hwy.

Saddle Rd.

19

'Anaeho'omalu Bay

'Anaeho'omalu

Ki'holo

Ki'holo Bay

Queen Ka'ahumanu Hwy.

Waiki'i

190

200

Puuanahulu

Hawai'i Belt Rd.

Hu'ehu'e Ranch

Kalaoa

NORTH KONA

Mt. Hualālai

0   5 miles
0   5 km

A Good Drive

If you're staying in Kona or at a Kohala Coast resort, begin this tour early in the morning by driving north on Queen Ka'ahumanu Highway 19 along the base of Mt. Hualālai. When you get to the split in the road 33 mi from Kailua-Kona, turn left on Highway 270 toward Kawaihae and stop at **Pu'ukoholā Visitor Center** ㊽. The park service ranger at this National Historic Site tells the history of three heiaus, two large ones on land and a third submerged just offshore, that King Kamehameha I had his men rebuild from 1790 to 1791. You can get a good photo of the two heiaus by driving a bit farther down the road and turning into **Samuel M. Spencer Beach Park.**

Retrace your route and continue east, climbing on Highway 19 through Parker Ranch land toward Waimea. (Note: Technically, the name of the Waimea post office is Kamuela, and the name of the town is Waimea. Some say the post office is named for the son of the founder of Parker Ranch.) Where the road divides and Kohala Mountain Road (Hwy. 250) makes a sharp left, you'll find **Kamuela Museum** ㊾, home to an impressive number of Hawaiian artifacts.

Upcountry Waimea can get cool and misty in the winter, but it's a bustling, affluent town. It doesn't seem to know the challenges the island's many plantation towns face. There are currently about 30 places where you can find a bite to eat and some of them are world-famous. A whole new complex with shops, High Country Traders, opened in 2000. It's to the right of Kawaihae Road as you enter town. Behind it, **Waimea Visitor Center** ㊿ has opened its doors in the historic old Lindsey House, listed on the Hawai'i Register of Historic Places. Stop in for detailed information on the cultural and historic sites of Kohala, then poke around and shop at adjacent Parker Square. Gallery of Great Things and Waimea General Store stock high-quality artwork and gifts. Just down the street is a shopping opportunity of a different sort. On weekends before 11:30, drop by the tiny swap meet (flea market) behind nearby St. James's Episcopal Church. On the far side of town, at Parker Ranch Shopping Center, a long-established visitor attraction is **Parker Ranch Visitor Center and Museum** (51). Mānā, the original koa-wood residence of the ranch founder, and the century-old Smart family home, Pu'u'ōpelu, which contains an extensive art collection, are on the outskirts of town. Wagon tours take you through the ranch paniolo-style (☞ Contacts and Resources *in* Big Island A to Z).

From Parker Ranch Visitor Center drive northeast on Highway 19 to pass the offices of the Keck Observatory, which has the world's largest mirrored telescope, at the top of Mauna Ke'a. Then drive by the first church on the left, but stop to peek into the cream-color **'Imiola Congregational Church** (52) to view its unique koa-wood interior. Make sure to browse through Cook's Discoveries at the third traffic light for exquisite local-themed gifts, then turn around.

Turn right on Kohala Mountain Road (Hwy. 250) for a scenic ride through the mountains to Hāwī. An overlook affords a view of the entire coastline, including the protective breakwater at **Kawaihae Harbor** (53) directly below. Farther on, through ironwood trees that act as windbreaks along the road, you'll see an exclusive country-home subdivision called Kohala Ranch. Here are the headquarters of Kohala Na'alapa, and just up the road, Paniolo Riding Adventures also guides horseback rides through the countryside (☞ Participant Sports *in* Outdoor Activities and Sports, *below*).

The road rises and then drops gradually from 3,564 ft. After about 20 mi it rejoins Highway 270 at the old sugar plantation village of **Hāwī** (54).

Turn right to **Kapa'au** ⑤ to visit the original **King Kamehameha Statue** ⑤ and browse through the many galleries and unusual gift shops nestled in restored historic buildings.

The road ends at an overlook with a stunning view of **Pololū Valley** ⑤. A hiking trail leads into the valley. Organized mule trail rides, waterfall hikes, and kayak cruises lead adventurers deeper into this hauntingly beautiful and historic area (☞ Contacts and Resources *in* Big Island A to Z, *below*). Drive back toward Hāwī to complete the loop via Highway 270, past Kapa'a Beach Park and Māhukona Beach Park. Feel free to pass up the two parks if you're short of time, as they do not have particularly enticing swimming beaches.

If you have a four-wheel-drive vehicle, turn off to remote 'Upolu Point and the 'Upolu Airport. A rough lane leads left at the airport to **Mo'okini Heiau** ⑤, a huge, impressive work of craftsmanship built about AD 480. About 1,000 yards away from the heiau is King Kamehameha I's birthplace.

If time permits, make a final stop at **Lapakahi State Historical Park** ⑤, where a 1-mi trail meanders through the site of once-prosperous Koai'e, an ancient fishing village. Lapakahi is also a Marine Life Conservation District and water activities are discouraged. The coral beach and welcoming cove offer shade, however, for a festive picnic lunch. Go for a cooling swim in the calm waters of Samuel M. Spencer Beach Park before returning to Kona via Highway 270.

TIMING

This is an all-day excursion covering a lot of miles over ground that ranges from lava-covered flatlands with glorious seaside views to lush mountain pastures. If you're short on time, head either straight for Waimea to shop and dine, and to visit the Parker Ranch Museum, or drive to Hāwī and Kapa'au via Highway 270 to see the dramatic history of these sugar towns. Allow half a day or more for the abbreviated trip, depending on how long you dally in shops and over lunch.

Sights to See

⑤ **Hāwī and Kapa'au.** These two old neighboring villages thrived during plantation days. There were hotels, saloons, and theaters—even a railroad. Today both towns are blossoming once again, honoring their past. Old historic buildings have been restored and are home to shops, galleries, and eateries. The latest project, the 1898 Old Nanbu Hotel, opened its doors to visitors in 1999. ⊠ *Kohala Mt. Rd. off Hwy. 270.*

NEED A BREAK?

It can get hot and humid in North Kohala. A great place to feel the breeze is on the lānai of the **Nanbu Courtyard** (☎ 808/889–6884) behind the historic Old Nanbu Hotel. Open as early as 6:30 on weekdays, this friendly espresso shop serves toasted bagels, salads, and grilled sandwiches alongside home-baked macadamia-nut cookies, specialty breads, and soft ice cream. And, of course, there are great lattes and other coffee delights.

⑤ **'Imiola Congregational Church.** Be careful not to walk in while a service is in progress, as the front entry of this church, which was established in 1832 and rebuilt in 1857, is behind the pulpit. Note the dark koa interior and the unusual wooden calabashes hanging from the ceiling. ⊠ *Off Hwy. 19, Waimea,* ☎ *808/885–4987.*

⑤ **Kamuela Museum.** Parker descendant Harriet Solomon and her husband, Albert, have amassed fascinating artifacts from Hawai'i and around the world in this privately owned museum. The Solomons have an eclectic collection including Hawaiian weapons, a satiny-smooth koa table that once graced 'Iolani Palace, and a stuffed black bear from British Columbia. ⊠ *Hwys. 19 and 250, Kamuela,* ☎ *808/ 885–4724.* 🖭 *$5.* ☉ *Daily 8–5.*

53 **Kawaihae Harbor.** Of Big Island harbors, this one near the Kawaihae Shopping Center is second in size only to Hilo Harbor on the east coast. King Kamehameha I and his men launched their canoes from here when they set out to conquer the island chain. Today, paddlers from all over the island gather here for races. ⊠ *Hwy. 270, Kawaihae.*

55 **King Kamehameha Statue.** This is the original of the statue in front of the Judiciary Building on King Street in Honolulu. It was cast in Florence in 1880 but lost at sea when the German ship transporting it sank near the Falkland Islands. A replica was shipped to Honolulu. Two years later an American sea captain found the original in a Port Stanley (Falkland Islands) junkyard and brought it to the Big Island. The legislature voted to erect it near Kamehameha's birthplace. Every year, on King Kamehameha Day (June 11), a magnificent abundance of leis adorns the image of Hawai'i's great king. ⊠ *Hwy. 270, Kapa'au.*

NEED A BREAK?   Across from the King Kamehameha statue in Kapa'au, **Jen's Kohala Café** (☎ 808/889–0099) serves imaginative wraps and large sandwiches all day long. Try the Greek spinach wrap—stuffed with organic baby greens, black olives, feta cheese, and pickled *peperoncini* (small, hot chili peppers). If something sweet is more to your taste, **Kohala Coffee Mill** (☎ 808/889–5577), an espresso café in bustling Hāwī, whips up Kona coffee, espresso drinks, and luscious iced *chai* (Indian tea). There is also a selection of pastries and Tropical Dreams ice cream in such island flavors as mango and white chocolate ginger.

58 **Lapakahi State Historical Park.** A self-guided walking tour (pick up a map at the entrance) leads you through the ruins of the ancient, once-prosperous fishing village Koai'e. Displays illustrate early Hawaiian fishing, salt gathering, legends, games, shelters, and crops, and a park guide is on-site to answer questions. Since the shores off Lapakahi are now mostly a Marine Life Conservation District, and part of the site itself is considered sacred, swimming is not encouraged. ⊠ *Makai side of Hwy. 270, midway between Kawaihae and Māhukona, North Kohala,* ☎ *808/882–6207.* 🖭 *Free.* ☉ *Daily 8–4.*

57 **Mo'okini Heiau.** Few people seek out this isolated *luakini* (sacrificial) heiau, but it is so impressive in size it will give you "chicken skin" (goose bumps), especially when you think that it was built about AD 480. A nearby sign marks the place where Kamehameha I was born in 1758. Take the turnoff to 'Upolu Airport on 'Upolu Point. A rough lane to the left of the airport leads to Mo'okini Heiau. ⊠ *Turn off Hwy. 270 at sign for 'Upolu Airport, near Hāwī.*

★ **51** **Parker Ranch Visitor Center and Museum.** The center chronicles the life of John Palmer Parker (and his descendants), who founded Parker Ranch in 1847 after befriending King Kamehameha, marrying his granddaughter, and buying 2 acres of land from the king for the sum of $10. A couple of miles south of town, **Mānā,** the original koa-wood family residence, is open, as is **Pu'u'ōpelu,** the century-old residence of the late Richard Smart, a sixth-generation Parker who was an avid art collector: Venetian glass, antiques, and oils by classic artists. A ride with Parker Ranch Wagon Tours allows you a comfortable albeit old-fashioned visit of the pastures. Tickets for all attractions can be purchased at the Parker Ranch Shopping Center, at the junction of Highways 19 and 190. ⊠ *Parker Ranch Shopping Center, Hwy. 19, Kamuela,* ☎ *808/885–7655.* 🖭 *Museum*

$5, homes $7.50, wagon tour $15; combined admissions less. ☉ *Museum daily 9–5, homes daily 10–5.* 🍃

NEED A
BREAK?
At the **Little Juice Shack** in the Parker Ranch Shopping Center (☎ 808/885–1686), you can treat yourself to fresh juices made with carrots, beets, or watermelon to name a few. Add a shot of wheatgrass juice from the crop grown in the windows. Sample an organic spinach salad or six-grain turkey sandwich, or, on a cold day, try the thick and spicy five-pepper chowder.

56 **Pololū Valley.** You'll want to have cameras ready for this view of rugged coastline pounded by relentless surf and ribboned by silver waterfalls. A hiking and mule trail leads into a valley that in ancient days was heavily populated. The valleys beyond provide water for the Kohala Ditch, the ingenious project that used to bring water to the sugar plantation. The former ditch trails have become inaccessible and dangerous. A kayak cruise, a mule ride, and a ditch-trail hike reveal more of this dramatic part of Kohala history (☞ Contacts and Resources *in* Big Island A to Z, *below*). ⊠ *End of Hwy. 270.*

★ **48** **Puʻukoholā Visitor Center.** In 1790 a prophet told King Kamehameha I to build **Puʻukoholā Heiau,** and dedicate it to the war god Kūkāʻilimoku by sacrificing his principal Big Island rival, Keoua Kuahuʻula. Thus, the king would achieve his goal of conquering the Hawaiian Islands. The sacrifice was made, and the prophecy was fulfilled in 1810. Weather permitting (the trail is closed on windy days at this National Historic Site), it is a short walk over arid landscape from the visitor center to Puʻukoholā Heiau and then across the road to the smaller **Mailekini Heiau,** constructed about 1550. The center organizes Hawaiian arts-and-crafts programs on a regular basis. You can get another good view of the two heiaus by driving a bit farther down the road and turning into **Samuel M. Spencer Beach Park** (⊠ Hwy. 270, uphill from Kawaihae Harbor, ☎ 808/961–5797), which is safe for children and has extensive facilities. ⊠ *Hwy. 270, Kawaihae,* ☎ *808/882–2401.* 🎫 *Free.* ☉ *Daily 7:30–4.* 🍃

50 **Waimea Visitor Center.** The old Lindsey House—a restored ranch cabin, and listed on the Hawaiʻi Register of Historic Places—reopened in 1999 as a visitor center with detailed information on Kohala's many historic and cultural sites. ⊠ *65-1291 Kawaihae Rd., behind High Country Traders,* ☎ *808/885–6707.* ☉ *Weekdays 9–5.*

NEED A
BREAK?
If you are in the mood for a mug of steaming caffe latte with a hot croissant, stop by at the **Waimea Coffee Company** (⊠ Parker Square, off Kawaihae Rd., ☎ 808/885–4472), where you'll also find a nice selection of gourmet gifts. At **Aioli's** (⊠ ʻOpelo Plaza, Hwy. 19 and ʻOpelo Rd., ☎ 808/885–6325) you can pick up ready-to-go gourmet box lunches or opt for a custom-made sandwich. Tuesday through Saturday evening, bistro-style dinners are served from 5 to 8. Not enough choices? Friendly **Tako Taco Taqueria** (☎ 808/887–1717) serves superb fresh, organic Mexican fare. You can get it to go or eat it in the small, boldly painted eatery.

BEACHES

Don't believe it if anyone tells you the Big Island lacks beaches. It actually has 80 or more, and new ones appear—and disappear—regularly. In 1989 a new black-sand beach, Kamoamoa, formed when molten lava shattered as it hit cold ocean waters. Kamoamoa was the largest of the black-sand beaches, more than ½ mi long and 25 yards wide, until it was closed by new lava flows in 1992. Some beaches are just a little hard to get to—several are hidden behind elaborate hotels or down unmarked roads for which you'll want a four-wheel-drive vehicle or dauntless hiking spirit (or both)—and others have dangerous undertows and should be used for sunning and fishing rather than swimming. In 1990, two of the Big Island's most popular beach parks—Harry K. Brown and Kaimū—were covered by lava flows from Kīlauea. In Kailua-Kona and even in Keauhou, it's true, there are no broad expanses of coral sand. The most beautiful, swimmable white-sand beaches stretch along the Kohala coastline. The surf tends to get rough in winter. To be safe, swim only when you see local people swimming in the area. Few public beaches have lifeguards or staffed beach centers. Beaches are listed in a counterclockwise direction around the island, starting from the northern tip.

Kēōkea Beach Park. Driving back from the end of Highway 270 at the Pololū overlook to the north, you'll see a curvy road angle off to the right. Follow it for a mile, pass the cemetery with the weathered old stones, and you'll come upon the green lawns and large picnic pavilion of Kēōkea Beach Park. The black-boulder beach is suited for fishing and snorkeling in the calm summer months, but heavy surf in the winter makes this a hazardous swimming beach. A shallow, protected cove on the northeastern side of the bay is great for children. Picnic tables, rest rooms, showers, drinking water, electricity, and a campsite make this a popular weekend destination for local folks. ⊠ *Off Hwy. 270 near Pololū overlook.*

Māhukona Beach Park. Next to the abandoned Port of Māhukona, in the Kohala District, where sugar was once shipped by rail to be loaded on boats, Māhukona Beach's old docks and buildings are a photographer's treat. Divers and snorkelers can view both marine life and remnants of shipping machinery in the clear water. Heavy surf makes water activities off-limits in the winter, however. This is a pleasant picnicking spot, with rest rooms, showers, and a camping area, but no sandy beach. ⊠ *Off Hwy. 270, Māhukona.*

Samuel M. Spencer Beach Park. This spot is popular with local families because of its reef-protected, gently sloping white-sand beach, and it is safe for swimming year-round. There are cooking and camping facilities, showers, mediocre tennis courts, and a large covered pavilion with electrical outlets. Mynah birds and sparrows make their homes in large shade trees on the grounds here. You can walk to see the Pu`ukoholā and Mailekini heiaus, midway between the park and Kawaihae Harbor, which is a mile to the north. ⊠ *Entry road off Hwy. 270, uphill from Kawaihae Harbor,* ☎ *808/882–2401.*

★ **Kauna`oa Beach at Mauna Kea Beach Resort.** It's a toss-up whether this or neighboring Hāpuna is the most beautiful beach on the island. Kauna`oa is long and white, and it slopes very gradually. It's a great place for snorkeling. In winter, when the surf is high, swimmers should consult beach attendants before taking a dip, as the powerful waves can be dangerous. Hotel guests generally congregate near the hotel's beach facilities. Amenities are hotel-owned. Public parking places are limited and it's first-come, first-served. ⊠ *Entry through gate to Mauna Kea Beach Resort, off Hwy. 19.*

★ **Hāpuna Beach State Park.** This beach is a ½-mi crescent of glistening sand guarded by rocky points at either end. The surf can be hazardous in winter, but in summer the gradual slope of the beach can stretch as wide as 200 ft into a perfectly blue ocean—ideal for swimming, snorkeling, and scuba diving. Children enjoy the shallow cove with tidal pools at the north end. Signs restrict the use of surfboards and similar beach equipment. State cabins and public facilities are available nearby, and there is a convenient snack bar. There are no lifeguards to rescue swimmers from rough seas in winter, so keep out of the water at that time. ✉ *Between Mauna Kea Beach and Mauna Lani resorts, off Hwy. 19,* ☎ *808/974–6200 or 808/882–6206.*

Holoholokai Beach Park. A rocky beach of black-lava formations and white-coral clinkers is fine for surfers and snorkelers, and a small grassy area is available to sunbathers. Bathrooms, picnic tables, and barbecue grills are nicely maintained. Just before the beach park, you can explore historic Puakō Petroglyph Park. Malama Trail meanders 7/10 mi through brush and kiawe trees to an area of lava covered with the ancient etchings of Hawaiian figures and animals. ✉ *Off Hwy. 19 at Mauna Lani Bay Hotel and Bungalows.*

'Anaeho'omalu Beach, at Outrigger Waikoloa Resort. This expansive beach on the west coast, also known as A-Bay, is perfect for swimming, windsurfing, snorkeling, and diving. Some equipment is for rent at the north end. Be sure to wander around the ancient fishponds and petroglyph fields. ✉ *Follow Waikoloa Beach Dr. to Royal Waikoloan Resort, then signs to park and beach right-of-way to south.*

Ki'holo Bay. The unmarked road across a vast lava field requires a four-wheel-drive vehicle. Private homes are built along the oceanfront. The huge, spring-fed Luahinewai Pond anchors the south end of the bay, and the three black-pebble beaches are fine for swimming in calm weather. At the northern end, Wainānāli'i Pond (a 5-acre lagoon) is a feeding site for green sea turtles. Kamehameha I had a well-stocked fishpond here that was destroyed by lava in 1859. The two ponds are off-limits to swimmers. Secluded areas of the 2-mi bay are sometimes sought out by nude sunbathers, although nudity is officially illegal on all Big Island beaches. You'll find good swimming here but no facilities. ✉ *Hwy. 19, Mile Marker 81.*

Kona Coast Beach Park. In a primitive setting, this sandy white beach nestles in a bay area with gentle surf. It has a limited number of picnic tables shaded by coconut trees but no drinking water. Portable toilets are the only additional facilities. ✉ *Sign about 1 mi north of Kona International Airport, off Hwy. 19, marks rough 1½-mi road to beach.*

Honokōhau and 'Alula. These two beaches are down the road to Honokōhau Harbor. 'Alula is a slip of white sand a short walk over the lava to the left of the harbor entrance. Honokōhau Beach is north of the harbor (turn right at Gentry Marina and go past the boat-loading dock). Follow the trail to the right through the bush until you come upon the ¾-mi beach and the ruins of ancient fishponds. The center portion of the beach is comparatively rock-free, though a shelf of lava along the water's edge lines most of the shore. The 'Aimakapā fishpond is directly inland. At the north end of the beach a trail leads mauka across the lava to a freshwater pool. The only public facilities are at the boat harbor. ✉ *Off Hwy. 19, Honokōhau Harbor.*

Old Kona Airport Park. The unused runway—great for jogging or running—is still visible above this beach at Kailua Park, which has picnic tables, showers, bathroom facilities, tennis courts, and palm trees strung out along the shore. The beach has a sheltered, sandy inlet for children, but for adults it's better for snorkeling and scuba diving than it is for swimming. An offshore surfing break known as Old Airport is popular with Kona surfers. ✉ *North end of Kuakini Hwy., Kona,* ☎ *808/327–4958.*

White Sands, Magic Sands, or Disappearing Sands Beach Park. Now you see it, now you don't. Overnight, winter waves wash away this small white-sand beach on Ali'i Drive just south of Kailua-Kona. In summer you'll know you've found it when you see the body- and board-surfers. Rest rooms, showers, a lifeguard tower, and a coconut grove create a favorite and convenient summer hangout, but this isn't a great beach for swimming. ✉ *4½ mi south of Kailua-Kona on Ali'i Dr.*

Kahalu'u Beach Park. This spot was a favorite of King Kalākaua, whose summer cottage is on the grounds of the Aston Keauhou Beach Resort next door. Kahalu'u is popular with commoners, too, and on weekends there are just too many people. On the other hand, this is one of the best snorkeling places. A strong riptide during high surf pulls swimmers away from shore. Facilities include a pavilion, rest rooms, showers, a lifeguard tower, and limited parking. A narrow path takes you directly to the Resort's Beach Bar & Grill which serves sandwiches and plate lunches. ✉ *5½ mi south of Kailua-Kona on Ali'i Dr.*

Ho'okena Beach Park. You'll feel like an adventurer when you come upon Ho'okena, at the northern end of Kauhakō Bay. When Mark Twain visited, 2,500 people populated the busy seaport village. You can still find gas lampposts dating from the 1900s. This dark-gray coral-and-lava-sand beach offers good swimming, snorkeling, and bodysurfing. Rest rooms, showers, and picnic tables are available at the park. The access road is narrow and bumpy. ✉ *2-mi drive down road bordered by ruins of stone wall off Hwy. 11, 23 mi south of Kailua-Kona.*

Nāpō'opo'o Beach Park. The best way to see this black-sand beach and marine preserve is to take a snorkel, scuba, or glass-bottom boat tour from Keauhou Bay, unless you don't mind the long, steep road down from the highway to the ocean. A 27-ft white obelisk indicates where Capt. James Cook was killed in 1779. This six-acre beach park has a picnic pavilion, tables, showers, rest rooms, and a basketball court. ✉ *Kealakekua Bay.*

Green Sand (Mahana) Beach. You need a four-wheel-drive vehicle to get to this beach, whose greenish tint is caused by an accumulation of the olivine that forms in volcanic eruptions. You can get to South Point (where you'll find ruins of a heiau and the winches once used to load cattle and produce onto boats from the cliffs) in a regular car, but it's a few rugged road miles to where the beach lies at the base of Pu'u o Mahana, a cinder cone formed during an early eruption of Mauna Loa. Swimming can be hazardous when the surf is up in this windy, remote area. There are no facilities and no shade trees. ✉ *2½ mi northeast of South Point, off Hwy. 11.*

Punalu'u Beach Park. The endangered Hawaiian green sea turtle nests in the black sand of this beautiful and easily accessible beach. Fishponds are just inland. At the northern end of the beach near the boat ramp lie the ruins of a heiau and a flat sacrificial stone. This used to be a sugar and army port until the tidal wave of 1946 destroyed the buildings. Offshore rip currents are extremely dangerous, though you'll see a few local surfers riding the waves. There are rest rooms across the road. Inland is a memorial to Henry Opukaha'ia. In 1809, when he was 17, Opukaha'ia swam out to a fur-trading ship in the harbor and asked to sail as a cabin boy. When he reached New England, he entered the Foreign Mission School in Connecticut, but he died of typhoid fever in 1818. His dream of bringing Christianity to the Islands inspired the American Board of Missionaries in 1820 to send the first Protestant missionaries to Hawai'i. ✉ *Hwy. 11, 27 mi south of Volcanoes National Park.*

Ahalanui Park. This three-acre beach park with a ½-acre pond heated by a volcanic steam opened in 1993 to replace earlier beach parks that were lost to lava flows. The pond here is good for swimming, but the nearby ocean is rough. Drinking water and a few tables are available for picnicking, and there are portable rest rooms. ✉ *Kapoho coast, southeast of Pāhoa, 2½ mi south of junction of Hwys. 132 and 137, Puna District,* ☎ *808/961–8311.*

MacKenzie State Recreation Area. This spacious, 13-acre park shaded by ironwoods is good for picnicking and camping. You can't swim here, but there are rest rooms and plenty of free parking. ⊠ *Off Hwy. 137 2 mi south of junction with Hwy. 132, Puna District.*

Isaac Hale Beach Park. Oceanfront park facilities include rest rooms and picnic areas. It's a good place for an afternoon nap. ⊠ *Puna district off Hwy. 137 just north of junction with Hwy. 132.*

Onekahakaha Beach Park. A protected, white-sand beach makes this a favorite for Hilo families with small children. Lifeguards are on duty year-round. The park has picnic pavilions, rest rooms, and showers. ⊠ *Follow Kalaniana'ole Ave. east 3 mi south of Hilo.*

Leleiwi Beach Park and Richardson Ocean Park. Near Hilo, along Hilo's Keaukaha shoreline laced with bays, inlets, lagoons, and pretty parks, these two beaches are adjacent to each other. Richardson's tiny beach, just beyond the seawall, allows entry to the water for good snorkeling and swimming. The grassy area is ideal for picnics. ⊠ *2349 Kalaniana'ole Ave.; follow Kalaniana'ole Ave. east along the water about 4 mi south of Hilo.*

Reeds Bay Beach Park. Rest rooms, showers, drinking water, calm and safe swimming, and proximity to downtown Hilo are the enticements of this cove. Most swimmers take a dip in the Ice Pond adjoining the head of Reeds Bay. Cold freshwater springs seep from the bottom of the pond and rise in the saltwater. ⊠ *Banyan Dr. and Kalaniana'ole Ave., Hilo.*

DINING

Choosing a place to eat in the western part of the Big Island is difficult. There are many good, established restaurants and a wide variety of ethnic eateries. All along Ali'i Drive in Kailua-Kona, sunny little restaurants and cafés with indoor-outdoor seating offer numerous cuisines as well as regular American/Hawai'i regional menus. Hotels along the Kohala Coast invest in top chefs and, between that and the opulent settings, diners are rarely disappointed. Upcountry Waimea—just a 40-minute drive inland from the resorts—also has an array of restaurants if you want a change from hotel dining. While Hilo's dining scene may seem less exciting, restaurants there are often lower-priced family places where good, substantial food makes up for lack of atmosphere. For price category explanations, *see* Smart Travel Tips A to Z at the back of the book.

Hilo

American/Casual

$$ ✕ **Harrington's.** A popular and reliable steak and seafood restaurant right on Reeds Bay, Harrington's has a dining lānai that extends over the water. The fresh mahimahi meunière, served with browned butter, lemon, and parsley, and the Slavic steak, thinly sliced and slathered with garlic butter, are two popular dishes. Daily specials might include lobster-stuffed 'ahi and chicken Florentine. ⊠ *135 Kalaniana'ole Ave.,* ☎ *808/961–4966. MC, V. No lunch weekends.*

$–$$ ✕ **Seaside.** This family-home eatery is casual and can get noisy at times. It's also one of the best fish restaurants around. Most of the fish served are raised in the 10-acre pond or are caught in Hawaiian-style fish traps when they swim in from the ocean via a connecting waterway. Fried *āholehole* (young Hawaiian flagtail) is a signature dish, as is mullet steamed in ti leaves. Trout, perch, and catfish are also on the menu. The restaurant offers steak, pasta, and chicken dishes as well. Bare wooden tables offer great water views on the patio or from a window-enclosed room. Beer, wine, and sake are available. ⊠ *1790 Kalaniana'ole Ave.,* ☎ *808/935–8825. MC, V. Closed Mon. No lunch.*

Big Island Dining

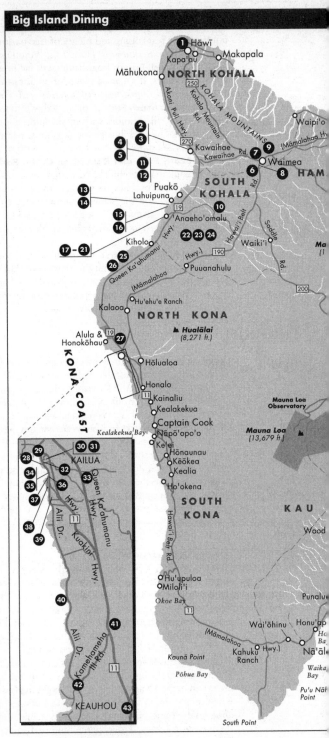

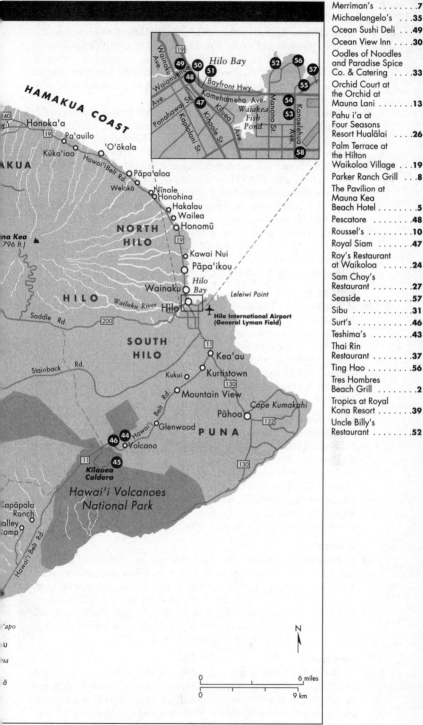

$–$$ ✕ **Uncle Billy's Restaurant.** The decor is pure Hawaiian kitsch—right out of 1930s Hollywood—but the thatched roofs, tinkling capiz-shell wind chimes, Tahitian print curtains, and plastic flowers in lauhala-covered planters add to the fun. There is a free nightly hula show as well. Choose fish presented in meunière sauce, macadamia-nut sauce, admiral sauce (with shallots), or shrimp-and-wine sauce; or teriyaki beef or shrimp Orientale. ⊠ *Hilo Bay Hotel, 87 Banyan Dr.,* ☎ *808/ 935–0861. AE, D, DC, MC, V. No lunch.*

$ ✕ **Fiasco's.** Booths with floor-to-ceiling dividers provide privacy in this restaurant with a something-for-everyone menu: fajitas, chicken wings, and an all-you-can-eat soup-and-salad bar. The place is famous for its margarita specials and 35 varieties of domestic and imported beer. There is live entertainment Thursday, Friday, and Saturday nights. ⊠ *200 Kanoelehua Ave.,* ☎ *808/935–7666. AE, D, MC, V.*

$ ✕ **Ken's House of Pancakes.** For years this 24-hour coffee shop between the airport and the Banyan Drive hotels has been a gathering place for Hilo residents for breakfast. Ken's serves good pancakes and omelets. They're cheap, too. With close to 180 items on the menu, a paniolo night, and a "Golden Oldies" Sunday, lunch and dinner can be fun as well. ⊠ *1730 Kamehameha Ave.,* ☎ *808/935–8711. Reservations not accepted. AE, D, DC, MC, V.*

Chinese

$–$$$ ✕ **Ting Hao.** This Mandarin restaurant emphasizes fresh island fish with offerings that change daily. Other entrées include spicy Szechuan and Hunan dishes and scrumptious specialties from Taiwan and Peking, including lobster with black-bean sauce and chicken with cashew nuts. All are cooked to your taste, from mild to searingly hot. Vegetarian dishes, such as eggplant with garlic sauce, round out the menu. ⊠ *Hawai'i Naniloa Resort, 93 Banyan Dr.,* ☎ *808/935–8888. AE, D, DC, MC, V. Closed Tues.*

Hawaiian

$ ✕ **Kuhio Grille.** There is no ambience and your water is served in unbreakable plastic, but if you are searching for local fare—that eclectic and undefinable fusion of ethnic cuisines—Kuhio Grille is a must. Sam Araki serves a one-pound *laulau* (ti-leaf steamed dishes) made with Waipi'o Valley–grown taro leaves and pork alongside "loco" plate lunches and grilled meats. It is a cafeteria-like place at the edge of Hilo's largest shopping mall, and is open 24 hours on weekends. ⊠ *Prince Kūhiō Shopping Plaza,* ☎ *808/959–2336. MC, V.*

Italian

$$ ✕ **Pescatore.** An intimate old-world atmosphere of dark wood and plush red chairs is the setting for traditional dishes such as eggplant parmigiana and lasagna. Pescatore's menu also includes veal with sage, prosciutto, and provolone, and a classic cioppino. It's right in downtown Hilo and is recommended for families. In addition to lunch and dinner daily, the restaurant serves breakfast on weekends. ⊠ *235 Keawe St., at Haili St.,* ☎ *808/969–9090. D, MC, V.*

Japanese

$–$$ ✕ **Ocean Sushi Deli.** Fresh seafood dishes and superb sushi rolls will make you quickly forget the mediocre ambience of Formica tables and neon lights. Authentic and affordable, sushi rolls start at just $2 each, and there are dozens to choose from. 'Ahi *poke* (seasoned raw tuna), fried limpets, and chewy *taco* (octopus) salad are favorites of the local crowd, but there are also more familiar, equally delectable dishes such as sake-steamed scallops. The place is popular and almost always crowded. ⊠ *239 Keawe St.,* ☎ *808/961–6625. MC, V.*

$ ✕ **Honu's Nest.** Overlooking Hilo Bay, this tiny restaurant (just four tables and a window bar) is a local favorite. A Japanese menu with a contemporary local twist includes luscious and spicy curries, tempura chicken or vegetables, and homemade ginger and teriyaki sauces. Each *donburi* (bowl of rice topped with your menu choice) or *teishaku* (plate with rice on the side) comes with fragrant miso soup. The staff is friendly, the ceramic bowls are exquisite, and the prices are hard to beat. Try to avoid Hilo's lunch rush hour. ✉ *270 Kamehameha Ave.,* ☎ *808/ 935–9321. No credit cards. Reservations not accepted. Closed Sun.*

Thai

$ ✕ **Royal Siam.** More than 50 Thai dishes are featured on the menu of this well-established restaurant situated in the heart of the old downtown district. Service is excellent. Many vegetarian choices are available. Try the Buddha Rama—chicken or tofu sautéed in peanut sauce and served on a bed of spinach—or one of the five fresh curries. ✉ *70 Mamo St.,* ☎ *808/961–6100. AE, D, DC, MC, V. Closed Sun.*

Kohala-Kona and Keauhou

American/Casual

$$$–$$$$ ✕ **The Grill at the Orchid at Mauna Lani.** Featuring an award-winning
★ wine list and a superb menu, this stellar restaurant has earned a top-notch reputation. Rich koa-wood paneling, a large koa bar, and a piano with a small dance floor give it an old-world ambience. Both appetizers and entrées expand on the fresh, local flavors of Hawai'i regional cuisine, adding robust dishes such as pan-seared Hudson Valley foie gras and grilled beef tenderloin with Kona lobster and creamed-corn potato. Seating out in the open air is available, and the service is impeccable. ✉ *Orchid at Mauna Lani, 1 N. Kanikū Dr., Kohala Coast,* ☎ *808/885–2000. Reservations essential. AE, D, DC, MC, V.*

$$–$$$$ ✕ **Kamuela Provision Company at the Hilton Waikoloa Village.** You'll have a spectacular view of the Kohala-Kona coastline as you sample light and flavorful salad selections, broiled and grilled steak, or seafood. Tables along the lānai open to sea breezes, and ceiling fans cool the rest of the dining room. It's a great place to sip cocktails. The fresh-fish menu includes all the Hawaiian favorites: Order your ono or 'ahi sautéed, grilled, poached, or blackened. An 18-ounce porterhouse leads the steak menu. ✉ *425 Waikoloa Beach Dr., Kamuela,* ☎ *808/ 886–1234. AE, D, DC, MC, V.*

$$–$$$ ✕ **Big Island Steak House.** The walls here are adorned with Hawaiian kitsch dating from the '30s, '40s, and '50s—'ukuleles, steamer trunks, a zany grass-skirted gorilla, and the like. As the name implies, the place serves steak—large portions in four different styles, straight from the grill and without much fanfare. On the menu are also seafood dishes such as coconut shrimp and vegetarian pastas. ✉ *King's Shops, Waikoloa Resort, Waikoloa Beach Dr., across from Royal Waikoloan Hotel, Waikoloa,* ☎ *808/886–8805. AE, D, MC, V. No lunch.*

$$–$$$ ✕ **Chart House at Waterfront Row.** This casual chain restaurant in the shopping and dining complex on Ali'i Drive overlooks the ocean. A cool gray, teal, and peach interior, and prints of old Hawaiian maps on the tables, complement the artwork displayed. Many come here for drinks and appetizers. The extensive menu is reliable and seldom changes. Dinners include thickly sliced prime rib, fresh local fish, and Alaskan king crab and are served with signature squaw and sourdough breads. ✉ *75-5770 Ali'i Dr., Kailua-Kona,* ☎ *808/329–2451. AE, DC, MC, V. No lunch.*

$$–$$$ ✕ **Jameson's by the Sea.** Sit outside next to the ocean or just inside the picture windows for glorious sunset views over Magic Sands Beach. When the ocean is calm this is a most romantic place. You can choose between three or four island fish specials daily, including Cajun-style

preparations. Stir-fried scallops and Jameson's special creamy clam chowder are popular as well. ✉ 77-6452 Ali'i Dr., Kailua-Kona, ☎ 808/329–3195. AE, D, DC, MC, V. No lunch weekends.

$$–$$$ ✕ **Kona Inn Restaurant.** This open-air restaurant, which faces a wide lawn with the ocean beyond, has been a longtime favorite for cocktails at sunset. Fresh fish—'ahi and mahimahi—and chicken entrées are consistently delectable. Burgers at lunch are generously sized and reasonably priced. The steak fries are just right. ✉ 75-5744 Ali'i Dr., Kailua-Kona, ☎ 808/329–4455. AE, MC, V.

$–$$$ ✕ **Bubba Gump Shrimp Company.** For all you shrimp lovers, or Forrest Gump fans, the Big Island now sports its own spin-off restaurant, right at the ocean's edge. In downtown Kailua-Kona, this was once an old-timers' restaurant but now attracts a rambunctious, young crowd. It's chaotic, it's fun, there's a lot of shrimp—for breakfast, lunch, and dinner every day—and you get the attention of your waiter with a sign that says: RUN FORREST FUN. ✉ 75-5776 Ali'i Dr., Kailua-Kona, ☎ 808/331–8442. AE, D, DC, MC, V.

$–$$ ✕ **Kona Beach Restaurant at King Kamehameha's Kona Beach Hotel.** The buffet-style meals offered at this Kailua-Kona hotel are themed and great for families: Monday and Tuesday it's Hawaiian; Wednesday and Thursday pasta; and Friday and Saturday prime rib and seafood. Tables look out on a torchlit lawn. Beyond is the beach, with outrigger canoes and a thatched house built on a restored heiau. A Sunday champagne brunch is served from 9 to 1. ✉ 75-5660 Palani Rd., Kailua-Kona, ☎ 808/329–2911. AE, D, DC, MC, V.

$ ✕ **Ocean View Inn.** To those on a tight budget, this local hangout facing the pier at Kailua Bay has been a lifesaver for breakfast, lunch, and dinner since the 1920s. Chinese and American food are on the plate-lunch menu, and you can get Hawaiian specialties à la carte. Although there is no atmosphere, the servings are ample. ✉ 75-5683 Ali'i Dr., Kailua-Kona, ☎ 808/329–9998. No credit cards. Closed Mon.

Chinese

$$–$$$ ✕ **Kirin.** This new addition to the Hilton Waikoloa Village restaurants serves authentic Cantonese fare in a classic Chinese restaurant setting. Over a hundred exotic dishes are featured on the menu, many with ingredient combinations you might not be used to, but which prove to be delicious. How about prawns with honey-glazed walnuts and a citrus dressing or sizzling beef tenderloin with peppercorns? More conventional noodle and rice dishes are also available. ✉ 425 Waikoloa Beach Dr., Kamuela, ☎ 808/886–1234. AE, D, DC, MC, V.

$–$$$ ✕ **Grand Palace Chinese Restaurant.** A reasonable alternative in a land of high-priced hotel dining, this successful and friendly Chinese restaurant is open for lunch and dinner. It is nicely decorated with a floral carpet and etched-glass panels. An extensive menu offers Chinese items from most regions, including such standards as egg foo young, wonton soup, chicken with snow peas, and beef with broccoli. More adventurous are local sautéed seafood, lobster, and sizzling scallops with a pepper-and-black-bean sauce. ✉ King's Shops, Waikoloa Resort, Waikoloa Beach Dr., Waikoloa, ☎ 808/886–6668. AE, DC, MC, V.

Contemporary/Hawaiian

$$$$ ✕ **Hale Samoa at Kona Village Resort.** Slightly formal, superbly romantic, this Kona Village restaurant has a magical atmosphere, especially in the glow of sunset. In a Samoan setting with tapa screens and candles you can feast on prix-fixe dinners that change daily. Specialties may include papaya and coconut bisque, duck stuffed with andouille sausage on a mango-and-orange coulis, or wok-charred prime strip loin. Reservations can be made only on the day you want to dine, and they are essential. The entry road to Kona Village is 6 mi out Highway 19

from Kailua. Resort wear is the norm here at dinner. ⊠ *Queen Ka'ahu-manu Hwy., Kailua-Kona,* ☎ *808/325–5555. Reservations essential. AE, DC, MC, V. Closed Wed., Fri., and 1 wk in Dec.*

$$$–$$$$ ✕ **The Batik at Mauna Kea Beach Resort.** For the hotel's signature restau-
★ rant—with a dining lānai and an ambience hinting of exotic India—executive chef Goran Streng has combined classical European flavors with neo-Asian dishes. The menu features tandoor-oven-baked nan bread, Thai and Indonesian curries, and Hawai'i regional creations using specialty produce such as Keāhole lobster. Irresistible desserts include Grand Marnier soufflé and warm Valhrona chocolate cake. Romantic dinner music complements the evening. Dress up a little for this place. Jackets for men are optional, but they must wear button-down shirts, and shorts are a no-no. ⊠ *62-100 Mauna Kea Beach Dr., Kamuela,* ☎ *808/882–7222. AE, D, DC, MC, V. Closed Tues. and Sat.*

$$$–$$$$ ✕ **Pahu i'a at Four Seasons Resort Hualālai.** The English translation
★ for the word *pahu i'a* is "aquarium." For sure, the 9-by-4-ft center-piece in the entrance casts a dreamy light on the wooden interior of this exquisite restaurant. The restaurant is closer to the ocean than any other, and outdoor deck seating is romantic even at breakfast. Meals are imaginative and beautifully presented. The daily tasting menu offers three courses and a dessert, or you may choose sophisticated à la carte entrées such as kiawe-wood smoked veal chop in Madeira jus or Keāhole lobster with a sauce made of macadamia nuts and ginger butter. ⊠ *Four Seasons Resort Hualālai, 100 Ka'ūpūlehu Dr.,* ☎ *808/325–8000. No lunch. AE, D, DC, MC, V.*

$$–$$$$ ✕ **CanoeHouse at the Mauna Lani Bay Hotel and Bungalows.** This open-
★ air beachfront restaurant, surrounded by fishponds and with its signature shining koa canoe, is widely hailed as one of Hawai'i's best. Its cuisine is Pacific Rim the way it used to be: a matching of pure Eastern and Western flavors with imaginative entrées such as grilled New York steak with a sauce of merlot and *panini* (local wild cactus fruit), and miso-sake–marinated mahimahi. Also consider the famous CanoeHouse *pūpū* (appetizer) platter, and finish your meal with the crème brûlée sampler. ⊠ *68-1400 Mauna Lani Dr., Kohala Coast,* ☎ *808/885–6622. AE, D, DC, MC, V.*

$$–$$$$ ✕ **Coast Grille at Hāpuna Beach Prince Hotel.** This spacious, high-ceil-
★ ing seafood restaurant has lānai overlooking the ocean—a great place to sit when the nights are balmy, but take a sweater when the trade winds are up. Oyster lovers should head to the oyster bar, which also offers clams, Dungeness crab, and lobster claws. The must-try fish here is the delicate farm-raised *moi*, a fish that in ancient times was savored only by chiefs. For dessert, sample the warm chocolate pudding while the stars rise over the ocean. ⊠ *62-100 Kauna'oa Dr., Kamuela,* ☎ *808/880–1111. AE, D, DC, MC, V.*

$$–$$$$ ✕ **Gallery Restaurant at Mauna Lani Resort.** Bordering the Francis H. I'i Brown Golf Course, the open-air Gallery has a comfortable club-house atmosphere with mahogany paneling and an impressive koa bar. Fresh island ingredients find their way into American-inspired dishes. An appealing menu includes five different preparations for island fish. Try it crusted with macadamia nuts or broiled with tomatoes and shrimp. There is also fillet with shiitake mushroom sauce. Desserts include superb apple cobblers. ⊠ *68-1400 Mauna Lani Dr., Kohala Coast,* ☎ *808/885–7777. AE, D, DC, MC, V. Closed Sun.–Mon.*

$$–$$$$ ✕ **The Pavilion at Mauna Kea Beach Resort.** Relax on the lānai over-looking the white sands of Kauna'oa Beach to savor a meal that makes you appreciate Hawai'i. This family-oriented restaurant serves traditional fare such as pastas and grilled items as well as sophisticated Hawai'i regional–style seafood. It also offers an elaborate, totally global breakfast buffet that includes everything from carrot juice and bagels with smoked salmon to miso soup. At night, below in the lapping waves,

you'll see manta rays swim underneath torch lights. ⊠ *62-100 Mauna Kea Beach Dr., Kamuela,* ☎ *808/882–7222. AE, D, DC, MC, V.*

$$–$$$ ✕ **Huggo's.** Open windows extend out over the rocks at the ocean's edge, and you can almost touch the manta rays drawn to the spotlights at night. Relax with a sensational flaming volcanic cocktail or feast on fresh local seafood, prepared to your taste or offered as a daily-changing special preparation. For lighter fare, try an exquisite dinner-size salad with fresh bread. This popular spot also offers nightly live entertainment and can get crowded. ⊠ *75-5828 Kahakai Rd., off Ali'i Dr., Kailua-Kona,* ☎ *808/329–1493. D, DC, MC, V. No lunch weekends.*

$$–$$$ ✕ **Roy's Restaurant at Waikoloa.** Roy Yamaguchi, one of the inven-
   ★   tors of Hawai'i regional cuisine, designs his restaurants as places to have fun. At Waikoloa's King's Shops, window tables overlook a golf course lake. There's an enormous selection of appetizers that you can order as starters or make a complete meal of: If you decide not to select an individual wood-oven pizza (hard choice!), try pūpū like blackened 'ahi with a hot soy-mustard butter sauce, Asian hibachi salmon, sweet onion tart, or three-cheese spinach polenta. There's an extensive wine list to go with Roy's innovative fare. Be forewarned that the place tends to get noisy, especially on weekends. ⊠ *King's Shops, Waikoloa Resort, Waikoloa,* ☎ *808/886–4321. AE, D, DC, MC, V.*

$$ ✕ **Bamboo Restaurant.** It's out of the way, the food is wonderful, and the service has a delightful country flair. The decor is inviting and artistic, combining such elements as bamboo finishes, bold art, and an old unfinished wooden floor. The restaurant's signature dish is chicken potsticker with peanuts, ginger, garlic, and lemongrass and a sweet chili-mint sauce. Creative entrées feature fresh island fish prepared several ways. The coconut-and-saffron bouillabaisse is exquisite. The restaurant has a large koa gallery, and Friday and Saturday nights local musicians entertain. ⊠ *Old Takata Store, Hwy. 270, Hāwī,* ☎ *808/889–5555. DC, MC, V. Closed Mon. No dinner Sun.*

$$ ✕ **Sam Choy's Restaurant.** In the Kaloko Industrial Park near Kona International Airport, Sam's attracts workers in the surrounding area for hearty, local-style breakfasts and lunches—saimin, stew omelets, and Hawaiian burritos. Tuesday through Saturday nights, the chef-owner puts out white tablecloths, and customers bring their own wine and settle in for some of the finest Hawai'i regional cuisine. The dinner menu changes weekly but almost always includes fresh fish, seafood laulau, Chinese honey duck, or macadamia-nut chicken. ⊠ *73-5576 Kauhola St., Bay 1, Koloko Industrial Park, Kailua-Kona,* ☎ *808/326–1545. D, MC, V. BYOB.*

Continental

$–$$ ✕ **Tropics at Royal Kona Resort.** At dusk, when the sun outlines the boats bobbing offshore, you'll have a lovely, peaceful view at this open-air dining room overlooking Kailua Bay and within walking distance of central Kailua-Kona. While the restaurant serves daily breakfast buffets and is open three nights a week for à la carte dinners, the place is known for its ample seafood and prime-rib buffets on Tuesday and Friday–Sunday nights, a good-value feast for big eaters. The hotel hosts lū'aus three times a week. ⊠ *75-5852 Ali'i Dr.,* ☎ *808/329–3111. AE, D, DC, MC, V.*

French

$$–$$$ ✕ **La Bourgogne.** A genial husband-and-wife team owns this relaxing, country-style restaurant with dark-wood walls and romantic blue-velvet booths. It's just 4 mi out of town. The traditional French menu features classics such as beef filet with a cabernet sauvignon sauce, escargots, rack of lamb with mustard sauce, and—less traditional—Lāna'i venison with a pomegranate glaze. ⊠ *Kuakini Plaza S. on Hwy.*

11, 77-6400 *Nālani, Kailua-Kona,* ☎ *808/329–6711. AE, D, DC, MC, V. Reservations essential. No smoking. Closed Sun. No lunch.*

Greek

$–$$ ✗ **Cassandra's Greek Taverna.** Sporting the blue and white colors of the Greek flag, Cassandra's offers plenty of authentic selections. Greek salads, a gyro plate of sliced beef with roast potatoes, *dolmades* (grape leaves stuffed with meat and rice), moussaka, and a variety of souvlaki (lamb, beef, chicken) keep dinners interesting, but the restaurant's main attraction is the belly dancer on Friday, Saturday, and Sunday nights. ✉ *75-5719 W. Ali'i Dr., Kailua-Kona,* ☎ *808/334–1066. AE, D, DC, MC, V. No lunch Sun.*

Indonesian

$–$$ ✗ **Sibu.** In the heart of Kailua-Kona and hidden by large potted plants inside a tiny shopping mall, this small Indonesian restaurant has been a favorite with locals for years. Try shrimp flavored with delicate lemongrass, coconut milk, and fragrant Indonesian spices or a hearty vegetable satay with lush cherry tomatoes grilled over an open flame. ✉ *75-5695 Ali'i Dr., Kailua-Kona,* ☎ *808/329–1112. No credit cards.*

Italian

$$–$$$ ✗ **Café Pesto.** Popular, and crowded at lunchtime, this harborside restaurant with its bold decor has earned a reputation for its innovative pizzas and other Mediterranean dishes prepared with Pacific Rim flair and island ingredients. Sample a pizza with chili-grilled shrimp, shiitake mushrooms and cilantro crème fraîche, or the popular seafood risotto made with sweet Thai chilies, jumbo scallops, and tiger prawns. A second location is in Hilo right across from the bay. ✉ *Kawaihae Shopping Center, Kawaihae,* ☎ *808/882–1071;* ✉ *New S. Hata Bldg., 308 Kamehameha Ave., Hilo,* ☎ *808/969–6640. AE, D, DC, MC, V.*

$$–$$$ ✗ **Donatoni's at the Hilton Waikoloa Village.** Lighter cuisine, shellfish, and the more subtle sauces of Italy, as well as *orecchiette* (little ear-shape) pasta and gnocchi, are served in this romantic restaurant. Reminiscent of an Italian villa and overlooking a lagoon, Donatoni's has tables on various levels and a wide lānai, so no view is obstructed. Be sure to look over the extensive Italian wine and champagne list, and treat yourself to an authentic tiramisu for dessert. ✉ *425 Waikoloa Beach Dr., Kamuela,* ☎ *808/886–1234. AE, D, DC, MC, V. No lunch.*

$$ ✗ **Michaelangelo's.** This Italian and seafood restaurant on the second level of Waterfront Row offers a superb oceanside dining view. Pastas, with various toppings such as steak Capri, lobster and garlic, and scallops in creamy macadamia-nut sauce, come with homemade focaccia. There are nice pizzas, too. The place rocks after 10 with a live DJ. ✉ *Waterfront Row, Kailua-Kona,* ☎ *808/329–4436. D, DC, MC, V.*

Japanese

$$$ ✗ **Imari at the Hilton Waikoloa Village.** This elegant Japanese restau-
★ rant, complete with waterfalls and a teahouse, serves sukiyaki and tempura aimed to please mainland tastes. Beyond the display of Imari porcelain at the entrance, you'll find beef and chicken cooked at your table, complete *teppan* (grilled) dinners, and an outstanding sushi bar. Impeccable service by kimono-clad waitresses adds to the quiet, refined ambience. ✉ *425 Waikoloa Beach Dr., Kamuela,* ☎ *808/886–1234. AE, D, DC, MC, V. No lunch.*

$$–$$$ ✗ **Hakone at Hāpuna Beach Prince Hotel.** It's hard not to start whis-
★ pering in this tranquil and graceful restaurant, open only at night, where exquisite specialty dishes such as *shirasu oroshi* (grated daikon radish) and *mozaku su* (marinated seaweed) compete with an elaborate sushi bar and the finest sashimi platters. You can choose a Japanese buffet or opt for an à la carte meal such as sukiyaki. A beautiful selection of

sake guarantees to enliven your meal. ⊠ *62-100 Kauna`oa Dr., Hāpuna Beach Prince Hotel,* ☎ *808/880–1111. AE, D, DC, MC, V. Closed Thur.–Fri. No lunch.*

$–$$ ✕ **Teshima's.** Local businesspeople show up at Teshima's whenever they're in the mood for reliable Big Island Japanese-American cooking. Service is so-so, but residents come for the sashimi, beef-tofu stir-fry, and puffy shrimp tempura. You might also want to try a *teishoku* (tray) of assorted Japanese delicacies. The restaurant is 15 minutes south of Kailua-Kona. ⊠ *Māmalahoa Hwy., Honalo,* ☎ *808/322–9140. No credit cards.*

Mexican

$–$$ ✕ **Tres Hombres Beach Grill.** Here's a less-expensive lunch and dinner alternative if you're staying at the Kohala Coast resorts. The casual Californian-Mexican restaurant offers burgers, sandwiches, and chilies *rellenos* (mildly roasted and stuffed with cheese) at lunch. Dinner items include bean-and-rice combinations, fresh fish, salads, steaks, and gazpacho. A "fit for life" menu features low-fat entrées. The separate bar has a '50s Surf City look and is known for its Mexican beer and tequila selection. ⊠ *Kawaihae Shopping Center,* ☎ *808/ 882–1031. MC, V.*

Mixed Menu

$$–$$$ ✕ **Edward's at Kanaloa.** This local favorite has delicious Mediterranean food with North African and Middle Eastern overtones, and dinner prices are within reason. The tagine chicken is Moroccan-spiced and comes atop a saffron couscous. The Aegean salmon and shrimp are served with a roasted red pepper sauce. Luscious desserts vary daily but always include a superb flourless chocolate cake. ⊠ *Kanaloa at Kona, 78-261 Manukai St., Kailua-Kona,* ☎ *808/322–1434 or 808/ 322–9625. AE, DC, MC, V.*

$$–$$$ ✕ **Orchid Court at the Orchid at Mauna Lani.** Bordering the resort's native gardens, this is a casual, family-oriented restaurant. Seafood fettuccine, salads and sandwiches, grilled vegetable wraps, and fresh fish that might be sesame wok-seared or served with ginger butter suit the light, fresh ambience. This is also a great place to start the day with a fine breakfast. ⊠ *The Orchid at Mauna Lani, 1 N. Kanikū Dr., Kohala Coast,* ☎ *808/885–2000. AE, D, DC, MC, V. No lunch.*

$–$$ ✕ **Oodles of Noodles and Paradise Spice Co. & Catering.** Renowned chef Amy Ferguson-Ota combines Southwestern flavors with Hawai`i regional cuisine and a touch of French. In her small restaurant, Hawaiian native woods like mango, `ōhi`a, and koa complement vivid blue, green, and yellow walls. The menu features noodles of all types, in all shapes, from all ethnic backgrounds—be it as delicate spring rolls or as a crisp garnish to an exquisite salad. ⊠ *Crossroads Shopping Center, 75-1129 Henry St., Kailua-Kona,* ☎ *808/329–9222. D, DC, MC, V.*

Thai

$$–$$$ ✕ **Thai Rin Restaurant.** The friendly owner, the quiet atmosphere, and the affordable prices make this an attractive spot for lunch or dinner. The restaurant, a few minutes walking from downtown Kailua-Kona, is modest, but the food is authentic and adequate. Thai spring rolls, green papaya salad, crab stir-fry, and Thai garlic shrimp or squid are favorites. ⊠ *75-5799 Ali`i Dr., Kailua-Kona,* ☎ *808/329–2929. AE, D, DC, MC, V.*

$–$$ ✕ **Palm Terrace at the Hilton Waikoloa Village.** This open-air restaurant sits next to a cascading waterfall and a pond with swans floating by. It is open for American-style breakfasts and offers affordable buffet dinners. ⊠ *425 Waikoloa Beach Dr., Kamuela,* ☎ *808/886–1234. AE, D, DC, MC, V. No lunch.*

Volcano

Contemporary

$$–$$$ ✕ **Kīlauea Lodge.** Albert Jeyte has incorporated trends of the new millennium with traditional cooking styles from his native Germany and from France and America. Built in 1938 as a scouting retreat, the restaurant still has the original stone "Friendship Fireplace" embedded with coins from around the world. The roaring fire, koa tables, and warm lighting create a cozy, intimate lodge ambience—just the thing after a day of hiking around the crater. Entrées are pricey, but they come with a delicious soup du jour, salad, and freshly baked three-grain bread. The signature dessert, a Grand Marnier custard, is sensational. ⊠ *Old Volcano Rd., Volcano Village,* ☎ *808/967–7366. AE, MC, V. No lunch.*

$$ ✕ **Surt's.** Given the Chaîne des Rôtisseurs approval, chef Surt Thammountha's fusion cuisine combines Asian fire with European traditions. In a contemporary setting of glass tables set with Fiesta ware and bold stemware, guests may enjoy such specialties as escargots on mushroom caps in creamy champagne sauce, lobster ravioli, and blackened 'ahi with a Mediterranean tomato sauce. A nice wine list adds to unexpectedly fine dining on top of a volcano. ⊠ *Old Volcano Rd.,* ☎ *808/967–8511. AE, D, DC, MC, V.*

Continental

$–$$$ ✕ **Ka 'Ōhelo Dining Room.** Perched right at the edge of Kīlauea Crater in a mountain-lodge setting, this restaurant serves up breakfast and luncheon buffets primarily for tour groups during the day. But at night it's quiet and has white tablecloths if water restrictions don't limit the laundry load. The setting, at the rim of a volcano, is the thing, but you can't go wrong with the fresh catch of the day or the prime rib. ⊠ *Volcano House, Hawai'i Volcanoes National Park,* ☎ *808/967–7321. AE, D, DC, MC, V.*

Waikoloa Village

Continental/Cajun/Creole

$$ ✕ **Roussel's.** This was Hilo's best restaurant before it moved to west to Waikoloa. Roussel's still serves Creole entrées that have made it popular, but bows to golfers' demands for burgers, club sandwiches, and chicken wings during much of the day. Peaceful golf course views through big white-frame windows that open to the trade winds go well with dishes such as shrimp Creole or blackened prime rib. ⊠ *68-1792 Melia St., Waikoloa Village Golf Club, Waikoloa,* ☎ *808/883–9644. AE, DC, MC, V. No dinner Sun.–Mon.*

Waimea

American/Casual

$$ ✕ **Parker Ranch Grill.** With cowhides serving as wallpaper and riding boots as doorknobs, this popular restaurant makes no mistake about its paniolo identity and unique Parker Ranch heritage. In front of a blazing hearth fire, the koa tables, set with hand towels instead of napkins, are a perfect setting for "kamuela pride" beef entrées such as citrus-and-herb ribsteak with pistachio-roasted chili butter or meat loaf with a sweet corn-cheddar casserole. The wine list is extensive, and a separate bar area offers a variety of pūpū. ⊠ *Parker Ranch Shopping Center, 67-1185 Mamalahoa Hwy.,* ☎ *808/887–2624. AE, D, MC, V.*

$–$$ ✕ **Koa House Grill.** In the heart of cowboy country, this family restaurant has developed into a busy lunch stop for Waimea's business crowd. Its down-to-earth dinners vary between bold, all-American flavors like garlic mashed potatoes and Asian accents such as passion fruit and ginger. Shrimp scampi is a favorite, and there are also large steaks and pastas on the menu. A full salad bar features fresh Waimea greens. Large windows open out onto the Keck Observatory headquarters and offer a glimpse of the mountains. ⊠ *Waimea Shopping Center, 65-1144 Mamalahoa Hwy.,* ☎ *808/885–2088. AE, MC, V.*

Contemporary

$$–$$$
★
✕ **Merriman's.** This is the signature restaurant of Peter Merriman, one of the pioneers of Hawai'i regional cuisine. Don't miss the opportunity to sample his imaginative and impeccable dishes featuring local and often organic produce. Merriman's is the home of the original wok-charred 'ahi, usually served with exquisite buttery Pāhoa corn and black-and-white Thai rice. Try the Kahuā Ranch lamb, raised to the restaurant's specifications. Selections—such as herb-roasted leg of lamb with a cabernet and plum sauce—vary daily. The extensive wine list includes 22 selections poured by the glass, and the staff is refreshingly knowledgeable. ⊠ *'Opelo Plaza, Hwy. 19 and 'Opelo Rd., Waimea,* ☎ *808/885–6822. Reservations essential. AE, MC, V.*

Continental

$$
✕ **Edelweiss.** Faithful local diners and visitors alike flock to this relaxed, family-oriented restaurant with rustic redwood furnishings. The chef's rack of lamb is always excellent. A varied menu includes more than 20 daily specials (such as a sausage platter and fresh seafood), many with a German flavor. Make reservations to avoid a long wait. There's a nice bar area for predinner drinks. ⊠ *Hwy. 19, entering Waimea,* ☎ *808/885–6800. MC, V. Closed Sun.–Mon. and Sept.*

LODGING

You'll almost always be able to find a room on the Big Island, but you might not get your first choice if you wait until the last minute. Make plans early if you're visiting during the winter season, December 15 through April 15. Amazingly enough, you will not be able to find a room in Hilo during the week after Easter Sunday, when the Merrie Monarch Festival (☞ Hula *in* Nightlife and the Arts, *below*) is in full swing. Kailua-Kona bursts at the seams in mid-October. Athletes and their support teams fill the hotels during the Ironman World Triathlon Championship. An even bigger problem than finding a room at these times is finding a rental car. Be sure to make reservations well in advance—six months to a year—if your stay coincides with the festival, the triathlon, or any major holiday.

Hotel, room, and car package deals are often available in all price categories; a reputable travel agent should be able to furnish up-to-date information. Some of the older hotels do not have air-conditioning, but they will almost always have fans, which should be adequate except during the hot summer and early fall seasons. All rooms have a TV and phone unless otherwise indicated.

If you choose a bed-and-breakfast, inn, or an out-of-the-way hotel, explain your expectations fully and ask plenty of questions before booking. Be clear about your travel and location needs. Many B&Bs close to Hawai'i Volcanoes National Park, for example, are not the perfect locations for beach and sun worshipers. Some require stays of two or three days. When booking, ask about car-rental arrangements, as many B&B networks can offer discounted rates. For B&B referrals, *see* Contacts and Resources *in* Big Island A to Z, *below.* For price category explanations, *see* Smart Travel Tips A to Z at the back of the book.

Hilo

$$–$$$$ ⊞ **Hawai'i Naniloa Resort.** Ask for a room with an ocean or bay view when you book here. The hotel has a clean and contemporary feel. Green rugs in the bedrooms contrast beautifully with the bird-of-paradise designs of the bedspreads. The premium rooms on the ninth floor are especially nice. The 10- and 12-story towers on the Puna side are connected by an open, modern lobby area with shops. A complete spa specializes in Hawaiian treatments. An executive golf course, the Naniloa Country Club, is across Banyan Drive. ⊠ *93 Banyan Dr., Hilo 96720,* ☏ *808/969–3333; 800/367–5360 from the mainland; 800/442–5845 interisland;* 𝔽𝔸𝕏 *808/969–6622. 308 rooms, 17 suites. 2 restaurants, bar, refrigerators, health club, dance club. AE, DC, MC, V.*

$$–$$$$ ⊞ **Hilo Hawaiian Hotel.** This is one of the most pleasant lodgings on Hilo Bay, with large bay-front rooms offering spectacular views of Mauna Ke'a and Coconut Island. Streetside rooms overlook the golf course. Beige carpets and rattan furniture enliven the decor, and most accommodations have private lānai. All rooms have refrigerators. Kitchenettes are available in one-bedroom suites. Views of the bay are showcased in the Queen's Court dining room, and the Wai'oli Lounge has entertainment Thursday through Saturday. ⊠ *71 Banyan Dr., Hilo 96720,* ☏ *808/935–9361; 800/367–5004 from the mainland; 800/272–5275 interisland;* 𝔽𝔸𝕏 *808/961–9642. 286 rooms, 6 suites. Restaurant, bar, refrigerators, pool, meeting rooms. AE, D, DC, MC, V.*

$$$
★ ⊞ **Shipman House Bed & Breakfast Inn.** Situated on 5½ acres of lush grounds on Reed's Island, and possibly Hilo's most-photographed mansion, the Shipman House is on the national and state registers of historic places. Restored by W. H. Shipman's great-granddaughter, Barbara Ann, and her husband, Gary Andersen, in 1997, the 100-year-old turreted "castle" has three gracious B&B rooms in the house and two separate cottage units that have a tropical feel. The house is furnished with antique koa and period pieces, some dating from the days when Queen Lili'uokalani came to tea. On Tuesday night guests are invited to watch the ancient dances of an authentic hula school. If you want to play music yourself, a concert grand piano is available. ⊠ *131 Ka'iulani St., Hilo 96720,* ☏ *808/934–8002 or 800/627–8447,* 𝔽𝔸𝕏 *808/934–8002. 3 rooms, 2 cottage units. Fans, refrigerators, library. AE, MC, V. CP.*

$$ ⊞ **Hale Kai Bjornen Bed & Breakfast.** On a bluff above Hilo Bay, just 2 mi from downtown Hilo, this 5,400-square-ft modern home has four impeccable rooms and a private loft that is ideal for families—all with grand ocean views and within earshot of lapping waves. Freshly painted and decorated, all units have private baths and patios, with access to a pool and a hot tub; fresh flowers and bedspreads from Portugal add a warm, European touch. The Norwegian-Hawaiian hosts, Evonne and Paul Bjornen, serve a gourmet breakfast—macadamia-nut waffles, Portuguese sausage, fruits, breads, and special egg dishes—on an outdoor deck or in the kitchen's bay-window dining area. ⊠ *111 Honoli'i Pali St., Hilo 96720,* ☏ *808/935–6330,* 𝔽𝔸𝕏 *808/935–8439. 4 rooms, 1 suite. Fans, pool, hot tub, laundry service. No credit cards.*

$$ ⊞ **Hilo Bay Hotel, Uncle Billy's.** This friendly, easygoing place is a popular stopover for Neighbor Islanders who enjoy proprietor Uncle Billy Kimo's Hawaiian hospitality. A nightly hula show and entertainment during dinner are part of the fun. ⊠ *87 Banyan Dr., Hilo 96720,* ☏ *808/935–0861; 800/367–5102 from the mainland; 800/442–5841 interisland;* 𝔽𝔸𝕏 *808/935–7903. 120 rooms. Restaurant, bar, kitchenettes, refrigerators, pool, meeting rooms. AE, D, DC, MC, V.*

$$ ⊞ **Hilo Seaside Hotel.** The most pleasant rooms here have private lānai and overlook the koi-filled lagoon or are situated around the pool. Lots of foliage along the walkways and friendly personnel create a very

Big Island Lodging

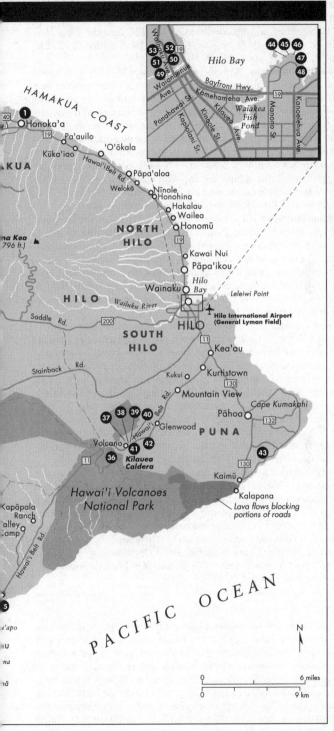

Hawaiian ambience. This is a peaceful place, except when planes take off and land, as the hotel is near the airport's flight path. Some units have kitchenettes and air-conditioning. ⊠ *126 Banyan Way, Hilo 96720,* ☎ *808/935–0821 or 800/367–7000,* ℻ *808/969–9195. 136 rooms. Restaurant, pool. AE, D, DC, MC, V.* ⊛

$$ 🏨 **The Inn at Kulaniapia.** With an awesome view of Hilo Bay 4 mi below, as well as access to a magnificent 120-ft waterfall that tumbles in a 300-ft-wide swimming pond, the inn is an oasis of beauty and tranquility. Trails meander to the river and it's close enough to the activities of both Hilo and Volcano (a 15-minute drive over sugarcane roads). Hosts Jane and Len Sutton added Asian accents, koa, and eucalyptus wood floors to the inn. A small generator must run two hours every day (it's a bit noisy). Buffet-style breakfasts are served and can be supplemented throughout the day with your own cooking on the barbecue and in the modern, tiled kitchen. ⊠ *Box 11338, Hilo 96721,* ☎ *808/966–6373 or 888/838–6373. 4 rooms. MC, V.* ⊛

$–$$ 🏨 **Dolphin Bay Hotel.** All units have kitchens in this clean, modest hotel in a lovely, green Hawaiian garden setting four blocks from Hilo Bay. Coffee and fresh fruits are offered daily. The staff is helpful and welcoming. The rooms do not have phones, but a pay phone is in the lobby. Guests of the hotel, which is away from the beach in a residential area called Pu'ue'o, return repeatedly. ⊠ *333 'Iliahi St., Hilo 96720,* ☎ *808/ 935–1466,* ℻ *808/935–1523. 13 rooms, 4 1-bedroom units, 1 2-bedroom unit. Kitchenettes. MC, V.* ⊛

$ 🏨 **Arnott's Lodge.** Owner Doug Arnott has created an ever-expanding budget lodge for backpackers, bicyclists, and other active visitors. You can choose from tenting, dormitory-style bunkbeds, or semiprivate or private rooms. Four rooms in a recently renovated adjacent house have private, tiled bathrooms. The lodge provides a shared kitchen and a separate gazebo with video facilities. Though it's minutes from the airport, the setting is lush, oceanside wilderness. A young international clientele takes advantage of guided hikes and barbecues offered by the lodge. ⊠ *98 'Apapane Rd., Hilo 96720,* ☎ *808/969–7097,* ℻ *808/961–9638. 12 semiprivate units, 6 private units, 36 bunks. Camping, coin laundry, travel services, airport shuttle. DC, MC, V.* ⊛

$ 🏨 **Wild Ginger Inn Bed & Breakfast.** This one-of-a-kind, 24-room inn is reminiscent of '40s Hawai'i plantation-style accommodations. Clean, simple rooms with Polynesian and plantation themes are in an old wooden building. A big lawn and a jungle garden run along a stream bank. Most rooms have double and twin beds. A complimentary buffet breakfast is served on the lānai lobby. There are no phones in the rooms, but pay phones are available. ⊠ *100 Pu'u'eo St., Hilo 96720,* ☎ *808/935–5556 or 800/882–1887,* ℻ *808/969–1225. 24 rooms. Refrigerators, coin laundry. D, MC, V. CP.* ⊛

Puna

$–$$$ 🏨 **Kalani Oceanside Eco-Resort.** This out-of-the way retreat is 5 mi east of Kalapana and 1 mi from Puna beach. A unique, tropical getaway, Kalani offers healthful cuisine, nearby thermal springs, and a variety of programs on Hawaiian culture, healing, gay spirituality, and ecology. Accommodations include campsites, shared rooms with shared bath, cottage units, and lodge rooms with private or shared bath. Bathing suits are optional both on the nearby beach and in the evenings at the resort's Olympic-size pool. ⊠ *Hwy. 137, Pahoa–Beach Rd., Pahoa 96778,* ☎ *808/965–7828 or 800/800–6886. 24 rooms, 9 cottages, guest house. Fans, pool, hot tubs, sauna, tennis court, camping, coin laundry. AE,D, MC, V.* ⊛

Volcano/South Point ↓ *www.volcano-hawaii.com*

$–$$$$ 🏨 **Chalet Kīlauea Collection.** A selection of theme rooms, suites, and vacation homes that range from the basic to the extravagant are offered here. Best-known is the Inn at Volcano—a "boutique resort." All in all, the Collection includes five inns and lodges and five vacation houses in and around Volcano Village. The two-story TreeHouse Suite, with wraparound windows, marble wet bar, and fireplace, gives one the impression of floating on the tops of tree ferns. Afternoon tea is served before a fireplace. A gourmet candlelit breakfast under a glittering chandelier adds class. ✉ *Wright Rd., Volcano Village 96785,* ☎ *808/967–7786 or 800/937–7786,* FAX *808/967–8660. 11 rooms, 9 suites, 5 houses. AE, D, DC, MC, V.* 🐾

$$$ 🏨 **Hydrangea Cottage & Mountain House.** About a mile from Hawai'i Volcanoes National Park, on an impeccably landscaped estate, the Cottage is a private retreat with a wraparound covered deck and floor-to-ceiling windows looking out over giant tree ferns—home to rare Hawaiian birds. Mountain House has three bedrooms, each with its own bath. Antique furnishings add to the rich, quiet atmosphere. Both units have a kitchen as well as fixings for a self-prepared breakfast. This luxurious and protected hideaway must be booked via Hawai'i's Best Bed & Breakfasts. ✉ *Reservations: Box 563, Kamuela 96743* ☎ *808/885–4550 or 800/262–9912,* FAX *808/885–0559. 1 3-bedroom house, 1 cottage. No credit cards.* 🐾

$$–$$$ 🏨 **Carson's Volcano Cottages.** You can choose the privacy of a romantic hideaway with a full kitchen and a hot tub in the midst of hapu ferns, or the intimate rooms and cottages on the property itself. Either way, you'll love the elaborate breakfasts in the main house's cozy dining room, featuring home-baked breads and dishes such as spinach quiche and poi doughnuts. Each unit has its own theme decor and comes with maid service and television. ✉ *Box 503, Volcano 96785,* ☎ *808/967–7683 or 800/845–5282,* FAX *808/967–8094. 5 rooms, 6 cottages. Dining room. AE, D, MC, V.* 🐾

$$–$$$ 🏨 **Colony One Sea Mountain.** With lodging hard to find in the Ka'u area, avid golfers and seekers of seclusion will enjoy the spacious Colony One condominiums, bordered by the ocean and fairways and a 25-minute drive away from Hawai'i Volcanoes National Park. The property is adjacent to the black-sand Punalu'u Beach Park, home of the green sea turtle preserve. Condominium units are not plush but have a country feel, rattan furnishings, complete kitchens, and lānai. There are cleaning services, and a two-day minimum stay is required. ✉ *95-789 Ninole Loop Rd. (turn off Hwy. 11 at Punalu'u), Punalu'u 96777,* ☎ *808/928–6200 or 800/344–7675,* FAX *808/928–8075. 23 studios, 36 1-bedroom units, 17 2-bedroom units. Kitchenettes, pool, 18-hole golf course, 4 tennis courts, meeting room. MC, V.* 🐾

$$–$$$ 🏨 **Hale Ohia Cottages.** Built in 1931 as a vacation house for the Dillingham family, this charming estate has a Japanese hot tub surrounded by ancient trees and glorious gardens. Antique furnishings and unique collectibles, fireplaces, and antique stained glass create a romantic ambience. The luxurious Ihilani cottage is an octagonal hideaway with private garden, but all the suites and cottages provide a place for restful, cozy hours spent close to Hawai'i Volcanoes National Park. ✉ *Hale Ohia Rd. off Hwy. 11, Volcano Village 96785,* ☎ *808/967–7986 or 800/455–3803,* FAX *808/967–8610. 4 suites, 3 cottages. Refrigerators, hot tub. D, DC, MC, V. CP.* 🐾

$$–$$$ 🏨 **Kīlauea Lodge.** A mile from the Hawai'i Volcanoes National Park
★   entrance, this country inn is possibly the most popular place to stay in the area. The original building dates from the 1930s, and its rooms have their own wood-burning fireplaces. All of the units reflect a

Hawaiian theme with rich quilts and photographs, and the antiques are distinctly European. There is a deluxe honeymoon suite, a separate cottage, and a gazebo on the front lawn that is great for weddings. Tutu's Place, a 1929 remodeled cottage with two bedrooms off the main property, is also available. The restaurant, run by chef-owner Albert Jeyte, has earned a reputation for excellent food (☞ Volcano *in* Dining, *above*). Breakfast is included in the price of the room. ⊠ *Old Volcano Hwy., about 1 mi northeast of Volcano Store, Volcano Village 96785,* ☎ *808/967–7366,* FAX *808/967–7367. 11 rooms, 2 cottages. Restaurant. MC, V.*

$$–$$$ **Volcano House.** The charm of the Volcano House is its location at the edge of Kīlauea Caldera, so if you choose to stay, plan on paying a bit extra to book one of the rooms with a crater view. The clean and comfortable rooms in the main building have period koa furniture. Dinner at the Ka 'Ōhelo Dining Room can stir romance, as can a walk in the cool, crisp air topped off with a nightcap in front of an 'ōhi'a-wood fire in the lobby's stone fireplace. ⊠ *Hawai'i Volcanoes National Park, Crater Rim Dr., 96718,* ☎ *808/967–7321,* FAX *808/967–8429. 42 rooms. Restaurant. AE, D, DC, MC, V.*

$–$$$ **My Island Bed & Breakfast Inn.** Gordon, Joann, and daughter Ki'i Morse opened their historic century-old house and 7-acre botanical estate to visitors in 1985. The house is the oldest in Volcano, built in 1886 by the Lyman missionary family. Three rooms, sharing two baths, are available in the main house. Scattered around the area are 17 additional units in private garden apartments, studios, guest houses, and cottages. A luxurious home on the golf course, which features an Italian-tile kitchen and a complete party patio, is also available. You won't start the day hungry after a gourmet all-you-can-eat breakfast. ⊠ *19-3896 Old Volcano Rd., Volcano Village (Box 100, Volcano 96785),* ☎ *808/967–7216 or 808/967–7110,* FAX *808/967–7719. 3 rooms without bath, 17 units. No credit cards.*

$ **Shirakawa Motel.** In the remote Ka'ū District, midway between Kona and Hilo near Nā'ālehu, the southernmost town in the United States, this bare and basic motel has been run by the same family since 1921. Families can get connecting units with cooking facilities, though there are places to eat nearby in town. A new, large one-bedroom unit offers a full kitchen. ⊠ *95-6040 Māmalahoa Hwy. 11, Wai'ōhinu (Box 467, Na'alehu 96772),* ☎ *808/929–7462. 12 rooms. No credit cards.*

Upcountry Kona District

$$$ **Hōlualoa Inn.** Six spacious rooms, each with private bath, are available in this cedar home situated on a 40-acre estate with glorious coastal views. It is in Upcountry Kona amid coffee bushes, fruit orchards, and rolling pastures 4 mi above Kailua Bay, and the artists' town of Hōlualoa is steps away. Each room has an island theme. The premium Balinese suite has wraparound windows with stunning views. A lavish breakfast includes estate-grown coffee as well as homemade breads and macadamia-nut butters. Rooftop gazebos inspire quiet, relaxing moments. For stargazers there's a telescope. Around sunset, platters of cheeses and tropical fruits are available. ⊠ *76-5932 Māmalahoa Hwy. (Box 222), Hōlualoa 96725,* ☎ *808/324–1121 or 800/392–1812,* FAX *808/322–2472. 6 rooms. Pool, hot tub, billiards. AE, D, MC, V.*

$$$ **Horizon Guest House.** About 30 miles south of Kona, on 40 acres overlooking the Kona Coast, this new luxury retreat offers quietness, comfort, sweeping views, and a state-of-the-art solar-heated pool. Hawaiian quilts, collectibles, and antiques give personality and warmth to the four rooms. A generous buffet breakfast starts your day. ⊠ *Reservations: Box 563, Kamuela 96743,* ☎ *808/885–4550 or 800/262–9912,* FAX *808/885–0559. 4 rooms. Pool, hot tub, library. No credit cards.*

$$–$$$ 🏠 **Hale Maluhia Country Inn B&B.** In Upcountry Kona, this friendly plantation estate, right off a winding coffee road and surrounded by macadamia and mango trees, offers guests many comforts, including family antiques, full use of a modern tiled kitchen, an inviting family and living room, and a Japanese slate Jacuzzi hot tub. A gourmet breakfast, including make your own omelets, is served on the lānai. A spacious, romantic cottage is also available. All rooms have private baths. There is a tiny waterfall and koi pond, with hideaway garden seats scattered around the property. ⊠ *76-770 Hualalai Rd., Kailua–Kona 96740,* ☎ *808/329–5773 or 800/559–6627,* FAX *808/326–5487. 5 rooms, 1 cottage. Hot tub. AE, D, MC, V.* ♨

$ 🏠 **Manago Hotel.** You'll get a great ocean view high above the Kona Coast in the newer wing of this family-run three-story hotel. There is one Japanese-style room with tatami instead of beds and a *furo* (deep bathtub), which the proprietor has kept in remembrance of his grandparents, who built the main hotel in 1917. The other rooms are nothing special, and none have phones, but the Manago has an authentic old Hawai'i ambience, especially in the bar and local-style restaurant. ⊠ *81-6155 Māmalahoa Hwy., Captain Cook (Box 145, Captain Cook 96704),* ☎ *808/323–2642,* FAX *808/323–3451. 65 rooms, 42 with bath. Restaurant. D, MC, V.* ♨

Kailua-Kona and Keauhou

$$$$ 🏠 **Aston Kona by the Sea.** Complete modern kitchens, tile lānai, and washers and dryers can be found in every suite of this comfortable oceanfront condo complex. An open-air lobby and a helpful reception desk add to the friendly atmosphere. Despite being near the bustling town of Kailua-Kona, the place is quiet and relaxing. The nearest sandy beach is 2 mi away, but the pool is next to the ocean. ⊠ *75-6106 Ali'i Dr., Kailua-Kona 96740,* ☎ *808/327–2300 or 800/922–7866,* FAX *808/ 327–2333. 35 1-bedroom units, 40 2-bedroom units. Pool, hot tub. AE, D, DC, MC, V.* ♨

$$$$ ★ 🏠 **Kanaloa at Kona.** The 13-acre grounds provide a verdant setting for this low-rise condominium complex bordering the Keauhou-Kona Country Club. Large one- and two-bedroom apartments feature koa-wood cabinetwork and washer-dryers. Oceanfront suites have private hot tubs. Edward's at Kanaloa Restaurant has a romantically tropical atmosphere in addition to excellent Mediterranean cuisine ⊠ *78-261 Manukai St., Kailua-Kona 96740,* ☎ *808/322–9625, 808/322–2272, or 800/688–7444;* FAX *808/322–3818. 79 1- and 2-bedroom condominiums. Restaurant, kitchenettes, 3 pools, 2 tennis courts. AE, D, DC, MC, V.* ♨

$$$–$$$$ 🏠 **Kailua Plantation House B&B.** At the ocean's edge just outside Kailua-Kona, this majestic two-story house was built in 1990 as a B&B, with four rooms upstairs (two overlooking the ocean) and one oceanfront suite downstairs. Rooms with private lānai are done in a unique range of styles and named to reflect their decor—Pilialoha (Friendship Room) or Ali'i Wikolia (Queen Victoria Room), for example. The house has a tropical ambience, and an extensive display of local art is displayed along the second-story stairwell. Delicious breakfasts may include avocado omelets and island-style pancakes. ⊠ *75-5948 Ali'i Dr., Kailua-Kona 96740,* ☎ *808/329–3727 or 888/357–4262,* FAX *808/ 326–7323. 5 rooms. AE, MC, V.* ♨

$$–$$$$ 🏠 **Kona Bali Kai.** Less than 2 mi from White Sands Beach, these older, family-style condominium units midway between Kailua-Kona and Keauhou Country Club all have kitchen-dining areas. Only the mountain-side ones have air-conditioning. Ask for a place makai rather than mauka of the road. ⊠ *76-6246 Ali'i Dr., Kailua-Kona 96740,* ☎ *808/ 329–9381 or 800/535–0085,* FAX *808/326–6056. 14 rooms, 62 con-*

dominiums (13 studios, 25 1-bedroom, 24 2-bedroom). Pool, hot tub, coin laundry. AE, D, DC, MC, V. ✍

$$$ 🏨 **Royal Kona Resort.** Of the major hotels, the spacious Royal Kona Resort is nearest to Kailua on the south side of town and right across from shops and restaurants. It has a distinctive profile and extends into a bay, giving the impression that it sits on the water. Rooms have new floors and bathrooms and a fresh aqua, violet, and sea-foam green color scheme. A large saltwater pond with a waterfall and ocean fish surrounds the hotel, and there is a private lagoon with a sandy beach. ⊠ *75-5852 Ali'i Dr., Kailua-Kona 96740,* ☎ *808/329–3111 or 800/919-8333,* 📠 *808/329–9532. 444 rooms, 8 suites. Restaurant, bar, in-room safes, refrigerators, pool, 4 tennis courts, health club, meeting rooms. AE, D, DC, MC, V.* ✍

30 **$$–$$$**   🏨 **Aston Keauhou Beach Resort.** This quiet oceanfront hotel, just 5 mi
Hotel   south of Kailua-Kona, has airy rooms overlooking the ocean and Keauhou's historic fishing grounds. Boutiques and gift shops line the open-air downstairs lobby, where several authentic racing canoes are on display. The hotel is adjacent to Kahalu'u, one of the Big Island's best snorkeling beaches. ⊠ *78-6740 Ali'i Dr., Kailua-Kona 96740,* ☎ *808/322–3441 or 800/922–7866,* 📠 *808/322–3117. 311 rooms, 1 suite. Restaurant, bar, 2 pools, 6 tennis courts, health club, meeting room. AE, D, DC, MC, V.* ✍

$$–$$$ 🏨 **King Kamehameha's Kona Beach Hotel.** This is the most convenient of the major hotels, and it's right next to Kailua Pier. Rooms are not particularly special (fifth- and sixth-floor oceanfront rooms are best), but it is the only central Kailua-Kona hotel with a white-sand beach. Free tours explore the grounds and Ahu'ena Heiau, which King Kamehameha I had reconstructed in the early 1800s. The hotel serves an ample champagne brunch every Sunday and hosts beachfront Polynesian dinner shows. ⊠ *75-5660 Palani Rd., Kailua-Kona 96740,* ☎ *808/329–2911 or 800/367–6060,* 📠 *808/329–4602. 450 rooms, 5 suites. 2 restaurants, 2 bars, pool, sauna, 4 tennis courts, beach. AE, D, DC, MC, V.* ✍

$$ 🏨 **Hale Kona Kai.** This small, three-story vacation condominium on the ocean's edge, next door to the Royal Kona Resort (☞ *above*), requires a three-day minimum stay. These privately owned units are all furnished differently. The corner units with wraparound lānai have the best views. It is within walking distance of restaurants and shops. ⊠ *75-5870 Kahakai Rd., Kailua-Kona 96740,* ☎ *808/329–2155 or 800/ 421–3696,* 📠 *808/329–2155. 25 condominiums. Pool. AE, MC, V.*

$$ 🏨 **Kona Bay Hotel, Uncle Billy's.** These two- and four-story motel-type units are right in the center of town, across the street from the ocean. The place is owned and managed by the same local family that owns the Hilo Bay Hotel, Uncle Billy's (☞ *Hilo, above*). The atmosphere is friendly and fun-loving. Open-air dining around the pool is casual. Some rooms have kitchenettes. ⊠ *75-5739 Ali'i Dr., Kailua-Kona 96740,* ☎ *808/329–1393, 800/367–5102, or 800/423–8733 ext. 220,* 📠 *808/329–9210. 146 rooms. Restaurant, bar, pool. AE, D, DC, MC, V.* ✍

$$ 🏨 **Kona Magic Sands.** This condo complex is near Magic Sands Beach, a plus for swimmers and sunbathers in summer (the sand washes away in winter). Units vary because they are individually owned, but all are oceanfront. Some have enclosed lānai. Four units have air-conditioning. ⊠ *77-6452 Ali'i Dr., Kailua-Kona 96740,* ☎ *808/329–9393 or 800/553–5035,* 📠 *808/326–4137. 17 rooms. Restaurant, bar, kitchenettes, pool. MC, V.* ✍

$$ 🏨 **Kona Seaside Hotel.** What you get here is location. This hotel, a combination of the old Hukilau Hotel and the adjoining Kona Seaside, is right across the street from Kailua Bay. Rooms nearest the main street are built around a pool. The small rooms have tiny bathrooms and showers but are completely adequate. ⊠ *75-5646 Palani Rd., Kailua-Kona 96740,*

☎ *808/329–2455 or 800/367–7000,* FAX *808/329–6157. 223 rooms, 1 suite. Restaurant, bar, 2 pools, meeting rooms. AE, D, DC, MC, V.* ✆

$ 🏨 **Kona Tiki Hotel.** The best thing about this three-story walk-up budget hotel, about a mile south of Kailua-Kona, is that all the units have lānai right next to the ocean. The rooms are modest but pleasantly decorated nonetheless. Guests can sunbathe by the seaside pool. There are no in-room TVs or phones. ⊠ *75-5968 Ali'i Dr., Kailua-Kona 96745,* ☎ *808/329–1425,* FAX *808/327–9402. 15 rooms. Grill, fans, refrigerators, pool. No credit cards. CP.*

Kohala Coast and Waikoloa

$$$$ 🏨 **Aston the Shores at Waikoloa.** These red-tile–roof villas are set amid
★ landscaped lagoons and waterfalls at the edge of the championship Waikoloa Village Golf Course. The spacious villas and condo units— ground floor and upper floor are available separately—are privately owned and have unique furnishings and interiors. Sliding glass doors open onto large lānai. Oversize tubs and large, separate, glassed-in showers add to the luxury. Units have washer-dryers and come with maid service. ⊠ *69-1035 Keana Pl., Waikoloa 96738,* ☎ *808/886–5001 or 800/922–7866,* FAX *808/886–8414. 75 1- and 2-bedroom units, 1 3-bedroom villa. Kitchenettes, pool, 2 hot tubs, 2 tennis courts. AE, D, DC, MC, V.* ✆

$$$$ 🏨 **Four Seasons Resort Hualālai.** At historic Ka'ūpūlehu, four clusters
★ of bungalows house six or eight luxurious rooms each in this romantic oceanfront hotel. Built in 1996, it is consistently rated among the best in the country. Natural china-matte slate floors, Hawaiian artwork, warm earth and cool-white tones, and large, two-sink bathrooms with glass-door showers create a peaceful haven. Ground-level rooms have outdoor garden showers. Natural ponds—attracting rare native birds— dot the property. The educational Hawaiian Cultural Center honors the grounds' spiritual heritage, and the Sports Club and Spa offers guests top-rate health and fitness options. The resort's golf course annually hosts the Senior PGA Tournament of Champions. The Kids for All Seasons program provides complementary child-care service. ⊠ *100 Ka'ūpūlehu Dr., Ka'ūpūlehu/Kona (Box 1269, Kailua-Kona 96745),* ☎ *808/325–8000 or 800/332-3442,* FAX *808/325–8100. 243 rooms, 31 suites. 4 restaurants, 5 pools, 18-hole golf course, 8 tennis courts, beach, children's programs (ages 5–11), concierge, meeting rooms, airport shuttle. AE, DC, MC, V.* ✆

$$$$ 🏨 **Hāpuna Beach Prince Hotel.** This Kohala Coast luxury hotel fronts
★ white-sand Hāpuna, one of the best beaches in the United States. The hotel is a glitzy beauty with floors of slate tile. The 350 oceanview rooms are decorated in cool, natural tones, and all have marble bathrooms and private lānai. Meandering pathways lead to restaurants, beach facilities, and a spectacular environmentally sensitive golf course. The showpiece of the hotel is the 8,000-square-ft, four-bedroom Hāpuna Suite with its own swimming pool and 24-hour butler service. ⊠ *62-100 Kauna'oa Dr., Kohala Coast 96743,* ☎ *808/880–1111 or 800/882–6060,* FAX *808/880–3142. 314 rooms, 36 suites. 5 restaurants, 2 bars, pool, beauty salon, hot tub, spa, 18-hole golf course, 13 tennis courts, health club, meeting rooms. AE, D, DC, MC, V.* ✆

$$$$ 🏨 **Hilton Waikoloa Village.** This 62-acre property on a rocky stretch
★ of coast is elaborately landscaped, with shaded pathways passing by items from a multimillion-dollar Pacific Island art collection and connecting three tower buildings. Shuttle trains and boats will take you to your destination if you don't want to walk. The resort recently added three new restaurants, including one at a boat-landing pavilion. The pool features a 175-ft water slide, a meandering river that connects smaller pools, and a man-made sand beach bordering a four-acre la-

goon. You can have an encounter with the resort's dolphins through a special lottery, or practice your swing at one of two golf courses or your putt on a new 18-hole putting course. The Kohala Spa has some of the finest fitness facilities on the island. ✉ *69-425 Waikoloa Beach Dr., Waikoloa 96738,* ☎ *808/886–1234 or 800/445–8667,* FAX *808/886–2901. 1,240 rooms, 57 suites. 8 restaurants, 7 bars, 3 pools, 2 18-hole golf courses, 8 tennis courts, beach, children's programs (ages 5–12). AE, D, DC, MC, V.*

$$$$ 🏨 **Islands at Mauna Lani.** Surrounded by saltwater ponds, streams, and waterfalls are two- and three-bedroom condominium town homes. Each air-conditioned unit has a private drive with two-car garage. Both the dining room downstairs and the second floor open onto private lānais with views of luxurious gardens. Rates include a welcome supply of groceries for a spacious kitchen and a rental car. Guests have access to the beach club at Mauna Lani Bay Hotel and Bungalows (☞ *below*) as well as the tennis courts and fitness facilities at the nearby racquet club. There are a variety of dining options throughout the resort. ✉ *Classic Resorts, 68-1310 Mauna Lani Dr., Kohala Coast 96743,* ☎ *808/885–5022 or 800/642–6284,* FAX *808/885–5015. 15 2-bedroom units, 1 3-bedroom unit. Pool, hot tub, 2 18-hole golf courses, 6 tennis courts, beach, cars. AE, DC, MC, V.*

$$$$ 🏨 **Kona Village Resort.** Without phones, TVs, or radios it is easy to
★   feel you are part of an extended Polynesian *ohana* (family), with your own thatched-roof *hale* (house) near the resort's sandy beach. Built on the grounds of an ancient Hawaiian village, the modern bungalows stay true to original, Polynesian colors and decorative themes. The extra-large rooms are cooled by ceiling fans. Hot tubs are in 23 of them. Rates include meals, an authentic Polynesian Friday night lū`au, history and petroglyph tours, tennis, sports activities, and rides in the resort's glass-bottom boat. Children's programs are offered, except in the months of May and September. ✉ *Queen Ka`ahumanu Hwy., Kailua-Kona 96745,* ☎ *808/325–5555 or 800/367–5290,* FAX *808/325–5124. 92 1-bedroom bungalows, 33 2-bedroom bungalows. 2 restaurants, 3 bars, 2 pools, hot tubs, health club, 3 tennis courts, beach, boating, children's programs (ages 6–17), meeting rooms, airport shuttle. AE, DC, MC, V. FAP.*

$$$$ 🏨 **Mauna Kea Beach Hotel.** This world-class oceanfront resort hotel
★   was developed by Laurence S. Rockefeller in 1965 and sits on one of the islands' finest white-sand beaches. Rare works of art, such as a 7th-century Buddha statue, enhance walkways and open spaces. The rooms have a natural look with beige tiles and carpets complemented by pastel colors. They all feature original artwork and antiques. The fitness center has cardiovascular machines and free-weights. Shuttles operate between the Mauna Kea and the adjacent Hāpuna Beach Prince Hotel (☞ *above*), allowing guests to use the facilities at both stellar hotels. Wine and food lovers might want to plan a stay during annual Winter Wine Escape in November. ✉ *62-100 Mauna Kea Beach Dr., Kohala Coast 96743,* ☎ *808/882–7222 or 800/882–6060,* FAX *808/882–5700. 300 rooms, 10 suites. 5 restaurants, in-room safes, pool, beauty salon, 2 18-hole golf courses, 13 tennis courts, health club, beach. AE, D, DC, MC, V.*

$$$$ 🏨 **Mauna Lani Bay Hotel and Bungalows.** Almost all the spacious rooms
★   in this modern hotel have ocean views, and all have a large lānai. Comfortable furnishings grace rooms with natural fabrics and teak. The resort is known for its two spectacular golf courses. Pacific Rim cuisine is served at the oceanfront CanoeHouse (☞ *Kohala-Kona and Keauhou in Dining, above*). Lighter eaters can graze on appetizers and enjoy live entertainment in the Honu Bar. The annual Cuisines of the Sun celebration in July brings celebrity guest chefs to the hotel for food-and-

wine events. ⊠ *68-1400 Mauna Lani Dr., Kohala Coast 96743,* ☎ *808/ 885–6622 or 800/367–2323,* FAX *808/885–6183. 335 rooms, 10 suites, 5 bungalows. 5 restaurants, 5 bars, in-room safes, refrigerators, in-room VCRs, pool, 2 18-hole golf courses, 10 tennis courts, children's programs (ages 5–12). AE, D, DC, MC, V.* ✎

$$$$ 🏨 **Mauna Lani Point Condominiums.** These elegant and roomy two-story suites are set off by themselves on one of the world's most beautiful oceanside golf courses. It's just a few steps away from the Mauna Lani Bay Hotel (☞ *above*), where guests may use the golf and tennis facilities. Rooms have a modern tropical decor and come with washer-dryers and maid service. ⊠ *68-1310 Mauna Lani Dr., Kohala Coast 96743,* ☎ *808/885–5022 or 800/642–6284,* FAX *808/885–5015. 24 1-bedroom units, 37 2-bedroom units, 1 3-bedroom unit. Kitchenettes, pool, hot tub, sauna. AE, DC, MC, V.* ✎

$$$$ 🏨 **The Orchid at Mauna Lani.** This classy, romantic hotel, situated ★ around botanical gardens and waterfall ponds, stretches along 32 beach-front acres. Rooms are elegant, with European luxury; marble bathrooms and fluffy robes are only part of the pampering. The Orchid's signature restaurant, the Grill, features a terrific wine list presented by a knowledgeable sommelier. The Spa without Walls blends ancient wisdom with modern fitness facilities and treatments—outdoors if you wish. There's a protected swimming lagoon, and, for those who wish to explore Polynesian navigational skills, the resort offers 2½–hour voyages aboard an authentic double-hulled sailing canoe. ⊠ *1 N. Kanikū Dr., Kohala Coast 96743,* ☎ *808/885–2000 or 800/845–9905,* FAX *808/885– 5778. 539 rooms, 54 suites. 3 restaurants, 4 bars, pool, sauna, spa, 2 18-hole golf courses, 10 tennis courts, health club, beach, snorkeling, boating, children's programs (ages 5–12). AE, D, DC, MC, V.* ✎

$$$–$$$$ 🏨 **Outrigger Waikoloa Beach.** On the site of ancient royal fishponds, historic trails, and petroglyph fields, this 15-acre resort reopened in 1999 after an extensive renovation. The new design honors the unique Hawaiian history of the grounds. Rooms feature Hawaiian art and bamboo-type furnishings and have private lānai with views of the ocean or of immaculate gardens. An additional 17 plush cabanas are near the ocean. Good, affordable dining is available at the Hawai'i Calls Restaurant. The hotel is next to a white-sand beach and 'Anaeho'omalu Bay—perfect for windsurfing and snorkeling. ⊠ *69-275 Waikoloa Beach Dr., Waikoloa 96738,* ☎ *808/886–6789 or 800/922–5533,* FAX *808/886–7852. 545 rooms, 17 cabanas. Restaurant, 2 bars, pool, 2 hot tubs, sauna, spa, 2 18-hole golf courses, 6 tennis courts, health club, beach, children's programs (ages 5–12), coin laundry, meeting rooms. AE, D, DC, MC, V.* ✎

$$$–$$$$ 🏨 **Waikoloa Villas at Waikoloa Village.** This is about the only moderately priced Waikoloa-area accommodation, although it's 6 mi inland. The wide-open spaces of cowboy country attract golfers and the horsey set. Individually owned condominium units are all decorated differently, but all are tasteful and have ceiling fans and washer-dryers. Two-night minimum stays are required. ⊠ *68-3840 Lua Kua St. (Box 38-5134), Waikoloa 96738,* ☎ *808/883–9144 or 800/535–0085,* FAX *808/883–8740. 3 1-bedroom units, 8 2-bedroom units, 2 3-bedroom units. 2 pools, 18-hole golf course, 2 tennis courts, horseback riding. AE, MC, V.* ✎

$–$$ 🏨 **Kohala Village Inn.** This simple, clean little hotel is the only one in the country town of Hāwī. Cable TV and friendly proprietors make this pleasant inn an adequate place to stay. It is close to many of Kohala's activities and is within walking distance of shops and galleries. Rooms have showers but not tubs. ⊠ *55-514 Hāwī Rd., Hāwī 96719,* ☎ *808/889–0419,* FAX *808/889–0419. 17 rooms, 1 suite. MC, V.*

Waimea/Hāmākua Coast

$$$ 🏨 **Waimea Gardens Cottage.** These two charming streamside coun-
try cottages have kitchens stocked with your choice of breakfast items.
French doors, antique furnishings, window boxes spilling over with
flowers, and a fireplace create a romantic ambience. It's 8 mi from the
island's beaches, on the sunny side of Waimea, and you can awake on
cool, Upcountry mornings to collect your own eggs from the quiet flock
of miniature hens outside. You'll be looked after by friendly hosts Charles
and Barbara Campbell. ⊠ *Reservations: Hawai'i's Best Bed and Break-
fasts, Box 563, Kamuela 96743,* ☎ *808/885–4550 or 800/262–9912,*
FAX *808/885–0559. 2 cottages. No credit cards. CP.* 🐾

$$ 🏨 **Waimea Country Lodge.** In cool Upcountry surroundings, this lodge
has rooms that look out onto green pastures. New furnishings and
Hawaiian print bedspreads make the lodge an adequate and friendly
place. Six of the rooms have their own kitchenette. ⊠ *65-1210 Lindsey Rd., Waimea (Box 2559, Kamuela 96743),* ☎ *808/885–4100,* FAX
808/885–6711. 21 rooms. AE, D, DC, MC, V. CP.

$–$$ 🏨 **Hotel Honoka'a Club.** This basic, bargain hotel is 45 minutes from
Hilo and close to Waipi'o Valley. Rustic rooms range from lower-level
hostel units with three or four beds and an adjoining shower per room
to upper-story units with queen-size beds and views of kukui, mango,
African tulip, and avocado trees. Collectors will enjoy poking through
the secondhand stores in the country town of Honoka'a. ⊠ *45-3480
Māmane St., Honoka'a (Box 247, Honoka'a 96727),* ☎ *808/775–0678
or 800/808–0678. 13 rooms, 5 hostel rooms. Restaurant. MC, V.* 🐾

$–$$ 🏨 **Kamuela Inn.** Twenty minutes from the island beaches, every room
in this modest inn is attractively designed. A penthouse suite sleeps six
and has a sunset lānai and full kitchen. Continental breakfast is served
at the breakfast lānai. The inn has a peaceful country setting, its own
art gallery, and is near shops, a theater, restaurants, and a museum.
Note that not all rooms have phones. ⊠ *65-1300 Kawaihae Rd., Kamuela (Box 1994, Kamuela 96743),* ☎ *808/885–4243 or 800/555–
8968,* FAX *808/885–8857. 20 rooms, 11 suites. AE, D, DC, MC, V.* 🐾

NIGHTLIFE AND THE ARTS

Clubs and Cabarets

If you're the kind of person who doesn't come alive until after dark,
you're going to be pretty lonely on the Big Island. In Hilo, the streets
roll up at dusk. Even on the visitor-oriented Kona-Kohala Coast, there
is not a lot doing after dark. Blame it on the plantation heritage. People did their cane-raising in the morning.

Breakwater. This disco at the Hawai'i Naniloa Resort in Hilo com-
petes with the crashing surf on Friday and Saturday nights from 10 PM
until around 3 AM. ⊠ *93 Banyan Dr., Hilo,* ☎ *808/969–3333.*
Fiasco's. This lively restaurant has margarita specials, a huge selection
of beers, and bands (blues, rock, soul) most Thursday through Saturday nights. ⊠ *200 Kanoelehua Ave., Hilo,* ☎ *808/935–7666.*
Honu Bar. Thursday through Saturday you'll find easy-listening jazz
at this elegant spot in the Mauna Lani Bay Hotel and Bungalows on
the Kohala Coast. Comfortable booths, a dance floor, sashimi prepared
tableside, imported cigars, and fine cognacs have made this a popular,
upscale gathering spot. ⊠ *68-1400 Mauna Lani Dr., Kohala Coast,*
☎ *808/885–6622.*
Huggo's. Jazz-style entertainment, accompanied by the sound of lapping waves, sets a romantic mood at this popular restaurant. Various
singers perform, sometimes country, sometimes rock, so call ahead of

time. ✉ *75-5828 Kahakai Rd., Ali'i Dr., Kailua-Kona,* ☎ *808/329–1493.*
Lulu's. A crowd dances every evening here to hot dance music selected by
a professional DJ. ✉ *75-5819 Ali'i Dr., Kailua-Kona,* ☎ *808/331–2633.*
Michaelangelo's.)n the second level of the Waterfront Row complex,
this Italian restaurant starts rocking after 10 every night with a live
DJ. ✉ *Waterfront Row, Kailua-Kona,* ☎ *808/329–4436.*

Dinner Cruise

Captain Beans' Polynesian Dinner Cruise. This is the ever-popular
standby in sunset dinner cruises. You can't miss it—as the sun sets in
Kailua, look out over the water and you'll see a big gaudy boat with
distinctive orange sails. This cruise is corny, and you would get a better full-course dinner (your choice of teriyaki steak or baked chicken)
elsewhere, but it's an experience, with unlimited drinks and a Hawaiian show. This is for adults only. ✉ *73-4800 Kanalani St., Suite 200,
Kailua-Kona,* ☎ *808/329–2955.* ✍ *$49, including dinner, entertain-
ment, and open bar.* ⊙ *Sails Sat.–Tues. and Thurs. at 5:15, Fri. at 7.*

Film

Hilo

Films are shown regularly at the new state-of-the-art **Prince Kuhio Stadium Cinemas** (✉ Prince Kūhiō Plaza, 111 E. Puainako Ave., ☎ 808/
959–4595); **Kress Cinemas** (✉ 174 Kamehameha Ave., ☎ 808/961–
3456), which offers art films; and the value-priced **Waiākea Theaters
1, 2, and 3** (✉ Waiākea Kai Shopping Plaza, 88 Kanoelehua Ave., ☎
808/935–9747).

Kailua-Kona

Find regular showings and current movies at **Hualālai Theaters 1, 2,
and 3** (✉ Hualālai Center, Kuakini Hwy. and Hualālai St., ☎ 808/329–
6641); **Kona Marketplace Cinemas** (✉ Kona Marketplace, across from
Kona Inn Shopping Center, 75-5725 Ali'i Dr., ☎ 808/329–4488);
Keauhou Theatres (✉ Keauhou Shopping Center, 78-6831 Ali'i Dr.,
☎ 808/324–7200), a splendid seven-theater complex; and at the new
10-screen **Makalapua Stadium Cinema** (✉ Makalapua Ave. next to K-
Mart), at press time under construction.

Around the Island

Akebono Theater (✉ Hwy. 130, Pāhoa, ☎ 808/965–9943) was built
in 1917 and is the oldest theater in the state. Visit this quaint building
to see classic movies or plays, dances, and shows run by the nonprofit
Hawai'i Island Theater.

Honoka'a Peoples Theaters (✉ Manane St., Honoka'a, ☎ 808/775–0000)
shows movies on weekends. **Kahei Theater** (✉ Hwy. 270, Hāwī, ☎ 808/
889–6831) shows first-run movies Friday, Saturday, and Sunday evenings.
And **Na'alehu Theater** (✉ Hawai'i Belt Rd., Hwy. 11, Na'alehu, ☎ 808/
929–9133) shows movies Friday, Saturday, and Sunday nights.

Hula

For hula lovers, the biggest show of the year and the largest event of
its kind in the world is the annual **Merrie Monarch Festival** (✉ Hawai'i
Naniloa Resort, 93 Banyan Dr., Hilo 96720, ☎ 808/935–9168). Honoring the legacy of King David Kalākaua, Hawai'i's last king, it is staged
in Hilo at the spacious Edith Kanakaole Auditorium during the first
week following Easter Sunday. Hula hālau compete in various classes
of ancient and modern dance styles. You need to reserve accommodations and tickets as much as a year in advance.

Lū'au and Polynesian Revues

Kohala Coast and Waikoloa

Hilton Waikoloa Village. The Hilton seats 400 outdoors at the Kamehameha Court, where the acclaimed Polynesian group Tihati offers a lively show. A buffet dinner provides samplings of Hawaiian food, as well as fish, beef, and chicken to appeal to all tastes. The price includes one tropical drink. ⊠ *425 Waikoloa Beach Dr., Waikoloa,* ☎ *808/886–1234.* ⊡ *$58.* ☉ *Tues. and Fri. from 5:45.*

Kona Village Resort. The lū'au here is one of the most authentic and traditional in the Islands. Activities include the steaming of a whole pig in the *imu* (ground oven). Mainland taste buds might reject some items, such as raw *'opihi* (a limpet, considered a chewy delicacy in Hawai'i), but there is plenty to appeal to the less adventuresome. A Polynesian show on a stage over a lagoon is magical. ⊠ *6 mi north of Kona International Airport, off Queen Ka'ahumanu Hwy., Kailua-Kona,* ☎ *808/325–5555.* ⊡ *$69.75 includes wine.* ☉ *Fri. from 5; walking tour 5:30, imu ceremony 6:30, dinner at 7, show at 8.*

Mauna Kea Beach Resort. Every Tuesday chefs come together here to create a traditional Hawaiian *pa'ina* (dinner feast), which includes the classic *kalua* (roasted in an underground oven) pig. On the gracious North Pointe Lu'au Grounds of the Mauna Kea Hotel, guests experience an awe-inspiring fire show and can sample the best of Hawaiian cuisine. The enchanting songs of Nani Lim and her spellbinding hula halau create a memorable ambience. ⊠ *62-100 Mauna Kea Beach Dr.,* ☎ *808/882–7222.* ⊡ *$68.* ☉ *Tues. from 5:30; dinner at 6, show at 8.*

Outrigger Waikoloa Beach. The Outrigger offers a great value Sunday- and Wednesday-night lū'au at the Lū'au Grounds, where the well-known Polynesian revue Tihati presents the entertainment. ⊠ *69-275 Waikoloa Beach Dr., Kamuela,* ☎ *808/886–6789.* ⊡ *$55 includes open bar.* ☉ *Wed. and Sun. 5:30–8:30.*

Kailua

In Kailua, two lū'au fill the bill, with Polynesian entertainment, kalua pig cooked in the traditional underground oven, pageantry, and an open bar.

King Kamehameha's Kona Beach Hotel's Island Breeze Lū'au. Witness the arrival of the Royal Court by canoe and have pictures taken at this beachfront evening that includes a 22-course buffet and a show. ⊠ *75-5660 Palani Rd., Kailua-Kona,* ☎ *808/326–4969 or 808/329–2911.* ⊡ *$53.* ☉ *Tues.–Thurs. and Sun. at 5:30.*

Royal Kona Resort. This resort lights lū'au torches for a full Polynesian show and a Hawaiian-style buffet three times a week in an oceanfront setting right on the water. ⊠ *75-5852 Ali'i Dr., Kailua-Kona,* ☎ *808/329–3111 ext. 4.* ⊡ *$52 includes beer and wine.* ☉ *Mon. and Fri.– Sat. at 5:30.*

Theater

Aloha Performing Arts Center. Near Kailua-Kona, check with the Arts Center for its schedule of musicals and Broadway plays performed by local talent. ⊠ *Aloha Theatre Café, Hwy. 11, Kainaliu,* ☎ *808/322–9924.*

Hilo Community Players. This group stages plays on an occasional basis. ⊠ *141 Kalākaua Ave., Hilo,* ☎ *808/935–9155.*

Kahilu Theater Foundation. For legitimate theater, the little town of Waimea is your best bet. The Kahilu Theater Foundation hosts internationally acclaimed performances, including theater, on a regular basis. ⊠ *Parker Ranch Center,* ☎ *808/885–6868.*

OUTDOOR ACTIVITIES AND SPORTS

Participant Sports

The Big Island attracts active people. Whether you like to run, ride, bicycle, hike, sail, or even ski, there is so much to explore. In North Kohala a new mule trail adventure takes you into historic Pololū Valley, and inaccessible pasture trails are now open to a mountain bike tour. In general, water-sports activities center on the Kailua-Kona area because of its calmer waters.

An increased number of eco-adventures around Volcano and in the Kona areas also focus on the island's wondrous eco-system of and its unique species. For information about these and other organized outdoor tours, *see* Contacts and Resources *in* Big Island A to Z, *below.*

Brochures that designate self-guided trails for mountain biking, driving, and walking tours are available at Hawai'i Visitor Bureau outlets.

Biking

Although pedalers should be fairly physically fit for extended bicycling tours, there seems to be no typical rider. Everyone from college students to retirees has completed tours of a week or longer. How much you ride is up to you, as generally the support van that carries gear will also stop to pick up tired riders. Helmets are strongly recommended, and some operators require them. Also, sheepskin seat covers and bicycle shorts add greatly to personal comfort on long trips.

Backroads Bicycle Touring. This company has been pushing pedaling in Hawai'i since 1985. It offers monthly eight-day, 320-mi circle-island biking trips. Lodgings, included in the fee, alternate between luxury resorts and old Hawaiian inns. The $2,200 fee includes meals, but bicycle and airfare are extra. ✉ *801 Cedar St., Berkeley, CA 94710-1800,* ☎ *510/527–1555 or 800/462–2848.* 🐾

Bicycle Adventures, Inc. Six- and eight-day winter or spring bicycle tours of the Big Island that cover 40 to 50 mi a day are offered. Pedalers enjoy beach time, snorkeling, hiking excursions, comfortable accommodations, and fine dining in addition to visits to Kīlauea Volcano and Pu'uhonua o Hōnaunau. The cost of $1,600 to $2,000 does not include bicycle rental. ✉ *Box 11219, Olympia, WA 98508,* ☎ *360/786–0989 or 800/443–6060.* 🐾

C&S Outfitters. These folks in Waimea offer guided tours, have a wealth of knowledge about the island's biking trails, and rent a range of bikes. They have a shop for accessories and repair needs, plus they rent kayaks and other beach equipment. ✉ *64-1066 Mamalahoa Hwy.,* ☎ *808/885–5005.* 🐾

Chris' Adventures Bike or Hike. Chris' offers six- to seven-hour biking excursions in which you cruise from 4,000-ft elevations down to Pololū Valley in North Kohala. Shorter hikes and bike-and-hike combinations in the area are also available. Morning tours include breakfast and a picnic lunch. Costs, including the bike, are around $85. ✉ *Box 869, Kula,* ☎ *808/326–4600.* 🐾

Journey of Discovery. This ecotour bike venture in North Kohala leads beginners downhill through historic pastures and a taro patch, past streams and waterfalls, all on private property. Skilled bikers go the extra mile uphill on a single track. The $90 fee includes a local Kohala snack. ✉ *Hwy. 270, at the old laundromat in Hāwī,* ☎ *808/889–0097 or 877/326–7646.* 🐾

Mauna Kea Mountain Bikes, Inc. Daily tours in the Hāmākua rain forest area as well as bike rentals are offered by this company in Kamuela.

Tour prices range from $45 to $80. ⊠ *Box 44672, Kamuela,* ☎ *808/883–0130 or 888/682–8687.* 🐾

BIKE RENTAL

If you want to strike out on your own, consider renting a bicycle in Kailua-Kona at **B&L Bike and Sports** (⊠ 75-5699 Kopiko Pl., ☎ 808/329–3309), **Dave's Bike & Triathlon Shop** (⊠ 75-5669 Ali'i Dr., ☎ 329–4522), or **Hawaiian Pedals Bicycle Rentals** (⊠ Kona Inn Shopping Village, 75-5744 Ali'i Dr., Kailua-Kona, ☎ 808/329–2294 or 808/326–2453). **Red Sail Sports** on the Kohala Coast rents mountain bikes by the hour, for hotel guests only, at the Hilton Waikoloa Village (☎ 808/886–2876).

Fitness and Spa Centers

With nine spas and several health clubs encircling the island, you can find rejuvenation easily. In Hilo, exercise addicts might try **Spencer Health and Fitness Center** (⊠ 197 Keawe St., ☎ 808/969–1511). The **Hawai'i Naniloa Resort** (⊠ 93 Banyan Dr., ☎ 808/969–3333) has a spa and fitness center open to nonguests for $15. Such specialties as herbal wraps and lomi lomi massages are available.

In Kona, the **Club** (⊠ 75-5699 Kopiko Rd., ☎ 808/326–2582) has high-tech fitness facilities at a daily rate of $10.

Five of the major hotels have spa facilities that may be used by nonguests. The Centre for Well Being and the Spa Without Walls program at **The Orchid at Mauna Lani** (⊠ 1 N. Kanikū Dr., ☎ 808/885–2000; $15 daily) offers luxurious treatments indoors and outdoors. The **Hilton Waikoloa Village** (⊠ 69-425 Waikoloa Beach Dr., ☎ 808/886–1234) is home to the well-known Kohala Spa ($20 daily) where you can even find a healthy smoothie at the Spa Café. The **Hāpuna Beach Prince Hotel** (⊠ 62-100 Kauna'oa Dr., ☎ 808/880–1111) has daily passes for $10. The new Hawaiian Rainforest Spa and Salon at the **Outrigger Waikoloa Beach** (⊠ 69-275 Waikoloa Beach Dr., ☎ 808/886–6789) as well as the **Mauna Lani Bay Hotel and Bungalows** (⊠ 68-1400 Mauna Lani Dr., ☎ 808/885–6622) welcome nonguests for massages and oceanside healing treatments.

Golf

If there is one thing the Big Island is known for, it's the beautiful golf courses. Like green oases they quicken the black, arid landscape of lava rock fields. Four of the Big Island's golf courses—two at the Mauna Kea Beach Resort and two at Mauna Lani Resort, the Francis H. I'i Brown golf courses (North and South)—are repeatedly chosen by golfing magazines as the best, the most spectacular, and the favorite. The course at Four Seasons hosts the Senior MasterCard Tournament. Costs are very reasonable at the municipal golf courses.

Ali'i Country Club. Known as the Mountain Course, the 18 holes here offer awesome views of the Kona Coast. The pros try to avoid the lava and play the high side. ⊠ *78-7000 Ali'i Dr., Kailua-Kona,* ☎ *808/322–2595.* 🏌 *Greens fee $150.*

Big Island Country Club. This course opened in 1997 as a private membership course. At a 2,500-ft elevation, it has a dramatic layout and stunning views. ⊠ *71-1420 Mamalahoa Hwy., Kailua-Kona,* ☎ *808/325–5044.* 🏌 *Call for fees.*

Discovery Harbor Golf Course. At this course on the southern end of the island you can play 18 holes, par 72. It's a public course designed by Robert Trent Jones, Sr. ⊠ *Kamaoa Rd., take South Point Rd. off Hwy. 11,* ☎ *808/929–7353.* 🏌 *Greens fee $28; cart included.*

Francis H. I'i Brown Golf Course at the Mauna Lani Resort. This demanding and stunningly beautiful course was redesigned in 1991 by Nelson Wright Haworth and is now two 18-hole courses (North and

South). The men's tee at the 15th hole of the South Co[ast] among golfers because they must carry their tee shot ov[er] open ocean to reach the green. ⊠ *68-1400 Mauna Lan[i] Coast,* ☎ *808/885–6655.* 🖼 *Greens fee for either course, для nonguests, $200, twilight $75; cart included.*

Hāmākua Country Club. This is a friendly 9-hole course, designed in 1925, where greens fees are deposited into a drop box on the honor system. ⊠ *41 mi north of Hilo on ocean side of Hwy. 19, Honoka'a,* ☎ *808/775–7244.* 🖼 *Greens fee $10; no carts available.*

Hāpuna Golf Course. Landscaped with indigenous plants, trees, and grasses, this course at the Hāpuna Beach Prince Hotel aims to be environmentally sensitive. It's also one of the best, a challenging par-72 designed by Arnold Palmer and Ed Seay in 1992. It has both the 1st and 18th holes in easy walking distance of Mauna Kea Beach Resort hotels. ⊠ *62-100 Kauna'oa Dr.,* ☎ *808/880–3000.* 🖼 *Greens fee for nonguests $135, twilight $85; cart included.*

Hilo Municipal Golf Course. On the east side of the island is this 18-hole, flat, Hilo-green course with four sets of tees. It's near the airport. Bring both water and an umbrella. ⊠ *340 Haihai St., Hilo,* ☎ *808/ 959–7711.* 🖼 *Greens fee nonresidents, weekdays $20, weekends $25; cart $14.50.*

Hualālai Golf Course. This Jack Nicklaus–designed course is a masterpiece. Players can see the ocean from every hole. Play here is a treat reserved for Four Seasons guests and resort residents, so the course is seldom crowded. ⊠ *100 Ka'ūpūlehu Dr., off Hwy. 19 10 mins north of Kona International Airport,* ☎ *808/325–8480.*

Kona Country Club. This Kailua-Kona club offers an adventurous 18-hole ocean course with panoramic views. ⊠ *78-7000 Ali'i Dr., Kailua-Kona,* ☎ *808/322–2595.* 🖼 *Greens fee $150; cart included.*

Mākālei Hawai'i Country Club. On the cool slopes of Hualālai Mountain, the course climbs from 1,800 to 2,800 ft and is home to peacocks, wild turkeys, and pheasants that wander across the bent-grass greens. ⊠ *72-3890 Hawai'i Belt Rd., Kailua-Kona,* ☎ *808/325–6625.* 🖼 *Greens fee $110; twilight $50; cart included.*

Mauna Kea Beach Resort Golf Course. This extremely challenging par-72, 18-hole course receives award after award from golf magazines. It was designed by Robert Trent Jones, Sr. ⊠ *62-100 Mauna Kea Beach Dr.,* ☎ *808/882–5400.* 🖼 *Greens fee $175; twilight $95; cart included.*

Naniloa Country Club Golf Course. The Naniloa is a 9-hole course convenient to Hilo's major hotels. ⊠ *120 Banyan Dr., Hilo,* ☎ *808/935–3000.* 🖼 *Greens fee nonguests $40; cart $7.*

Sea Mountain Golf Course. This course is above the shores of a black-sand beach about 30 mi south of Volcano Village. The 18-hole, par-72 course stretches from the Pacific Coast up the slopes of Mauna Loa. ⊠ *Hwy. 22, Ninole Loop Rd., Punalu'u,* ☎ *808/928–6222.* 🖼 *Greens fee $40; cart included.*

Volcano Golf & Country Club. This 18-hole, par-72 course perches on the rim of Kilauea Volcano, an elevation of 4,000 ft. It is comfortably cool, and on clear days you'll have glamorous views. It was originally built in 1922, and four ponds have been added since. ⊠ *Hawai'i Volcanoes National Park (Box 46),* ☎ *808/967–7331.* 🖼 *Greens fee $60; cart included.*

Waikoloa Beach Golf Club. Designed by Robert Trent Jones, Jr., in 1981, this course sprawls over historical grounds at the two Waikoloa resorts. An 18-hole, par-70 course with three sets of tees, it wends through lava formations and has beautiful ocean views. ⊠ *Waikoloa Beach Dr.,* ☎ *808/886–6060.* 🖼 *Greens fee nonguests $120; twilight $60; cart included.*

Waikoloa King's Golf Course. This par-72 Tom Weiskopf/Jay Morrish–designed 18-hole course features four large lakes and is adjacent to the Hilton Waikoloa Village. ⊠ *600 Waikoloa Beach Dr.*, ☎ *808/886–7888.* 🎫 *Greens fee nonguests $120; twilight $60; cart included.*

Waikoloa Village Golf Club. The second of the two Robert Trent Jones, Jr.–designed Waikoloa courses, the Waikoloa Village Golf Club is 6 mi up from the resorts. You'll have beautiful views at this 1,000-ft elevation. ⊠ *68-1792 Melia St., Waikoloa Village*, ☎ *808/883–9621.* 🎫 *Greens fee $80, twilight $45; cart included.*

Waimea Country Club. Wedged inside a eucalyptus forest is this 18-hole, bent-grass greens, par-72 course that opened in 1994. It borders Waipi'o Valley in the cool, misty highlands on the Hilo side of Waimea. ⊠ *47-5220 Māmalahoa Hwy., Kamuela*, ☎ *808/885–8053.* 🎫 *Greens fee $65, twilight $45; cart included.*

Hiking and Camping

For the fit adventurer, hiking is a great way to explore the Big Island's natural beauty. Trails crisscross the slopes of Mauna Ke'a and plunge into Kīlauea Iki Crater (☞ Hawai'i Volcanoes National Park *in* Exploring, *above*). A challenging, little-known trek leads to the top of 13,680-ft **Mauna Loa.** It's 20 mi one-way, with overnight stops at two cabins, one at 10,000 ft and the other at the summit. You should count on three to four days. The cabins are free, but you must obtain a permit before setting out at the visitor center in Hawai'i Volcanoes National Park. Here you can also get permits for two other backcountry hikes—along the coast or across the East Rift Zone. ⊠ *Hawai'i Volcanoes National Park, Volcano 96785*, ☎ *808/985–6000.* 🐾

Nāmakani Paio Cabins, at the 4,000-ft level, 3 mi beyond the Volcano House, are managed by Volcano House, a concession of the National Park Service. Each cabin has a double bed, two bunk beds, and electric lights. Guests should bring extra blankets, because it gets cold in these simple but adequate units. Each cabin has a grill outside, but you must bring your own firewood. ⊠ *Volcano House, Box 53, Hawai'i Volcanoes National Park, 96718*, ☎ *808/967–7321*, ⨳ *808/967–8429.* 🎫 *Single or double $40; a $32 refundable deposit allows guests to pick up bedding and keys (for cabins and separate bath facilities) at Volcano House.*

For information on camping at county parks, including Spencer Beach Park, contact the **Department of Parks and Recreation** (⊠ 25 Aupuni St., Hilo 96720, ☎ 808/961–8311, 🐾).

The **Department of Land and Natural Resources** handles cabin reservations for the island's many state parks, including Hāpuna Beach Park and Kalopa Park. ⊠ *75 Aupuni St., Hilo 96720*, ☎ *808/974–6200.*

For general hiking information, topographic and other maps, as well as up-to-date guidebooks, contact **Hawai'i Geographic Society** (⊠ Box 1698, Honolulu 96806, ☎ 800/538–3950). A hiking information package is available for $7.

Horseback Riding

In addition to the companies listed below, the Mauna Kea Beach Resort (☞ Kohala Coast and Waikoloa *in* Lodging, *above*) maintains stables in Upcountry Waimea. Most other hotels offer transportation to commercial stables. Ask at your hotel activities desk.

King's Trail Rides O'Kona, Inc. Riders take a 4½-hour excursion to Captain Cook monument in Kealakekua Bay. The trip includes snorkeling and lunch for $95. Custom rides can also be arranged. ⊠ *Hwy. 11, Mile Marker 111, Kealakekua*, ☎ *808/323–2388.*

Kohala Na'alapa. Here, adjacent to the white fence of Kohala Ranch, riders of all levels are invited to take open-pasture rides on historic Kahua Ranch. Forested areas alternate with splendid panoramic views. Excursions range from $55 to $75. ⊠ *Kohala Mountain Rd., Hwy. 250,* ☎ *808/889–0022.*

Paniolo Riding Adventures. Paniolo leads trail rides for beginners to buckaroos through lush Kohala ranch land. You'll never be nose-to-tail on these rides. Two-and-a-half–hour rides are $85. A four-hour Paniolo Picnic Adventure (bring your own lunch) is $125. ⊠ *Kohala Mountain Rd., Hwy. 250,* ☎ *808/889–5354.*

Waipi'o Na'alapa Trail Rides. Twice-daily rides through the Waipi'o Valley are offered for $75. Departure point is at Waipi'o Valley Artworks (☎ 808/775–0958) in Kukuihaele, past Honoka'a, where a four-wheel-drive vehicle takes riders to the horses. ☎ *808/775–0419.*

Waipi'o Ridge Stables. Two different rides around the rim of Waipi'o are offered, one for $75 and one for $145. Riders meet at Waipi'o Valley Artworks (☎ 808/775–0958) in Kukuihaele and are shuttled by four-wheel-drive to the horses. ☎ *808/775–1007.*

Skiing
Skiing on Mauna Ke'a is for experienced skiers only. Currently the ski area has no lodge or lifts.

Ski Guides Hawai'i. Christopher Langan of Mauna Kea Ski Corporation is the only outfit currently licensed to furnish transportation, guide services, and ski equipment on Mauna Ke'a. Snow can fall from Thanksgiving through June, but the most likely months are February and March. For an eight-hour day trip for up to six people, Langan charges $250 per person, including refreshments and a mountaintop lunch, equipment, guide service, transportation from Waimea, and four-wheel-drive shuttle back up the mountain after each ski run. ⊠ *Box 1954, Kamuela,* ☎ *808/885–4188 in ski season; 808/884–5131 off-season.* ⌘

Tennis
School and park courts are free and open to anyone who wishes to play, though students have first priority during school hours at high school courts. In Hilo you will find courts at the **University of Hawai'i–Hilo** (⊠ 200 Kawili St., ☎ 808/974–7520). There are four free, lighted courts at **Lincoln Park** (⊠ Kino'ole and Ponahawai Sts., ☎ 808/961–8311 for a full list of all island park courts). The eight courts (three lighted for night play) at **Hilo Tennis Stadium** (⊠ Pi'ilani and Kalanikoa Sts., ☎ 808/961–8720) charge a small fee. **Waiākea Racket Club** (⊠ 400 Hualani St., ☎ 808/961–5499) is also open to the public for a reasonable fee.

Across the island the Keauhou-Kona resorts have become renowned for their beautiful tennis courts. **Hōlua Stadium** is a headquarters for exhibition tennis. Two of the few courts where not-so-heavy hitters can play free are at **Kailua Playground**—the wait may be long, however—and at the **Old Kona Airport.** Nonguests can play for a fee at the **Kona Surf Hotel's Racquet Club** and on the four courts at the **Royal Kona Resort** (☞ Kailua-Kona and Keauhou *in* Lodging, *above*). At **King Kamehameha's Kona Beach Hotel** (☞ Kailua-Kona and Keauhou *in* Lodging, *above*) nonguests may purchase memberships to play. Farther afield, there are two free, lighted courts at **Waimea Park** (on Hwy. 19) in Waimea. Courts at the **Outrigger Waikoloa Beach, Hilton Waikoloa Village** (two of its eight courts are clay), and **Colony One Sea Mountain at Punalu'u** (☞ Volcano/South Point *in* Lodging, *above*) are open at an hourly charge. The **Orchid at Mauna Lani** (☞ Kohala Coast and Waikoloa *in* Lodging, *above*) has 10 courts (including one exhibition court). **Mauna Kea Beach Resort**'s (☞ Kohala Coast and Waikoloa *in* Lodging, *above*) 13 courts are in a beautiful 12-acre oceanside tennis park. The pro shop carries the most complete line of tennis wear on the Kohala Coast.

Water Sports

DEEP-SEA FISHING

Along the Kona Coast you'll find some of the world's most exciting "blue water" fishing. Although July, August, and September are peak months, with a number of tournaments, charter fishing goes on year-round. You don't have to compete to experience the thrill of landing a big Pacific blue marlin or a mahimahi, tuna, wahoo, or other game fish. More than 50 charter boats, averaging 26 to 54 ft, are available for hire, most of them out of **Honokōhau Harbor** just north of Kailua. Prices for a full day of fishing range from $150 for shared charters to $900 for private trips. Half-day charters are also available in the $70 to $550 range and might be preferable if you have never experienced the hypnotic effect of sun, wind, and waves on a small boat. Tackle, bait, and ice are furnished, but you'll have to bring your own lunch. Most boats do not allow you to keep your entire catch, although if you ask, many captains will send you home with a few fish fillets.

Make arrangements for deep-sea fishing at your hotel activities desk or stop by at **Kona Marlin Center** (☎ 808/329–7529) at Honokōhau Harbor, where you can get a lunch-to-go as well. You can also book charters or get information about tournaments at **Kona Charters Skippers Association** (☎ 808/329–3600 or 800/762–7546, ✍), **Charter Services Hawai'i** (☎ 808/334–1881 or 800/567–5662,✍), or **Jack's Kona Charters** (☎ 808/325–7558 or 888/584–5662). **Kona Activities Center** (☎ 808/329–3171 or 800/367–5288) also provides bookings and information.

The biggest of the fishing competitions is the **Hawaiian International Billfish Tournament** at the beginning of August, which attracts teams from around the world. Since tournament participants rate boats' cleanliness, crew, and equipment, the listing can serve as a helpful guide in choosing which boat to charter. In addition, be sure to describe your expectations when you book your charter so the booking agent can match you with a captain and a boat you will like.

Big fish are sometimes still weighed in at **Kailua Pier** adjacent to the King Kamehameha's Kona Beach Hotel in Kailua-Kona, but most of the activity has moved up to Honokōhau Harbor's Fuel Dock. Try to be there in the afternoon between 4 and 5 to watch the weigh-in of the day's catch.

PARASAILING AND WINDSURFING

Parasailers sit in a harness attached to a parachute that lifts off from the boat deck and sails aloft. Passengers can choose to glide 7 or 10 minutes at 400- or 800-ft heights. Call **UFO Parasail** (⊠ Across the street from Kailua Pier, Kailua-Kona, ☎ 808/325–5836) to make arrangements for parasailing. Costs range from $45 to $55.

One of the best windsurfing locations on the Big Island is at 'Anaeho'omalu Bay, on the beach in front of **Outrigger Waikoloa Beach.** Call Ocean Sports at the Royal Waikoloan Resort (☎ 808/886–6666) to obtain information.

SCUBA DIVING

Two-tank dives should cost from $80 to $100, depending on whether they are in one or two locations and if they are dives from a boat or from the shore. Many dive outfits have underwater cameras for rent, in case you are lucky enough to glimpse humpback whales and their calves during the winter months or simply want to capture colorful reef fish on film. Instruction with PADI certification in three to five days is $250–$550. The Kona Coast has calm waters for diving, and dive operators are helpful about suggesting dive sites. Most companies also rent out dive equipment, snorkel gear, and other water toys. Many organize otherworldly manta ray dives at night. Some offer additional whale-watch cruises.

Reputable scuba charters to consider in Kailua-Kona are **Big Island Divers** (✉ 75-5467 Kaiwi St., ☎ 808/329–6068, ✎), **Sandwich Isle Divers** (✉ 75-5729 I Ali'i Dr., ☎ 808/329–9188, ✎), and **Kona Coast Divers** (✉ 74-5614 Palani Rd., ☎ 808/329–8802, ✎).

Body Glove Cruises (☎ 808/326–7122 or 800/551–8911, ✎) has a 55-ft catamaran that sets off from the Kailua Pier daily for a 4½-hour dive and snorkel cruise, which includes breakfast and a buffet lunch.

At 'Anaeho'omalu Bay at the Outrigger Waikoloa Beach on the Kohala Coast, **Red Sail Sports** (☎ 808/885–2876) organizes scuba dives from the 38-ft *Lanikai*. Farther north, in Kawaihae, **Kohala Divers Ltd.** (✉ Kawaihae Shopping Center, downstairs, ☎ 808/882–7774, ✎) offers a complete package of diving services.

SNORKELING

Colorful tropical fish frequent the lava outcroppings along many Big Island shorelines, so it's easy to arrange a do-it-yourself snorkeling tour by renting masks and snorkels from any of the many diving outfits in Kona or at the resorts. If you are island hopping and want to drop off your equipment on O'ahu, Maui, or Kaua'i, consider **Snorkel Bob's** (✉ Ali'i Dr. next to the Royal Kona Resort, Kailua-Kona, ☎ 808/329–0770), where prices start at $29 a week for a simple set.

Many snorkel cruises are available. Shop for prices, ask about the size of the boat, and make sure you know what is included and how much the extras (e.g., underwater cameras) cost.

Among the Big Island's wet-and-wild offerings is the **Captain Zodiac Raft Expedition** (✉ Honokōhau Harbor, Kailua-Kona, ☎ 808/329–3199, ✎) along the Kona Coast. The exciting four-hour trip on this inflatable raft explores gaping lava-tube caves, searches for dolphins and turtles, and drifts through Kealakekua Bay, where passengers can snorkel and float. Take a towel, sunscreen, and camera. Cost is $65.

At Keauhou Bay **Fair Wind and Orca Raft Adventure** sail for 4½-hour morning and 3½-hour afternoon excursions. *Fair Wind* is a 60-ft double-decker catamaran, which supplies snorkel gear, a 15-ft waterslide, a dive tower, estate coffee, and even prescription lenses. Morning sails include a barbecue lunch. The *Orca*, a 28-ft inflatable raft, cleaves the waves in a high-thrill, fast-paced ride not for the weak at heart. It also takes time for snorkeling and gentler floating opportunities. ✉ *Keauhou Bay, Kailua-Kona,* ☎ *808/322–2788.* ▣ *Morning sail $79, afternoon $48.* ✎

Spectator Sports

Golf

Ample opportunities for celebrity spotting exist at a growing number of golf tournaments held at resort golf courses in the Kohala area. The biggest and best attended is the **Senior Skins Game** (☎ 800/556–5400), which attracts competitors the caliber of Arnold Palmer, Jack Nicklaus, and Lee Trevino, all competing for their share of the $540,000 purse. This tournament kicks off the year in January, always on Super Bowl weekend. At press time, course selection had not been decided for the year 2001.

In January the Four Seasons Resort Hualālai hosts the **MasterCard Championship** (☎ 800/417–2770), a Senior PGA Tour event.

Polo

Mauna Kea Polo Club. Matches sponsored by the club are scheduled every Sunday October through mid-December. ✉ *Waiki'i Ranch, off Saddle Rd., 6½ mi from Māmalahoa Hwy.,* ☎ *808/322–3880.* ✆ *$3.*

Triathlon

The highly popular **Ironman Triathlon** (☎ 808/329–0063, ✎) is not for amateurs. The $250,000-purse race is limited to 1,500 competitors, who swim 2.4-mi, bicycle 112 mi, and run a 26.2-mi marathon. Most entrants must qualify through other international competitions, though a few slots are awarded by lottery. The annual grueling event begins with the ocean swim from Kailua Pier at 7 AM on a Saturday in October. Spectators cheer contestants on from vantage points along Ali'i Drive, Queen Ka'ahumanu Highway, and the turnaround in Hāwī. The course closes at midnight.

SHOPPING

Residents like to complain that there isn't much to shop for on the Big Island, but unless you're searching for career clothes or high-tech computer toys, you'll find plenty to deplete your pocketbook. Kailua-Kona has a range of souvenirs from far-flung corners of the globe. Resorts along the Kohala coast have high-quality goods. Visit, for example, Collections, at the Mauna Lani Bay Hotel and Bungalows (☞ Kohala Coast and Waikoloa *in* Lodging, *above*) for exclusive clothing and accessories. Galleries and boutiques, many with the work of award-winning local artists, fill historic buildings in Waimea and North Kohala.

In general, stores and shopping centers on the Big Island open at 9 or 10 AM and close by 6 PM. Hilo's Prince Kūhiō Shopping Plaza (☞ *below*) stays open until 9 weekdays. In Kona, most of the stores at the Kona Coast Shopping Center are open daily 9–9, though the KTA Super Stores outlet (a supermarket) is open from 6 AM to midnight. Many small grocery stores also maintain longer hours, as do the shops along Kona's main Ali'i Drive, which are geared toward tourists.

Shopping Centers

In Hilo the most comprehensive mall, similar to mainland malls, is **Prince Kūhiō Shopping Plaza** (✉ 111 E. Puainako, at Hwy. 11). Here you'll find Liberty House and Sears for fashion, Ku'uipo Heirloom Jewelers for jewelry, Safeway for food, and Longs Drugs for just about everything else.

The older **Hilo Shopping Center** (✉ 70 Kekuanaoa St., at Kīlauea Ave.) has several air-conditioned shops and restaurants, great cookies at Lanky's Bakery, and plenty of free parking. The **Kaiko'o Mall** (✉ 777 Kīlauea Ave., Hilo) has inexpensive restaurants and service stores. The new **Waiakea Center** (✉ Makaala, across Prince Kuhio Shopping Plaza, Hwy. 11) is home to Borders Books & Music, Island Naturals, and Wal-Mart.

On the western side of the island, **Keauhou Shopping Center** (✉ 78-6831 Ali'i Dr.) has a value-for-the-money steak-and-seafood restaurant, Drysdale's Two. A variety of stores and boutiques; and a post office where you can drop off postcards.

Shopping in Kailua-Kona has begun to go the way of mainland cities with Wal-Mart, a huge Safeway, and Borders Books & Music at **Crossroads Shopping Center** (✉ 75-1000 Henry St.), which opened in 1997 on Queen Ka'ahumanu Highway. Right in Kailua-Kona, however, there are so many small shopping malls along Ali'i Drive that they tend to blend into one another. Virtually all of them offer merchandise to appeal to visitors. On the makai side of Ali'i Drive, extending an entire block, is

Kona Inn Shopping Village (☎ 808/329–6573), crammed with boutiques offering bright pareos (beach wraps) and knickknacks as well as coffee shops and restaurants. Here Island Salsa (☎ 808/329–9279) has great tropical toppers, sandals, and ethnic and Hawaiian clothes, and Honolua Surf Company (☎ 808/329–1001) is filled with cool beachwear.

Kona Marketplace, across the street from Kona Inn Shopping Village in Kailua-Kona, is a valuable find simply for the fact that public rest rooms are upstairs.

A block off Ali'i Drive, **Kopiko Plaza** and **Lanihau Center** (✉ 75-5595 Palani Rd.) house Longs Drug and several other stores, including a budget-friendly Sack 'n Save Foods.

Just outside Kona, off Highway 19, islanders find bargains at Kmart (✉ Makalapua Ave.) in the new **Makalapua Center.** Of more interest might be the large Liberty House, a statewide chain store with nice selections in apparel, bedding, lingerie, and gifts.

King's Shops (✉ 250 Waikoloa Beach Dr., ☎ 808/886–8811) houses Under the Koa Tree and Pacific Rim Collections, which both carry gift items by artisans, as well as Crazy Shirts and Malia and Kane by Malia for quality clothing; Kona Wine Market to find celebratory drinks; and a complete Gecko Store. There are several restaurants for all tastes and budgets.

The harborside **Kawaihae Center** (✉ Hwy. 270) houses restaurants, a dive shop, a bathing suit store, and the Harbor Gallery, which carries an eclectic spread of paintings, jewelry, and gift items. In Waimea, browse around exciting boutiques in **Parker Square** (✉ Kawaihae Rd., Waimea ☎ 808/885–7178) and in the adjacent brand-new building High Country Traders. **Waimea Center** (✉ Hwy. 19), with the area's first McDonald's, plus shops for all your needs, has a good health-food store and an unusual, San Francisco–style gift shop, Without Boundaries.

Specialty Stores

Books and Maps

Kohala Book Shop (✉ 54-3885 Akoni Pule Hwy., ☎ 808/889–6400) in the historic Old Nanbu Hotel in Kapa'au is the largest used bookstore in the state with one of the most complete Hawaiian and Pacific collections in the nation. Rare first editions include maps, work by Mark Twain, Captain Cook's personal journals, and 19th-century annexation documents.

In Hilo, **Basically Books** (✉ 160 Kamehameha Ave., ☎ 808/961–0144 or 800/903–6277) stocks one of Hawai'i's largest selection of maps and charts, including USGS, topographical, and raised relief maps. It also has Hawaiiana books with great choices for *keikis* (children).

Hawaiian Art and Crafts

In Hilo, **Mauna Kea Galleries** (✉ 276 Keawe St., ☎ 808/969–1184) specializes in rare vintage collectibles, including hula dolls, prints, and koa furniture. You'll find exquisite ceramics, Japanese tea sets, and affordable bamboo ware at **Ets'ko** (✉ 35 Waiānuenue Ave., ☎ 808/961–3778). The **Most Irresistible Shop** (✉ 256 Kamehameha Ave., ☎ 808/935–9644) lives up to its name with unique gifts, all from the Pacific. Be it ginger soap or guava butter, there is something for everyone. Walk into **Dragon Mama** (✉ 266 Kamehameha Ave., ☎ 808/934–9081) and marvel over expensive Japanese fabrics and antiques.

On your way to Hawai'i Volcanoes National Park, be sure to visit the workshop of **Dan DeLuz's Woods, Inc.** (✉ Hwy. 11, Mile Marker 12,

Mountain View, ☎ 808/968–6607; ⊠ 64-1013 Mamalahoa Hwy., Waimea, ☎ 808/885–5856), where master bowl-turner Dan DeLuz creates works of art from 50 types of exotic wood grown on the Big Island.

In the National Park, **Volcano Art Center** (☎ 808/967–7565) remains a favorite with everyone. The Art Center represents more Hawai'i island artists than any other gallery and carries a selection of fine art prints and oils as well.

If you're driving around the Big Island via the South Point route, stop at **Wood Works** (☎ 808/323–2247) next to the Manago Hotel in Captain Cook for rocking chairs, wooden pens, boxes, clocks, and frames, almost all made of koa wood. It's closed Sunday.

If you're driving north from Hilo, take time to browse through the remote **Waipi'o Valley Artworks** (⊠ Off Hwy. 240, Kukuihaele, ☎ 808/ 775–0958) gallery. You'll find finely crafted wooden bowls; oils, pastels, and watercolors by local artists; as well as jewelry and accessories. You can also make arrangements here for tours into and around Waipi'o Valley.

Waimea is home to the **Waimea Arts Council** (⊠ 67-1201 Mamalahoa Hwy., Kamuela 96743, ☎ 808/887–1052), dedicated to promoting the arts in the towns of Waimea, Hāmākua, Kohala, and Waikoloa. The council sponsors free *kaha ki'is* (one-person shows) at the Waimea Art Center, in the old fire station near the main stoplight in Waimea. The gallery is open Tuesday through Thursday and Saturday 10–2.

Also in Waimea, at **Parker Square** (⊠ Kawaihae Rd., ☎ 808/885–7178), in Gallery of Great Things (☎ 808/885–7706), you might fall in love with the Ni'ihau shell leis ($200–$4,000) they occasionally have. More affordable perhaps are koa mirrors and other high-quality artifacts from all around the Pacific basin.

In a red-roof, ranch-green building in Waimea, **Cook's Discoveries** (⊠ 64-1066 Mamalahoa Hwy., Waimea, ☎ 808/885–3633) is one of the best places in the state to shop for the work of local artisans.

If you're on a budget, don't forget to browse the **Waimea Craft Mall** (⊠ 67-1167 Mamalahoa Hwy.), ☎ 808/887–0020, at the second traffic light, where shelves are packed with wood products, quilt work, and other finds.

Remote North Kohala is home to dozens of artists and hosts a remarkable number of galleries in its old restored plantation buildings along the main street through Hāwī and Kapa'au. Start toward the Pololū end and visit **Rankin Gallery** (☎ 808/889–6849) in the old Wo On Store, next to the Chinese temple. At **Ackerman Gallery** (☎ 808/889–5971), painter Gary Ackerman, his wife, Yesan, and their daughter, Camille, have a fine and varied collection of gifts for sale in two locations near the King Kamehameha statue. Make sure to stop at the Old Nanbu Hotel, a historic building, which was rescued from demolition in 1999. Here, working in the front window of his new store **Elements** (☎ 808/ 889–0760), John Flynn creates exquisite, delicate jewelry such as silver maile lei and gold waterfalls. He and his wife also sell other carefully chosen gifts, including tabletop fountains filled with local river rocks. **Nanbu Gallery** (☎ 808/889–0997) features the paintings of owner Patrick Sweeney and other island artists.

Inside the Bamboo Restaurant in Hāwī, **Kohala Koa Gallery** (☎ 808/ 889–0055) seduces visitors with koa-wood pieces such as rocking chairs and writing desks. It also has a wealth of more affordable gift items such as boxes, jewelry, and Hawaiian wrapping paper. Just upcountry of Kailua-Kona nestles the little coffee town of Hōlualoa. The **Kona Arts center,** established years ago, has drawn an entire community of artists and is open to curious drop-in visitors. Many galleries crowd the narrow street. Especially wonderful for browsing are **Kimura's Lauhala Shop** (☎ 808/324–0053), where all men should get themselves an authentic lauhala hat for some top-level sun protection and **Hōlualoa Gallery** (☎ 808/322–8484), which has stunning raku (Japanese lead-glazed pottery). Most shops in Hōlualoa close at 4 or 5 PM and are closed all day Sunday and Monday.

In downtown Kailua-Kona, at **Rift Zone** (✉ Coconut Plaza, 75-5801 Ali'i Dr., ☎ 808/331–1100), owned by ceramist Robert Joiner and his wife, Kathy, you'll find ceramics but also exquisite jewelry, bowls, ornaments, hand-blown glass, and items created by local artists. For hula instruments, intricate feather headbands, and other original art drive to **Alapaki's Hawaiian Gifts** (✉ Keauhou Shopping Village, 78-6831 Ali'i Dr., ☎ 808/322–2007).

Resort Wear

Hotel shops generally offer the most attractive and original resort wear. **Kona Inn Shopping Village** (✉ 75-5744 Ali'i Dr.), that long boardwalk on the ocean side of Ali'i Drive, is stuffed with intriguing shops. Looking for an aloha shirt, a silk slipdress, or a vintage scarf? Try Flamingo's (☎ 808/329–4122).

In Keauhou Shopping Center (☞ *below*) look for **Borderlines** (☎ 808/322–5003) for colorful women's apparel.

Upcountry in the one-street town of Kainaliu, **Paradise Found** (✉ Māmalahoa Hwy. 11, ☎ 808/322–2111) has contemporary silk and rayon clothing. If you'd like to take home some of Hawai'i's splashy material, try Kainaliu's main street for **Kimura's Fabrics** (✉ Māmalahoa Hwy. 11, ☎ 808/322–3771).

In North Kohala, in the historic 1932 Toyama Building, **As Hāwī Turns** (☎ 808/889–5023) adds a sophisticated touch to breezy resort wear, pareos, and hand-painted silk clothing. There are vintage and secondhand treasures, crafts, and gifts as well.

Across the island in Hilo, **Sig Zane** (✉ 122 Kamehameha Ave., ☎ 808/935–7077), a popular designer, sells his distinctive island wearables, bedding, and gifts. Also in Hilo, **Kristina Lilleeng** (✉ 140 Keawe St., ☎ 808/961–0838) sells contemporary designer wear, such as pants and vests of natural-fiber fabrics or hand-painted silk.

In recent years, **Hilo Hattie** (✉ Prince Kuhio Plaza, 111 E. Puainako St., Hilo, ☎ 808/961–3077; ✉ Kopiko Plaza., Kailua-Kona, ☎ 808/329–7200 for free transportation from selected hotels), an old standby, has gone beyond matching his-and-her aloha wear to carry a huge selection of casual clothes, slippers, jewelry, and souvenirs.

Tropical Flowers and Produce

Akatsuka Orchid Gardens. You can buy tropical blooms here and have them shipped home. The nursery is in Glenwood, 22 mi from Hilo. ✉ *Hwy. 11, Glenwood,* ☎ *808/967–8234.* ☉ *Daily 8:30–5.*

Fuku-Bonsai Cultural Center. In addition to selling and shipping miniature brassaia lava plantings and other bonsai plants, this nursery on the way to Volcano has free educational exhibits of different ethnic styles of pruning. ✉ *Ola'a Rd., Kurtistown,* ☎ *808/982–9880.* ☉ *Mon.–Sat. 7:15–4.*

Hilo Farmers' Market. Individual entrepreneurs hawk a profusion of tropical flowers, high-quality produce, and gourmet macadamia nuts at this colorful, open-air market—the most popular in the state. ✉ *Kamehameha Ave. and Mamo St.* ☉ *Wed. and Sat. 6–2.*

Kona Inn Farmers' Market. This is a low-key farmers' market filled with colorful tropical flowers and locally grown produce, including macadamia nuts and coffee. ⊠ 75-7544 Ali'i Dr., Kona Inn Village Parking Lot ☉ Wed. and Sat. 7–3.

Volcano Store. The old stone store near Hawai'i Volcanoes National Park has excellent bargains in cut flowers and will ship them for you as well. ⊠ Old Volcano Hwy., ☎ 808/967–7210.

THE BIG ISLAND A TO Z

Arriving and Departing

By Plane

The Big Island has two main airports. Visitors whose accommodations are on the west side of the island, at Keauhou, Kailua-Kona, or the Kohala Coast, normally fly into **Keāhole–Kona International Airport** (☎ 808/329–2484; 808/329–3423 for visitor information), 7 mi from Kailua. Those staying on the eastern side, in Hilo or near the town of Volcano, fly into **Hilo International Airport** (General Lyman Field) (☎ 808/934–5801; 808/934–5840 for visitor information), just 2 mi from Hilo's Banyan Drive hotels.

In addition, one Maui-based airline, **Pacific Wings** (☎ 888/575–4546), has flights into and out of **Waimea-Kohala Airport** (☎ 808/885–4520). Midway between Hilo and Kailua-Kona, Kamuela Airport is used primarily by residents of Waimea to commute between islands. Another airstrip, at 'Upolu Point, services small private planes only.

FLIGHTS FROM THE MAINLAND UNITED STATES

United (☎ 800/241–6522) offers daily direct flights from San Francisco and Los Angeles to Kona International Airport. **Hawaiian Airlines** (☎ 800/882–8811) has one flight direct daily from Los Angeles; daily service from San Francisco, Portland, Los Angeles, Las Vegas, and Seattle flies into Honolulu Airport, where you can transfer to the Big Island. **Aloha Airlines** (☎ 800/367–5250 or 808/935–5771) initiated direct service in 2000 with two daily trips connecting Oakland, California, with both Maui and Honolulu. You need to transfer from there to reach the Big Island. **Canada 3000** (☎ 808/327–9485) offers a direct flight into Kona from Vancouver.

FLIGHTS FROM HONOLULU

Between the Neighbor Islands, both **Aloha Airlines** (☎ 808/935–5771 or 800/367–5250) and **Hawaiian Airlines** (☎ 800/882–8811) offer jet flights, which take about 45 minutes from Honolulu to Hilo International Airport and 34 minutes from Honolulu to Kona. Fares are approximately $100. Aloha Airline's sister commuter carrier **Island Air** (☎ 800/323–3345 or 800/652–6541) provides flights to Hawai'i's resort and smaller community destinations—the islands' more exotic locations. **Pacific Wings** (☎ 888/575–4546) offers daily service between Waimea and Honolulu and Waimea and Maui. Flights depart once a day, and seating is limited.

BETWEEN THE AIRPORT AND HOTELS

By Car. Kona International Airport is about 7 mi (a 10-minute drive) from Kailua, the resort area on the western side of the Big Island. The Keauhou resort area stretches another 6 mi to the south beyond Kailua. Visitors staying at the upscale resorts along the Kona-Kohala Coast should allow 30 to 45 minute to reach their hotels.

On the eastern side of the island, Hilo International Airport is just 2 mi, or a five-minute drive, from Hilo's Banyan Drive hotels. If you have chosen a B&B near the little mountain town of Volcano, plan on a half-hour drive from Hilo International Airport.

If you have booked out-of-the-way accommodations near Waimea, you might want to fly into Kamuela Airport, but be sure to arrange your rental car in advance (☞ Car Rentals *in* Contacts and Resources, *below*) because few car-rental companies service that airport.

By Limousine. Limousine service with a chauffeur who will act as your personal guide is $75–$80 an hour, with a two-hour minimum. **Luana** (☎ 808/326–5466) in Kona provides all the extras—TV, bar, and narrated tours, plus Japanese-speaking guides.

By Minibus. Roberts Hawai'i offers group services in both Kailua-Kona (✉ 73-4800 Kanalani St., Suite 200, Kailua-Kona, ☎ 808/329–1688 or 800/767–7551) and Hilo (✉ Shipman Industrial Park, Hilo, ☎ 808/966–5483). You'll need to make arrangements well in advance.

By Shuttle. There is no regularly scheduled shuttle service from either main airport, although private service is offered by the Kohala Coast resorts to the north of Kona International Airport. Transportation includes a lei greeting and costs less than a taxi. The rates vary depending on the distance each resort is from the airport. Arriving guests can check in at the **Kohala Coast Resort Association** counters at the Aloha and Hawaiian airlines arrival areas.

Guests staying in Kailua or at the Keauhou resort area to the south of the airport should check with their individual hotels upon booking to see if shuttle service is available.

By Taxi. Taxis are generally on hand for plane arrivals at both major airports. Some services from Hilo's Airport include **A-1 Bob's Taxi** (☎ 808/959–4800), **Ace One** (☎ 808/935–8303), and **Hilo Harry's** (☎ 808/935–7091). Taxis from Hilo International Airport to Hilo charge about $9 for the 2-mi ride to the Banyan Drive hotels. Often drivers will charge an extra $1 for large bags.

A number of taxis service Kona International Airport. The following also offer guided tours: **Aloha Taxi** (☎ 808/325–5448), **Paradise Taxi** (☎ 808/329–1234), and **Marina Taxi** (☎ 808/329–2481). From the airport to King Kamehameha's Kona Beach Hotel, taxi fares are about $20; to the Kona Surf in Keauhou, the cost is about $33. Taxis to South Kohala from the airport are even more expensive: approximately $40 to the Royal Waikoloan and $56 to the Mauna Kea Beach Resort. **SpeediShuttle** (☎ 808/329–5433) arranges shared rides and is less pricey, but you must call ahead of time.

By Ship from Honolulu

American Hawai'i Cruises. The cruise line runs eight-day excursions departing Honolulu Harbor every Saturday on the S.S. *Independence*. You visit Hilo and Volcano on Thursday, then Kona on Friday, before returning to Honolulu the following day. Rates range from $1,390 to $3,580. Pre- and post-cruise hotel packages are offered at a variety of rates. ✉ *American Hawai'i Cruises, 1380 Port of New Orleans Pl., New Orleans, LA 70130-1890,* ☎ *800/765–7000.* ✎

Getting Around

By Bus and Shuttle

A locally sponsored **Hele-On Bus** (☎ 808/961–8744) operates Monday through Saturday between Hilo and Kailua-Kona. (*Hele* translates roughly as "go.") The bus goes from Kailua-Kona to Hilo and back again, at $5.25 each way. An additional $1 is charged for luggage and backpacks that do not fit under the seat. Hele-On departs from Lani-hau Center on Palani Road in Kailua-Kona at 6:45 AM, arriving in Hilo at 9:45 AM. It leaves from the Mo'oheau Bus Terminal, between Kame-hameha Avenue and Bayfront Highway in Hilo, at 1:30 PM and arrives in Kailua-Kona at 4:30 PM. **Roberts Hawai'i** (☎ 808/329–1688) of-fers a shuttle service linking the Waikoloa resorts with downtown Kailua-Kona. Buses run every two hours from 7 to 7. Ask for a sched-ule at your hotel. Rates are $10 one-way, $20 round-trip.

The Hele-On operates also in the Hilo and Kailua-Kona town areas themselves for 75¢ and up, with exact fare required. Within Keauhou, a **free shuttle** (☎ 808/322–3500) runs from hotels and condos to Keauhou Shopping Center and the Kona Country Club golf course.

By Car
An automobile is necessary to see the sights of the Big Island in any reasonable amount of time. Even if you're solely interested in relax-ing at your self-contained megaresort, you may still want to rent a car, simply to travel to Kailua-Kona or to the restaurants in Waimea.

Though there are perhaps two dozen car-rental companies from which to choose, cars can be scarce during holiday weekends, special events, and peak seasons—from mid-December through mid-March. It is best to book well in advance (☞ Car Rentals *in* Contacts and Resources, *below*).

By Motorcycle
Scooters and motorcycles can be rented in Kailua-Kona from **DJ's Rentals** (☎ 808/329–1700 or 800/993–4647), across from King Kame-hameha Kona Beach Hotel. Some words of warning: Big Island roads often have narrow shoulders, and the drafts from oversize tour buses swooping by can double the excitement of a simple Sunday ride. Hel-mets are advised but not mandatory in Hawai'i.

By Plane
Big Island Air (☎ 808/329–4868 or 800/303–8868) can make ar-rangements for charters from Kona International Airport in nine-pas-senger aircraft at hourly rates starting at $770. "Wait time" (for example, if you fly to Waimea for lunch and the plane sits on the ground) is about $100 per hour.

By Taxi
Several companies advertise guided tours by taxi, but it is an expen-sive way to travel, with a trip around the island totaling about $350. Meters automatically register $2 on pickup, and most click off another $2 with each passing mile. If you have the urge to splurge on a taxi, *see* By Taxi *in* Arriving and Departing, *above*.

Contacts and Resources

B&B Information and Reservation Services
Members of the Big Island–based Hawai'i Island Bed and Breakfast As-sociation are listed with phone numbers and rates online or in a leaflet avail-able from the **Hawai'i Island B & B Association** (✉ Box 1890, Honoka'a 96727,✎). These Big Island–based networks will help you find a B&B to meet your needs and make reservations for you: **Hawai'i's Best Bed and Breakfasts** (✉ Box 563, Kamuela 96743, ☎ 808/885–4550 or 800/262–9912, FAX 808/885–0559,✎), and **Bed & Breakfast Honolulu (Statewide)** (✉ 3242 Kaohinani Dr., Honolulu 96817, ☎ 800/288–4666, FAX 808/595–2030,✎). On the mainland: **Go Native Hawai'i** (✉ 2009 Westholmes Rd., Suite 9, Lansing MI 48910, ☎ 800/662–8483,✎).

Car Rentals

If you pick up an auto at either airport and drop it off at the other, be aware that it could cost you as much as $75 extra. If you decide to return a car to the original pickup point, allow 2½ hours to drive the 96-mi Hāmākua Coast route. To get the best rate on a rental car, book it in conjunction with an interisland Hawaiian or Aloha airlines flight, or ask your travel agent to check out room-and-car packages.

The national car-rental firms represented on the Big Island are **Alamo** (☎ 800/327–9633), **Avis** (☎ 800/333–1212), **Budget** (☎ 800/527–0700), **Dollar** (☎ 800/800–4000), **Hertz** (☎ 800/654–3011), **National** (☎ 800/227–7368), and **Thrifty** (☎ 800/367–2277).

Harper Car & Truck Rentals (✉ 456 Kalanianaole Ave., Hilo 96720, ☎ 808/969–1478 or 800/848–8999), a Hawai'i-based company at both Hilo and Kona airports, is the only agency with a rental contract that allows its four-wheel-drive vehicles to be taken on Saddle Road—the inland route from Waimea to Hilo—although a number of other agencies have four-wheel-drive vehicles in their fleets. Driving on Saddle Road can be dangerous, and there are no gas stations or emergency phones. You might also need a four-wheel-drive vehicle to reach rugged shoreline sites. Use of the $100-a-day, five-passenger Isuzu Rodeos, Trooper IIs, and Toyota Four-Runners is restricted to those 25 years and older. Also available are seven- and nine-passenger vehicles.

Doctors and Dentists

Hilo Medical Center (✉ 1190 Waiānuenue Ave., Hilo, ☎ 808/974–4700).

Kona Community Hospital (✉ Hwy. 11 at Hau Kapila St., Kealakekua 96750, ☎ 808/322–9311).

North Hawai'i Community Hospital (✉ 67-1125 Mamalahoa Hwy., Kamuela 96743, ☎ 808/885–4444).

Dentist: Ask personnel at the locations above to refer you or to call a dentist who will take emergency patients.

Emergencies

Ambulance or fire (☎ 911). **Police** (☎ 808/935–3311 or 911). **Poison Control Center** (☎ 800/362–3585). **Volcano updates** (☎ 808/985–6000 for 24-hr recorded information).

Guided Tours

AERIAL TOURS

Gazing at a waterfall that drops a couple of thousand feet into multiple pools is absolutely breathtaking. You can fly above the lava lake on Kīlauea, then follow the flow to the ocean, where clouds of steam billow into the air. (The lava flow has been changing locations and sometimes goes underground, so ask exactly what you'll see when you book your flight.) Expect to pay anywhere from $140 for 45 minutes flights to $300-plus for 2 hours, and make reservations in advance as the flights are well booked.

Big Island Air. One-hour and 1¾-hour circle-island tours are offered in nine-passenger planes for $135–$185 per person. Flights depart daily from Kona International Airport starting at 6:30 AM. Weight is critical on these smaller planes, so be prepared to divulge your true body weight. ☎ *808/329–4868 or 800/303–8868.*

Blue Hawaiian. This reputable company will film a video of your helicopter flight if you wish to purchase one. Blue Hawaiian flies over Kīlauea and Hawai'i Volcanoes National Park, as well as over waterfalls from either point of origin. Departure is from the Hilo International Airport or the Waikoloa Helipad. ☎ *808/961–5600 or 800/745–2583.* ✐

Hawai'i Helicopters. Twin-engine jet helicopters are used for several tours from both Hilo and Kona. ☎ 800/994–9099. ✍

Island Hoppers Hawai'i. Island Hoppers offers a one-hour flight-seeing tour over the volcano and a waterfall on four passenger planes from Hilo. Everyone gets a window seat and a headset to talk to the pilot. Two longer flights—a 2½-hour circle-island tour and a 2-hour volcano tour—depart from Kona. ☎ 808/969–2000 or 800/538–7590. ✍

Mauna Kea Helicopters. Flights take off from a private helicopter pad at the Mauna Lani Resort, as well as from Kamuela Airport and Hilo International Airport. ☎ 808/885–6400 or 800/400–4354. ✍

Sunshine Helicopters. Sunshine flies from the helipad at the Hapuna Beach Prince Hotel for tours to the volcano and the waterfalls of Kohala. ☎ 808/882–1223 or 800/469–3000. ✍

Volcano Heli-Tours. This is the only helicopter company that departs from the volcano area, right near the golf course. Flying time over the lava lake and to the ocean is minimized, so the 45-minute flights are somewhat cheaper than those on other helicopter tours. ✉ Box 626, Volcano 96785, ☎ 808/967–7578.

ASTRONOMY TOURS

Mauna Ke'a. The clearest place in the world for viewing the heavens is reputedly the summit of 13,796-ft Mauna Ke'a. The trick is getting there. It takes a four-wheel-drive vehicle to reach the top, and you must traverse Saddle Road on the way. Make your first stop the Onizuka Center for International Astronomy Visitor Information Station (☎ 808/961–2180), about 34 mi from Hilo. To reach this station from Hilo, take Highway 200, Saddle Road, turning right at the 28-mi marker onto the Summit Access Road. The center is about 6 mi from the intersection on the right side of the road, at a 9,300-ft elevation, and can be reached in a standard automobile. From the visitor station, for those 16 and older, an escorted summit tour of four-wheel-drive vehicles makes free tours to the Mauna Ke'a observatories on weekends. Departure is at 1 PM. Reservations are not required. You must be in good health and not pregnant.

Freezing temperatures are common at the summit, even when the heat is high at the seashore, so you must take along warm parkas. The Visitor Information Station offers stargazing programs (for gazers of all ages) Thursday–Sunday at 6 PM.

Five companies take all the worry out of a trip to the top. You may book a van tour with knowledgeable Pat Wright of Paradise Safaris (☎ 808/322–2366 or 888/322–2366, ✍). The excursion starts at about 2 PM, includes dinner, and ends around 10 PM. Warm parkas are provided. Pickup is at three locations. Waipi'o Valley Shuttle (☎ 808/775–7121) conducts Mauna Ke'a summit tours that leave from Parker Ranch Shopping Center in Waimea for a minimum of four passengers. Waipi'o on Horseback (☎ 808/775–7291) furnishes transportation up Mauna Ke'a by four-wheel-drive van for a minimum of four passengers. Hawaiian Eyes Land Tours (☎ 808/937–2530) will pick you up from your hotel on the Kohala Coast for an insightful nine-hour excursion, which includes lunch, snacks, and warm clothing. Arnott's Lodge & Hiking Adventures (☎ 808/969–7097, ✍) offers two inexpensive summit/observatory tours on Tuesdays and Fridays. Doug Arnott even takes his own telescopes along. Prices among the various companies are $75–$135.

ALL-TERRAIN-VEHICLE TOURS

A different way to experience the Big Island's rugged coastline and wild ranchlands is an option with **ATV Outfitters Hawai'i** (✉ Old Sakamoto Store, Hwy. 270, Kapa'au, ☎ 808/889–6000, ✍) in North Kohala. The 1½-hour ride takes you to old plantation roads and railroad passways, ocean bluffs, and mountain trails. The company provides helmets, goggles, and gloves. You must be over 16 years of age and weigh between 90 and 220 pounds (✉ $75).

COFFEE TOURS

In addition to the tour listings below, you're also welcome at other farms, mills, and co-ops along the Upcountry coffee belt from Hōlualoa to Hōnaunau, including the **Coffee Shack** (✉ 83-5799 Māmalahoa Hwy. 11, near Mile Marker 109, Captain Cook, ☎ 808/328–9555) and **Bay View Farms** (✉ ½ mi past St. Benedict's Painted Church, Painted Church Rd., Hōnaunau, ☎ 808/328–9658) to sample coffee and see how it is farmed and milled.

Greenwell Farms. This is a modern coffee mill, although many of the trees are more than 90 years old. Coffee and macadamia nuts from the estate are sold here, and several kinds of coffee are available to sample. The farm offers free tours. ✉ *81-6581 Māmalahoa Hwy. 11, Kealakekua,* ☎ *808/323–2862.* ☉ *Mon.–Sat. 8–4:30.*

Holualoa-Kona Coffee Company. Visitors to Upcountry can tour this mill and roasting establishment and see coffee processing from green beans to packaging. ✉ *77-6261 Old Māmalahoa Hwy., Hwy. 180, Hōlualoa,* ☎ *808/322–9937 or 800/334–0348.* ✉ *Free.* ☉ *Weekdays 8–4.*

Kona Coffee Living History Farm. Known as the D. Uchida Farm, this old farm has been preserved and restored by the Kona Historical Society. Interpretive guides share a rare glimpse of the days of the coffee pioneers—the 1926 farm house surrounded by coffee trees; a Japanese bath house; Kuriba (coffee processing mill), and Hoshidana (traditional drying platform). Tours of the farm are available by reservations only. ✉ *Kona Historical Society, 81–6551 Māmalahoa Hwy., Kealakekua,* ☎ *808/323–2006.* ✉ *$20, children $10.* ☉ *Tues. and Thurs. 8:30 and 10:30* AM *or by special arrangement for groups.*

Royal Kona Coffee Museum and Coffee Mill. If you prefer a self-guided tour, drop by this mill for displays of coffee trees and photos, plus a three-minute video detailing the history and processing of coffee. ✉ *83-5427 Māmalahoa Hwy. 11, next to the tree house in Hōnaunau,* ☎ *808/328–2511.* ☉ *Daily 8–5.*

FOUR-WHEEL-DRIVE TOURS

Hawaiian Eyes Land Tours. Geologist Lee Meyerson and his wife, Betty, may be the only Big Islanders who'll take you to the volcanic landscapes at the 11,000-ft level of Mauna Loa. Informal "talk story" sessions along the way furnish insights into Hawai'i's geology and culture. Prices range from $99 to $119 per person. Excursions last from 9 to 12 hours. The van will pick you up at your hotel along the Kohala coast. ☎ *808/937–2530 or 808/332–5661.*

GARDEN TOUR

Amy B. H. Greenwell Ethnobotanical Garden. You'll find a wealth of Hawaiian cultural traditions here. It is home to 250 plants, including food and fiber crops, on 12 acres that were typical in an early Hawaiian *ahupua'a,* a pie-shape land division that ran from the mountains to the sea. It is open all day weekdays to walk-in visitors, and there's a guided tour on the second Saturday of each month at 10. ✉ *82-6188 Māalahoa Hwy., Captain Cook,* ☎ *808/323–3318.* ✉ *Donation.*

KOHALA MULE TRAIL ADVENTURE

Hawai'i Forest and Trail. This company has restored part of the historic trails at the end of Highway 270 in North Kohala. Mules take riders into Pololū Valley and experienced guides recount the ancient history of this mesmerizing land. The cost is $95. ✉ *680 Iwilei Rd., Honolulu,* ☎ *808/329–1688 or 800/767–7551.*

ORIENTATION TOUR

Roberts Hawai`i. Roberts conducts a Hilo–Volcano–Kalapana tour out of Hilo, and an 11-hour circle-island tour from Kona. Both cost $55. ✉ *680 Iwilei Rd., Honolulu,* ☎ *808/329–1688 or 800/767–7551.*

SUBMARINE TOURS

Atlantis IV **Submarine.** A boat shuttles passengers from Kailua Pier to the 65-ft *Atlantis IV* submarine, which, with its clean plastic seats, feels more like an amusement-park ride than the real thing. A large glass dome in the bow and 13 viewing ports on the sides allow clear views of the watery world, where coral formations are filled with colorful sea creatures. You may even see a turtle or a shark. Children must be at least 3 ft tall. Sign up across from King Kamehameha's Kona Beach Hotel. ✉ *75-5669 Ali`i Dr., Kailua-Kona,* ☎ *808/329–6626 or 800/ 548–6262.* 💳 *$79.*

WAIPI`O VALLEY TOURS

This Edenlike refuge in the north of the island, once the vacation spot for Hawaiian royalty, is accessible via a number of means if you don't have your own four wheel drive. **Waipi`o on Horseback** (✉ Box 183, Honoka`a 96727, ☎ 808/775–7291) hosts horseback rides and van trips into Waipi`o Valley with pickup at the Last Chance Store in Kukuihaele. **Waipi`o Valley Shuttle** (✉ Box 5128, Kukuihaele 96727, ☎ 808/775– 7121) leaves Waipi`o Valley Artworks daily on 1½-hour tours. **Waipi`o Valley Wagon Tours** (✉ Box 1340, Honoka`a 96727, ☎ 808/775–9518) departs from the Last Chance Store, also for 1½-hour excursions. Costs range from $25 to $75.

WAGON TOURS

☺ **Parker Ranch Wagon Tours.** In true paniolo-style, a covered wagon pulled by a pair of draft horses leads you through a portion of the 225,000-acre Parker Ranch. During the 45-minute tour you can see cattle and horses as they roam green, rolling pastures. Dexterous paniolo may ride by as well. ✉ *Parker Ranch Visitor Center, Hwy. 19, Kamuela,* ☎ *808/885–7655.* 💳 *$15.* ☉ *Tue. through Sat., every hour between 10 and 2.*

WALKING AND HIKING TOURS

In addition to the companies below, you can take a self-guided walking tour of downtown Hilo with the help of a map from the Lyman Mission House and Museum (☞ Hilo *in* Exploring the Big Island, *above*). The **Big Island Visitors Bureau** (250 Keawe St., ☎ 808/961–5797 or 808/886–1655) has excellent free walking-tour brochures and maps for the Hilo and Kona areas.

Hawaiian Walkways. Since 1984, Hugh Montgomery has been custom-designing hikes to suit the individual's skill level and choice of scenery. A full-day hike averages $110 per person. He also offers fully catered and equipped hikes around Waipi`o, Kona, and the volcano. ✉ *Waimea Office Center, Bldg. 2, Suite 1, Kamuela,* ☎ *808/775–0372 or 800/457–7759.*

**Hawai`i Earth Guides Eco-Adventures.** In its own category, Earth Guides specializes in custom adventures and hikes. Depending on your ambitions and your fitness level, your guides will take you up Hualalai Mountain, down to pristine Makalawena Beach, or to the summit of Mauna Ke`a. The hikes include meals and may be part of a snorkeling or kayak experience. Adventure spas of three or seven days are also available. Prices vary and your best bet is to visit the Web site to see the current offerings. ✉ *Box 2639, Kailua-Kona,* ☎ *800/949–3483 or 808/329–7116.*

Hawai'i Forest and Trail. Personable founder Rob Pacheko organizes nature hikes to 500-ft Kalopa Falls along a historic trail carved into sheer cliffs 1,000 ft above the valley floor. An expert naturalist guide, he also offers adventures through normally inaccessible areas of Hawai'i Volcanoes National Park and Hawaiian rain forests. ☎ *808/331–8505 or 800/464–1993.* ✎

Kona Historical Society. Interpretive guides lead 1½-hour historic Kailua-Kona village walking tours starting at the King Kamehameha Kona Beach Hotel. Tours cover the history of the Ahu'ena Heiau, Moku'aikaua Church, Kona Inn (the town's first hotel), and end at Hulihe'e Palace. Make reservations 24 hours in advance. ✉ *81-6551 Mamalahoa Hwy., Kealakekua,* ☎ *808/323–2005.* 🎫 *$10.* ☉ *Tues.– Thurs. 9:30, Fri. 9:30 and 1:30.* ✎

WATER-SPORTS TOURS

Fluming the Ditch. "Fluming the ditch" in an inner tube used to be a dangerous and exciting pastime for sugar plantation children. The pitch-black, eerie tunnels of the 22½-mi Kohala Ditch, emerging now and then to pristine rain forests, are now accessible in inflatable double-hulled kayaks. The history of these irrigation ditches, built in 1905 by Japanese workers, adds magic to the 3-mi Kohala Mountain kayak cruise. ✉ *55-519 Hāwī Rd., Hwy. 250, Hāwī,* ☎ *808/889–6922,* 🗚 *808/889–6944.* 🎫 *Twice daily, $75.* ✎

Hawaiian Adventure Tours. Six-day inn-to-inn, hike-swim-kayak-snorkel excursions are offered for $1,050 on the Big Island. A similar 10-day, three-island package for $1,800 includes the Big Island, Kaua'i, and Maui. ✉ *Box 1269, Kapa'au, 96755,* ☎ *808/889–0227 or 800/659–3544.* ✎

WHALE-WATCHING

Captain Dan McSweeney's Year-Round Whale Watching Adventures. Although most Hawaiian whale-watching cruises focus on the migratory humpbacks that are seen here only from December through April, this company offers three-hour trips year-round to find six other species of whales that rarely stray far from the Kona Coast. McSweeney has spent 20 years researching these local creatures, and his cruises offer a close-up and informative look at all Hawai'i's whales. The 38-ft double-decker boat is specially equipped for listening to the whales while they are underwater. A sighting is guaranteed, or you cruise again for free. ✉ *Honokōhau Harbor, Kailua-Kona,* ☎ *808/322–0028 or 888/ 942–5376,* 🗚 *808/322–2732.* 🎫 *$52.* ✎

Visitor Information

Information and brochures are dispensed at the **Big Island Visitors Bureau** (BIVB) booths at Big Island airports and at the two offices in Hilo and King's Shops. ✉ *250 Keawe St., Hilo,* ☎ *808/961–5797,* 🗚 *808/ 961–2126; 250 Waikoloa Beach Dr., B12, Kings' Shops, Waikoloa, 96738,* ☎ *808/886–1655.* ✎

For detailed street maps, **Basically Books** (✉ 160 Kamehameha Ave., Hilo, ☎ 808/961–0144) is a complete map shop. Good maps are also available at the **Middle Earth Bookshoppe** (✉ 75-5719 Ali'i Dr., Kailua-Kona, ☎ 808/329–2123) and **Borders Books & Music** (✉ 75-1000 Henry St., Kailua-Kona, ☎ 808/331–1668; ✉ 301 Maka'ala, Hilo, ☎ 808/ 933–1410). If you rent a car, be sure to get a **"Drive Guide."** These handy booklets have all the maps you'll probably need to navigate the island.

Another helpful source of information is the **Kona–Kohala Resort Association** (✉ HC02, Box 5300, Waikoloa 96743, ☎ 808/886–4915), a group of resorts and luxury hotels cooperating to promote the Kohala Coast as a resort destination. For information about Kona Coast attractions, contact **Destination Kona Coast** (✉ Box 2850, Kailua-Kona 96745, ☎ 808/329–6748). For questions about east Hawai'i, write to **Destination Hilo** (✉ 400 Hualani Bldg., Hilo 96720, ☎ 808/935–5294). For general information, visit the Web site of the **Hawai'i Visitors and Convention Bureau** at www.visit.hawaii.org.

Weather: For daily reports call ☎ 808/961–5582.

4 KAUA'I
THE GARDEN ISLE

Greenest and most tropical of all, Kaua'i is the only Hawaiian island with sizable rivers. Polynesians first chose to settle here on the banks of the bubbling Wailua, on the east coast. The lushness of the misty, magical north shore is a startling contrast to the west coast's Waimea Canyon—the "Grand Canyon of the Pacific"—with its rich, vivid coloration of copper, rust, and gold.

By Betty
Fullard-Leo

NICKNAMED THE GARDEN ISLE, Kaua'i is Eden epitomized. In the mountains of Kōke'e, lush swamps ring with the songs of rare birds, and the heady aroma of ginger blossoms sweetens the cool rain forests of Hā'ena. Time and nature carved the elegant spires along the remote northwestern shore known as the Nā Pali (cliffs) Coast as seven coursing rivers gave life to the valleys where ancient Hawaiians once dwelled. Today visitors can explore this Pacific paradise by land, sea, and air—hiking along the Kalalau Trail, kayaking up the Hanalei River, or hovering in a helicopter high above 5,148-ft Wai'ale'ale, the wettest spot on earth.

Though devastating hurricanes are rare in Hawai'i, in September 1992 Hurricane 'Iniki swept right across the island and caused hundreds of millions of dollars' worth of damage. The people of Kaua'i were quick to rebuild and revitalize their communities, and today Kaua'i looks better than ever thanks to extensive renovations and improvements.

The Garden Isle is a laid-back, restful retreat—an island of unmatched physical beauty that easily rewards those who love the great outdoors. You can take a boat trip up Nā Pali Coast to snorkel in azure waters; ride a horse-drawn coach around a plantation-era sugar estate; or play golf on the world-class greens of Princeville Resort, where a majestic mountain peak, nicknamed Bali Hai, rises just beyond the fairways. Then again, you might just want to saddle up and go horseback riding into Waimea Canyon and see why these steep ridges and ravines are often called the "Grand Canyon of the Pacific."

One road runs almost all the way around the island but dead-ends on either side of a 15-mi stretch of the rugged Nā Pali Coast. Driving from one end to the other takes you past lustrous green stands of sugarcane, which are gradually being replaced with coffee and macadamia-nut orchards. Sugar was a key economic force on the island from the 1990s dating from 1836, when Hawai'i's first sugar mill was built in Kōloa. Patches of taro are found around Hanalei Valley. This longtime staple of the Hawaiian diet is grown for its root (to make *poi,* a puddinglike accompaniment for fish and meat) as well as its leaves (used to wrap and cook food). Traveling around the island, you'll see such movie settings as the Hulē'ia River, where Indiana Jones made his daring escape at the beginning of *Raiders of the Lost Ark.* Other locations on the island were used in filming *Honeymoon in Vegas, Jurassic Park,* and *Six Days, Seven Nights.*

Kaua'i, the fourth-largest island in the Hawaiian chain, has its capital in Līhu'e, a town whose government buildings resemble a small New England village. Līhu'e is the island's commercial center, yet its collection of businesses—a pair of banks, a library, a school, a museum, some family-run restaurants, and hotels—is small enough to keep the pace unhurried.

On the south coast the sunny beaches and clear skies around Po'ipū have spawned a crop of classy condos and resort hotels. The area has also come into its own as a golf destination, and several fine restaurants have found a home here as well. Head west, beneath the slopes of the Hoary Head Mountains, to encounter such storybook plantation villages as Hanapēpē, Kalāheo, and Waimea—where Capt. James Cook first landed back in 1778. Beyond Waimea lies Polihale Beach, an idyllic stretch of golden sand sprawled beneath the cool highlands of Kōke'e State Park.

From the southwestern part of Kaua'i you can see the island of Ni'ihau 17 mi off the coast. Until 1987 no uninvited guests were allowed to visit this family-owned island. Most people who live in Hawai'i still consider

Niʻihau off-limits, but its mysteries can now be breached by helicopter—Kauaʻi-based tours touch down each weekday for three-hour visits.

North of Līhuʻe the climate turns cooler and wetter, and everything sparkles in luxuriant shades of green. In Wailua and Kapaʻa several resort complexes huddle along a picturesque shoreline called the Royal Coconut Coast for its abundant array of palms. As you head farther north to Anahola, Kīlauea, Princeville, and Hanalei, vines and flowers flourish. At the end of the road, in Hāʻena, you'll encounter a misty otherworldliness conjuring up the legends of the ancients.

More myths are attached to the natural landscape of Kauaʻi than to any other Hawaiian island. A favorite among locals is the legend of the Menehune, a community of diminutive yet industrious workers said to have lived on Kauaʻi before the Polynesians. Few people actually saw the Menehune because they worked in privacy at night—practicing, it seems, their impressive stoneworking skills. There are bridges, walls, fishponds, and other solid constructions attributed to the engineering skill of these mysterious mythical stonemasons.

Kauaʻi is the oldest of the Hawaiian Islands, and its 550 square mi are rich in natural history and the resonance of past cultures. A sense of relaxation and unaffected natural beauty calmly welcomes all who step off the plane at the Līhuʻe Airport and wraps them in a lei of traditional Hawaiian hospitality. The people in the tourism and hospitality industry here work hard to keep visitors and guests satisfied, and the aloha spirit reigns everywhere. In fact, many feel that Kauaʻi's people are the friendliest in all the Islands and that this splendid jewel of an island harbors all that nature allows from a tropical paradise.

Pleasures and Pastimes

Beaches
As the oldest of the Hawaiian Islands, Kauaʻi has had more time to develop—and perfect—its beaches. The Garden Isle is embraced by stretches of magnificent ivory sands, many with breathtaking mountain backdrops. Poʻipū, on the south shore, has the sandiest, most consistently sunny beaches for water lovers. Here is some of the island's best swimming, snorkeling, and bodysurfing, in waters that are generally safe year-round. You do need to look out for occasional patches of coral, which can leave a nasty cut on your foot when stepped on.

The north shore is a different story altogether. Although some of Kauaʻi's most scenic beaches can be found here, they are treacherous in winter. In summer, however, they are safe for swimming.

The beaches that front the hotels and condominiums along the eastern shore are conducive to seaside strolling but less favorable for swimming. The strong surf and rip currents of the winter months are unpredictable, and it's often windy. If you want beaches with plenty of wide open spaces, drive to the west coast beyond Waimea. This is where many locals go to fish and swim, and you'll catch the best sunsets from this vantage point. Waimea has a black-sand beach where sunsets are dramatic, while the Kekaha and Barking Sands beaches are a dazzling white-sand continuation of the beach that starts beneath the cliffs at Polihale.

Beaches along the northwest shore are inaccessible except to those who hike the rugged Nā Pali trail from the opposite end of the road at Hāʻena or who book a boat tour along the north shore. Some tour operators (☞ Contacts and Resources *in* Kauaʻi A to Z, *below*) offer a hiker-camper drop-off service from May through September, transporting passengers one way so they can enjoy a secluded beach, then hike back on their own.

HAWAIIAN MYTHS AND LEGENDS

THE BEST-KNOWN DEITY IN HAWAIIAN lore is Pele, the volcano goddess. Although visitors are warned not to remove lava rocks from Pele's domain without her permission, some do and find themselves dogged by bad luck until they return the stolen items. The Hawai'i Volcanoes National Park Service often receives packages containing chunks of lava along with letters describing years of misfortune.

Tales of Pele's fiery temper are legion. She battled Poli'ahu, ruler of snowcapped Mauna Ke'a on the Big Island, in a fit of jealousy over the snow goddess's extraordinary beauty. She picked fights with her peace-loving sister, Hi'iaka, turning the younger goddess's friends into pillars of stone. And her recurring lava-flinging spats with suitor Kamapua'a, a demigod who could change his appearance at will, finally drove him into the sea, where he turned into a fish to escape from her wrath.

But Pele can be kind if the mood suits her. It is said that before every major eruption, she appears in human form as a wrinkled old woman walking along isolated back roads. Those who pass her by find their homes devastated by molten lava. Those who offer her a ride home return home to find a river of boiling magma abruptly halted inches from their property or diverted around their houses. Many hula *hālau* (schools) still make pilgrimages to the rim of Kīlauea—Pele's home—where they honor the fickle goddess with prayers, chants, and offerings of gin and flower leis.

A less volatile but equally intriguing figure in Hawaiian lore is Māui, a demigod who is credited with pulling the Hawaiian Islands up from the bottom of the sea with a magic fishhook, pushing the sky away from the treetops because it had flattened all the leaves, and, his most prestigious feat—lassoing the sun as it came up over the top of Haleakalā and demanding that it move more slowly across the sky in summer so that Māui's mother would have longer daylight hours to dry her *kapa* (cloth made from bark).

In addition to battling the elements and each other, gods were thought to have intervened in the daily lives of early Hawaiians. Storms that destroyed homes and crops, a fisherman's poor catch, or a loss in battle were blamed on the wrath of angry gods. And according to legend, an industrious race of diminutive people called *menehune* built aqueducts, fishponds, and other constructs requiring advanced engineering knowledge unavailable to early Hawaiians. Living in remote hills and valleys, these secretive workers toiled only in darkness and completed complex projects in a single night. Their handiwork can still be seen on all the islands.

Also at night, during certain lunar periods, a traveler might inadvertently come across the Night Marchers—armies of dead warriors, chiefs, and ancestral spirits whose feet never touch the ground as they tread the ancient highways, chanting and beating their drums, and pausing only to claim the spirits of their brethren who died that night. It was believed that such an encounter would mean certain death unless a relative among the marchers pleaded for the victim's life.

The moral? Leave the lava rocks as they are and pick up any elderly hitchhikers you might come across. Straightforward enough. But I'd still hightail it in the other direction if I heard mysterious chanting or drum beating.

Dining

The sugar plantations of 19th-century Kaua'i brought together a universe of cultures as workers from other countries sought new jobs in Hawai'i. With them came an international array of foods, reflected in the cuisines found today on Kaua'i. You can choose from among Hawai'i regional restaurants or those preparing Chinese, Japanese, Thai, Mexican, Italian, and French specialties, mixed with a heavy dose of traditional Hawaiian food, available in just about any town on the island. When it's time for a snack, look for the carryout wagons that are often parked at major beaches. They serve local foods, such as the "plate lunch"—two scoops of rice served with such entrées as teriyaki beef or chicken, veal cutlet, or luncheon meat. Another standard component is a mound of either macaroni salad or potato salad, with a few token greens thrown in for show. The "mixed plate" is a plate lunch with two or sometimes three entrée selections.

Lodging

Part of the appeal of the Garden Isle is its range of hotel properties—from swanky and pricey resorts to rustic mountaintop cabins to barebones lodgings whose main appeal is a rock-bottom price. Sunshine seekers often head south to the shores of Po'ipū, where three- and four-story condos line the coast and the gentle surf offers ideal swimming. Po'ipū has more condos than hotels, with prices in the moderate to expensive range, although several oceanfront cottages are in demand with budget travelers. Guests interested in the history of the islands often stay on the east coast near the Wailua River, home to Kaua'i's first inhabitants. Many of the hotels here place an emphasis on the legends and lore of the area. The beaches are so-so for swimming but nice for sunbathing. Farther north are the swanky hotels and condominiums of Princeville Resort. You can't go wrong here, because just about any accommodation offers views of the bay or the chiseled mountain peaks of Hanalei. Golfers find the courses here a paradise. Bed-and-breakfasts are an attractive option if you are looking for a more settled-in and residential experience. There are a range of private homes scattered around the island. A good booking service (☞ Contacts and Resources *in* Kaua'i A to Z, *below*) can help you locate one.

Outdoor Activities and Sports

GOLF

Princeville Resort's stunning Robert Trent Jones–designed Prince Course is rated the second most difficult course in Hawai'i. The resort's (and Jones's) neighboring Makai Course is also beautiful, with the so-called Zen bunker (a boulder in the middle of a huge sand trap) and an eighth hole played across an ocean chasm. Jack Nicklaus's Kiele course has many greens positioned diagonally to the fairway. Nicklaus's adjacent Lagoons course is less dramatic and wider. As you play the four closing holes of Jones's Po'ipū Bay course you will hear the crashing surf on your left. Endangered wildlife, such as the nēnē goose, monk seal, and sea turtle, can often be spotted—the geese in ponds on the back nine, and the seals and turtles on the beach or in the water below. Kiahuna Plantation is Jones's fourth course on Kaua'i. It's a challenging inland course that winds over streams, through woods, and past lava formations.

HIKING

Best known for the challenging north shore Kalalau Trail, Kaua'i is also a mecca for hikers. Trails at Kōke'e State Park range from easy to difficult. They overlook the green ramparts of the Nā Pali coastline or showcase views of the painted wonders of Waimea Canyon. Easy excursions through Keāhua Forestry Arboretum, Limahuli Garden, and other tropical gardens appeal to all ages.

HORSEBACK RIDING

Kaua'i offers possibly the broadest selection of equestrian outings of all the Islands. You can saddle up to ride along the rim of Waimea Canyon, to a secluded waterfall, along the edge of a moonlit beach, or through the greenest of mountain pastures.

WATER SPORTS

Safe yet exciting water adventures are possible through a vast number of companies. Kayaks can be rented for do-it-yourself or guided excursions. This is the only island where you have the choice of kayaking on rivers, ancient fishponds, or in the ocean. Fishing, scuba, and snorkel guides are quick to locate the spots where the biggest and most colorful array of fish hang out, and surfing and windsurfing instructors can help you soar like a tropical bird across the cresting waves.

There are three great dive sites on Kaua'i. Cannon's Reef, on the north shore, drops quickly from the shoreline, forming a long ledge permeated with lava tubes. Plate coral is found here, and turtles are a common sight. You may come across white tip sharks sleeping in caverns or patrolling the ledge. Depths range from 30 ft to 60 ft, and you can only dive here in summer. General Store, at Kukui'ula, is the site of a 19th-century shipwreck. The horseshoe-shape ledge and two caverns teem with schools of lemon butterfly fish that follow divers around. There are also green moray eels and black coral at this site, which runs to depths of 65 ft to 80 ft. Sheraton Caverns, off Po'ipū, are formed by three immense, parallel lava tubes. There is a lobster nursery in one cavern, sea turtles swim in all three, and the occasional white tip shark cruises by. Depths range from 35 ft to 60 ft.

EXPLORING KAUA'I

The main road tracing the island's perimeter takes you past a variety of easily explored landscapes and attractions. There are magical mountains, cascading waterfalls, verdant fern grottoes, mist-shrouded caves, and a lighthouse designated a National Historic Landmark. All around the island are beautiful overlooks where you can stop to take a breath and soak up the fragrant beauty.

Mauka means on the mountain side of the road, and *makai* means on the ocean side.

Great Itineraries

With Līhu'e as your point of departure, it's easy to explore the island by traveling to sights along its eastern and northern coasts, then visiting attractions around Līhu'e itself, and finally striking out toward the southern and western coasts. Each of these routes can easily fill a day of sightseeing. Allow one day for the north and east sections of the island and another day for sights to the south and west. To fully enjoy the sunning, surfing, hiking, golfing, and other activities and adventures on Kaua'i, plan on spending at least five or six days.

Numbers in the text correspond to numbers in the margin and on the Kaua'i map.

IF YOU HAVE 2 DAYS

In two full days you can barely scratch the surface of Kaua'i's idyllic beauty. Plan to stay along the southeast shoreline, anywhere from Po'ipū to Kapa'a, and then spend one day exploring in either direction. Beginning your trek in **Līhu'e** ⑮, drive around **Nāwiliwili** ⑰ Harbor, then head up the hill to the lookout for an encompassing view of **Menehune Fishpond** ⑱, connecting with Highway 50 until a left turn on Highway 520 takes you through the Tunnel of Trees to **Kōloa** ㉑ for shopping and

Po'ipū ㉒ for sightseeing. Follow the signs to **Spouting Horn** ㉕ for a quick look at this natural waterspout and then continue on through Po'ipū for a beach break at Brennecke's. Head back to Highway 50, stopping at the ruins of **Ft. Elisabeth** ㉛ for a glimpse of Russia's influence on this island. Then proceed directly to **Waimea Canyon** ㉟ to revel in colorful vistas and fresh, cool air. It's a 36-mi return to Līhu'e.

On your second day, make your goal the end of the road at Hā'ena, 40 mi north of Līhu'e. On the way, stretch your legs at the **Kīlauea Lighthouse and Kīlauea Point National Wildlife Refuge** ⑧. Check out the orchard and have some juice at Guava Kai Plantation, pause at the **Maniniholo Dry Cave** ⑪ and at **Waikapala'e and Waikanaloa Wet Caves** ⑬ before turning around and heading to Hanalei for lunch. Spend the afternoon at the beach before heading back.

IF YOU HAVE 4 DAYS

Basically you'll want to cover the same ground as you would in two days, but you'll have more leisure time to enjoy beach and shopping breaks. Spend day one exploring **Līhu'e** ⑮ more thoroughly. Get a feeling for Kaua'i's history at the **Kaua'i Museum** ⑯, then drive south to **Po'ipū** ㉒ for some leisurely shopping in **Kōloa** ㉑, and then have lunch and sun on the beach in Po'ipū before calling it a day.

A drive directly to Kōke'e on day two will allow time for longer hikes and perhaps a stop at a west-side beach as well as a trek around the ruins of **Ft. Elisabeth** ㉛ on the return leg.

Make day three a full day's exploration of Kaua'i's north shore. Take in **Kīlauea Lighthouse and Kīlauea Point National Wildlife Refuge** ⑧, examine **Maniniholo Dry Cave** ⑪ and **Waikapala'e and Waikanaloa Wet Caves** ⑬, and amble through **Limahuli Garden** ⑫. Then stop in Hanalei for lunch before stretching out at **Ke'e Beach State Park** ⑭ in the afternoon sun.

On your fourth day stick close to Kapa'a. In the morning, make the Fern Grotto your destination, either going aboard one of the Wailua river boats or renting a kayak and asking directions before paddling off on the river. On your return, pick up a plate lunch or a few picnic supplies. Then drive up Mā'alo Road to see the **Pōhaku-ho'ohānau and Pōhaku Piko** ④ (royal birthing stones) and **'Ōpaeka'a Falls** ⑤. If you follow the road nearly to its end, you'll come upon the Keāhua Forestry Arboretum, where picnic tables and a freshwater pool offer a soothing respite, before returning to Kapa'a for some last-minute shopping at the Coconut Marketplace.

IF YOU HAVE 6 DAYS

With six days you might want to split your vacation nights into two hotels, spending the first two nights on the south side and the last three at Princeville on the north shore. On day one, explore the **Waimea Canyon** ㉟ area, also stopping at **Ft. Elisabeth** ㉛ and perhaps walking the main street (one block off the highway) of **Hanapēpē** ㉙, a quiet town with an extraordinary number of art galleries. Spend the morning of day two in **Līhu'e** ⑮, touring **Grove Farm Homestead** ⑲ (with prior reservations) and/or the **Kaua'i Museum** ⑯. In the afternoon take time to explore the main street of **Kōloa** ㉑ and see **Spouting Horn** ㉕ in Po'ipū. Then relax during the late afternoon at the beach.

Pack and get away early on day three, so you can take in the Fern Grotto, the **Pōhaku-ho'ohānau and Pōhaku Piko** ④, and **'Ōpaeka'a Falls** ⑤, with a little time for having lunch or shopping in Kapa'a on your way to your new north-shore location.

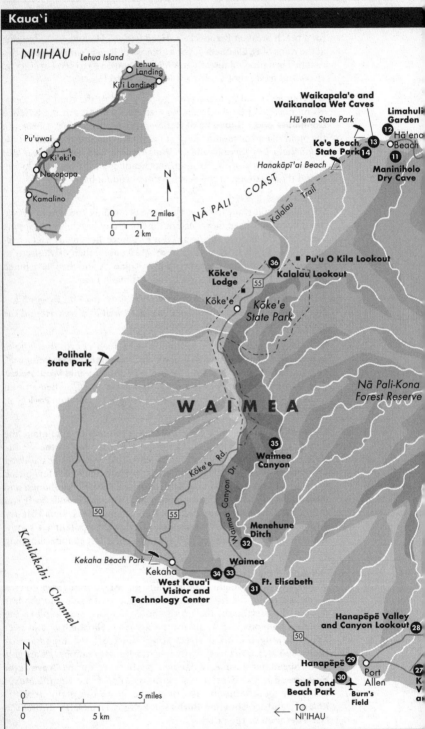

NI'IHAU   Lehua Island

Lehua
Landing
Ki'i Landing

Pu'uwai
Ki'eki'e
Nonopapa

Kamalino

N

0   2 miles
0   2 km

Waikapala'e and
Waikanaloa Wet Caves

Hā'ena State Park

Limahuli
Garden

Ke'e Beach
State Park ⑭

⑫

⑬

Hā'ena
○ Beach

⑪

Maniniholo
Dry Cave

Hanakāpī'ai Beach

NĀ PALI COAST

Kalalau Trail

■ Pu'u O Kila Lookout

Kōke'e
Lodge

⑯

55

Kalalau Lookout

Kōke'e ○

*Kōke'e
State Park*

Polihale
State Park

*Nā Pali-Kona
Forest Reserve*

W A I M E A

⑮

Waimea
Canyon

Kōke'e Rd.

Waimea Canyon Dr.

Menehune
Ditch

⑫

50

55

Kekaha Beach Park

Kekaha

West Kaua'i
Visitor and
Technology Center

⑭ ⑬

Waimea

Ft. Elisabeth

⑪

Kaulakahi Channel

N

0   5 miles
0   5 km

Hanapēpē Valley
and Canyon Lookout

⑱

50

Hanapēpē ⑲

Salt Pond
Beach Park

⑳

Port
Allen

K.
V.
a

⑰

Burn's
Field

← TO
NI'IHAU

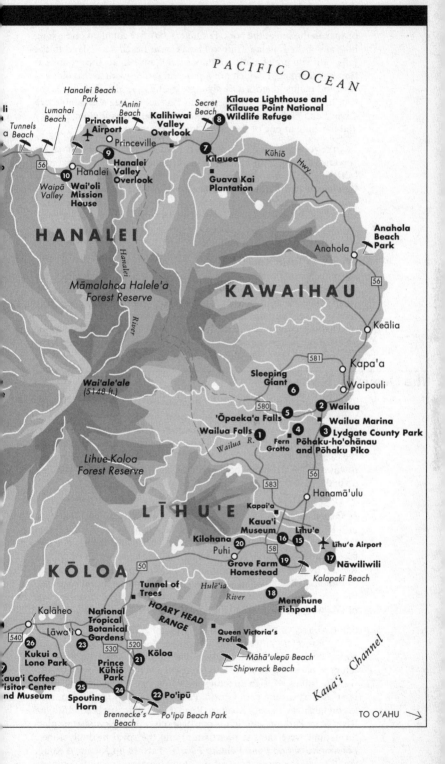

PACIFIC OCEAN

Hanalei Beach Park

Lumahai Beach

'Anini Beach

Kalihiwai Valley Overlook

Secret Beach

Kīlauea Lighthouse and Kīlauea Point National Wildlife Refuge

8

Tunnels a Beach

Princeville Airport

Princeville

9

7

Kīlauea

Kūhiō

Hwy.

56

10 Hanalei

Hanalei Valley Overlook

Wai'oli Mission House

Guava Kai Plantation

Waipā Valley

HANALEI

Hanalei River

Anahola Beach Park

Anahola

Māmalahoa Halele'a Forest Reserve

KAWAIHAU

Keālia

56

Wai'ale'ale (5148 ft.)

Sleeping Giant

6

581

Kapa'a

Waipouli

580

'Ōpaeka'a Falls

5

2 **Wailua**

Wailua Falls

1

4

3 **Wailua Marina**

Lydgate County Park

Wailua R.

Fern Grotto

Pōhaku-ho'ohānau and Pōhaku Piko

Lihue-Koloa Forest Reserve

583

56

Hanamā'ulu

LĪHU'E

Kapai'a

Kaua'i Museum

Kilohana

20

Puhi

16

15

Līhu'e

✈ Līhu'e Airport

17 **Nāwiliwili**

KŌLOA

50

58

19

Grove Farm Homestead

Kalapakī Beach

Tunnel of Trees

Hule'ia River

18

Menehune Fishpond

Kalāheo

Lāwa'i

National Tropical Botanical Gardens

HOARY HEAD RANGE

Queen Victoria's Profile

540

26

530

520

Kōloa

Māhā'ulepū Beach

Kukui o Lono Park

23

21

Shipwreck Beach

aua'i Coffee isitor Center nd Museum

25

24

Prince Kūhiō Park

22 **Po'ipū**

Spouting Horn

Brennecke's Beach

Po'ipū Beach Park

Kaua'i Channel

TO O'AHU →

On day four you might simply want to revel in the beauty of your new surroundings: Play golf, visit the spa, paddle a kayak up Hanalei River, or soak in the sun at the pool. For hikers, day five could involve a long hike along the Kalalau Trail to Hanakāpiʻai Beach and inland to the falls, or if you prefer a less-strenuous stroll, investigate the grounds at **Limahuli Garden** ⑫, which are a peaceful retreat with archaeological sites and plants identified by signage. In any case, this fifth day is the time to drive to the end of the road at Hāʻena, visiting **Maniniholo Dry Cave** ⑪ and **Waikapalaʻe and Waikanaloa Wet Caves** ⑬ along the way and lunching at one of the casual little restaurants in Hanalei.

Reserve your sixth and final day to accomplish activities and see sights you missed along the northeast shore. You might discover Secret Beach (officially called Kauapea Beach), which is just to the left of **Kīlauea Lighthouse and Kīlauea Point National Wildlife Refuge** ⑧; shop at Kong Lung Center in Kiʻlauea; seek out a farmers' market; or explore a side road to ʻAnini Beach. Of course, if you've had enough sightseeing, day six could be a repeat of day four—a day to relax and to dream about repeating day four endlessly.

When to Tour Kaua'i

Kaua'i is beautiful in every season; however, if it's hot beach weather you prefer, you might schedule your visit from June through October, when rainfall is at its lightest. The northern coast of Kaua'i generally receives more rainfall than the rest of the island, particularly during the December–February span. To avoid family crowds, time a visit for pre- and postschool months, May or October, for example, when the weather is generally fine and plenty of rooms are available.

The Heavenly Northeast

Traveling north from Līhuʻe, you'll encounter green pastureland, lush valleys, and untamed tropical wilderness. An area rich in history and legend, it was one of the first communities of the Polynesians who settled here more than 1,000 years ago. As the road turns west, tracing the island's north shore, you'll time-travel through historic plantation towns and the definitely here-and-now resort of Princeville, winding up in the mist-shrouded primeval wilds around Keʻe Beach and Nā Pali Coast State Park.

A Good Drive

Head north out of Līhuʻe on Highway 56, the main artery that traces the eastern and northern coasts of Kaua'i and forms the main artery for a tour of the region. For an early scenic side trip turn left on Māʻalo Road (Hwy. 583) at the bottom of the hill in Kapaia. Then drive 4 mi to **Wailua Falls** ①, one of the Aloha State's most beautiful cascades. Backtrack 4 mi to Highway 56 and continue north to the historic town of **Wailua** ②, the island's early capital.

Before you reach Wailua, a short drive makai at Kaua'i Resort will take you to a former "city of refuge," **Lydgate County Park** ③. Today the park's community-built Kamalani Playground offers a present-day refuge to parents with active kids in the car. On the mauka side of Highway 56, follow the sign directing you to Wailua Marina, where cruise boats depart for the Fern Grotto. Past the mouth of the Wailua, turn left off Highway 56 onto Kuamoʻo Road (Hwy. 580). Just beyond Wailua River State Park on your left is one of seven revered *heiau* (stone platforms that were the site of worship) and the royal birthing stones, **Pōhaku-hoʻohānau and Pōhaku Piko** ④. Farther up Kuamoʻo Road, you'll reach the most intact of the stone temples, Poliʻahu, complete with story boards. On clear days you can see Waiʻaleʻale, the misty peak that is the source of the Wailua River. Across the road are the spectacular **'Ōpaeka'a Falls** ⑤. For a look at this beautiful cascade, return to Kuamo'o Road and drive 1 mi to the lookout on the right.

Adventurers can follow Kuamo'o Road another 7 or 8 mi to its end in Keāhua Forestry Arboretum for a picnic amid aromatic yellow ginger. A huge, shady mango tree on a riverbank in the arboretum comes equipped with a dangling rope, so take your bathing suit, because the spirit of Tarzan is sure to surface when you see the inviting pool below.

Head back to Highway 56 and drive north toward the historic village of Waipouli, now famous for its Coconut Marketplace (☞ Shopping Centers *in* Shopping, *below*), a low-rise shopping complex with storefronts that open invitingly onto a large central mall. On your left you'll pass a mountain ridge resembling a mythical **Sleeping Giant** ⑥. It's thought to be the body of a sleeping warrior. Follow the meandering highway along the eastern coast to Kapa'a, Kaua'i's largest town. Its quaint storefronts and buildings house boutiques and eateries.

To the north you'll pass Keālia and the turnoff to Anahola Beach Park. Seven miles farther is **Kīlauea** ⑦, another former plantation town worth a brief stop if only to check out Kong Lung, a one-of-a-kind boutique filled with Hawaiiana and other fine treasures, or to buy pastries or a loaf of fresh-baked bread from Kīlauea Bakery and Pizza. Turn right on Kolo Road when you see the post office, next to which is Christ Memorial Episcopal Church. Take the first left off Kolo Road, onto Kīlauea Road, and follow it to the end, where you'll find **Kīlauea Lighthouse and Kīlauea Point National Wildlife Refuge** ⑧.

Return through Kilauea and continue until you reach Mile Marker 25 on Highway 56. You'll be at Kalihi Wai Valley Overlook, a splendid point for photographing the valley and the glimmering waterfall across the road. As you drive farther along you'll pass Princeville Airport (on the mauka side of the road) before you reach **Hanalei Valley Overlook** ⑨, across the street from the Princeville Shopping Center. From here you can look out across vast acres of taro fields in the valley below. The road descends and switches back to cross a rustic, arched one-lane bridge dating from 1912, then switches back again into the town of Hanalei, home to the 19th-century **Wai'oli Mission House** ⑩.

West of Hanalei the highway (now labeled 560 on street signs) winds its way between the mountains and the sea and crosses a series of old one-lane bridges. As the road rises and curves left, look for the marker to Lumaha'i Beach (☞ Beaches, *below*), where some scenes in *South Pacific* were filmed amid a spectacular setting of majestic cliffs, black lava rocks, and hala trees.

Continuing west, just past Mile Marker 8, you'll see a right turn through a grove of trees. This takes you to Tunnels Beach. A little farther, on the mauka side, is **Maniniholo Dry Cave** ⑪. Just across the way is Hā'ena State Park. A few miles farther, also on the mauka side, is a national tropical botanical garden, **Limahuli Garden** ⑫, with its ancient taro *loi* (terraces), stone walls, and well-marked, peaceful paths. Less than ½ mi up the highway, a five-minute walk uphill takes you to **Waikapala'e and Waikanaloa Wet Caves** ⑬. When you reach the end of Highway 560 in Hā'ena, you'll be at the Kalalau trailhead near **Ke'e Beach State Park** ⑭. Here, where an ancient stone hula platform is still intact, Laka, Hawaiian goddess of the hula, did most of her dancing. You might still be able to catch her spirit here . . . then come away with a sway in your hips!

TIMING

Without stopping, you can drive the 40 mi from Līhu'e to Hā'ena in less than 90 minutes. You'll probably want to allow a full day, however, including meal breaks, to stop and explore at least some of the sights along the way, take a short hike around Hā'ena's caves, and pause for some photos. The northeast is green year-round, but profusions of unusual wildflowers are a sure sign of spring.

Sights to See

following the text of a review is your signal that the property has a Web site where you will find details and, usually, images; for a link, visit www.fodors.com/urls.

Fern Grotto. A 3-mi boat ride up the Wailua River culminates at a yawning lava tube covered with enormous fishtail ferns. You can rent a kayak, hire a boat and captain, or take one of the popular boat tours (☞ Contacts and Resources *in* Kaua'i A to Z, *below*) to this site, which is only approachable via the river.

OFF THE
BEATEN PATH

GUAVA KAI PLANTATION – Try a free sample of juice and jelly at the visitor center. Then stretch your legs with a nature walk through a 480-acre guava orchard with displays of medicinal plants beside a heart-shape fishpond. The nearest sight is Kīlauea (☞ *below*). ✉ *Hwy. 56, 34 mi north of Līhu'e; turn mauka onto Kuawa Rd. off Hwy. 56, near turnoff to Kīlauea, and follow signs.* ☎ *808/828–6121.* ☑ *Free.* ☉ *Daily 9–5.*

⑨ Hanalei Valley Overlook. One of the state's red-caped Hawaiian-warrior site markers identifies this spot. In the 1850s Robert Wyllie attempted to establish a coffee plantation here. After that failed the Chinese farmed rice in the valley until the early 1900s. Now the valley floor is a patchwork of taro, a staple of the traditional Hawaiian diet. From this panoramic overlook you can see more than a half mile of taro, plus the 900 acres that compose a National Wildlife Refuge for endangered waterfowl. ✉ *Hwy. 56, Princeville.*

★ ⑭ **Ke'e Beach State Park.** You can view the spectacular Nā Pali coastline from this idyllic beach. This is also where you'll find the start of the difficult 11-mi **Kalalau Trail** (☞ Hiking and Camping *in* Outdoor Activities and Sports, *below*). Another path leads from the beach to an open, grassy meadow with a stone altar called **Lohi'au's Hula Platform.** Treat this beautiful site with reverence, for it is full of historical and spiritual *mana* (power). It's said that Laka, goddess of the hula, did most of her dancing on this very spot. Today's hula practitioners sometimes leave offerings here for her. ✉ *Western end of Hwy. 56, Hā'ena.*

⑦ Kīlauea. This former plantation town is known today for its aquacultural successes, especially with prawns. It has also distinguished itself as the guava capital of the world. One of Kīlauea's most notable buildings, **Christ Memorial Episcopal Church** (✉ Kolo St.), dates from 1941. The church is constructed of native lava rock, and its stained-glass windows came from England. ✉ *Hwy. 56, 25 mi north of Līhu'e.*

★ ⑧ **Kīlauea Lighthouse and Kīlauea Point National Wildlife Refuge.** A beacon for passing air and sea traffic since it was built in 1913, the lighthouse, a National Historic Landmark, still has the largest clamshell lens of any lighthouse in the world, but it has laid its traffic responsibilities aside. It is surrounded by the Kīlauea Wildlife Refuge, home to eight species of seabirds, some of them endangered. ✉ *Kīlauea Lighthouse Rd., Kīlauea,* ☎ *808/828–1413.* ☑ *$2.* ☉ *Daily 10–4.*

NEED A
BREAK? **Banana Joe's Tropical Fruit Farm** (✉ 5-2719 Kūhiō Hwy., Kīlauea, ☎ 808/828–1092) occupies a rustic yellow shelter with a distinctly Polynesian look to it on the mauka side of Highway 56, just past the turnoff to Kīlauea. Sample the native Kaua'i-grown fruit here (fresh or dehydrated, or in smoothies and salads). It's the perfect tropical energy booster. Banana Joe's also sells fresh corn and other vegetables in season.

★ ⑫ **Limahuli Garden.** This lovely, natural garden is one of five gardens and three preserves known as the National Tropical Botanical Garden. Limahuli's sometimes steep ¾-mi trail passes ancient taro loi, labeled plants and trees, and mountain streams. Picnicking is not allowed here, and reservations are required for guided tours. ✉ *Hwy. 56, Hā'ena,* ☎ *808/826–1053.* ✑ *Self-guided tour $10, guided tour $15.* ☾ *Tues.–Fri. and Sun. 9:30–4.* ✎

☙ ❸ **Lydgate County Park.** Named for the Rev. J. M. Lydgate, founder of the Līhu'e English Union Church, the park houses a children's playground and the remains of a heiau. In pre–Captain Cook days, the area was a city of refuge for Hawaiians who had violated one of the religious *kapu* (taboos). If they made their way to this beachfront haven, they could escape banishment or death by remaining until their families arranged for their forgiveness. ✉ *Near the mouth of Wailua River, turn makai off Hwy. 56 onto Lehu Dr. and left onto Nalu Rd.* ✑ *Free.* ☾ *Daily.*

⓫ **Maniniholo Dry Cave.** An eerie grotto said to have been dug by a Menehune chief searching for an evil spirit, this cave was a site of ancient worship. Walk 75 yards into it—if you dare—but don't be spooked; some or another Hawaiian goddess removed the traces of evil that lurked here long ago, most likely Laka and her hula followers. Across the highway from Maniniholo Dry Cave is **Hā'ena State Park,** a fine beach for swimming when there's no current. The well-protected **Tunnels Beach** adjoins Hā'ena State Park. A lunch wagon stands ready to feed hungry surfers and sightseers. ✉ *Hwy. 56, Hā'ena.*

OFF THE
BEATEN PATH
NĀ PALI COAST AND STATE PARK – This is Kaua'i's ultimate adventure hike, so even if you plan only to complete the first 2 mi of the hike from Ke'e Beach to Hanakāpī'ai, start early, wear rugged shoes, and carry a picnic lunch and plenty of drinking water. The Kalalau Trail dips and rises along the misty, fluted oceanside cliffs, leaving you breathless—and not just from the climbing. A white-sand beach at the head of Hanakāpī'ai Valley is a fine stopping point for day hikers. Those in good shape may want to follow an unmaintained trail an additional 2 mi to the waterfall and freshwater pool at the back of the valley. A campsite exists at Hanakāpī'ai, but the waiting list for permits is long.

Serious backpackers can complete an 11-mi trek—if they can make the initial 800-ft climb out of the valley. The hike crosses streams that bisect a series of valleys, passes waterfalls and wild fruit trees until 4 mi later you reach another campsite at Hanakoa Valley. A ⅓ mi inland, Hanakoa Falls provides a refreshing cool shower. Campsites are on old Hawaiian agricultural terraces that still have coffee trees, planted in the 1800s, growing on them.

The last 5 mi of the trail culminates at Kalalau Valley and Beach. Nearby, after the final stream crossing, a red-dirt trail leads upslope to an old heiau. A nearby campsite can be crowded in fine weather when many adventurers seek out Kalalau's legendary beauty.

Backpackers must obtain permits from the Department of Land and Natural Resources (☞ Hiking and Camping *in* Outdoor Activities and Sports, *below*) and are limited to five nights in the Nā Pali State Park. Hiking the trail during the rainy winter season should not be attempted as flash floods are a danger. Tour boats no longer take passengers along the Nā Pali shore from Hanalei on the north side of the island, but in the summer months, when the ocean is calm, boats run from Port Allen on the west coast, and kayakers can take a guided tour or explore the coast line in their own rental kayaks (☞ Water Sports *in* Outdoor Activities and Sports, *below*).

★ ❺ **'Ōpaeka'a Falls.** This dramatic waterfall plunges hundreds of feet to the pools below. 'Ōpaeka'a means "rolling shrimp," which refers to the little creatures that are said to have been so abundant at one time that they could be seen tumbling in the falls to the pool below. ⌧ *Hwy. 580 (Kuamo'o Rd.), Wailua.*

❹ **Pōhaku-ho'ohānau and Pōhaku Piko.** These two rocks make Wailua one of the most sacred sites in all Hawai'i, as it was here that all the royal births of Kaua'i took place. An expectant royal mother supported her back against the birthing stone Pōhaku-ho'ohānau. After the newborn's umbilical cord fell off, it was wrapped in kapa and deposited in the crevices of the Pōhaku Piko for safekeeping. Just up the road is Poli'ahu Heiau, where story boards tell about the heiau, the Wailua River area, and its former inhabitants. ⌧ *Hwy. 580 (Kuamo'o Rd.), Wailua.*

❻ **Sleeping Giant.** This formation on Mount Nounou is said to be the mythical giant Puni. Sleeping face-up, his back outlining the mountain ridge, he has dozed here undisturbed since hungry villagers fed him stones after he ate all their taro and fish. ⌧ *Hwy. 56, about 1 mi north of Wailua River.*

🄲 **Smith's Tropical Paradise.** Right next to Wailua Marina on the east side of the island, Smith's Tropical Paradise is 30 acres of family fun, with orchards, jungle paths, exotic foliage, tropical birds, ethnic village settings, and tranquil lagoons. A lū'au banquet and live show are offered Monday, Wednesday, and Friday from 5 to 9, and there is free shuttle service from Wailua. Reservations are essential for the lū'au, shuttle, and show. ⌧ *174 Wailua Rd., Kapa'a,* ☏ *808/821–6895.* ⌧ *$5, lū'au and show $54.* ⊙ *Daily 8:30–4.*

OFF THE   **SUNSHINE MARKETS** – If you want to rub elbows with the locals and get
BEATEN PATH   an eyeful of homegrown produce and flowers, head for one of these
               County of Kaua'i–sponsored outdoor markets, held once a week at five
               locations around the island, including sessions in Kapa'a and Kīlauea.
               Hours and locations change frequently. Call County of Kaua'i (☏ 808/
               241–6303) for a current schedule.

🄳 **Waikapala'e and Waikanaloa Wet Caves.** Said to have been dug by Pele, goddess of fire, these watering holes used to be clear, clean, and great for swimming. Now stagnant, they're nevertheless a photogenic example of the many haunting natural landmarks of Kaua'i's north shore. Across the road from a small parking area, a five-minute uphill walk leads to Waikapala'e. Waikanaloa is visible right beside the highway. ⌧ *Western end of Hwy. 56, Hā'ena.*

❷ **Wailua.** Kaua'i's first communities were built along the Wailua River. Among Wailua's historic treasures, tucked away along the riverbanks, are remnants of important heiau. The town itself was the island's early capital. Its name means "two waters" in Hawaiian. ⌧ *Hwy. 56, 7 mi north of Līhu'e.*

NEED A
BREAK?

Every bebopper who remembers the '50s fondly will love **Beezers** (⊠ 1380 Kūhiō Hwy., Kapa'a, ☎ 808/822–4411), just a few miles north of Wailua. Its jukebox plays tunes you can sing to, the walls are decked with pictures of Marilyn and Elvis, and the counter has red leatherette stools. Malts, root-beer floats, and a Mustang Sally (chocolate brownie topped with ice cream and smothered in hot fudge, whipped cream, and nuts) make this a great haven on hot days.

❶ **Wailua Falls.** You may recognize this impressive cascade from the opening sequences of the *Fantasy Island* television series. Kaua'i has plenty of picturesque waterfalls, but this one surpasses most. ⊠ *End of Hwy. 583, Ma'alo Rd., 4 mi from Hwy. 56.*

❿ **Wai'oli Mission House.** This 1837 mission was once the home of missionary teachers Lucy and Abner Wilcox. Its prim and proper koa-wood furnishings are straight out of missionary Hawai'i, and its tidy architecture feels like it belongs back in New England. Half-hour guided tours are available. ⊠ *Kūhiō Hwy., Hanalei,* ☎ *808/245–3202.* 🎫 *Donations accepted.* ☉ *Tues., Thurs., and Sat. 9–3.*

NEED A
BREAK?

Bubba's (⊠ Hanalei Center, Hanalei, ☎ 808/826–7839) is where you can find the "Slopper" (open-face burger with chili) or a "Hubba Bubba" (burger, hot dog, chili, and rice). Burgers range in size from ⅙ pound to the three-patty Big Bubba, and there are chicken burgers, fish burgers, corn dogs, and fish-and-chips, too. Orders, filled quickly and with just the irreverent humor you'd expect at a place called Bubba's, may be eaten at the four picnic tables on the lawn right out front.

Līhu'e and Southward

As you follow the main road south from Līhu'e the air seems to become gradually warmer and drier. This is one way to tell you're nearing the region called Po'ipū, named after the south-shore resort town that is its unofficial center. The sun shines steadily on the populated, friendly beaches here. A string of condominiums and hotels lines the coastline, and an impressive variety of water sports is available.

A Good Drive

Begin in **Līhu'e** ⑮, the commercial and political center of Kaua'i, and visit the **Kaua'i Museum** ⑯, where displays and an exciting aerial movie provide an overview of this tropical isle. Head south on Rice Street, the town's main road, until it dead-ends; then turn right onto Wa'apā Road, which takes you to **Nāwiliwili** ⑰, Kaua'i's major port. From Wa'apā Road, turn right onto Hulemalu Road and follow the Hulē'ia River to view **Menehune Fishpond** ⑱.

Return to Nāwiliwili, take a left on Nāwiliwili Road (Hwy. 58), and begin to look on your right for **Grove Farm Homestead** ⑲. This 80-acre plantation estate and living museum affords a wonderful look at 19th-century agricultural life on the island. At the intersection of Nāwiliwili Road and Highway 50, turn left and head west on Highway 50. Two miles farther on your right you'll find the entrance to **Kilohana** ⑳, another attraction with shops and galleries that will enrich your experience of earlier plantation days.

Continuing west on Highway 50, you'll pass the majestic slopes of the Hoary Head Mountains. On the top of the range to your right is a formation called Queen Victoria's Profile, indicated by a Hawaiian-warrior marker. When you get to the intersection of Highways 50 and 520, you have reached Kōloa Gap, a natural pass between Mt. Wai'ale'ale on your right and the Hoary Heads on your left. Turn left on Highway 520 (Maluhia Rd.), also known as the Tunnel of Trees because of the eucalyptus trees that border the road to form a canopy overhead.

Highway 520 takes you to **Kōloa** ㉑, site of Kauai'i's first sugar mill, dating from 1835. Kōloa's main street is lined with old buildings that have been preserved to house shops, art galleries, and restaurants. Head south on Highway 520, which here is also called Po'ipū Road. At the fork stay to the left.

From here turn right onto Honowili Road, which takes you through the heart of sunny **Po'ipū** ㉒, the major resort area of Kaua'i's south shore. On the makai side of the road are Po'ipū Beach Park and Brennecke's Beach, prime spots for sunbathers and bodysurfers. Return to Po'ipū Road and follow it past the stunning Hyatt Regency Kaua'i, which fronts Shipwreck Beach. The road abruptly turns to dirt, but 3 mi farther awaits beautiful Māhā'ulepū Beach. To reach it, follow the road to the T intersection, turn right, stop at the gates to sign in (this is private property), and park at the end of the dirt road to walk to the beach. Explorers willing to search can find an interesting cave site at the far end of this beach if they hike inland beside a little stream. When you head back on Po'ipū Road, instead of turning to Kōloa go left onto Lāwa'i Road just after you cross the bridge over Waikomo Stream. On the mauka side of the road, you'll spot the visitor center for the **National Tropical Botanical Gardens** ㉓, a botanical research center and showcase for a multitude of rare and endangered plant species. Farther on, you'll pass **Prince Kūhiō Park** ㉔, honoring the birthplace of one of Hawai'i's most beloved members of Congress. At the end of this beachfront road is **Spouting Horn** ㉕, a waterspout that shoots up out of an ancient lava tube. Its rising plume signals your drive's end.

TIMING

From Līhu'e to Po'ipū it's only 14 mi, but since there is plenty to see, you can easily devote a day or two to this itinerary. If you have only a half day, try to make it an afternoon, so you can watch the sunset from Brennecke's Beach. The bodysurfers on this legendary beach are something to see, especially if it's big-wave season—summer.

Sights to See

⑲ **Grove Farm Homestead.** One of Kaua'i's oldest plantation estates, founded in 1864 by George Wilcox, today offers a look at 19th-century life on Kaua'i. On the 80 acres composing this living museum are the original family home (filled with turn-of-the-century memorabilia), workers' quarters, and elaborate gardens of tropical flowers and tall palm trees. Tours are limited to six people, and reservations are essential. ⊠ *Hwy. 58, ½ mi south of Nāwiliwili Rd., Līhu'e,* ☎ *808/245–3202.* 🕾 *$5 donation.* ☉ *Tour Mon. and Wed.–Thurs. at 10 and 1.*

⑯ **Kaua'i Museum.** A permanent display, "The Story of Kaua'i," provides an overview of the Garden Isle and traces its mythology and its geological and cultural history. It's highlighted by a 30-minute aerial movie. Ni'ihau is also represented in the museum. Works by local artists are on display in the Mezzanine Gallery, and the gift shop offers a good selection of books and souvenirs. ⊠ *4428 Rice St., Līhu'e,* ☎ *808/245–6931.* 🕾 *$5.* ☉ *Weekdays 9–4, Sat. 10–4.*

★ ⑳ **Kilohana.** Dating from 1935, this is the site of the old Wilcox sugar plantation, which has been transformed into a 35-acre visitor attraction. The estate is a beautiful showpiece from plantation days, with agricultural exhibits, local arts and crafts, horse-and-carriage rides, specialty shops, and a garden courtyard restaurant called Gaylord's, which is pleasant for breakfast or Sunday brunch. ⊠ *3-2087 Kaumuali'i*

Hwy. (Hwy. 50), Līhu'e, ☎ *808/245–5608.* ☒ *Free.* ☉ *Mon.–Sat. 9:30–9:30, Sun. 9:30–5.*

㉑ **Kōloa.** Kaua'i's first sugar mill began operating here in 1835. You can see the remains of its old stone smokestack on the right side of the road. A sculpture depicting the various ethnic groups that made their mark on the sugar industry on Kaua'i sits on a small green nearby. The main street of Kōloa is lined with old buildings that have been preserved to house expensive boutiques, an old general store, and a selection of restaurants. Placards outside each building describe its original tenants and tell about life in the old mill town. ☒ *Hwy. 520.*

NEED A BREAK?	An open-air establishment called **Pizzetta/La Griglia** (☒ 5408 Old Kōloa Rd., Kōloa, ☎ 808/742–8881) concocts the best *mai tai* cocktail (rum with orange and lime juice) on the island. A rustic wood-panel room at the back, with an open deck, makes up the bar area. Sit by one of the huge open windows and watch the world go by. When you're ready for dinner, order a pizza or choose a freshly made fettuccine.

★ ⑮ **Līhu'e.** The commercial and political center of Kaua'i County, which includes the islands of Kaua'i and Ni'ihau, Līhu'e is the home of the island's major airport and harbor. Its main thoroughfare, Rice Street, offers a short, pleasant stroll from the War Memorial and Convention Hall (Rice and Hardy Sts.), past government offices, to the Līhu'e Shopping Center (Rice St. and Hwy. 50). ☒ *Hwys. 56 and 50.*

NEED A BREAK?	If you're looking for a down-home Kaua'i-style meal or a filling snack, stop by **Hamura Saimin** (☒ 2956 Kress St., Līhu'e, ☎ 808/245–3271), a ramshackle diner with booths and counter seating. Each day the Hiraoka family serves about 1,000 orders of saimin, a steaming bowl of broth and noodles with varying garnishes. This little landmark also turns out tasty chicken and beef grilled on barbecue sticks, as well as *liliko'i* (passion fruit) chiffon pie.

⑱ **Menehune Fishpond.** Secretive little workers are said to have built these intricate walls, 4 ft thick and 5 ft high, for a princess and prince. Today the walls of this ancient aquaculture structure, also known as *'alekoko,* still contain placid waters where mullet thrive and kayakers enjoy blissful serenity. ☒ *Hulemalu Rd., Niumalu.*

㉓ **National Tropical Botanical Gardens.** A good example of a tropical green thumb can be found at this 252-acre scientific research center (Lawa'i Gardens) and 100-acre estate property (Allerton Gardens) for botany and horticulture. The visitor center showcases 2,600 different plant species, some of them rare and endangered Hawaiian varieties. There's a gift shop, too. The grounds are open only for visitors with reservations for the guided 2½-hour walking tour. ☒ *Meet at the visitor center across from Spouting Horn parking lot, Lāwa'i, Po'ipū,* ☎ *808/332–7361.* ☒ *$25.* ☉ *Tours Tues.–Sat. at 9, 11:30, and 2.*

⑰ **Nāwiliwili.** At Kaua'i's major port a host of fishing and recreational boats come and go, and tour boats offer snorkeling and sightseeing adventures along the coast. This is a port of call for container ships, U.S. Navy vessels, and the American Hawai'i Cruise line. Nearby there's protected swimming and sunbathing at **Kalapakī Beach** (☞ Beaches, *below*). ☒ *Makai end of Wa'apā Rd., Līhu'e.*

㉒ **Po'ipū.** The major resort town of the south shore remains irrepressibly sunny despite the shadowy hulk of an empty hotel looming eerily on the beach. Although the Stouffer Waiohai resort has not reopened since Hurricane 'Iniki blew through in 1992, the Sheraton Kaua'i Resort and a half dozen condominiums, including Kiahuna Plantation, rim the beach's golden sands. Boogie-boarders, swimmers, and families enjoy the good-time atmosphere. ⊠ *Hwy. 520.*

㉔ Prince Kūhiō Park. The park behind the Prince Kūhiō condominium honors the birthplace of one of Hawai'i's most beloved congressional representatives, Prince Jonah Kūhiō Kalaniana'ole, a man who might have become Hawai'i's king if Queen Lili'uokalani had not been overthrown in 1893. ⊠ *Lāwa'i Rd., Po'ipū.*

★ **㉕ Spouting Horn.** Kaua'i's natural wonders never cease. This one is a waterspout that shoots up like Old Faithful out of an ancient lava tube. Follow the paved walkways around this area, because the rocks are slippery and people have been known to fall in. Vendors sell inexpensive souvenirs and costume jewelry here, but you'll also find one of the best selections of rare and treasured Ni'ihau shell necklaces. When purchasing a Ni'ihau shell lei, ask for a certificate of authenticity and an address in case you need to reorder or repair your purchase at a later date. ⊠ *Lāwa'i Bay, Po'ipū.*

The Western Route and Kōke'e

Heading west along Kaua'i's south shore, you'll pass through one former plantation town after the next, each with its own story to tell: Hanapēpē, whose salt ponds have been harvested since ancient times; Ft. Elisabeth, from which an enterprising Russian tried to take over the island in the early 1800s; and Waimea, home of the Menehune Ditch, supposedly built by the legendary race of little people.

From Waimea you can drive up along the rim of magnificent Waimea Canyon to reach the crisp, cool climate of Kōke'e, 3,000 ft above sea level. Here you'll discover another facet of this ancient island: Sequoia forests and swamp lands provide a home to remarkable indigenous birds and plants, and a mountain lodge welcomes guests with old-style warmth and hospitality.

From the Burns Field airstrip here on the western side of the island, helicopter tours depart for the "Forbidden Isle" of Ni'ihau and snorkeling excursions can be planned from Port Allen harbor. By land, sea, or air, this part of Kaua'i is worth exploring.

A Good Drive

The west side of the island offers a look at the sleepiest—as well as the most dramatic—sections of Kaua'i. Begin this tour by heading west on Highway 50 out of Līhu'e. The first town you come to is Lāwa'i. This tiny town once housed the Kaua'i Pineapple Cannery. In its wake, Lāwa'i has emerged as a significant producer of tropical fruits and plants. The next town along Highway 50 is Kalāheo. Turn left on Pāpālina Road to make the climb to **Kukui o Lono Park** ㉖, where you can bliss out on Japanese gardens and spectacular scenic vistas before you depart.

Beyond Kalāheo, a left turn onto Highway 540 will take you to the **Kaua'i Coffee Visitor Center and Museum** ㉗, where a minimuseum is housed in two restored camp houses. Highway 540 loops back to 50. Either way you'll see acres of shiny-leaf coffee trees, but if you travel the loop, you'll miss the **Hanapēpē Valley and Canyon Lookout** ㉘. This dramatic divide holds a place in Hawaiian history as the site of Kaua'i's last battle in 1824.

Hanapēpē ㉙, the "Biggest Little Town on Kaua'i," lies just west of the lookout. At the fork turn right to drive down Hanapēpē's dusty main street, or angle left and follow Highway 50 past the town. Then turn makai on Lele Road to reach **Salt Pond Beach Park** ㉚. Early Hawaiians harvested salt here. Nearby is Burns Field, Kaua'i's first airfield and the departure point for flightseeing adventures and helicopter trips to Ni'ihau. It's a taste of a more primitive Hawai'i (☞ Contacts and Resources *in* Kaua'i A to Z, *below*). Just around the bend and across the bay from the airstrip is Port Allen Harbor, the shipping center for the west side of the island and home base for snorkeling excursions from September to May (☞ Water Sports *in* Outdoor Activities and Sports, *below*).

Head west again on Highway 50 and look on the makai side of the road for the Hawaiian-warrior marker to **Ft. Elisabeth** ㉛. The ruins of this stone fort are testament to a time when Imperial Russia had designs on conquering the Islands. Cross the Waimea River Bridge and take your first right on Menehune Road, which leads you 2½ mi up Waimea Valley to **Menehune Ditch** ㉜, a stone aqueduct carved with the mysterious markings of an earlier era. As you enter **Waimea** ㉝ you might spot the statue commemorating Captain Cook's arrival here in 1778. The remains of a missionary church built here in 1846 will hold your interest as well. On the right, **West Kaua'i Visitor and Technology Center** ㉞ houses attractive photo displays and computers that download information—simply touch the screen indicating your field of interest.

Highway 50 meanders through the sugar town of Kekaha. Eventually it passes the Pacific Missile Range Facility. Take the right fork after you pass the missile range and you can follow Highway 50 to where it ends near Polihale State Park. The park is accessible only by a dirt road through sugarcane fields. During or after heavy rain, you might want to skip it. When the road is passable, though, it's worth a visit to this immense stretch of glistening golden sand fringed by dramatic mountains.

As you return to Līhu'e you have two choices for visiting **Waimea Canyon** ㉟, the "Grand Canyon of the Pacific." The main route, Kōke'e Road (Hwy. 550), makes a steep climb from Kekaha. The other, more scenic option is Waimea Canyon Drive, which you pick up near the western edge of Waimea, by the church. It's narrow but well paved and climbs quickly for immediate views of the town and ocean below. A few miles up, the roads converge and continue the steep ascent; spectacular birds'-eye views out over the canyon encompass you. Be sure to stop at the Pu'u-ka-Pele and Pu'u-hinahina lookouts for the most appealing vistas. As the road rises to 4,000 ft it passes through Kōke'e State Park with its cozy Kōke'e Lodge. The road out of the park leads past the NASA Tracking Station.

Waimea Canyon Drive ends 4 mi above the park at the **Kalalau Lookout** ㊱. This is the beginning of a beautiful hiking trail that passes Pu'u-o-Kila Lookout. Be sure to bring a jacket for the cool weather here.

TIMING

The 36-mi drive from Līhu'e to Waimea Canyon takes about 90 minutes with no stops for botanical gardens, beaches, or quaint little towns. If you want to spend a half day or more hiking in the canyon, you might save south-shore sightseeing for another day. Save at least a half day for your air adventure over to Ni'ihau. In winter be prepared for chilly temperatures in the heights above the canyon, especially in the early morning.

Sights to See

★ ㉛ **Ft. Elisabeth.** The ruins of this stone fort, built in 1816 by an agent of the Imperial Russian government named Anton Scheffer, are reminders of the days when Scheffer tried to conquer the island for his homeland . . . and the czar! King Kaumuali'i eventually chased the foreigner off the island. The crumbling walls of the fort, at the ocean's edge, are cleared of brush intermittently and cover about an acre. ⊠ *Hwy. 50, Waimea.*

29 Hanapēpē. This quiet farming town on the south coast supplies Kaua'i with much of its produce and all the islands with Lappert's ice cream. **Hanapēpē Road** had a featured role (as an Australian town) in the television miniseries *The Thorn Birds*. Today shops sell koa wood and other crafts. Talented artist James Hoyle has his art gallery here. **Burns Field,** Kaua'i's first airfield and now the base of operations for several helicopter companies, is nearby. Just to the east is **Port Allen** harbor, still the shipping center for the west side of Kaua'i and headquarters of the McBryde Company, which has replaced its cane fields with coffee trees. If you want further proof that Hanapēpē was once a power center, check out **'Ele'ele Shopping Center** on Lele Road. It was the first "modern" shopping center built on Kaua'i. ⊠ *Hwy. 50, Hanapēpē.*

NEED A
BREAK?
You can sit at the spiffy black-and-white bar for a quick espresso or relax at a dozen tables while you dine on vegetarian food with French-Italian flair. You'll find garden burgers, Caesar salads, soup, croissants, and calzones at **Hanapēpē Café and Espresso** (⊠ 3830 Hanapēpē Rd., Hanapēpē, ☎ 808/335–5011). There is a vegetarian breakfast and lunch menu Tuesday through Saturday, with coffee and pastries served until 3. Dinner, with live music by local guitarists, is served Friday and Saturday 6 to 9.

28 Hanapēpē Valley and Canyon Lookout. This dramatic divide once housed a thriving Hawaiian community, and some remains of its taro patches still exist. Hanapēpē is a historic canyon. It's the site of Kaua'i's last battle, led in 1824 by Humehume, son of the island's King Kaumuali'i. ⊠ *Hwy. 50.*

★ **36 Kalalau Lookout.** Kalalau Lookout, near the end of the road high above Waimea Canyon, marks the head of a challenging hiking trail that also passes **Pu'u-o-Kila Lookout.** On a clear day at either spot you can gaze right down into the gaping valley at sawtooth ridges and waterfalls. But stick around for a few minutes if clouds are obscuring the view. Winds are strong up here and just might blow away the clouds so you can snap a photo. If you turn your back to the valley and look to the northwest, you might pick out the shining sands of Kalalau Beach, gleaming like a tiny golden thread against the vast blue Pacific. ⊠ *Waimea Canyon Dr., 4 mi north of Kōke'e State Park.*

27 Kaua'i Coffee Visitor Center and Museum. Two restored camp houses dating from the days when sugar was the main agricultural crop in the islands house a museum–visitor center and gift shop. About 3,400 acres of McBryde sugar land have become Hawai'i's largest coffee plantation. Visitors can walk among the trees, view old grinders and roasters and a video to learn how coffee is processed, and sample the various estate roasts. ⊠ *870 Halawili Rd., off Hwy. 50, west of Kalāheo,* ☎ *808/335–0813.* ▣ *Free.* ☼ *Daily 9–5.*

NEED A
BREAK?
Ten kinds of hot dogs, burgers made with such fresh fish as mahimahi, and a big condiment bar make **Mustard's Last Stand** (⊠ Corner of Hwy. 50 and Old Kōloa Rd., Lāwa'i, ☎ 808/332–7245) an appropriate, if not essential, stop while you're touring. After you eat, the kids can be photographed riding a curling fiberglass wave while you shop for deals in the adjacent Old Hawaiian Trading Company.

26 Kukui o Lono Park. Translated as "light of the god Lono," Kukui o Lono has serene Japanese gardens and a display of significant Hawaiian stones—an anchor stone and salt pan—collected by Walter McBryde, the sugar-plantation heir who founded the estate in the 1900s. Spectacular panoramic views make this one of Kaua'i's most scenic park areas and an ideal picnic spot. There is also a golf cour[se], a 9-acre expanse. ⊠ *Pāpālina Rd., Kalāheō.* 🎫 *Free*

③② **Menehune Ditch.** Archaeologists claim that this aqueduct was b[e]fore the first Hawaiians lived on Kaua'i, and it is therefore attributed to the industrious hands of the tiny Menehune. The way the flanged and fitted cut-stone bricks are stacked and assembled indicates a knowledge of construction that is foreign to Hawai'i, and the ditch is inscribed with mysterious markings. Until someone comes up with a better suggestion, the Menehune retain the credit for this engineering feat. ⊠ *Menehune Rd., Waimea Valley.*

③⓪ **Salt Pond Beach Park.** Here you can see how the Hawaiians harvested salt for almost 200 years. They let the sun evaporate the seawater in mud-lined drying beds, then gathered the salt left behind. This is a safe area for swimming. ⊠ *Lele Rd., Hanapēpē.*

③③ **Waimea.** This is the town that first welcomed Capt. James Cook to the Sandwich Islands in 1778. An easy-to-miss monument on the mauka side of the road commemorates his landfall, as does a statue near the entry to town. Waimea was also the place where Kaua'i's King Kaumuali'i ceded his island to the unifying efforts of King Kamehameha. Waimea played host to the first missionaries on the island, and you can still see what's left of their old **Waimea Christian Hawaiian and Foreign Church** on Mākeke Road. Constructed in 1846, the church was made of huge timbers brought down from the mountains 8 mi away, as well as limestone blocks from a nearby quarry. The church suffered severe damage from Hurricane 'Iniki, but the beautiful stonework of its front and side walls is worth a photo. ⊠ *Hwy. 50.*

★ ③⑤ **Waimea Canyon.** Created by an ancient fault in the earth's crust, the canyon has been eroding over the centuries due to weather, wind, and the water of its rivers and streams. The "Grand Canyon of the Pacific" is 3,600 ft deep, 2 mi wide, and 10 mi long. Its deep reds, greens, and browns are ever changing in the light. Be sure to allow time to soak up the views from **Pu'u-ka-Pele** and **Pu'u-hinahina** lookouts.

Kōke'e State Park, at the north end of Waimea Canyon, is 4,000 ft above sea level. Here the air is cool and crisp, and the vegetation turns to evergreens and ferns. This 4,345-acre wilderness park is full of wild fruit, heady flowers, and colorful rare birds that make their home in these forests. A 45-mi network of hiking trails takes you to some of Kaua'i's most remote places. Before you set off, ask about trail conditions. ⊠ *Hwy. 550 (contact Kōke'e Natural History Museum, below, or Division of State Parks, Box 1671, Līhu'e 96766),* ☎ *808/335–5871.* ♽

Kōke'e Natural History Museum in the park holds displays of plants, native birds, and other wildlife, as well as a weather exhibit that describes the formation of hurricanes. ⊠ *Kōke'e State Park, 96766,* ☎ *808/335–9975,* 𝔽𝔸𝕏 *808/335–6131.* 🎫 *Donation suggested.* ☉ *Daily 10–4.*

NEED A BREAK?

Treat yourself to a cup of coffee or a sandwich at **Kōke'e Lodge** (⊠ 3600 Kōke'e Rd., Mile Marker 15, Kōke'e State Park, ☎ 808/335–6061), a comfortably rustic mountaintop inn. With temperatures almost always nippy outside, this is a warm retreat for breakfast or lunch from 9 to 3:30. Peruse the gift shop for T-shirts, postcards, or Kōke'e memorabilia.

③④ **West Kaua'i Visitor and Technology Center.** This visitor center is a state-of-the-art facility where computers with touch screens bring alive the island's history and attractions. ⊠ *9565 Kaumualii Hwy., Waimea,* ☎ *808/338–1332.* 🎫 *Free.* ☉ *Daily 9–5.*

EACHES

The waters that hug the island are clean, clear, and inviting, but be careful to go in only where it's safe. All beaches on Kaua'i are free and open to the public, and none have a phone number. For information about beaches around the island, call the **County Department of Parks and Recreation** (☎ 808/241–6670) and the **Department of Land and Natural Resources** (☎ 808/274–3446).

The list of beaches below starts from the western end of Highway 50 and goes counterclockwise around the island to the end of the road on the north shore.

★ **Polihale Beach Park.** This magnificent stretch of sand, flanked by impressive sea cliffs, stretches from the town of Kekaha to end miles away within 140-acre Polihale State Park. The beach is beautiful for sunbathing, beachcombing, and surfcasting, but the rip currents are often too rough for swimming. Locals dune-buggy here on the weekends. Polihale has no lifeguards. ⊠ *Drive to end of Hwy. 50 and turn left at Hawaiian-warrior marker onto dirt road, which leads several miles through sugarcane fields; turn left at small national park sign.*

Kekaha Beach Park. Stretching for miles along the south shore, this strip of sand brings to mind the long beaches of southern California. Dune-buggying is popular here. If you don't like the noise, stay away. There are no lifeguards, rest rooms, or showers. ⊠ *Hwy. 50 west of Kekaha.*

Salt Pond Beach Park. A protected bay here is particularly safe for swimmers, so this is a real family spot. There are picnic tables under covered pavilions, showers, rest rooms, lifeguards, and a large grassy lawn. Camping is allowed. ⊠ *Follow Lele Rd., on makai side off Hwy. 50 in Hanapēpē.*

Po'ipū Beach Park. A prime bodysurfing and sunbathing spot, Po'ipū Beach has clean white sand. It's a fun place for a picnic or a barbecue under the palm trees. There are lifeguards, showers, rest rooms, and a take-out deli across the street. A walk on the beach takes strollers past a half dozen condominiums to the Sheraton Kaua'i Resort, which has an inviting cocktail lounge overlooking the beach—a cool respite from the hot sun. ⊠ *Po'ipū Rd. on south shore, opposite Ho'ōne and Pane Rds.*

Brennecke's Beach. A steady stream of small- to medium-size waves makes this a bodysurfer's heaven. Waves are bigger here in summer than in winter. Showers, rest rooms, and lifeguards are on hand, and there are several food stands nearby. ⊠ *Po'ipū Rd. on south shore.*

Keoneloa, or Shipwreck Beach. Nicknamed Shipwreck Beach for an old wooden boat that wrecked on the 2-mi stretch of sand fronting the Hyatt Regency Po'ipū, this beach is popular with surfcasters who fish from Makawehi Point on the east side of the beach. Sea turtles and monk seals like the coves, but strong rip currents and shore break can make swimming dangerous for human water lovers, and there are no lifeguards. Showers, rest rooms, and a walkway can be found along the dunes. ⊠ *Turn into Hyatt Regency Po'ipū Resort, drive along the east side of the hotel, and turn right.*

Kalapakī Beach. This sheltered bay is ideal for swimming, surfing, and windsurfing in the small waves. It fronts the Kaua'i Marriott Resort and Beach Club. There are rest rooms, lifeguards, showers, and food and drink nearby. ⊠ *Nāwiliwili off Wapa'a Rd., which runs from Līhu'e.*

Lydgate County Park. Depending on the wind, this is a good spot for family picnicking and swimming (there are lifeguards here), with a swimming area protected by a rock wall and a covered pavilion. Any time of year it's a nice place for beachcombing and reflecting on the days when this was a Hawaiian city of refuge. Rest rooms and showers are available, and there's a large playground for kids. ✉ *Before mouth of Wailua River turn makai off Hwy. 56 onto Lehu Dr. and left onto Nalu Rd.*

Anahola Beach Park. This quiet stretch of sand edged by a grassy park on the east shore offers calm waters for swimming and snorkeling. The Makalena Mountains are your backdrop here. There are rest rooms and showers but no lifeguards. ✉ *After Mile Marker 13 on Hwy. 56, turn makai on Anahola Rd.*

★ **'Anini Beach County Park.** Safest of the north-shore beaches, this 3-mi stretch of golden sand lies beside a reef-protected blue lagoon, making it ideal for beginning windsurfers, snorkelers, and swimmers. A beach-side park, polo field, campground, public rest rooms, showers, grills, and picnic tables keep families happy year-round. There are no lifeguards here. ✉ *Turn makai off Hwy. 56 onto Kalihi Wai Rd. on Hanalei side of Kalihi Wai Bridge; road angles left along beach onto 'Anini Rd.*

Hanalei Beach Park. With views of Nā Pali Coast and shady trees over picnic tables, this is beach-bum heaven. But swimming here can be treacherous. Stay near the old pier, where the water is a bit calmer. There are rest rooms and showers. ✉ *In Hanalei turn makai at Aku Rd. and right at dead end.*

Lumaha'i Beach. Known for its striking natural beauty, Lumaha'i is flanked by high mountains and lava rocks. In the movie *South Pacific,* this is where Mitzi Gaynor sang "I'm Gonna Wash That Man Right Outta My Hair." Swimming is good only in summer. There are no lifeguards, showers, or rest rooms. ✉ *On winding section of Hwy. 56 west of Hanalei between Mile Markers 4 and 5. Park on makai side of road and walk down a steep path to the beach.*

★ **Tunnels Beach.** Kaua'i's best-protected, big, deep lagoon for swimming and snorkeling is rimmed by a beach shaded with ironwood trees. There are no lifeguards, showers, or rest rooms. ✉ *¹⁄₁₀ mi past Mile Marker 8 on Hwy. 56. Turn makai onto dirt road that runs through grove of trees. If parking lot is full, continue ½ mi to Hā'ena Beach Park and walk back.*

Hā'ena Beach Park. This beach on Maniniholo Bay is good for swimming when the surf is down, which means summertime. There are rest rooms, showers, camping facilities, picnic tables, and food wagons but no lifeguards. ✉ *On north shore near end of Hwy. 56 across from lava-tube sea caves.*

★ **Ke'e Beach.** In summer this is a fine swimming beach, with a reef just made for snorkeling. In winter, big waves wash away the sand, so stay out of the water and enjoy the views of the Nā Pali Coast. This is where the Kalalau Trail begins. Changing facilities are available, as are showers and rest rooms, but there are no lifeguards. ✉ *Northern end of Hwy. 56, 7 mi from Hanalei.*

Hanakāpī'ai Beach. It's a 2-mi hike to this crescent of beach, which changes length and width throughout the year as fierce winter waves rob the shoreline of sand and summer's calm returns it. Be very careful swimming here in summer, and don't even think of going in during the winter swells. Hike an additional 2 mi inland beside the adjacent stream and you'll find Hanakāpī'ai Falls, which splashes into a fresh-water pool perfect for shutterbugs or a cool dip. ✉ *Mi 2 of Kalalau Trail, which begins near Ke'e Beach, at northern end of Hwy. 56.*

DINING

In addition to preparing all kinds of ethnic dishes, a growing contingent of independent restaurateurs experiment with Hawai'i regional cuisine, using the best produce grown on native soil. On Kaua'i there is an especially heavy emphasis on local fruits. Thanks to the abundance of fish in the waters surrounding Kaua'i, the catch of the day is always well worth trying.

Restaurants are open daily unless otherwise noted. Reservations are rarely required on Kaua'i, but it's never a mistake to avoid disappointment and call ahead. For an explanation of price categories, *see* Dining *in* Smart Travel Tips A to Z at the back of the book.

The East Coast

American

$ ✕ **Eggbert's.** If you are big on breakfasts, try indoor or outdoor dining at Eggbert's, in the Coconut Marketplace. It's a great spot for omelets, banana pancakes, and eggs Benedict. You can even create your own Benedicts, adding mushrooms, spinach, or other meats and veggies as you please. Such kid-size meals as "pigs in a blanket" keep down the cost of family outings here. ⊠ *Coconut Marketplace, Kapa'a,* ☎ *808/822–3787. MC, V.*

Contemporary

$$$ ✕ **A Pacific Cafe.** With its East-meets-West atmosphere and cutting-
★ edge cuisine, chef Jean-Marie Josselin's restaurant has won high acclaim and numerous awards. He combines a love of Asian cooking with a commitment to fresh, homegrown ingredients. The menu changes daily. In true nouvelle fashion he might present grilled moonfish with black-olive polenta, sun-dried tomatoes, pancetta, and shiitake mushrooms, or lamb with a red wine–mint glaze and garlic mashed potatoes. The macadamia-nut torte comes topped with toasted coconut, and the crème brûlée, a huge portion served in a pastry shell, is deliciously creamy. ⊠ *Kaua'i Village Shopping Center, Hwy. 56, Kapa'a,* ☎ *808/822–0013. AE, D, DC, MC, V. No lunch.*

$ ✕ **Caffé Coco.** A riot of tropical foliage surrounds this little restored plantation cottage and hangs from an overhead arbor in an outdoor dining area. The café, an attached black-light art gallery, and an artful shop called Bambulei make this a fun stop for any meal. Tasty dishes made from island products range from coco-custard French toast at breakfast to pot-sticker appetizers, *'ahi* (yellowfin tuna) nori wraps, and Greek salads. "Fresh from the Garden" jams, salsas, and condiments are available to sample or take home. ⊠ *4-369 Kūhiō Hwy., Wailua,* ☎ *808/822–7990. MC, V. Closed Mon.*

Japanese

$$ ✕ **Restaurant Kintaro.** This pretty restaurant with sliding shoji-screen doors and Asian prints on the walls serves complete sukiyaki dinners in an iron pot and tempura combinations that use fresh local fish. *Teppan* (grilled) dinners include tender hibachi shrimp sautéed in lemon butter and served with bean sprouts and steamed rice. Dinners come with chilled buckwheat noodles, miso soup, rice, Japanese pickles, and tea. A sushi bar is also on hand. ⊠ *4-370 Kūhiō Hwy., Kapa'a,* ☎ *808/ 822–3341. AE, D, DC, MC, V. Closed Sun. No lunch.*

Mixed Menu

$–$$ ✕ **Wailua Family Restaurant.** You can't miss this place. It's lit up like a Christmas tree with 25,000 lights hanging from the ceiling. You can order a 22-ounce prime rib and other entrées from the menu, but buffets are the most reasonable at under $10 for either lunch or dinner. Kids can order Mickey Mouse–shape pancakes for breakfast, and the dinner buffet is stocked with something for everyone: soba noodles, poi, taco salads, and *lomilomi* salmon (massaged until tender and served with minced onions and tomatoes). A seafood bar is featured at dinner but best of all, the kids will love creating their own cake with toppings at the dessert bar. ⊠ *4-361 Kūhiō Hwy., Kapa'a,* ☎ *808/822–3325. MC, V.*

Natural Foods

$ ✕ **Papaya's.** Courtyard dining is the draw at this well-stocked natural foods market, which is also a restaurant under the whale tower at Kaua'i Village. Sit beneath a pretty blue umbrella and enjoy grilled fish, a vegetarian burger, pasta with pesto, or Thai and Mexican fare. Takeout is also available. ⊠ *Kaua'i Village Shopping Center, 4-831 Kuhio Hwy. 56, Kapa'a,* ☎ *808/823–0190. MC, V. Closed Sun.*

Steak and Seafood

$$ ✕ **Kapa'a Fish & Chowder House.** The gray-and-blue color scheme of this open-air restaurant is punctuated by thick hanging ferns and nautical memorabilia. Fish selections offered daily are served sautéed or broiled with a variety of sauces. Try sautéed sea scallops or the baked tiger prawns stuffed with shrimp and crab. The seafood fettuccine is also recommended. Ask for a table in the Edenlike Orchid Room. ⊠ *4-1639 Kūhiō Hwy., Kapa'a,* ☎ *808/822–7488. AE, D, DC, MC, V. No lunch.*

$–$$ ✕ **Bull Shed.** The A-frame design of this popular restaurant imparts a distinctly rustic feel, but the interior is brightened with light-color walls and unobstructed ocean views. Although it is known especially for prime rib, teriyaki sirloin, and fresh fish, the Alaskan king crab and homemade desserts are also good. Entrées come with salad from a rather basic salad bar and bread, but in true local style, plates are light on vegetables. ⊠ *796 Kūhiō Hwy., Kapa'a,* ☎ *808/822–3791. AE, D, DC, MC, V. No lunch.*

$–$$ ✕ **Wailua Marina Restaurant.** Dockside views of boats chugging along the Wailua River make this an ideal stop before or after a trip to the Fern Grotto. An open-air dining lānai is perched right on the water, next to shores where ancient Hawaiian communities once stood. For the large number of people it serves, the restaurant has a surprisingly thoughtful menu. Baked stuffed chicken is cooked in plum sauce and served with a lobster salad, and there's a good choice of steak, stuffed pork chops, and fresh seafood dishes. ⊠ *Wailua River State Park, Wailua Rd., Wailua,* ☎ *808/822–4311. AE, DC, MC, V. Closed Mon.*

Thai

$–$$ ✕ **Mema, Thai Chinese Cuisine.** Such menu items as broccoli with oyster sauce and cashew chicken reveal their Chinese origins, but the emphasis in this attractive restaurant is on Thai dishes. A host of curries—red, green, yellow, and house—made with coconut milk and kaffir lime leaves runs from mild to mayhem in spiciness. You have a choice of chicken, beef, pork, or shrimp with several side dishes, such as stir-fried eggplant with fresh basil. Orchids, torch ginger, and Asian memorabilia highlight a pretty-in-peach interior. ⊠ *Wailua Shopping Plaza, 4-361 Kuhio Hwy., Kapa'a,* ☎ *808/823–0899. AE, D, DC, MC, V. No lunch weekends.*

The North Coast

American/Casual

$–$$ ✕ **Hanalei Gourmet.** A casual north-shore atmosphere has made this a popular hangout. There is bar and table seating and big open windows. The TV over the bar is usually tuned to sports and music programs, but the clientele is generally too busy eating and talking to watch. Breakfasts include lox and bagels with cream cheese, and croissant sandwiches with bacon and scrambled eggs. Lunch and dinner menus feature hot sandwiches, burgers, salads, soups, fresh catch, big *pūpū* (appetizer) platters, and picnic items to go. There's live music of one

286

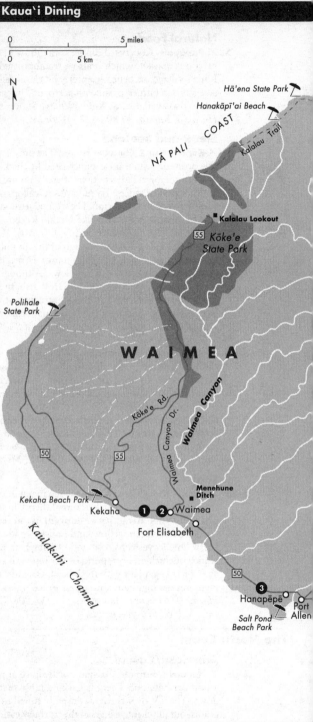

Kaua'i Dining

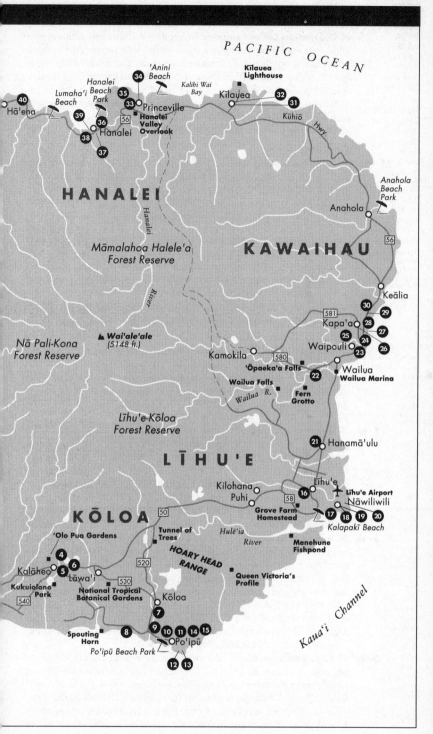

PACIFIC OCEAN

HANALEI

Lumaha'i Beach
Hā'ena
'Anini Beach
Hanalei Beach Park
Kalihi Wai Bay
Kīlauea Lighthouse
Princeville
Kīlauea
Hanalei Valley Overlook
Hanalei
Kūhiō Hwy.

KAWAIHAU

Māmalahoa Halele'a Forest Reserve
Hanalei River
Anahola Beach Park
Anahola

Nā Pali-Kona Forest Reserve
Wai'ale'ale (5148 ft.)
Keālia
Kamokila
'Ōpaeka'a Falls
Kapa'a
Wailua Falls
Waipouli
Wailua
Wailua R.
Fern Grotto
Wailua Marina

Līhu'e-Kōloa Forest Reserve

LĪHU'E
Hanamā'ulu

Kilohana
Puhi
Grove Farm Homestead
Līhu'e
Līhu'e Airport
Nāwiliwili
Kalapakī Beach

KŌLOA
'Olo Pua Gardens
Tunnel of Trees
Hulē'ia River
Menehune Fishpond
Kalāheo
Lāwa'i
Kukuiolono Park
National Tropical Botanical Gardens
HOARY HEAD RANGE
Queen Victoria's Profile
Kōloa
Kaua'i Channel
Spouting Horn
Po'ipū
Po'ipū Beach Park

sort or another every night. ✉ *5-5161 Kūhiō Hwy., across from Ching Young Center, Hanalei,* ☎ *808/826–2524. D, DC, MC, V.*

$ ✕ **Old Hanalei Coffee Company.** In a restored 1920s home, this green-and-white emporium provides a wake-up call with its specialty coffees, waffles, and egg dishes. Pastries include aloha bars made with chocolate chips and macadamia nuts, and the fresh fruit smoothie of the day is reliably yummy. Visits here can be habit-forming and relatively inexpensive. Relax on the pretty white porch, sip your cappuccino, and watch the Hanalei scene drift by. ✉ *5-5183 Kūhiō Hwy., across from Ching Young Center, Hanalei,* ☎ *808/826–6717. D, MC, V.*

Contemporary

$$–$$$ ✕ **Cafe Hanalei and Terrace.** Indoor and outdoor tables take full ad-
★   vantage of glorious views of Hanalei Bay and the peak popularly known as Bali Hai. The Sunday brunch and daily breakfast buffet are a feast of made-to-order omelets, crêpes, and fresh fruit, but the vanilla Belgian waffles and smoked peppered salmon with bagels, cream cheese, and capers are equally tasty. Luncheon selections include Japanese specialties in addition to lobster bisque, Cobb salad, and super sandwiches. For dinner try steamed *'ōpakapaka* (snapper) with ginger, cilantro, and mushrooms, or sample Friday night's seafood buffet. ✉ *Princeville Hotel, Princeville Resort, 5520 Haku Rd.,* ☎ *808/826–9644. Reservations essential. AE, D, DC, MC, V.*

$$ ✕ **Postcards Cafe.** In what was once an old house in the rice fields, this "Old Hawai'i" restaurant is decorated with vintage photos and postcards to capture the mood of an earlier era, but the food is deliciously up-to-date. Smoothies and salads made with organic fruits and vegetables, vegan dishes, Thai coconut curry, and taro fritters highlight a varied menu that emphasizes local seafood. Desserts, often made with macadamia nuts and in-season fruits, have an island flavor. Brunch is great, but service can be slow. ✉ *5-5075A Kūhiō Hwy.,* ☎ *808/826–1191. AE, MC, V. Closed Mon. No lunch.*

$–$$ ✕ **Lighthouse Bistro.** This out-of-the-way restaurant has a comfortable plantation look with windows that open wide to the outdoors, terracotta floors, bamboo chairs, and Hawaiian artwork on the walls that's for sale. Some entrées have an Italian flair, such as seafood linguine or tortellini. Others, like stuffed shrimp in phyllo and chicken satay with Thai peanut sauce, are more Pacific Rim. Hank Curtis is at the piano Friday through Saturday nights. ✉ *2484 Kaneke St., at Lighthouse Rd.,* ☎ *808/828–0480. Reservations recommended. MC, V.*

$–$$ ✕ **Surt's on the Beach.** Spacious and gracious with in-your-face views of breaking surf just beyond the Mexican tile floors, Surt's is Kaua'i's northernmost restaurant. The attached Lava Vent deli provides fresh take-out sandwiches if you're planning to picnic on a hike to Hanakāpī'ai Beach at the end of the road. French-Asian influences are found in entrées such as green curry pork and lemongrass-grilled *shutome* (swordfish) steak sandwich, but there's also hearty Dutch steaks with potatoes and light liliko'i-mango tiramisu for dessert. ✉ *5-7132 Kuhio Hwy., Hanalei,* ☎ *808/826–0060. AE, D, MC, V.*

$–$$ ✕ **Zelos Beach House.** Call the menu eclectic—what else could you say about its American-Italian-Thai-Creole leanings? The decor, however, is strictly South Pacific at this "beach-blanket bingo goes to the South Seas" kind of place. A bamboo bar, *lau hala* (pandanus leaf) mats on the walls, a kayak overhead, and Tahitian-print bar stools add to the fun—and the food is good. Burgers and burritos are served on an open-air deck. For dinner, large salads, fresh fish, pasta, steaks, and chicken pesto tortellini fill the bill. ✉ *5-5156 Kūhiō Hwy., Hanalei,* ☎ *808/826–9700. MC, V.*

SEE THE WORLD
IN FULL COLOR

Fodor's Exploring Guides bring all the great sights vividly to life with hundreds of photographs, fascinating historical background, and colorful anecdotes. Detailed maps and practical information keep you headed in the right direction.

Pair a **Fodor's** Exploring Guide with your trusted Gold Guide for a complete planning package.

When it Comes to Getting Local Currency at an ATM,

Same Thing.

Whether you're in Yosemite or Yemen, using your Visa® card or ATM card with the PLUS symbol is the easiest and most convenient way to get local currency. For example, let's say you're in France. When you make a withdrawal, using your secured PIN, it's dispensed in francs, but is debited from your account in U.S. dollars. This makes it easy to take advantage of favorable exchange rates. And if you need help finding one of Visa's 627,000 ATMs in 127 countries worldwide, visit **visa.com/pd/atm**. We'll make finding an ATM as easy as finding the Eiffel Tower, the Pyramids or even the Grand Canyon.

It's Everywhere You Want To Be®.

Italian

$$$ ✕ **La Cascata.** Terra-cotta floors, hand-painted murals, and trompe l'oeil paintings give La Cascata an Italian villa flair, and picture windows offer dazzling views of Hanalei Bay. The menu emphasizes light sauces; plenty of pastas; plus fresh seafood, beef, and lamb. Savor smoked Hawaiian marlin with fresh asparagus and caviar or sample sautéed shrimp, lobster, clams, and scallops on pasta with a spicy tomato-fennel sauce. Top it off with an airy tiramisu or the day's sorbet selection. ✉ *Princeville Hotel, Princeville Resort, 5520 Haku Rd.,* ☎ *808/826–9644. Reservations essential. AE, D, DC, MC, V. No lunch.*

$$–$$$ ✕ **Café Luna.** In a historic schoolhouse converted into shops and restaurants, Café Luna has indoor and outdoor garden-patio dining, an exhibition kitchen, and a good wine selection. For lunch or dinner, individual pizzas from the wood-burning oven come with toppings ranging from the tried-and-true (pepperoni and black olives) to the adventurous (smoked fish, caramelized onion, capers, and béchamel). Polenta with shrimp and 'ahi, *ono* (wahoo), and crab bisque are all flavorful starters, and for entrées the seared fresh fish on organic greens with wasabi vinaigrette or shrimp pasta with porcini mushrooms are recommended. Mocha mousse and tiramisu are satisfying desserts. ✉ *Hanalei Center, 5-5161 Kūhiō Hwy., Hanalei,* ☎ *808/826–1177. AE, MC, V.*

Mexican

$–$$ ✕ **Roadrunner Bakery and Café.** Casual with a capital "C," the Roadrunner has a counter where you can order fresh-baked taro rolls or bread in addition to breakfast pastries and espresso coffee. Vegetarian selections are available at lunch and dinner. The huevos rancheros have tomatillo sauce, beans, cheese, salsa, guacamole, rice, and tortillas. Burritos are huge. The filling for the "black dog" is pork, grilled taro, and black beans. Mexican scenes painted on the walls, hanging plants, ceiling fans give it a let-it-all-hang-out atmosphere. ✉ *2430 Oka St., Kīlauea,* ☎ *808/828–8226. MC, V.*

Steak and Seafood

$$–$$$ ✕ **Bali Hai.** Views of the bay are as memorable as the cuisine at this openair, tropical restaurant that is richly appointed with natural wood. A specialty is Kaua'i onion soup topped with melted provolone cheese and croutons. For entrées you have a choice of a wide variety of preparations for three types of fresh seafood served nightly. Lamb, filet mignon, and vegetarian offerings are also on the menu. For breakfast there are poi pancakes, fried taro, eggs, and griddle fare. In the adjacent Happy Talk Lounge there's nightly entertainment. ✉ *Hanalei Bay Resort, 5380 Honoiki Rd., Princeville,* ☎ *808/826–6522. AE, D, DC, MC, V.*

$$ ✕ **Chuck's Steak House.** A *paniolo* (Hawaiian cowboy) feeling permeates this split-level eatery, and saddles and blankets hang from the open-beam ceiling. Barbecue pork ribs, lobster, chicken, and Alaskan king crab are all good, but fresh island seafood and Black Angus beef is what Chuck's is known for. Can't make up your mind? They can put steak alongside almost any other entrée on a combination platter. The salad bar comes with all entrées. If you saved room for dessert, Chuck's special mud pie is a winner. ✉ *Princeville Shopping Center, Princeville,* ☎ *808/826–6211. AE, D, DC, MC, V. No lunch weekends.*

Līhu'e and Vicinity

Contemporary

$–$$ ✕ **JJ's Broiler.** Easy to find, with dining on an open deck overlooking Kalapakī Bay, this is a nautically natty place to stop for lunch or dinner. The Caesar salad could use a little spicing up, but thick and crispy french fries, potato skins, burgers, and pastrami-and-Swiss club sandwiches are reliable favorites for lunch. Dinners—herbed seafood linguine, coconut shrimp—are fancier and come with a salad bar rolled to your table. The house specialty is Slavonic steak, a broiled sliced tenderloin dipped in a buttery wine sauce. There's a shuttle bus from the harbor to take you here—a nice touch for those arriving by sea. ⊠ *Anchor Cove, Nāwiliwili,* ☎ *808/246–4422. D, MC, V.*

$–$$ ✕ **Whalers Brew Pub.** The view of the ocean and Kalapakī Bay is breathtaking whether you sit inside or outside under umbrella-shaded tables. Some diners like to sit at high "chronie bars" while they chomp down on beer-battered fish-and-chips, a 20-ounce whale of a burger, or deep-fried onion flowers. Others choose regular tables and healthier family fare: Whaler's salad bar, island-style barbecue ribs with cole slaw, or mahimahi sandwiches with french fries. Eight handcrafted ales brewed in the gleaming tanks near the entry are on offer. Seating for 300 includes separate areas for private parties. A 400-gallon aquarium adds an airy ambience. ⊠ *3132 Ninini Point St., Lihu'e,* ☎ *808/245–2000,* FAX *808/245–6580. AE, D, DC, MC, V.*

Italian

$$ ✕ **Café Portofino.** Dining here affords a panorama of mountain, sea, and sky across from Kalapakī Bay; get a table out on the lānai for the best views. The award-winning northern Italian cuisine includes such fresh pasta dishes as fettuccine in tomato, mushroom, garlic, and herb sauce. Specialties include rabbit with white wine, black olives, and herbs; and sweetbreads in a cream sauce on a bed of linguine. Italian gelati is made fresh daily. Entertainment is offered nightly. ⊠ *Pacific Ocean Plaza, 3501 Rice St., Nāwiliwili,* ☎ *808/245–2121. AE, D, DC, MC, V. No lunch weekends.*

Japanese

$–$$ ✕ **Hanam'āulu Restaurant, Tea House, Sushi Bar and Robatayaki.** The first dining room with adjacent bar that you enter in this old brown building is unexciting, but make reservations and ask for seating in one of the traditional Japanese rooms around the garden complete with carp in a peaceful pond. Chinese plate lunches with soup, salad, fried chicken, chop suey, crisp wonton, and spare ribs are the best deal, but traditional Japanese fare like sashimi, sushi, and *teishoku* (set meal) platters with miso soup, tempura shrimp, fish, and vegetables, chicken *katsu* (cutlet), and *robatayaki* (grilled seafood and meat) are the main attractions. ⊠ *1-4291 Kūhiō Hwy. 58, Hanamā'ulu,* ☎ *808/245–2511 or 808/245–3225. MC, V. Closed Mon.*

Mixed Menu

$$–$$$ ✕ **Kukui's Poolside Restaurant and Bar.** An imaginative marriage of Asian, Hawaiian, Mexican, and Continental tastes characterizes the menu at this comfortable restaurant. Open-air tables face the hotel's sprawling pool—a perfect spot to enjoy a lunch or an afternoon snack of *kālua* (roasted) pork quesadillas or Thai chicken pizza. A more formal atmosphere prevails at dinner, when the menu features selections with a Pacific Rim twist. Try lemon-rosemary chicken or a barbecued rack of lamb with shiitake risotto. At breakfast the temptations are twofold: a buffet or a full à la carte menu. ⊠ *Kaua'i Marriott Hotel Resort and Beach Club, 3610 Rice St., Lihu'e,* ☎ *808/246–5171. AE, D, DC, MC, V.*

$ ✕ **Dani's Restaurant.** Kaua'i residents frequent this big and bare local eatery near the Lihu'e Fire Station. Owners Tsutao and Harriet Morioka have created a friendly "come as you are" ambience for breakfast or lunch. Dani's is a good place to try lū'au food without commercial lū'au prices. You can order Hawaiian-style *laulau* (pork wrapped in ti leaves and steamed) or kālua pig and rice. Other island-style dishes include Japanese-prepared *tonkatsu* (pork cutlet) and teriyaki beef, and there's an all-American New York steak. ⊠ *4201 Rice St., Līhu'e,* ☎ *808/245–4991. No credit cards. Closed Sun. No dinner.*

Seafood

$$–$$$ ✕ **Duke's Canoe Club.** This popular club is a feast of beautiful native woods, greenery, and Duke Kahanamoku memorabilia, enhanced by the sound of a waterfall running alongside the staircase that leads from the upstairs dining room to the beachside Barefoot Bar. Prime rib, seafood coconut curry, smoked marlin, and linguine are available if you like, but the best order here is the fresh catch of the day—prepared as you like it, from broiled plain to firecracker Thai-chili-glazed. Hula pie (Oreo cookie crust with ice cream) is the star of the dessert menu—with strolling musicians as an accompaniment. A bar menu and lunch are available. ⊠ *Kalapakī Beach, Līhu'e,* ☎ *808/246–9599. AE, D, DC, MC, V.*

The South and West Coasts

American

$–$$ ✕ **Camp House Grill.** A simple plantation-style camp house on the road to Waimea Canyon has been transformed into a quaint little restaurant with creaky wooden floors. The food is equally down-home, with hamburgers, cheeseburgers, chicken, pork ribs, and fresh fish aimed to please families. Barbecued specialties include chicken and ribs, and huge sandwiches are served at lunchtime. Home-style breakfasts are served, and pies are baked fresh daily. As you enter Kalāheo heading west, look for the blue building on the right. There are also two other locations: 1-3959 Kaumuali'i Hwy. (Hwy. 50) in Hanapēpē (☎ 808/335–5656), and Kaua'i Village in Kapa'a (☎ 808/822–2442). ⊠ *Kaumuali'i Hwy. (Hwy. 50), Kalāheo,* ☎ *808/332–9755. MC, V.*

Contemporary

$$–$$$
★ ✕ **The Beach House.** This may have the best ocean view of any restaurant on the south shore. It's equally possible to get swept away by the cuisine here now that chef Jean-Marie Josselin (owner of the highly acclaimed A Pacific Café on Kaua'i, Maui, and O'ahu) oversees the kitchen, with chef Linda Yamada on-site. The menu changes more often than the work of local artists on the walls, but you might find grilled salmon with spinach wonton and shrimp tomato broth; wok-charred sesame-crusted mahimahi with ginger-lime beurre blanc; or grilled Black Angus fillet with tumbleweed shrimp and a port-Gorgonzola sauce. ⊠ *5022 Lawai Rd., Kōloa,* ☎ *808/742–1424. AE, D, DC, MC, V. No lunch.*

$$–$$$ ✕ **Shells Restaurant.** You'll hear the surf as you dine here on the lānai or inside the high-ceilinged restaurant. The dining room is lighted by big shell chandeliers salvaged after Hurricane 'Iniki, and the airy, tropical room has rattan furnishings that make it easy to relax. Menu highlights include crab cakes; rack of lamb with herb and hoisin crust; and fresh fish and prawns with spicy pineapple, baked sweet potato, Kaua'i slaw, and steamed rice. A great tropical topper is Mount Wai'ale'ale chocolate mousse cake with sorbet and fresh fruit, or a choice of desserts from the buffet. Adjacent is a lounge called the Point, which also features an ocean view and has indoor and outdoor seating for predinner cocktails at sunset. ⊠ *Sheraton Kaua'i Resort, 2440 Ho'onani Rd., Po'ipū Beach, Kōloa,* ☎ *808/742–1661. AE, D, DC, MC, V. No lunch.*

$–$$ ✕ **Plantation House Café.** This is a friendly family restaurant in Po'ipū Shopping Village with wooden floors, green shutters, and white decks that look like those on early plantation homes. Sit-down, takeout, and delivery service are offered for lunch and dinner, and they also serve espresso and bakery goods at breakfast. You can order eight kinds of pizza, including Hawaiian with fresh pineapple. Besides pizza, there is something on the menu to suit anyone's taste—from Chinese chop salad to barbe-

cued half chicken to hot-and-spicy sweet chili shrimp to desserts of coconut macadamia-nut bread pudding—and everything is delicious. Wine
and beer are served. ⊠ *Po'ipū Shopping Village, 2360 Kiahuna Plantation Dr., Kōloa,* ☎ *808/742–7373. AE, D, DC, MC, V.*

$–$$ ✕ **Tomkats Grille.** This casual drop-in eatery keeps kids happy during
lunch or early dinner hours with tropical ponds, a little waterfall, and
a section of the menu geared to young tastes. Adults might pass up the
PB&J for chicken marinara, barbecue pork ribs, a burger, or a Reuben
accompanied by a glass of wine or a choice of 35 ales, stouts, ports,
and lagers. Plenty of Tomkats' Nibblers—buffalo wings, stuffed mushrooms, jalapeño poppers—enliven happy hour from 4 to 6. ⊠ *5402
Kōloa Rd., Kōloa,* ☎ *808/742–8887. DC, MC, V.*

$–$$ ✕ **Waimea Brewing Company.** This Kaua'i brew pub fits the laid-back
ambience of Waimea Plantation Cottages, where it is housed in a spacious,
airy room with hardwood floors surrounded by open-air decks. Entrées
served in two sizes and reasonable prices attract Islanders and visitors on
their way to Waimea Canyon. Dine indoors amid rattan furnishings or
at a bar decorated with petroglyphs and colored with Kaua'i red dirt. The
chef turns out smoked chicken quesadillas, grilled Portobellos, hamburgers, kalbi beef short ribs, and fresh fish. It's a good place to pick up
a picnic basket on the way to the canyon, or stop on the way back for a
Wai'ale'ale Golden Ale or Alakai Stout and a little live music on weekends. ⊠ *9400 Kaumuali'i Hwy., Waimea,* ☎ *808/338–9733. MC, V.*

Italian

$$–$$$ ✕ **Casa di Amici.** Casa di Amici means "house of friends," and with
rattan furnishings under ceiling fans inside and deck seating with
sweeping ocean views outside, it feels like the kama'aina home the building once was. The menu is broader than Italian-Mediterranean, including
French, Thai, Japanese, and Vietnamese touches, but you'll find traditional *antipasti* (starters), *zuppe* (soup), pasta, *insalata* (salads), and
pietanza maggiore (main courses). You can mix your favorite pasta with
your choice of sauce, including pesto and *salsa arrabiatta* (a spicy
tomato sauce with sautéed pancetta and crushed chili pepper), or savor
the house scampi. Most entrées can be ordered in "light" or regular
portions. ⊠ *2301 Nalo Rd., Po'ipū,* ☎ *808/742–1555. Reservations
recommended. AE, D, DC, MC, V.*

$$–$$$ ✕ **Dondero's at the Hyatt Regency Kaua'i.** Inlaid marble floors, ornate
green tile work, and ivy and Italianate murals make it difficult to choose
between indoor and outdoor dining in this elegant restaurant. Porcini
mushroom crêpes with Parmesan sauce, a perfectly seasoned Caesar salad,
and *spiedini* (skewered lobster, scallops, and shrimp suspended over tender gnocchi pillows) might have sprung from an artist's palate. Chocolate hazelnut torte and sinfully rich crème brûlée are decadent indulgences
to close the meal. ⊠ *Hyatt Regency Kaua'i Resort and Spa, 1571 Po'ipū
Rd., Kōloa,* ☎ *808/742–1234. AE, D, DC, MC, V. No lunch.*

$$–$$$ ✕ **Piatti.** This historic home, once the residence of a plantation man-
ager, now offers Italian food served in a Polynesian atmosphere—a tri-
partite mix you'll find only in Aloha Land. Gardens with torchlit paths,
rich wood interiors, and veranda dining will spark romance. Fresh
herbs come from the manager's garden, and the island fish might have
been caught only hours before reaching your table. Flavors are outstanding
in such dishes as marinated grilled eggplant filled with goat cheese and
sun-dried tomatoes; pizza with Portobello mushrooms, pancetta, and
fontina cheese baked in the wood-burning oven; or the meltingly tender osso buco served with saffron risotto. ⊠ *2253 Po'ipū Rd., Kiahuna
Plantation, Kōloa,* ☎ *808/742–2216. AE, DC, MC, V. No lunch.*

$$–$$$ ✕ **Pomodoro.** This intimate, family-run restaurant is brightened by pink
linens, rattan chairs, and two walls of windows. Begin with prosciutto

and melon, and then proceed directly to the lasagna (a favorite of the chefs, who are two Italian-born brothers). Other menu highlights include eggplant or veal parmigiana and scampi in a garlic, caper, and white-wine sauce. Freshly baked garlic bread and seasonal vegetables come with each meal. ⊠ *Upstairs at Rainbow Plaza, Kaumuali'i Hwy. (Hwy. 50), Kalāheo,* ☎ *808/332–5945. MC, V. No lunch.*

Mixed Menu

$$–$$$ ✕ **Roy's Po'ipū Bar & Grill.** Hawai'i's culinary superstar Roy Yamaguchi
★ opened his sleek Kaua'i restaurant in 1994, and it quickly became a mecca for fans of his Euro-Asian Pacific cuisine. Who but Roy would turn smoked duck into *gyoza* (Japanese dumplings) and serve the appetizer with star-fruit passion sauce, or team fresh seared *'ōpakapaka* (snapper) with orange shrimp butter and Chinese black bean sauce? There are 15 to 20 or more specials nightly. Dark chocolate soufflé and volcanic puffed pastry are regulars on the dessert menu. ⊠ *Po'ipū Shopping Village, 2360 Kiahuna Plantation Dr., Po'ipū Beach,* ☎ *808/742–5000. AE, D, DC, MC, V. No lunch.*

$–$$ ✕ **Green Garden.** Hanging and standing plants throughout characterize this aptly named family-run restaurant, a favorite dining spot for Kaua'i residents and visitors since 1948. The Green Garden is very low-key, and the waitresses treat you like longtime friends. The food is no-frills local fare. Come here for the atmosphere first and the meals second. Dinner includes some 30 items of local, Asian, and American influence. The seafood special is breaded mahimahi fillet, scallops, oysters, and deep-fried shrimp. The homemade desserts are the best part of a meal here, particularly the liliko'i chiffon pie. ⊠ *Hwy. 50, Hanapēpē,* ☎ *808/335–5422. AE, MC, V. Closed Tues.*

Steak and Seafood

$$–$$$ ✕ **House of Seafood.** Tropical vines wrap themselves around the handsome exposed beams of this restaurant overlooking the Po'ipū Resort tennis courts. Under this establishment's soaring ceilings try island seafood, from 'ahi to *weke* (goatfish). Preparations for 10 types of fish vary nightly. A variety of shellfish is also available, including lobster. Caesar salad is made fresh at your table, and all entrées come with fresh vegetables, almond rice pilaf, and freshly baked rolls. Delicious kiwi crêpes flambées and bananas Foster garner raves for dessert. ⊠ *Po'ipū Kai Resort, 1941 Po'ipū Rd., Po'ipū,* ☎ *808/742–6433. AE, D, DC, MC, V. No lunch.*

$$–$$$ ✕ **Tidepools.** The Hyatt Regency Kaua'i has three superb restaurants, but this one delivers the most tropical atmosphere. Dine in one of the grass-thatched huts that float on a koi-filled pond, and enjoy views of the romantic torchlit grounds and starry Po'ipū skies. A major advocate of Hawai'i regional cuisine, which utilizes Kaua'i-grown products, the chef prepares fish with a variety of local flavors. Specialties include macadamia-crusted fish, prime rib, and filet mignon. ⊠ *Hyatt Regency Kaua'i, 1571 Po'ipū Rd., Kōloa,* ☎ *808/742–6260. AE, D, DC, MC, V. No lunch.*

$–$$$ ✕ **Brennecke's Beach Broiler.** Right across from Po'ipū Beach Park, this place has been around for years, and happily so. Large open windows look out onto palm trees and the ocean, and pretty window boxes filled with petunias further brighten the scene. The restaurant specializes in kiawe-wood broiled foods—New York steak covered with mushrooms and beef ribs smothered in barbecue sauce. Brennecke's also serves fresh clams, catch of the day, Hawaiian spiny lobster, and gourmet burgers. The well-stocked all-you-can-eat salad bar with bread and chowder is a good deal. ⊠ *Ho'one Rd., Po'ipū,* ☎ *808/742–7588. AE, D, DC, MC, V.*

$$ ✕ **Kalāheo Steak House.** It's the huge cut of prime rib, the tender top sirloin, the Cornish game hen in spicy herb and citrus marinade, and the succulent Alaskan king crab legs that make locals seek out this restaurant. Ceiling fans stir the air through open wooden louvers in the dark wood-paneled interior of this old building. Dinners are served with salad, rolls, and a choice of rice or baked potato. Rum cake, baked fresh daily, comes with Lappert's ice cream (made at a factory just up the road). Wines range from $8 to $25 a bottle. Children up to 11 can order from a separate low-priced menu. ⊠ *4444 Papalina Rd., Kalāheo,* ☎ *808/ 332–9780. D, MC, V. No lunch.*

$–$$ ✕ **Keoki's Paradise.** Seafood stars at this Po'ipū favorite, styled to resemble a dockside boathouse. Though it sits in a corner of the inland Po'ipū Shopping Village, tinkling streams, lush foliage, and thatched roofs over the bar create an outdoor Polynesian atmosphere. Even the appetizers have an ocean flavor—from sashimi to fisherman's chowder. There is a sampling of beef and pork entrées for committed carnivores, but the day's fresh catch is what brings patrons to Keoki's. Choose from a half-dozen preparation styles and sauces, and save room for the hula pie. ⊠ *Po'ipū Shopping Village, Po'ipū Beach,* ☎ *808/742–7534. AE, D, DC, MC, V.*

$–$$ ✕ **Wrangler's Steakhouse.** Wrangler's seems right out of the Wild West, with wooden floors and tables, denim-upholstered seating, and saddles and a stagecoach on display. Steak—sizzling and prepared with either garlic, capers, peppers, or teriyaki—can be ordered in a he-man 16-ounce size, but if meat is not your thing, opt for the fresh catch, scampi, or one of the Mexican entrées. Local folks love the kaukau tin lunch: soup, rice, beef teriyaki, and shrimp tempura served in a three-tiered tin lunch pail (the kind that sugar plantation workers once carried). A gift shop features local crafts (and sometimes a craftsperson), a deck out back allows open-air dining, and the adjoining Pacific Pizza and Deli (with some of the most imaginative pizzas around) is part of the same family-run complex. ⊠ *98-52 Kaumuali'i Hwy., Waimea,* ☎ *808/338–1218. AE, MC, V. Closed Sun.*

LODGING

Whether you choose to stay at a plush Po'ipū resort or condo, where you can bask all day in the sun; at the posh Princeville Resort, where you can enjoy world-class golfing; or at a Coconut Coast guest house, where you can take advantage of an abundance of nearby shops and restaurants, plan to make advance reservations. Peak months are February and August. When booking your accommodations, ask about such extras as special tennis, golf, honeymoon, and room-and-car packages. For explanations of price categories, *see* Dining *in* Smart Travel Tips A to Z at the back of the book.

The East and North Coasts

$$$$ 🛏 **Princeville Hotel.** As you walk through the enormous, grand lobby
★   you can't miss the sweeping views across Hanalei Bay and the majestic backdrop of Bali Hai's mountain peaks. You feel as if you've truly arrived in the Land of the Lotus Eaters. Almost all guest rooms take advantage of this jaw-dropping vista. All have marble bathrooms, gold-plated fixtures, handsome appointments, and a bathroom feature called a privacy window, which can be opaque or, with a flip of a switch, clear so you can see the view outside while in the shower. A drink at sunset at the Living Room, the lobby bar, is an event, complete with a traditional Hawaiian ceremony. There's often entertainment, such as a jazz trio, here in the evening. There are two top-ranked 18-hole golf courses, one of which was voted one of the 10 best in country in 1998 by *Golf Digest*. There is an exercise room in the hotel and a health

club that can be reached by shuttle. The pool area, with several hot tubs and a swim-up bar, is stunning. The hotel has a convenient check-in procedure: The valet parking attendant has your room key, and the bellman who delivers your bags checks you in. ✉ *5520 Ka Haku Rd. (Box 3069), Princeville 96722,* ☎ *808/826–9644 or 800/826–4400,* FAX *808/826–1166. 201 rooms, 51 suites. 3 restaurants, 2 bars, minibars, room service, pool, massage, 2 18-hole golf courses, 8 tennis courts, exercise rooms, health club, beach, children's programs (ages 5–12), dry cleaning, laundry service, concierge, business services, meeting rooms, travel services. AE, D, DC, MC, V.* 🐾

$$$$ 🏨 **Secret Beach Hideaway.** You could start a romance or write the great American novel—anything seems possible at four sumptuous, very private retreats offered here. Two one-bedroom, one-bath cottages with kitchens and indoor-outdoor garden showers have marble and granite touches. Picture windows in the living rooms of each cottage frame 11 acres of landscaped grounds—one with a natural waterfall, the other with a freshwater stream—that slope to Secret Beach; few find these hidden sands, a haven for families and privacy-seekers. Two other larger, luxury houses, which attract Hollywood types, are on separate properties. There's a onetime cleaning fee of $100. ✉ *2884 Kauapea Rd. (Box 781), Kīlauea 96754,* ☎ *808/828–2862 or 970/925–7445,* FAX *971/ 925–1662. 2 cottages, 2 houses. Fans, hot tubs.*

$$$–$$$$ 🏨 **Hanalei Bay Resort.** The clifftop location of these 16 low-rise buildings overlooks Hanalei Bay and the north shore. Units are extremely spacious, some as large as 2,000 square ft. They have high, sloping ceilings and large private lānai with mountain or bay views. Rattan furniture and island art add a casual feeling to rooms that come with kitchens. Studios, which have kitchenettes that are not meant for serious cooking, have rattan furniture and forest green decor. There's a lava-rock waterfall by the hot tub. ✉ *5380 Honoiki Rd., Princeville 96722,* ☎ *808/826–6522 or 800/367–5004,* FAX *808/826–6680. 161 rooms, 75 suites. Restaurant, lobby lounge, kitchenettes (some), pool, hot tub, 18-hole golf course, 4 tennis courts, coin laundry. AE, D, DC, MC, V.* 🐾

$$$–$$$$ 🏨 **Hanalei Colony Resort.** This 5-acre beachfront property has an ideal location near the mysterious and verdant north end of the island. It sits on the road heading north, with magnificent mountains on one side and the ocean on the other. Each two-bedroom unit has a private lānai and kitchen, but no TVs or phones will interrupt the peaceful splendor of your visit. Free daily workshops teach guests about Hawaiian culture and art, from stringing lei to weaving lau hala mats. A barbecue gazebo is handy when you don't want to dine in the restaurant next door. ✉ *5-7130 Kūhiō Hwy. (Box 206), Hā'ena 96714,* ☎ *808/ 826–6235 or 800/628–3004,* FAX *808/826–9893. 52 suites. Kitchenettes, pool, hot tub, coin laundry. AE, MC, V.* 🐾

$$$–$$$$ 🏨 **Holiday Inn SunSpree Resort.** This hotel has ocean views, but it's a short walk via Lydgate Park to the beach. Kids love the playground at the park and the beach has a protected area so it's safe for youngsters. A bubbling waterfall and exotic flowers enhance the lobby, and rooms have dark green carpets, pastel colors, rattan furnishings, and large windows. A complimentary children's program and such adult activities as shuffleboard, tennis, and beach volleyball are part of the package, as are free local phone calls and in-room coffee. ✉ *3-5920 Kūhiō Hwy., Kapa'a 96746,* ☎ *808/246–6976 or 888/823–5111,* FAX *808/823–6666. 188 rooms, 2 suites, 26 cabana suites. Restaurant, deli, lobby lounge, 2 pools, hot tub, 2 tennis courts, exercise room, shuffleboard, volleyball, children's programs (ages 4–12). AE, D, DC, MC, V.* 🐾

$$$–$$$$ 🏨 **Kaua'i Coast Resort.** Eight miles north of Līhu'e Airport, this condominium resort is well situated for east- and north-shore sightseeing. It's also a five-minute drive from the Wailua Municipal Golf Course

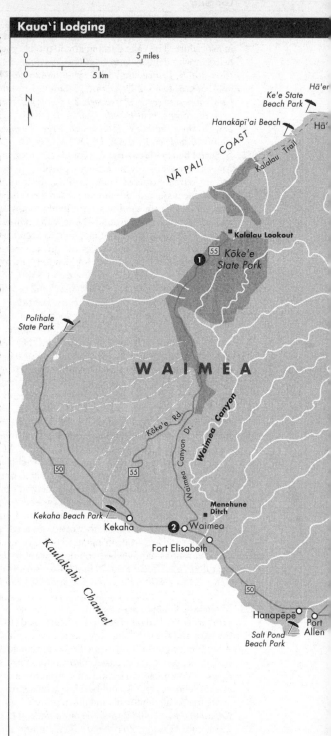

Kaua'i Lodging

PACIFIC OCEAN

Beach Park

Hanalei Beach Park

Lumaha'i Beach

'Anini Beach

Kalihi Wai Bay

34 33

32

Kīlauea Lighthouse

Kīlauea

Maniholo Dry Cave

35

Princeville

Hanalei Valley Overlook

56

Hanalei

Kūhiō Hwy.

Anahola

Anahola Beach Park

H A N A L E I

Hanalei River

Māmalahoa Halele'a Forest Reserve

K A W A I H A U

56

Nā Pali-Kona Forest Reserve

▲ Wai'ale'ale (5148 ft.)

Keālia

581

31

Kapa'a

30

Kamokila

580

Waipouli

27

24

29

'Ōpaeka'a Falls

Wailua

Wailua Marina

28

Wailua Falls

Fern Grotto

23

26

Wailua R.

25

22

Hanamā'ulu

L Ī H U ' E

Kilohana

Puhi

Līhu'e

Līhu'e Airport

Nāwiliwili

21

Līhu'e-Kōloa Forest Reserve

Grove Farm Homestead

58

20

K Ō L O A

50

Kalapakī Beach

'Olo Pua Gardens

Tunnel of Trees

Hulē'ia River

Menehune Fishpond

19

Kalāheo

Lāwa'i

520

H O A R Y   H E A D   R A N G E

Kukuiolono Park

530

National Tropical Botanical Gardens

Kōloa

Queen Victoria's Profile

Kaua'i Channel

540

7

Spouting Horn

3 4

5

Po'ipū

18

Mahaulepu

6

17

Shipwreck Beach

11

8

9

10

Po'ipū Beach Park

12

13 14

15

16

and within walking distance of the Coconut Marketplace. The three-building, three-story resort is set along an uncrowded stretch of Waipouli Beach. The property was purchased by Shell Vacations and remodeled in 2000 to create one- and two-bedroom condos and some time-share units. They are decorated in rich sage, persimmon, and golds following the theme of "My Old Hawaiian Home." A pool with bridge and waterfall is visible from the spacious lānai of many rooms. ☒ *4-484 Kūhiō Hwy., Kapa'a 96746, ☎ 808/822–3441 or 800/922–7866, FAX 808/822–0843. 108 1- and 2-bedroom condos and time-shares, 6 hotel rooms. Restaurant, lobby lounge, refrigerators, 2 pools, hot tub, tennis court. AE, D, DC, MC, V.* ✸

$$$–$$$$ 🏨 **Kaua'i Coconut Beach Resort.** On 11 acres of beachfront property midway between north- and south-shore attractions and within walking distance of three major shopping centers, this full-service resort's location can't be beat. Its award-winning nightly lū'au is considered the most authentic by many, and free hula and torch-lighting shows at sunset perpetuate aloha spirit. Rooms have pale green walls, peach accents, and floral bedspreads. ☒ *Kūhiō Hwy., Box 830, Kapa'a 96746, ☎ 808/822–3455 or 800/222–5642, FAX 808/822–1830. 309 rooms, 2 suites. Restaurant, lobby lounge, air-conditioning, refrigerators, room service, pool, hot tub, 3 tennis courts, jogging, shuffleboard, meeting rooms. AE, D, DC, MC, V.* ✸

$$$–$$$$ 🏨 **Outrigger Lae Nani.** Ruling Hawaiian chiefs once returned from ocean voyages to this spot, now host to condominiums comfortable enough for minor royalty. An oceanside heiau and hotel-sponsored Hawaiiana programs, with a booklet for self-guided historical tours, are a special plus. Units are all decorated differently, with full kitchens and expansive lānai. Your view of landscaped grounds is interrupted only by a large pool before ending at a sandy ocean beach. A barbecue and picnic area is on-site as well. ☒ *410 Papaloa Rd., Kapa'a 96746, ☎ 808/822–4938 or 800/688–7444, FAX 808/822–1022. 84 condominiums (60 rentals). Picnic area, kitchenettes, pool, tennis court, beach. AE, MC, V.* ✸

$$$ 🏨 **Plantation Hale Resort.** Across from the beach and near Coconut Marketplace, these attractive units have kitchens, garden lānai, and a homey feel. Rooms are clean and pretty, with rose carpets, white rattan furnishings, and pastel colors. You couldn't ask for a more convenient location for dining, shopping, and sightseeing on either end of the island. Ask for a unit on the makai side, away from Kūhiō Highway. ☒ *484 Kūhiō Hwy., Kapa'a 96746, ☎ 808/822–4941 or 800/775–4253, FAX 808/822–5599. 160 condominiums (143 rentals). Air-conditioning, in-room safes, kitchenettes, 3 pools, hot tub, putting green. AE, D, DC, MC, V.* ✸

$$–$$$ 🏨 **Islander on the Beach.** The eight three-story buildings of this pleasant 6-acre beachfront property have a low-key Hawai'i plantation look. Rooms have showers but not tubs; dark carpeting is brightened by open-air lānai and lovely green lawns outside. A free-form pool is right next to a golden-sand beach, and you can take the lounge chairs to the ocean's edge. Shops, restaurants, and a cinema are at the adjacent Coconut Marketplace. ☒ *484 Kūhiō Hwy., Kapa'a 96746, ☎ 808/822–7417 or 800/847–7417, FAX 808/822–1947. 194 rooms, 2 suites. Restaurant, bar, pool, hot tub, tennis court, volleyball, coin laundry, meeting room. AE, D, DC, MC, V.*

$$–$$$ 🏨 **Kaua'i Sands.** For money-saving beachfront accommodations this establishment might serve you well. The green-and-blue decor of the rooms may seem outdated, but carpets were replaced in 1999. With the ocean right outside and your need to get wet and tan primary . . . who cares about colors? Wide lawns to the beach look inviting for playing or unwinding, and for shade you'll find a restaurant and lounge up-close to sunswept seas and ocean vistas. Units in the two two-story buildings are air-conditioned; those with kitchenettes cost a few extra dollars. ⊠ *420 Papaloa Rd., Kapa'a 96746,* ☎ *808/822–4951 or 800/367–7000,* FAX *808/922–0052. 198 rooms, 2 suites. Restaurant, lobby lounge, kitchenettes, 2 pools. AE, D, DC, MC, V.* 😊

$$ 🏨 **Kapa'a Sands.** With only 20 condominiums, the Kapa'a Sands is an intimate gem. At seaside on the eastern coast, it's on the site of an old Japanese Shinto temple—an old rock etched with Japanese characters is a remnant of its presence. Small rooms are equipped with ceiling fans, appropriate for beachside bungalows, and have full kitchens, all with dishwashers and garbage disposals. Ask for an oceanfront room to get an open-air lānai. The landscaping around the eight two-story buildings includes meandering pathways lined with palms, gingers, and other tropical flora. ⊠ *380 Papaloa Rd., Kapa'a 96746,* ☎ *808/822–4901 or 800/222–4901,* FAX *808/822–1556. 20 condominiums. Fans, in-room VCRs, pool. MC, V.*

$–$$ 🏨 **Hotel Coral Reef.** This older, well-maintained hotel is right on the sand's edge, although the swimming in front of the hotel is not as good as at the public beaches nearby. Colorful bedspreads liven up the bare-minimum furnishings. Upper units have carpeting. Ground-level rooms are done in terrazzo tile with patios that lead directly to the beach, where there are barbecue grills. Oceanfront accommodations have private lānai and refrigerators. Continental breakfast is served. The property is ideally situated, near shopping, dining, and sightseeing, and the rates are attractive. ⊠ *1516 Kūhiō Hwy., Kapa'a 96746,* ☎ *808/822–4481 or 800/843–4659,* FAX *808/822–7705. 24 rooms, 2 suites. Beach, coin laundry. MC, V.* 😊

Līhu'e and Vicinity

$$$$ 🏨 **Kaua'i Marriott Resort & Beach Club.** Public areas here impart a sense
★ of grandeur, carried out by an elaborate tropical garden, luxuriant plantings, and waterfalls right off the lobby, plus there's a huge, cinematic pool worthy of Xanadu. Poolside dining makes use of this two-tier, templelike extravaganza. The hotel nestles in the 800-acre, independently owned Kaua'i Lagoons Resort. There's a lovely beach and lagoon to rest beside as well. ⊠ *3610 Rice St., Kalapakī Beach, Līhu'e 96766,* ☎ *808/245–5050 or 800/220–2925,* FAX *808/245–5049. 356 rooms, 11 suites, 232 time-share units. 2 restaurants, lobby lounge, minibars, room service, pool, 5 outdoor hot tubs, spa, 2 18-hole golf courses, 7 tennis courts, health club, beach, children's programs (ages 5–12). AE, D, DC, MC, V.* 😊

$$$ 🏨 **Outrigger Kaua'i Beach Hotel.** Designed with sensitivity to the history of the nearby Wailua River area, this low-rise, horseshoe-shape hotel surrounds a pool complex designed with rock-sculpted slopes, waterfalls, tropical flowers, and a cave resembling the Fern Grotto. Each night at sunset, staff in native dress light 100 tiki torches around the pools. Guest rooms are decorated in muted tones of peach, mauve, teal, and off-white, and lānai have views of mountains, gardens, or the sea. ⊠ *4331 Kaua'i Beach Dr., Līhu'e 96766,* ☎ *808/245–1955 or 800/ 688–7444,* FAX *808/246–9085. 341 rooms, 5 suites. 2 restaurants, 2 lobby lounges, room service, 3 pools, hot tub, 18-hole golf course, 4 tennis courts. AE, D, DC, MC, V.* 😊

$–$$ 🏨 **Garden Island Inn.** This handy three-story inn, across the road from Kalapakī Beach and Anchor Cove shopping center, is a bargain. The facilities and fantasy of the elegant Kaua'i Marriott are just down the beach. Orchid suites on the top floor and tropical rooms on the second have lānai and glimpses of the ocean. Budget rooms are on the ground floor. Rooms have linoleum tile and queen or two twin beds. Innkeepers Steve and Susan Layne loan boogie boards and snorkeling and golf equipment and give away fruit from their trees. ⊠ *3445 Wilcox Rd., Kalapakī Bay 96766,* ☎ *808/245–7227 or 800/648– 0154,* FAX *808/245–7603. 21 rooms, 2 suites. Air-conditioning, fans, kitchenettes. AE, DC, MC, V.* ☜

$ 🏨 **Hale Līhu'e Motel.** Nearly all the sights of the north, south, and west portions of the island are within an easy hour's drive of this well-situated Līhu'e motel. And the price can't be beat. From the outside the low-rise building looks run-down, but the inside is clean though the no-frills rooms are small. Kitchenettes are available. Ask in advance for one of the air-conditioned rooms. ⊠ *2931 Kalena St., Līhu'e 96766,* ☎ *808/245–2751. 18 rooms. No credit cards.*

The South Coast

$$$$ 🏨 **Embassy Vacation Resort Po'ipū Point.** Kaua'i's most luxurious
★   condominium complex combines hotel services with such condo-style amenities as kitchens, washers and dryers, and a barbecue area. Large suites have plush carpeting, European-style cabinetry, and granite kitchen countertops. The 22-acre grounds include lily ponds, reflecting pools, and a swimming pool surrounded by sand. Complimentary Continental breakfast and evening cocktail reception are hosted in the club room. ⊠ *1613 Pe'e Rd., Kōloa 96756,* ☎ *808/742–1888 or 800/ 426–3350,* FAX *808/742–1924. 210 2-bedroom suites. Bar, kitchenettes, pool, 2 hot tubs, health club, concierge. AE, D, DC, MC, V.* ☜

$$$$ 🏨 **Hyatt Regency Kaua'i Resort and Spa.** This superbly designed, dra-
★   matically handsome, classic Hawaiian low-rise hotel has airy courtyards and gardens. Rooms, two-thirds with ocean views, further the plantation theme with bamboo and wicker furnishings and island art. Five acres of meandering fresh- and saltwater swimming lagoons are beautifully set amid landscaped grounds. The Anara Spa and Fitness Center, with a food bar, lap pool, hot tub, and massage rooms, covers 25,000 square ft. ⊠ *1571 Po'ipū Rd., Kōloa 96756,* ☎ *808/742– 1234 or 800/233–1234,* FAX *808/742–6265. 60 rooms, 37 suites. 5 restaurants, 2 bars, 3 lobby lounges, minibars, room service, 3 pools (1 saltwater), spa, 18-hole golf course, 4 tennis courts, health club, beach, nightclub. AE, D, DC, MC, V.* ☜

$$$$ 🏨 **Po'ipū Shores.** These three low-rise buildings, with a pool in front of the middle one, sit right on a rocky point above pounding surf—a perfect spot for whale- or turtle-watching. Weddings are staged on a little lawn beside the ocean. A sandy swimming beach is a 10-minute walk away. Units are all decorated differently by individual owners. Two share a sundeck, the rest have lānai, but all have great windows and many of them have bedrooms on the ocean side. Kitchens have microwaves and washer and dryers. In addition, there are two barbecue areas on the property. ⊠ *1775 Pe'e Rd., Kōloa 96756,* ☎ *808/742– 7700 or 800/367–5004,* FAX *808/742–9720. 39 condominium suites. Fans, kitchenettes, pool. AE, MC, V.* ☜

$$$$ 🏨 **Sheraton Kaua'i Resort.** Returning guests will recognize a few touches from the old Sheraton Kaua'i, which was reopened late in 1997 after rebuilding due to Hurricane 'Iniki. The lobby opens onto a central courtyard surrounded by shops and an area under a banyan tree where Hawaiian artisans stage demonstrations. Four-story guest wings are right on the beach or in a garden cluster. Beachfront rooms in muted sand and eggshell colors are highlighted with tapa dividers, and garden rooms have a brighter palette. A wedding gazebo has an ocean backdrop. There's a children's pool, and children's programs are free in summer. ⊠ *2440 Ho'onani Rd., Po'ipū Beach, Kōloa 96756,* ☎ *808/ 742–1661 or 888/847–0208,* FAX *808/742–9777. 399 rooms, 14 suites. 4 restaurants, bar, room service, 2 pools, massage, 3 tennis courts, ex-*

ercise room, beach, water slide, children's programs (ages 5–12), meet-ing rooms. AE, D, DC, MC, V. 🖎

$$$$ 🏨 **Whalers Cove.** All 38 one- and two-bedroom condos in two low-rise buildings face the water and share a swimming pool, which is al-most near enough to the surf to cast out a fishing line. The rocky beach is good for snorkeling, but a short drive or brisk walk will get you to a sandy stretch. A handsome koa-bedecked reception area offers full services for the plush units. The grandest bathrooms have whirlpool tubs on a raised platforms, separate showers, and twin sinks. Two bar-becue areas, big picture windows, spacious living rooms, lānai, and mod-ern kitchens with washer-dryers make this a place to leave home for. ✉ *2640 Puʻuholo Rd., Kōloa 96756,* 🕾 *808/742–7571 or 800/225–2683,* 𝔽𝔸𝕏 *808/742–1185. 38 1- and 2-bedroom condominiums. Kitch-enettes, fans, pool, hot tub. AE, MC, V.* 🖎

$$$–$$$$ 🏨 **Kiahuna Plantation.** This 35-acre oceanfront resort's expansive lawns hold 42 plantation-style, low-rise buildings. The one- and two-bedroom units have pastel color schemes and rattan furnishings. The administrative office and an excellent Italian restaurant, Piatti, are in a lovely sugar-plantation manor house dating from the early 1900s. Lily ponds and Hawaiian gardens with plant labels enhance the set-ting. ✉ *2253 Poʻipū Rd., Kōloa 96756,* 🕾 *808/742–2200 or 800/367–5004,* 𝔽𝔸𝕏 *800/477–2329 or 808/742–1047. 333 condominium units. Restaurant, kitchenettes, pool, 18-hole golf course, 6 tennis courts. AE, DC, MC, V.* 🖎

$$$–$$$$ 🏨 **Makahuena at Poʻipū.** These extra large, tastefully decorated suites with white tile and sand-color carpets are housed in two- and three-story white wooden buildings surrounded by well-kept lawns. Suites have kitchens and washer-dryers. There's a barbecue area on the prop-erty. Situated near the center of Poʻipū on a rocky point over the ocean, Shipwreck Beach is several blocks to the east and Poʻipū Beach is also close by. ✉ *1661 Peʻe Rd., Poʻipū 96756,* 🕾 *808/742–2482 or 800/367–5004,* 𝔽𝔸𝕏 *808/742–2379. 79 2- and 3-bedroom suites. Pool, hot tub, tennis court. AE, MC, V.* 🖎

$$$–$$$$ 🏨 **Poʻipū Kapili.** Ultraspacious one- and two-bedroom units, minutes from Poʻipū restaurants, enjoy garden and across-the-street ocean views combined with privacy. Architects managed to give a plantation look to the two-story, white-frame exteriors and double-pitched roofs, which complement the tropical landscaping. Decorator-designed inte-riors include full kitchens and entertainment centers. Guests can choose to mingle at a weekly morning coffee hour held beside the ocean-view pool. There is an herb garden and an on-site library stocked with videos and books. ✉ *2221 Kapili Rd., Kōloa 96756,* 🕾 *808/742–6449 or 800/443–7714,* 𝔽𝔸𝕏 *808/742–9162. 60 condominiums. In-room VCRs, pool, 2 tennis courts, library. MC, V.* 🖎

$$$ 🏨 **Garden Isle Cottages.** The theme of each of these reasonably priced, spacious oceanside accommodations is Hawaiian, and tropical flower gardens surround the cottages for an exotic touch. It's a five-minute walk to the restaurants of nearby Poʻipū. Five of seven units have kitchens with microwaves, ceiling fans, and washers and dryers, so request this when you reserve if it's important to you. Units do not have tele-phones. There's also a barbecue area. ✉ *2666 Puʻuholo Rd., Kōloa 96756,* 🕾 *808/742–6717 or 800/742–6711. 7 cottages. Fans. No credit cards.* 🖎

$$$ 🏨 **Gloria's Spouting Horn Bed & Breakfast.** The classiest oceanfront bed-★ and-breakfast on Kauaʻi, this cedar home was built by owners Gloria and Bob Merkle specifically to house guests. Breakfast, snacks, and a chilled beverage are available in the comfortable common room with its soaring A-frame ceiling and ocean-immediate deck. Waves dash the black rocks below, while just above the ocean's edge a man-made sand

beach invites sunbathers. All three bedrooms have four-poster beds with romantic canopies, oceanside lānai, and bathrooms with deep soaking tubs and separate showers. ⊠ *4464 Lawai Rd., Po'ipū,* ☎ *808/742–6995. 3 rooms. Refrigerators, in-room VCRs, pool. No credit cards.* ✍

$$$ 🏨 **Suite Paradise Po'ipū Kaī.** Luxuriously appointed apartments, many with cathedral ceilings and all with big windows surrounded by spreading lawns, give this property the feeling of a spacious, quiet retreat inside and out. Big furnished lānai have views to the ocean and across the 110-acre landscaped grounds. Some units are two level, some have sleeping lofts, all are furnished with modern kitchens. There are barbecue facilities as well. House of Seafood Restaurant is on the property. ⊠ *1941 Po'ipū Rd., Kōloa 96756,* ☎ *808/742–6464 or 800/367–8020,* ℻ *808/ 742–9121. 130 condominiums. Restaurant, fans, in-room safes, in-room VCRs, 6 pools, hot tub, 9 tennis courts. AE, D, DC, MC, V.* ✍

$$$ 🏨 **Sunset Kahili.** Of 36 suites, 26 in this five-story ocean-edge building are available for vacationers. The hotel is situated on a bluff and built around a circular swimming pool. Views from the lānai take in great ocean sunsets, and you can catch a glimpse of the spray from Spouting Horn. Privately owned apartments are individually furnished in an island motif. Narrow kitchens are equipped with everything right down to hotpads, and include microwaves and washers and dryers. There's a barbecue area on the grounds. ⊠ *1763 Pe'e Rd., Po'ipū 96756,* ☎ *808/742–7434 or 800/827–6478,* ℻ *808/742–6058. 24 condominium units. Fans, in-room VCRs, kitchenettes, pool. AE, D, DC, MC, V.* ✍

$$–$$$ 🏨 **Po'ipū Plantation.** Pretty 1-acre grounds planted with plumeria, ti, and other tropical foliage surround three two-story cottage-style buildings. Upper-level units have ample decks with ocean views. Many have hardwood floors, vaulted ceilings, and are decorated in light, airy shades of white and pale pink. A full breakfast is served, and the hosts provide beach towels, mats, some children's toys, and free local phone calls. Two units are equipped for disabled travelers. ⊠ *1792 Pe'e Rd., Kōloa 96756,* ☎ *808/742–6757 or 800/634–0263,* ℻ *808/742–8681. 3 rooms, 9 1- and 2-bedroom units. Air-conditioning, fans, in-room VCRs, kitchenettes, hot tub, coin laundry. D, MC, V.* ✍

$$ 🏨 **Kaua'i Cove Cottages.** Three modern cottages sit side by side at the mouth of Waikomo Stream beside an ocean cove that offers super snorkeling. The studios, each with complete kitchen, have an airy tropical decor under cathedral ceilings. Private patios on the ocean side have their own gas grills. There is a $25 cleaning fee for stays of less than three nights. VCRs are available upon request. ⊠ *2672 Pu'uholo Rd., Po'ipū 96756,* ☎ *808/742–2562 or 800/624–9945. 3 cottages. Kitchenettes, snorkeling. D, MC, V.* ✍

$$ 🏨 **Kūhiō Shores.** Every unit in this four-story waterfront condo has an ocean view, with large windows and spacious lānai to help you enjoy it whenever you can tear yourself away from the surfing and snorkeling activity right outside. Accommodations are large—a sure sign that individual owners enjoy vacationing here themselves—with tropical-tone rattan furniture and kitchens. ⊠ *5050 Lāwa'i Beach Rd., Kōloa 96756,* ☎ *808/742–7555, 808/742–1391, or 800/367–8022,* ℻ *808/ 742–1559. 75 condominium suites. Restaurant, kitchenettes, beach, coin laundry. MC, V.* ✍

$–$$ 🏨 **Kōloa Landing Cottages.** Guests are treated like family here by the helpful owners, who came to Hawai'i from Holland. Kōloa Landing has five cottages including a studio about a 10-minute walk from a swimming beach. Accommodations sleep two to six. Open-beam ceilings, fans, and light-color decor keep the interiors cool. Book well in advance for these in-demand, comfortably spacious, but not overly fancy accommodations with kitchens and phones. Barbecue grills are available as well. ⊠ *2704-B Ho'onani Rd., Kōloa 96756,* ☎ *808/742–1470* *or 800/779–8773, FAX 808/332–9584. 5 cottages, 2 rooms. Kitch-enettes, fans, coin laundry. No credit cards.* ❧

The West Side

$$$ 🏠 **Waimea Plantation Cottages.** Tucked into a coconut grove, these reconstructed sugar-plantation cottages, near the stunning Waimea Canyon and many beautiful beaches, make for a laid-back vacation experience. The one- to five-bedroom cottages are unpretentious to the point of being a bit rough around the edges, but they're spacious and all have porches. Wooden floors, ceiling fans (no air-conditioning), rattan furniture, and claw-foot bathtubs are mixed with modern kitchens and cable TVs. Barbecue grills, hammocks, porch swings, a gift shop, and museum are on the property. Cottages are steps away from a black-sand beach with equally murky water. ⊠ *9400 Kaumuali'i Hwy. (Box 367), Waimea 96796,* ☎ *808/338–1625 or 800/992–4632,* FAX *808/338–2338. 48 cottages. Restaurant, bar, pool, horseshoes, beach. AE, D, DC, MC, V.* ❧

$ 🏠 **Kōke'e Lodge.** Outdoors-oriented visitors can experience Kaua'i's mountain wilderness at this lodge that's a little different from the usual beachfront property one expects on a tropical isle. Twelve rustic cabins have wood-burning stoves (wood is a few dollars extra) to ward off any chill from the mountain air. The Lodge restaurant serves a light breakfast and lunch between the hours of 9 and 3:30 daily. Many residents head for Kōke'e for the weekend, so make your reservations in advance. Advance payment is required. Credit cards are accepted for bookings 10 days in advance. Otherwise, personal checks are preferred. ⊠ *3600 Kōke'e Rd., Mile Marker 15, Kekaha (Box 819, Waimea 96796),* ☎ *808/335–6061. 12 cabins. Restaurant.*

NIGHTLIFE AND THE ARTS

People on Kaua'i take great pride in their culture and enjoy sharing their unique traditions with those who come to call. As a result, on the Garden Isle you will find more traditional Hawaiiana and less razzmatazz and glitz than on neighboring O'ahu.

Most of the island's dinner and lū'au shows take place within a hotel or resort; major credit cards are accepted. Hotel lounges and restaurant bars offer live music with no cover charge.

Check the local newspaper, the *Garden Island Times,* for listings of weekly happenings. Free publications like *Kaua'i Gold, This Week on Kaua'i,* and *Kaua'i Magazine* also list entertainment events. You can pick them up at the Hawai'i Visitors Bureau and at Līhu'e Airport.

Bars and Clubs

For the most part, discos never fit into the serenity of Kaua'i, and the bar scene is extremely limited. The major resorts generally host their own live entertainment and happy hours. The drinking age in Hawai'i is 21, and if you look younger than that, you may be asked to show some identification. All bars and clubs that serve alcohol must close at 2 AM, except for those with a cabaret license, which allows them to close at 4 AM.

The following establishments present dance music on a regular basis.

Duke's Barefoot Bar. Contemporary Hawaiian music is performed in the beachside bar on Thursday and Friday, and upstairs a traditional Hawaiian trio plays nightly for diners. ⊠ *Kalapakī Beach, Līhu'e,* ☎ *808/246–9599.* ⊘ *Barefoot Bar Thurs.–Fri. 10–12:30.*

Gilligan's. At the Outrigger Kaua'i Beach near Wailua, Gilligan's has varying entertainment, including line dancing, request night, and 70's night (call ahead to confirm). ✉ *Outrigger Kaua'i Beach Hotel, 4331 Kaua'i Beach Dr., Līhu'e,* ☎ *808/245–1955.* ⊘ *Thurs.–Sat. 8:30–midnight.*

Hanalei Gourmet. The sleepy north shore comes alive each evening in this small, convivial setting. The emphasis here is on local jazz, rock, and folk music. ✉ *5-5161 Kūhiō Hwy., Hanalei Center, Hanalei,* ☎ *808/826–2524.* ⊘ *Mon.–Sat. 8–10:30, Sun. 4–9.*

Tropics. A sports bar on the weekends, this funky hangout presents live island-style music nightly. ✉ *4-1330 Kūhiō Hwy., at Kauwila St., Kapa'a,* ☎ *808/822–7330.* ⊘ *Music nightly 8–11.*

Whalers Brew Pub. In Līhu'e, you can dance to live music (usually reggae or contemporary Hawaiian) on most Friday nights. ✉ *3132 Ninini Point St., Līhu'e,* ☎ *808/245–2000.*

Lū'au

Drums of Paradise Lū'au. More than just music and dance, this hotel lū'au features displays of Hawaiian artwork, as well as a traditional and contemporary menu to suit all tastes and the dances of Polynesia. ✉ *Hyatt Regency Kaua'i Resort and Spa, 1571 Po'ipū Rd., Kōloa,* ☎ *808/742–1234.* ⊠ *$60.* ⊘ *Thurs. and Sun. 5–8.*

Kaua'i Coconut Beach Resort Lū'au. The music, dance, and food of Polynesia come together at this hotel-based lū'au, regarded by many as the island's best. It takes place in a lovely setting of flaming tiki torches. ✉ *Coconut Plantation, Kapa'a,* ☎ *808/822–3455, ext. 651.* ⊠ *$55.* ⊘ *Nightly 6–9.*

Pa'ina o Hanalei. The blowing of the conch calls guests to the beach at Hanalei Bay for a Hawaiian feast and "A Show of Splendor by the Sea" with local entertainers. ✉ *Princeville Hotel, Princeville Resort,* ☎ *808/826–9644.* ⊠ *$59.50.* ⊘ *Mon. and Thurs. 6–9.*

Reflections of Paradise. Set at an historic estate-turned-shopping center, this lū'au, catered by Gaylords, captures the feeling of an old-time family party. Sip mai tais before sampling the buffet line, then relax for a vibrant Polynesian review. ✉ *3-2087 Kaumuali'i St., Līhu'e,* ☎ *808/821–6895.* ⊠ *$49.* ⊘ *Mon. and Thurs. 6:30.*

Smith's Tropical Paradise Lū'au. Amid 30 acres of tropical flora and fauna, this lū'au begins with the traditional blowing of the conch shell and *imu* (underground oven) ceremony, followed by cocktails, an island feast, and an international show in the Lagoon Amphitheater. ✉ *174 Wailua Rd., Kapa'a,* ☎ *808/821–6895.* ⊠ *$52.* ⊘ *Mon., Wed., and Fri. 5–9:15.*

Tahiti Nui Lū'au. This venerable institution is a welcome change from the standard commercial lū'au. It's smaller (about 40 guests) and put on by a family that really knows how to party. The all-you-can-eat buffet includes kālua pig that has been slow-roasted in an imu, and the show features plenty of dancing, music, and laughs. ✉ *Kūhiō Hwy., Hanalei,* ☎ *808/826–6277.* ⊠ *$40.* ⊘ *Wed. 6.*

Music

Very little classical arts activity takes place on laid-back Kaua'i.

Kaua'i Community College Performing Arts Center (✉ 3-1901 Kaumuali'i Hwy., Līhu'e, ☎ 808/245–8311) provides a venue for Hawaiian music and dance as well as visiting performers. Call to find out what's on the bill.

The **Kaua'i Concert Association** (☎ 808/245–7464) offers a seasonal program at the Arts Center.

In Līhu'e, the **Līhu'e Public Library** (⊠ 4344 Hardy St., ☎ 808/241–3222) sometimes plays host to storytelling, musical presentations, and arts-and-crafts events.

Theater

The **Kaua'i Community Players** (⊠ Līhu'e Parish Hall, 4340 Nāwiliwili Rd., Līhu'e, ☎ 808/245–7700) is a talented local group that presents a variety of plays throughout the year.

The **Kaua'i International Theatre** (⊠ Kaua'i Village, 4831 Kūhiō Hwy., Kapa'a, ☎ 808/821–1588) presents six shows per season plus other entertainment in a 62-seat, air-conditioned theater.

OUTDOOR ACTIVITIES AND SPORTS

Participant Sports

Biking

Kaua'i Coasters. You can coast for four hours starting at dawn from the Waimea Canyon Rim. It's a scenic 12 mi—all downhill—with a Continental breakfast included. ⊠ *Box 3038, Līhu'e 96766,* ☎ *808/ 639–2412.*

Outfitters Kaua'i. Here you can rent bikes and get information on how to do a self-guided tour of Kōke'e State Park and Waimea Canyon. The company also leads coasting tours (under the name Bicycle Downhill, Canyon to Coast) from Waimea Canyon to the island's west-side beaches. ⊠ *2827-A Po'ipū Rd., Po'ipū 96756,* ☎ *808/742–9667.*

Pedal 'n' Paddle. This company rents bicycles for $20 a day. Hourly and weekly rates are also available. ⊠ *Ching Young Village, Hanalei,* ☎ *808/826–9069.*

MOUNTAIN BIKING

Triathletes need to train to conquer the 12-mi Power Line Trail, which begins in the mountains above Wailua in Keāhua Arboretum—you'll see the poles heading across the mountains—and ends mauka of Princeville Resort. You're sure to be covered in red clay mud from head to toe by the time you're halfway into the ride, but you'll have views of Waialeale that are usually seen only from the air. Be sure your mountain bike is in top condition, take plenty of water and high-energy bars, and let someone know when and where you are going. If you rent a mountain bike, explain what you've got in mind and heed any advice offered by the experts.

Fitness Centers

Anara Spa at the Hyatt Regency Kaua'i. This resort in the Po'ipū area opens its spa facilities to visitors. For $25 per day you'll have use of the weight room, lap pool, steam, sauna, and hot tub in the deluxe 25,000-square-ft facility. ⊠ *1571 Po'ipū Rd., Po'ipū,* ☎ *808/742–1234.*

Kaua'i Athletic Club. Centrally located, this facility has saunas, racquetball, aerobics classes, swimming, cardio-fitness instruction, and a hot tub. ⊠ *4370 Kukui Grove, Līhu'e,* ☎ *808/245–5381.*

Princeville Health Club & Spa. You'll find state-of-the-art equipment here in a workout room surrounded by inspiring views of mountains, sea, and sky. A variety of facials and body and massage treatments are available for total relaxation. ⊠ *53-900 Kūhiō Hwy., Princeville,* ☎ *808/826–5030.*

Spa and Tennis Club at the Kaua'i Lagoons. Here you'll find separate facilities for men and women. The weight room, sauna, steam room, and hot tub are in elegant pink marble surroundings. ⊠ *3351 Ho'olaulea Way, Līhu'e,* ☎ *808/246–2414.*

Golf

Grove Farm Golf Course. This is Kaua'i's newest course, opened in 1997. It's a 10-hole beauty, and made *Sports Illustrated*'s list of the top 10 nine-hole courses in the country. ⊠ *4315 Kalepa St., Līhu'e,* ☎ *808/245–8756.* ⊒ *Greens fee $40 for 10 holes, $65 for 20 holes; cart included.*

Kaua'i Lagoons Golf Club. Two Jack Nicklaus–designed par-72 courses adjoin the Kaua'i Marriott Resort and Beach Club. The championship Kiele course challenges golfers of all levels. The links-style Mokihana course promises a satisfying round for everyone. Forty acres of tropical lagoons provide breathtaking views. ⊠ *3351 Ho'olaulea Way, Līhu'e,* ☎ *808/241–6000.* ⊒ *Greens fee Kiele $150, Mokihana $100; shared cart and same-day use of practice facility included.*

Kiahuna Plantation Golf Club. On the southern part of the island is this Robert Trent Jones, Jr.–designed 18-hole course. There's a pro shop, equipment rentals, a restaurant, and a bar. ⊠ *2545 Kiahuna Plantation Dr., Kōloa,* ☎ *808/742–9595.* ⊒ *Greens fee nonresidents $75, $55 after 11; shared cart included.*

Kukui-o-lono Golf Course. You can play nine holes or a full round here in a peaceful wooded hilltop setting with spectacular views of Kaua'i's eastern shore. ⊠ *854 Pu'u Rd., Kalāheo,* ☎ *808/332–9151.* ⊒ *Greens fee $7; cart $6 for 9 holes, club rental $6.*

Po'ipū Bay Resort Golf Course. This 18-hole links-style course has been the site of the PGA Grand Slam for many years. It's next to the Hyatt Regency Kaua'i. ⊠ *2250 'Ainakō St., Kōloa,* ☎ *808/742–8711.* ⊒ *Greens fee $100 for Hyatt Regency guests, $145 nonguests; shared cart included.*

Princeville Resort Makai Course. Kaua'i's best-known golf facility, the Makai Course was designed by Robert Trent Jones, Jr. and features a pro shop, driving range, practice area, lessons, club rental and storage, and snack bar. This course has been the setting for the LPGA Women's Kemper Open, including the Helene Curtis Pro-Am. ⊠ *Hwy. 56, Princeville,* ☎ *808/826–3580.* ⊒ *Greens fee $97 guests, $115 nonguests; shared cart included.*

Princeville Resort Prince Course. This 18-hole, Robert Trent Jones–designed course has spectacular ocean and mountain views and is also rated Kaua'i's toughest course. A restaurant and bar are open for breakfast and lunch. ⊠ *Off Hwy. 56, Princeville,* ☎ *808/826–5000.* ⊒ *Greens fee $124 guests, $155 nonguests; cart included.*

Wailua Municipal Golf Course. This municipal course sits next to the Wailua River and beach. Its 18 holes have hosted national tournaments, and there's a pro shop, driving range, and restaurant. ⊠ *3-5351 Kūhiō Hwy., Wailua,* ☎ *808/241–6666.* ⊒ *Greens fee $25 weekdays, $35 weekends; carts $14.*

Hiking and Camping

Before planning any hike or camping trip on Kaua'i, contact the **Department of Land and Natural Resources** (⊠ State Parks Division, 3060 Eiwa St., Room 306, Līhu'e 96766, ☎ 808/274–3446) for information on which campsites and trails are open and what condition they are in. For your safety, wear sturdy shoes, bring plenty of water, never hike alone, stay on the trail, and avoid hiking when it's wet and slippery. All hiking trails on Kaua'i are free.

Kaua'i's prize hiking venue is the **Kalalau Trail,** which begins at the western end of Highway 56 and proceeds 11 mi to Kalalau Beach. With hairpin turns, sometimes very muddy conditions, and constant ups and downs, this hike is a true test of endurance and can't be tackled round-trip in one day. For a good taste of it, hike just the first 2 mi to Hanakāpī'ai Beach (☞ Beaches, *above*). For the best trail and weather conditions, hike Kalalau between May and September.

If you plan to hike beyond Hanakāpīʻai to Kalalau (☞ Heavenly Northeast *in* Exploring Kauaʻi, *above*), a camping permit must be obtained from the Department of Land and Natural Resources. Permits must also be obtained to camp at Miloliʻi, Kokeʻe, and Polihale. Permits, which are issued for five nights maximum, are free and can be requested up to a year in advance. These state campsites assess a charge of $10 for those along the Kalalau trail, $5 for other locations.

Kōkeʻe State Park is a glorious 45-mi network of hiking trails of varying difficulty, all worth the walk. Its acres of native forests, home to many species of birds, are a wonder to behold. The Kukui Trail takes hikers right down the side of Waimea Canyon. Awaʻawapuhi Trail leads 4 mi down to a spectacular overlook into the canyons of the north shore. Pleasant, shaded campsites can be reserved through the Parks Department. All hikers should register at Kōkeʻe Park headquarters, which offers trail maps and information. ⊠ *Kōkeʻe Rd., 20 mi north of Hwy. 50, Kekaha,* ☎ *808/335–9975 Kōkeʻe Museum.*

Horseback Riding

Kauaʻi's scenic mountain pastures and shorelines can be explored on escorted rides along panoramic oceanside cliffs and beaches.

CJM Country Stables. This company in Poʻipū charges $65 to $90 for three guided rides: a two-hour ranch ride with ocean scenery, a three-hour hidden-valley beach breakfast ride, and a 3½-hour swim and picnic ride. ☎ *808/742–6096.*

Esprit de Corps. In Kapaʻa, Esprit de Corps offers private lessons, pony parties for children, and half-day horse camps, as well as trail rides that range from three-hour jaunts for $99 to eight-hour excursions for $350 that include lunch. Group trail rides require some experience as they allow trotting and cantering. Private custom rides for less experienced riders are available. ☎ *808/822–4688.*

ʻŌmaʻo Country Stables. Experienced riders eight and older are allowed to let their horses run freely. You can choose a 1½-hour sunset beach ride for $125 or book an exclusive 2½-hour custom ride through pasturelands with panoramic ocean and mountain views. ʻŌmaʻo is on southern Kauaʻi, not far from Lāwaʻi. ☎ *808/822–4688.*

Princeville Ranch Stables. Guided horseback tours from this very professional operation take riders into the less-explored reaches of the island. A 90-minute country ride is $55 per person. A scenic three-hour bluff ride is $100 and includes a snack. A 4-hour waterfall picnic ride is $110, including lunch. ☎ *808/826–6777.*

Silver Falls Ranch. At this Kīlauea ranch you can take an individual excursion or private lesson, or join a two-hour Hawaiian Discovery ride with refreshments ($75) or a three-hour Silver Falls ride ($99) that includes picnicking by a waterfall and a swim in a secluded freshwater pool. ☎ *808/828–6718.*

Tennis

Kauaʻi has 20 lighted public tennis courts and more than 70 private courts at the hotels.

Hanalei Bay Resort (⊠ 5380 Honoiki Rd., Princeville, ☎ 808/826–6522) has eight courts. Guests play free; nonguests pay $6 per hour.
Hyatt Regency Kauaʻi (⊠ 1571 Poʻipū Rd., Kōloa, ☎ 808/742–1234) has four courts, a pro shop, and a tennis pro. The cost is $20 per hour.
Kauaʻi Coconut Beach Resort (☎ 808/822–3455) offers three courts. Guests play free; nonguests pay $7.
Princeville Tennis Center (⊠ 4080 Lei-o-papa Rd., Princeville, ☎ 808/826–9823) has six courts. The cost is $10 for 90 minutes.

Spa and Tennis Club at the Kaua'i Lagoons (⊠ 3351 Ho'olaulea Way, Līhu'e, ☏ 808/246–2414) has the island's only tennis stadium and seven courts for mere mortals. Unlimited court time costs $20 per day, private lessons are $50 per hour, lessons for two are $60 per hour, and a 75-minute daily clinic is $15.

Water Sports

FISHING

For freshwater fishing, head for the bass- and trout-filled streams near Kōke'e and Waimea Canyon. A 30-day visitor license for freshwater fishing, costing $20, must be obtained from the **Department of Land and Natural Resources** (⊠ 1151 Punchbowl St., Room 131, Honolulu 96815, ☏ 808/587–0109).

No matter which company you choose for ocean fishing, plan to spend $125–$150 for a full day of charter fishing on a shared basis, $85–$90 for a half day on a shared basis, $600–$700 for an exclusive full day, and $400–$450 for an exclusive half day. The following are reliable enterprises:

Anini Fishing Charters (⊠ Box 594, Kīlauea 96754, ☏ 808/828–1285) has a 33-ft sport cruiser, *Sea Breeze V,* that skipper Bob Kutkowski completed himself for sport or bottom-fishing charters.
Sportfishing Kaua'i (⊠ Box 1195, Kōloa 96756, ☏ 808/639–0013) runs 28-ft and 38-ft six-passenger custom sportfishers.
True Blue (⊠ Box 1722, Kalapakī Beach, Līhu'e 96766, ☏ 808/246–6333) offers charters on a roomy 55-ft Delta certified to carry 33, and a Rainbow Runner sailboat that carries 18, but fishing trips are limited to 10 anglers. A 4-hour share charter runs $90 per person. A 6-hour share charter is $120. A 4-hour exclusive charter is $600. A ¾-day charter is $700.

KAYAKING

Kayak Kaua'i. In addition to renting kayaks to individuals, this outfit also offers half- and full-day guided kayak tours along the Nā Pali Coast and up the Hanalei and Wailua rivers with snorkeling included (☞ Contacts and Resources *in* Kaua'i A to Z, *below*). ☏ *808/826–9844 or 800/437–3507.* ▢ *$48–$130.*
Outfitters Kaua'i. This company offers guided kayak excursions for novices as well as longer Nā Pali Coast and jungle-stream paddles. Experienced paddlers can rent a kayak, grab a plastic-coated map, and discover a romantic waterfall on their own. ⊠ *2827-A Po'ipū Rd., Po'ipū 96756,* ☏ *808/742–9667, 888/742–9887.*
Paradise Outdoor Adventures. Paradise provides topographical maps and motorboat and kayak rentals and guided excursions. A half-day guided Wailua Jungle-River Safari includes a hike to a waterfall and a snack for $59. A longer tour including lunch is $80. ⊠ *1-56 Kūhiō Hwy., Kapa'a 96746,* ☏ *808/822–1112 or 877/422–6287.* ▢ *2-person kayak $50 per day.*

SCUBA DIVING

Dive Kaua'i Scuba Center. This shop offers an introductory half-day scuba excursion for $98. Two-tank shore dives for certified divers cost $98, a refresher course is $83, and a five-day PADI (scuba-diving certification) course is $395. A boat dive with two tanks costs $115, including equipment. ⊠ *976 Kūhiō Hwy., No. C, Kapa'a 96746,* ☏ *808/822–0452 or 800/828–3483.*
Ocean Odyssey. Ocean Odyssey will arrange lessons, shore dives, night dives, and even underwater videotaping for you. Packages range from a simple one-tank shore dive starting at $65 for certified divers to three- to five-day PADI certification courses. ⊠ *Outrigger Kaua'i Beach Hotel, 4331 Kaua'i Beach Dr., Līhu'e 96766,* ☏ *808/245–8681.*

Seasport Divers. This full-service PADI, NAUI, and SSI training facility has a full range of dive options, from beginner lessons and introductory dives to private charters. It also offers equipment rental and repair service. ⊠ *2827 Poʻipū Rd., Kōloa 96756,* ☎ *808/742–9303 or 800/685–5889.*

SNORKELING

The following experts operate entertaining and well-run snorkeling cruises. Several companies depart from the north shore for snorkeling trips along the scenic Nā Pali Coast. Schedules vary with the weather. Call in advance for details.

Blue Water Sailing (☎ 808/828–1142) ferries snorkelers to south-shore sites on a 12-passenger, 42-ft, luxury Pearson sailing yacht, the *Lady Leanne II.* A fun excursion for all ages and the only monohull sailing charter on Kauaʻi, this four-hour snorkeling voyage includes gear, instruction, swimming, fishing, a gourmet picnic lunch, snacks, and beverages. In winter you might catch glimpses of whales. Trips leave from Port Allen mid-September–mid-May and from other ports during the rest of year. The cost is $105. A two-hour sunset sail that carries 15 is $60. A 42-ft power boat, *Blue Water Express,* also cruises Kauaʻi's waters. From May through September, Blue Water is one of the few operations that depart from Hanalei.

Captain Andy's Sailing Adventures (☎ 808/335–6833) takes up to 49 passengers on its 55-ft catamaran *Spirit of Kauaʻi;* cruises depart from Kukuiʻula Harbor in Poʻipū. The rate for the four-hour morning snorkel-picnic tour is $85, including gear and lunch. Whale-watching excursions are run during the winter months. Seasonal Nā Pali Coast tours are offered that include Continental breakfast, lunch, snorkeling gear, and instruction for $109.

Catamaran Kahanu (☎ 808/826–4596) offers a 4½-hour Nā Pali Coast cruise on a 36-ft power catamaran. The trip includes snorkeling, whale- or dolphin-watching, lunch, and a bit of Hawaiian history and culture presented by the Hawaiian owner/operators. The price is $105 for adults.

Hanalei Sea Tours (☎ 808/826–7254 or 800/733–7997) runs marine ecology whale-watching tours during the winter and year-round snorkeling tours on Power Cats and rigid-hull inflatable rafts. Narrated sightseeing trips range from $60 to $130 and take from two hours to a full day. Longer cruises include snorkeling gear, lunch, and cold drinks.

Hanalei Watersports (☎ 808/826–7509) offers scuba and surfing lessons in addition to guided kayak and snorkel tours. These accommodating guides can craft a full day's land-and-sea adventure to suit your every whim. They also offer an idyllic sunset cruise from the Princeville Resort aboard a Hawaiian outrigger canoe equipped with a traditional sail and a paddling canoe. Prices run the gamut.

Nā Pali EcoAdventures (☎ 808/826–6804 or 800/659–6804) takes groups on five-hour snorkeling and snack excursions, four-hour sightseeing trips along the north shore, and two-hour winter whale-watch cruises in power catamarans that hold 26 or 35 people. Rates are $60 and up.

SURFING AND WINDSURFING

ʻAnini Beach Windsurfing (☎ 808/826–9463) stands ready to help you get started as a windsurfer. An introductory group lesson and certification lesson include equipment; each of three one-hour sessions is $65. Private lessons are available, and sailboard rentals are $25 per hour, $50 per day.

Margo Oberg Surfing Lessons (⊠ Nukumoi Surf Shop, Poʻipū Beach, next to Brennecke's Beach Broiler, ☎ 808/742–8019). Here seven-time world surfing champion Margo Oberg furnishes surfboards, and she and her staff give dry-land and wave instruction to beginning surfers. Lessons are $45 for 1½ hours.

SHOPPING

Kaua'i may not have the myriad shopping alternatives of its cosmopolitan neighbor, O'ahu, but what it does have is character. Along with a few major shopping malls, Kaua'i has some of the most delightful mom-and-pop shops and family-run boutiques imaginable.

Kaua'i also offers one-of-a-kind options for souvenirs. For instance, the famous shell jewelry from nearby Ni'ihau is sometimes sold on Kaua'i for less than it is on other islands. The Garden Isle is also known for its regular outdoor markets where you find bargain prices on various souvenirs and produce and get a chance to mingle with island residents.

Kaua'i's major shopping centers are open daily from 9 or 10 to 5, although some stay open until 9. Stores are basically clustered around the major resort areas and Līhu'e.

Department Stores

Mainland-style department stores on the island, carrying an all-inclusive selection of moderately priced merchandise, include **Big Kmart** (⊠ Kukui Grove Center, 3-2600 Kaumuali'i Hwy., ☎ 808/245–7742); **Sears** (⊠ Kukui Grove Center, 3-2600 Kaumuali'i Hwy., ☎ 808/246–8301); **Wal-Mart** (⊠ 3-3300 Kūhiō Hwy., ☎ 808/246–1599).

Shopping Centers

Ching Young Village. In the heart of Hanalei, Ching Young draws people to its Village Variety Store with cheap prices on beach towels, macadamia nuts, film and processing, wet suits—you name it. There's also a well-stocked Hanalei Natural Foods store; a few steps away is Evolve Love Artists Gallery, where you can find work by local artisans. ⊠ *Kūhiō Hwy., Hanalei.*

Coconut Marketplace. This is part of a larger complex of resort hotels and restaurants; more than 70 shops sell everything from snacks and slippers to scrimshaw. ⊠ *4-484 Kūhiō Hwy., Waipouli.*

'Ele'ele Shopping Center. Kaua'i's west side has a scattering of stores, including those at this no-frills shopping center. It's a good place to rub elbows with local folk or to grab a quick bite to eat at the casual restaurant called Grinds. ⊠ *Hwy. 50 near Hanapēpē.*

Hanalei Center. The old Hanalei School, a building listed on the Historic Register, that has been refurbished and rented out to boutiques and restaurants. After you dig through a wonderful collection of '40s and '50s vintage clothing and memorabilia in the Yellow Fish Trading Company or search for that unusual gift at Sand People, you can grab a shave ice and relax on the front deck or lawn or go Italian for lunch at a charming courtyard restaurant called Café Luna. ⊠ *5-5016 Kūhiō Hwy., Hanalei,* ☎ 808/826–7677.

Kaua'i Village Shopping Center. In this Kapa'a shopping village the buildings are built in the style of 19th-century plantation towns. ABC Discount Store sells sundries, Safeway sells groceries and alcoholic beverages, Wyland Gallery sells island art, and Kaua'i One-Hour Photo provides speedy film processing. ⊠ *4-831 Kūhiō Hwy., Kapa'a.*

Kilohana Plantation. A unique collection of plantation-style shops and galleries are housed on both levels of the main house as well as in quaint guest cottages. Here you'll find an emphasis on the handcrafted goods of the islands; for example, the Artisans Room, in the plantation's guest bedroom, sells paintings by Rosalie Rupp Prussing, carvings by Russ

Graff, and collages by Cece Rodriguez, as well as limited-edition prints, ceramics, and glass. The Hawaiian Collection Room, in the restored cloak room, focuses on unusual crafts, with Ni'ihau shell leis and scrimshaw. ⊠ *3-2087 Kaumuali'i Hwy., 1 mi west of Līhu'e.*

Kinipopo Shopping Village. On Kūhiō Highway in Kapa'a, across from Wailua Family Restaurant, is this tropical-garden setting for casual shopping. Here you'll find the Goldsmith's Gallery, which sells handcrafted Hawaiian-style gold jewelry, and Tin Can Mailman bookstore, filled with old collectible and new Hawaiian books and paper ephemera. You can also rent water skis and beach paraphernalia here at Kaua'i Water Ski & Surf Co. ⊠ *4-356 Kūhiō Hwy., Kapa'a.*

Kong Lung Center. The center houses Kong Lung Co., a gift shop filled with special treasures from around the world, and around its grassy courtyard are a couple of shops, including Island Soap and Candle Works and Plantation Pottery, where you can view the production process. Kīlauea Bakery, also in the courtyard, is legendary for pizza and bread sticks. ⊠ *2490 Keneke St., Kīlauea,* ☎ *808/828–1822.*

Kukui Grove Center. This is Kaua'i's largest assemblage of shops. Besides the island's major department stores, it offers a Longs Drugs for personal needs and Star Market for groceries. You'll find island-inspired garb at Hawaiian Islands Creations, Kaua'i-made gifts at Kaua'i Products Store, and athletic footwear at Foot Locker. ⊠ *3-2600 Kaumuali'i Hwy. on Hwy. 50, just west of Līhu'e.*

Old Kōloa Road. Not really a shopping center, but this, the main street of Old Kōloa, concentrates several boutiques and eateries in one handy location. Favorites are Kōloa Ice House and Deli, which sells shave-ice fantasies laced with tropical syrups; Koloa Fish Market, for a take-out taste of poke or sashimi; and Progressive Expressions, which offers surfing and windsurfing accessories, swimwear, and beachwear.

Po'ipū Shopping Village. Catering mainly to guests in nearby hotels and condos the two dozen shops here offer resort wear, gifts, souvenirs, sundries, jewelry, and art, and there are half a dozen restaurants as well. The upscale Black Pearl Kaua'i and Hale Manu, with "gifts for the spirited," are particularly appealing. ⊠ *2360 Kiahuna Plantation Dr., Po'ipū.*

Princeville Shopping Center. This is an upscale little gathering of such trendy shops as Kaua'i Kite and Hobby Shop, Pretty Woman, and JM's Jewels. If you're vacationing in a nearby condo and want to shop for dinner, you'll also find a Foodland, where you can pick up not only dinner but a bottle of wine to sip at sunset. ⊠ *5-4280 Kūhiō Hwy., Princeville.*

Waimea Canyon Plaza. The little town of Kekaha is proud of its tidy complex of shops offering local foods, souvenirs, and gifts. ⊠ *Kōke'e Rd. at Hwy. 50, Kekaha.*

Waipouli Town Center. On the east coast of the island in Kapa'a you'll find a modest collection of 10 shops where you can buy a T-shirt at Waipouli Variety and then grab a good-value plate lunch or other local food at Waipouli Restaurant. ⊠ *4-901 Kūhiō Hwy., Kapa'a.*

Specialty Stores

Books

Borders Books & Music. A healthy section of books focused on Hawai'i are on offer, plus plenty of magazines for beach reading. ⊠ *4303 Nāwiliwili Rd., Līhu'e,* ☎ *808/246–0862.*

Kaua'i Museum. The gift shop at the museum sells some fascinating books, maps, and prints. ⊠ *4428 Rice St., Līhu'e,* ☎ *808/245–6931.*

Clothing

Crazy Shirts. This chain has a wide variety of shirts, from classy to crazy designs. It's a good place for active wear. ⊠ *Po'ipū Shopping Village,*

2360 Kiahuna Plantation Dr., ☎ *808/742–9000;* ⊠ *Anchor Cove, 3416 Rice St., Līhu'e,* ☎ *808/245–7073;* ⊠ *Kaua'i Village, 4-831 Kūhiō Hwy., Kapa'a,* ☎ *808/823–6761;* ⊠ *Kōloa,* ☎ *808/742–7161.*

Liberty House. This island chain carries high-quality designer labels as well as nice resort wear. ⊠ *Kukui Grove Center, 3-2600 Kaumuali'i Hwy.,* ☎ *808/245–7751*

M. Miura Store. This is a great assortment of clothes for the outdoor fanatic, including tank tops, visors, swimwear, and Kaua'i-style T-shirts. ⊠ *4-1419 Kūhiō Hwy., Kapa'a,* ☎ *808/822–4401.*

Paradise Sportswear. This is the retail outlet of the folks who invented Kaua'i's popular "red dirt" shirts: do let the salesperson tell you the charming story behind these shirts. Sizes from infants up to 5X are available. ⊠ *4350 Waialo Rd., Port Allen,* ☎ *808/335–5670.*

RESORT WEAR

Hilo Hattie Fashion Factory. This is the big name in inexpensive aloha wear for tourists throughout the Islands. You can visit the factory, a mile from Līhu'e Airport, to pick up cool, comfortable aloha shirts and mu'umu'u in bright floral prints, and other souvenirs. ⊠ *3252 Kūhiō Hwy., Līhu'e,* ☎ *808/245–3404.*

Tropical Shirts. Come here for the beautiful clothing embroidered by local artists. There is also a selection of the island's unique "red dirt" T-shirts, dyed and printed with the characteristic local soil. ⊠ *Po'ipū Shopping Village, 2360 Kiahuna Plantation Dr.,* ☎ *808/742–6691.*

Flowers

Kaua'i Tropicals. This company ships heliconia, anthuriums, ginger, and other tropicals directly from the flower farm in 5-ft boxes. ⊠ *3870 Waha Rd., Box 449, Kalāheo 96741,* ☎ *808/332–9071 or 800/303–4385.*

Food

Kaua'i has its own yummy specialties that you won't be able to resist while on the island. The **Kaua'i Products Council** (⊠ Box 3660, Līhu'e 96788, ☎ 808/823–8714) will tell you the best places to find Kaua'i Kookies, taro chips, Kaua'i boiled peanuts, salad dressings, and jams and jellies made from locally grown fruit, as well as nonfood items handcrafted on the island.

Kaua'i now produces more coffee than any other island in the state, and the local product, somewhat milder than the Big Island's better-known Kona coffee, makes a worthy souvenir. Coffee can be purchased at the source, **Kaua'i Coffee Visitor Center and Museum** (⊠ 870 Halawili Rd., off Hwy. 50, west of Kalāheo, ☎ 808/335–0813).

Near Līhu'e, you can buy fresh pineapple, sugarcane, ginger, coconuts, local jams, jellies, and honey, plus Kaua'i-grown papayas, bananas, and mangos in season—all at **Kaua'i Fruit and Flower Company** (⊠ 3-4684 Kūhiō Hwy., ☎ 808/245–1814). Special gift packs are available, inspected and certified for shipment out of the state.

Don't forget to try a big scoop of **Lappert's Ice Cream** (⊠ 1-3555 Kaumuali'i Hwy., ☎ 808/335–6121; ⊠ Coconut Marketplace, 4-484 Kūhiō Hwy., ☎ 808/822–0744; ⊠ Kōloa, ☎ 808/742–1272; ⊠ Princeville Shopping Center, ☎ 808/826–7393), created by Walter Lappert in Hanapēpē in 1983 and now a favorite all over Hawai'i. The Lappert shops also sell locally produced gourmet coffees, which are easier to ship home than the ice cream.

Some of the best prices on Hawai'i's famous macadamia nuts are available at **Star Market** (⊠ Kukui Grove Center, 3-2600 Kaumuali'i Hwy., ☎ 808/245–7777).

Gifts

Hilo Hattie Fashion Factory. If you've neglected shopping for take-home gifts while you were sightseeing, hiking, and diving, this is the place where you can buy all the hats, baskets, inexpensive shell jewelry, rubber slippers, golf towels, and other trinkets you need to carry home to friends and family. The location is perfect for a last-minute stop en route to Līhu'e Airport. ⊠ *3252 Kūhiō Hwy., Līhu'e,* ☎ *808/245–3404.*

Kong Lung Co. This elegant gift shop, sometimes called the Gump's of Kaua'i, combines clothing, glassware, books, and artwork. It is housed in a beautiful 1892 stone structure on the way to the lighthouse in out-of-the-way Kīlauea. Thriftier souls might find the "gently used and new fashions" upstairs at Reinventions to their liking. ⊠ *2490 Keneke St., Kīlauea,* ☎ *808/828–1822.*

Lee Sands' Eelskin. Eelskin is popular in the Islands, and you can buy it wholesale here at this spot in the Hawaiian Trading Post. It's an unusual store, with other skin lines such as sea snake, chicken feet, and frog. A lizard card case is available for about $12. ⊠ *Hwy. 50 at Kōloa Rd., Lāwa'i,* ☎ *808/332–7404.*

Village Variety Store. How about a fun beach towel for the folks back home? That's just one of the gifts you can find here, along with shell leis, Kaua'i T-shirts, macadamia nuts, and other great souvenirs at low prices. ⊠ *Ching Young Village, Kūhiō Hwy., Hanalei,* ☎ *808/826–6077.*

Hawaiian Arts and Crafts

Art Shop. This intimate gallery in Līhu'e sells original oils, photos, and sculptures. ⊠ *3196 'Akahi St.,* ☎ *808/245–3810.*

Kahn Galleries. You can purchase the works of many local artists—including seascapes by George Sumner and Roy Tabora—at this gallery's locations. ⊠ *Coconut Marketplace, 4-484 Kūhiō Hwy., Kapa'a,* ☎ *808/822–3636;* ⊠ *Kilohana Plantation, Līhu'e,* ☎ *808/246–4454;* ⊠ *Kaua'i Village Shopping Center, Kapa'a,* ☎ *808/822–4277;* ⊠ *Old Koloa Town,* ☎ *808/742–2277;* ⊠ *Hanalei Center, 5-5161 Kūhiō Hwy., Hanalei,* ☎ *808/826–6677.*

Kapaia Stitchery. Featured here are quilting and other fabric arts, plus kits for trying your own hand at various crafts; the kits are great gifts for crafters. ⊠ *Kūhiō Hwy. in a red building ½ mi north of Līhu'e,* ☎ *808/245–2281.*

Kaua'i Heritage Center. Authentic reproductions of old (and new) Hawaiian crafts by Kaua'i artisans are featured here. Sales of feather hatbands, nose flutes, konane gameboards and playing pieces, calabashes, and woven lau hala hats and pocketbooks help to support the center's cultural workshops and programs, which sometimes take place in the courtyard by the clock tower. ⊠ *Kaua'i Village, 4-831 Kūhiō Hwy., No. 838, Kapa'a,* ☎ *808/821–2070.*

Kaua'i Products Store. Every seed lei, every finely crafted koa-wood box, every pair of tropical flower earrings in this boutique is handcrafted on Kaua'i. ⊠ *Kukui Grove Center, 3-2600 Kaumuali'i Hwy., Līhu'e,* ☎ *808/246–6753.*

Wyland Galleries. This gallery showcases the work of Wyland, a famed artist of marine life. You can buy his original works, lithographs, prints, and sculptures, plus pieces by other island artists. Wyland is known for his massive wall murals, and you can see an example of his work on Kūhiō Highway, on the side of a building fronting Kaua'i Village. ⊠ *Kaua'i Village, 4-831 Kūhiō Hwy., Kapa'a,* ☎ *808/822–9855; Po'ipū Shopping Village, Po'ipū,* ☎ *808/742–6030.*

Ye Olde Ship Store & Port of Kaua'i. Kaua'i artist Peter Kinney specializes in scrimshaw pocket and army knives, and they are available at this store in the Coconut Marketplace. The shop also carries the work of nearly 40 other scrimshaw artists and sponsors an annual contest celebrating the art form. ⊠ *Coconut Marketplace, 4-484 Kūhiō Hwy., Waipouli,* ☎ *808/822–1401.*

Jewelry

Jim Saylor Jewelers. A good selection of gems from around the world is showcased here with black pearls, diamonds, and unique settings. Jim Saylor has been designing these pretty keepsakes for more than 20 years on Kauaʻi. ⊠ *1318 Kūhiō Hwy., Kapaʻa,* ☎ *808/822–3591.*

Kauaʻi Gold. A wonderful selection of rare Niʻihau shell leis ranging from $20 to $200 and up is available here. Take time to ask about these remarkable necklaces before you buy; you'll appreciate the craftsmanship, understand the sometimes high prices, and learn to care for and preserve their fragile beauty. The store also has a selection of 14-karat gold jewelry. ⊠ *Coconut Marketplace, 4-484 Kūhiō Hwy., Waipouli,* ☎ *808/822–9361.*

Remember Kauaʻi. Mementos of your trip in the form of fashion jewelry, gifts, and Niʻihau shell necklaces are offered here. They also run a booth at Poʻipū Spouting Horn. ⊠ *Outrigger Kauaʻi Beach Hotel, 4331 Kauaʻi Beach Dr., Līhuʻe,* ☎ *808/245–6650.*

KAUAʻI A TO Z

Arriving and Departing

By Plane

The **Līhuʻe Airport** (☎ 808/246–1400) handles most of the air traffic in and out of Kauaʻi. Three miles east of the town of Līhuʻe, the terminal is spacious and contemporary. It easily accommodates the growing number of visitors to the Garden Isle. Once you arrive, if you have any immediate questions, stop by the Līhuʻe Airport Visitor Information Center (☎ 808/246–1440), outside each baggage claim area. It's open daily.

North of Līhuʻe is **Princeville Airport,** a tiny strip in the middle of rolling ranch lands and sugarcane fields today used primarily by private planes. Princeville Airport is just a five-minute drive from the Princeville development area, which plays home to condos and a luxurious accommodation called the Princeville Hotel. The airport is also about a 10-minute drive from the shops and accommodations of sleepy Hanalei.

FLIGHTS FROM HONOLULU

Carriers flying from Honolulu International Airport to Līhuʻe Airport include **Aloha Airlines** (☎ 808/245–3691 or 800/367–5250) and **Hawaiian Airlines** (☎ 808/245–1813 or 800/367–5320). The rates go up and down depending on which airline is trying to outdo the other, ranging from about $70 to $100 one-way. Aloha offers more than 20 round-trip flights a day between Honolulu and Līhuʻe, while Hawaiian has 14 round-trips. It's a 30- to 40-minute flight.

BETWEEN THE AIRPORT AND HOTELS

The driving time from Līhuʻe Airport to the town of Līhuʻe is a mere five minutes. If you're staying in Wailua or Kapaʻa, your driving time from Līhuʻe is 15 minutes, and to Princeville and Hanalei it takes about 45 minutes. If you're staying in Hanalei, flying into Princeville Airport can save you some driving time.

To the south, it's a 30-minute drive from Līhuʻe to Poʻipū, the major resort area. To Waimea it takes one hour, and if you choose the rustic accommodations in the hills of Kōkeʻe, allow a good hour and a half of driving time from Līhuʻe.

Check with your hotel or condo to see if it offers free shuttle service from the airport.

By Car. Car-rental companies have offices at both airports. They'll also provide you with driving directions to your hotel or condo (☞ Car Rentals *in* Contacts and Resources, *below*).

By Limousine. For luxurious transportation between the airport and your accommodations, contact **Custom Limousine Service** (✉ Box 3267, Līhu'e 96766, ☎ 808/246–6318). Rates are $73.50 per hour, with a two-hour minimum. **North Shore Limousine** (✉ Box 757, Hanalei 96714, ☎ 808/826–6189) can pick you up at Princeville Airport.

By Taxi. Fares around the island are $2 at the meter drop plus $2 per mile. That means a taxicab from Līhu'e Airport to Līhu'e town runs about $6 and to Po'ipū about $32, excluding tip.

A taxi company that will take you to Līhu'e and Po'ipū is **Po'ipū Taxi** (☎ 808/639–2042 or 808/639–2044). Cabs are also available from **Scotty Taxi** (☎ 808/245–7888) and **Akiko's Taxi** (☎ 808/822–7588).

From the Princeville Airport to Hanalei, you'll pay about $12 when you ride with the **North Shore Cab Company** (☎ 808/826–6189), which serves only the northeast portion of the island.

By Ship

A romantic way to visit Kaua'i for a short time is to book passage on an interisland cruise ship. The massive white "love boat," the S.S. *Independence,* and the M.S. *Patriot* leave Honolulu each Saturday and stop at Kaua'i, as well as Maui and Hilo and Kona on the Big Island. At each port of call you may get off the ship for sightseeing and shore excursions. At Kaua'i, the ships dock at Nāwiliwili on the east coast. Optional extension packages allow you to add a hotel stay before or after the cruise in the port of your choice. **American Hawai'i Cruises** (✉ Robin St. Wharf, 1380 Port of New Orleans Pl., New Orleans, LA 70130-1890, ☎ 800/765–7000) has been presenting these successful seven-day excursions for years. The S.S. *Independence* was refurbished in 1997. The 1,214-passenger MS*Patriot* was added to the fleet in 2000.

Getting Around

By Bike

A two-wheeler is an exciting way to cruise around the Garden Isle. Its country roads are generally uncrowded, so you can ride along at your own pace and enjoy the views. This is a safe island to explore by bicycle, as long as you exercise caution on the busier thoroughfares. Guests can rent bikes from the activities desks of certain hotels around the island. Check with your concierge or front desk. *See* Biking *in* Outdoor Activities and Sports, *above,* for information on where to rent bikes.

By Bus

Excursion buses take visitors to such specific commercial attractions as the Fern Grotto, Waimea Canyon, Spouting Horn, Ft. Elisabeth, 'Ōpaeka'a Falls, and Menehune Fishpond (☞ Guided Tours *in* Contacts and Resources, *below*).

By Car

Although Kaua'i is relatively small, its sights reach from one end of the island to the other. You can walk to the stores and restaurants in your resort area, but the important attractions of the island are generally not within walking distance of each other. As a result, you'll probably want to rent a car, unless you plan to do all your sightseeing with tour companies (☞ Car Rentals *in* Contacts and Resources, *below*).

It's easy to get around on Kaua'i, for it has one major road that almost encircles the island. Your rental-car company will supply you with a map with enlargements of each area of the island. The traffic on Kaua'i is pretty light most of the time, except in the Līhu'e and Kapa'a areas during rush hour (6:30 AM–8:30 AM and 3:30 PM–5:30 PM). Major attractions are indicated by a Hawaiian-warrior marker on the side of the road.

As is the case throughout Hawai'i, a seat-belt law is enforced on Kaua'i for front-seat passengers. Children under the age of three must be in a car seat, which you can get from your car-rental company. Although Kaua'i looks like paradise, it has its fair share of crime. Play it safe and lock your car whenever you park it. Don't leave valuables in the car, and pay attention to parking signs, particularly in Līhu'e.

By Limousine

One doesn't see many limousines cruising the country roads of Kaua'i, but if the idea intrigues you, contact **Custom Limousine Service** (⊠ Box 3267, Līhu'e 96766, ☎ 808/246–6318). Among its options are airport service, touring, wedding packages, lei greetings, and complete ground handling. **North Shore Limousine** (⊠ Box 757, Hanalei 96714, ☎ 808/826–6189) specializes in service in the Hanalei and Princeville areas.

By Taxi

A taxicab will take you all around the island, but you'll pay dearly for the service. The cost for each mile is $2, after a $2 meter drop, so from Līhu'e to Po'ipū the price is $32; from Līhu'e to Princeville, $60, excluding tip. Your best bet is to call a cab for short distances only (to a restaurant, for instance). A 5-mi cab ride will run you about $12 plus tip. The drivers are often from Kaua'i, which means they'll give you information about the island.

Two reliable cab companies on the island are **City Cab** (☎ 808/245–3227) and **Akiko's Taxi** (☎ 808/822–7588). Based in Princeville is the **North Shore Cab Company** (☎ 808/826–6189), which provides complete ground handling services for the north and east sections of the island.

Contacts and Resources

B&B Reservation Services

The following are two Kaua'i-based services: **Bed and Breakfast Kaua'i** (⊠ 105 Melia St., Kapa'a 96746, ☎ 808/822–1177 or 800/822–1176, FAX 808/822–5757, ✆) and **Bed and Breakfast Hawai'i** (⊠ Box 449, Kapa'a 96746, ☎ 808/822–7771 or 800/733–1632, ✆).

Island-wide reservations services include the following: **All Islands Bed and Breakfast** (⊠ 463 'Iliwahī Loop, Kailua 96734, ☎ 808/263–2342 or 800/542–0344, FAX 808/263–0308, ✆), **Bed and Breakfast Honolulu** (⊠ 3242 Kā'ohinani Dr., Honolulu 96817, ☎ 808/595–7533 or 800/288–4666, FAX 808/595–2030, ✆), and **Hawaiian Islands Bed and Breakfasts and Vacation Rentals** (⊠ 1277 Mokulua Dr., Kailua 96734, ☎ 808/261–7895 or 800/258–7895, ✆).

Car Rentals

Unless you plan to do all of your sightseeing as part of guided van tours, you will want a rental car on Kaua'i. The vast beauty of the island begs to be explored, and its attractions are sprinkled from one end to the other. Reserve your vehicle in advance, especially if you will be on Kaua'i during the peak seasons of summer, the Christmas holidays, and February.

Right across from the baggage-claim area at Līhu'e Airport you'll find several rental-car firms, as well as vans that will shuttle you to offices nearby. Rental companies also have desks at Princeville Airport. There are also several lesser-known and local companies that offer slightly lower rates. Daily prices for a car from the major-name companies begin at $38, unless you rate a discount through AAA, AARP, or by other means. A fly-drive deal can sometimes reduce that cost, and many hotels and even some condos offer packages that include rental cars. There is a $3 daily surcharge on all rentals.

Car-rental companies with offices at or near Līhu'e Airport are **Alamo** (☎ 800/462–5266), **Avis** (☎ 800/831–8000), **Budget** (☎ 800/527–0700), **Dollar** (☎ 800/342–7398; 800/800–4000 from outside HI), **Hertz** (☎ 800/654–3011), and **National** (☎ 800/227–7368).

Companies with Princeville Airport offices are **Avis** and **Hertz.** Several companies also operate reservation desks at the major hotels on the island, including **Avis** (⊠ Hyatt Regency Kaua'i, ☎ 808/742–1627).

You can get some good deals on a car if you book with one of Kaua'i's budget or used-car rental companies. These include the reliable **Westside Enterprises** (☎ 808/332–8644), which rents cars from $21.95 and jeeps from $69.95. It keeps its vehicles in good shape and offers free delivery and pickup of your car at your hotel or condo in Po'ipū.

Doctors

The **Kaua'i Medical Clinic** (KMC) has a staff with 32 different specialties, so it can handle all medical problems. It has lab and X-ray facilities, physical therapy, optometry, and emergency rooms. The main clinic (⊠ 3420-B Kūhiō Hwy., ☎ 808/245–1500) is in Līhu'e. Other KMC clinics are in Kīlauea (⊠ North Shore Clinic, ☎ 808/828–1418), Kukui Grove (☎ 808/246–0051 or 808/742–1621), 'Ele'ele (☎ 808/335–0499), Kōloa (☎ 808/246–0051 or 808/742–1621), and Kapa'a (☎ 808/822–3431). Physicians are on call 24 hours (☎ 808/245–1831).

Emergencies

Police, ambulance, or fire department (☎ 911).

HOSPITALS

Wilcox Memorial Hospital (⊠ 3420 Kūhiō Hwy., Līhu'e, ☎ 808/245–1100). **Kaua'i Veterans Memorial Hospital** (⊠ 4643 Waimea Canyon Dr., Waimea, ☎ 808/338–9431).

Guided Tours

There are three major methods for getting a good guided look at the Garden Isle: by land, by sea, and by air. You can book these tours through the travel desk of your hotel or call directly.

GREAT OUTDOORS TOURS

Aloha Kaua'i Tours. You'll get *way* off the beaten track on this four-wheel-drive van excursion through Nā Pali–Kona Forest Preserve and the rugged side of Waimea Canyon. The price includes picnic lunch and hotel pickup. Also offered is a half-day backroads tour and a "Sea-Fun" snorkeling tour. ⊠ *Box 3069, Līhu'e 96766,* ☎ *808/245–7224 or 800/452–1113.* 🖃 *$88.*

Kayak Kaua'i. Hawai'i's forests and marshes are the home of rare and exceptional flora and fauna that often go unseen. In addition to kayak rentals and half-day tours for intrepid explorers that traverse mountains, rivers, and ocean, Kayak Kaua'i also offers a Discovery Tour of Kaua'i: a seven-day paddling and hiking adventure with six nights spent in out-of-the-way inns and cottages. ⊠ *Box 508, Hanalei 96714,* ☎ *808/826–9844 or 800/437–3507.* 🖃 *Discovery Tour $1,350, including accommodations, transportation, boats, and meals.*

HELICOPTER TOURS

Kaua'i from the air is mind-boggling. In an hour you can see waterfalls, craters, and places that are inaccessible even by hiking trails. Expect to pay $125 or more per person for the longest, most comprehensive tours, but call around for itineraries. A shorter, less-expensive flight might suit your needs. Don't be afraid to ask about the pilot's experience and safety record. The companies use top-of-the-line equipment, and the operators listed below each have reliable flight experience.

Bali Hai Helicopters (☎ 808/335–3166 or 800/325–8687). Around-the-island, photographer's delight tours are aboard four- and six-passenger choppers from Port Allen Airport on Kaua'i's west side.

Hawai'i Helicopters (☎ 808/826–6591 or 800/994–9099). This company flies out of Princeville on the north shore and offers three tours ranging from 30 minutes to 60 minutes and from $99 to $179.

Island Helicopters (☎ 808/245–8588 or 800/829–5999). Island Helicopters flies out of Līhu'e Airport for 55-minute tours over stunning valleys and waterfalls. Ask about special discounts sometimes available with coupons from free visitors' pamphlets.

South Sea Tour Co. (☎ 808/245–2222 or 800/367–2914). A choice of tours are available from Līhu'e.

Will Squyres Helicopter Tours (☎ 808/245–8881 or 888/245–4354). This company offers group rates and charters from Līhu'e Airport.

ROUND-THE-ISLAND TOURS

Sometimes called the **Wailua River/Waimea Canyon Tour,** this is a good overview of the island, because you get to see all the sights, including Ft. Elisabeth, 'Ōpaeka'a Falls, and Menehune Fishpond. Guests are transported in air-conditioned 17-passenger minivans. The trip includes a boat ride up the Wailua River to Fern Grotto, then a drive around the island to scenic views above Waimea Canyon. The tour stops at a casual restaurant for lunch (not included in tour price). Companies offering round-the-island ground tours include Polynesian Adventure Tours and Roberts Hawai'i Tours (☞ Tour Companies, *below*).

Best of Kaua'i Tour. This whirlwind day-long tour, sponsored by the North Shore Cab Company, focuses on the highlights of the east and north shores. It includes a visit to Kilohana, a refurbished plantation mansion in Līhu'e, followed by a boat ride to the Fern Grotto. Later, you take a tour of Kīlauea Lighthouse and end with a helicopter tour out of Līhu'e Airport. Ground transportation is in 15-passenger, air-conditioned vans. North Shore Cab will pick you up at Līhu'e Airport or at your hotel if it's on the north or east side of the island. ⊠ *Box 757, Hanalei 96714,* ☎ *808/826–6189.* ☞ *$139 per person with minimum 6 people.*

SPECIAL-INTEREST TOURS

Fern Grotto. Cruise boats depart Wailua Marina at the mouth of the Wailua River for the Fern Grotto. Round-trip excursions, on 150-passenger flat-bottom riverboats, take an hour and a half, including time to walk around the grotto and environs. During the boat ride, guitar and 'ukulele players regale you with Hawaiian melodies and tell the history of the river. The 3-mi upriver trip culminates at a yawning lava tube that is covered with enormous fishtail ferns. Two companies offer several trips daily to Fern Grotto: **Wai'ale'ale Boat Tours** (⊠ Wailua Marina, Kapa'a, ☎ 808/822–4908) and **Smith's Motor Boat Service** (⊠ 174 Wailua Rd., Kapa'a, ☎ 808/821–6892). Both charge $15 for the trip.

Gay and Robinson Sugar Mill Tours. This tour takes you first into the heart of a cane field where you learn about the history and the cultivation of sugar in Hawai'i, then concludes with a hard-hat tour in one of the few remaining working sugar mills in the islands. The roar of the giant gears, crushing machines, and centrifuges would strike joy in the heart of any "Tim the Toolman" type. ⊠ *423 Kauamakani Ave., Kaumakani 96747,* ☎ *808/335–2824,* FAX *808/335–6852.* ☞ *$30* ☉ *Weekdays 8:45–12:45.*

Hawai'i Movie Tours. Comfortable minibuses with big television screens carry 14 passengers from the southeast end of the island to the north shore to see movie locations filmed in *Jurassic Park, Raiders of the Lost Ark, South Pacific, Blue Hawaii, Gilligan's Island,* and more. One stop is for a picnic lunch at 'Anini Beach. A deluxe tour includes helicopter viewing, a boat trip to the Fern Grotto, lunch, and a lū'au. ✉ *Box 659, Kapa'a 96746,* ☎ *808/822–1192, or 800/628–8432.* 🎫 *$85, deluxe tour $295.*

Kamokila Hawaiian Village. This replica of an old Hawaiian village actually sits on an early village site. The Fernandez family offers a cultural tour with explanations about the sleeping *hale* (house), men's and women's eating hales, plants, and skills such as coconut frond weaving. The village is on the bank of the Wailua River, so guests can also rent a kayak for the day and paddle to a swimming hole with a rope swing and to a hiking trail that leads to a waterfall. Bring your own drinks and picnic lunches. ✉ *5443 Kuamo'o Rd., Wailua 96746,* ☎ *808/823–0559 or 800/628–8432.* 🎫 *$5, kayak rental $25.*

Ni'ihau Tours. Once it was called the Forbidden Isle. Now it takes only 12 minutes to fly from Kaua'i to an island that few outsiders have set foot on since Elizabeth Sinclair bought it from King Kamehameha V in 1864. This 72-square-mi island just 17 mi from Kaua'i is now run by the Robinson family, who raise cattle and sheep on the barren, arid land. The Robinsons continue to preserve Ni'ihau as a refuge of primitive Hawai'i. Island residents speak Hawaiian and do not use electricity, plumbing, or telephones. They get around on bikes and horses. Bruce Robinson initiated Ni'ihau Helicopters in 1987 in order to boost the struggling island economy. Tours avoid the western coastline, where Pu'uwai village—home to the island's 200 residents—is. Flights depart from and return to Kaua'i's Burns Field, near Hanapēpē, and are conducted in an Agusta 109 twin-engine, seven-passenger, single-pilot helicopter. The first touchdown on the two-stop tour is near the sunken crater of Lehua. The second takes you to a cliff overlooking the beach coves of Keanahaki Bay. It's the perfect tour for those with a yen to explore untrammeled territory. There is a four-passenger minimum for each flight, and reservations are essential. Ground transportation is not available. ✉ *Ni'ihau Helicopters, Box 370, Makaweli 96769,* ☎ *808/335–3500.* 🎫 *3-hr tour with 2 stops $280 per person.*

Plantation Lifestyles Walking Tour. To see a lifestyle that is rapidly vanishing, take this unique, volunteer-led walking tour through the residential housing of a real mill camp. In the shadow of the old sugar mill, the dirt lanes of the 70-year-old camp are shaded by fruit trees and tropical gardens, and sometimes elderly residents come out to say aloha. Reservations are needed for the 1½- to 2-hour tours that begin at 9 AM every Tuesday, Thursday, and Saturday at Waimea Plantation Cottages. ✉ *Box 1178, Waimea 96796,* ☎ *808/335–2824,* FAX *808/337–9449.* 🎫 *$10.*

SUNSET CRUISES

Blue Water Sailing. Up to 12 passengers can board a 42-ft luxury Pearson sailing yacht in Port Allen for a two-hour sunset cruise in the turquoise waters of the southern shore. Juice, sodas, and snacks are included in the $60 cost. A half-day snorkel sail is $105, including a deli lunch. ✉ *Box 1318, Hanalei 96714,* ☎ *808/828–1142.*

Captain Andy's Sailing Adventures. The 55-ft catamaran *Spirit of Kaua'i* takes passengers on a two-hour sunset sail along the south shore. Hors d'oeuvres and beverages are included in the $45 cost. Captain Andy also offers a four-hour snorkeling excursion with snacks for $75 and a five-hour Nā Pali cruise from Port Allen with breakfast and lunch for $95. ✉ *Box 1291, Kōloa 96756,* ☎ *808/822–7833.*

Royal Hawaiian Cruises. This catamaran *Navatek II* is equipped with special twin hulls that provide the smoothest ride possible, making it easy to enjoy a gourmet buffet dinner, two cocktails, and live entertainment during the sunset and early evening ($150). Also offered is a champagne brunch cruise five days a week ($85). ✉ *4469 Waialo Rd., #23, 'Ele'ele 96705,* ☎ *808/335–9909, or 800/852–4183.*

TOUR COMPANIES

The companies that take you on guided ground tours of Kaua'i use big air-conditioned buses and stretch limousines as well as smaller vans. The latter seem to fit in more with the countrified atmosphere of Kaua'i. Whether you choose a bus or van tour, the equipment will be in excellent shape, because each of these companies wants your business. When you make your reservations, ask what kind of vehicle you'll be riding in and which tours let you get off and look around. The guides are friendly and generally know their island inside out. It's customary to tip them $2 or more per person for their efforts.

If you're interested in a north-shore sea excursion, be forewarned that big winter waves often cause trips to be canceled, so call first to find out if the company you're interested in is operating. The best-known and most reliable land, sea, and air tour companies on Kaua'i are the following:

Captain Zodiac Raft Expeditions (✉ Box 456, Hanalei 96714, ☎ 808/826–9371 or 800/422–7824) has long been known for its three-, four-, and five-hour boat trips and in-season whale-watch cruises along the Nā Pali Coast.

Kaua'i Island Tours (✉ Box 1645, Līhu'e 96766, ☎ 808/245–4777 or 800/733–4777) takes you around Kaua'i in 11-, 21-, 45-, and 57-passenger vans and 4-passenger Lincoln Town Cars.

Liko Kaua'i Cruises (✉ Box 18, Waimea 96796, ☎ 808/338–0333 or 888/732–5456) tour the northern coastline in a 49-ft powered catamaran while captains share Hawaiian history and legends. Boats depart for 4½-hour tours from Kīkīaola Harbor in Waimea.

Nā Pali Explorer (✉ 9600 Kaumuali'i Hwy., Waimea 96796, ☎ 808/335–9909) departs at 7:30 am from Port Allen to tour the Nā Pali Coast (weather permitting) in a 48-ft adventure craft with an onboard toilet and shade canopy. During the winter months, whale-watching can get up close and personal, as the boat gets you down close to the water. Scenic 2½-hour cruises include a snack; longer snorkel trips include Continental breakfast and picnic lunch, snorkel gear, and a Hawaiian cultural specialist to answer questions. Rates range from $65 to $118. Charters are available.

Polynesian Adventure Tours (✉ 3113-B Oihana St., Līhu'e 96766, ☎ 808/246–0122 or 800/622–3011) specializes in full- and half-day mini-coach tours of Waimea Canyon, Wailua River, and Kaua'i's north shore.

Roberts Hawai'i Tours (✉ Box 3389, Līhu'e 96766, ☎ 808/245–9558 or 888/472–4729) has top-of-the-line air-conditioned vehicles for tours to four different locations.

Trans Hawaiian Services (✉ 1770 Haleukana St., Puhi 96766, ☎ 808/245–5108 or 800/533–8765) offers English- and Japanese-language tours of Waimea Caynon and Hanalei.

Pharmacies

Except for Long's Drugs, most pharmacies close about 5 PM on Kaua'i. The **Kaua'i Medical Clinic** (✉ 3-3420-B Kūhiō Hwy., Līhu'e 96766, ☎ 808/245–1500) has a well-stocked pharmacy at its main clinic (☞ Doctors, *above*). In Līhu'e, try **Long's Drugs** (✉ Kukui Grove Center, Hwy. 50, Līhu'e, ☎ 808/245–8871); in Kapa'a, try **Shoreview Pharmacy** (✉ 4-1177 Kūhiō Hwy., Suite 113, Kapa'a, ☎ 808/822–1447); and in Hanapēpē, **Westside Pharmacy** (✉ 1-3845 Kaumuali'i Hwy., Hanapēpē, ☎ 808/335–5342).

Visitor Information

The **Hawai'i Visitors and Convention Bureau** (⊠ 4334 Rice St., Suite 101, Līhu'e 96766, ☎ 808/245–3971 or 800/262–1400, FAX 808/246–9235, ✎) is easy to find on Rice Street, Līhu'e's main thoroughfare, right near the Kaua'i Museum. The bureau has a good selection of brochures and other visitor's literature, including such free weekly visitor's magazines as *Spotlight Kaua'i* and *This Week on Kaua'i,* and the quarterly *Menu* magazine.

Po'ipū Resort Association (⊠ Box 730, Koloa 96756, ☎ 808/742–7444, or 888/744–0888, FAX 808/742–7887, ✎) is the central source of information about the south shore. Maps and brochures are sent on request.

The **Kaua'i Visitor Center** (⊠ Kaua'i Village, Kapa'a, ☎ 808/639–6175, FAX 808/332–8676) is another good source of information about the Garden Isle. It handles reservations for a variety of activities and has current brochures and schedules on hand.

Several activity centers will help visitors book tours, arrange sporting excursions, rent cars, reserve rooms in hotels and condos, and even plan weddings. These centers include **Pahiō Activities** (⊠ 4331 Kaua'i Beach Dr., Līhu'e, ☎ 808/246–0111), and the **Chopper Shop** (⊠ Po'ipū Shopping Village, 2360 Kiahuna Plantation Dr., Po'ipū, ☎ 808/742–1263).

5 MOLOKAʻI

Something about this island makes it stand
out from its neighbors. You can see it in
the way the sun hits the water of ancient
fishponds or hear it as the waves break
on Pāpōhaku Beach. There's a mysterious
sensuality here that springs from the island's
history and inspires its present.

By Marty
Wentzel

Updated by
Betty Fullard-Leo

NICKNAMES FOR MOLOKA'I have come and gone. In ancient times it was called "Moloka'i of the Potent Prayers," for its powerful *kahuna* (priests) who worshiped in solitude. During the late 1800s it was dubbed the "Forbidden Isle," because Hawai'i's lepers were banished here to a remote peninsula on the northern shore called Kalaupapa. Only in the last few decades has it worn the nickname "Friendly Isle."

Today those who visit the Friendly Isle's shores quickly become aware of its down-to-earth charm. As its neighboring islands become crowded with high-rise hotels, Moloka'i greets its guests modestly with a handful of basic accommodations and unusual sightseeing alternatives.

The Friendly Isle seduces visitors to explore its enveloping tropical outdoors. You can ride a mule or hike a switchback trail down a steep mountain to Kalaupapa, the historic colony once reserved for sufferers of Hansen's disease (leprosy). Tours of the settlement begin at the base of towering sea cliffs. To the east, a horse-drawn wagon tour takes you to Hawai'i's largest *heiau* (stone platforms that were the sites of worship) and through enormous mango and coconut groves. In the island's highest reaches you can explore the Kamakou Preserve atop Mt. Kamakou, the 2,774-acre refuge for endangered birds, plants, and wildlife. Moloka'i also appeals to visitors who enjoy adventure at a personal pace. Plenty of opportunities are available for snorkeling, swimming, hiking, and sunbathing, but there are fewer facilities for organized sports such as fishing, horseback riding, tennis, and golf. The more creative you are, the more you will enjoy your stay.

A major plus of the Friendly Isle is that it is uncluttered. You can drive your rental car down any road and take your time looking around without fear of someone honking at you to maintain the speed limit. Sometimes yours is the only car on the road. There are no buildings higher than three stories, no elevators, no traffic jams, and no stoplights. The fanciest hotel is a 22-room lodge in tiny Maunaloa town.

Moloka'i has miles and miles of undeveloped countryside, like the picturesque farmlands of Moloka'i Ranch (the island's largest local landholder) and the acres of abandoned pineapple fields. Pineapples—seemingly synonymous with Hawai'i in the popular imagination—were once big business for the Dole and Del Monte companies, but the crop's significance to the island's economy has sharply diminished in the face of foreign competition.

At night from beaches on the western shore, you can see the twinkling lights of O'ahu 25 mi across the channel. In spirit, however, Moloka'i is much, much farther away from its highly developed neighbor. With its slow pace and simple beauty, Moloka'i drowses in another era, and, if its 6,861 proud people have their way, it's likely to continue to.

Pleasures and Pastimes

Dining

The choice of restaurants on Moloka'i is limited. During a week's stay, you might easily hit all the dining spots worth a visit, then return to your favorites for a second round. The dining scene is fun, nevertheless, because it is a microcosm of Hawai'i's diverse cultures. You'll find locally grown vegetarian foods, spicy Filipino cuisine, and Hawaiian-style fish—such as *'ahi* or *aku* (types of tuna), mullet, and moonfish, grilled, sautéed, or sliced and mixed with seaweed and eaten raw as *poke* (marinated raw fish)—all on Ala Malama Street in Kaunakakai, with pizza, pasta, and ribs only a block away. What's more, the price is right. Most eateries fall into our least expensive category ($). For something a bit fancier (but casual just the same), try dinner at the Lodge at Moloka'i Ranch, or Kaluako'i Hotel and Golf Club's Ohia Lodge.

Festivals and Seasonal Events

The island has several events around which you might want to plan a trip. For more information, *see* When to Go *in* Smart Travel Tips A to Z at the back of the book. The year kicks off with the Ka Moloka'i Makahiki Festival in January, a day when Islanders and visitors get together to compete in ancient Hawaiian games. Translated, Moloka'i Ka Hula Piko means a "Celebration of the Birth of Hula on Moloka'i." The annual daylong event in May brings performances by some of the state's best hula troupes, musicians, singers, lecturers, and storytellers. It's all in tribute to Kā'ana, on the slopes of Maunaloa Mountain, which is reputed to be the birthplace of the hula. The Moloka'i-to-O'ahu Canoe Race is the world's major long-course outrigger canoeing event. It begins near the harbor of Haleolono. After paddling across the rough Kaiwi Channel, participants finish at Ft. DeRussy Beach in Waikīkī. The event takes place each September (women) and October (men). Thanksgiving Day weekend, the Moloka'i Ranch Rodeo draws cowpokes for contests ranging from bull riding to barrel racing.

Lodging

Moloka'i appeals less to travelers who like impeccable furnishings and swanky amenities than to those who appreciate genuine Hawaiian hospitality in down-home surroundings. Hotel and condominium properties range from adequate to funky. Kaluako'i Hotel and Golf Club has the best larger hotel, whereas Kaunakakai's accommodations lend themselves to visitors on a tight budget and to those who want a central location. There is also a handful of bed-and-breakfasts, as well as the luxury Camps at Moloka'i Ranch, where you can stay in a bungalow-size tent, complete with a queen-size bed and a private bathroom.

Your interest in sports might influence your lodging choice. The Camps at Moloka'i Ranch is the place for people who want to be active: Horseback riding, mountain biking, snorkeling, kayaking, and other activities are in close proximity, and guests are given priority when it comes to availability. For those interested in spa treatments and additional comforts, the Lodge at Moloka'i Ranch in Maunaloa is the island's newest and most luxurious accommodation. Ke Nani Kai and Wavecrest have tennis courts available only to guests.

Outdoor Activities and Sports

Moloka'i's unspoiled beauty, sunny skies, and fragrant winds constantly beckon outdoors lovers. Moloka'i's leading adventure, by far, is a mule ride down a narrow 1,664-ft cliff over a 3-mi, 26-switchback trail to Kalaupapa National Historical Park. You can also take a guided trek through Kamakou Preserve, a Hawai'i Nature Conservancy for endangered plants and birds, but arrangements must be made in advance. Kayakers and hikers can head out on their own or try a guided excursion. At Kaunakakai Wharf, you can arrange a fishing charter, a sailing-snorkeling-scuba outing, or book a whale-watching cruise. Divers should try Mokuho'oniki Island, at the east end of the island. It was once a military bombing target, and artifacts from World War II are scattered throughout its many pinnacles and drop-offs. The area is home to barracuda and gray reef sharks. Black coral is also found here. Depths range from 30 ft to 100 ft.

EXPLORING MOLOKA'I

Moloka'i is long and shaped like a slipper, with the "heel" facing west and the "toe" pointing to the east. The imaginary dividing line is the town of Kaunakakai, which is right in the center of the island's southern shore. West, Central, and East Moloka'i are used as natural divisions in this chapter.

You'll have the most fun if you explore at your own pace in a rental car. Most of the highlights are natural landmarks—waterfalls, valleys, overlooks, and the like—and it's nice to get out and wander around an area at your leisure without worrying that you'll miss the tour bus.

Directions on Moloka'i are often referred to as *mauka* (toward the mountains) and *makai* (toward the ocean).

Great Itineraries

Moloka'i is small enough that you can drive it end to end in a single day. There are no traffic jams to hold you up—unless you get behind a horseback rider or a couple of friendly locals who have stopped their vehicles in the middle of the road to chat. The essence of Moloka'i is the "hang loose" attitude, so to experience the island properly, pace yourself—focus on visiting just a few sights per day.

Numbers in the text correspond to numbers in the margin and on the Moloka'i map.

IF YOU HAVE 1 DAY

Book a **Moloka'i Mule Ride** ④ and a tour of **Kalaupapa** ⑥ prior to leaving home. Fly into Ho'olehua Airport and drive to Ka La'e, where the steep, 26-switchback trail begins. The tour of the former leper colony, where some 43 people live with the now manageable disease currently known as Hansen's disease, is the most emotionally moving experience on Moloka'i, and if you ask nicely, you might be able to convince your driver to stop at **Pālā'au State Park** ⑤ for a photo of the Phallic Rock before you head back to the airport in the afternoon. For less-adventurous souls, flights directly to Kalaupapa can be arranged, thereby eliminating the grueling mule ride.

IF YOU HAVE TWO DAYS

Maunaloa ③ on West Moloka'i makes a good starting point, particularly because many visitors stay in the hotel or condominiums at **Kaluako'i Hotel and Golf Club** ① or in Moloka'i Ranch's luxurious camping facilities. Spend a little time poking through the jumble of treasures at the Plantation Gallery and the adjacent Big Wind Kite Factory, then explore town. Stop for lunch at the Village Grill. On Moloka'i, one of the first orders of business for any vacation ought to be to relax, so by afternoon you'll want to head for the nearest beach. This could be Kaluako'i Hotel and Golf Club's own Kawākiu Beach or, if you prefer privacy, **Pāpōhaku Beach** ②, a few miles southwest of the hotel. When the lengthening rays of the sun signal dinnertime, the resort's Ohia Lodge is a natural choice. Reserve day two for the **Moloka'i Mule Ride** ④ and a tour of **Kalaupapa** ⑥, taking in **Pālā'au State Park** ⑤ and the Phallic Rock afterward. If you've got the stamina after the ride, stop by **Coffees of Hawai'i** ⑧, **R. W. Meyer Sugar Mill and Moloka'i Museum** ⑦, and **Purdy's Macadamia Nut Farm** ⑨. If not, pause for chocolate macadamia-nut cheesecake at the Kualapu'u Cookhouse before heading back to your resort.

IF YOU HAVE FOUR DAYS

Follow the itinerary above for your first two days, and then visit **Kaunakakai** ⑫ on your third day to pick up souvenirs, sample ethnic foods, and stop at the Kanemitsu Bakery for the basis of a picnic later in the day. Try the *lavosh*, a Kanemitsu specialty flavored with sesame, Maui onion, Parmesan cheese, or jalapeño; or a round Moloka'i bread—a sweet, pan-style white loaf. Check out **Kaunakakai Wharf** ⑬ (you might rent a kayak to take along, or set out on a fishing or scuba excursion from here). Otherwise, continue on a leisurely drive to Moloka'i's east end. Along the way, you'll find such sightseeing points as **Kaloko'eli Fishpond** ⑭, St. Joseph's church near **Kamalō** ⑮, and 'Ili'ili'ōpae Heiau, turning around for the return drive when you reach **Hālawa Valley** ⑱. Your final day should be reserved for your own pleasures—perhaps a morning game of golf, an easy hike, a return to the beach, or an easy drive to see anything you might have missed.

When to Tour Moloka'i

Moloka'i's weather is good year-round, and you'll seldom encounter crowds. At any time of year the west end of the island is relatively dry and free of rain—hence its arid landscape. The island gets an influx of visitors during special events and festivals, but for a real taste of old Hawai'i you might want to visit during these weekends anyway. Just be sure you make reservations well in advance if you schedule a trip during the Moloka'i Ka Hula Piko in May, Moloka'i Ranch's Rodeo Days over Thanksgiving weekend, or the Moloka'i Mule Drag at the end of September.

West Moloka'i

Much drier than the east, the western region of the island is largely made up of Moloka'i Ranch, a 53,000-acre tract. Its rolling pastures and farmlands are presided over by Maunaloa, a sleepy little plantation town with a dormant volcano of the same name. West Moloka'i has two additional claims to fame: Kaluako'i Hotel and Golf Club and Pāpōhaku, the island's best beach.

A Good Drive

This driving tour focuses on two of Moloka'i's areas of "civilization." If you're approaching the west end from Kaunakakai on Highway 460 (also called the Kamehameha V Highway), turn right down Kaluako'i Road and right again at the sign for **Kaluako'i Hotel and Golf Club** ①. Park in one of the many small public lots in front of the resort and then stroll the grounds. Stop on the hillside above the beach for gorgeous ocean views, particularly at sunset. If you need information about touring the island, ask at the activities desk in the lobby.

Back behind the wheel, turn right out of Kaluako'i Hotel and Golf Club and follow Kaluako'i Road 2 mi to the west until it dead-ends. This shoreline drive takes you past a number of lovely beach parks, including **Pāpōhaku Beach** ②, the largest white-sand beach in the islands. To find a place to get out and stroll in the sand, look for a big sign for the beach on the makai side of the road.

Turn around and follow Kaluako'i Road back past the resort entrance, and continue uphill to its intersection with Highway 460. Turn right and drive 2 mi on Highway 460 (Maunaloa Highway) to **Maunaloa** ③, a former plantation town with a colorful past, a charming present, and controversial plans for the future. In 1997, the island's first cinema was opened by Moloka'i Ranch in Maunaloa, and in 1998 the first fast-food restaurant—a KFC—started serving. A 22-room lodge complete with spa facilities was completed in August of 1999, and for those interested in country living at its best, Moloka'i Ranch has subdivided house lots and opened model homes in Maunaloa. All these changes are in the name of employment and economic opportunity.

If you follow this excursion at a leisurely Moloka'i pace, it will take you the better part of a day, particularly if your accommodations are not on the west end of the island. A walk around Kaluako'i Hotel and Golf Club, with stops in its shops, can take an hour or more. Most stores are open 9–5.

Another hour can fly by at Pāpōhaku Beach as you dig your toes in its sands and picnic (that KFC in Maunaloa could come in handy) on its shady grassy area. Avoid sitting or walking on the beach between 11 and 1, when the sun is at its peak. Allow one hour for exploring Maunaloa's main street to shop for souvenirs and chat with local shop owners. Do your shopping Monday through Saturday, or you will likely find CLOSED signs on the doors.

Sights to See
✎ *following the text of a review is your signal that the property has a Web site where you will find details and, usually, images; for a link, visit www.fodors.com/urls.*

❶ Kaluako'i Hotel and Golf Club. Moloka'i's only major resort (☞ West Moloka'i *in* Lodging, *below*) covers approximately 6,700 acres of beachfront property, including 5 mi of coastline. Developed in 1968, it looks tame and manicured compared to the surrounding wilds of Moloka'i Ranch. Kaluako'i comprises three bungalow-style condominiums and a hotel, plus residences, ranch properties, a 10-acre beach park, and an 18-hole golf course. ⊠ *Kaluako'i Rd., Maunaloa,* ☎ *808/552–2555 or 888/552–2550.*

★ **❸ Maunaloa.** This blink-and-you'll-miss-it town anchoring the west end of Moloka'i was established in 1923 to support the island's pineapple plantation. Although the fields of golden fruit have gone fallow, many of the workers' dwellings still stand and new homes springing up at the far end of town evoke an earlier plantation-style architecture. Colorful local characters run the half-dozen businesses (including a kite shop and a classic old market) along the town's short main street. This is also headquarters for Moloka'i Ranch, with its Outfitters Center and rodeo arena. ⊠ *Western end of Maunaloa Hwy. (Hwy. 460).*

❷ Pāpōhaku Beach. The most splendid beach on Moloka'i, and perhaps in all Hawai'i, Pāpōhaku, the islands' biggest beach, stretches 3 mi along the island's western shore. On busier days you're likely to see only a handful of other people. If the waves are up, stay out of the water; sunbathe, relax in the shade of its grassy area, or take a walk along the sand. ⊠ *Kaluako'i Rd., 2 mi from Kaluako'i Hotel and Golf Club.*

Central Moloka'i

The center of the island is where the action is, relatively speaking. If you opt to do the Moloka'i Mule Ride in the morning and still feel up to exploring afterward, you can make quick stops at the places along the drive that follows. Central Moloka'i has the shops and eateries of Kaunakakai, the water sports based at Kaunakakai Wharf, and the attractions and natural beauty of the central highlands.

A Good Drive
Driving from Kaluako'i Hotel and Golf Club in West Moloka'i toward the center of the island, you can see how the island is laid out: two dormant volcanoes connected by a vast plain. If you have reserved the **Moloka'i Mule Ride** ④, go directly to Kala'e. Head mauka on Highway 460 and north on Highway 470 to reach the ride. The highway

Moloka'i

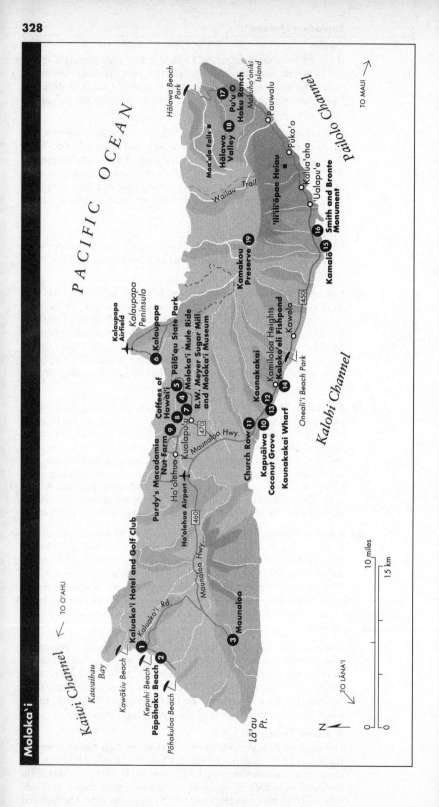

PACIFIC OCEAN

Kaiwi Channel

TO O'AHU

Kawaihau Bay

Kalaupapa Airfield

Kalaupapa Peninsula

Kalaupapa

6 Pālā'au State Park

Coffees of Hawai'i

5 Moloka'i Mule Ride

4 R.W. Meyer Sugar Mill and Moloka'i Museum

8 **7**

9

Purdy's Macadamia Nut Farm

Kualapu'u

Ho'olehua

Maunaloa Hwy.

470

Ho'olehua Airport

1 Kaluako'i Hotel and Golf Club

Kaluako'i Rd.

Kepuhi Beach

2 Pāpōhaku Beach

Kawākiu Beach

Pōhakuloa Beach

Lā'au Pt.

Maunaloa Hwy.

460

3 Maunaloa

TO LĀNA'I

Hālawa Beach Park

17 Pu'u O Hoku Ranch

Moku'ohooniki Island

Pauwalu

18 Hālawa Valley

Mo'oula Falls

Pāilolo Channel

TO MAUI

Pūko'o

Kalua'aha

Wailau Trail

'Ualapu'e

'Ili'ili'ōpae Heiau

16 Smith and Bronte Monument

15 Kamalō

19 Kamakou Preserve

450

Kamiloloa Heights

Kalokoʻeli Fishpond

14

Kawela

12 Kaunakakai

13

11 Church Row

10 Kapuāiwa Coconut Grove

Kaunakakai Wharf

Oneali'i Beach Park

Kalohi Channel

N

10 miles

15 km

0

0

ends at **Pālā'au State Park** ⑤, where you can admire knockout views of **Kalaupapa** ⑥ and the Kalaupapa Peninsula. Bring along a light jacket.

On the way back down the hill on Highway 470, stop at the **R. W. Meyer Sugar Mill and Moloka'i Museum** ⑦ to see photos and machinery from earlier times. Then turn right on Farrington Highway to visit the minuscule town of Kualapu'u, where **Coffees of Hawai'i** ⑧ has a plantation store and espresso bar and offers tours of its coffee fields and processing plant. A five-minute drive west takes you to **Purdy's Macadamia Nut Farm** ⑨ in Ho'olehua.

Head back on Farrington Highway, and then take a right onto Highway 470; go down the rest of the hill and turn left on Highway 460. Near the ocean on Highway 460 are two stops of note that are practically right across the road from each other: **Kapuāiwa Coconut Grove** ⑩ and **Church Row** ⑪. Follow Highway 460 east to reach **Kaunakakai** ⑫, Moloka'i's "big city." Folks who love the ocean will want to locate **Kaunakakai Wharf** ⑬, home base for deep-sea fishing excursions and other adventures.

TIMING

If you save the Moloka'i Mule Ride for another day, there's no need to rush. Otherwise many shops in Kaunakakai may be closed by the time you get there. Allow at least a day to explore this part of the island. If you like big breakfasts, reserve an hour for the Kualapu'u Cookhouse. During your tour of the highlands, take an hour to visit the sugar museum and another hour or more for the macadamia-nut farm and plantation store. Enjoy these activities Monday through Saturday, since they're closed on Sunday. Once you hit Kaunakakai, indulge yourself: Take an hour or two to stroll around town and "talk story" (chat) with the locals. Be sure to save a half hour for snacks at the Kanemitsu Bakery, a local institution.

Sights to See

⑪ **Church Row.** Standing cheek by jowl along the highway are several houses of worship with primarily native Hawaiian congregations. Notice the unadorned, boxlike style of architecture so familiar to missionary homes. ⊠ *Mauka side of Hwy. 460, 5½ mi southwest of airport.*

⑧ **Coffees of Hawai'i.** Tour 500 acres of shiny-leaf coffee trees in a mule-drawn wagon, and then move indoors for an illuminating tour of the coffee processing plant. ⊠ *Farrington Hwy., off Hwy. 470, Kualapu'u,* ☎ *808/567–9241.* ⌨ *$14.* ☺ *Tours Mon.–Sat.*

NEED A BREAK?

In a green plantation-style country store with a big front lānai and fields of coffee trees across the road is **Coffees of Hawai'i Espresso Bar and Gift Shop** (⊠ Farrington Hwy., Kualapu'u, ☎ 808/567–9023), where you can sample the two coffee varieties grown on 450 acres of central Moloka'i land. Try a mango biscotti and wash it down with an espresso or cappuccino.

⑥ **Kalaupapa.** Kalaupapa is the name of a peninsula, a town, and a park. Views of the peninsula from Kalaupapa Lookout in Pālā'au State Park are a standout. Founded in the 1860s and now a National Historical Park, the town of Kalaupapa was once a community of about 1,000 victims of Hansen's disease (leprosy), banished from other parts of Hawai'i. A Belgian man named Joseph de Veuster, ordained in Hawai'i in 1864 and known as Father Damien, committed himself to the care of the afflicted until he died here of the same disease in 1889. At press time there were 43 patients still living in Kalaupapa—now by choice, as the disease is controlled by drugs and patients are no longer carriers. Visitors will most likely not see any patients other than perhaps the tour guide, who might be a bit disfigured, with missing fingers or something unusual about the face. The history of the community is fascinating and heart wrenching. The settlement is accessible via the ☞ **Moloka'i Mule Ride** in Kualapu'u or by guided tour (☞ Contacts and Resources *in* Molokai A to Z, *below*). ⊠ *North end of Hwy. 470.*

❿ Kapuāiwa Coconut Grove. At first glance this looks like a sea of coconut trees. Close-up you'll see that the tall, stately palms are planted in long, elegant rows leading down to the sea. This is one of the last surviving royal groves planted by Prince Lot, who ruled Hawai'i as King Kamehameha V from 1863 to 1872, the year of his death. ⊠ *Hwy. 460, 5½ mi south of airport.*

★ ⓬ Kaunakakai. Moloka'i's commercial hub is a quiet center—not as much commercial commotion as the other links in this island chain. What Kaunakakai does have is personality: It looks like an Old West movie set. Along its one-block main drag is a cultural grab bag of restaurants and shops. People are friendly and willing to supply directions, and no one dresses in anything fancier than a mu'umu'u or aloha shirt. More often, the preferred dress is shorts and a tank top. ⊠ *Hwy. 460, about 3 blocks north of Kaunakakai Wharf.*

NEED A BREAK?	Stop by **Kanemitsu Bakery and Restaurant** (⊠ 79 Ala Malama St., ☎ 808/553–5855) for a taste of its *lavosh* (flatbread) or its round Moloka'i bread, which makes excellent French or cinnamon toast. There is also an assortment of rolls, buns, doughnuts, pies, and cakes. You can sit right at the counter and have a diner-style breakfast or lunch. Kanemitsu is closed Tuesday.

⓭ Kaunakakai Wharf. The docks, once bustling with watercraft exporting pineapples, now ship out potatoes, tomatoes, baby corn, herbs, and other produce. The wharf is also the starting point for various excursions, including deep-sea fishing, sailing, snorkeling, whale-watching, and scuba diving. ⊠ *Hwy. 450 and Ala Malama St.; drive makai on Kaunakakai Pl., which dead-ends at the wharf.*

★ ❹ Moloka'i Mule Ride. To reach the town of Kalaupapa, do it on the back of a sure-footed, stubborn steed. Mount a friendly mule and wind your way along a 3-mi, 26-switchback trail built in 1886 as a supply route to the settlement below. Once in Kalaupapa, you'll get a guided tour of the town and a picnic lunch. No one under the age of 16 is allowed to visit Kalaupapa, and everyone—even those who walk down—must be part of a tour. The trail is very steep, down some of the highest sea cliffs in the world. It's narrow and has no rails, so if it's muddy, the ride is cancelled. Only those in good shape should attempt the ride, as two hours each way on a mule can take its toll. The entire tour takes seven hours. Hikers need to start walking by 8 to coordinate with the guided tour of the facility. It's wise to make reservations for the tour before arrival, as mules are limited. ⊠ *100 Kala'e Hwy. (Hwy. 470), Kualapu'u,* ☎ *808/567–6088.* ☜ *$150, including picnic lunch, Damien Tour, and completion certificate.* ☉ *Tour Mon.–Sat. 8–3:30.*

★ ❺ Pālā'au State Park. One of the island's few formal recreation areas, this cool retreat commands 233 acres at a 1,000-ft elevation. A short path through a heady pine forest leads to **Kalaupapa Lookout**, a magnificent overlook with views of the town of Kalaupapa and the 1,664-ft-high sea cliffs protecting it. Informative plaques have facts about leprosy, Father Damien, and the colony itself. The park is also the site of **Phallic Rock**, known as Kauleonānāhoa to the ancient Hawaiians. It is said that if women sit by this large rock formation they will become more fertile. The park, open daily, is well maintained, with camping facilities, washrooms, and picnic tables. ⊠ *Take Hwy. 460 west from Kaunakakai and then head mauka on Hwy. 470, which dead-ends at the park.* ☜ *Free.*

❾ Purdy's Macadamia Nut Farm. Moloka'i's only working macadamia-nut farm is open for tours. A family business on Hawaiian homestead land in Ho'olehua, it takes up 1½ acres with a flourishing grove of some 50 trees more than 70 years old. Taste a fresh, delicious nut right out of its shell. Then try the farm's fresh macadamia blossom honey. Look for Purdy's sign behind Moloka'i High School. ⊠ *Lihipali Ave., Ho'olehua,* ☎ *808/567–6495.* ☜ *Free.* ☉ *Weekdays 9:30–3:30, Sat. 10–2.*

❼ R. W. Meyer Sugar Mill and Moloka'i Museum. Built in 1877, this old mill has been reconstructed to signify Moloka'i's agricultural history. The old equipment is still in working order, including a mule-driven cane crusher, redwood evaporating pans, some copper clarifiers, and a steam engine. There is also a museum with exhibits on the island's early history and a gift shop. ⊠ *Rte. 470, Kala'e, 2 mi southwest of Pālā'au State Park,* ☎ *808/567–6436.* ☜ *$2.50.* ☉ *Mon.–Sat. 10–2.*

East Moloka'i

On the beautifully undeveloped eastern end of Moloka'i, you'll find ancient fishponds, a magnificent coastline, splendid ocean views, and a gaping valley that's been inhabited for centuries. The east is flanked by Mt. Kamakou, at 4,961 ft the island's highest point, and home to the Nature Conservancy's Kamakou Preserve. There are miles of rain forests burgeoning with tropical fruit, misty valleys with waterfalls, and ancient lava cliffs jutting out from the sea.

A Good Drive

The road from Kaunakakai east on Highway 450 is 30 mi long, and much of it runs next to the ocean. The farther east you drive, the wilder the coastline, changing from white sandy beaches to rocky shores. Be forewarned that the road, which hugs the shore as it twists and turns, is wrought with bumps and potholes. However, there are several bays beside which you can stop and take a breather. Keep your eyes open for mile markers along the side of the road. At times, they'll be your only references for locating the sights of the east side.

Six miles east of Kaunakakai, look offshore to see **Kaloko'eli Fishpond** ⑭, surrounded by the most picturesque of Moloka'i's historic rock walls. After another 5 mi you reach the natural harbor of **Kamalō** ⑮, followed a mile later by the easy-to-miss **Smith and Bronte Monument** ⑯, dedicated to a pair of transpacific pilots. At Mile Marker 15, a hidden trail leads to the enormous 'Ili'ili'ōpae Heiau. Close to Mile Marker 20 the road climbs and winds through **Pu'u O Hoku Ranch** ⑰, a vast Upcountry expanse with sparkling ocean panoramas.

The road east dead-ends at **Hālawa Valley** ⑱, a lush destination beckoning you to explore its inner reaches on foot. Please don't. Although there is a gorgeous 3-mi trail to the back of the valley, landowners here are known to chase away unsuspecting hikers. You're better off heading for the luscious, tropical **Kamakou Preserve** ⑲. Hiking tours can be arranged in advance.

TIMING

Give yourself a full day for this meandering drive, especially if you want to break it up with a picnic at one of the beach parks. From Kaunakakai, you can complete the tour in a half day. If you're going to tour the Kamakou Preserve allow a full day. The sights on the east of the island are natural, so opening hours don't apply. You might want to save this excursion for a weekend and visit the shops and attractions of East and Central Moloka'i during the week, when they're open.

Sights to See

⑱ Hālawa Valley. As far back as AD 650, a busy community lived in this valley, the oldest recorded habitation on Moloka'i. Hawaiians grew fruit and taro and fished here until 1946, when a fierce tidal wave struck. Now much of the valley is overrun with lush vegetation, though you can still see the remains of house platforms and garden walls. At the base of the road into Hālawa Valley is the beginning of a 3-mi trail that leads back to Moa'ula Falls, a 250-ft cascade. Exploring the trail is not recommended unless you are with an authorized guide (☞ Hiking *in* Outdoor Activities and Sports, *below*), as the valley landowners are not hiker-friendly. ✉ *Eastern end of Hwy. 450.*

OFF THE
BEATEN PATH

'ILI'ILI'ŌPAE HEIAU – Human sacrifices once took place at this impressive, hard-to-find heiau, listed on the National Register of Historic Places. As long as a football field, it is a well-preserved example of Hawai'i's ancient outdoor shrines. This revered site is said to hold great power to this day. Please act with respect by speaking in a soft voice. The sacrifices were introduced by Tahitian immigrants who came between AD 1090 and 1240, but the heiau could have existed before then—as early as AD 650, the time of the first island habitation. The old religion, which included human sacrifice, was no longer practiced as of 1819. Don't wander off the designated trail. The whole area is private property. The owners don't object to people simply visiting the heiau, but permission should be requested by phoning 808/558–8132. ✉ *15 mi east of Kaunakakai and ½ mi inland of Hwy. 450; park on the side of road, look for Wailau Trail sign, and walk about 10 min mauka until you see sign on left for heiau.*

★ **⑭ Kaloko'eli Fishpond.** With its narrow rock walls connecting two points of the shore, Kaloko'eli is typical of the numerous fishponds that define southern Moloka'i. Many of them were built around the 13th century. This early type of aquaculture, unique to Hawai'i, exemplifies the ingenuity of precontact Hawaiians. Fishpond walls were built of lava rocks or coral or both. You can see the tops of the dark circular stone walls a foot or two above the surface of the water all along the coast. Usually they were built on fringing reefs. One or more openings were left in the wall, where gates with grills (wooden slats side by side) called *makaha* were installed. These gates could be opened and closed. They allowed seawater and tiny fish to enter the enclosed pond, kept larger predators out, and allowed water to circulate so the pond didn't get stagnant. The ponds were stocked with fish too big to escape through the slats, but tiny fish that entered and were not eaten by bigger ones often grew too big to get out. When fish were needed, they were harvested by net. At one time there were 62 fishponds around Molokai's coast. ✉ *Hwy. 450 about 6 mi east of Kaunakakai.*

★ **⑲ Kamakou Preserve.** Tucked away on the slopes of Mt. Kamakou, Moloka'i's highest peak, is a Hawai'i Nature Conservancy property affording a safe haven for endangered birds and plants. With its 2,774 lush acres, the preserve is a dazzling wonderland full of wet 'ohi'a (hardwood trees of the myrtle family, with red blossoms called lehua flowers) forests, rare bogs, and native trees and wildlife. Guided hikes can be arranged in advance. Hikers meet at Ho'olehua Airport at 8:30 and return by 4. About 12 hikes, limited to eight people, are held each year on Saturdays. Reservations in writing are required well in advance. You can visit the park without the tour, but you need a four-wheel-drive vehicle, and the Nature Conservancy requests that you sign in first and get directions at the following address. ✉ *The Nature Conservancy, 23 Pueo Pl. (Box 220), Kualapu'u 96757,* ☎ *808/553–5236.* 🎫 *Free; donation suggested for guided hike, $10 members, $25 nonmembers (includes one-year membership).*

⓯ Kamalō. A natural harbor for small cargo ships during the 19th century, this is also the site of St. Joseph's, a tiny white church built by Father Damien (☞ Kalaupapa *in* Central Molokai, *above*) in the 1880s. ✉ *Hwy. 450 about 11 mi east of Kaunakakai, on makai side.*

⓱ Pu'u O Hoku Ranch. A 14,000-acre private spread in the highlands of East Moloka'i, Pu'u O Hoku was developed in the '30s by wealthy industrialist Paul Fagan. Highway 450 cuts right through this rural gem with its green pastures and grazing horses and cattle. As you drive along enjoy the splendid views of Maui and Lāna'i. The small island off the coast is **Mokuho'oniki,** where the military practiced bombing techniques during World War II. ✉ *Hwy. 450 about 20 mi east of Kaunakakai.*

⓰ Smith and Bronte Monument. This humble sight tucked away in a grove of trees and bushes is dedicated to Ernest Smith and Emory Bronte, Americans who crash-landed here in 1927. They were the first civilians to complete a transpacific flight from California, a noteworthy feat even if it did have a bumpy ending. They ran out of fuel over Moloka'i and ended up in a grove of kiawe trees, both wings having been sheared off the airplane and the fuselage broken in two. Amazingly, the aviators walked away with only scratches from the trees. ✉ *Hwy. 450, 12 mi east of Kaunakakai, makai side.*

NEED A
BREAK?

The best place to grab a snack or stock up on picnic supplies is the **Neighborhood Store 'N Counter** (✉ Hwy. 450, 16 mi east of Kaunakakai, Puko'o, ☎ 808/558–8498). It's the last store on your drive heading east from Kaunakakai on Highway 450.

BEACHES

Moloka'i has numerous beaches, many of them quite remote and undisturbed, so don't be surprised if you're the only person sunbathing for miles. The largest and most beautiful beaches are along the west coast, but steer clear of their high winter waves. Beaches fronting the Kaunakakai hotels and condominiums are narrow and less appealing, yet the shallow waters are almost always calm for wading. At the extreme east end of the island is the beach fronting Hālawa Valley, a nice place to relax after the long drive it takes to get there. All of the beaches are free and open to the public. None have telephones. To find out more about them, contact the **Department of Parks, Land and Natural Resources** (✉ Box 153, Kaunakakai 96746, ☎ 808/567–6083).

West Moloka'i

Kawākiu Beach. One of the best swimming beaches on Moloka'i, Kawākiu is part of the Kaluako'i Hotel and Golf Club. It has also been set aside as a beach park in honor of its archaeological sites, including house platforms and structures from an ancient Hawaiian settlement. Outdoor showers are available at the resort, but there are no lifeguards. ✉ *Kaluako'i Rd., northern end of bay in front of Kaluako'i Hotel and Golf Club.*

Kapukahehu Bay. Local people like to surf just out from this bay in a break called Dixie's or Dixie Maru. The sandy protected cove is usually completely deserted during the weekdays but can fill up when the surf is up. There are no facilities. ✉ *Drive about 3½ mi beyond*

Pāpōhaku Beach to end of coastal road on northwest end of island; beach access sign on makai side of road points to parking lot.

Kepuhi Beach. Ideal for strolling, sunbathing, and watching the sunset, this white-sand beach stretches about ½ mi in front of Kaluako'i Hotel and Golf Club. However, it is fairly windy here all year long, which makes the swimming somewhat dangerous during high tide. There are outdoor showers at the resort but no lifeguards. ⊠ *Kaluako'i Hotel and Golf Club, Kaluako'i Rd.*

★ **Pāpōhaku Beach.** Perhaps the most sensational beach in Hawai'i, Pāpōhaku is a 3-mi-long strip of white sand, the longest of its kind on the island. It's also quite wide, so you can sunbathe at a comfortable distance from your neighbor. Some places are too rocky for swimming; look carefully before entering the water and go in only when the waves are small (generally in summer). Between the parking lot and the beach are outdoor showers, picnicking facilities, and a rest room. There are no lifeguards. ⊠ *Kaluako'i Rd.; 2 mi beyond Kaluako'i Hotel and Golf Club, look for sign on makai side of road.*

Central Moloka'i

Oneali'i Beach Park. From this spot there are smashing views of Maui and Lāna'i across the Pailolo Channel. It's also the only decent beach park on the island's south-central shore. A narrow and long beach, Oneali'i has adequate swimming in calm waters year-round, along with rest rooms, outdoor showers, and tree-shaded picnic tables. There are no lifeguards. ⊠ *Hwy. 450 east of Hotel Moloka'i.*

East Moloka'i

Hālawa Beach Park. The long drive to Hālawa Valley is worth it, in part because it culminates in this pretty, curving beach flanked by cliffs. Swimming is safe only during the summer. Watch out for the hazardous currents and high surf in winter. A small pavilion with grassy areas on either side is popular with locals for family picnics. An outdoor shower is available, but there aren't any lifeguards. ⊠ *Drive east on Hwy. 450 until it dead-ends at beach.*

DINING

Moloka'i is not the dining hub of the islands. For example, East Moloka'i only has one dining establishment, Neighborhood Store 'N Counter (☞ East Moloka'i *in* Exploring Moloka'i, *above*). Still, with low prices and a host of local specialties to try, most diners are happy and enjoy the laid-back island atmosphere. Restaurants listed are open daily unless otherwise noted. For an explanation of price categories, *see* Dining *in* Smart Travel Tips A to Z at the back of the book.

West Moloka'i

$$–$$$$ ✕ **Maunaloa Room.** Bar none, the Maunaloa Room serves the finest
★ (and priciest) haute cuisine on the island. The chef describes his menu as "Moloka'i regional" and buys as many ingredients as possible locally. This is one of the few places you can order such fancy dishes as a Moloka'i 'opihi (a crunchy limpet) appetizer and pan-seared venison as an entrée. Corn and crab bisque and macadamia nut–crusted catch of the day on spinach with lobster coconut curry sauce and pineapple ginger relish are delicately and deliciously flavored. Views from an open-air deck stretch 3 mi to the ocean. Inside the decor follows a ranch theme with wooden tables and wagon-wheel chandeliers with electric candles. ⊠ *Lodge at Moloka'i Ranch, 8 Maunaloa Hwy., Maunaloa,* ☎ *808/660–2725. Reservations recommended. AE, MC, V.*

$$ ✕ **Ohia Lodge.** Although one of the most formal restaurants on Moloka'i, this '70s-style dining room at the Kaluako'i Hotel and Golf Club (☞ West Moloka'i *in* Lodging, *below*) is still pretty casual. Dark wood is offset by bright ocean vistas during the day. Ask for a table on the lower level, close to the picture windows. The menu is American with island overtones—kalua pork, pot stickers, tempura, and Portuguese bean soup with Moloka'i bread. Fresh catch of the day is either sautéed with soy sauce and butter or broiled with lemon. ⊠ *Kaluako'i Hotel and Golf Club, Kaluako'i Rd., Maunaloa,* ☎ *808/552–2555. Reservations essential. AE, D, DC, MC, V. No lunch.*

$–$$ ✕ **The Village Grill.** Diners might arrive on horseback, Harley, or Honda rent-a-car to the Village Grill, but they're all bound to get a real taste of local favorites—prime rib, New York steak, pizza—flavored with locally grown herbs. Half the fun is cooking your own on a stone grill, brought to the table so your meal is guaranteed hot. Try a "cow pie" for dessert, a mound of vanilla, macadamia-nut, and coffee ice cream in a graham-cracker crust with three sweet sauces. The restaurant sports a historic bar that once graced O'ahu's Pearl City Tavern. ⊠ *Mauka side of Maunaloa Hwy., Maunaloa,* ☎ *808/552–0012. AE, DC, MC, V.*

Central Moloka'i

$$–$$$ ✕ **Pu'u Ho'omaha (Hotel Moloka'i Restaurant).** An earlier Hawai'i seems palpable as you sit at open-air, candlelit tables and gaze across outrigger canoes to the ocean a few feet away. It's a toss-up whether to order Moloka'i coconut shrimp deep-fried in a tempura batter, or the broiled baby-back ribs smothered in barbecue sauce. Friday and Saturday nights a combination of prime rib specials and island entertainers make this a local gathering place. Continental breakfast gives way to a full breakfast service on Saturday and Sunday. ⊠ *Makai side of Kamehameha Hwy, Kaunakakai,* ☎ *808/553–5347. MC, V.*

$ ✕ **Moloka'i Drive Inn.** Open since 1960, this simple eatery in the heart of Kaunakakai is Moloka'i's answer to McDonald's. You'll find the usual take-out staples—hot dogs, fries, and sundaes. But locals come here for the food they grew up on, like *min* (chicken soup), shave ice (snow cone with flavored syrup), and the beloved *loco moco* (rice topped with a hamburger and fried egg, covered in gravy). ⊠ *857 Ala Malama St., Kaunakakai,* ☎ *808/553–5655. No credit cards.*

$ ✕ **Moloka'i Pizza Cafe.** This cheerful order-at-the-counter restaurant is a popular gathering spot for visitors and locals. Pizza, sandwiches, salads, pasta, soft-serve ice cream, homemade pies, and fresh fish are simply prepared and tasty. ⊠ *Kaunakakai Pl. on the Wharf Rd., Kaunakakai,* ☎ *808/553–3288. Reservations not accepted. No credit cards.*

$ ✕ **Outpost Natural Foods.** Vegetarian cuisine has made its way to Kaunakakai in the form of this unpretentious natural foods store and carryout. Just off Ala Malama Street, it stocks good salads as well as vegetarian burritos, tempeh burgers, and a daily special hot entrée such as curried vegetables. Its fruit smoothies are delicious, and it sells fresh produce. ⊠ *70 Makaena St., Kaunakakai,* ☎ *808/553–3377. Reservations not accepted. No credit cards. Closed Sat.*

$ ✕ **Oviedo's.** Kaunakakai may seem lacking in ways, but it does have two authentic Filipino diners, Oviedo's and Rabangs. Oviedo's, where the waitresses treat you like family, is the better of the two. It specializes in *adobos* (stews) with traditional Filipino spices and sauces. Try the tripe, pork, or beef adobo for a real taste of tradition. You can eat in or take out. ⊠ *145 Ala Malama St., Kaunakakai,* ☎ *808/553–5014. Reservations not accepted. No credit cards.*

$ ✕ **Sundown Deli.** This clean little rose-color deli serves primarily freshly made take-out food. Sandwiches can be ordered on a half-dozen types of bread, and the Portuguese bean soup and chowders are rich and filling. Some specials, perhaps vegetarian quiche, change daily. The chiffonlike *liliko'i* (passion fruit) pie is great with an espresso. Vitamins and locally themed T-shirts are also found here. ⊠ *145 Ala Malama Ave., Kaunakakai,* ☎ *808/553–3713. Reservations not accepted. AE, MC, V. Closed Sun.*

LODGING

Several of the lodging establishments listed in this chapter arrange outdoor excursions and have sports facilities that aren't accessible to nonguests and are hard to find elsewhere. Check each review to find the accommodation that best suits your needs. Some properties also offer free shuttle transportation from the airport—ask when you book your room. For an explanation of price categories, *see* Lodging *in* Smart Travel Tips A to Z at the back of the book.

West Moloka'i

$$$–$$$$ ⚠ **The Camps at Moloka'i Ranch.** Comfortable camping is the name
    ★   of the game at these one- and two-unit tents managed by Moloka'i Ranch. Canvas and yurt tents are grouped in distinct locations. Upcountry near Maunaloa and the rodeo arena—with views of Cook pines, grassy pasturelands, and the ocean—is Paniolo Camp, which is the most economical; Kolo Cliffs Camp, on a bluff overlooking the ocean and a short distance from the beach, is good for couples; and Kaupoa Beach Camp has all double units (good for families or groups) right on the beach. Mounted on wooden platforms, tents have solar-powered running water and lights and self-composting flush toilets. Three meals are served family-style each day in an open-air pavilion for an additional fee. Box lunches are also available, and individual ice chests are restocked with soft drinks daily. Extensive outdoor activities, including snorkeling, kayaking, and sporting clays, are available with discounted rates to guests. In addition, a ropes course includes cooperative activities that build trust and communication among guests. A 980-ft "zipline" over a ravine is one of many elements that challenge participants. There's free shuttle transport to the beach. ⊠ *Maunaloa Hwy. (Box 259), Maunaloa 96770,* ☎ *808/552–2791 or 877/726–4656,* ℻ *808/534–1606. 100 tents. Hiking, horseback riding, snorkeling, boating, mountain bikes. AE, MC, V.* ✎

$$$–$$$$ ▥ **The Lodge at Moloka'i Ranch.** This plantation-style lodge with
    ★   wraparound lānai is Moloka'i's newest and plushest accommodation. Each of the 22 suites sports its own name and decor, as well as its own private lānai. Some rooms have skylights for stargazing at night. Ranching memorabilia reminiscent of the 1930s and '40s and artwork by local artists decorate guest room walls. An impressive stone fireplace in the central great room and a games room make socializing pleasant during cool Moloka'i evenings, and pathways and a greenhouse make the grounds worth exploring during the day. Spa facilities here exude a tranquil, country feeling with massage rooms, juice bar, and separate sauna facilities for men and women. Guests can reserve Moloka'i Ranch activities (horseback rides, fishing, mountain biking, etc.). ⊠ *Maunaloa Hwy., Maunaloa 96770,* ☎ *808/660–2725 or 877/ 726–4656,* ℻ *808/534–1606. 22 suites. Restaurant, bar, air-conditioning, pool, sauna, spa, recreation room. AE, MC, V.* ✎

$$$ ▥ **Ke Nani Kai.** This well-managed condominium complex is set back from the water. Views are of the gardens and golf course, but the beach is a mere five-minute walk away. Furnished lānai have flower-laden trellises, and the spacious interiors are decorated with tropical rattans and pastels. Each unit has a washer-dryer and a completely equipped kitchen. ✉ *Kaluako'i Rd. (Box 289), Ke Nani Kai Resort, Maunaloa 96770,* ☎ *808/552–2761 or 800/888–2791,* FAX *808/552–0045. 120 condominiums (37 rentals). Kitchenettes, pool, 18-hole golf course, 2 tennis courts. AE, D, DC, MC, V.* ⌨

$$–$$$ 🏨 **Paniolo Hale.** Perched high on a ledge overlooking the beach, Pan-
★ iolo Hale is one of Moloka'i's best condominium properties. Some units have spectacular ocean views. Guests can choose from among studios and one- or two-bedroom units, all with screened lānai and kitchens; some have hot tubs for an additional charge. Kitchens are well equipped, and the rooms are tidy and simple. Adjacent to the Kaluako'i Golf Course and a stone's throw from the Kaluako'i Hotel and Golf Club, the property is some nights a playground for wild turkeys and deer. ✉ *Lio Pl. (Box 190), Maunaloa 96770,* ☎ *808/552–2731 or 800/367–2984,* FAX *808/552–2288. 77 condominiums (23 rentals). Kitchenettes, pool, 18-hole golf course, paddle tennis. AE, MC, V.* ⌨

$$ 🏨 **Kaluako'i Hotel and Golf Club.** This property does its best to pro-
vide a sense of laid-back elegance for its guests, but it's showing signs of wear and tear. Two-level complexes are set on ultragreen lawns shaded by immense palm trees and brightened by bougainvillea bushes. Rooms have high ceilings with exposed-wood beams, rattan furnishings, and bright tropical colors. Some units have kitchenettes and furnished lānai. ✉ *Kaluako'i Rd. (Box 1977), Maunaloa 96770,* ☎ *808/552–2555 or 888/552–2550,* FAX *808/552–2821. 104 rooms. Restaurant, bar, snack bar, in-room VCRs, refrigerators, pool, 18-hole golf course. AE, D, DC, MC, V.* ⌨

$$ 🏨 **Kaluako'i Villas.** Studios and one-bedroom ocean-view suites are decorated in blue and mauve, with island-style art, rattan furnishings, and private lānai. Units are spread out in 21 two-story buildings covering 29 acres. Guests can take advantage of Kaluako'i Hotel and Golf Club's many activities, though there are no signing privileges. ✉ *1131 Kaluako'i Rd. (Box 200), Maunaloa 96770,* ☎ *808/552–2721 or 800/367–5004,* FAX *808/552–2201. 56 rooms, 11 suites, 2 1-bedroom cottages. Kitchenettes, in-room VCRs, pool, 18-hole golf course, shops. AE, MC, V.* ⌨

Central Moloka'i

$$$ 🏨 **Moloka'i Shores.** Every room in this oceanfront, three-story prop-
erty has a view of the water. Guests can stay in either one-bedroom, one-bath units or two-bedroom, two-bath units. All have furnished lānai, which look out on 4 acres of tropical gardens. In addition, picnic ta-
bles and barbecue areas are available. ✉ *Kamehameha Hwy., No. 450 (Box 1037), Kaunakakai 96748,* ☎ *808/553–5954 or 800/535–0085,* FAX *800/633–5085. 100 units (30 1-bedroom rentals, 2 2-bedroom rentals). Kitchenettes, pool, shuffleboard. AE, D, MC, V.*

$ 🏨 **A Hawaiian Getaway.** Guests in the two bedrooms here use the same
entrance, bathroom, and living room as the proprietors. But for those wanting to learn about Moloka''is history and culture, gracious hosts Lawrence and Catherine Aki have an extensive library and also con-
duct cultural hikes (☞ Hiking *in* Outdoor Activities and Sports, *below*). The two rooms are small and simply decorated. Both have double beds, and one has a television and VCR. You're within walk-
ing distance of Kaunakakai. ✉ *270 Kaiwi St., Kaunakakai 96748,* ☎ *808/553–9803, 800/274–9303. 2 rooms with shared bath. Library, coin laundry. No credit cards.*

$ 🏨 **Hotel Moloka'i.** This hotel is right on the beach, but the pool on
premises is a better alternative for swimming. Furnishings are tropi-
cal, with basket swings on the lānai, white rattan accents in the rooms, and wood beams on the ceiling. The hotel often offers overnight

deals in conjunction with airlines and rental-car companies. Ask
about this when you make your reservation. The Hotel Moloka'i
Restaurant serves Continental breakfast, lunch, dinner, and libations.
⊠ *Box 1020, Kamehameha V Hwy., Kaunakakai 96748,* ☎ *808/553–
5347 or 800/367–5004,* ⅢX *808/553–5047. 45 rooms. Restaurant, fans,
pool. AE, D, DC, MC, V.* ⊛

East Moloka'i

$$$ ⊞ **Dunbar Beachfront Cottages.** Two 2-bedroom, 2-bath cottages, each
with it's own secluded beach, are right on the ocean about a quarter mile
apart. It's a good spot for swimming and snorkeling and great for whale-
watching during the winter months. Covered lānais have panoramic vis-
tas of Maui, Lana'i, and Kaho'olawe across the ocean. These spotlessly
clean, serene cottages with complete kitchens are hard to leave at the
end of a three-night minimum stay. ⊠ *HC01, Box 901, Kauanakakai
96748,* ☎ *808/558–8153, 800/673–0520,* ⅢX *808/558–8153. 2 cot-
tages. Kitchenettes, fans, in-room VCRs, beach. No credit cards.* ⊛

$$–$$$ ⊞ **Hale Kawaikapu.** A cottage and a house, both fully furnished, are
available for weekly or longer rentals on a 10-acre oceanfront site. The
house sleeps six and has a large lānai with a queen-size sofa bed and
large dining-room table. The two bedrooms have Polynesian decor. The
cottage, which has grass mats on the floor, sleeps four with two sofa
beds in a downstairs living area and a queen bed in an upstairs loft
cooled by a ceiling fan. ⊠ *Reservations: 532 'Elepaio St., Honolulu
96816,* ☎ *808/521–9202. 1 house, 1 cottage. Fans. No credit cards.*

$$–$$$ ⊞ **Wavecrest.** An oceanfront, south-shore condominium 13 mi east of
★ Kaunakakai, this property is suited to travelers who want to explore
the east side of the island. Individually decorated one- and two-bed-
room condominiums have full kitchens. Each has a furnished lānai, some
with views of Maui and Lāna'i. The shallow water here is bad for swim-
ming but good for fishing. Car-and-room package rates are sometimes
available. ⊠ *Hwy. 450 near Mile Marker 13 (HC 1, Box 541), Kau-
nakakai 96748,* ☎ *808/558–8101 or 800/535–0085,* ⅢX *800/558–
8102. 126 1- and 2-bedroom condominiums (8 rentals). Kitchenettes,
pool, 2 tennis courts, shuffleboard. AE, D, MC, V.*

$–$$$ ⊞ **Kamalo Plantation Bed and Breakfast.** At this tropical paradise 15
minutes east of Kaunakakai, guests can stay either in two cottages or
in the guest suite in a separate wing of the main house. Each Polyne-
sian-style cottage has a fully equipped kitchen, living room, dining room,
and deck. One cottage is set right beside the ocean and has great views
from its huge deck. The large, airy suite, accessed by a private entrance,
has picture windows, a sitting room, and a deck overlooking the gardens. Home-grown fruit and fresh-baked bread are provided at breakfast. ⊠ *10½ mi east of Kaunakakai off Hwy. 450, (HC 1, Box 300),
Kaunakakai 96748,* ☎ ⅢX *808/558–8236. 2 cottages, 1 suite. Kitchenettes. No credit cards.* ⊛

$$ ⊞ **Honomuni House.** A tropical garden setting, complete with water-
falls and a freshwater stream, awaits you 17 mi east of Kaunakakai
on Highway 450. Inside there's an equipped kitchen, one bedroom,
one bath, and a large living-dining room. ⊠ *HC 1, Box 700, Kaunakakai
96748,* ☎ *808/558–8383. 1 room. Kitchenette. No credit cards.*

$$ ⊞ **Kumu'eli Farms.** Floor-to-ceiling windows offer a spectacular view
of the peaks of Ka'apahu and Kamakou and the 8-acre garden surrounding
this property. Several pathways lead to old Hawaiian archaeological sites.
The separate-entry guest room available here is connected to the main
house by a covered deck. It has its own deck, kitchenette, and a big shower
and separate tub with a 6-ft window that opens onto the garden deck.
Hosts Dorothe and David Curtis have decorated the high-ceiling room

with cheerful Hawaiian prints. A 75-ft-long, 8-ft-wide lap pool is on the grounds. Full breakfast is included. ⊠ *10½ mi east of Kaunakakai off Hwy. 450, Box 1829, Kaunakakai 96748,* ☎ *808/558–8284 or 808/ 558–8281,* ℻ *808/558–8284. 1 room. Fan, kitchenette, in-room VCR, refrigerator, pool. No credit cards.* ☜

$$ 🏠 **Puʻu O Hoku Ranch.** At the east end of Molokaʻi, near Mile Marker 25, are two ocean-view accommodations on 14,000 isolated acres of pastures and forestland. The draws here are the views and the peaceful surroundings. The Country Cottage has basic wicker furnishings and lau hula matting on the floors. The lodge, which has 11 rooms opening off a main hallway and seven bathrooms, is similarly decorated. Rooms here are for groups only. A pool and horseback riding are available on the property. ⊠ *HC 1, Box 1889, Kaunakakai 96748,* ☎ *808/558–8109,* ℻ *808/558– 8100. 2-bedroom cottage sleeps 6, 11 rooms. No credit cards.* ☜

NIGHTLIFE AND THE ARTS

Molokaʻi doesn't have much of a nightlife in the traditional sense. Locals enjoy simply sitting around with friends and family, sipping a few cold ones, strumming ʻukulele and guitars, singing old songs, and talking story. Still, opportunities are available to kick up your heels for a festive night out. Go into Kaunakakai, pick up a copy of the weekly *Molokaʻi Dispatch,* and see if there's a church supper or square dance taking place where you can mix and mingle.

Bars and Clubs

Ohia Lodge Lounge. A few steps away from the Ohia Lodge dining room, this laid-back lounge delivers mellow island music by Molokaʻi's own. The *pūpū* (appetizers) menu is strictly local, from pot stickers to spring rolls. ⊠ *Kaluakoʻi Hotel and Golf Club, Kaluakoʻi Rd.,* ☎ *808/552– 2555.* ◷ *Live music Fri.–Sat. 8–11.*

Film

Maunaloa Town Cinemas (⊠ Maunaloa town, ☎ 808/552–2707). Folks from all around Molokaʻi come here nightly for current blockbusters.

OUTDOOR ACTIVITIES AND SPORTS

Golf

Compared with the more commercialized Neighbor Islands, Molokaʻi has a relatively mellow golf scene. The best option is the **Kaluakoʻi Golf Course** at the Kaluakoʻi Hotel and Golf Club. The 18-hole, 6,564-yard course was designed by Ted Robinson and includes five holes next to the beach. ⊠ *Kaluakoʻi Hotel and Golf Club, Kaluakoʻi Rd., 3½ mi from intersection with Hwy. 460,* ☎ *808/552–2739.* ☒ *Greens fee $80; cart included (hotel guests and late-afternoon players pay less).*

The **Ironwood Hills Golf Club** in Upcountry Kalaʻe is a public nine-hole course. This was pastureland until the Del Monte Corporation turned it into a golf course for plantation workers in 1928. The course was redesigned in 1990. It gets windy in the afternoons, so it's a good idea to call for a morning tee time. ⊠ *Turn off Hwy. 460 onto 470 and go north uphill 3½ mi; the dirt road to the golf course is on the left side; Kualapuʻu,* ☎ *808/567–6000.* ☒ *Greens fee $14; cart $14.*

Hiking

You can make a day of hiking to Kalaupapa and back along the 3-mi, 26-switchback trail that is also used for the Molokaʻi Mule Ride (☞ Central Molokaʻi *in* Exploring Molokaʻi, *above*). The trail is well maintained by the National Park Service. You will need a permit to hike the trail, as well as a confirmed reservation with **Damien Tours**

(☞ Contacts and Resources *in* Moloka'i A to Z, *below*) to tour Kalaupapa. For further information contact the **National Park Service** (✉ Box 2222, Kalaupapa 96742, ☎ 808/567–6802).

Hālawa Falls Cultural Hike is a guided trek through private property on the east end of Moloka'i in the lush and lovely Hālawa Valley. Along the way the guide points out a heiau, old rock walls, house sites, and native fruit trees. At Moa'ula Falls you can swim in the pool and eat food you have brought yourself. Hikers meet at 8:30, begin hiking by 9:45, and return by 2. ✉ *Meet at Neighborhood Store, beyond Mile Marker 15 on Hwy. 450*, ☎ *808/553–4355 after 5.* ☞ *$25.*

At **Historical Hikes of West Moloka'i**, Lawrence and Catherine Aki of A Hawaiian Gateway (☞ Central Moloka'i *in* Lodging, *above*) guide four hikes ranging from two to six hours that focus on Moloka'i's cultural past. One hike treks to an ancient adze quarry, another explores the ruins of a village where Hawaiian chiefs played games during the makahiki season, and another follows the remains of an ancient paved trail. Lunch is provided on intermediate and advanced hikes. ✉ *Meet at Moloka'i Ranch Outfitters Center, Maunaloa Hwy., Maunaloa*, ☎ *808/552–2797, 808/553–9803 or 800/274–9303.* ☞ *$40–$90.*

Horseback Riding

Moloka'i Horse and Wagon Ride is a 1½-hour ride that takes in a heiau, a mountain lookout to search for whales in the ocean below, a mango grove, and a beach. Trips take six riders and start at 10. Call to make arrangements. ✉ *15 mi east of Kaunakakai off Hwy. 450 (Box 1528), Kaunakakai*, ☎ *808/558–8380.* ☞ *$40.*

Water Sports

FISHING

Based at Kaunakakai Wharf, the four-passenger, 31-ft twin-diesel cruiser **Alyce C.** (✉ Kaunakakai, ☎ 808/558–8377) runs excellent sportfishing excursions. Shared cost is about $200 a day, $150 a half day. On an exclusive basis, the full-day cost runs approximately $400, $300 for a half day.

Also departing from Kaunakakai Wharf, **Fun Hogs Hawai'i** (✉ Box 424, Ho'olehua 96729, ☎ 808/567–6789) runs the 27-ft *Ahi* for ¾-day and full-day sportfishing for $325 and $400. Fly-fishing excursions are also available (bring your own rods for fly-fishing).

SAILING

The 42-ft Cascade sloop *Satan's Doll* is your craft with **Moloka'i Charters** (✉ Box 1207, Kaunakakai 96748, ☎ 808/553–5852). The company arranges two-hour sails for $40 per person. Half-day sailing trips cost $50 per person, including soft drinks and snacks. A minimum of four people is required, but shared charters can be arranged.

SNORKELING AND SCUBA DIVING

Moloka'i Charters (✉ Box 1207, Kaunakakai 96748, ☎ 808/553–5852) takes people via sailboat on full-day snorkeling excursions to the island of Lāna'i for $90 per person. Soft drinks and a picnic lunch are included.

Bill Kapuni's Snorkel & Dive (✉ Box 1962, Kaunakakai 96748, ☎ 808/553–9867 or 877/553–9867) leaves Kaunakakai Wharf daily for two-hour snorkeling excursions. Whale-watching cruises in season, underwater massages, and diving certification can all be arranged. Prices vary with the length of dive and number of people involved.

You can book a snorkeling excursion or, in season, a whale-watch cruise for $50 per person with **Fun Hogs Hawai'i** (✉ Box 424, Ho'olehua

96729, ☎ 808/567–6789). Fun Hogs' boat *Ahi* also conducts custom-designed cruises. During the calmer summer months, north-shore sight-seeing trips are offered.

Jim Brocker, owner of **Moloka'i Fish and Dive** (☞ Central Moloka'i *in* Shopping, *below*) in Kaunakakai, can fill you in on how to find the best snorkel sites and can rent you the gear.

SHOPPING

Moloka'i has two major commercial drags: Maunaloa Road in Maunaloa and Ala Malama Street in Kaunakakai. Happily, there are no department stores or shopping malls, and the fanciest clothes you'll find are pretty mu'umu'u and colorful aloha shirts. But now that you've gone totally "native," could you ask for anything more?

Each tiny hamlet has emporiums with flair and diversity; the best bargains are locally made artwork and jewelry. Kaluako'i Hotel and Golf Club shops are higher priced and more tourist oriented than the family-run shops in other parts of the island.

Most stores in Kaunakakai are open Monday through Saturday between 9 and 6. In Maunaloa most shops close by 4 in the afternoon and all day Sunday. Call ahead to confirm hours.

West Moloka'i

There is a handful of family-run businesses along the main drag of Maunaloa, a rural plantation town. Shop proprietors always extend the aloha spirit to visitors.

Arts and Crafts
Plantation Gallery (⊠ 120 Maunaloa Hwy., Maunaloa, ☎ 808/552–2364) is Maunaloa's best arts-and-crafts emporium, crammed with everything from clothes to sculpture to musical instruments.

Clothing
A Touch of Moloka'i (☎ 808/552–2555), at Kaluako'i Hotel and Golf Club, sells resort wear with tropical prints.

Grocery Store
Victuals and travel essentials are available at the **Maunaloa General Store.** It's convenient for guests staying at the nearby condos of Kaluako'i Hotel and Golf Club, who shop here for meat, produce, dry goods, and the fixings for their holiday libations. ⊠ *200 Maunaloa Hwy.,* ☎ *808/552–2346.* ☉ *Mon.–Sat. 8–6.*

Kites
The **Big Wind Kite Factory** (⊠ 120 Maunaloa Hwy., ☎ 808/552–2364), a fixture of the Maunaloa community, has custom-made, appliquéd kites you can fly or display. Designs range from hula girls to tropical fish. Also in stock is a wide variety of kite kits, paper kites, minikites, and wind socks. Ask to go on the factory tour, and then take a free kite-flying lesson.

Central Moloka'i

You can walk from one end of Kaunakakai's main street (Ala Malama) to the other in about five minutes—unless you like to peruse, of course. Ho'olehua has just one must-shop stop, the Plantation Store, next to Coffees of Hawai'i.

Clothing
Casual, knockabout island wear is available at the **Imports Gift Shop** (⊠ 82 Ala Malama St., Kaunakakai, ☎ 808/553–5734), across from Kane-

mitsu Bakery. **Moloka'i Island Creations** (✉ 62 Ala Malama St., Kaunakakai, ☎ 808/553–5926) carries exclusive swimwear, beach cover-ups, sun hats, and tank tops. **Moloka'i Surf** (✉ 130 Kamehameha Hwy., Kaunakakai, ☎ 808/553–5093) is known for its wide selection of Moloka'i T-shirts, swimwear, and sports clothing.

Grocery Stores

Friendly Market Center in Kaunakakai is the best-stocked supermarket on the island. Its slogan—"Your family store on Moloka'i"—is truly credible: Hats, T-shirts, and sun-and-surf essentials keep company with fresh produce, meat, groceries, liquor, and sundries. ✉ 93 *Ala Malama St., Kaunakakai,* ☎ *808/553–5595.* ☉ *Weekdays 8:30–8:30, Sat. 8:30–6:30.*

Misaki's Inc. is a grocery with authentic island allure. It has been in business since 1922. Pick up housewares and beverages here, as well as your food staples. ✉ 78 *Ala Malama St., Kaunakakai,* ☎ *808/553–5505.* ☉ *Mon.–Sat. 8:30–8:30, Sun. 9–noon.*

Don't let the name **Moloka'i Wines 'n' Spirits** fool you. Along with a surprisingly good selection of fine wines and liquors, it also carries gourmet cheeses and snacks. ✉ 77 *Ala Malalma St., Kaunakakai,* ☎ *808/553–5009.* ☉ *Sun.–Thurs. 9 AM–10 PM, Fri.–Sat. 9 AM–10:30 PM.*

Island Goods

The Plantation Store is the only shop of interest in Kualapu'u. Once inside, you'll find the most complete range of Moloka'i-made products on the island, particularly 100% Moloka'i coffee. In the market for seed bracelets, or perhaps some jewelry made from coconut shells and wiliwili seeds? This is your place. You'll also find local artwork, homemade jellies and jams, island soaps, pen-and-ink drawings of Moloka'i landscapes, and handcrafted pottery. ✉ *Kualapu'u Base Yard, Farrington Hwy.,* ☎ *808/567–9023.* ☉ *Daily 10–3.*

Jewelry

Along with casual clothing, the **Imports Gift Shop** (✉ 82 Ala Malama St., Kauanakai, ☎ 808/553–5734) has a decent collection of 14-karat-gold chains, rings, earrings, and bracelets, plus a jumble of Hawaiian quilt pillows, books, and postcards. It also carries Hawaiian Heirloom Jewelry, unique replicas of popular Victorian pieces. These stunning gold pieces are made to order with your Hawaiian name inscribed on them. **Moloka'i Island Creations** (✉ 62 Ala Malama St., Kaunakakai, ☎ 808/553–5926) carries its own unique line of jewelry, including sea opal, coral, and sterling silver, as well as other gifts and resort wear.

Sporting Goods

Moloka'i Bicycle. This shop sells and rents mountain and road bikes as well as jogging strollers, kids trailers, helmets, and racks. It supplies maps and information on biking and hiking, and will drop off and pick up equipment for a fee nearly anywhere on the island. ✉ 80 *Mohala St., Kaunakakai,* ☎ *808/553–3931.* ☉ *Weekdays.*

Moloka'i Fish and Dive. Make this the main source for your sporting needs, from snorkeling rentals to free and friendly advice. Owner Jim Brocker knows the island inside out and can recommend the best spots for fishing and diving. Ask to see his original-design Moloka'i T-shirts, and the best books about Moloka'i. ✉ 61 *Ala Malama St., Kaunakakai,* ☎ *808/553–5926.* ☉ *Weekdays 8:30–6, Sat. 8–6, Sun. 8–2.*

MOLOKA'I A TO Z

Arriving and Departing

By Plane

Moloka'i's transportation hub is **Ho'olehua Airport** (☎ 808/567–6140), a tiny airstrip 8 mi west of Kaunakakai and about 15 mi east of Kaluako'i Hotel and Golf Club. If you're flying in from the mainland United States, you must first make a stop in Honolulu. From there, it's a 25-minute trip to the Friendly Isle.

Hawaiian Airlines (☎ 800/367–5320) flies its DC-9 jet aircraft daily between O'ahu and Moloka'i. A round-trip ticket can cost up to $200 per person. **Island Air** (☎ 800/323–3345) provides daily flights on its 18-passenger deHaviland Dash-8 Twin Otters. **Pacific Wings** (☎ 808/873–0877 or 888/575–4546) flies an eight-passenger Cessna three times daily between O'ahu and Moloka'i.

An even smaller **airstrip** (☎ 808/567–6331) serves the little community of Kalaupapa on the north shore. Island Air flies here directly from Honolulu for $180 round-trip, and for $180 round-trip from Ho'olehua Airport. However, you must first have a land-tour confirmation for Kalaupapa. Your arrival should coincide with one of the authorized ground tours of the area (☞ Guided Tours *in* Contacts and Resources, *below*). Otherwise you'll be asked to leave.

BETWEEN THE AIRPORT AND HOTELS

From Ho'olehua Airport, it takes about 10 minutes to reach Kaunakakai and 25 minutes to reach the hotels and condominiums of Kaluako'i Hotel and Golf Club by car. Since there's no rush hour on the Friendly Isle, traffic won't be a problem. There is no bus service.

By Car. From the Ho'olehua Airport, it's easy to find your way on the island's roads. Turn right on the main road, Highway 460 (also called Maunaloa Highway), to reach Kaluako'i Hotel and Golf Club and left if you're staying in Kaunakakai. **Budget** and **Dollar** are the two rental companies with offices at Ho'olehua Airport, while **Island Kine Rent-a-Car** offers airport pickup (☞ Car Rentals *in* Contacts and Resources, *below*).

By Shuttle. For shuttle service call **Moloka'i Off-Road Tours and Taxi** (☎ 808/553–3369) or **Kukui Tours and Limousines** (☎ 808/552–2282 or 808/660–2859). Drivers are on call 24 hours a day. The shuttle service for two passengers costs about $18 from Ho'olehua Airport to Kaunakakai and about $18 to Kaluako'i Hotel and Golf Club.

Getting Around

By Car

If you want to explore Moloka'i from one end to the other, it's best to rent a car (☞ Car Rentals *in* Contacts and Resources, *below*). With just a few main roads to choose from, it's a snap to drive on Moloka'i. You'll find gas stations in Kaunakakai and Maunaloa. If you park your car somewhere, be sure to lock it. Thefts aren't unknown. Drivers must wear seat belts or risk a $42 fine. Children under three must ride in a federally approved child passenger restraint device, easily leased at the rental agency. Ask your rental agent for a free *Moloka'i Drive Guide*.

By Shuttle

Kukui Tours and Limousines (☎ 808/553–3369 or 808/660–2859) offers half-day and full-day tours to various points of interest in seven-passenger vehicles (☞ Arriving and Departing, *above*). **Moloka'i**

Off-Road Tours and Taxi (☎ 808/553–3369) provides personalized service to any point on the island.

Contacts and Resources

Car Rentals
Both **Budget** (☎ 800/350–0540) and **Dollar** (☎ 800/367–7006) have offices at Ho'olehua Airport. Expect to pay between $30 and $50 per day for a standard compact and from $36 to $55 for a midsize car. Rates are seasonal and may run higher during the peak winter months. It's best to make rental arrangements in advance. If you're flying on Island Air or Hawaiian Airlines, see whether fly-drive package deals are available—you might luck out on a less-expensive rate.

Locally owned **Island Kine Rent-a-Car** (☎ 808/553–5242) offers airport pickup and sticks to one rate year-round for vehicles in a broad spectrum from two- and four-wheel drives to 15-passenger vans.

Doctors
Round-the-clock medical attention is available at **Moloka'i General Hospital** (✉ 280A Puali St., Kaunakakai 96748, ☎ 808/553–5331).

Emergencies
Ambulance (☎ 911). **Coast Guard** (☎ 808/244–5256). **Fire** (☎ 808/553–5601 in Kaunakakai; 808/567–6525 at Ho'olehua). **General emergencies** (☎ 911). **Police** (☎ 808/553–5355).

Guided Tours

ADVENTURE TOURS
Moloka'i Action Adventures. Walter Naki is a friendly, knowledgeable guide who custom-designs tours to Moloka'i's outdoors attractions. One of his most popular excursions is a north-shore cruise aboard a 21-ft Boston Whaler. He is also a competent guide for year-round fishing and hunting excursions for deer, wild boar, and goats. Prices vary. ✉ *Box 1269, Kaunakakai 96748,* ☎ *808/558–8184.*

FOUR-WHEEL-DRIVE VEHICLE AND WAGON TOURS
Moloka'i Off-Road Tours and Taxi. Visit Hālawa Valley, Kalaupapa Lookout, Maunaloa town, and other points of interest in the comfort of an air-conditioned Jeep Cherokee or Ford Ranger pickup. Pat and Alex Pua'a are your personal guides. They'll even help you mail a coconut back home. ☎ *808/553–3369 or 808/552–2218.* ☞ *$50.* ☉ *Daily; pickup at 9, return at 2:30, but other arrangements are possible.*
Moloka'i Wagon Ride. Island residents Junior and Nani Rawlins take folks on a scenic and informative amble in a horse-drawn wagon. First stop is 'Ili'ili'ōpae Heiau, the largest outdoor shrine in Hawai'i. Next, tour the largest mango grove in the world before hitting the beach for coconut husking, barbecuing, and fishing. Call for arrangements and directions. ☎ *808/558–8132 or 808/558–8380.* ☞ *$50 including lunch.* ☉ *Daily.*

KALAUPAPA TOURS
Damien Tours. These tours are operated by longtime residents of Kalaupapa who are well versed in its history. The four-hour van tour begins and ends at Kalaupapa Airport if you arrive by air or at the foot of the 3-mi trail if you hike down the mountain. Tours depart at 10:15. No one under 16 is allowed. Bring your own lunch and water. ☎ *808/567–6171.* ☞ *$30.*

MO'OMOMI DUNES
The Nature Conservancy. The Conservancy conducts about 12 tours annually of Mo'omomi Dunes, a fine example of a pristine coastal ecosystem on West Moloka'i. The educational walks are for those interested

in geology, archaeological sites, rare plants, snails, and Hawai'i's extinct bird species. Tours are on Saturday and must be booked months in advance. ⊠ *The Nature Conservancy, 23 Pueo Pl. (Box 220), Kualapu'u 96757,* ☎ *808/553–5236.* ➦ *Donation suggested: $10 members, $25 nonmembers (includes one-year membership).*

Visitor Information

You can pick up free brochures and tourist information in kiosks and stands at the airport in Ho'olehua or at the Moloka'i Visitors Association at 10 Kam V Highway in Kaunakakai. Car-rental agencies distribute the free *Moloka'i Drive Guide* along with maps and other up-to-date information.

Moloka'i Visitors Association (⊠ Box 960, Kaunakakai 96748, ☎ 808/553–3876 or 800/800–6367) and **Maui Visitors Bureau** (⊠ Box 580, Wailuku, Maui 96793, ☎ 808/244–3530) can offer advice on accommodations and tours and provide other visitor information.

6 LĀNAʻI

Lānaʻi's only population center is Lānaʻi City, smack in the middle of the island. The town is surrounded by natural wonders: Garden of the Gods, strewn with colorful boulders, to the northwest; breathtaking Hulopoʻe Beach to the south; and Lānaʻihale, the highest point on the island, to the east. Rugged and isolated, with two championship golf courses, one of the world's best diving spots, and hiking and riding trails, Lānaʻi offers both serenity and adventure.

By Marty
Wentzel

Updated by
Sophia
Schweitzer

FOR DECADES, LĀNA'I WAS KNOWN as the Pineapple Island, with hundreds of acres of fields filled with the golden fruit. Today this 141-square-mi island has been renamed Hawai'i's Most Secluded Island, and the pineapple fields have given way to sophisticated hotels and guest activities. In 1990, Dole Foods Inc.—now Castle & Cooke, Inc.— which owns 98% of the island, opened the luxurious 102-room Lodge at Kō'ele, and, the following year, the 250-room Mānele Bay Hotel, plus two championship golf courses. Despite these new additions, Lāna'i remains the most remote and intimate visitor destination in Hawai'i.

Most of the island's population is centered in Lāna'i City, an old plantation town of 2,800 residents, whose tiny houses have colorful façades, tin roofs, and tidy gardens. Although the weather across much of the island is hot and dry, the tall Cook pines that line Lāna'i City's streets create a cool refuge. Here you'll encounter descendants of those who came in the 1920s from the Philippines, Korea, China, and Japan to work in Lāna'i's pineapple fields. Mainland *haole* (Caucasians) have also moved in. Though Lāna'i City has a few family-run shops and stores, its options are limited. You'll find a couple of diner-style eateries; an art center; and the comfy old Hotel Lāna'i, an 11-room hostelry that serves as a gathering place for locals and tourists. The town adds a hint of civilization to a mostly wild island.

Lāna'i City, however, is not the primary reason for visiting the island. Among the unique outdoor attractions is the Garden of the Gods in Kānepu'u, where rocks and boulders are scattered across a crimson landscape as if some divine being had placed them there as a sculpture garden. Adjacent is a self-guided nature trail leading through the Kānepu'u Preserve, a unique dryland forest hosting some 48 native species, including endangered the Hawaiian gardenia. The waters at Hulopo'e Beach are so clear that within a minute of snorkeling you can see fish the colors of turquoise and jade. After hiking or driving to the summit of Lāna'ihale, a 3,370-ft-high windswept perch, you'll find a splendid view of nearly every inhabited Hawaiian island.

Although today it is an island that welcomes visitors with its friendly, rustic charm, Lāna'i has not always been so amiable. The earliest Polynesians believed it to be haunted by evil ghosts who gobbled up unsuspecting visitors. In 1836 a pair of missionaries named Dwight Baldwin and William Richards came and went after failing to convert the locals to their Christian beliefs. In 1854 a group of Mormons tried to create the City of Joseph here, but they were forced to abandon their mission after a drought in 1857.

One of Lāna'i's more successful visitors was a man named Jim Dole (1877–1958). In 1922 Dole bought the island for $1.1 million and began to grow pineapples on it. He built Lāna'i City on the flatlands, where the crater floor is flanked by volcanic slopes. Then he planned the harbor at Kaumālapa'u, from which pineapples would be shipped. Four years later, as he watched the first harvest sail away to Honolulu, this enterprising businessman could safely say that Dole Plantation was a success. But in the late 1980s pineapples ceased to be profitable because of global competition. The solution? The company built two new hotels and developed a tourism industry which is starting to thrive.

Isolated as it may seem, Lāna'i has found a powerful way to connect with the outside world through its hotel-hosted Visiting Artist Program. Pulitzer Prize–winning authors, celebrity chefs, and world-famous actors enliven the island with complimentary performances for guests and residents. You can meet inspirational people such as author Armistead Maupin or jazz guitarist Bucky Pizzarelle.

A visit to Lāna'i can be either simple or elegant. Solitude is easily acquired, though you may encounter the occasional deer on the hillsides, the spirits that linger in the ancient fishing village of Kaunolū, and the playful dolphins of Mānele Bay. On the other hand, you can rub elbows with sophisticated travelers during a game of croquet at the Lodge at Kō'ele or a round of golf. Bring casual clothes because many of your activities will be laid-back, whether you're riding the unpaved roads in a four-wheel-drive vehicle or having a drink on the porch of the Hotel Lāna'i. Come, take your time, and enjoy it before the island changes too much more.

Pleasures and Pastimes

Dining

Lāna'i's has developed its own unique version of Hawai'i regional cuisine. The upscale menus at the two resorts reflect the fresh-flavored products provided by local hunters and fishermen—everything from Mānele *'ahi* (yellowfin tuna) to Lāna'i venison. Lāna'i City's eclectic fare ranges from hamburgers to Cajun dishes and pizzas with organic toppings. Pricing is straightforward: Hotel dining rooms are expensive, and family-run eateries are much more affordable.

Golf

Lāna'i's two championship golf courses compete with the finest in the world. The pine-covered fields of the Experience at Kō'ele stretch across rolling hills. At the top-ranking oceanfront Challenge at Mānele, dolphins and whales have been known to distract even the most serious golfer.

Hiking

Only 30 mi of Lanai'i's roads are paved. But red-dirt, four-wheel-drive roads and walking trails will take you to abandoned villages and historic *heiau* (stone platforms that were the site of worship), isolated beaches and forest preserves. Follow a self-guided walk through Hawai'i's largest native dryland forest or hike the 8 mi of the Munro trail over Lāna'ihale with views of plunging canyons and all of Hawai'i Nei. Before you go, fill a water bottle and arm yourself with provisions and maps.

Lodging

Lāna'i offers several lodging options on its limited number of properties. The Lodge at Kō'ele and Mānele Bay Hotel are luxury resorts, and their rates reflect this. If you're on a tighter budget, seek out a bed-and-breakfast or consider the Hotel Lāna'i. House rentals, although expensive, give you a taste of what it's like to live here.

Snorkeling and Scuba Diving

With Cathedrals (pinnacle formations) for a dive site and angelfish among the marine, it's no wonder that snorkeling and scuba-diving buffs call the waters off Lāna'i a religious experience. For the best underwater viewing, try Hulopo'e Beach (☞ Beaches, *below*), a marine conservation area, or go on an excursion with Lāna'i Ecoadventure Centre (☞ Contacts and Resources *in* Lāna'i A to Z, *below*).

EXPLORING LĀNA'I

Most of Lāna'i's sights are out of the way. You have to search, but it's worth it. Ask your hotel's concierge for a road and site map, fill up on gas if you have a four-wheel-drive vehicle, and bring along a cooler with drinks and snacks. Admission is free to all sights mentioned.

Great Itineraries

Lāna'i is small enough to explore in a couple of days of leisurely travel. Be selective with your time, for it goes by fast here.

Numbers in the text correspond to numbers in the margin and on the Lāna'i map.

IF YOU HAVE 1 DAY

If you can only tear yourself away from your lounge chair for one day of exploring, rent a four-wheel-drive vehicle and get to know the back roads of Lāna'i, where the power of the landscape is immense. If you're staying at the Lodge at Kō'ele or Hotel Lāna'i, allow yourself enough time to see the **Garden of the Gods** ⑦ and the **Kānepu'u Preserve** ⑥ in the morning. After lunch in **Lāna'i City** ⑩, drive down to **Lu'ahiwa Petroglyphs** ② and **Kaunolū** ③, followed by a late-afternoon swim at Hulopo'e Beach (☞ Beaches, *below*). Guests of the Mānele Bay Hotel should reverse the itinerary, with the beach, petroglyphs, and Kaunolū in the morning and Garden of the Gods in the afternoon.

IF YOU HAVE 3 DAYS

Follow the one-day itinerary above. On day two, take an adventurous tour of the undeveloped north and east shores. Pack a picnic and start the day with a drive to **Shipwreck Beach** ⑨ for a morning walk and some sunbathing. Then drive along the bumpy coastal road to **Keōmuku** ⑪, **Kahe'a Heiau** ⑫, **Naha** ⑬, and Lōpā Beach, where you can picnic. After retracing your route, relive the day's adventures over tropical drinks at your hotel's lounge. Start your third day with a cool morning hike atop Lāna'ihale, stopping midway for a picnic. In the afternoon, how about a spa treatment or some time in the swimming pool and hot tub?

IF YOU HAVE 5 DAYS

Follow the three-day itinerary and then dedicate day four to the sport of your choice, be it golf on the championship courses, tennis at the Mānele Bay Hotel or the Lodge at Kō'ele, horseback riding from the Stables at Kō'ele, or sporting clays in the highlands; or sign up for a lesson and learn a new sport. On day five, see the island from the sea by going on a half-day fishing trip or snorkeling–scuba diving expedition. In the afternoon, stroll around Lāna'i City, talk story (chat) with the residents and shop owners, and pick up some island souvenirs like hand-carved pine bowls.

When to Tour Lāna'i

The weather on Lāna'i is warm and clear throughout the year. It's sunniest at sea level, while in Upcountry Lāna'i City the nights and mornings can feel chilly and the fog can settle in on the tops of the pine trees. As in all of Hawai'i, winter weather is cooler and less predictable. For a taste of local arts, crafts, and entertainment, time your trip with an island event such as autumn's Aloha Festivals.

South and West Lāna'i

Pineapples once blanketed the Pālāwai Basin, the flat area south of Lāna'i City. Today it is used primarily for agriculture and grazing and holds historic and natural treasures worth exploring. In the Islands, the directions *mauka* (toward the mountains) and *makai* (toward the ocean) are often used.

A Good Drive

From Lāna'i City, drive south on Highway 440 a few blocks until you reach a major intersection. Go straight, following the highway west to **Kaumālapa'u Harbor** ①, the island's main seaport. Backtrack to the intersection, turn right, and take Highway 440 south (also called Mānele Road). After about a mile you'll see a dirt road on your left leading to the **Lu'ahiwa Petroglyphs** ② and its ancient rock carvings.

Lāna'i

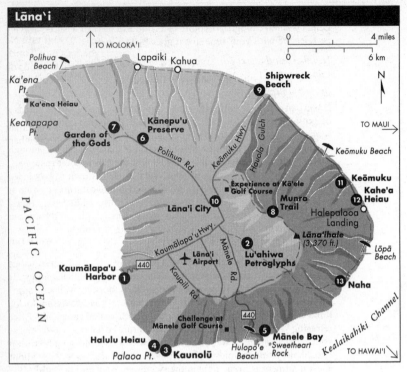

Return to Highway 440 and drive another 2 mi south until the road veers left. Here, go straight on bumpy and unpaved Kaupili Road (you'll need a four-wheel-drive vehicle for this). Then take the fourth left onto another unnamed dirt road. All of this four-wheeling pays off when you reach your destination: the well-preserved archaeological sites of **Kaunolū** ③ and **Halulu Heiau** ④.

Back on Highway 440, drive down the long, steep hill. At the bottom awaits **Mānele Bay** ⑤, with its boat harbor. Take a look at Pu'upehe (Sweetheart Rock) and its sheer 50-ft-high cliffs. The road ends at the island's only true swimming area, Hulopo'e Beach (☞ Beaches, *below*).

TIMING

Although it's a small area, south and west Lāna'i deserves a full day of exploration. If you're a fan of water sports, you'll want to spend half the day at Hulopo'e Beach and use the rest for visiting the other attractions. The south is almost always sunny, clear, and warm, so wear sunscreen and head for shade in the middle of the day.

Sights to See

✍ *following the text of a review is your signal that the property has a Web site where you will find details and, usually, images; for a link, visit www.fodors.com/urls.*

④ **Halulu Heiau.** The carefully excavated remains of an impressive heiau attest to the sacred history of this spot, which was actively used by the earliest residents of Lāna'i. As late as 1810, this hilltop sight was also considered a place of refuge for wayward islanders. ⊠ *From Lāna'i City, follow Hwy. 440 (Mānele Rd.) south; when road makes sharp left, continue straight on Kaupili Rd.; turn makai onto fourth dirt road.*

❶ Kaumālapa'u Harbor. Built in 1926 by the Hawaiian Pineapple Company, which later became Dole, this is the principal seaport for Lāna'i. The cliffs flanking the western shore are as much as 1,000 ft tall. No water activities are allowed here, but if you are in the area on a Thursday, be sure to witness the arrival of the barge. The Island depends on its weekly deliveries. ⊠ *From Lāna'i City, follow Hwy. 440 (Kaumālapa'u Hwy.) west as far as it goes; turn left and drive about 7 mi makai.*

❸ Kaunolū. Set atop the island's highest sea cliffs, Kaunolū was a prosperous fishing village in precontact times. This important Hawaiian archaeological site includes terraces, stone floors, and platforms where 86 houses and 35 shelters once stood. You'll also see petroglyphs, a series of intricate rock carvings that have been preserved. Kaunolū has additional significance because Hawai'i's King Kamehameha I sometimes lived here. ⊠ *From Lāna'i City follow Hwy. 440 (Mānele Rd.) south; when road makes sharp left, continue straight on Kaupili Rd. through pineapple fields; turn makai onto fourth dirt road.*

❷ Lu'ahiwa Petroglyphs. On a steep slope overlooking the Pālāwai Basin, in the flatlands of Lāna'i, are 34 boulders with ancient rock carvings inscribed on them. Drawn in a mixture of ancient and historic styles, the simple stick-figure drawings represent humans, nature, and life on Lāna'i. ⊠ *From Lāna'i City, follow Hwy. 440 (Mānele Rd.) south 1 mi to an unmarked dirt road that leads left through pineapple fields; at end of that road, walk up unmarked trail to petroglyphs.*

❺ Mānele Bay. The site of an ancient Hawaiian village dating back to AD 900, Mānele Bay is flanked by lava cliffs that are hundreds of feet high. A Marine Life Conservation District, it is the only public boat harbor on Lāna'i, and it was the location of most post-contact shipping until Kaumālapa'u Harbor was built in 1926. The ferry to and from Maui also pulls in here.

Just offshore you can catch a glimpse of **Pu'upehe.** Often called Sweetheart Rock, the islet is an isolated 50-ft-high formation that carries a sad Hawaiian legend. To make a long story short, a man hid his wife Pehe here, she drowned, and he then buried her on the summit of this rock with the help of the gods. ⊠ *From Lāna'i City, follow Hwy. 440 (Mānele Rd.) south to bottom of hill and look for harbor on your left.*

North and East Lāna'i

With a ghost town and heiau to its credit, the north and east section of Lāna'i is wild and untamed. The best way to explore the area's distinctive beauty is by hiking or four-wheel-vehicle driving, since most attractions are accessible only by rugged dirt roads.

A Good Drive

From Lāna'i City, take Keōmuku Highway north. Turn left on the road that runs between the Stables at Kō'ele and tennis courts. This leads you to a dirt road, which cuts through hay fields for a couple of miles. At the crossroad, turn right onto Polihua Road, which heads upward through the dryland forest of **Kānepu'u Preserve** ⑥ and, 1½ mi beyond, to the **Garden of the Gods** ⑦. Red and black lava rocks are scattered across this unique landscape. Beyond is a crystal-blue seascape.

Return to Keōmuku Highway, turn left, and drive toward the top of the hill. If you're in a four-wheel-drive vehicle, make a right onto the only major dirt road in sight, and you're on your way to the **Munro Trail** ⑧, an 8-mi route that runs over the top of Lāna'ihale, the mountain that rises above Lāna'i City.

After enjoying the stunning views from the trail, head back to Keōmuku Highway, and follow its long descent to **Shipwreck Beach** ⑨, an 8-mi expanse of sand. Here, stretch your legs and look for glass balls (used as flotation devices for fishing nets) and other washed-up treasures. Return to **Lāna'i City** ⑩ for an afternoon drink and some browsing in its gift stores. Or if you feel adventurous, head southeast (the opposite direction from Shipwreck Beach, but only if you have a four-wheel-drive vehicle). At the end of the paved road (Keōmuku Highway, which dead-ends at Shipwreck Beach), turn right and follow the very bumpy dirt road. Five miles later you will see dozens of tall coconut trees and a historic church. This is the site of **Keōmuku** ⑪, an abandoned town where 2,000 people once lived. A mile and a half farther down the road, you can see the ruins of a temple called **Kahe'a Heiau** ⑫. The road ends 3 mi later at the remnants of an old Hawaiian fishpond at **Naha** ⑬ and the often-deserted Lōpā Beach. To get back to Keōmuku Highway, retrace your route.

TIMING

Give yourself a day to tour the north and east reaches of the island. You can visit all of the following sights any day of the year, but keep your eye on the sky. It's more apt to rain in the highlands than in Lāna'i City. If you're a hiker, you'll want a day just to enjoy the splendors of Lāna'ihale. Bring a jacket because it gets cool up there. A walk along Shipwreck Beach makes a nice morning outing, with stops for shell-collecting, picture-taking, and picnicking. Since most of the driving is on rugged roads, it takes more time to reach such places as the Garden of the Gods and Keōmuku than it does actually to experience them. Relax. On Lāna'i, getting there is half the fun.

Sights to See

★ ❼ **Garden of the Gods.** This heavily eroded landscape is scattered with boulders of different sizes, shapes, and colors that seem to have been placed here for some divine purpose. This lunar appearance is unmatched in Hawai'i. Anyone who's a geology buff will want to photograph the area, which presents magnificent views of the Pacific Ocean, Moloka'i, and, on clear days, O'ahu. Stand quietly and you might spot a deer here. ⊠ *From the Stables at Kō'ele, follow dirt road through hay fields 2 mi; turn right at crossroads and head through ironwood forest 1½ mi.*

⑫ **Kahe'a Heiau.** This ancient temple was once a place of worship for the people of Lāna'i. Today you must look hard to find its stone platforms and walls, for they have succumbed to an overgrowth of weeds and bushes. There are also remnants here of an old wharf used for shipping sugarcane. ⊠ *6½ mi southeast from where Keōmuku Hwy. dead-ends at Shipwreck Beach, on dirt road running along north shore.*

❻ **Kānepu'u Preserve.** The 590 acres of this native dryland forest have been under the stewardship of the Nature Conservancy of Hawai'i since 1991. Kānepu'u is the largest remnant of this unique forest type. More than 45 native species of plants, including endangered Hawaiian gardenia, grow in the shade of such rare trees as Hawaiian sandalwood, olive, and ebony. A short self-guided loop trail with carefully illustrated signs reveals the beauty of this ecosystem and the challenges it faces today. ⊠ *Polihua Rd.,* ☎ *808/537–4508.*

⑪ **Keōmuku.** During the late-19th century, this busy Lāna'i community of some 2,000 residents served as the headquarters of the Maunalei Sugar Company. The company failed, and Keōmuku shut down in 1901. The land was used for ranching, but by 1954 the area had been abandoned. Its church, built in 1903, making it the oldest on the island, is currently being restored by volunteers. There's an eerie beauty about Keōmuku, with its crumbling stone walls and once-stately homes now reduced to weed-infested ruins. ⊠ *5 mi along unpaved road southeast of Shipwreck Beach.*

🔟 **Lāna'i City.** This neat plantation town—Lāna'i's only population center—was built in 1924 by Jim Dole. Remarkably organized, it reflects his wish to create a model plantation village: a tidy grid work of roads lined with tall Cook pines and all the basic services a person might need. Visit the **Lāna'i Arts & Culture Center** to get a glimpse of this Island's creative abundance, then relax with a drink at the vintage **Hotel Lāna'i**, built in 1923 for Dole's VIPs.

★ ❽ **Munro Trail.** This 8-mi path winds through a lush tropical rain forest. It was named after George Munro, ranch manager of the Lāna'i Ranch Co., who began a reforestation program in the 1950s. Use caution if it has been raining, as the roads get very muddy. The trail winds over the top of **Lāna'ihale**, which means House of Lāna'i in Hawaiian. At 3,370 ft, it's the highest point of the island and offers spectacular views of nearly all the Hawaiian Islands. ⊠ *From Lodge at Kō'ele head north on Keōmuku Hwy. for 1¼ mi, then turn right onto tree-lined dirt road; trailhead is ½ mi past cemetery on right.*

⓭ **Naha.** An ancient rock-walled fishpond can be seen clearly here at low tide, where the sandy shorelines end and the cliffs begin their rise along the south, west, and north shores of the island. Local fishermen come here to fish, but the treacherous tide and currents make this a dangerous place for swimming. ⊠ *East side of Lāna'i, at end of dirt road that runs from end of Keōmuku Hwy. along the eastern shore.*

★ ❾ **Shipwreck Beach.** Beachcombers come for its shells and washed-up treasures, photographers love the spectacular view of Moloka'i across the Kalohi Channel, and walkers enjoy its broad, 8-mi-long stretch of sand—in all, a beach to explore. It's not, however, for swimmers. Have a look at the tanker rusting offshore and you'll see that these are not friendly waters. ⊠ *End of Keōmuku Hwy. heading north.*

BEACHES

Only a few beaches on Lāna'i are worth seeking out, and only one has good swimming in protected waters. If you need more information, try **Destination Lāna'i** (⊠ 730 Lāna'i Ave., Suite 102, Lāna'i City 96763, ☎ 808/565–7600) or ask at your hotel. The beaches below are listed clockwise from the south.

★ **Hulopo'e Beach.** Lāna'i's only swimming beach, the sparkling crescent of this Marine Life Conservation District beckons with its perennially clear waters, great snorkeling reefs, and views of spinner dolphins at play. Here was once an ancient village dating back to AD 900. The tide pools, like natural aquariums, are fascinating to explore. One of the best beaches in all of Hawai'i, it also has shady trees and grassy expanses perfect for picnics, and there are showers, rest rooms, and changing facilities. It's a five-minute walk from the Mānele Bay Hotel via a short path. ⊠ *From Lāna'i City follow Hwy. 440 (Mānele Rd.) south to bottom of hill; road dead-ends at beach's parking lot.*

Polihua Beach. Due to its more obscure location and frequent high winds, this beach is often deserted, except for the turtles that nest here. That makes it all the more spectacular, with its long white-sand strand and glorious views of Moloka'i. Because of strong currents, swimming is dangerous. To get here you need a four-wheel-drive vehicle. ⊠ *Northwest shore, 11 mi from Lāna'i City, past Garden of the Gods.*

Shipwreck Beach. A nice beach for walking but not swimming, Shipwreck is an 8-mi stretch of sand on the 9-mi wide Kalohi Channel between Lāna'i and Moloka'i. The beach has no lifeguards, no changing rooms, and no outdoor showers. ⊠ *North shore, 10 mi north of Lāna'i City at end of Keōmuku Hwy.*

DINING

Although Lāna'i's restaurant choices are limited, the menus are wide-ranging. If you dine at the Lodge at Kō'ele or Mānele Bay Hotel, you'll be treated to unique preparations of ingredients harvested or caught locally and served in upscale surroundings. Dining in Lāna'i City is a different story. Its restaurants have simple fare, homey atmospheres, and nondescript service. For an explanation of price categories, *see* Dining *in* Smart Travel Tips A to Z at the back of the book.

South and West Lāna'i

$$$$ ✕ **'Ihilani.** The Mānele Bay Hotel's (☞ South and West Lāna'i *in* Lodg-
★ ing, *below*) dining room shimmers with crystal, exquisite china, and sil-
ver. Moonlight filters through the glass ceiling of its open-air terrace. Executive chef Edwin Goto uses fresh island ingredients to create a cuisine he calls Mediterranean gourmet. The changing menu may include such dishes as grilled filet mignon with seared foie gras and a sauce of wild mushrooms, port, and truffles. You can opt for a five-course food-and-wine pairing menu. The dessert menu features such taste explosions as a white chocolate and pistachio dome with *liliko'i* (passion fruit) sauce. ⊠ *Mānele Bay Hotel, Lāna'i City,* ☎ *808/565–7700. Reservations essential. AE, DC, MC, V. No lunch.*

North and East Lāna'i

$$$$ ✕ **Formal Dining Room.** Reflecting the elegant country atmosphere of
★ the Lodge at Kō'ele (☞ North and East Lāna'i *in* Lodging, *below*), this romantic octagonal-shape restaurant offers intimate tables close to a roaring fireplace. The walls are hand-stenciled by local artists. The chef expands on the concept of Hawai'i regional cuisine with a changing menu that includes specialties such as roasted Lāna'i venison loin with pineapple-cider sauce or potato-wrapped Hawaiian *moi,* a fish that in ancient times was savored only by chiefs. The wine list has selections from small, unique wineries. ⊠ *Lodge at Kō'ele,* ☎ *808/565–7300. Reservations essential. Jacket required. AE, DC, MC, V. No lunch.*

$$–$$$ ✕ **Henry Clay's Rotisserie.** Don't overlook this popular spot at the Hotel Lāna'i (☞ North and East Lāna'i *in* Lodging, *below*). Louisiana-style ribs, Cajun-style dishes, and seafood jalapeño over fettuccine add up to what Chef Henry Clay Richardson calls American country, but he brings it back home with such fresh local ingredients as venison, Hawaiian-caught seafood, and island produce. A redbrick fireplace and the paintings of a local artist add to the country ambiance. ⊠ *Hotel Lāna'i, 828 Lāna'i Ave.,* ☎ *808/565–7211. MC, V.*

$ ✕ **Blue Ginger Cafe.** This small, no-frills eatery may look run-down with its bare floor and plastic tablecloths, but the menu is diverse and the wonderful owner, Georgia Abilay, has turned this place into the town's most popular hangout. At breakfast enjoy a three-egg omelet with rice or a big plate of French toast. Blue Ginger also has fresh pastries each morning. Lunchtime selections include burgers, chef's salad, pizza, and saimin. Try the stir-fry fish or some Mexican fare for dinner. ⊠ *409 7th Ave.,* ☎ *808/565–6363. No credit cards.*

$ ✕ **Pele's Other Garden.** Call it a juice bar, a deli, or a pizzeria. By any name, this white building with blue trim adds a healthy twist to the Lāna'i City dining scene with mile-high sandwiches, vegetarian dishes, and fresh-baked breads. The signature 16-inch whole wheat–crust pizza is a great reward after an arduous hike. You can also order tantalizing picnic lunches, which come with your choice of salad, dessert, and juice—all in a convenient cooler bag. There are just four tables in the cramped space inside, so it's better to have a seat on the porch or on the new terrace, or to order carryout. ⊠ *811 Houston St.,* ☎ *808/565–9628. Reservations not accepted. AE, D, DC, MC, V.*

LODGING

In years past the only accommodation on the island was the no-fuss Hotel Lāna'i in Lāna'i City. Today you can choose among two classy resorts, pleasant bed-and-breakfasts, and a few house rentals. Let your tastes and your budget determine which place you select. For an explanation of price categories, *see* Lodging in Smart Travel Tips A to Z at the back of the book.

South and West Lāna'i

$$$$ 🏨 **Mānele Bay Hotel.** This elaborate beachfront property on historic
★ land has spectacular views of Lāna'i's dramatic coastline and beyond. Open arcades, breezeways, and bridges connect guest-room buildings with the main entrance, and five courtyard gardens are lavishly landscaped in different themes. The design combines elements both Mediterranean and traditionally Hawaiian. Asian art as well as work by local artists fills the common areas, and a library is a quiet, inviting escape for guests. For parents with kids, the hotel offers a unique children's program with daily adventures. The crescent of Hulopo'e Bay is just minutes away. ⊠ *Box 310, Lāna'i City 96763,* ☎ *808/565–7700 or 800/321–4666,* 🖷 *808/565–3868. 222 rooms, 28 suites. 4 restaurants, bar, minibars, room service, pool, spa, 18-hole golf course, 6 tennis courts, health club, children's programs. AE, DC, MC, V.* 🐾

North and East Lāna'i

$$$$ 🏨 **Captain's Retreat.** Single-room bookings are not available here, but if its rate is split between four couples or a family, this two-story private home turns out to be a reasonably priced lodging alternative. Within walking distance of town, it's the ultimate group getaway, with 3,000 square ft, four bedrooms, a redwood deck, an outside shower, and a roomy kitchen. ⊠ *Okamoto Realty, 730 Lāna'i Ave., Lāna'i City 96763,* ☎ *808/565–7519. 1 unit. MC, V.* 🐾

$$$$ 🏨 **Jasmine Garden.** The Hunters, who run the Dreams Come True B&B (☞ *below*), rent out several houses. One of them is this three-bedroom residence in the older section of Lāna'i City. It sleeps six, so three couples can share it. It has a well-equipped kitchen. Weekly and monthly rates are available. Call to find out more about their other properties. They rent four-wheel-drive vehicles as well. ⊠ *Jasmine St. at 13th Ave., Lāna'i City 96763,* ☎ *808/565–6961 or 800/566–6961,* 🖷 *808/565–7056. 1 unit. Car rental. AE, D, MC, V.*

$$$$ 🏨 **Lodge at Kō'ele.** Situated on 21 acres in the highlands on the edge
★ of Lāna'i City, this grand country estate feels like a luxurious private mountain retreat. Secluded by old pines, 1 ½ mi of pathways meander through theme gardens, along a pond and waterfall, and past an orchid greenhouse. Inside, beamed ceilings, stone fireplaces, a music room, a tea room, and the magnificent Great Hall (where afternoon tea with scones and clotted cream is served) create an Old World ambiance. A generous porch offers views of spectacular sunsets, and unique artworks and artifacts are on display. The Lodge has been called the most romantic getaway in America, and if you have *keiki* (children) with you, they'll love the children's program. ⊠ *Box 310,*

Lāna'i City 96763, ☎ 808/565–7300 or 800/321–4666, ⅢⅩ 808/565–3868. 88 rooms, 14 suites. 2 restaurants, bar, lobby lounge, minibars, room service, pool, 18-hole golf course, 3 tennis courts, croquet, health club, horseback riding, children's programs. AE, DC, MC, V. ⊜

$$–$$$ ⓣ **Hotel Lāna'i.** Built in 1923 to house visiting plantation executives, this quaint 11-room inn was once the only accommodation on the island. Today even though two luxury hotels may tempt you, you shouldn't overlook this island institution. The old front porch with the big wicker chairs has long been a meeting place for residents and locals, who gather to read the paper, order a drink, and talk story. The rooms, with country quilts and original plantation-era pictures, make you feel like you're in a country home. A Continental breakfast with fresh-baked breads is included in the rate. ⊠ 828 Lāna'i Ave., Lāna'i City 96763, ☎ 808/565–7211 or 800/795–7211, ⅢⅩ 808/565–6450. 11 rooms. Restaurant. AE, MC, V. ⊜

$$ ⓣ **Blue Ginger Vacation Rental.** Georgia Abilay, of Blue Ginger Cafe (☞ North and East Lāna'i in Dining, above) fame, owns this vacation home in a newer neighborhood of Lāna'i City. Grounds are landscaped with tropical plants and roses, and room decor is modern. One of the bedrooms has a double bed, the other has twin beds, and the living room's overstuffed couch converts to a bed. Breakfast can be arranged courtesy of the café. ⊠ 421 Lama St., Lāna'i City 96763, ☎ 808/565–6363 or 808/565–6666. 1 unit. No credit cards.

$$ ⓣ **Dreams Come True.** Michael and Susan Hunter's bed-and-breakfast in the heart of Lāna'i City has canopy beds, antique furnishings, and memorabilia from their many years in Asia and on Lāna'i. Fresh fruit from their own trees enhances the big morning meal. Susan is a trained massage therapist and provides in-house massage for $35 an hour. Vehicle rental is also available. ⊠ 547 12th St., Lāna'i City 96763, ☎ 808/565–6961 or 800/566–6961, ⅢⅩ 808/565–7056. 3 rooms. Massage. AE, D, MC, V.

NIGHTLIFE AND THE ARTS

Locals entertain themselves by gathering on the front porch of the **Hotel Lāna'i** (⊠ 828 Lāna'i Ave., Lāna'i City, ☎ 808/565–7211) for drinks and conversation. The classy lounge at the **Mānele Bay Hotel** (⊠ Lāna'i City, ☎ 808/565–7700), Hale Aheahe (House of Gentle Breezes) offers entertainment every evening. The cozy cocktail lounge at the **Lodge at Kō'ele** (⊠ Lāna'i City, ☎ 808/565–7300) stays open until 11 PM. The lodge also features music in its Great Hall. The 153-seat **Lāna'i Theater and Playhouse** (☎ 808/565–7500), a '30s landmark, presents first-run movies. Lāna'i's **Visiting Artist Program** brings world-renowned authors and musicians to the island once a month for free, informal presentations. Past visitors have included author Armistead Maupin, the Irish folk music band Gaelic Storm, and jazz guitarist Bucky Pizzarelle. These events take place at either the Lodge at Kō'ele or the Mānele Bay Hotel.

OUTDOOR ACTIVITIES AND SPORTS

Participant Sports

Golf

Cavendish Golf Course. This nine-hole course in the pines is free, but a donation for upkeep is requested. Call the Lodge at Kō'ele concierge (☎ 808/565–7300) for information and directions. Bring your own clubs.

Challenge at Mānele. This 18-hole world-class course was designed by Jack Nicklaus. The clubhouse here serves lunch. ⊠ Mānele Bay Hotel, ☎ 808/565–2222 or 800/321–4666. ▧ Greens fee $125 for guests of the Lodge at Kō'ele or Mānele Bay Hotel, $150 nonguests; cart included.

Experience at Kō'ele. The Lodge at Kō'ele has this 18-hole championship course designed by Greg Norman. There's also an 18-hole executive putting course, free to guests but not accessible to nonguests. The clubhouse serves lunch. ✉ *Lodge at Kō'ele,* ☎ *808/565–4653.* ✎ *Greens fee $125 guests, $150 nonguests; cart included.*

Hiking and Camping

Lāna'i is a hiker's paradise with trails roaming through unique forests, over rugged grasslands and along splendid shores. The most popular Lāna'i hike is the **Munro Trail,** a strenuous 9-mi trek that takes about eight hours. There is an elevation gain of 1,400 ft, leading you to the lookout at Lāna'i's highest point, Lāna'ihale.

The remote 8-mi trail along **Shipwreck Beach** is an adventure for beachcombers.

There are lesser known treks with whimsical names, such as **Eucalyptus Ladder, Old Cowboy Trail,** and **Ancient Graveyard.** It's a good idea to get one of the guidebooks described below, and a good map. Also make sure—especially if you want to camp—to call the folks at Destination Lāna'i (☎ 808/565–7600 or 800/947–4774, ✍) or to stop by at the **Lāna'i Ecoadventure Centre** (☞ Contacts and Resources *in* Lāna'i A to Z, *below*) in town, where you can rent camping gear as well.

Horseback Riding

The **Stables at Kō'ele** (☎ 808/565–4424) take you to scenic high-country trails. They have a corral full of well-groomed horses for riders of all ages and skill levels. Group rides cost $40 for one hour, $65 for two hours. Lessons start at $30. Private rides start at $70 for the first hour. Customized rides, with lunch, can be arranged as well.

Mountain Biking

The **Lodge at Kō'ele** (☎ 808/565–7300) rents mountain bikes only to guests of the lodge and of the Mānele Bay Hotel for $8 per hour or $40 per day. John and Kris, the friendly couple at **Lāna'i Ecoadventure Centre** (☞ Contacts and Resources *in* Lāna'i A to Z, *below*), rent out mountain bikes starting at $19.95 per day.

Sporting Clays

Lāna'i Pine Sporting Clays Range is the only target course of its kind in Hawai'i. The rustic, 14-station course is in a pine-wood valley overlooking the sea. A single shooter can complete the course in an hour. Cost is $125 for 100 targets and $65 for 50 targets. Beginners can start with an introductory lesson—25 targets—for $55. Each October, celebrities—Arnold Schwarzenegger and Tom Selleck have been among them—host the cash-winning Open Play Target Shoot. You have to arrange to play the course through your hotel.

Water Sports

DEEP-SEA FISHING

Spinning Dolphin Fishing Charters (☎ 808/565–6613) handles both heavy and light tackle fishing on its 28-ft diesel-powered Omega sport fisher. The half-day ($400) and full-day ($800) charters are private, with a six-person maximum. Bring your own lunch. Juice and ice are provided.

SCUBA DIVING

Trilogy Excursions (☎ 808/667–7721 or 888/628–4800, ✍) offers introductory and one-tank dives for $55. Scuba diving is also available on Trilogy's daily snorkel sail (☞ Snorkeling, *below*). There's a free diving session for novices at the Mānele Bay Hotel pool. It's best to book this through your hotel concierge.

The dive site **Cathedrals,** off the south shore, gets its name from the spacious caverns created by numerous pinnacles that rise from depths of 60 ft to just below the water's surface. In these beautiful chambers lurk spotted moray eels, lobster, and ghost shrimp.

Sergeant Major Reef, on the south shore, is made up of three parallel lava ridges, a cave, and an archway, with rippled sand valleys between the ridges. It's home to several large schools of sergeant major fish. Depths range from 15 to 50 ft. Other nearby sites include Lobster Rock, Menpachi Cave, Grand Canyon, Sharkfin Rock, and Monolith.

SNORKELING

Hulopo'e Beach (☞ Beaches, *above*) is one of Hawai'i's outstanding snorkeling destinations. It attracts brilliantly colored fish to its protected cove, in which you can also marvel at underwater coral and lava formations. Ask at your hotel about renting equipment. The companies also offer snorkeling tours.

Spinning Dolphin Fishing Charters (☞ Deep-Sea Fishing, *above*) offers private snorkel and sightseeing tours. When the whales are here (December through April), three-hour whale-watching tours are also available.

Trilogy Excursions (☞ Deep-Sea Fishing, *above*) presents a daily 4-hour morning snorkel sail on a 51-ft catamaran for $95. Continental breakfast, lessons, equipment, and lunch are included. Make arrangements with the concierge at the Mānele Bay Hotel (☎ 808/565–7700) in Lāna'i City.

SHOPPING

Except for the boutiques at the Lodge at Kō'ele and Mānele Bay Hotel, Lāna'i City is the island's only place to buy what you need. Its main streets, 7th and 8th avenues, have a scattering of shops straight out of the '20s. In the most literal sense, the main businesses in town are what you would call general stores. They do offer personal service and congenial charm. Stores open their doors Monday through Saturday between 8 and 9 and close between 5 and 6. Some shops are closed on Sunday and between noon and 1:30 on weekdays.

General Stores

International Food and Clothing Center. You may not find everything the name implies, but this old-fashioned emporium does stock many items for your everyday needs. ⊠ 833 'Ilima Ave., ☎ 808/565–6433.

Lāna'i City Service. In addition to being a gas station, taxi company, and car-rental operation, this outfit sells fast food and sodas, sundries, T-shirts, and island crafts. ⊠ 1036 Lāna'i Ave., ☎ 808/565–7227.

Pine Isle Market. You can get everything from cosmetics to canned vegetables here at one of Lāna'i City's two supermarkets. It's a great place to buy fresh fish. ⊠ 356 8th Ave., ☎ 808/565–6488.

Richard's Shopping Center. Richard Tamashiro founded this place in 1946, and the Tamashiro clan continues to run the place. Along with groceries, the store has a fun selection of Lāna'i T-shirts. ⊠ 434 8th Ave., ☎ 808/565–6047.

Crafts

Akamai Trading. Akamai Trading sells such unique Lāna'i crafts as pinetree bowls and flower-dyed gourds alongside its island posters, T-shirts, and tropical jellies and jams. It's also the only place in town that serves cappuccino and espresso. ⊠ 408 8th Ave., ☎ 808/565–6587.

Gifts With Aloha. In addition to a tasteful selection of gift items and casual resort wear, the work of Lāna'i and Hawai'i artists here includes ceramic ware, raku (Japanese-style lead-glazed pottery), fine hand-blown glass, and watercolor prints. ⊠ 811-B Houston St., ☎ 808/565–6589.

Lāna'i Art Studio. This is the home of the Lāna'i Art Program, which offers art classes to residents and visitors. Its gift shop sells unique Lāna'i handicrafts, from painted silk scarves to beaded jewelry. ✉ *339 7th Ave.,* ☎ *808/565–7503.*

Hotel Shops

The **Lodge at Kō'ele** (☎ 808/565–7300) and the **Mānele Bay Hotel** (☎ 808/565–7700) have sundries shops that are handy for guests who need to stock up on suntan lotion, aspirin, and other vacation necessities. It also carries classy logo wear, resort clothing, books, and jewelry.

LĀNA'I A TO Z

Arriving and Departing

By Ferry

Expeditions (☎ 808/661–3756 or 800/695–2624) crosses the channel five times daily departing from Lahaina on Maui and Mānele Bay Harbor on Lāna'i. The crossing takes 45 minutes and costs $25.

By Plane

The small **Lāna'i Airport** (☎ 808/565–6757) is centrally located in the southwest area of the island. There is a gift shop, food concession, plenty of parking, and a federal agricultural inspection station so that departing guests can check luggage directly to the mainland.

In order to reach Lāna'i from the mainland United States, you must first stop at O'ahu's Honolulu International Airport or at Maui's Kahului Airport. From there it takes about a half hour to fly to Lāna'i. **Hawaiian Airlines** (☎ 800/882–8811) offers two round-trip flights daily between Honolulu and Lāna'i. A round-trip on one of its DC-9 jets costs $194. **Island Air** (☎ 808/484–2222 or 800/323–3345) offers about 12 flights daily on its 18-passenger Dash-6s and 37-seat Dash-8s, also at a cost of $194.

BETWEEN THE AIRPORT AND HOTELS

Lāna'i Airport is a 10-minute drive from Lāna'i City. If you're staying at the Hotel Lāna'i, the Lodge at Kō'ele, or the Mānele Bay Hotel, you will be met by a complimentary shuttle. Don't expect to see any public buses at the airport, because there aren't any on the island.

By Car. With public transportation virtually nonexistent and attractions so far apart, you'll want to rent a car while on Lāna'i. Make your reservation for a car or four-wheel-drive vehicle way in advance of your trip, because Lāna'i's fleet of vehicles is limited (☞ Car and Four-Wheel-Drive-Vehicle Rentals *in* Contacts and Resources, *below*).

By Taxi. Taxi transfers between Lāna'i City and the airport are handled by **Lāna'i City Service,** a subsidiary of Dollar Rent-A-Car (☎ 808/565–7227 or 800/533–7808). One-way charges are $5 per person for the Lodge at Kō'ele and $15 for Mānele Bay Hotel.

Getting Around

Private transportation is advised on Lāna'i, unless you plan to stay in one place during your entire visit. Avoid that urge, because the island has natural splendors from one end to the other.

By Car

Driving around Lāna'i isn't as easy as on other islands. Secondary roads aren't marked. But renting a car can be fun (☞ Car and Four-Wheel-Drive Vehicle Rentals *in* Contacts and Resources, *below*). From town, the streets extend outward as paved roads with two-way traffic. Keōmuku Highway runs north to Shipwreck Beach, and Highway 440 leads south down to Mānele Bay and Hulopo'e Beach and west to Kaumālapa'u Harbor. The rest of your driving takes place on bumpy, muddy roads best navigated by a four-wheel-drive vehicle or van.

The island doesn't have traffic lights, and you'll never find yourself in a traffic jam. However, heed these words of caution: Before heading out on your explorations, ask at your hotel desk for a road and site map, and ask for confirmation that you're headed in the right direction. Some attractions don't have signs, and it's easy to get lost.

By Taxi

It costs $5 to $15 per person for a cab ride from Lāna'i City to almost any point on the paved roads of the island. Call **Lāna'i City Service** (☏ 808/565–7227 or 800/533–7808).

Contacts and Resources

Car and Four-Wheel-Drive-Vehicle Rentals

Two companies on Lāna'i rent vehicles. **Lāna'i City Service** (✉ Lāna'i Ave. at 11th St., Lāna'i City, ☏ 808/565–7227 or 800/533–7808) is the Dollar Rent-a-Car affiliate on the island. Fees are $60 a day for a compact car, $80 a day for a midsize vehicle, $129 a day for a seven-passenger minivan or a four-wheel-drive Jeep Wrangler, and $145 a day for a four-wheel-drive Cherokee. There's an additional charge if you want to pick your car up or drop it off at the airport. **Lāna'i Ecoadventure Centre** (☞ Guided Tours, *below*) also has a fleet of reliable jeeps.

Emergencies

Police, fire, or **ambulance** (☏ 911).

HOSPITAL

The **Lāna'i Community Hospital** (✉ 628 7th Ave., Lāna'i City, ☏ 808/565–6411) is the health-care center for the island. It has 24-hour ambulance service and a pharmacy.

Guided Tours

Lāna'i Ecoadventure Centre (✉ 8th Ave., next to the police station, ☏ 808/565–7737 or 808/565–7373, 🐾) takes all the worries about getting lost or stuck in the mud away with its popular 4x4 Trek. They'll stop where and when you want as they take you to Lāna'i's most scenic places. Guides talk story about island history and the unique plants and animals. They even provide binoculars, snorkel gear, snacks, and drinks. Call John or Kris for costs.

Tours of the island's two major hotels and properties are free to the public upon request. Contact the concierge at **Mānele Bay Hotel** (☏ 808/565–7700) or the **Lodge at Kō'ele** (☏ 808/565–7300).

Visitor Information

Your best contact for general information, and for brochures and maps, is Lāna'i's visitors bureau **Destination Lāna'i** (✉ 730 Lāna'i Ave., Suite 102, Lāna'i City 96763, ☏ 808/565–7600, 🐾); feel free to stop in (although it has erratic opening hours), or e-mail or write ahead of time. The **Maui Visitors Bureau** (✉ 1727 Wili Pa Loop, Wailuku, Maui 96793, ☏ 808/244–3530, FAX 808/244–1337, 🐾) has some information about Lāna'i as well as Maui. Once you're on the island, the **information desks** of the two major hotels—the Lodge at Kō'ele and the Mānele Bay Hotel—are useful sources if you are a guest at either of these properties.

7 BACKGROUND AND ESSENTIALS

Portraits of Hawai'i

Books and Videos

Chronology

Smart Travel Tips A to Z

Hawaiian Vocabulary

Menu Guide

Map of Hawaiian Islands

THESE VOLCANIC ISLES

Dawn at the crater on horseback. It's cold at 10,023 ft above the warm Pacific—maybe 45°F. The horses' breath condenses into a smoky cloud, and the riders cling against their saddles. It's eerily quiet except for the creak of straining leather and the crunch of volcanic cinders under foot, sounds that are absurdly magnified in the vast empty space that yawns below.

This is Haleakalā, the "house of the sun." It's the crown of east Maui and the largest dormant volcano crater in the world. Every year thousands of visitors shake themselves awake at three in the morning to board vans that take them from their comfortable hotels and up the world's most steeply ascending auto route to the summit of Haleakalā National Park. Sunrise is extraordinary here. Colors from the palest pink to the most fiery red slowly spread across the lip of the summit. Mark Twain called it "the sublimest spectacle" he had ever witnessed.

But sunrise is only the beginning. The park encompasses 28,665 acres, and the valley itself is 21 mi in circumference and 19 square mi in area. At its deepest, it measures 3,000 ft from the summit. The two towers of Manhattan's World Trade Center could be placed one atop the other and still not reach the top. While Haleakalā is dormant, the vast, wondrous valley here isn't a single crater created by some devastating explosion. Misnamed by the first European explorers, Haleakalā's huge depression would be more properly called an "erosional valley," the result of eons of wind and rain wearing down what was likely a small crater at the mountain's original summit. The small hills within the valley are volcanic cinder cones, each the site of an eruption.

More than anything, entering Haleakalā is like descending to the moon. Trails for hiking and horseback riding crisscross the crater for some 32 mi. The way is strewn with volcanic rubble, crater cones, frozen lava flows, vents, and lava tubes. The colors you see on your descent are muted yet dramatic—black, yellow, russet, orange, lavender, brown, and gray, even a pinkish-blue. It seems as if nothing could live here, but in fact this is an ecosystem that sustains, among other, more humble life forms, the surefooted mountain goat, the rare nēnē goose (no webbing between its toes, the better to negotiate this rugged terrain with), and the strange and delicate silversword. The silversword, a spiny, metallic-leaf plant, once grew abundantly on Haleakalā's slopes. Today it survives in small numbers at Haleakalā and at high elevations on the Big Island of Hawai'i. The plants live up to 20 years, bloom only once, scatter their seeds, and die.

The valley's starkness is overwhelming. Even shadows cast in the thin mountain air are flinty and spare. It's easy to understand why in the early days of this nation's space program moon-bound astronauts trained in this desolate place.

It is also not difficult to see this place as a bubbling, sulfurous cauldron, a direct connection not to the heavens but to the core of the earth. Haleakalā's last—and probably final—eruption occurred in 1790, a few years after a Frenchman named La Perouse became the first European to set foot on Maui. That fiery outburst was only one of many in Hawai'i over the millennia, just as Maui and its now-cold crater are just one facet of the volcanic variety of the Aloha State.

Large and small, awake or sleeping, volcanoes are Hawai'i's history and its heritage. Behind their beauty is the story of the flames that created this ethereal island chain. The tale began some 25 million years ago, yet it is still unfinished.

The islands in the Hawaiian archipelago are really only the very crests of immense mountains rising from the bottom of the sea. Formed by molten rock known as magma, the islands were slowly pushed up from the earth's volatile, uneasy mantle, forced through cracks in the thin crust that is the ocean floor. The first ancient eruptions cooled and formed pools on the Pacific bottom. Then, as more and more magma spilled from the vents over millions of years, the pools became ridges and grew into crests. The latter built upon themselves over the eons, until finally, miles high, they towered above the surface of the sea.

As the islands cooled in the Pacific waters, the stark lava slopes slowly bloomed, over centuries, with colorful flora—exotic, jewellike species endemic only to these islands, with their generous washings of tropical rain and abundant sunshine. Gradually, as seeds, spores, or eggs of living creatures were carried by the winds and currents to these isolated volcanic isles more than 2,000 mi from the closest continental land mass, the bare and rocky atolls became a paradise of greenery.

This type of volcano, with its slowly formed, gently sloping sides, is known as a shield volcano, and each of the Hawaiian isles is composed of them. As long as the underwater vents spew the lifeblood lava out from the earth's core and into the heart of the mountain, a shield volcano will continue to grow.

The Hawaiian Islands rest on an area called the Pacific Plate, and this vast shelf of land is making its way slowly to the northwest, creeping perhaps 2–3 inches every year. The result is that contact between the submarine vents and the volcanoes' conduits for magma is gradually disrupted and closed off. Slowly, the mountains stop growing, one by one. Surface eruptions slow down and finally halt completely, and these volcanoes ultimately become extinct.

That, at least, is one explanation. Another—centuries older and still revered in Hawaiian art and song—centers upon Pele, the beautiful and tempestuous daughter of Haumea, the Earth Mother, and Wakea, the Sky Father. Pele is the Hawaiian goddess of fire, the maker of mountains, melter of rocks, eater of forests, and burner of land—both creator and destroyer. Legend has it that Pele came to the Islands long ago to flee from her cruel older sister, Na Maka o Kahai, goddess of the sea. Pele ran first to the small island of Ni'ihau, making a crater home there with her digging stick. But Na Maka found her and destroyed her hideaway, so Pele again had to flee. On Kaua'i she delved deeper, but Na Maka chased her from that home as well. Pele ran on—from O'ahu to Moloka'i, Lana'i to Kaho'olawe, Molokini to Maui—but always and ever Na Maka pursued her.

Pele came at last to Halema'uma'u, the vast firepit crater of Ki'lauea, and there, on the Big Island, she dug deepest of all. There she is said to remain, all-powerful, quick to rage, and often unpredictable; the mountain is her impenetrable fortress and domain— a safe refuge, at least for a time, from Na Maka o Kahai.

Interestingly, the chronology of the old tales of Pele's flight from isle to isle closely matches the reckonings of modern volcanologists regarding the ages of the various craters. Today, the Big Island's Ki'lauea and Mauna Loa retain the closest links with the earth's superheated core and are active and volatile, though three other volcanoes that shaped the island are not. The remainder of the Hawaiian volcanoes have been carried beyond their magma supply by the movement of the Pacific Plate. Those farthest to the northwest in the island chain are completely extinct. Those at the southeasterly end of the island chain— Haleakalā, Mauna Kea, and Hualālai—are dormant and slipping away, so that the implacable process of volcanic death has begun.

Eventually, experts say, in another age or so, the same cooling and slow demise will overtake all of the burning rocks that are the Hawaiian Islands. Eventually, the sea will claim their bodies and, to Pele's rage, Na Maka o Kahai will win in the end. Or will she? Off the Big Island of Hawai'i a new island is forming. It's still ½ mi below the water's surface. Several thousand years more will be required for it to break into the sunlight. But it already has a name: Loihi.

By far the largest island of the archipelago, the Big Island of Hawai'i rises some 13,796 ft above sea level at the summit of Mauna Kea. Mauna Loa is nearly as high at 13,667 ft. From their bases on the ocean floor, these shield volcanoes are the largest mountain masses on the planet. Geologists believe it required more than 3 million years of steady volcanic activity to raise these peaks up above the waters of the Pacific.

Mauna Loa's little sister, Ki'lauea, at about 4,077 ft, is the most active volcano in the world. Between the two of them, they have covered nearly 200,000 acres of land with their red-hot lava flows over the past 200 years or so. In the process, they have ravished trees, fields, meadows, villages, and more than a few unlucky human witnesses. For generations, Ki'lauea, in a continually eruptive state, has pushed molten lava up from the earth's magma at 1,800°F and more. But as active as she and Mauna Loa are, their eruptions are comparatively safe and gentle, producing continuous small and especially liquid lava flows rather than dangerous bursts of fire and ash. The exceptions were two violently explosive displays during recorded history—one in 1790, the other in 1924. During these eruptions, Pele came closest to destroying the Big Island's largest city, Hilo. She also gave residents another scare as recently as 1985.

It is around these major volcanoes that the island's Hawai'i Volcanoes National Park was created. A sprawling natural preserve, the park attracts geology experts, volcanologists, and ordinary wide-eyed visitors from all over the world. They come for the park's unparalleled opportunity to view, up close and in person, the visual wonders of Pele's kingdom of fire and fantasy. They come to study and to improve methods for predicting the times and sites of eruptions. They have done so for a century or more.

Thomas Augustus Jaggar, the preeminent volcanologist and student of Ki'lauea, built his home on stilts wedged into cracks in the volcanic rock of the crater rim. Harvard-trained and universally respected, he was the driving force behind the establishment of the Hawaiian Volcano Observatory at Ki'lauea. When he couldn't raise research funds from donations, public and private, he raised pigs to keep the scientific work going. After Jaggar's death, his wife scattered his ashes over the great fiery abyss.

The park is on the Big Island's southeastern flank, about 30 minutes out of Hilo on the aptly named Volcano Highway. Wear sturdy walking shoes and carry a warm sweater. It can be a long hike across the lava flats to see Pele in action, and at 4,000 ft above sea level, temperatures can be brisk, however hot the volcanic activity. So much can be seen at close range along the road circling the crater that Ki'lauea has been dubbed the "drive-in volcano."

At the park's visitor center sits a large display case. It contains dozens of lava-rock "souvenirs"—removed from Pele's grasp and then returned, accompanied by letters of apology. They are sent back by visitors who say they regret having broken the *kapu* (taboo) against removing even the smallest grain of native volcanic rock from Hawai'i. A typical letter might say: "I never thought Pele would miss just one little rock, but she did, and now I've wrecked two cars . . . I lost my job, my health is poor, and I know it's because I took this stone." The letters can be humorous, or poignant and remorseful, requesting Pele's forgiveness.

It is surprisingly safe at the crater's lip. Unlike Japan's Mount Fuji or Washington State's Mount St. Helens, Hawai'i's shield volcanoes spew their lava downhill, along the sides of the mountain. Still, the clouds of sulfur gas and fumes produced during volcanic eruptions are noxious and heady and can make breathing unpleasant, if not difficult. It has been pointed out that the chemistry of volcanoes—sulfur, hydrogen, oxygen, carbon dioxide—closely resembles the chemistry of the egg.

It's an 11-mi drive around the Ki'lauea crater via the Crater Rim Road, and the trip takes about an hour. But it's better to walk a bit. There are at least eight major trails in the park, ranging from short 15-minute strolls to the three-day, 18-mi (one way) Mauna Loa Trail, which is, as you might expect, only for the seasoned hiker. A comfortable walk is Sulfur Banks, with its many vast, steaming vents creating halos of clouds around the rim of Ki'lauea. The route passes through a seemingly enchanted forest of sandalwood, flowers, and ferns.

Just ahead is the main attraction: the center of Pele's power, Halema'uma'u. This yawning pit of flame and burning rock measures some 3,000 ft wide and is a breathtaking sight. When Pele is in full fury, visitors come here in droves, on foot and by helicopter, to see her crimson expulsions coloring the dark earth and smoky sky. Recently, however, Ki'lauea's most violent activity has occurred along vents in the mountain's sides instead of at its summit crater. Known as rift zones, they are lateral conduits that often open in shield volcanoes.

Ki'lauea has two rift zones, one extending from the summit crater toward the southwest, through Kau, the other to the east-northeast through Puna, past Cape Kumakahi, and into the sea. In the last two decades, repeated eruptions in the east rift zone have blocked off 12 mi of coastal road—some under more than 300 ft of rock—and have covered a total of 10,000 acres with lava. Where the flows entered the ocean, roughly 200 acres have been added to the Big Island.

Farther along the Crater Rim Road (about 4 mi from the visitor center) is the Thurston Lava Tube, an example of a strangely beautiful volcanic phenomenon common on the Islands. Lava tubes form when lava flows rapidly downhill. The sides and top of this river of molten rock cool, while the fluid center flows on. Most formations are short and shallow, but some measure 30 ft–50 ft high and hundreds of yards long. Dark, cave-like places, lava tubes were often used to store remains of the ancient Hawaiian royalty—the *ali'i*. The Thurston Lava Tube sits in a beautiful prehistoric fern forest called Fern Jungle.

Throughout the park, new lava formations are continually being created. Starkly beautiful, these volcanic deposits exhibit the different types of lava produced by Hawai'i's volcanoes: *'a'ā*, the dark, rough lava that solidifies as cinders of rock; and the more common *pāhoehoe*, the smooth, satiny lava that forms the vast plains of black rock in ropy swirls known as lava flats, which in some areas go on for miles. Other terms that help identify what may be seen in the park include *caldera*, which are the open, bowl-like lips of a volcano summit; *ejecta*, the cinders and ash that float through the air around an eruption; and olivine, the semiprecious chrysolite (greenish in color) found in volcanic ash.

But it isn't all fire and flash, cinders, and devastation in this volcanic landscape. Hawai'i Volcanoes National Park is also the home of some of the most beautiful of the state's black-sand beaches; humid forest glens full of lacy butterflies and colorful birds like the dainty flycatcher, called the *'elepaio*; and exquisite grottoes sparked with bright wild orchid sprays and crashing waterfalls. Even as the lava cools, still bearing a golden, glassy skin, lush, green native ferns—*ama'uma'u, kupukupu,* and *'ōkupukupu*—spring up in the midst of Pele's fallout, as if defying her destructiveness or simply confirming the fact that after fire she brings life.

Some 12 centuries ago, in fact, Pele brought humans to her verdant islands: The fiery explosions that lit Ki'lauea and Mauna Loa like twin beacons in the night probably guided to Pele's side the first stout-hearted explorers to Hawai'i from the Marquesas Islands, some 2,400 mi away across the trackless, treacherous ocean.

Once summoned, they worshiped her from a discreet distance. Great numbers of religious *heiau* (outdoor stone platforms) dot the landscapes near the many older and extinct craters scattered throughout Hawai'i, demonstrating the great reverence the native islanders have always held for Pele and her creations. But the ruins of only two heiau are to be found near the very active crater at Halema'uma'u.

There, at the center of the capricious Pele's power, native Hawaiians caution one even today to "step lightly, for you are on holy ground."

For all the teeming tourism and bustle that are modern Hawai'i, no one today steps on the ground that Pele may one day claim for her own. In future ages, when mighty Ki'lauea is no more, this area will still be a volcanic isle. Beneath the blue Pacific waters, fiery magma flows and new mountains form and grow. Just below the surface, Loihi waits.

–Gary Diedrichs

THE ALOHA SHIRT: A COLORFUL SWATCH OF ISLAND HISTORY

Elvis Presley had an entire wardrobe of them in the '60s films *Blue Hawaii* and *Paradise, Hawaiian Style*. During the '50s, entertainer Arthur Godfrey and bandleader Harry Owens often sported them on television shows. John Wayne loved to lounge around in them. Mick Jagger felt compelled to buy one on a visit to Hawai'i in the 1970s. Dustin Hoffman, Steven Spielberg, and Bill Cosby avidly collect them.

From gaudy to grand, from tawdry to tasteful, aloha shirts are Hawai'i's gift to the world of fashion. It has been more than 50 years since those riotously colored garments made their first appearance as immediately recognizable symbols of the Islands.

The roots of the aloha shirt go back to the early 1930s, when Hawai'i's garment industry was just beginning to develop its own unique style. Although locally made clothes did exist, they were almost exclusively for plantation workers and were constructed of durable palaka or plain cotton material.

Out of this came the first stirrings of fashion: Beachboys and schoolchildren started having sport shirts made from colorful Japanese kimono fabric. The favored type of cloth was the kind used for children's kimonos— bright pink and orange floral prints for girls; masculine motifs in browns and blues for boys. In Japan, such flamboyant patterns were considered unsuitable for adult clothing, but in the Islands such rules didn't apply, and it seemed the flashier the shirt, the better—for either sex. Thus, the aloha shirt was born.

It was easy and inexpensive in those days to have garments tailored to order; the next step was moving to mass production and marketing. In June 1935, Honolulu's best-known tailoring establishment, Musa-Shiya, advertised the availability of "Aloha shirts—well tailored, beautiful designs and radiant colors. Ready-made or made to order . . . 95¢ and up." This is the first known printed use of the term that would soon refer to an entire industry. By the following year, several local manufacturers had begun full-scale production of "aloha wear." One of them, Ellery Chun of King-Smith, registered as local trademarks the terms "Aloha Sportswear" and "Aloha Shirt" in 1936 and 1937, respectively.

These early entrepreneurs were the first to create uniquely Hawaiian designs for fabric as well—splashy patterns that would forever symbolize the Islands. A 1939 *Honolulu Advertiser* story described them as a "delightful confusion (of) tropical fish and palm trees, Diamond Head and the Aloha Tower, surfboards and leis, ukuleles and Waikīkī beach scenes."

The aloha wear of the late 1930s was intended for—and mostly worn by—tourists, and interestingly, a great deal of it was exported to the mainland and even Europe and Australia. By the end of the decade, for example, only 5% of the output of one local firm, the Kamehameha Garment Company, was sold in Hawai'i.

World War II brought this trend to a halt, and during the postwar period, aloha wear really came into its own in Hawai'i itself. A strong push to support local industry gradually nudged island garb into the workplace, and kama'āina began to wear the clothing that previously had been seen as attire for visitors.

In 1947, for example, male employees of the City and County of Honolulu were first allowed to wear aloha shirts "in plain shades" during the summer months. Later that year, the first observance of Aloha Week started the tradition of "bankers and bellhops . . . mix(ing) colorfully in multihued and tapa-designed Aloha shirts every day," as a local newspaper's Sunday magazine supplement noted in 1948. By the 1960s, "Aloha Friday," set aside specifically for the wearing of aloha attire, had become a tradition. In the following decade, the suit and tie practically disappeared as work attire in Hawai'i, even for executives.

Most of the Hawaiian-theme fabric used in manufacturing aloha wear was designed in the Islands, then printed on the mainland or in Japan. The glowingly vibrant rayons of the late '40s and early '50s (a period now seen as aloha wear's heyday) were at first printed on the East Coast, but manufacturers there usually required such large orders, local firms eventually found it impossible to continue using them. By 1964, 90% of Hawaiian fabric was being manufactured in Japan—a situation that still exists today.

Fashion trends usually move in cycles, and aloha wear is no exception. By the 1960s, the "chop suey print" with its "tired clichés of Diamond Head, Aloha Tower, outrigger canoes (and) stereotyped leis" was seen as corny and garish, according to an article published in the *Honolulu Star-Bulletin*. But it was just that outdated aspect that began to appeal to the younger crowd, who began searching out old-fashioned aloha shirts at the Salvation Army and Goodwill thrift stores. These shirts were dubbed "silkies," a name by which they're still known, even though most of them were actually made of rayon.

Before long, what had been 50¢ shirts began escalating in price, and a customer who had balked at paying $5 for a shirt that someone had already worn soon found the same item selling for $10—and more. By the late 1970s, aloha-wear designers were copying the prints of yesteryear for their new creations.

The days of bargain silkies are now gone. The few choice aloha shirts from decades past that still remain are offered today by specialized dealers for hundreds of dollars apiece, causing many to look back with chagrin to the time when such treasures were foolishly worn to the beach until they fell apart. The best examples of vintage aloha shirts are now rightly seen as art objects, worthy of preservation for the lovely depictions they offer of Hawai'i's colorful and unique scene.

— DeSoto Brown

"The Aloha Shirt: A Colorful Swatch of Island History" first appeared in *Aloha* magazine. Reprinted with permission of Davick Publications.

WHAT TO READ & WATCH BEFORE YOU GO

Books

If you like your history in novel form you'll enjoy James A. Michener's weighty *Hawaii* for its overall perspective; it's also available on audiocassette. Capt. James Cook's *A Voyage to the Pacific Ocean,* one of the first guidebooks to the Islands, contains many valid insights; *Shoal of Time,* by Gavan Daws, chronicles Hawaiian history from Cook's time to the 1960s. History also comes to life in the pages of *Travels in Hawaii,* by Robert Louis Stevenson; *History Makers of Hawaii,* by A. Grove Day, is a biographical dictionary of people who shaped the territory from past to present. To gain familiarity with the gods and goddesses who have also had a hand in this land's development, read *Hawaiian Mythology* by Martha Beckwith. *Hawaiʻi's Story by Hawaiʻi's Queen,* the tale of the overthrow of the Hawaiian monarchy in Queen Liliʻuokalani's own words, is poignant and thought-provoking. For a glimpse at military history, *Pearl Harbor: Fact and Reference Book* by Terrance McCombs, is a collection of both well-known facts and lesser-known trivia. For a truly Hawaiian perspective, *Voices of Wisdom: Hawaiian Elders Speak* by M. J. Harden shares interviews with some of Hawaiʻi's most respected elders, Hawaiʻi's traditional keepers of knowledge and wisdom.

A whole new genre of Hawaiian writing offers insights into island lifestyles through the use of pidgin prose and local settings. Paul Wood's essays, collected in *Four Wheels, Five Corners: Facts of Life in Upcountry Maui,* convey a real sense of place. Recent novels that capture the South Seas texture include *Shark's Dialogue,* by Kiana Davenport; this book weaves together multi-ethnic stories, legends, and ancient beliefs to create a mystical air. *Wild Meat and the Bully Burg-*

ers, by Lois Ann Yamanaka, is a tale of growing up on the Big Island, told in an authentic native voice. Writers Paul Theroux, Barbara Kingsolver, and Maxine Hong Kingston are among those who share stories about the Islands in *Hawaii: True Stories of the Island Spirit,* a collection edited by Rick and Marcie Carroll.

Those interested in the outdoors will want to pick up *A Guide to Tropical and Semitropical Flora,* by Loraine Kuck and Richard Tongg. The *Handbook of Hawaiian Fishes,* by W. A. Gosline and Vernon Brock, is great for snorkelers. *Hawaii's Birds,* by the Hawaiʻi Audubon Society, is perfect for bird-watchers. *Hawaiian Hiking Trails,* by Craig Chisholm, is just the guide for day hikers and backpackers. Find your perfect place in the sand with *Hawaii's Best Beaches* by John R. K. Clark, a guide to the 50th State's 50 best beaches. *Surfing: The Ultimate Pleasure,* by Leonard Lueras, covers everything about the sport, from its early history to the music and films of its later subculture.

Preparing your palate for an upcoming visit, or have you returned from the Islands in love with haute Hawaiian cuisine? *The New Cuisine of Hawaii,* by Janice Wald Henderson, is beautifully designed and features recipes from the 12 chefs credited with defining Hawaiʻi regional cuisine. One of these pioneers, celebrity chef Roy Yamaguchi, has opened a veritable empire of restaurants across the Islands. His cookbook *Roy's Feasts from Hawaii* provides an in-depth taste of the island in addition to some gorgeous photography and island background. Rachel Laudan's *The Foods of Paradise* describes local foods and their histories in addition to providing recipes. *Hawaiian Country Tables* by Kaui Philpotts spotlights vintage Island recipes and dishes

Books and Videos

and gives readers an unusual entrée into Hawai'i's history.

For swaying musicologists, there's *Hula Is Life, The Story of Maiki Aiu and Hālau Hulo o Maiki,* by Rita Aryioshi; it's the definitive book on hula's origins and development. Hawaiian music lovers might take note of the ideas presented in *Strains of Change: Impact of Tourism on Hawaiian Music* by Elizabeth Tatar. *Hawaiian Traditions in Hawaii,* by Joan Clarke, is an illustrated book detailing ethnic celebrations in the Islands. Robert Shaw traces the history of the Islands through its tradition of quilting in this artful book *Hawaiian Quilt Masterpieces.* Instead of just taking home a lei, learn how to make one: *Hawaiian Lei Making,* by Laurie Shimizu Ide, offers a photographic guide and reference tool for making of floral leis. Albert J. Schütz's souvenir-worthy paperback, *All About Hawaiian,* is a good introduction to the authentic language of the Islands and recent efforts to preserve it. *Hawai'i Magazine* (✉ Box 55796, Boulder, CO 80322, ☎ 800/365–4421; subscription $17.97 for six issues) is an attractive bimonthly magazine devoted to the 50th state.

Videos

To view Hawai'i on video before your arrival, take a look at *Forever Hawaii,* a video portrait of Hawai'i's six major islands.

For hikers the video *Hawaii on Foot* with Robert Smith gives hikers a peek at some of the best trails on O'ahu, Maui, the Big Island, and Kaua'i. It is available from H.O.A. Publications (✉ 102-16 Kaui Pl., Kula 96796, ☎ 808/678–2664). For lovers of dance, hula comes alive in the *1999 Merrie Monarch Festival Highlights.* This hula festival, held each spring on the Big Island, is Hawai'i's most prestigious competition. The video is available from www.BooklinesHawaii.com, or by phone by calling ☎ 800/828–4852.

Movie buffs will enjoy *Made in Paradise: Hollywood's Films of Hawaii and the South Seas,* by Luis Reyes. It points out movie locations and pokes gentle fun at some of the misinformation popularized by Tinseltown's version of Island life. Guided tours of Kaua'i locations used in filming are provided by **Hawai'i Movie Tours** (☎ 800/628–8432). Its tours are highly recommended.

Most people automatically think of Elvis when the words "Hawai'i" and "movie" are mentioned in the same sentence. Elvis Presley's Hawaiian-filmed movies are *Girls! Girls! Girls!* (1962), *Paradise, Hawaiian Style* (1966), and *Blue Hawaii* (1962), which showcases O'ahu's picturesque Hanauma Bay and Kaua'i's Coco Palms Resort, the site of Elvis's celluloid wedding.

Films such as Shirley Temple's *Curly Top* (1935); *Waikiki Wedding* (1937), with Bing Crosby; and *Gidget Goes Hawaiian* (1962) feature Hawai'i's beaches, palm trees, and hula dancers. The Islands' winter waves have taken center stage in a legion of hang-ten films of which only *North Shore* (1987) is on video.

Military-theme movies filmed in Hawai'i include *Mister Roberts* (1955), starring Henry Fonda, Jack Lemmon, and James Cagney; and *Lt. Robin Crusoe, USN* (1966), with Dick Van Dyke. Some serious military films, often dealing with WWII, with Hawaiian locales frequently posing as the South Pacific, include *Between Heaven and Hell* (1956), starring Robert Wagner; *The Enemy Below* (1957), with Robert Mitchum; and John Wayne's *Donovan's Reef* (1963). *Tora! Tora! Tora!* (1971) re-created the December 7, 1941, bombing of Pearl Harbor. For *Flight of the Intruder* (1991), director John Milius turned taro farms at the base of Kaua'i's Mount Wai'ale'le into the rice paddies of Southeast Asia.

Hawai'i has repeatedly doubled for other places. Kaua'i's remote valleys and waterfalls and O'ahu's Kualoa Ranch portrayed a Costa Rican dinosaur preserve in Steven Spielberg's *Jurassic Park* (1993). The opening beach scene of that movie's sequel, *The Lost World* (1997), was also filmed on Kaua'i. Spielberg was no stranger to Kaua'i, though, having filmed Harrison Ford's escape via seaplane from Kaua'i's Menehune Fishpond in *Raiders of the Lost Ark* (1981). The fluted cliffs and gorges of Kaua'i's rugged Nā Pali coastline play the misunderstood beast's island home in *King Kong* (1976), and a jungle dweller of another sort, in *George of the Jungle* (1997), frolicked on Kaua'i. Harrison Ford returned to the island for 10 weeks during the filming of *Six Days, Seven Nights* (1998), a romantic adventure set in French Polynesia.

Mitzi Gaynor washed that man right out of her hair on Kaua'i's Lumaha'i Beach in *South Pacific* (1958). And the tempestuous love scene between Burt Lancaster and Deborah Kerr in *From Here to Eternity* (1954) took place on O'ahu's Halona Cove beach.

James Michener's story *Hawaii* (1967) chronicles the lives of the Islands' missionary families. *Picture Bride* (1995) tells the story of a young Japanese girl who arrives on the Islands to face harsh realities as the wife of a sugar plantation laborer she has only seen in a photograph. And in *Race the Sun* (1996), a group of Big Island high school students build a solar-powered car and go on to win an international competition.

Other movies with Hawai'i settings include *Black Widow* (1987), in which journalist Debra Winger travels to the Big Island's lava fields to prevent a murder; *Honeymoon in Vegas* (1992); *Under the Hula Moon* (1995); and *A Very Brady Sequel* (1997).

HAWAI'I AT A GLANCE

ca. AD 500 The first human beings to set foot on Hawaiian shores are Polynesians, who travel 2,000 mi in 60- to 80-ft canoes to the islands they name Havaiki after their legendary homeland. Researchers today believe they were originally from Southeast Asia, and that they discovered the South Pacific Islands of Tahiti and the Marquesas before ending up in Hawai'i.

ca. 1758 Kamehameha, the Hawaiian chief who unified the Islands, is born.

1778 In January, Capt. James Cook, commander of the H.M.S. *Resolution* and the consort vessel H.M.S. *Discovery*, lands on the island of Kaua'i. He names the archipelago the Sandwich Islands after his patron, the Earl of Sandwich. In November, he returns to the Islands for the winter, anchoring at Kealakekua Bay on the Big Island.

1779 In February, Cook is killed in a battle with Hawai'i's indigenous people at Kealakekua.

1785 The isolation of the Islands ends as British, American, French, and Russian fur traders and New England whalers come to Hawai'i. Tales spread of thousands of acres of sugarcane growing wild, and farmers come in droves from the United States and Europe.

1790 Kamehameha begins his rise to power with a series of bloody battles.

1791 Kamehameha builds Pu'ukoholā Heiau (temple) and dedicates it by sacrificing a rival chief he has killed.

1795 Using Western arms, Kamehameha wins a decisive confrontation on O'ahu. Except for Kaua'i (which he tries to invade in 1796 and 1804), this completes his military conquest of the Islands.

1810 The chief of Kaua'i acknowledges Kamehameha's rule, giving him suzerainty over Kaua'i and Ni'ihau. Kamehameha becomes known as King Kamehameha I, and he rules the unified Kingdom of Hawai'i with an iron hand.

1819 Kamehameha I dies, and his oldest son, Liholiho, rules briefly as Kamehameha II, with Ka'ahumanu, Kamehameha I's favorite wife, as co-executive. Ka'ahumanu persuades the new king to abandon old religious taboos, including those that forbade women to eat with men or to hold positions of power. The first whaling ships land at Lahaina on Maui.

1820 By the time the first missionaries arrive from Boston, Hawai'i's social order is beginning to break down. First, Ka'ahumanu and then Kamehameha II defy *kapu* (taboo) without attracting divine retribution. Hawaiians, disillusioned with their own gods, are receptive to the ideas of Christianity. The influx of Western visitors also introduces to Hawai'i Western diseases, liquor, and what some view as moral decay.

1824 King Kamehameha II and his favorite wife die of measles during a visit to England. Honolulu missionaries give both royals a Christian burial outside Kawaiaha'o Church, inspiring many Hawaiians to convert to the Protestant faith. The king's younger brother, Kau'ikea'ōuli, becomes King Kamehameha III, a wise and gentle sovereign who reigns for 30 years with Ka'ahumanu as regent.

1832 Ka'ahumanu is baptized and dies a few months later.

1840 The Wilkes Expedition, sponsored by the U.S. Coast and Geodetic Survey, pinpoints Pearl Harbor as a potential naval base.

1845 Kamehameha III and the legislature move Hawai'i's seat of government from Lahaina, on Maui, to Honolulu, on O'ahu.

1849 Kamehameha III turns Hawai'i into a constitutional monarchy, and the United States, France, and Great Britain recognize Hawai'i as an independent country.

1850 The Great Mahele, a land commission, reapportions the land to the crown, the government, chiefs, and commoners, introducing for the first time the Western principle of private ownership. Commoners are now able to buy and sell land, but this great division becomes the great dispossession. By the end of the 19th century, white men own four acres for every one owned by a native. Some of the commission's distributions continue to be disputed to this day.

1852 As Western diseases depopulate the Islands, a labor shortage occurs in the sugarcane fields. For the next nine decades, a steady stream of foreign labor pours into Hawai'i, beginning with the Chinese. The Japanese begin arriving in 1868, followed by Filipinos, Koreans, Portuguese, and Puerto Ricans.

1872 Kamehameha V, the last descendent of the king who unified the Islands, dies without heirs. A power struggle ensues between the adherents of David Kalākaua and William Lunalilo.

1873 Lunalilo is elected Hawai'i's sixth king in January. The bachelor rules only 13 months before dying of tuberculosis.

1874 Kalākaua vies for the throne with the Dowager Queen Emma, the half-Caucasian widow of Kamehameha IV. Kalākaua is elected by the Hawai'i Legislature, against protests by supporters of Queen Emma. American and British marines are called in to restore order, and Kalākaua begins his reign as the "Merrie Monarch."

1875 The United States and Hawai'i sign a treaty of reciprocity, assuring Hawai'i a duty-free market for sugar in the United States.

1882 King Kalākaua builds 'Iolani Palace, an Italian renaissance–style structure, on the site of the previous royal palace.

1887 The reciprocity treaty of 1875 is renewed, giving the United States exclusive use of Pearl Harbor as a coaling station. Coincidentally, successful importation of Japanese laborers begins in earnest (after a false start in 1868).

1891 King Kalākaua dies and is succeeded by his sister, Queen Lili'uokalani, the last Hawaiian monarch.

1893 After a brief two-year reign, Lili'uokalani is removed from the throne by American business interests led by Lorrin A. Thurston (grandson of the missionary and newspaper founder Asa Thurston). Lili'uokalani is imprisoned in 'Iolani Palace for nearly eight months.

1894 The provisional government converts Hawai'i into a republic and proclaims Sanford Dole president.

1898 With the outbreak of the Spanish-American War, president William McKinley recognizes Hawai'i's strategic importance in the Pacific and moves to secure the Islands for the United States. On August 12, Hawai'i is officially annexed by a joint resolution of Congress.

1901 Sanford Dole is appointed first governor of the territory of Hawai'i. The first major tourist hotel, the Moana (now called the Sheraton Moana Surfrider), is built on Waikīkī Beach.

1903 James Dole (a cousin of Sanford Dole) produces nearly 2,000 cases of pineapple, marking the beginning of Hawai'i's pineapple industry. Pineapple eventually surpasses sugarcane as Hawai'i's number-one crop.

1907 Fort Shafter Base, headquarters for the U.S. Army, becomes the first permanent military post in the Islands.

1908 Dredging of the channel at Pearl Harbor begins.

1919 Pearl Harbor is formally dedicated by the U.S. Navy. Representing the Territory of Hawai'i in the U.S. House of Representatives, Prince Jonah Kūhiō Kalaniana'ole, the adopted son of Kapi'olani, the wife of Kalākaua, and with his brother one of the designated heirs to the throne of the childless Lili'uokalani, introduces the first bill proposing statehood for Hawai'i.

1927 Army lieutenants Lester Maitland and Albert Hegenberger make the first successful nonstop flight from the mainland to the Islands. Hawai'i begins to increase efforts to promote tourism, the industry that eventually dominates development of the Islands. The Matson Navigation Company builds the Royal Hawaiian Hotel as a destination for its cruise ships.

1929 Hawai'i's commercial interisland air service begins.

1936 Pan American World Airways introduces regular commercial passenger flights to Hawai'i from the mainland.

1941 At Pearl Harbor the U.S. Pacific Fleet is bombed by the Japanese, forcing U.S. entry into World War II. Nearly 4,000 men are killed in the surprise attack.

1942 James Jones, with thousands of others, trains at Schofield Barracks on O'ahu. He later writes about his experience in *From Here to Eternity*.

1959 Congress passes legislation granting Hawai'i statehood. In special elections the new state sends to the U.S. House of Representatives its first American of Japanese ancestry, Daniel Inouye, and to the U.S. Senate its first American of Chinese ancestry, Hiram Fong. Later in the year, the first Boeing 707 jets make the flight from San Francisco in a record five hours. By year's end 243,216 tourists visit Hawai'i, and tourism becomes Hawai'i's major industry.

1986 Hawai'i elects its first native Hawaiian governor, John Waihe'e.

1992 Hurricane 'Iniki, the most devastating hurricane to hit Hawai'i, tears through Kaua'i on September 11. The island's people, infrastructure, gardens, and tourism industry have happily all since recovered.

1993 After native Hawaiians commemorate the 100th anniversary of the overthrow of Queen Lili'uokalani with a call for sovereignty, Congress issues an apology to the Hawaiian people for the annexation of the Islands.

1997 After 34 years of planning, construction, and endless litigation, Oahu's H-3 "Trans-Koolau" freeway linking Pearl Harbor to the Windward side of O'ahu finally opens. Opposition to the highway centered on the route through the Hālawa and Haiku valleys, areas of historical and religious significance to native Hawaiians. The price tag for this scenic roadway with a million-dollar view? $1.3 billion in state and federal tax dollars.

1998 The U.S.S. *Missouri* comes to her final resting place in Pearl Harbor. The battleship, on whose decks the Japanese signed their surrender agreement in World War II, is now a floating museum, permanently docked at Ford Island.

2000 Kilauea Volcano on the Big Island of Hawai'i greets the new year with a show of lava, making this the 18th year of its current eruptive phase and the longest phase of such activity in recorded volcanic history.

ESSENTIAL INFORMATION

AIR TRAVEL

Hawai'i is a major destination link for flights traveling to and from the U.S. mainland, Asia, Australia, New Zealand, and the South Pacific. When traveling to the Islands, remember that many of the major airline carriers serving Honolulu now fly direct to the islands of Maui, Kaua'i, and the Big Island, allowing visitors to bypass connecting flights out of Honolulu. For the more spontaneous traveler, island hopping is still easy, with flights departing Honolulu every 20 to 30 minutes daily until mid-evening. International travelers also have options. Two of Hawai'i's islands are gateways from foreign destinations into the United States—O'ahu and the Big Island. Entering into the islands via the Big Island's Kona International airport can save international visitors a considerable amount of time spent clearing U.S. Customs, which during peak arrival times at Honolulu International Airport can be considerable.

BOOKING

When you book look for nonstop flights and remember that "direct" flights stop at least once. Try to avoid connecting flights, which require a change of plane.

CARRIERS

➤ MAJOR AIRLINES: American (☎ 800/433–7300) to Honolulu and Maui. Continental (☎ 800/525–0280) to Honolulu and Kaua'i. Delta (☎ 800/221–1212) to Honolulu and Maui. Northwest (☎ 800/225–2525) to Honolulu. TWA (☎ 800/221–2000) to Honolulu and the Big Island. United (☎ 800/241–6522) to Honolulu, Maui, the Big Island, and Kaua'i.

➤ SMALLER AIRLINES: Hawaiian Airlines (☎ 800/367–5320) to Honolulu, Kaua'i, Maui, the Big Island, Moloka'i, and Lāna'i.

➤ DIRECT FLIGHTS FROM THE U.K.: Air New Zealand (☎ 0181/741–2299). American (☎ 0345/789–789). Continental (☎ 0800/776–464). Delta (☎ 0800/414–767). United (☎ 0800/888–555). Trailfinders (✉ 42–50 Earls Court Rd., Kensington, London, W8 6FT, ☎ 020/7937–5400) can arrange bargain flights.

➤ WITHIN HAWAI'I: Aloha Airlines (☎ 800/367–5250), Hawaiian Airlines (☎ 800/367–5320), Island Air (☎ 800/323–3345), Trans Air (☎ 800/634–2094). Pacific Wings (☎ 888/575–4546).

CHECK-IN & BOARDING

Plan to arrive at the airport 45 to 60 minutes before departure for interisland flights, 60 to 90 minutes for domestic flights, and at least 2 hours prior to departure for travel to international destinations. Although the neighbor island airports are smaller and more casual than Honolulu International, during peak times they can also be quite busy. Allot extra travel time to all airports during morning and afternoon rush-hour traffic periods. Prior to check-in, all luggage being taken out of Hawai'i must pass agricultural inspection. Fruit, plants, and processed foods that have been labeled and packed for export (including pineapples, papaya, coconuts, flowers, and macadamia nuts) are permitted. Fresh fruit and other agricultural items, including seed leis are not, and will be confiscated.

Assuming that not everyone with a ticket will show up, airlines routinely overbook planes. When everyone does, airlines ask for volunteers to give up their seats. In return, these volunteers usually get a certificate for a free flight and are rebooked on the next flight out. If there are not enough volunteers, the airline must choose who will be denied boarding. The first

...mped are passengers who ... in late and those flying on ...ted tickets, so **get to the gate** ...eck in as early as possible, especially during peak periods.

Always **bring a government-issued photo I.D. to the airport.** You may be asked to show it before you are allowed to check in.

CUTTING COSTS

The least-expensive airfares to Hawai'i must usually be purchased in advance and are nonrefundable. It's smart to **call a number of airlines, and when you are quoted a good price, book it on the spot.** The same fare may not be available the next day. Always **check different routings** and look into using different airports. Travel agents, especially low-fare specialists (☞ Discounts & Deals, *below*), are helpful.

Consolidators are another good source. They buy tickets for scheduled international flights at reduced rates from the airlines, then sell them at prices that beat the best fare available directly from the airlines, usually without restrictions. Sometimes you can even get your money back if you need to return the ticket. Carefully read the fine print detailing penalties for changes and cancellations, and **confirm your consolidator reservation with the airline.**

When you **fly as a courier,** you trade your checked-luggage space for a ticket deeply subsidized by a courier service. There are restrictions on when you can book and how long you can stay.

In Hawai'i, both **Aloha Airlines** and **Hawaiian Airlines** offer travelers multi-island air passes that allow unlimited interisland travel during a specific time period at a reduced rate.

➤ CONSOLIDATORS: **Cheap Tickets** (☎ 800/377–1000). **Discount Airline Ticket Service** (☎ 800/576–1600). **Unitravel** (☎ 800/325–2222). **Up & Away Travel** (☎ 212/889–2345). **World Travel Network** (☎ 800/409–6753).

➤ DISCOUNT PASSES: **Aloha Airlines** (☎ 800/367–5250). **Hawaiian Airlines** (☎ 800/367–5320).

ENJOYING THE FLIGHT

For more legroom, **request an emergency-aisle seat.** Don't sit in the row in front of the emergency aisle or in front of a bulkhead, where seats may not recline. If you have dietary concerns, **ask for special meals when booking.** These can be vegetarian, low-cholesterol, or kosher, for example. On long flights, try to maintain a normal routine, to help fight jet lag. At night, **get some sleep.** By day, **eat light meals, drink water** (not alcohol), and **move around the cabin** to stretch your legs.

FLYING TIMES

Flying time is about 10 hours from New York, 8 hours from Chicago, and 5 hours from Los Angeles.

HOW TO COMPLAIN

If your baggage goes astray or your flight goes awry, complain right away. Most carriers require that you **file a claim immediately.**

➤ AIRLINE COMPLAINTS: U.S. Department of Transportation **Aviation Consumer Protection Division** (✉ C-75, Room 4107, Washington, DC 20590, ☎ 202/366–2220, airconsumer@ost. dot.gov, www.dot.gov/airconsumer). **Federal Aviation Administration Consumer Hotline** (☎ 800/322–7873).

AIRPORTS

Hawai'i's major airport is **Honolulu International,** on O'ahu, 20 minutes (9 mi) west of Waikīkī. To travel interisland from Honolulu, visitors depart from either the interisland terminal or the commuter-airline terminal, located in two separate structures adjacent to the main overseas terminal building. **A free bus service, the Wiki Wiki Shuttle, operates between terminals.**

Maui has two major airports: **Kahului Airport,** in the island's central town of Kahului, and **Kapalua-West Maui Airport.** For visitors to West Maui, the easiest arrival point is the Kapalua facility; it saves about an hour's drive from the Kahului airport. The tiny town of Hāna in East Maui also has an airstrip, but it is only serviced by one commuter airline.

On Kaua'i, visitors fly into Līhu'e Airport, on the east side of the island.

Those flying to the Big Island of Hawai'i regularly land at one of two fields. Kona's **Kona International Airport,** on the west side, best serves Kailua-Kona, Keauhou, and the Kohala Coast. **Hilo International Airport** is more appropriate for those going to the east side. One O'ahu-based airline has regular flights into **Waimea-Kohala Airport,** called Ka-muela Airport by residents, who use it when commuting between islands.

Moloka'i's **Ho'olehua Airport** is small and centrally located, as is **Lāna'i Airport** on that island. Both rural airports handle a limited number of flights per day. Visitors to these islands must first stop in O'ahu and change to an interisland flight.

➤ AIRPORT INFORMATION: O'ahu: **Honolulu International Airport** (☎ 808/836–6413 or 808/836–6411). Maui: **Kahului Airport** (☎ 808/872–3894 or 808/872–3830), **Kapalua–West Maui Airport** (☎ 808/669–0623), **Hāna Airport** (☎ 808/248–8208). The Big Island: **Kona International Airport** (☎ 808/329–2484 or 808/329–3423), **Hilo International Airport** (☎ 808/934–5801), **Waimea-Kohala Airport** (☎ 808/885–4520). Kaua'i: **Līhu'e Airport** (☎ 808/246–1400). Moloka'i: **Ho'olehua Airport** (☎ 808/567–6140). Lāna'i: **Lāna'i Airport** (☎ 808/565–6757).

BIKE TRAVEL

Hawai'i's natural beauty, breathtaking coastal routes, and year-round fair weather make it attractive to explore by bike. However, on many roads, bicycle lanes are limited or nonexistent, and **on the more populated islands, cyclists must contend with heavy traffic.** While biking on O'ahu may require some skillful maneuvering, bike routes on the neighbor islands include the challenge of the Big Island's 225-mi circle-island route, cycling downhill at Maui's Haleakala crater, exploring the lush routes of tropical Kaua'i, and mastering off-road mountain biking on Lāna'i and Moloka'i. **Visitors can rent bikes for some solo cruising, join local cycling clubs for their weekly rides, or hit the road with outfitters** for tours that go beyond the well-traveled paths.

➤ BIKE MAPS: **Honolulu City and County Bike Coordinator** (☎ 808/527–5044). **Big Island Mountain Bike Association** (☎ 808/961–4452). **Mayor's Advisory Committee on Bicycling, Maui** (☎ 808/871–6886). **The Division of Forestry and Wildlife, Kaua'i** (☎ 808/274–3433).

➤ BIKE RENTALS: **Blue Sky Rentals** (O'ahu, ☎ 808/947–0101). **Dave's Triathlon Shop** (Big Island, ☎ 808/329–4522). **Kaua'i Cycle and Tour** (Kaua'i, ☎ 808/821–2115). **West Maui Cycles** (Maui, ☎ 808/661–9005).

BIKES IN FLIGHT

Most airlines accommodate bikes as luggage, provided they are dismantled and boxed. For bike boxes, often free at bike shops, you'll pay about $5 from airlines (at least $100 for bike bags). International travelers can sometimes substitute a bike for a piece of checked luggage at no charge; otherwise, the cost is about $100. Domestic and Canadian airlines charge $25–$50.

BOAT & FERRY TRAVEL

Ferry travel in the islands is limited to daily service between Lahaina, Maui, and Manele Bay, Lāna'i. The 9-mi crossing costs $50 round-trip and takes about 45 minutes or so, depending on ocean conditions (which can make this trip a rough one). Reservations are essential.

➤ BOAT & FERRY INFORMATION: **Excursions/Lāna'i Passenger Ferry** (☎ 808/661–3756).

BUS TRAVEL

Getting around the islands by bus is an option on O'ahu, but on neighbor island services are limited and car rental is recommended. O'ahu's transportation system, known just as "TheBus," is one of the island's best bargains. Fares per ride are $1, and with more than 68 bus routes you can even do a O'ahu circle-island tour that will only cost you a buck.

The Big Island's county bus, called "The Hele-On" Bus, travels a Kailua-Kona–to–Hilo route once daily except Sunday. There are limited routes to other areas. On the island of Kaua'i, the "Kaua'i Bus" travels two main routes, one going north to Hanelei from Lihue and one going south from Lihue to Koloa and Poipu. Routes don't come close to many of the island's resorts or best-known attractions, but do wind through residential towns. Maui has no public bus service, but a private commercial company does have regular bus routes within various resort areas and to popular attractions. Check with your hotel desk upon arrival for schedules. Neighbor island public transportation does not run on Sundays.

➤ BUS INFORMATION: "TheBus"on O'ahu (☎ 808/848–5555 or 296–1818, then press 8287). "Hele-On" Bus on the Big Island (☎ 808/961–8744). Kaua'i Bus on Kaua'i (☎ 808/241–6410). Trans-Hawaiian Services on Maui (☎ 808/877–0380).

BUSINESS HOURS

Even in paradise, people must work. Local business hours are generally 8 to 5 weekdays. Banks are generally open Monday through Thursday 8:30 to 3 and until 6 on Friday. Some banks have Saturday morning hours. Twenty-four-hour money access is available through ATM machines, which are plentiful. You'll find machines within many of the major resorts, at shopping centers, and within close proximity to major attractions.

Many self-serve gas stations now stay open around the clock, with full-service stations usually open from around 7 AM until 9 PM. U.S. postal offices are open from 8:30 AM to 4:30 PM weekdays, 8:30 to noon on Saturdays. On O'ahu, the Ala Moana post office branch is the only branch, other than the main Honolulu International Airport facility, that stays open till 4 PM on Saturday.

MUSEUMS & SIGHTS

Museum opening hours throughout the islands vary depending on the size of the museum. Most generally open their doors between 9 AM and 10 AM and stay open till 5 PM Tuesday through Saturday. Many museums operate with afternoon hours only on Sundays and close on Monday. Visitor attractions hours vary throughout the state, but most are open daily with the exception of major holidays like Christmas. **Check local newspapers upon arrival if for attraction hours and schedules if visiting over holiday periods.** The local dailies carry a listing of "What's Open/What's Not" for those time periods.

SHOPS

Stores in resort areas can open as early as 8, with shopping-center opening hours varying from 9:30 to 10 on weekdays and Saturdays, a bit later on Sundays. Bigger malls stay open until 9 weekdays and Saturdays and close at 5 on Sundays. Boutiques in resort areas may stay open as late as 11.

CAMERAS & PHOTOGRAPHY

While you are traveling in Hawai'i, it's important to remember to **keep film out of direct sunlight and away from high-temperature areas** like the trunk of your car. Carry extra film and batteries for those jaunts to less-populated island spots. **For underwater photography, today's "disposable" cameras can provide terrific photos** for those once-in-a-lifetime underwater experiences, at a fraction of the cost of purchasing equipment.

Film developing is available on all islands. Many hotel-resort sundry stores offer the service, and larger department stores, like Long's Drugs, offer one-hour service for regular film developing and overnight service for panoramic film.

➤ PHOTO HELP: Kodak Information Center (☎ 800/242–2424). *Kodak Guide to Shooting Great Travel Pictures* is available in bookstores or from Fodor's Travel Publications (☎ 800/533–6478; $16.50 plus $5.50 shipping).

EQUIPMENT PRECAUTIONS

Always **be prepared to turn on your camera or camcorder** to prove to security personnel that the device is real. Always **ask for hand inspection of film,** which becomes clouded after repeated exposure to airport X-ray machines, and **keep videotapes away from metal detectors.**

CAR RENTAL

You can rent anything from a $26-a-day econobox to a $1,100-a-day

Ferrari. It's wise to **make reservations in advance,** especially if visiting the islands during peak seasons or when coming for a major convention or sporting event. This is especially true on the neighbor islands, where rental fleets are smaller and cars can sell out quickly.

Rates in Honolulu begin at $38 a day ($164 a week) for an economy car with air-conditioning, automatic transmission, and unlimited mileage. Rates on Maui begin at $32 a day ($144 a week) for the same. This does not include tax, insurance, and a $2-per-day road tax.

➤ MAJOR AGENCIES: **Alamo** (☎ 800/ 327–9633; 0181/759–6200 in the U.K.). **Avis** (☎ 800/331–1212; 800/ 879–2847 in Canada; 02/9353–9000 in Australia; 09/525–1982 in New Zealand). **Budget** (☎ 800/527–0700; 0144/227–6266 in the U.K.). **Dollar** (☎ 800/800–4000; 0181/897–0811 in the U.K., where it is known as Eurodollar; 02/9223–1444 in Australia). **Hertz** (☎ 800/654–3131; 800/ 263–0600 in Canada; 0181/897–2072 in the U.K.; 02/9669–2444 in Australia; 03/358–6777 in New Zealand). **National InterRent** (☎ 800/227–7368; 0345/222525 in the U.K., where it is known as Europcar InterRent).

CUTTING COSTS

For a better rental deal, **check out local and national promotions as well as discounts offered through frequent-flyer programs, automobile clubs, or business or military affiliations.** Many rental companies in Hawai'i also offer customers coupons for discounts at various attractions that could save you money later on in your trip. To get the best deal, **book through a travel agent who will shop around.** Also **price local car-rental companies,** although the service and maintenance may not be as good as those of a major player. Remember to ask about required deposits, cancellation penalties, and drop-off charges if you're planning to pick up the car in one city and leave it in another. If you're traveling during a holiday period, also make sure that a confirmed reservation guarantees you a car.

Do **look into wholesalers,** companies that do not own fleets but rent in bulk from those that do and often offer better rates than traditional car-rental operations.

➤ LOCAL AGENCIES: **Thrifty Car Rental** (☎ 808/831–2277) on O'ahu, Kaua'i, the Big Island, and Maui. **VIP Car Rentals** (☎ 808/922–4605) on O'ahu. **JN Car and Truck Rentals** (☎ 808/831–2724) on O'ahu.

➤ WHOLESALERS: **Auto Europe** (☎ 207/842–2000 or 800/223–5555, FAX 800–235–6321, www.autoeurope. com). **Kemwel Holiday Autos** (☎ 800/ 678–0678, FAX 914/825–3160, www. kemwel.com).

INSURANCE

When driving a rented car you are generally responsible for any damage to or loss of the vehicle as well as for any property damage or personal injury that you may cause. Before you rent see what coverage your personal auto-insurance policy and credit cards already provide.

For about $15 to $20 per day, rental companies sell protection, known as a collision- or loss-damage waiver (CDW or LDW), that eliminates your liability for damage to the car. In most states you don't need a CDW if you have personal auto insurance or other liability insurance. However, **make sure you have enough coverage to pay for the car.** If you do not have auto insurance or an umbrella policy that covers damage to third parties, purchasing liability insurance and a CDW or LDW is highly recommended.

REQUIREMENTS & RESTRICTIONS

In Hawai'i you must be 25 years of age to rent a car and have a valid driver's license and a major credit card. There is no upper age limit on car rentals, though one agency said they would not rent to anyone over 99 years of age. You'll pay extra for child seats (about $3 per day), which are compulsory for children under five, and for additional drivers (about $2 per day). Non-U.S. residents will need a reservation voucher, a passport, a driver's license, and a travel policy that covers each driver, when picking up a car.

In Hawai'i your unexpired mainland driver's license is valid for up to 90 days. If you plan to stay in the Islands for extended periods, apply for a Hawai'i driver's license (cost $18) at the State Department of Motor Vehicles office in Honolulu. You'll also have to take a $2 written exam. For drivers from foreign destinations, most car rental companies will accept a foreign driver's license printed in English. An international driver's license is readily accepted.

SURCHARGES

Before you pick up a car in one city and leave it in another, **ask about drop-off charges or one-way service fees**, which can be substantial. Note, too, that some rental agencies charge extra if you return the car before the time specified in your contract. To avoid a hefty refueling fee, **fill the tank just before you turn in the car,** but be aware that gas stations near the rental outlet may overcharge.

CAR TRAVEL

Technically, the Big Island of Hawai'i is the only island you can completely circle by car, but each island offers plenty of sightseeing from its miles of roadways. O'ahu can be circled except for the roadless west-shore area around Ka'ena Point. Elsewhere, major highways follow the shoreline and traverse the island at two points. Rush-hour traffic (6:30–8:30 AM and 3:30–6 PM) can be frustrating around Honolulu and the outlying areas, as many thoroughfares allow no left turns due to contra-flow lanes. Parking along many streets is curtailed during those times, and towing is strictly practiced. **Read curbside parking signs** before leaving your vehicle, even at a meter.

GASOLINE

Regardless of today's fluctuating gas prices, you can pretty much count on having to pay about 20% more at the pump for gasoline in the islands, self-serve or not, than on the U.S. mainland.

ROAD CONDITIONS

It's difficult to get lost in most of Hawai'i. Roads and streets, although they may challenge the visitor's tongue (Kalaniana'ole Highway, for example), are well marked. **Keep an eye open for** the Hawai'i Visitors and Convention Bureau's red-caped warrior signs that mark major visitor attractions and scenic spots. Ask for a map at the car-rental counter. Free visitor publications containing good-quality road maps can be found on all islands, too.

Kaua'i has a well-maintained highway running south from Līhu'e to Barking Sands Beach; a spur at Waimea takes you along Waimea Canyon to Koke'e State Park. A northern route also winds its way from Līhu'e to end at Hā'ena, the beginning of the rugged and roadless Nā Pali Coast. Maui also has its share of impenetrable areas, although four-wheel-drive vehicles rarely run into problems on the island. Saddle roads run between the east and west landmasses composing Maui. Other highways follow the western coasts of East and West Maui. Although Moloka'i and Lāna'i have fewer roadways, car rental is still worthwhile and will allow plenty of interesting sightseeing. **Opt for a four-wheel-drive vehicle** if dirt-road exploration holds any appeal.

RULES OF THE ROAD

Be sure to **buckle up.** Hawai'i has a strictly enforced seat-belt law for front-seat passengers. Children under 4 must be in a car seat (available from car-rental agencies). Children 18 and under, riding in the backseat, are also required by state law to use seat belts. The highway speed limit is usually 55 mph. In-town traffic moves from 25 to 40 mph. Jaywalking is very common, so be particularly watchful for pedestrians, especially in congested areas such as Waikīkī. Unauthorized use of a parking space reserved for persons with disabilities can net you a $150 fine.

Asking for directions will almost always produce a helpful explanation from the locals, but you should be prepared for an island term or two. Instead of using compass directions, remember that Hawai'i residents refer to places as being either *mauka* (toward the mountains) or *makai* (toward the ocean) from one another. Other directions depend on your location: in Honolulu, for example, people say to "go Diamond Head," which means toward that famous landmark, or to "go *'ewa,*" meaning in the opposite direction. A shop on the mauka–Diamond Head corner of a street is on the mountain side of the street on the corner closest to Diamond Head. It all makes perfect sense once you get the lay of the land.

CHILDREN IN HAWAI'I

Its sunny beaches and many family-oriented cultural sites, activities, and attractions make the islands a very *keiki* (child) friendly place. Here kids can swim with a dolphin, surf with a boogie board, visit an active volcano, or ride a sugarcane train. Parents should **use caution on beaches and during water sports.** Even waters that appear calm can harbor powerful rip currents. And remember that the sun's rays are in operation full-force year-round here. Sunblock for children is essential. If you are renting a car, don't forget to **arrange for a car seat** when you reserve.

➤ LOCAL INFORMATION: Most major resort chains in Hawai'i offer children's activity programs for kids ages 5–12. These kid clubs offer kids opportunities to learn about local culture, make friends with children from around the world, and to experience age-appropriate activities while giving moms and dads a "time-out." Upon arrival, **check out the daily local newspapers for children's events.** The Honolulu Advertiser's "TGIF" section each Friday includes a section on keiki activities with a local flavor.

FLYING

If your children are two or older, **ask about children's airfares.** As a general rule, infants under two not occupying a seat fly at greatly reduced fares or even for free. Experts agree that it's a good idea to use safety seats aloft for children weighing less than 40 pounds. Airlines set their own policies: U.S. carriers usually require that the child be ticketed, even if he or she is young enough to ride free, since the seats must be strapped into regular seats. Do **check your airline's policy about using safety seats during takeoff and landing.** And since safety seats are not allowed just everywhere in the plane, get your seat assignments early.

When reserving, **request children's meals or a freestanding bassinet** if you need them. But note tha[t] head seats, where you must the bassinet, may lack an o[v]er bin or storage space on the [...]

LODGING

Families cannot go wrong choosing resort locations on each island that are part of larger hotel chains like Hilton, Sheraton, and Outrigger. Many of these resorts are located on the best beaches on each island, have an array of activities created for kids, and are centrally located for visits to popular attractions. Outrigger's new "Ohana" brand hotels are off the beachfront, but provide great value at good prices. Many condominium resorts now also offer children's activities and amenities during holiday periods. Bed-and-breakfast lodgings on the neighbor islands give families some unique options, from Upcountry ranchland locations to private beachfront estates. Note that most hotels allow children under a certain age to stay in their parents' room at no extra charge, but others charge for them as extra adults. Be sure to **find out the cutoff age for children's discounts. Also check for special seasonal programs, like "kids eat free" promotions.**

➤ BEST CHOICES: **Aston Hotels** (☎ 800/922–5533,www.aston-hotels.com). **Four Seasons Resorts** (☎ 800/819–5053, www.fshr.com). **Hilton Hawaii** (☎ 800/445–8667, www.hilton.com/hawaii). **Hyatt Hawaii** (☎ 800/554–9288, www.hyatt.com). **Lanai Resorts** (☎ 800/321–4666, www.lanai-resorts.com). **Moloka'i Ranch** ☎ (800/254–8871, www.molokai-ranch.com). **Outrigger Hotels** (☎ 800/922–5533, www.outrigger.com). **Sheraton Resorts** (☎ 800/325–3535, www.sheraton-hawaii.com).

SIGHTS & ATTRACTIONS

Top picks for children run the gamut from the natural attractions that kids can enjoy for free to some fairly expensive amusements. On O'ahu, kid favorites include hiking Diamond Head, snorkeling Hanauma Bay, learning about marine life at Sea Life Park, playing ancient Hawaiian games at Waimea Valley Adventures Park, and touring through South Pacific cultures at the Polynesian Cultural Center. On

Maui, kid favorites include the Sugar Cane Train in Kā'anapali, snorkeling at Molokini Island, watching the sunrise atop Haleakala crater, driving the Road to Hāna with mom and dad for a dip in one of the Seven Sacred Pools, or whale-watching after a visit to the Maui Ocean Center. Kids "lava" the Big Island of Hawai'i's Volcano National Parks, touring the Mauna Loa macadamia-nut factory near Hilo, swimming with dolphins at the Hilton Waikoloa, or horseback riding at Parker Ranch.

Kaua'i is where kids go to explore film locations like Peter Pan's Never-Never Land and Jurassic Park. They can learn to waterski on the Wailua River, visit Kokee National Park (known as "the Grand Canyon of the Pacific"), or just spend the day swimming Poipu's sunny south shores. Lāna'i and Moloka'i are great islands for adventurous kids. At Moloka'i Ranch, families can sleep in "tentalows" and tackle the rope-challenge course for excitement. On Lāna'i, four-wheel-drive off-road adventure tours take families to destinations like Shipwreck Beach and Manele Bay, where the dolphins sometimes come to play. Read through the pages of this book for a myriad of other sights and activities. Places that are especially appealing to children are indicated by a rubber-duckie icon in the margin.

COMPUTERS ON THE ROAD

Since Hawai'i is isolated in the middle of the Pacific Ocean, staying connected electronically to the world has always been a priority. New hotels and resorts, or those who have recently renovated in the islands, now offer in-room dataports. Many hotels that cater to the business traveler also have business centers with full computer setups that allow even the leisure traveler to check e-mail while away from home. **Check out the islands' new crop of Internet cafés,** where you can get a steaming cup of Kona coffee while checking your e-mail or surfing the Web for a small hourly fee. If you don't want to travel with your laptop computer but want to have access to your e-mail while on the road, **open an account with a Web-based e-mail system like Hotmail that gives you access to your mail through any Internet connection.**

CONSUMER PROTECTION

Whenever shopping or buying travel services in Hawaii, **pay with a major credit card** so you can cancel payment or get reimbursed if there's a problem. If you're doing business with a particular company for the first time, **contact your local Better Business Bureau and the attorney general's offices** in your own state and the company's home state as well. Have any complaints been filed? Finally, if you're buying a package or tour, always **consider travel insurance** that includes default coverage (☞ Insurance, *below*).

➤ BBBs: **Council of Better Business Bureaus** (✉ 4200 Wilson Blvd., Suite 800, Arlington, VA 22203, ☎ 703/276–0100, ℻ 703/525–8277, www.bbb.org).

CRUISE TRAVEL

When Pan Am's amphibious *Hawai'i Clipper* touched down on Pearl Harbor's waters in 1936, it marked the beginning of the end of regular passenger-ship travel to the Islands. From that point on, the predominant means of transporting visitors would be by air, not by sea. Today, however, cruising to Hawai'i still holds a special appeal for those with the time and money to spare, and with a bit of research you can arrange passage aboard the luxury liners that call on Honolulu.

No regularly scheduled American ships steam between the mainland and Hawai'i. Although foreign-owned vessels often ply the Pacific, the Jones Act of 1896 prohibits them from carrying passengers between two U.S. ports unless the ships first stop at an intervening foreign port or carry the passengers to a foreign destination. What that means to those wishing for the relaxing ways of ship travel is that they'll have to book with one of the major lines passing through Honolulu.

Cruises within the islands are available on the 1,021-passenger ship the S.S. *Independence,* under the direction of American Hawai'i Cruises. The liner's parent company, American Classic Voyages, has added a second vessel, under its new United States Lines brand, the 1,212-passenger M.S. *Patriot.* At press time, the ship was expected to begin its inaugural cruise December 9, 2000. Two additional cruise vessels are scheduled to be added to Island waters in 2002 and 2003. Seven-day cruises will now originate from both Honolulu and Maui, for visits to both these islands as well as ports of call on the Big Island and Kaua'i. To get the best deal on a cruise, **consult a cruise-only travel agency.**

Even if you choose, as most travelers do, to travel by air to the islands, you can get the flavor of what the luxury cruise era in Hawai'i was like by checking out Aloha Tower Marketplace's Boat Day Celebrations. Vessels having Hawai'i as a port of call are met upon arrival by hula dancers and the kind of entertainment and floral festivities that once greeted travelers almost a century ago. Contact the Aloha Tower Marketplace for a boat-day schedule upon arrival.

➤ CRUISE LINES: For details on cruises that pass through Honolulu: **American Hawai'i Cruises** (☎ 800/765–7000). **Cunard** (☎ 800/221–4770). **Holland America** (☎ 800/426–0327). **Princess** (☎ 800/421–0522). **Royal Caribbean Cruise Line** (☎ 800/327–6700). **Royal Cruise Line** (☎ 415/956–7200).

CUSTOMS & DUTIES

When shopping, **keep receipts** for all purchases. Upon reentering the country, **be ready to show customs officials what you've bought.** If you feel a duty is incorrect or object to the way your clearance was handled, note the inspector's badge number and ask to see a supervisor. If the problem isn't resolved, write to the appropriate authorities, beginning with the port director at your point of entry.

IN AUSTRALIA

Australian residents who are 18 or older may bring home $A400 worth of souvenirs and gifts (including jewelry), 250 cigarettes or 250 grams of tobacco, and 1,125 ml of alcohol (including wine, beer, and spirits). Residents under 18 may bring back $A200 worth of goods. Prohibited items include meat products. Seeds, plants, and fruits need to be declared upon arrival.

➤ INFORMATION: **Australian Customs Service** (Regional Director, ✉ Box 8, Sydney, NSW 2001, ☎ 02/9213– 2000, FAX 02/9213–4000).

IN CANADA

Canadian residents who have been out of Canada for at least 7 days may bring home C$500 worth of goods duty-free. If you've been away less than 7 days but more than 48 hours, the duty-free allowance drops to C$200; if your trip lasts 24–48 hours, the allowance is C$50. You may not pool allowances with family members. Goods claimed under the C$500 exemption may follow you by mail; those claimed under the lesser exemptions must accompany you. Alcohol and tobacco products may be included in the 7-day and 48-hour exemptions but not in the 24-hour exemption. If you meet the age requirements of the province or territory through which you reenter Canada, you may bring in, duty-free, 1.14 liters (40 imperial ounces) of wine or liquor *or* 24 12-ounce cans or bottles of beer or ale. If you are 16 or older you may bring in, duty-free, 200 cigarettes and 50 cigars. Check ahead of time with Revenue Canada or the Department of Agriculture for policies regarding meat products, seeds, plants, and fruits.

You may send an unlimited number of gifts worth up to C$60 each duty-free to Canada. Label the package UNSOLICITED GIFT—VALUE UNDER $60. Alcohol and tobacco are excluded.

➤ INFORMATION: **Revenue Canada** (✉ 2265 St. Laurent Blvd. S, Ottawa, Ontario K1G 4K3, ☎ 613/993–0534; 800/461–9999 in Canada, FAX 613/ 957–8911, www.ccra-adrc.gc.ca).

IN HAWAI'I

Plants and plant products are subject to regulation by the Department of Agriculture, both on entering and leaving Hawai'i. Pineapples and coconuts with the packer's agricultural inspection stamp pass freely; papayas must be treated, inspected, and stamped. All other fruits are banned for export to the U.S. mainland. Flowers pass except for gardenia, rose leaves, jade vine, and mauna loa. Also banned are insects, snails, soil, cotton, cacti, sugarcane, and all berry plants.

You should **leave dogs and other pets at home.** A strict 30-day quarantine is imposed to keep out rabies, which is nonexistent in Hawai'i.

IN NEW ZEALAND

Homeward-bound residents 17 or older may bring back $700 worth of souvenirs and gifts. Your duty-free allowance also includes 4.5 liters of wine or beer; one 1,125-ml bottle of spirits; and either 200 cigarettes, 250 grams of tobacco, 50 cigars, or a combination of the three up to 250 grams. Prohibited items include meat products, seeds, plants, and fruits.

➤ INFORMATION: **New Zealand Customs** (Custom House, ✉ 50 Anzac Ave., Box 29, Auckland, New Zealand, ☎ 09/359–6655, FAX 09/359–6732).

IN THE U.K.

From countries outside the EU, including the United States, you may bring home, duty-free, 200 cigarettes or 50 cigars; 1 liter of spirits or 2 liters of fortified or sparkling wine or liqueurs; 2 liters of still table wine; 60 ml of perfume; 250 ml of toilet water; plus £136 worth of other goods, including gifts and souvenirs. If returning from outside the EU, prohibited items include meat products, seeds, plants, and fruits.

➤ INFORMATION: **HM Customs and Excise** (✉ Dorset House, Stamford St., Bromley, Kent BR1 1XX, ☎ 0171/202–4227).

IN THE U.S.

➤ INFORMATION: **U.S. Customs Service** (✉ 1300 Pennsylvania Ave. NW, Washington, DC 20229, www.customs.gov; inquiries, ☎ 202/354–1000; complaints c/o ✉ Office of Regulations and Rulings; registration of equipment c/o ✉ Resource Management, ☎ 202/927–0540).

DISABILITIES & ACCESSIBILITY

The Society for the Advancement of Travel for the Handicapped has named Hawai'i the most accessible vacation spot for people with disabilities. Ramped visitor areas and specially equipped lodgings are relatively common in the Islands. The Hawai'i Center for Independent Living publishes the "Aloha Guide to Accessibility" listing addresses and telephone numbers for support-service organizations and rates the Islands' hotels, beaches, shopping and entertainment centers, and major visitor attractions. The guide costs $15 but is available in sections for $3–$5 per section. Part I (general information) is free. Vision-impaired travelers who use a guide dog no longer have to worry about quarantine restrictions. All you need to do is present documentation that the animal is a trained guide dog and has a current inoculation record for rabies.

➤ LOCAL RESOURCES: **Hawai'i Center for Independent Living** (✉ 414 Kauwili St., Suite 102, Honolulu 96817, ☎ 808/522–5400). For accessibility information on Neighbor Islands: **Disability and Communications Access Board** offices on Kaua'i (✉ 3060 'Eiwa St., Room 207, Līhu'e 96766, ☎ 808/274–3308), and Maui (✉ 54 High St., Wailuku 96793, ☎ 808/984–8219).

LODGING

Travelers with disabilities and people using wheelchairs will find it easy to get around Hawai'i's resorts and hotels, with indoor/outdoor layouts that are easily accommodated. If choosing a smaller hotel or a condo or apartment rental, inquire about ground-floor accommodations and **always check to see if rooms will accommodate wheelchairs and if bathrooms are accessible.** Many hotels now offer special-needs rooms featuring larger living spaces and bathrooms equipped for guests who require additional assistance.

RESERVATIONS

When discussing accessibility with an operator or reservations agent, **ask hard questions.** Are there any stairs, inside *or* out? Are there grab bars next to the toilet *and* in the shower/tub? How wide is the doorway to the room? To the bathroom? For the most extensive facilities meeting the latest legal specifications, **opt for newer accommodations.**

SIGHTS & ATTRACTIONS

Many of Hawai'i's sights and attractions are accessible to travelers with disabilities. The state's number-one visitor attraction, Hawai'i Volcanoes National Park, includes a drive-through volcano; in Waikīkī, the City and County Department of Parks and Recreation can assist in obtaining an "all-terrain" wheelchair for strolls down the beach, and on Maui, **Accessibility Vans of Hawaii** can help travelers plan activities from snorkeling to whale-watching.

TRANSPORTATION

Paratransit Services (HandiVan) (☎ 808/456–5555) will take you to a specific destination—not on sightseeing outings—in vans with lifts and lock-downs. With a HandiVan Pass, one-way trips cost $1.50. Passes are free and can be obtained from the **Department of Transportation Services** (✉ 711 Kapi'olani Blvd., Honolulu 96819, ☎ 808/523–4083; ⊘ weekdays 7:45–4:30); you'll need a doctor's written confirmation of your disability or a paratransit ID card. **Handi-Cabs of the Pacific** (☎ 808/524–3866) also operates ramp-equipped vans with lock-downs in Honolulu. Fares are $9 plus $2.25 per mile for curbside service. Reservations at least one day in advance are required by all companies, so do advance planning.

Those who prefer to do their own driving may rent hand-controlled cars from **Avis** (☎ 800/331–1212; reserve 24 hrs ahead) and **Hertz** (☎ 800/654–3131; 24- to 72-hr notice required). You can use the windshield card from your own state to park in spaces reserved for people with disabilities.

➤ COMPLAINTS: **Disability Rights Section** (✉ U.S. Department of Justice, Civil Rights Division, Box 66738, Washington, DC 20035-6738, ☎ 202/514–0301 or 800/514–0301; TTY 202/514–0301 or 800/514–0301, FAX 202/307–1198) for general complaints. **Aviation Consumer Protection Division** (☞ Air Travel, *above*) for airline-related problems. **Civil Rights Office** (✉ U.S. Department of Transportation, Departmental Office of Civil Rights, S-30, 400 7th St. SW, Room 10215, Washington, DC 20590, ☎ 202/366–4648, FAX 202/366–9371) for problems with surface transportation.

TRAVEL AGENCIES

In the United States, the Americans with Disabilities Act requires that travel firms serve the needs of all travelers. Some agencies specialize in working with people with disabilities.

➤ TRAVELERS WITH MOBILITY PROBLEMS: **Access Adventures** (✉ 206 Chestnut Ridge Rd., Rochester, NY 14624, ☎ 716/889–9096, dltravel@prodigy.net), run by a former physical-rehabilitation counselor. **Accessible Vans of the Rockies** (✉ 2040 W. Hamilton Pl., Sheridan, CO 80110, ☎ 303/806–5047 or 888/837–0065, FAX 303/781–2329, www. access-able.com/avr/avrockies.htm). **Accessible Vans of Hawaii, Activity and Travel Agency** (✉ 296 Alamaha St., Suite C, Kahului, HI 96732, ☎ 808/871–7785 or 800/303–3750, FAX 808/871–7536, avavans@maui.net, www.accessiblevanshawaii.com). **CareVacations** (✉ 5-5110 50th Ave., Leduc, Alberta T9E 6V4, ☎ 780/986–6404 or 877/478–7827, FAX 780/986–8332, www.carevacations.com), for group tours and cruise vacations. **Flying Wheels Travel** (✉ 143 W. Bridge St., Box 382, Owatonna, MN 55060, ☎ 507/451–5005 or 800/535–6790, FAX 507/451–1685, thq@ll.net, www. flyingwheels.com). **Hinsdale Travel Service** (✉ 201 E. Ogden Ave., Suite 100, Hinsdale, IL 60521, ☎ 630/325–1335, FAX 630/325–1342, hinstrvl@ interaccess.com).

➤ TRAVELERS WITH DEVELOPMENTAL DISABILITIES: **New Directions** (✉ 5276 Hollister Ave., Suite 207, Santa Barbara, CA 93111, ☎ 805/967–2841 or 888/967–2841, FAX 805/964–7344, newdirec@silcom.com, www.silcom. com/~newdirec/). **Sprout** (✉ 893 Amsterdam Ave., New York, NY 10025, ☎ 212/222–9575 or 888/222–9575, FAX 212/222–9768, sprout@interport.net, www.gosprout.org).

DISCOUNTS & DEALS

Be a smart shopper and **compare all your options** before making decisions. A plane ticket bought with a promotional coupon from travel clubs, coupon books, and direct-mail offers may not be cheaper than the least-expensive fare from a discount ticket agency. And always keep in mind that what you get is just as important as what you save.

DISCOUNT RESERVATIONS

To save money, **look into discount reservations services** with toll-free numbers, which use their buying power to get a better price on hotels, airline tickets, even car rentals. When booking a room, always **call the hotel's local toll-free number** (if one is available) rather than the central reservations number—you'll often get a better price. Always ask about special packages or corporate rates.

➤ AIRLINE TICKETS: ☎ **800/FLY–4–LESS.** ☎ **800/FLY–ASAP.**

➤ HOTEL ROOMS: **Players Express Vacations** (☎ 800/458–6161, www.playersexpress.com). **RMC Travel** (☎ 800/245–5738, www.rmcwebtravel.com). **Steigenberger Reservation Service** (☎ 800/223–5652, www.srs-worldhotels.com). **Turbotrip.com** (☎ 800/473–7829, www.turbotrip.com).

PACKAGE DEALS

Don't confuse packages and guided tours. When you buy a package, you travel on your own, just as though you had planned the trip yourself. Fly/drive packages, which combine airfare and car rental, are often a good deal.

ECOTOURISM

Hawai'i's connection to its environment is spiritual, cultural, and essential to its survival. You'll find a rainbow of natural attractions to explore, from the ribbon of beaches that surround her shorelines to the summits of her volcanoes, where lava shows after dark are nothing less than spectacular. There are 13 climatic regions in the world and the Big Island of Hawai'i offers ecotravelers a glimpse of 11 of them. Much of Kaua'i's natural beauty can only be seen on foot. Its Nā Pali Coast/Waimea Canyon/Koke'e trail network includes 28 trails totaling some 45 miles rich in flora and fauna found nowhere else on earth. Maui offers travelers the sophistication of shoreline resorts at Kaanapali and Wailea, the exhilaration of a rain-forest hike in Hana, and the cool Upcountry climes of Kula at the base of Haleakala crater. Moloka'i and Lāna'i, two of the least-developed islands, offer adventures best experienced on foot and by four-wheel-drive vehicle, or even by mule. Eco-touring in Hawai'i gives visitors the opportunity to learn from local guides who are familiar with the *aina* (land) and Hawai'i's unique cultural heritage. Many of these tours take clients to locations less traveled, so it helps to **be in good physical shape.** The views at the ends of these roads are and exceedingly rich reward.

➤ LOCAL RESOURCES: **Hawai'i Ecotourism Association** (☎ 877/300–7058). **Alternative-Hawai'i** (www.Alternative-Hawaii.com) offers an ecotravel cyberguide.

ETIQUETTE AND BEHAVIOR

In 2001, Hawai'i celebrates 42 years of statehood, so residents can be pretty sensitive to visitors who refer to their own hometowns "back in the States." In a destination as exotic as Hawai'i, this slip of the tongue is easy to make. But remember, **when in Hawai'i, refer to the contiguous 48 as "the mainland" and not as the United States.** When you do, people will think of you as less of a *malahini* (newcomer).

FOOD & DRINK

Dining out in Hawai'i can be a vacation all its own. The islands are home to a world of cuisines, and restaurants range from casual to gorgeously gourmet. A new emphasis on Hawai'i regional cuisine is a boon, giving you a chance to seek out the chefs and restaurants who put an emphasis on the islands unique and abundant harvest.

Price categories are as follows:

CATEGORY	COST*
$$$$	over $60
$$$	$40–$60
$$	$20–$40
$	under $20

per person for a three-course meal, excluding drinks, service, and 4.17% sales tax

RESERVATIONS & DRESS

Go tropical when dressing up to dine out in Hawai'i. Aloha shirts and long pants for men and island-style dresses or casual resort wear are standard attire for evenings in most hotel restaurants and local eateries at dinner. For breakfast and lunch, T-shirts, shorts, and footwear are acceptable.

Reservations are always a good idea: we mention them only when they're essential or not accepted. Book as far ahead as you can, and reconfirm as soon as you arrive. We mention dress only when men are required to wear a jacket or a jacket and tie.

SPECIALTIES

Fish, fruit, and fresh island-grown products are at the heart of a cuisine that was born here, known as both Pacific Rim and Hawai'i regional cuisine. Expect to find an array of traditional world cuisines enhanced by island chefs to add the flavor of the tropics to the mix. Here, *pūpū* are appetizers, and a "plate lunch" is standard midday fare which, be it fish or beef, is accompanied by two scoops rice and a side of macaroni salad.

WINE, BEER & SPIRITS

Hawai'i has of a new generation of microbreweries that can be found throughout O'ahu, the Big Island, and Maui. Many restaurants also have on-site microbreweries. If visiting Maui, check out the Tedeschi Vineyards. There you can tour a beautiful island estate and get a taste of that sweet pineapple wine. The drinking age in Hawai'i is 21 years of age, and a photo ID must be presented to purchase alcoholic beverages. Bars are open until 2 AM, and venues with a cabaret license can stay open until 4 AM. No matter what you might see in the local parks, drinking alcohol in public parks or on the beaches is illegal. It is also illegal to have open containers of alcohol in motor vehicles.

GAY & LESBIAN TRAVEL

➤ LOCAL RESOURCES: **Pacific Ocean Holidays** (✉ Box 88245, Honolulu 96830, ☎ 808/923–2400 or 800/735–6600, www.gayHawaii.com) not only arranges independent travel in the Islands, but publishes the *Pocket Guide to Hawai'i,* distributed free in the state at gay-operated venues and available for $5 by mail for one issue, $12 for a yearly subscription of three issues.

A few small hotels and some bed-and-breakfasts in Hawai'i are favored by gay and lesbian visitors. A computerized Gay Community listing compiled by **GLEA** (Gay & Lesbian Education Advocacy Foundation, ✉ Box 37083,

Honolulu 96837, ☎ 808/532-
is available by contacting them b
phone or at the address listed above.

➤ GAY- & LESBIAN-FRIENDLY TRAVEL AGENCIES: **Different Roads Travel** (✉ 8383 Wilshire Blvd., Suite 902, Beverly Hills, CA 90211, ☎ 323/651–5557 or 800/429–8747, FAX 323/651–3678, leigh@west.tzell.com). **Kennedy Travel** (✉ 314 Jericho Turnpike, Floral Park, NY 11001, ☎ 516/352–4888 or 800/237–7433, FAX 516/354–8849, main@kennedy-travel.com, www.kennedytravel.com). **Now Voyager** (✉ 4406 18th St., San Francisco, CA 94114, ☎ 415/626–1169 or 800/255–6951, FAX 415/626–8626, www.nowvoyager.com). **Skylink Travel and Tour** (✉ 1006 Mendocino Ave., Santa Rosa, CA 95401, ☎ 707/546–9888 or 800/225–5759, FAX 707/546–9891, skylinktvl@aol.com, www.skylink-travel.com), serving lesbian travelers.

HEALTH

Hawai'i is known as the Health State. The life expectancy here is 79 years, the longest in the nation. Balmy weather makes it easy to remain active year-round, and the low-stress aloha attitude certainly contributes to general well-being. When visiting the Islands, however, here are a few health issues to keep in mind.

The Hawaii State Department of Health recommends that, **when hiking or spending time in the sun, drink 4 ounces of water every 15 minutes to avoid dehydration.** Use sunblock, wear sunglasses and protect your head with a visor or hat for shade. Visitors not acclimated to warm, humid weather should allow plenty of time for rest stops and liquid refueling. When visiting freshwater streams, be aware of the tropical disease leptospirosis which is spread by animal urine and carried into streams and mud. Symptoms include fever, headache, nausea, and red eyes. If left untreated it can cause liver and kidney damage, respiratory failure, internal bleeding, and death. To avoid this, don't swim or wade in freshwater streams or ponds if you have open sores and don't drink from any freshwater steams and ponds you encounter.

In the islands, fog is a rare occurrence, but there can often be "vog." This is the haze that is airborne by gases released from the volcanos. During certain weather conditions like "Kona Winds," the vog can settle like smog over island skies. These volcanic pollutants can play havoc with respiratory and other health conditions. If susceptible, plan indoor activities, drink plenty of warm fluids, and get emergency assistance if needed.

DIVERS' ALERT

Do not fly for 24 hours after scuba diving.

PESTS AND OTHER HAZARDS

The islands have their share of bugs and insects who enjoy the tropical climate as much as visitors do. Most are harmless but annoying. When planning to spend time outdoors in hiking areas, **use a strong mosquito repellant and wear long-sleeved clothing and long pants.** In very, damp wet places you may encounter centipedes. In the islands they usually come in two colors—brown and blue. Their sting can be powerful, and the reaction is similar to a bee- and wasp-sting reactions. If planning on hiking or traveling in remote areas, always carry a first-aid kit and appropriate medications for sting reactions.

HOLIDAYS

Major national holidays include New Year's Day (Jan. 1); Martin Luther King, Jr., Day (3rd Mon. in Jan.); President's Day (3rd Mon. in Feb.); Memorial Day (last Mon. in May); Independence Day (July 4); Labor Day (1st Mon. in Sept.); Thanksgiving Day (4th Thurs. in Nov.); Christmas Eve and Christmas Day (Dec. 24 and 25); and New Year's Eve (Dec. 31). In addition, Hawai'i celebrates Prince Kuhio Day (March 26); King Kamehameha Day (June 11); and Admission Day (3rd Fri. in August). State, city, and county offices as well as many local companies are closed for business.

INSURANCE

The most useful travel-insurance plan is a comprehensive policy that includes coverage for trip cancellation and interruption, default, trip delay, and medical expenses (with a waiver for preexisting conditions).

Without insurance you will lose all or most of your money if you cancel your trip, regardless of the reason. Default insurance covers you if your tour operator, airline, or cruise line goes out of business. Trip-delay covers expenses that arise because of bad weather or mechanical delays. Study the fine print when comparing policies.

British and Australian citizens need extra medical coverage when traveling overseas. Always **buy travel policies directly from the insurance company**; if you buy them from a cruise line, airline, or tour operator that goes out of business you probably will not be covered for the agency or operator's default, a major risk. Before making any purchase, **review your existing health and home-owner's policies** to find what they cover away from home.

➤ TRAVEL INSURERS: In the U.S.: **Access America** (⊠ 6600 W. Broad St., Richmond, VA 23230, ☎ 804/285–3300 or 800/284–8300, ℻ 804/673–1583, www.previewtravel.com), **Travel Guard International** (⊠ 1145 Clark St., Stevens Point, WI 54481, ☎ 715/345–0505 or 800/826–1300, ℻ 800/955–8785, www.noelgroup. com). In Canada: **Voyager Insurance** (⊠ 44 Peel Center Dr., Brampton, Ontario L6T 4M8, ☎ 905/791–8700; 800/668–4342 in Canada).

➤ INSURANCE INFORMATION: In the U.K.: **Association of British Insurers** (⊠ 51–55 Gresham St., London EC2V 7HQ, ☎ 0171/600–3333, ℻ 0171/ 696–8999, info@abi.org.uk, www.abi. org.uk). In Australia: **Insurance Council of Australia** (☎ 03/9614–1077, ℻ 03/9614–7924).

LANGUAGE

Studying the Hawaiian language is not needed for a vacation in the islands as English is spoken here. Despite the length of many Hawaiian words, the Hawaiian alphabet is actually one of the shortest in the world, comprising 12 letters. The five vowels, *a, e, i, o, u,* and 7 consonants, *h, k, l, m, n, p, w.* The Hawaiian words you are most likely to encounter during your visit to the Islands are *aloha, mahalo* (thank you), *keiki* (child), *haole* (Caucasian or foreigner), *mauka* (toward the mountains), *makai* (toward the ocean) and *pau* (finished, all done). The history of Hawai'i includes waves of immigrants who have settled here over centuries, each bringing with them their own language. To communicate with each other, they developed a sort of slang known as "pidgin." If you listen closely, you will know what is being said by the inflections and by the extensive use of body language. For example, when you know what you want to say, but don't know how to say it, just say "you know, da kine." For an informative and somewhat-hilarious view of things Hawaiian, check out Jerry Hopkins's series of books titled, Pidgin to the Max and Fax to the Max, available at most local bookstores in the Hawaiiana sections.

LEI GREETINGS

When you walk off a long flight, perhaps a bit groggy and stiff, nothing quite compares with a Hawaiian lei greeting. The casual ceremony ranks as one of the fastest ways to make the transition from the worries of home to the joys of your vacation. Though the tradition has created an expectation that everyone receives this floral garland when they step off the plane, the state of Hawai'i cannot greet each of its nearly 7 million annual visitors. Still, it's easy to **arrange for a lei ceremony for yourself or your companions before you arrive.** Contact one of the companies below if you are not part of a package that provides it.

➤ LEI GREETERS: **Greeters of Hawai'i** (✉ Box 29638, Honolulu 96820, ☎ 808/836–0161; 808/834–7667 for airport desk, FAX 800/736–5665); 48-hours' notice needed, $19.95 to $29.95 per person, add $10 for late notification. **Aloha Lei Greeters** (☎ 808/951–9990 or 800/367–5255 FAX 808/951–9992); $12 to $29 per person, one week's notice needed. **Kama'āina Ali'i, Flowers & Greeters** (✉ 3159-B Koapaka St., Honolulu, ☎ 808/836–3246 or 800/367–5183 FAX 808/836–1804); $11.50 for a standard greeting on O'ahu, and $13.50 for the neighbor islands.

LODGING

No matter what your budg[...] a place for you in Hawai'i. La[...] size resorts grace the islands' mo[...] scenic shores. Family-style condo-miniums offer spaciousness and many of the amenities of fine hotels, and it's possible to find many at reasonable prices. The islands offers visitors an opportunity to experience some of the world's most beautiful hotel locations, along with more intimate accommodations like bed and break-fasts. A number of hostel-style accommodations, ranches, and tent camps are good for those seeking an off-the-beaten path vacation.

The lodgings we list are the cream of the crop in each price category. We always list the facilities that are available, but we don't specify whether they cost extra. When pricing accommodations, always ask what's included and what costs extra.

CATEGORY	COST*
$$$$	over $200
$$$	$125–$200
$$	$75–$125
$	under $75

All prices are for a standard double room, excluding 11.41% tax and service charges.

APARTMENT & VILLA RENTALS

If you want a home base that's roomy enough for a family and comes with cooking facilities, **consider a furnished rental.** These can save you money, especially if you're traveling with a group. Home-exchange directories sometimes list rentals as well as exchanges.

➤ INTERNATIONAL AGENTS: **Europa-Let/Tropical Inn-Let** (✉ 92 N. Main St., Ashland, OR 97520, ☎ 541/482–5806 or 800/462–4486, FAX 541/482–0660). **Hideaways International** (✉ 767 Islington St., Portsmouth, NH 03801, ☎ 603/430–4433 or 800/843–4433, FAX 603/430–4444 info@hideaways.com www.hide-aways.com; membership $99).

Hometours International (✉ Box 11503, Knoxville, TN 37939, ☎ 865/690–8484 or 800/367–4668, home-tours@aol.com, www.thor.he.net/~hometour/). **Vacation Home Rentals**

Worldwide (✉ 235 Kensington Ave., Norwood, NJ 07648, ☎ 201/767–9393 or 800/633–3284, FAX 201/767–5510, vhrww@juno.com, www.vhrww.com). Villas and Apartments Abroad (✉ 1270 Avenue of the Americas, 15th floor, New York, NY 10020, ☎ 212/897–5045 or 800/433–3020, FAX 212/897–5039, vaa@altour.com, www.vaanyc.com).

B&BS

B&Bs have made heavy inroads into the Hawaiian market in the past several years, and offer visitors an accommodations alternative that is unique, charming, intimate, and spotlights Hawai'i's diverse cultural melting pot. Tucked away from traditional resort areas, you will find most located on the neighbor islands, with only a select few on O'ahu due to governmental regulations.

Before you choose this alternative, however, **decide exactly how much privacy you desire and what amenities you require** to be comfortable. Most of these accommodations book well in advance, require a 50% deposit prior to arrival, and do not accept credit cards. Utilizing a reservations service in the islands can assist you in finding the bed and breakfast that will meet your personal expectations. There is a small fee for these services, but they provide you a professional point of contact should something go wrong. These services can also assist with interisland travel and car-rental arrangements.

➤ RESERVATION SERVICES: **Bed and Breakfast Hawai'i** (✉ Box 449, Kapa'a, Kaua'i 96746 ☎ 800/733–1632, ☎ 808/822–7771, FAX 808/822–2723). **Bed and Breakfast Honolulu** (statewide) (✉ 3242 Kā'ohinani Dr., Honolulu 96817, ☎ 808/595–7533 or 800/288–4666, FAX 808/595–2030). **Go Native Hawai'i** (2009 W. Holmes Rd., Suite #9, Lansing, MI 48910, ☎ 800/662–8483). **Hawai'i's Best B&Bs** (✉ Box 563, Kamuela 96743, ☎ 808/885–0550 or 800/262–9912, FAX 808/885–0559), specializing in upscale properties. **Pacific Hawai'i Bed and Breakfast** (✉ 99-1661 Aiea Heights Dr., Aiea, O'ahu 96701, ☎ 808/261–0532 or 800/999–6026). **Volcano Reservations–Select Statewide Accom-**

modations (✉ Box 998, Volcano Village, 96785, ☎ 808/967–7244 or 800/937–7786, FAX 808/967–8660).

CAMPING

A variety of national, state, and county parks are available, some with bathroom and cooking facilities, others a bit more primitive. The National Park Service and Division of State Parks of the Hawai'i Department of Land and Natural Resources (☞ National and State Parks, *below*) can provide more information; details on local camping are available from the individual counties.

➤ CAMPING AND RV FACILITIES: The **City and County of Honolulu** (☎ 808/523–4525) can provide information about camping at county sites on O'ahu, and the **State Parks Division, Hawai'i State Department of Land and Natural Resources** (☎ 808/587–0300) handles the same questions for state camping sites. You can pack up your own sleeping bag and bring it along, or you can rent camping equipment at companies such as **Omar the Tent Man** (✉ 94-158 Leo'ole St., Waipahu, 96797, ☎ 808/677–8785) on O'ahu; **Pacific Rent-All** (✉ 1080 Kilauea Ave., Hilo, 96720, ☎ 808/935–2974) on the Big Island; and **Pedal 'n' Paddle** (✉ Box 1413, Ching Young Village, Hānalei, 96714, ☎ 808/826–9069) on Kaua'i.

CONDOMINIUMS

Hawai'i is known for developing the resort condominium concept in the early 1970s and continues to maintain its status as a leader in the field. Besides large living areas and full kitchens, many condos now offer front-desk and daily maid services. Nearly 100 companies in Hawai'i and around the U.S. rent out condominium space in the islands. Your travel agent will be the most helpful in finding the condo you desire.

➤ RESOURCES: **Hawai'i Condo Exchange** (✉ 1817 El Cerrito Pl., Los Angeles, CA 90068, ☎ 323/436–0300 or 800/442–0404, FAX 323/435–0331). **Castle Resorts and Hotels** (✉ 1150 S. King St., Honolulu, 96814, ☎ 800/367–5004, FAX 800/477–2329).

HOME EXCHANGES

If you would like to exchange your home for someone else's, **join a home-**

exchange organization, which will send you its updated listings of available exchanges for a year and will include your own listing in at least one of them. It's up to you to make specific arrangements.

➤ EXCHANGE CLUBS: **HomeLink International** (✉ Box 650, Key West, FL 33041, ☎ 305/294–7766 or 800/638–3841, 𝐅𝐀𝐗 305/294–1448, usa@homelink.org, www.homelink.org; $98 per year). **Intervac U.S.** (✉ Box 590504, San Francisco, CA 94159, ☎ 800/756–4663, 𝐅𝐀𝐗 415/435–7440, www.intervac.com; $89 per year includes two catalogues).

HOSTELS

No matter what your age, you can **save on lodging costs by staying at hostels.** In some 5,000 locations in more than 70 countries around the world, Hostelling International (HI), the umbrella group for a number of national youth-hostel associations, offers single-sex, dorm-style beds and, at many hostels, rooms for couples and family accommodations.

Membership in any HI national hostel association, open to travelers of all ages, allows you to stay in HI-affiliated hostels at member rates; one-year membership is about $25 for adults (C$26.75 in Canada, £9.30 in the U.K., $30 in Australia, and $30 in New Zealand). Hostels run about $10–$25 per night. Members have priority if the hostel is full. They're also eligible for discounts around the world, even on rail and bus travel in some countries.

➤ ORGANIZATIONS: **Hostelling International—American Youth Hostels** (✉ 733 15th St. NW, Suite 840, Washington, DC 20005, ☎ 202/783–6161, 𝐅𝐀𝐗 202/783–6171, www.hiayh.org). **Hostelling International—Canada** (✉ 400–205 Catherine St., Ottawa, Ontario K2P 1C3, ☎ 613/237–7884, 𝐅𝐀𝐗 613/237–7868, www.hostelling-intl.ca). **Youth Hostel Association of England and Wales** (✉ Trevelyan House, 8 St. Stephen's Hill, St. Albans, Hertfordshire AL1 2DY, ☎ 01727/855215 or 01727/845047, 𝐅𝐀𝐗 01727/844126, www.yha.uk). **Australian Youth Hostel Association** (✉ 10 Mallett St., Camperdown, NSW 2050,

☎ 02/9565–1699, 𝐅𝐀𝐗 02/9565–1325, www.yha.com.au). **Youth Hostels Association of New Zealand** (✉ Box 436, Christchurch, New Zealand, ☎ 03/379–9970, 𝐅𝐀𝐗 03/365–4476, www.yha.org.nz).

HOTELS

You can find most major hotel brands in Hawai'i, plus large, locally based operators, such as Aston Hotels and Resorts and Outrigger Hotels Hawai'i, as well as a number of independents. The result is an extensive range of rooms, from rock-bottom economy units to luxurious suites. All hotels listed have private bath unless otherwise noted.

➤ TOLL-FREE NUMBERS: **Best Western** (☎ 800/528–1234, www.bestwestern.com). **Choice** (☎ 800/221–2222, www.hotelchoice.com). **Colony** (☎ 800/777–1700. www.colony.com), **Days Inn** (☎ 800/325–2525. www.daysinn.com). **Doubletree and Red Lion Hotels** (☎ 800/222–8733, www.doubletreehotels.com). **Embassy Suites** (☎ 800/362–2779, www.embassysuites.com). **Fairfield Inn** (☎ 800/228–2800, www.marriott.com). **Four Seasons** (☎ 800/332–3442, www.fourseasons.com). **Hilton** (☎ 800/445–8667, www.hiltons.com). **Holiday Inn** (☎ 800/465–4329, www.holiday-inn.com). **Howard Johnson** (☎ 800/654–4656, www.hojo.com). **Hyatt Hotels & Resorts** (☎ 800/233–1234, www.hyatt.com). **La Quinta** (☎ 800/531–5900, www.laquinta.com). **Marriott** (☎ 800/228–9290, www.marriott.com). **Nikko Hotels International** (☎ 800/645–5687, www.nikko.com). **Radisson** (☎ 800/333–3333, www.radisson.com). **Ramada** (☎ 800/228–2828. www.ramada.com), **Renaissance Hotels & Resorts** (☎ 800/468–3571, www.hotels.com). **Sheraton** (☎ 800/325–3535, www.sheraton.com).

MEDIA

Although Hawai'i sits in the middle of the Pacific Ocean, it remains connected globally with a variety of media, including network television, cable television, Web-based media, newspapers, magazines, and radio. Many of the resorts and hotels throughout the islands include an additional **visitor-information channel on your in-room television.** Consult your in-room directory for channel and scheduling information and to find out the special activities or events that might be happening during your visit.

NEWSPAPERS & MAGAZINES

Each of the islands has its own daily newspapers. They can be picked up through many hotel bell desks, in sundry stores, restaurants, cafés and at newspaper stands located throughout the islands. Many hotels will deliver one to your room upon request. *The Honolulu Advertiser* is O'ahu's morning and Sunday paper; *The Honolulu Star-Bulletin* is O'ahu's evening paper. *West Hawai'i Today* is the Big Island's Kona Coast newspaper, while the *Hawai'i Tribune-Herald* serves the Hilo side of the Island. On Maui, it's *The Maui News*. On Kaua'i, it's *The Garden Island* and *Kaua'i Times*. *The Honolulu Weekly* is a great guide for arts and alternative events, and the *Pacific Business News* provides the latest in business news. There are a variety of free visitor publications and guides available throughout the islands. In addition, *Honolulu Magazine* is a monthly that focuses on island issues and happenings. Check out local bookstores for neighbor island magazines, some of which publish on a quarterly schedule.

RADIO & TELEVISION

Radio airwaves on the islands are affected by natural terrain, so don't expect to hear one radio station islandwide. Sometimes, just driving from the leeward to the windward coasts on each island is enough to lose the signal. For Hawaiian music, tune your FM radio dials to 105.7 KINE (O'ahu), 100 KINE (O'ahu), 97.9 KKBG (East Hawai'i), 106.1 KLEO (West Hawai'i), 93.5 KPOA (Maui), and 95.7 KSRF (Kaua'i). News junkies can get their fill of news and talk by tuning to the AM radio dial and the following island stations: 590 KSSK (O'ahu), 650 KHNR (O'ahu), 670 KPUA (East Hawai'i), 620 KIPA (West Hawai'i), 1110 KAOI or 1570 KUAU (Maui), 570 KONG (Kaua'i). National Public Radio enthusiasts can tune to the FM dial for NPR programming on 88.1 KHPR (O'ahu) and 90.7 KKUA (Maui).

Most Hawaiians wake up with Perry and Price on KSSK AM 59 or FM 92. The lively duo provides news, traffic updates, and weather reports between "easy-listening music" and phone calls from listeners from 5 to 10 AM.

Television channels in the islands are plentiful between network and cable channels. Channel allocation varies by island and location, so check daily island newspapers or your in-room hotel television guide for station selection. On O'ahu, you can find the following network programming with its channel and local affiliate call sign: FOX (2) KHON, ABC (4) KITV, UPN/WB (5) KHVE, CBS (9) KGMB, PBS (10) KHET, and NBC (13) KHNL.

MONEY MATTERS

Many of the islands' most memorable attractions and activities can be found in its natural beauty and cost nothing to view. Expect to pay 50¢ for a daily newspaper, $1 to ride the bus anywhere on O'ahu, and from $45 on up to attend a luau. Museums throughout the islands vary in size and admission fees, the large ones cost between $8 and $15 per entry. Smaller ones can cost from $3 to $6. Prices throughout this guide are given for adults. Substantially reduced fees are almost always available for children, students, and senior citizens. For information on taxes, *see* Taxes, *below.*

ATMS

Automatic teller machines for easy access to cash are everywhere on the islands. ATMS can be found in shopping centers, small convenience and grocery stores, inside hotels and resorts, as well as outside most bank branches. For a directory of locations, call 800/424–7787 for the Cirrus network or 800/843–7587 for the Plus network.

CREDIT CARDS

Most major credit cards are accepted throughout the islands and are required to rent a car. When making reservations, double-check to ensure that the lodging, restaurant, or attraction you are planning to visit accepts them. In smaller concessions, bed-and-breakfasts, and fast-food outlets, expect to pay cash. Throughout this guide, the following abbreviations are used: **AE,** American Express; **D,** Discover; **DC,** Diner's Club; **MC,** Master Card; and **V,** Visa.

➤ REPORTING LOST CARDS: **American Express** (☎ 800/528–4800). **Discover** (☎ 800/347–2683). **Diner's Club** (☎ 800/234–6377). **Master Card** (☎ 800/307–7309). **Visa** (☎ 800/847–2911).

NATIONAL AND STATE PARKS

Hawai'i is home to seven national parks. On Maui, Haleakala National Park houses Haleakala volcanic crater and some of the world's most beautiful sunrises. Moloka'i's Kalaupapa National Historical Park is the site of what was once a leper colony where victims of Hansen's disease were sent to exile in the late 1800s. On the island of O'ahu, the U.S.S. *Arizona* Memorial at Pearl Harbor is overseen by the National Park Service.

The Big Island, Hawai'i's largest island, boasts four national parks. Hawai'i Volcanoes National Park is the 50th state's number-one visitor attraction. The other three are Puuhonua O Honaunau National Historical Park, Puukohola Heiau National Historical Site, and Kaloko-Honokohau National Historical Park, each of which offers visitors a glimpse into Hawai'i's rich cultural history.

Hawaii's 52 state parks encompass over 25,000 acres on five islands, and include many of its most beautiful beaches and coastal areas.

Look into discount passes to save money on park entrance fees. The Golden Eagle Pass ($50) gets you and your companions free admission to all national parks for one year. (Camping and parking are extra). Both the Golden Age Passport ($10), for those 62 and older, and the Golden Access Passport (free), for travelers with disabilities, entitle holders to free entry to all national parks, plus 50% off fees for the use of many park facilities and services. You must show proof of age and of U.S. citizenship or permanent residency (such as a U.S. passport, driver's license, or birth certificate) and, if requesting Golden Access, proof of disability. All three passes are available at all national parks wherever entrance fees are charged. Golden Eagle and Golden Access passes are also available by mail.

➤ PASSES BY MAIL: **National Park Service** (✉ National Park Service National Office, 1849 C St. NW, Washington, DC 20240-0001, ☎ 202/208–4747).

➤ STATE PARKS: Details of state parks and historic areas come from the **State Parks Division, Hawai'i State Department of Land and Natural Resources** (✉ 1151 Punchbowl St., Room 310, Honolulu, 96813; ✉ Box 621, Honolulu, 96809, ☎ 808/587–0300).

PACKING

Hawai'i is casual: Sandals, bathing suits, and comfortable, informal clothing are the norm. In summer synthetic slacks and shirts, although easy to care for, can be uncomfortably warm. You'll easily find a bathing suit in Hawai'i, but **bring a bathing cap with you if you wear one.** You can waste hours searching for one.

Probably the most important thing to tuck in your suitcase is sunscreen. This is the tropics, and the ultraviolet rays are much more powerful. Doctors advise putting on sunscreen when you get up in the morning. Don't forget to **reapply sunscreen periodically during the day,** since perspiration can wash it away. Consider using sunscreens with a sun protection factor (SPF) of 15 or higher. There are many tanning oils on the market in Hawai'i, including coconut and *kukui* (the nut from a local tree) oils, but doctors warn that they merely sauté your skin. Too many Hawaiian vacations have been spoiled by sunburn, and even sun poisoning. Hats and sunglasses offer important sun protection, too. Both are easy to find in island shops, but if you already have a favorite packable hat or sun visor, bring it with you, and don't forget to wear it. All major hotels in Hawai'i provide beach towels.

As for clothing, in the Hawaiian Islands there's a saying that when a man wears a suit during the day, he's either going for a loan or he's a lawyer trying a case. Only a few upscale restaurants require a jacket for dinner, and none require a tie. The aloha shirt is accepted dress in Hawai'i for business and most social occasions. Shorts are acceptable daytime attire, along with a T-shirt or polo shirt. Golfers should remember that many courses have dress codes requiring a collared shirt; call courses you're interested in for details. If you're not prepared, you can pick up appropriate clothing at resort pro shops. If you're visiting in winter or planning to visit a volcano area, **bring a sweater or light- to medium-weight jacket.** Trade winds cool things off when the sun goes down, and things get chilly above 10,000 ft.

In your carry-on luggage, **pack an extra pair of eyeglasses or contact lenses** and **enough of any medication you take** to last the entire trip. You may also ask your doctor to write a spare prescription using the drug's generic name, since brand names may vary from country to country. In luggage to be checked, **never pack prescription drugs or valuables.** To avoid customs delays, carry medications in their original packaging. And don't forget to carry with you the addresses of offices that handle re-funds of lost traveler's checks.

CHECKING LUGGAGE

How many carry-on bags you can bring with you is up to the airline. Most allow two, but not always, so make sure that everything you carry aboard will fit under your seat or in the overhead bin, and get to the gate early. Note that if you have a seat at the back of the plane, you'll probably board first, while the overhead bins are still empty.

If you are flying internationally, note that baggage allowances may be determined not by piece but by weight—generally 88 pounds (40 kilograms) in first class, 66 pounds (30 kilograms) in business class, and 44 pounds (20 kilograms) in economy.

Airline liability for baggage is limited to $1,250 per person on flights within the United States. On international flights it amounts to $9.07 per pound or $20 per kilogram for checked baggage (roughly $640 per 70-pound bag) and $400 per passenger for unchecked baggage. You can buy additional coverage at check-in for about $10 per $1,000 of coverage, but it excludes a

rather extensive list of items, shown on your airline ticket.

Before departure, **itemize your bags' contents** and their worth, and label the bags with your name, address, and phone number. (If you use your home address, cover it so potential thieves can't see it readily.) Inside each bag, **pack a copy of your itinerary.** At check-in, **make sure that each bag is correctly tagged** with the destination airport's three-letter code. If your bags arrive damaged or fail to arrive at all, file a written report with the airline before leaving the airport.

PASSPORTS & VISAS

➤ CONTACTS: **U.S. Embassy Visa Information Line** (☎ 01891/200–290; calls cost 49p per minute, 39p per minute cheap rate) for U.S. visa information. **U.S. Embassy Visa Branch** (✉ 5 Upper Grosvenor Sq., London W1A 1AE) for U.S. visa information; send a self-addressed, stamped envelope. **U.S. Consulate General** (✉ Queen's House, Queen St., Belfast BTI 6EO) if you live in Northern Ireland. **Office of Australia Affairs** (✉ 59th floor, MLC Centre, 19–29 Martin Pl., Sydney, NSW 2000) if you live in Australia. **Office of New Zealand Affairs** (✉ 29 Fitzherbert Terr., Thorndon, Wellington) if you live in New Zealand.

PASSPORT OFFICES

The best time to apply for a passport or to renew is in fall and winter. Before any trip, check your passport's expiration date, and, if necessary, renew it as soon as possible.

➤ AUSTRALIAN CITIZENS: **Australian Passport Office** (☎ 131–232, www.dfat.gov.au/passports).

➤ CANADIAN CITIZENS: **Passport Office** (☎ 819/994–3500 or 800/567–6868, www.dfait-maeci.gc.ca/passport).

➤ NEW ZEALAND CITIZENS: **New Zealand Passport Office** (☎ 04/494–0700, www.passports.govt.nz).

➤ U.K. CITIZENS: **London Passport Office** (☎ 0990/210–410) for fees and documentation requirements and to request an emergency passport.

SAFETY

Hawai'i is one of the world's safer tourist destinations, but do remember that crimes do occur. It is wise to **follow the same commonsense safety precautions you would normally follow** in your own hometown. There are some spots on every island that are definitely "local" and you might wish to avoid. Hotel and visitor center staff can provide information should you decide to head out on your own to more of the remote areas. Rental cars are magnets for break-ins, so don't leave any valuables in the car, not even in a locked trunk. Avoid less lit areas, beach parks, and isolated areas after dark as a precaution. When hiking, **stay on marked trails,** no matter how alluring the temptation might be to stray. This prevents accidental meetings with illegal marijuana growers. Also, since weather conditions can cause landscapes to become muddy, slippery, and tenuous, staying on marked trails will lessen the possibility of a fall or getting lost. Ocean safety is of utmost importance when visiting an island destination. Don't swim alone, and **follow the international signage posted at beaches that alert swimmers** to strong currents, man-of-war jellyfish, sharp coral, high surf, and dangerous shorebreaks. At coastal lookouts along cliff tops, heed the signs indicating that waves can climb over the ledges. Check with lifeguards at each beach for current conditions, and if the red flags are up, indicating swimming and surfing is not allowed, **don't attempt to swim.** Waters that look calm on the surface can harbor strong currents and undertows.

LOCAL SCAMS

Be wary of those hawking "too good to be true" prices on everything from car rentals to visitor attractions. Many of these offers are just a lure to get you in the door for time-share presentations. When handed a flyer, read the fine print before you make your decision to participate.

WOMEN IN HAWAI'I

Women traveling alone are generally safe in the Islands, but always follow the safety precautions you would use in any major destination. When booking hotels, inquire about concierge or club floors that offer executive services, request rooms closest to the elevator, and always keep your hotel room door and balcony doors locked. Stay away from isolated areas after dark, and inquire about safety if planning to camp. If you stay out late visiting nightclubs and bars, use caution when exiting the night spot and returning to your lodging.

SENIOR-CITIZEN TRAVEL

Hawai'i is steeped in a tradition that gives great respect to elders, or *kapuna,* and considers them "keepers of the wisdom." For seniors, traveling in Hawai'i offers discounts, special senior-oriented activities, and easy access. Many lodging facilities offer discounts for members of the American Association of Retired Persons (AARP). No matter where you visit, be it visitor attractions, museums, restaurants, or movie theatres, **inquire about their senior-citizen discounts.** They can save you a bundle. To qualify for age-related discounts, **mention your senior-citizen status up-front** when booking hotel reservations (not when checking out) and before you're seated in restaurants (not when paying the bill). When renting a car, ask about promotional car-rental discounts, which can be cheaper than senior-citizen rates.

➤ EDUCATIONAL PROGRAMS: **Elderhostel** (✉ 75 Federal St., 3rd floor, Boston, MA 02110, ☎ 877/426–8056, ₣ᴀX 877/426–2166, www.elderhostel.org).

SHOPPING

KEY DESTINATIONS

On O'ahu, Ala Moana Center is one of the largest shopping spots; it's within easy walking distance of the west end of Waikīkī. The Royal Hawaiian Shopping Center is centrally located in Waikīkī itself. Farther away, you'll find Ward Warehouse, Aloha Tower Marketplace, the Kahala Mall, and Pearlridge Center.

The Neighbor Islands offer more in the way of smaller strips of shops. Still, it's possible to find larger stores grouped in areas such as Kaua'i's Kukui Grove Center in Līhu'e, Maui's Ka'ahumanu Shopping Center, and the Big Island's Prince Kūhiō Shopping Plaza in Hilo, and Keauhou Shopping Village and Lanihau Center in Kailua-Kona. Exclusive shops can often be found in the lobbies of luxury hotels on all the Islands.

SMART SOUVENIRS

Aloha shirts and resort wear, Hawaiian music recordings, shell leis, coral jewelry, traditional quilts, island foods, Kona coffee, and koa-wood products are just a few of the gifts that visitors to Hawai'i treasure. For the more elegant gift items, check out the Hawaiian boutiques located in major island shopping centers as well as those tucked away in smaller shopping areas in residential districts. Island craft fairs and swap meets offer a bargain bazaar of standard items like T-shirts and tiki statues as well as the original works of local artisans.

STUDENTS IN HAWAI'I

Hawai'i is a popular destination for exchange students from around the world. Contact your hometown university about study and internship possibilities. To check out the student scene in the islands, stop by any of the University of Hawai'i campuses, the community college campuses, and read the *Honolulu Weekly* upon arrival for club and event information. Be sure to ask about discounts for students at all museums and major attractions and be prepared to show ID to qualify.

➤ I.D.s & SERVICES: **Council Travel** (CIEE; ✉ 205 E. 42nd St., 14th floor, New York, NY 10017, ☎ 212/822–2700 or 888/268–6245, ℻ 212/822–2699, info@councilexchanges.org, www.councilexchanges.org) for mail orders only, in the U.S. **Travel Cuts** (✉ 187 College St., Toronto, Ontario M5T 1P7, ☎ 416/979–2406 or 800/667–2887, www.travelcuts.com) in Canada.

TAXES

There is a 4.17% state sales tax on all purchases, including food. A hotel room tax of 7.25%, combined with the sales tax of 4.17%, equals an 11.42% rate added onto your hotel bill. A $2-per-day road tax is also assessed on each rental vehicle.

TIME

Hawai'i is on Hawaiian Standard Time, 5 hours behind New York, 2 hours behind Los Angeles, and 10 hours behind London.

When the U.S. mainland is on daylight saving time, Hawai'i is not, so add an extra hour of time difference between the islands and U.S. mainland destinations.

TIPPING

Upon arrival, tipping can begin with your taxi ride from the airport. Tip cab drivers 15% of the fare. Standard tips for restaurants and bar tabs runs from 15% to 20% of the bill, depending on the standard of service. Bellman at hotels usually receive $1 per bag, more if you have bulky items like bicycles and surfboards. Tip the hotel room maid $1 per night, paid daily. Tip doorman $1 for assistance with taxis and tips for concierge vary depending on the service. For example, tip more for "hard-to-get" event tickets or dining reservations.

TOURS & PACKAGES

Because everything is prearranged on a prepackaged tour or independent vacation, you'll spend less time planning—and often get it all at a good price. Packages that include any combination of lodging, airfare, meals, sightseeing, car rental, and even sports activities and entertainment are popular in Hawai'i and are often considerably cheaper than piecing the vacation together à la carte. Just do your research, and make sure that the options offered (especially when it comes to lodging and meals) are really the ones you want. Honeymoon packages that include everything from the actual wedding ceremony to extras like special suites, champagne, flowers, and romantic dinners are offered by some resorts and hotels. Again, **do some homework, ask questions, and make sure that the package suits your tastes and budget.**

BOOKING WITH AN AGENT

Travel agents are excellent resources. But it's a good idea to collect brochures from several agencies as some agents' suggestions may be influenced by relationships with tour and package firms that reward them for volume sales. If you have a special interest, **find an agent with expertise in that area.** American Society of Travel Agents

(☞ Travel Agencies, *below*) has a database of specialists worldwide.

Make sure your travel agent knows the accommodations and other services of the place they're recommending. Ask about the hotel's location, room size, beds, and whether it has a pool, room service, or programs for children, if you care about these. Has your agent been there in person or sent others whom you can contact?

Do some homework on your own, too: local tourism boards can provide information about lesser-known and small-niche operators, some of which may sell only direct.

BUYER BEWARE

Each year consumers are stranded or lose their money when tour operators—even large ones with excellent reputations—go out of business. So **check out the operator.** Ask several travel agents about its reputation, and try to **book with a company that has a consumer-protection program.** (Look for information in the company's brochure.) In the United States, members of the National Tour Association and the United States Tour Operators Association are required to set aside funds to cover your payments and travel arrangements in the event that the company defaults. It's also a good idea to choose a company that participates in the American Society of Travel Agents' Tour Operator Program (TOP); ASTA will act as mediator in any disputes between you and your tour operator.

Remember that the more your package or tour includes the better you can predict the ultimate cost of your vacation. Make sure you know exactly what is covered, and **beware of hidden costs.** Are taxes, tips, and transfers included? Entertainment and excursions? These can add up.

➤ TOUR-OPERATOR RECOMMENDA-TIONS: **American Society of Travel Agents** (☞ Travel Agencies, *below*). **National Tour Association** (NTA; ✉ 546 E. Main St., Lexington, KY 40508, ☎ 606/226–4444 or 800/682–8886, www.ntaonline.com). **United States Tour Operators Association** (USTOA; ✉ 342 Madison Ave., Suite 1522, New York, NY 10173,

☎ 212/599–6599 or 800/468–7862, FAX 212/599–6744, ustoa@aol.com, www.ustoa.com).

TRANSPORTATION AROUND HAWAI'I

Renting a car is definitely recommended for those who plan to move beyond their hotel beach chair. With the exception of O'ahu, public transportation is extremely limited, and even if you are staying in Honolulu or Waikīkī you may want a car if you plan to do widespread exploring or if you have time constraints. **Reserve your vehicle in advance,** particularly during peak travel times and on the smaller islands, where the car-rental fleets are limited. Most major companies have airport counters and complimentary transportation for pickup/drop-off back at the airport upon departure.

Taxis can also be found at island airports, through your hotel doorman, in the more popular resort areas, or by contacting local taxi companies by telephone. Flag-down fees are $2 and each additional mile is $1.70. Most companies will also provide a car and driver for half-day or day-long island tours if you absolutely don't want to rent a car, and a number of companies also offer personal guides. Remember, however, that rates are quite steep for these services, ranging from $100 to $200 dollars and up.

TRAVEL AGENCIES

A good travel agent puts your needs first. Look for an agency that has been in business at least five years, emphasizes customer service, and has someone on staff who specializes in your destination. In addition, **make sure the agency belongs to a professional trade organization.** The American Society of Travel Agents (ASTA), with 27,000 agents in some 170 countries, is the largest and most influential in the field. Operating under the motto "Integrity in Travel," it maintains and enforces a strict code of ethics and will step in to help mediate any agent-client disputes if necessary. ASTA also maintains a Web site that includes a directory of agents. (If a travel agency is also acting as your tour operator, *see* Buyer Beware *in* Tours & Packages, *above*.)

AGENT REFERRALS: **American Travel Agents** (ASTA; ☎ 2782 24-hr hot line, FAX 703/ 19, www.astanet.com). **Association of British Travel Agents** (✉ 68– 71 Newman St., London W1P 4AH, ☎ 0171/637–2444, FAX 0171/637– 0713, abta.co.uk, www.abtanet.com). **Association of Canadian Travel Agents** (✉ 1729 Bank St., Suite 201, Ottawa, Ontario K1V 7Z5, ☎ 613/521–0474, FAX 613/521–0805, acta.ntl@sympa- tico.ca). **Australian Federation of Travel Agents** (✉ Level 3, 309 Pitt St., Sydney 2000, ☎ 02/9264–3299, FAX 02/9264–1085, www.afta.com.au). **Travel Agents' Association of New Zealand** (✉ Box 1888, Wellington 10033, ☎ 04/499–0104, FAX 04/499– 0827, taanz@tiasnet.co.nz).

VISITOR INFORMATION

Before you go, contact the Hawai'i Visitors & Convention Bureau for general information on each island, free brochures that include an accom- modations and car-rental guide, and an entertainment and dining listing con- taining one-line descriptions of bureau members. Take a virtual visit to Hawai'i on the Web, which can be most helpful in planning your vaca- tion. The HVCB site has a calendar section that allows you to see what local events are in place during the time of your stay.

➤ TOURIST INFORMATION: **Hawai'i Visitors & Convention Bureau** (✉ 2270 Kalakaua Ave., Suite 801, Honolulu, 96817, ☎ 808/923–1811). For brochures, ☎ 800/464–2924. In the U.K. contact the **Hawai'i Visitors & Convention Bureau** (✉ Box 208, Sunbury, Middlesex, TW16 5RJ, ☎ 020/8941–4009). Send a £2 check or postal order for an information pack.

WEB SITES

Do check out the World Wide Web when you're planning. You'll find everything from current weather forecasts to virtual tours of famous cities. Fodor's Web site, www.fodors. com, is a great place to start your on-line travels. When you see a 🐝 in this book, go to www.fodors.com/urls for an up-to-date link to that destina- tion's site. For more information on Hawai'i, visit www.goHawaii.com,

the official Web site of the Hawai'i Convention and Visitors Bureau.

Other sites to check out include www.bigisland.org (Big Island Visitors Bureau); www.visitmaui.com (Maui County Visitors Bureau); www.visit- Oahu.com (O'ahu Visitors Bureau); www.Kauaivisitorsbureau.org (Kaua'i Visitors Bureau); www.Molokai- Hawaii.com (Moloka'i Visitor Infor- mation); www.cruiseHawaii.com (for information on cruise vessels sailing interisland); www.thebus.org (O'ahu's public transportation sys- tem); and www.alohaboatdays.com (for a schedule and information about cruise arrival celebrations at Aloha Tower, Honolulu Harbor).

www.Hawaii.net has links to more than 100 Hawaiian sites (click on Visitor Center). www.search- Hawaii.com has an engine that can search all linked Hawaiian Web pages by topic or word.

Visit www.hsHawaii.com for the Hawai'i State vacation planner; www.Kauai-Hawaii.com for Kaua'i visitors information; www.honolu- luweekly.com for a weekly guide to the arts, entertainment, and dining in Honolulu; www.Hawaii.gov, the state's official Web site, for all infor- mation on the destination, including camping; and www.nps.gov for national parks information.

WHEN TO GO

Hawai'i's long days of sunshine and fairly mild year-round temperatures make it an all-seasons destination. In resort areas near sea level, the average afternoon temperature during the coldest winter months of December and January is 75°F; during the hottest months of August and September the temperature often reaches 92°F. Cold weather (30°F) can occur in Hawai'i in winter, but only near the summit of the Big Island's Mauna Ke'a crater, where skiing is possible.

Winter is the season when most travelers prefer to head for the is- lands. From mid-December through mid-April, visitors from the mainland and other areas covered with snow find Hawai'i's sun-splashed beaches and balmy trade winds particularly appealing. Not surprisingly, this high season also means that fewer travel bargains are available; room rates average 10%–15% higher during this season than the rest of the year.

The only weather change most areas experience during the December–February span is rainfall, though the sun is rarely hidden behind the clouds for a solid 24-hour period. Visitors should remember that regardless of the season, the northern shores of each island usually receive more rain than those on the south. Kaua'i and the Big Island's northern sections get more annual rainfall than the rest of Hawai'i.

CLIMATE

The following are average maximum and minimum temperatures for Honolulu; the temperatures throughout the Hawaiian Islands are similar.

➤ FORECASTS: **Weather Channel Connection** (☎ 900/932–8437), 95¢ per minute from a Touch-Tone phone.

HONOLULU, O'AHU

Jan.	80F	27C	May	85F	29C	Sept.	88F	31C
	65	18		70	21		73	23
Feb.	80F	27C	June	86F	30C	Oct.	87F	31C
	65	18		72	22		72	22
Mar.	81F	27C	July	87F	31C	Nov.	84F	29C
	69	21		73	23		69	21
Apr.	83F	28C	Aug.	88F	31C	Dec.	81F	27C
	69	21		74	23		67	19

FESTIVALS AND SEASONAL EVENTS

➤ DEC.: **Triple Crown of Surfing** (O'ahu; ☎ 808/638–7266): The world's top pro surfers gather on the North Shore during November and December for the big winter waves and some tough competition. **Nā Mele O Maui** (Maui; ☎ 808/661–3271): The first week of December, this Hawaiiana festival at Kā'anapali features arts and crafts, and schoolchildren competing in Hawaiian song and hula performances. **Honolulu Marathon** (O'ahu; ☎ 808/734–7200): Watch or run in one of the country's most popular marathons. **Bodhi Day** (all islands; ☎ 808/522–9200): The traditional Buddhist Day of Enlightenment is celebrated at temples statewide; visitors are welcome. **Jeep Aloha/Jeep O'ahu Bowls** (O'ahu; ☎ 808/947–4141): Four top college football squads meet in this annual football doubleheader held at Aloha Stadium on Christmas Day. **Festival of Lights** (all islands; ☎ 808/547–4397 O'ahu, ☎ 808/828–0014 Kaua'i, ☎ 808/667–9175 Maui). Islands deck out the lights to celebrate the season, with electric light parades, decorated city buildings, and events that last throughout December. **Christmas** (all islands): Hotels outdo each other in such extravagant exhibits and events as Santa arriving by outrigger canoe. **Rainbow Classic** (O'ahu; ☎ 808/956–6501): The UH Rainbows and seven top-ranked college basketball teams from the mainland compete at the University of Hawai'i between Christmas and New Year's Day. **First Night Maui** (Maui; ☎ 808/244–9166): An alcohol-free New Year's Eve street festival of arts and entertainment at dozens of downtown locations.

➤ JAN.: **Rivals.com Hula Bowl Game** (Maui; ☎ 808/947–4141): This annual college all-star football classic is followed by a Hawaiian-style concert. **Morey Boogie World Body Board Championships** (O'ahu; ☎ 808/396–2326): Competition days for the world's best body boarders are determined by the wave action at Banzai Pipeline. **Cherry Blossom Festival** (O'ahu; ☎ 808/949–2255): This popular celebration of all things Japanese includes a run, cultural displays, cooking demonstrations, music, and crafts. It runs through the end of March.

➤ JAN.–FEB.: **Chinese New Year Celebrations** (all islands; ☎ 808/533–3181 O'ahu, ☎ 808/667–9175 Maui, and ☏ 808/245–6931 Kaua'i): The Chinese New Year is welcomed with a Narcissus Festival pageant, coronation ball, cooking demonstrations, fireworks, and lion dances.

➤ FEB.: **NFL Pro Bowl** (O'ahu; ☏ 808/486–9300): This annual pro-football all-star game is played at Aloha Stadium a week after the Super Bowl. It culminates NFL Week (☏ 808/233–4635) with events on each island. **Sony Open Golf in Hawa'i Tournament** (O'ahu; ☏ 808/831–5400): Top golf pros tee off at the Wai'alae Country Club. **Punahou Carnival** (O'ahu; ☏ 808/944–5711): Hawai'i's most prestigious private school stages an annual fund-raiser with rides, arts and crafts, local food, and a great white-elephant tent. **Sand-Castle Building Contest** (O'ahu; ☏ 808/956–7225): Students of the University of Hawai'i School of Architecture take on Hawai'i's professional architects in a friendly competition; the result is some amazing and unusual sand sculpture at Kailua Beach Park.

➤ FEB.–MAR.: **Buffalo's Annual Big Board Surfing Classic** (O'ahu; ☏ 808/695–8935): The event features surfing as it used to be, on old-fashioned 12- to 16-ft boards, plus food and entertainment.

➤ MAR.: **Opening Day of Polo Season** (O'ahu; ☏ 808/637–6688): Games are held every Sunday through August at 2 PM at Mokule'ia and Waimānalo. **Hawai'i Challenge International Sportkite Championships** (O'ahu; ☏ 808/735–9059): Spectacular kite-flying demonstrations, workshops, and competitions at Kapi'olani Park. **East Maui Taro Festival** (Maui; ☏ 808/248–8972): Held in Hana, this festival focuses on all things taro, including poi. **Prince Kuhio Day** (all islands; ☏ 808/822–5521): March 26, a local holiday, honors Prince Kuhio, a member of Congress who might have become king if Hawai'i had not become a U.S. territory and later a state. **Twilight Tattoo** (O'ahu; ☏ 808/655–9759): Professional band competition at Fort DeRussy Park in Waikīkī, featuring bands from the U.S. military forces, the Royal Hawaiian Band, Celtic Pipes and Drums, and additional guest bands

➤ APR.: **Merrie Monarch Festival** (Big Island; ☏ 808/935–9168): A full week of ancient and modern hula competition begins with a parade the Saturday morning following Easter Sunday. Tickets must be purchased (and hotel rooms reserved) months in advance; the competition is held at the Edith Kanaka'ole Auditorium in Hilo. **Celebration of the Arts** (Maui; ☏ 808/669–6200): For three days the Ritz-Carlton Kapalua pays tribute to Hawai'i's culture with hula and chanting demonstrations, art workshops, a lū'au, and Hawaiian music and dance concerts. Most activities are free.

The 'Ulupalakua Thing! (Maui; ☏ 808/875–0457): Maui County holds its annual agriculture trade show and sampling, hosted by Tedeschi Winery, on the lovely grounds of 'Ulupalakua Ranch. **Buddha Day** (all islands; ☏ 808/536–7044): Flower pageants are staged at Island Buddhist temples to celebrate Buddha's birth. **Honolulu International Bed Race and Parade** (O'ahu; ☏ 808/696–6262): Big names in town turn out for this wild event centered in Waikīkī. The race and after-dark electric light parade are part of a charity fund-raiser.

➤ MAY: **Lei Day** (all islands; ☏ 808/547–7393): This annual flower-filled celebration on May 1 includes music, hula, food, and lei-making competitions, with lots of exquisite leis on exhibit and for sale. **Prince Lot Music Festival** (Kaua'i; ☏ 808/826–9644): Princeville's signature event attracts local musicians and distinguished American composers, plus there are hula performances and art and cultural exhibits. **Ka Hula Piko** (Moloka'i; ☏ 800/800–6367): A community celebration of the birth of hula marked by performances, storytelling, Hawaiian food, crafts, and lectures. **Hawai'i Fisherman's Festival** (O'ahu; ☏ 808/254–3474): This two-day event includes exhibits, forums, demonstrations from both governmental and state agencies who play a role in the preservation of Hawai'i's fisheries.

➤ MAY–JUNE: **50th State Fair** (O'ahu; ☏ 808/486–8300): Produce exhibits, food stands, amusement rides, and live entertainment at Aloha Stadium over several weekends. **Hawaiʻian Airlines Oʻahu Oceanfest** (Oʻahu; ☎ 808/521–4322): Ocean-based competitions, entertainment, international lifeguard competitions, as well as beach sports like volleyball.

➤ MAY–AUG.: **The Wildest Show in Town** (Oʻahu; ☎ 808/531–0101): Popular local entertainers perform free early-evening concerts Wednesday at the Honolulu Zoo.

➤ JUNE: **King Kamehameha Day** (all islands; ☎ 808/586–0333): Kamehameha united all the Islands and became Hawaiʻi's first king. Parades and fairs abound, and twin statues of the king—in Honolulu on Oʻahu and in Hāwī on the Big Island—are draped in giant leis. **Taste of Honolulu** (Oʻahu; ☎ 808/536–1015): One of this island's best food events, it features two days of sampling from the best restaurants in town, entertainment outdoors on the grounds of the Honolulu Civic Center.

➤ JULY: **Puʻuhonua O Hōnunau Festival** (Big Island; ☎ 808/328–2288): Ancient Hawaiian games, hula performances, food tasting, and lau hala and coconut-frond weaving demonstrations take place at the historic City of Refuge. **Kapalua Wine and Food Symposium** (Maui; ☎ 800/669–0244): Wine and food experts and enthusiasts gather for tastings, discussions, and gourmet dinners at the Kapalua Resort. **Makawao Statewide Rodeo** (Maui; ☎ 808/572–1895): This old-time Upcountry rodeo, held at the Oskie Rice Arena in Makawao on the July 4th weekend, includes a parade and three days of festivities. **Parker Ranch Rodeo** (Big Island; ☎ 808/885–7311): In beautiful Waimea, at the largest privately owned ranch in the United States, see how the Hawaʻian cowboy, the *paniolo*, works the circuit. **Independence Day** (all islands): The national holiday on July 4 is celebrated with fairs, parades, and, of course, fireworks. Special events include an outrigger canoe regatta featuring 30 events held on and off Waikīkī Beach. **Prince Lot Hula Festival** (Oʻahu; ☎ 808/839–5334): A whole day of hula unfolds beneath the towering trees of Oʻahu's Moanalua Gardens. **International Festival of the Pacific** (Big Island;

☎ 808/934–0177): This event features music, dance, a lantern parade, floats, sporting events, and food from Japan, China, Korea, Portugal, Tahiti, New Zealand, and the Philippines. **Kīlauea Volcano Wilderness Marathon and Rim Runs** (Big Island; ☎ 808/967–8222): More than 1,000 athletes from Hawaiʻi, the mainland, and Japan run 26.2 mi across Kaʻū desert, 5 mi around the Kīlauea Caldera rim, and 5.5 mi into Kīlauea Iki Crater. The event takes place in Hawaiʻi Volcanoes National Park. **Cuisines of the Sun** (Big Island; ☎ 808/885–6622): Well-known guest chefs present imaginative cuisine paired with fine wines at cooking classes and evening galas during a five-day celebration of food at the Mauna Lani Bay Hotel & Bungalows. **Kaneʻohe BayFest** (Oʻahu; ☎ 808/254–7679): This event is the largest military festival of its kind in Hawaiʻi—with rides, contests, food, and entertainment.

➤ JULY–AUG.: **Bon Odori Season** (all islands; ☎ 808/661–4304): Buddhist temples invite everyone to festivals that honor ancestors and feature Japanese o-bon dancing.

➤ AUG.: **Hawaiʻi State Farm Fair** (Oʻahu; ☎ 808/848–2074): Farm products, agricultural exhibits, arts and crafts, a petting zoo, contests, and a country market are featured on the grounds of Aloha Stadium. **Hawaiian International Billfish Tournament** (Big Island; ☎ 808/329–6155): This international marlin fishing tournament, held in Kailua-Kona, includes a parade with amusing entries. **Made In Hawaiʻi Festival** (Oʻahu; ☎ 808/533–1292): This three-day showcase of all products made in Hawaiʻi gives visitors an overview of what is available in the Islands; it's the perfect opportunity to get your Christmas shopping done early. **Queen Liliʻuokalani Keiki Hula Competition** (Oʻahu; ☎ 808/521–6905): Tickets for this popular children's hula competition, held over three days, are usually available at the end of June and sell out soon after. The **Maui Onion Festival** (Maui; ☎ 808/875–0457): This lighthearted and food-filled celebration of Maui's most famous crop takes place at Whalers Village, Kāʻanapali. **Admission Day** (all Islands): The state holiday, the third

Friday in August, recognizes Hawai'i's attainment of statehood in 1959.

➤ SEPT.: **Maui Music Festival** (Maui; ☎ 800/245–9229): On Labor Day weekend, well-known contemporary jazz, Hawaiian, and other musicians converge on the Kā'anapali Beach Resort for two days of nonstop music on several outdoor stages. **Big Island Bounty Festival** (Big Island; ☎ 800/845–9905): Hawai'i's top chefs celebrate Hawai'i Regional cuisine with cooking demonstrations, wine tastings, an outdoor market, dinners, and receptions at The Orchid at Mauna Lani on Labor Day weekend. **Maui Writers Conference** (Maui; ☎ 808/879–0061): Best-selling authors and powerhouse agents and publishers offer advice—and a few contracts—to aspiring authors and screenwriters at this Labor Day Weekend gathering. **Taste of Lahaina** (Maui; ☎ 808/667–9175): Maui's best chefs compete for top cooking honors, and samples of their entries are sold at a lively open-air party featuring live entertainment.

➤ SEPT.–OCT.: **Aloha Festivals** (all islands; ☎ 808/545–1771): This traditional celebration, started in 1946, preserves Hawaiian native culture. Crafts, music, dance, pageantry, street parties, and canoe races are all part of the festival. **Bankoh Moloka'i Hoe** (Moloka'i and O'ahu; ☎ 808/261–6615): Two annual canoe races from Moloka'i to O'ahu finish in Waikīkī. The women's race is in September; the men's is in October.

➤ OCT.: **Talking Island Festival** (O'ahu; ☎ 808/592–7029): Storytellers share legends and myths of Polynesia at Ala Moana Park's McCoy Pavilion. **Ironman Triathlon World Championships** (Big Island; ☎ 808/329–0063): This popular annual sporting event is limited to 1,250 competitors who swim, run, and bicycle. **Aloha Classic World Wavesailing Championships** (Maui; ☎ 808/575–9151): Top windsurfers from around the globe gather at Hookipa Beach for this professional tour's final event of the season. **Maui Country Fair** (Maui; ☎ 808/875–0457): This decades-old annual event is very popular. Rides, games, entertainment, and exhibits are at the War Memorial Complex, Kahului.

➤ NOV.: **King Kalakaua Kupuna and Keiki Hula Festival** (Big Island; ☎ 808/329–1532): This big, popular hula contest features both a children's competition and one for *kupuna*—adults 55 years and older. **Kona Coffee Cultural Festival** (Big Island; ☎ 808/326–7820): A weeklong celebration, including two parades and a family day with ethnic foods and entertainment at Hale Halawai Recreation Pavilion, follows the coffee harvest. **Winter Wine Escape** (Big Island; ☎ 800/880–1111): Three days of food and wine pairings, cooking demonstrations, receptions, dinners, and a farmers' market showcase Hawai'i Regional cuisine at the Hāpuna Beach Prince Hotel. **Mission Houses Museum Annual Christmas Fair** (O'ahu; ☎ 808/531–0481): Artists and craftspeople sell their creations in an open market. **Hawai'i International Film Festival** (O'ahu and Neighbor Islands; ☎ 808/528–3456): The visual feast showcases films from the United States, Asia, and the Pacific and includes seminars with filmmakers and critics.

WORDS AND PHRASES

Although an understanding of Hawaiian is by no means required on a trip to the Aloha State, a *malihini,* or newcomer, will find plenty of opportunities to pick up a few of the local words and phrases. Traditional names and expressions are widely used in the Islands, thanks in part to legislation enacted in the early '90s to encourage the use of the authentically spelled Hawaiian language. Visitors are likely to read or hear at least a few words each day of their stay. Such exposure enriches a trip to Hawai'i.

With a basic understanding and some uninhibited practice, anyone can have enough command of the local tongue to ask for directions and to order from a restaurant menu. One visitor announced she would not leave until she could pronounce the name of the state fish, the *humuhumunukunukuāpua'a.* Luckily, she had scheduled a nine-day stay.

Simplifying the learning process is the fact that the Hawaiian language contains only eight consonants—*H, K, L, M, N, P, W,* and the silent *'okina,* or glottal stop, written '—plus the five vowels. All syllables, and therefore all words, end in a vowel. Each vowel, with the exception of a few diphthongized double vowels such as *au* (pronounced "ow") or *ai* (pronounced "eye"), is pronounced separately. Thus *'Iolani* is four syllables (ee-oh-la-nee), not three (yo-la-nee). Although some Hawaiian words have only vowels, most also contain some consonants, but consonants are never doubled.

Pronunciation is simple. Pronounce *A* "ah" as father; *E* "ay" as in weigh; *I* "ee" as in marine; *O* "oh" as in no; *U* "oo" as in true.

Consonants mirror their English equivalents, with the exception of *W.* When the letter begins any syllable other than the first one in a word, it is usually pronounced as a *V.* *'Awa,* the Polynesian drink, is pronounced "ava"; *'ewa* is pronounced "eva."

Nearly all long Hawaiian words are combinations of shorter words; they are not difficult to pronounce if you segment them into shorter words. *Kalaniana'ole,* the highway running east from Honolulu, is easily understood as *Kalani ana 'ole.* Apply the standard pronunciation rules—the stress falls on the next-to-last syllable of most two- or three-syllable Hawaiian words—and Kalaniana'ole Highway is as easy to say as Main Street.

Now about that fish. Try *humu-humu nuku-nuku āpu a'a.*

The other unusual element in Hawaiian language is the *kahakō,* or macron, written as a short line (ˉ) placed over a vowel. Like the accent (´) in Spanish, the kahakō puts emphasis on a syllable that would normally not be stressed. The most familiar example is probably *Waikīkī.* With no macrons, the stress would fall on the middle syllable; with only one macron, on the last syllable, the stress would fall on the first and last syllables. Some words become plural with the addition of a macron, often on a syllable that would have been stressed anyway. No Hawaiian word becomes plural with the addition of an *S,* since that letter does not exist in *'ōlelo Hawai'i* (which is Hawaiian for "Hawaiian language").

What follows is a glossary of some of the most commonly used Hawaiian words. Don't be afraid to give them a try. Hawaiian residents appreciate visitors who at least try to pick up the local language.

ʻaʻā: rough, crumbling lava, contrasting with *pāhoehoe,* which is smooth.

ʻae: yes.

aikane: friend.

akamai: smart, clever, possessing savoir faire.

akua: god.

ala: a road, path, or trail.

aliʻi: a Hawaiian chief, a member of the chiefly class.

aloha: love, affection, kindness. Also a salutation meaning both greetings and farewell.

ʻānuenue: rainbow.

ʻaʻole: no.

ʻauwai: a ditch.

auwē: alas, woe is me!

ʻehu: a red-haired Hawaiian.

ʻewa: in the direction of ʻEwa plantation, west of Honolulu.

hala: the pandanus tree, whose leaves (*lau hala*) are used to make baskets and plaited mats.

halau: school.

hale: a house.

hale pule: church, house of worship.

hana: to work.

haole: originally a stranger or foreigner. Since the first foreigners were Caucasian, *haole* now means a Caucasian person.

hapa: a part, sometimes a half; often used as a short form of *hapa haole,* to mean a person who is part-Caucasian; thus, the name of a popular local band, whose members represent a variety of ethnicities.

hauʻoli: to rejoice. *Hauʻoli Makahiki Hou* means Happy New Year. *Hauʻoli lā hānau* means Happy Birthday.

heiau: an outdoor stone platform; an ancient Hawaiian place of worship.

holo: to run.

holoholo: to go for a walk, ride, or sail.

holokū: a long Hawaiian dress, somewhat fitted, with a yoke and a train. Influenced by European fashion, it was worn at court, and at least one local translates the word as "expensive muʻumuʻu."

holomū: a post–World War II cross between a *holokū* and a *muʻumuʻu,* less fitted than the former but less voluminous than the latter, and having no train.

honi: to kiss, a kiss. A phrase that some tourists may find useful, quoted from a popular *hula,* is *Honi Kaʻua Wikiwiki:* Kiss me quick!

honu: turtle.

hoʻomalimali: flattery, a deceptive "line," bunk, baloney, hooey.

huhū: angry.

hui: a group, club, or assembly. A church may refer to its congregation as a *hui* and a social club may be called a *hui.*

hukilau: a seine; a communal fishing party in which everyone helps to drive the fish into a huge net, pull it in, and divide the catch.

hula: the dance of Hawaiʻi.

iki: little.

ipo: sweetheart.

ka: the. This is the definite article for most singular words; for plural nouns, the definite article is usually *nā.* Since there is no *S* in Hawaiian, the article may be your only clue that a noun is plural.

kahuna: a priest, doctor, or other trained person of old Hawaiʻi, endowed with special professional skills that often included the gift of prophecy or other supernatural powers; plural: *kāhuna.*

kai: the sea, saltwater.

kalo: the taro plant from whose root poi is made.

kamaʻāina: literally, a child of the soil, it refers to people who were born in the Islands or have lived there for a long time.

kanaka: originally a man or humanity in general, it is now used to denote a male

Hawaiian or part-Hawaiian, but is occasionally taken as a slur when used by non-Hawaiians. *Kanaka maoli,* originally a full-blooded Hawaiian person, is used by some native Hawaiian rights activists to embrace part-Hawaiians as well.

kāne: a man, a husband. If you see this word on a door, it's the men's room. If you see *kane* on a door, it's probably a misspelling; that is the Hawaiian name for the skin fungus, Tinea.

kapa: also called by its Tahitian name, *tapa,* a cloth made of beaten bark and usually dyed and stamped with a repeat design.

kapakahi: crooked, cockeyed, uneven. You've got your hat on *kapakahi.*

kapu: keep out, prohibited. This is the Hawaiian version of the more widely known Tongan word *tabu* (taboo).

kapuna: grandparent.

keiki: a child; *keikikāne* is a boy, *keikiwahine* a girl.

kona: the leeward side of the Islands, the direction (south) from which the *kona* wind and *kona* rain come.

kula: upland.

kuleana: a homestead or small plot of ground on which a family has been installed for some generations without necessarily owning it. By extension, *kuleana* is used to denote any area or department in which one has a special interest or prerogative. You'll hear it used this way: If you want to hire a surfboard, see Moki; that's his *kuleana.* And conversely: I can't help you with that; that's not my *kuleana.*

lā: sun.

lamalama: to fish with a torch.

lānai: a porch, a balcony, an outdoor living room. Almost every house in Hawai'i has one. Don't confuse this two-syllable word with the three-syllable name of the island, Lāna'i.

lani: heaven, the sky.

lau hala: the leaf of the *hala* or pandanus tree, widely used in Hawaiian handicrafts.

lei: a garland of flowers.

limu: sun.

lolo: stupid.

luna: a plantation overseer or foreman.

mahalo: thank you.

makai: toward the ocean.

malihini: a newcomer to the Islands.

mana: the spiritual power that the Hawaiian believed inhabited all things and creatures.

manō: shark.

manuwahi: free, gratis.

mauka: toward the mountains.

mauna: mountain.

mele: a Hawaiian song or chant, often of epic proportions.

Mele Kalikimaka: Merry Christmas (a transliteration from the English phrase).

Menehune: a Hawaiian pixie. The *Menehune* were a legendary race of little people who accomplished prodigious work, such as building fishponds and temples in the course of a single night.

moana: the ocean.

mu'umu'u: the voluminous dress in which the missionaries enveloped Hawaiian women. Now made in bright printed cottons and silks, it is an indispensable garment in a Hawaiian woman's wardrobe. Culturally sensitive locals have embraced the Hawaiian spelling but often shorten the spoken word to "mu'u." Most English dictionaries include the spelling "muumuu," and that version is a part of many apparel companies' names.

nani: beautiful.

nui: big.

ohana: family.

'ono: delicious.

pāhoehoe: smooth, unbroken, satiny lava.

Pākē: Chinese. This *Pākē* carver makes beautiful things.

palapala: document, printed matter.

pali: a cliff, precipice.

pānini: prickly pear cactus.

paniolo: a Hawaiian cowboy, a rough transliteration of *español,* the language of the Islands' earliest cowboys.

pau: finished, done.

pilikia: trouble. The Hawaiian word is much more widely used here than its English equivalent.

puka: a hole.

pupule: crazy, like the celebrated Princess Pupule. This word has replaced its English equivalent in local usage.

puʻu: volcanic cinder cone.

waha: mouth.

wahine: a female, a woman, a wife, and a sign on the ladies' room door; plural: *wāhine.*

wai: freshwater, as opposed to saltwater, which is *kai.*

wailele: waterfall.

wikiwiki: to hurry, hurry up. (Since this is a reduplication of *wiki,* quick, neither *W* is pronounced as a *V.*).

Note: Pidgin is the unofficial language of Hawaiʻi. It is a Creole language, with its own grammar, evolved from the mixture of English, Hawaiian, Japanese, Portuguese, and other languages spoken in 19th-century Hawaiʻi, and it is heard everywhere: on ranches, in warehouses, on beaches, and in the hallowed halls (and occasionally in the classrooms) of the University of Hawaiʻi.

KEY WORDS
ON THE MENU

Much of the Hawaiian language encountered during a stay in the Islands will appear on restaurant menus and lists of lūʻau fare. Here's a quick primer.

ʻahi: locally caught yellowfin tuna.

aku: skipjack, bonito tuna.

ʻamaʻama: mullet; it's hard to get but tasty.

bento: a box lunch.

chicken lūʻau: a stew made from chicken, taro leaves, and coconut milk.

haupia: a light, gelatinlike dessert made from coconut.

imu: the underground ovens in which pigs are roasted for lūʻau.

kālua: to bake underground.

kaukau: food. The word comes from Chinese but is used in the Islands.

kim chee: pickled Chinese cabbage made with garlic and hot peppers.

Kona coffee: coffee grown in the Kona district of the Big Island.

laulau: literally, a bundle. *Laulau* are morsels of pork, butterfish, or other ingredients wrapped with young taro shoots in ti leaves for steaming.

lilikoʻi: passion fruit, a tart, seedy yellow fruit that makes delicious desserts, jellies, and sherbet.

lomilomi: to rub or massage; also a massage. Lomilomi salmon is fish that has been rubbed with onions and herbs, commonly served with minced onions and tomatoes.

lūʻau: a Hawaiian feast, also the leaf of the taro plant used in preparing such a feast.

lūʻau leaves: cooked taro tops with a taste similar to spinach.

mahimahi: mild-flavored dolphinfish, not the marine mammal.

mai tai: fruit punch with rum, from the Tahitian word for "good."

malasada: a Portuguese deep-fried doughnut without a hole, dipped in sugar.

manapua: dough wrapped around diced pork.

manō: shark.

niu: coconut.

ʻōkolehao: a liqueur distilled from the ti root.

onaga: pink or red snapper.

ono: a long, slender mackerel-like fish; also called wahoo.

ʻono: delicious; also hungry.

ʻopihi: a tiny shellfish, or mollusk, found on rocks; also called limpets.

pāpio: a young ulua or jack fish.

pohā: Cape gooseberry. Tasting a bit like honey, the pohā berry is often used in jams and desserts.

poi: a paste made from pounded taro root, a staple of the Hawaiian diet.

poke: chopped, pickled raw fish and seafood, tossed with herbs and seasonings.

pūpū: Hawaiian hors d'oeuvre.

saimin: long thin noodles and vegetables in broth, often garnished with small pieces of fish cake, scrambled egg, luncheon meat, and green onion.

sashimi: raw fish thinly sliced and usually eaten with soy sauce.

ti leaves: a member of the agave family, used to wrap food in cooking and removed before eating.

uku: deep-sea snapper.

ulua: a member of the jack family that also includes pompano and amber-jack. Also called crevalle, jack fish, and jack crevalle.

Hawaiian Islands

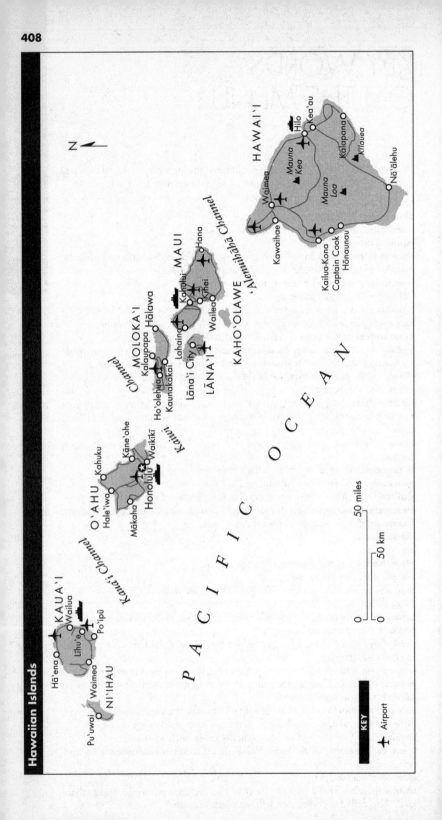

N

KAUA'I
Hā'ena
Wailua
Pu'uwai
Waimea
Līhu'e
Po'ipū
NI'IHAU

Kaua'i Channel

O'AHU
Kahuku
Kāne'ohe
Hale'iwa
Waikīkī
Mākaha
Honolulu

Kaiwi Channel

MOLOKA'I
Hālawa
Kalaupapa
Ho'olehua
Kaunakakai
Lahaina
Lāna'i City
LĀNA'I

MAUI
Kahului
Hana
Kīhei
Wailea

KAHO'OLAWE

'Alenuihāhā Channel

HAWAI'I
Hilo
Kea'au
Waimea
Mauna Kea
Kīlauea
Kalapana
Mauna Loa
Nā'ālehu
Kawaihae
Kailua-Kona
Captain Cook
Hōnaunau

PACIFIC OCEAN

0   50 miles
0   50 km

KEY
✈ Airport

INDEX

FODOR'S HAWAI'I 2001

EDITOR: Alice K. Thompson

Editorial Contributors: DeSoto Brown, Gary Diedrichs, Betty Fullard-Leo, Pablo Madera, Helayne Schiff, Sophia Schweitzer, Marty Wentzel, Paul Wood, Margaret M. Wunsch
Editorial Production: Frank Walgren
Maps: David Lindroth, *cartographer;* Rebecca Baer and Bob Blake, *map editors*
Design: Fabrizio La Rocca, *creative director;* Guido Caroti, *art director;* Jolie Novak, *photo editor;* Melanie Marin, *photo researcher*
Cover Design: Pentagram
Production/Manufacturing: Mike Costa

IMPORTANT TIP

Although all prices, opening times, and other details in this book are based on information supplied to us at press time, changes do occur all the time in the travel world, and Fodor's cannot accept responsibility for facts that become outdated or for inadvertent erros or omissions. So **always confirm information when it matters,** especially if you're making a detour to visit a specific place.

PHOTOGRAPHY

Catherine Karnow, *cover* (*Nā Pali Coast, Kaua'i*).

Alexander & Baldwin Sugar Museum, *p. 28 top.*

Big Island Visitors Bureau: *Bob Abraham, p. 2 top left. Robert Coello, p. 3 top right. Robert Miller, p. 3 center right. John Penisten, p. 2 top right, 30I. Red Sail Sports, p. 17H.*

Currents-Hawaii's Big Island, *p. 16E.*

John DeMello, *p. 23D, 30G.*

Dole Pineapple Plantation, *p. 2 bottom right.*

Sheila Donnelly & Associates: *Arnold Savrann, p. 30F.*

Robert Holmes, *15C.*

The Image Bank: *Alan Becker, p. 20 center, 20F. Andy Caulfield, p. 7D, 28 bottom. Angelo Cavalli, p. 15 bottom left, 16F, 29. David Hamilton, p. 1. Jeff Hunter, p. 15D. Marcel Isy-Schwart, p. 24 bottom right. John Kelly, p. 17I. Don King, p. 6A. A. Lanzellotto, 30H. Paul McCormick, p. 23E, 27 bottom. Michael Melford, p. 9H. Kaz Mori, p. 7C. Bernard Roussel, p. 11B. Joseph Szkodzinski, p. 8F, 20E, 30B. John Lewis Stage, p. 12G. Harald Sund, p. 7B, 11C. Cindy Turner, p. 17G. Pete Turner, p. 12E. Turner & De Vries, p. 9G, 13I, 19D, 21G, 27 top. Alvis Upitis, p. 16 top. Ulf Wallin, p. 13H. Stephen Wilkes, p. 30A.*

The Island of Lanai: *Jeffrey Asher, p. 25D, 30E.*

Kahala Mandarin Oriental, *p. 30C.*

Kaua'i Visitors Bureau: *David Boynton, p. 18A.*

Maui Ocean Center, *p. 13J.*

Maui Visitors Bureau: *William Waterfall, p. 3 bottom left, 3 bottom right. Phil Spalding III, p. 22B.*

Robert Miller, *p. 30J.*

PhotoDisc, *p. 26 bottom, 28 center.*

Photo Resource Hawaii: *David Boynton, p. 18C. John Callahan, p. 32. Jim Cazel, p. 4–5, 10A, 11D, 12F. Linny Morris Cunningham, p. 18B. Tammy Dawson, p. 21 bottom. Brad Lewis, p. 14A, 14B. Jon K. Ogata, p. 23C. Franco Salmoiraghi, p. 22A, 24A, 24B.*

Polynesian Cultural Center: *p. 2 bottom left, 3 top left, 8E, 9I. Dana Edmunds, p. 26 top.*

Princeville Resort: *Paul Barton, p. 21H, 30D.*

Trilogy Excursions: *Ron Dahlquist, p. 2 bottom center, 25C, 25E.*

ABOUT OUR WRITERS

Every trip is a significant trip. Acutely aware of that fact, we've pulled out all stops in preparing *Fodor's Hawai'i*. To help you zero in on what to see in Hawai'i, we've gathered some great color photos. To show you how to put it all together, we've created great itineraries and neighborhood walks. And to direct you to the places that are truly worth your time and money, we've rallied the team of endearingly picky know-it-alls we're pleased to call our writers. Having seen all corners of Hawai'i, they're real experts on the subjects they cover for us. If you knew them, you'd poll them for tips yourself.

Betty Fullard-Leo, a resident of the Islands since 1962, writes extensively about destinations, lifestyle, art, food, and culture in the Aloha State. Her work on *Fodor's Hawai'i* over the years has been invaluable. This year she was responsible for the Kaua'i and Moloka'i chapters. She's a contributing food editor for *Hawai'i* magazine, and previously she was editor of *Pacific Art & Travel* and associate editor of *ALOHA Magazine*. She has recently begun writing for travel sites on the Internet, including Insight2.com.

Pablo Madera, our Maui updater, is a freelance journalist, jazz drummer, and ethnobotanist who has made Maui his home base for 25 years. When he's not pursuing projects on various Pacific islands, he tries to keep up with banana production on his small farm, which is off the road to Hāna.

Big Island resident **Sophia Schweitzer** is our updater for that chapter as well as for Lāna'i. Sophia is a freelance food, wine, health and fitness, and travel writer whose work has appeared in magazines across the country. She is educational writer for *Wine X,* a lifestyle magazine for the new generation, and has just finished coauthoring a book about the Big Island.

Maggie Wunsch, our O'ahu updater, is a 27-year resident of Hawai'i whose writings about the Islands have appeared on radio, local and national television, and in both consumer and travel-trade publications. Wunsch grew up in Asia and Europe and fell in love with Hawai'i in 1961 when, at the age of 6, she first met the Pacific Ocean on the beach fronting the Halekūlani Hotel. Her fascination with Hawai'i and the Pacific continues to this day.

Don't Forget to Write

We love feedback—positive and negative—and follow up on all suggestions. So contact the Hawai'i editor at editors@fodors.com or c/o Fodor's, 280 Park Avenue, New York, NY 10017. Have a wonderful trip!

Karen Cure

Karen Cure
Editorial Director